MAESTRO

MAESTRO
Encounters with Conductors of Today

HELENA
MATHEOPOULOS

1817

HARPER & ROW, PUBLISHERS, New York
Cambridge, Philadelphia, San Francisco, London
Mexico City, São Paulo, Sydney

FIRST U.S. EDITION

Library of Congress Cataloging in Publication Data

Matheopoulos, Helena.
  Maestro: encounters with conductors of today.

  Bibliography: p.
  Includes index.
  1. Conductors—Interviews. I. Title.
ML402.M37   1982   785'.092'2 [B]   82-48125
ISBN 0-06-015103-X

---

83 84 85 86 87 10 9 8 7 6 5 4 3 2 1

To the memory of my Father
and of T.S.

"Love is not changed by death, and nothing is lost,
and all in the end is harvest."

(EDITH SITWELL)

"When talking about music, words are sometimes not enough..."
MAURIZIO POLLINI

CONTENTS

Independent Spirit

Soloist-Conductors

The Younger Generation

ILLUSTRATIONS

AUTHOR'S
ACKNOWLEDGEMENTS

When this book was first conceived, even in my wildest dreams I had not dared hope for the endless encouragement and help I was to receive from so many people. First and foremost, my thanks and gratitude are to the conductors themselves, who proved unstintingly generous both with their time and their thoughts and helped me in every way they could. Secondly to the many singers, soloists, orchestral players, managers and administrators who agreed to share some of their opinions and experiences of the conductors with me. All are named in the text itself before they are quoted, but I would like to use this space to thank them again, collectively, for their time and contributions.

After them, my greatest debt of gratitude is to Mary Jo Little (Promotions Manager, Deutsche Grammophon and Archiv Production, London), who believed in the book right from its conception and without whose active and moral support, constant help and friendship it would not, and could not, have been written; to Katharine Wilkinson (Press Officer, The Royal Opera, Covent Garden) an enthusiastic helper from the beginning, whose suggestions and occasional criticisms invariably proved constructive and fruitful; to Robert Leslie, who helped smooth many difficulties, cut many corners and bypass many obstacles, thus enabling me to get the book off the ground much more easily and quickly than would otherwise have been possible; to Dr Uli Märkle (Classical A & R Head of International Artists' Promotion, Polydor International) whose help and decisive intervention was instrumental in making the book what it is; to Savina Lykiardopoulos for introducing me to Gillon Aitken who was instantly taken with the idea of the book, took endless trouble to get it commissioned and has looked after it ever since; to Roddy Bloomfield (a Director of Hutchinson) and Kevin McDermott (formerly of Hutchinson and currently of The Royal Opera House) for thinking it worth commissioning and for creating a wonderfully relaxed and friendly working relationship; to my editor at Hutchinson, Antony Wood, who was landed in it halfway and took infinite pains thereafter; to Miss Mary Cohen and Miss Alison Cochrane of Knightsbridge Secretarial Services and Mrs Gwen Margrie of Secretarial Assistance, who typed the manuscript (invariably at short notice!); to Gennadi Zalkowitch for supplying invaluable material and information; to my cousin, Nicky Broudo; and to Mrs Helga Laptev for translating countless documents from German.

I should also like to thank many of my friends whose hospitality all over the world made it possible occasionally to work away from the monotony of my own surroundings or the unrelievable gloom of hotel rooms. They are: Ambassador and Mrs Sumner Gerard and Dorothy Hales-Gary in New York; Aleco and Marietta Goulandris on the *Anemos*; Effie Nomikos on the *Pegasus*; Nadia Stancioff in Venice; Irene Sculi-Logotheti in Paris; Bettina Hackelsberger, who also helped steer both people and material my way, in Munich; Lady Fraser in Hampshire; Stanley Falconer in Gloucestershire; Robin and Barbara Mackichan in Berkshire; George and Baba Boudi in Zakynthos, Daphne Manussis in Skiathos, David and Inga Smith.

I would also like to thank the following for their help:
Sir John Tooley, General Director, The Royal Opera House, Covent Garden
Dr Peter Girth, Intendant, the Berlin Philharmonic Orchestra
Michel Glotz
Matthias Vogt and Elisabeth De Géry of Musicaglotz
Terry McEwen, General Director, the San Francisco Opera
Dr R. Bächi, Director, Tonhalle Gesellschaft, Zurich
Humphrey and Christina Burton
John Denison
Peter Diamand
Christopher Bishop, Managing Director, the Philharmonia Orchestra
Ernest Fleischmann, Executive Director, the Los Angeles Philharmonic Orchestra
Lore Salzburger, Personal Assistant to Herbert von Karajan
Charles Kaye, Personal Assistant to Sir Georg Solti
Wolfgang von Karajan
Harold Rosenthal, Editor, *Opera* Magazine
Lothar Knessl, Press Officer, the Vienna State Opera
Gisela Huwe, Press Officer, the Berlin Philharmonic Orchestra
Brigitte Grabner, Press Officer, the Vienna Philharmonic
Patrizia Bissi, Ufficio Stampa, La Scala, Milan
Carolyn Moody, former Personal Assistant to James Levine
Maria Zimmel, formerly Press Officer, the Bavarian State Opera; currently Press Officer, Bühnen der Stadt Bonn
Henrietta Lloyd, formerly Press Officer, the Bavarian State Opera
Libby Rice, Press Officer, the London Symphony Orchestra
Hilary Sheard, Assistant Press Officer, the London Symphony Orchestra
Peter Cripps, Orchestral Manager, the London Philharmonic Orchestra
Quita Chavez, Editor, the *Gramophone* Magazine
Martha Anne Glantz, Press Officer, Berliner Festwochen

Professor Alfred Altenburger, Vorstand, the Vienna Philharmonic Orchestra

Friedrich Kleinknecht, Vorstand, the Bavarian State Orchestra

Bram Gay, Orchestra Director, The Royal Opera House, Covent Garden

Peter Gelb of Columbia Artists, formerly Director of Public Relations, the Boston Symphony Orchestra

Norma Flynn, Director of Publicity and Promotion, the Los Angeles Philharmonic

Kenneth Utz, Director of Public Relations, the Chicago Symphony Orchestra

Philippe de Bros, Assistant Manager, Opernhaus, Zurich

Rolf Trouwborst, Chefdramaturg, Deutsche Oper am Rhein, Düsseldorf

Gerda Plumacher, Librarian, Deutsche Oper am Rhein

Martin Campbell White, Director of Harold Holt Ltd

Jasper Parrott, Manager and impresario

John Walker

Inge Kühe

Alan Sievewright

Marina Rovera

Michael Kaye, General Administrator, the Royal Festival Hall

Gaia Servadio Mostyn Owen

Jane Lambert, formerly Assistant to Katharine Wilkinson, the Royal Opera, Covent Garden

Liza Hobbs

Gertraud Hemedinger, Ticket Office, Salzburg Easter Festival

Brigitte Baier, Ticket Office, Salzburg Summer Festival

Peter Andry, Director, International Classical Division, EMI Music

Peter Alward, Co-ordinator for International Classical Division, EMI Europe

Barry Malcomber, Manager, Merchandising Services, International Classical Division, EMI Music

Charles Rodier, Manager, Contracts and Business Affairs, International Classical Division, EMI Music

John Mordler, Recording Producer, EMI Music

Audrey Newman, Personal Assistant to Peter Andry

Hannelore Ilse, Assistant to Peter Alward

Sarah Green, Assistant to Barry Malcomber

Judith Barber, Photographic Librarian, International Classical Division, EMI Music

John Patrick, General Manager, Classical Division, EMI Records, U.K.

Joan Coulson, Classical Promotions, EMI Records, U.K.

Ray Minshull, Executive Vice Chairman, Decca International

David Rickerby, International Classical Marketing Manager, Decca International

John Kehoe, International Promotions Manager, Decca International

Richard Rollefson, Vice President, London Records, Polygram Classics Inc., New York

James Lock, Manager, Classical Recordings, Decca
Christopher Raeburn, Recording Producer, Decca
Rosalind Leitch, formerly Promotions Assistant, Decca
Graham Turnbull, formerly Marketing Assistant, Decca
Günther Breest, Head of Classical Artists & Repertoire Managers and Producers, Polydor International
Professor Dr Hans Hirsch, Director, Classical Artists & Repertoire, Deutsche Grammophon, Polydor International
Rainer Brock, Classical A & R Manager and Producer, Polydor International
Peter Russell, General Manager, Polygram Classics, London
Annemarie Nicol, Label Manager, Deutsche Grammophon and Archiv Productions
Gillian Finn, Promotions Assistant, Deutsche Grammophon
Antje Henneking, Head of Press Department, Polydor International (Classical Repertoire)
Ilse Koefod, Assistant to Antje Henneking
Eva Steck, Press Archive, Polydor International (Classical Repertoire)
Eike Kaessens, Photo Archive and Art Buyer, Polydor International (Classical Repertoire)
Gianfranco Rebulla, President, Polygram Classics, Inc., New York
Alison Ames, Vice President, Deutsche Grammophon and Archiv Production; Polygram Classics, Inc., New York
Claudia Hamann, Assistant to Günther Breest
Hildegard Heyse, Classical A & R Liaison Officer, Berlin, Polydor International
Marina Meynier, Classical A & R Liaison Officer, Vienna, Polydor International
Helen Kuzaj, Classical A & R Liaison Officer, Munich, Polydor International
Elisabeth Koehler, Press & Promotion, Classical Repertoire, Polydor France
Carol Felton, Promotions Manager, Philips Records
Vivienne Taylor, Manager, Artists' & Repertoire Adminstration, Europe, CBS Masterworks

PUBLISHER'S ACKNOWLEDGEMENTS

Grateful acknowledgement is due to the following publishers for their permission to quote passages from books published by them: Messrs Bertelsmann Verlag, Munich (*Herbert von Karajan* by Ernst Haeusserman, 1968); Messrs Diogenes Verlag AG, Zurich (*Ich erinnere mich ganz genau (Autobiographie)* by Karl Böhm, 1968); Harper & Row, New York (*Zubin: The Zubin Mehta Story* by Messrs Martin Bookspan and Ross Yockey, 1978); Messrs Severin und Siedler, West Berlin (*Grosse Deutsche Dirigenten*, 1981).

INTRODUCTION
The Mystery of Conducting

"In our profession, someone can be very brilliant and acquire total technical mastery. Yet in the last resort, the only thing that really counts is his quality as a human being. For music is created by Man for Man. And if someone sees nothing more than notes in it, this can perhaps be very interesting, but it cannot enrich him. And music should exist for one purpose only: to enrich Man and give him something he has lost in most respects."

(Herbert von Karajan) *

The mystery—as opposed to the so-called 'mystique'—of conducting has fascinated and intrigued me since my mid-teens when I first had an opportunity to observe the conductor's work at close quarters through numerous rehearsals and recording sessions. But paradoxically, the more familiar I became with the technicalities of conducting as a craft—stick technique, cueing, achieving a good ensemble and good balance between the various sections of the orchestra—the less I felt I understood the essence of this most elusive of arts.

For how can one explain the fact that a man who has no physical contact with sound can nevertheless make the same music played by the same orchestra sound totally different from the way it does when conducted by his colleagues? This happens even in German repertory theatres where conductors are tied to beating scores in the standard, traditional manner always practised in each particular opera house. One would think that this should result in uniform performances, no matter who is waving the stick. But it doesn't. It results in as many different interpretations as there are conductors. Why? What is this special ingredient 'x' that the conductor contributes to the realization of music? And how is it communicated to the players? And what is it about a conductor's personality that hypnotizes and compels over a hundred players, many of whom may be better musicians than he,

* from Joachim Kaiser's chapter in *Grosse Deutsche Dirigenten*, Severin und Siedler, 1981.

many of whom may disagree with his interpretation, many of whom may even dislike him, to submit to his will?

It was my curiosity about these questions that, many years later, prompted me to undertake this exploration of the art of conducting, through the best known conductors of our day. For it was obvious that some of the answers lay in their personalities both as artists and as human beings. And indeed their insights and thoughts about their profession and about music in general helped elucidate several of those questions.... Yet even after three years of constant thinking and talking about conducting, and of observing twenty-three conductors at work, the essence of this art remains and always will remain a mystery, "nearly unexplainable" according to Herbert von Karajan who understands it better than most—not only to me but even to those who practise it.

Of course some aspects of conducting are hardly mysterious at all and easily explainable. The fact that the conductor functions as both interpreter and master technician, for instance. As an interpreter, he has to form an opinion about the musical and spiritual meaning of each work and acquire a mental image of the sound contained in the score. And it goes without saying that the quality of his musicianship, his personality, his depth (or lack of depth) and quality as a human being will greatly affect his perceptions of what lies behind those black dots. For musical notation is an inexact, ambiguous and mysterious language and even instructions written in words—like *allegro* or *pianissimo*—are subject to different and highly individual interpretations. For what is the fastest or slowest possible speed, or the softest or loudest possible volume? There are no objective criteria. It all depends on the conductor's feeling and understanding. Recent research has shown that it also depends on biological factors like his heart beat, pulse and metabolic rate, in other words on his own inner rhythm.... And while every conductor is passionately convinced that he is faithfully following the composer's wishes, the fact remains that his own reading of a score is unique.

Having acquired his interpretation, the conductor then sets about his step by step preparation of the orchestra through a series of rehearsals at which he explains what kind of sound he wants both verbally and through his stick. Of course, conductors differ as widely in their rehearsal techniques as they do in their interpretations. Some use their time well, others not so well; some command good discipline, others not; some insist on performance-like tension at every rehearsal, while others (and these include the greatest conductors) prefer to leave something extra for the performance itself. But however they set about it, their work at rehearsal is 'tangible' and easy to understand. Except for one thing: the fact that the moment a new conductor steps onto the podium for his first rehearsal with an orchestra new to him, the players instantly sense whether or not he is a born conductor; and after a few bars, they have sized him up both as a musician and as a man. Indeed sometimes, as Riccardo Muti pointed out, the first rehearsal determines whether the concert will be good or not.

Because this is when the musicians first come into contact, albeit in a rather subdued form, with that mysterious ingredient 'x' which will play such a vital role at the performance, when the conductor's interpretation is transmitted to the players through channels that transcend the confines of technique and are extremely difficult to pinpoint, let alone define. They have, as all the artists in this book testify, to do with magnetism and electric emanation; and the ability to project his personality in this way is the most essential, crucial quality in the conductor's chemical make-up. "All other things he can learn. This he cannot. And every time someone steps onto a podium, I can immediately tell whether or not he has it," says Karajan. Therefore this ingredient must be innate, and conductors are therefore born, not made. And while several maestri pinpointed some of the other psychological qualities necessary for conducting, all of them were unanimous that these were secondary to this ingredient 'x', i.e. the ability to transmit his interpretation through the intangible ways mentioned above.

But apart from this *sine qua non* ingredient, a conductor needs "a terrific combination of both musical and non-musical qualities, especially if he wants to be an orchestra-builder as well," explains Zubin Mehta. "From the musical point of view, he is often the only person aware of the entire expanse of a given work—orchestral players usually learn only their own parts—and must know exactly where he is going, so that he can guide the music and plan its climaxes accordingly; he must also have a knowledge of style, every composer's style, plus total conviction that what he is doing is right, even if it sometimes isn't, in order to suggest it to a hundred people and expect them to follow him. From the human point of view, he must be good at handling people, which calls for some psychology, diplomacy and tact, plus considerable organizing skills. For he has to plan not only his own career, but all the orchestra's tours and recordings, the auditioning and hiring of players and the choice of guest conductors as well. *And* find time for private study, which is absolutely crucial."

Apart from this admirably clear and succinct summary of the qualities needed by a conductor, the other attributes mentioned most often were: a desire and capacity for leadership; and a considerable Ego that alone can bestow the confidence and will to impose his interpretation on a hundred players. ("Modest? *Of course* I'm not modest! If I were, I wouldn't be a conductor," says Bernard Haitink.)

"All conductors must have a big Ego," confirms Kenneth Goode, double bass player in the London Philharmonic. "But sometimes, some of them seem to love the music itself so much and get so completely absorbed in the work they are re-creating that they lose their Ego while conducting. And that's a bonus for us—that uplift we get when we feel that all of us are One with the music. This is what we are looking for. But it doesn't always happen. In fact with some conductors it *never* happens! In such cases well ... at least we have the consolation of our individual instruments and just concentrate on playing them as well as we can; but without feeling *part* of anything; we merely feel like individual players trying to do their best."

What this player means is that no conductor can be truly great unless his Ego is coupled with humility towards the composer and a willingness to be his servant but, as Carlo Maria Giulini explained, "a servant who serves with love, not because he has to". And this fusion, this one-ness, this merging together of identities—the conductor's, the players', the composer's imagination—that Kenneth Goode described above lies at the heart of the mystery of conducting. All great conductors experience and consider it the ultimate goal of their art: "In those performances which *I* call good, I feel I'm composing the piece as we go along—now we bring in the basses, next the trombones, now the chorus," says Leonard Bernstein. "At the end of such perform-ances, it takes minutes before I know where I am—in what hall, in what country—or who I am.... For you are in a sort of ecstasy which is nothing less than a loss of Ego: *You* don't exist." Karajan feels that "these are some of the great moments we experience. And we wait for them, and we prepare for them, but we cannot summon them the way that you can summon a waiter. This ... something just comes, and it's the grace of the moment."

But he went on to point out that first a conductor must ensure that he is completely free, i.e. that he must acquire technical mastery, first through his musical studies and secondly through experience. Yet one of the sad paradoxes of our time is that while the high standards of musical education and of conducting classes at musical academies and conservatoires the world over have produced a generation of 'virtuoso conductors' (the term was coined by Professor Thomas Brandis, Concertmaster of the Berlin Philharmonic) whose technical brilliance and clarity of beat is indeed dazzling and unprecedented in the history of conducting, this has been at the expense of, and in inverse proportion to, the general level of musical understanding, which has dropped dramatically, especially so in the interpretation of the works of the Classical and Romantic eras. The artist to voice this most forcibly is Simon Rattle, a generation removed from the 'virtuosos' and hence able to feel and pinpoint their and the preceding generations' plusses and minuses all the more accurately.

The main reason for this decline seems to be that nowadays, instead of being allowed to learn their craft and make their mistakes in relative seclusion, conductors are launched into the deep long before they are ready for it. The proliferation of opera houses and orchestras is such that the moment a promising talent appears on the scene, it is immediately snatched up, pressured into doing too much too soon, promoted and publicized far in excess of its merits, and tempted into lucrative recording contracts. No wonder then, that the result should be an abundance of performances which, however technically competent, glossy, polished and superficially rousing, nevertheless succeed in communicating little more than mere energy and fail to reveal the true musical content of the works they so shamelessly abuse. No one disputes the fact that there is a first time for everything and that therefore a young conductor has to conduct his first *Tristan* or *Parsifal* *somewhere*. But ideally this should be at as small and as remote an opera house as possible, and only after he has had enough time to reflect on and absorb not merely the notes, but what lies behind the notes. Otherwise he risks doing his homework in, and at the expense of, the public (a frequent occurrence today!).

And perhaps the most depressing aspect of the situation is the fact that this debasement of standards and depth of musical understanding is happening at a time when the cult of the conductor is at its zenith. Like the prima donnas of old, nowadays conductors are lionized and adulated, receive maximum material rewards and maximum media exposure. Possibly because this highly esoteric profession also happens to be a very glamorous one, able to entice and ignite the public imagination, which is dazzled mainly by the visible power that the conductor exerts over orchestras and over institutions. After all, the Italian word for conductor, _Maestro_—which all players, singers and soloists use when addressing a conductor at work—means 'master', and no conductor, however modest, is unaware of his power on the podium. ("Conducting an orchestra is a fantastic experience. Me and a magnificent one-hundred-and-five-horse carriage working together. I can rein them in or release them to go with the music," says Zubin Mehta.) Yet as everybody knows, power corrupts, and absolute power corrupts absolutely. And, as Carlo Maria Giulini has explained, the trap facing every conductor is that the podium—which after all is a technical necessity that enables all the players to see him and his stick—can easily also become a mental podium, a place which he comes to consider the rightful place from which to survey the world. In other words, instead of being the composer's servant, he might be tempted to serve himself.

It is a trap that many conductors have fallen into: some have come out of it again, some remain there, while a choice few have managed to avoid it altogether. This, as well as the depth and extent of their musical understanding and penetration, became immediately apparent during my encounters with them. Which is why I let them talk ... and talk ... and talk and why I have tried to reproduce their speech pattern as accurately as possible, and to preserve its rhythm and tempo even in cases where our conversations took place in a foreign language. Their merits or demerits as conductors are testified to by numerous orchestral players, singers and soloists. But their quality as musicians and as human beings can, I feel, only be transmitted through their own words; and not merely through _what_ they said but also in _how_ they said it. For one of the initial and delightful surprises about my encounters was the fact that they all talk exactly as they conduct: Karajan in one long, seamless line almost devoid of full stops (ideally all his sentences should end in '...' and begin with 'and') and reminiscent of the way that his musical interpretations are free of the tyranny of bar-lines; Solti in short, staccato sentences punctuated by almost audible exclamation marks; Bernstein with great immediacy, sincerity and punch, occasionally digressing from the main point by pursuing a relevant side line.... With one or two exceptions, I have refrained from 'judgements' of any kind, firstly because I don't believe that anyone sitting in a chair in front of a typewriter is fit or qualified to pronounce judgements on artists, and secondly because I know that readers confronted by these men as directly as possible can immediately sense their true value and draw their own conclusions about the level each of them has reached on his journey towards what Wilhelm Furtwängler called the ultimate aim of conducting: "The sensualization of the spiritual and the spiritualization of the sensual."

AUTHOR'S NOTE

Throughout, conductors' first names are used in the context of their childhood and early youth, and surnames in that of their work and careers.

Titles of works are given in the original language, for consistency's sake, even when, as at the English National Opera, for instance, operas are performed in translation. Thus *Mary Stuart* is referred to as *Maria Stuarda*.

In the case of symphonies and concertos, initial capitals are used when the formal title is given, e.g. 'The Mozart G minor Symphony, No. 40', but not in informal conversational references, e.g. 'the Brahms fourth', 'the Mahler ninth'.

To my lasting regret, technical reasons made it impossible for me to include Rafael Kubelik, a conductor I much admire, in the book. I had not realized until too late that Mr Kubelik now spends long periods in California; by the time I did find out, it was too late as my remaining time was already fully committed. This omission of an artist many of whose performances, especially of Schumann symphonies, are still vivid in my memory, is the single thing to do with this book that I am profoundly unhappy about.

Daniel Barenboim is omitted because he did not wish to be included.

As the chapters of this book were written to be read individually as well as continuously, certain general comments about aspects of contemporary musical life and practice recur from time to time.

H. M.
February 1982

COMPOSER-
CONDUCTORS

LEONARD BERNSTEIN
"A Sometime Conductor"

My first interview with Leonard Bernstein is hardly likely to prove instantly forgettable. It was supposed to take place at his suite at the Hotel Crillon in Paris at noon; it was to last an hour, after which I would accompany him to that afternoon's recording session at the Salle Wagram. Or so I thought.

But I waited in vain for three-quarters of an hour, with increasing resentment, amidst profuse apologies from his staff, and was just on the point of leaving when finally he burst, or rather, pirouetted in at ten to one, fresh from his "ballet class with Rudi", clad in baby-blue dungarees and a brown leather cap he had just "stolen" from Nureyev as a mascot. I couldn't resist laughing, which infuriated me. And I couldn't help liking him, which infuriated me even more.

After a few more pirouettes, he proceeded to show us the new dance steps he had just learnt in the first ballet class of his life—the *5ème* and *13ème* positions—and attempted to demonstrate how he had picked up and poised a ballerina on his left shoulder by doing the same thing with his valet, which didn't quite work out. After so much exercise, it was time for a shower. But, he added before disappearing into the bathroom, we could now talk as long as I liked, in the car on the way to the sessions, over dinner during the break, and again tomorrow, if necessary.

So instead of an hour's interview, we ended up having a two days' on-and-off conversation which, unlike the usual formal question-and-answer sessions, was allowed to wander off to personal and general topics as well as purely musical questions. It is in any case impossible to be formal with Lenny, even if one were so inclined. For, unless he takes one of his rare immediate dislikes to someone, he has the gift of creating instant informality and of making easy contacts with people. I feel therefore that the best way of 'putting him across' is to try and capture the unusual, unpredictable and rather disorganized character of our encounters in a way that preserves his speech pattern and conveys the indisputable sincerity and the erratic, slightly undisciplined, slightly self-indulgent but utterly compelling and unique genius of this composer/conductor/ pianist/writer/educator/celebrity. Of course, a life as varied and as turbulent as his and a talent so many-sided that it once caused John Dankworth to label him "the most notable jack-of-all-trades in music today" cannot be contained in a chapter of this size. For which Leonard Bernstein should one concentrate on in the first place?

The conductor with eleven years' experience as Music Director of the New York Philharmonic, the youngest and the first American-born conductor to 'make it' in a big way; the unstuffy, approachable maestro who became as famous for his extrovert, flamboyant podium mannerisms as for his often controversial musical interpretations, who has done more than any other living musician to make classical music accessible to ever-increasing numbers of people, and whose name has become a household word all over the world. That would be the obvious answer. But no, he protests. He is not a conductor. Only "a sometime" conductor. He is an "all-the-time musician".

So on to Leonard Bernstein the composer, with three symphonies,[1] choral works[2], songs and cantatas, ballets[3], three musicals[4], an Oscar-winning movie score[5] and an opera[6] to his credit. A composer who, much to his detractors' fury, remains firmly rooted in tonality and who draws his inspiration from the musical, cultural and emotional characteristics and traditions of his racial and national environment. Few composers, apart from Gershwin, have captured the American spirit and musical heritage as accurately and successfully as Bernstein has, in his musicals, while—another pointer to the essential dichotomy in the man and in his talent—his serious symphonic and choral works reflect the "Jewishness" of his ancestral roots. Yet one of the few records that he is proudest to have made features him neither as a composer nor as a conductor, but as a pianist.

So to Bernstein the pianist, whose recordings of Mozart, Ravel and Shostakovich concertos as well as Schumann quintets and Schubert quartets have been highly acclaimed, and who spent forty minutes at

---

[1] *Jeremiah* (1944), *The Age of Anxiety* (1949) and *Kaddish* (1963).
[2] *Chichester Psalms* (1965) and *Mass* (1971).
[3] *Fancy Free* (1946) and *Dybbuk* (1974).
[4] *On the Town* (1944), *Candide* (1956) and *West Side Story* (1957).
[5] *On the Waterfront.*
[6] *Trouble in Tahiti.*

the piano in the early hours of one morning trying to explain to me the specific difficulties and problems in interpreting Mozart.

Which brings us to Bernstein the teacher and educator, a former Professor of Music at Brandeis University, Head of the Conducting Department of the Berkshire Music Center at Tanglewood, the brilliant communicator and creator of "Leonard Bernstein's Young People's Concerts" through which an entire generation of Americans discovered and grew to love music. These concerts and the talks that accompanied them were conceived, written and presented by him alone, and in a style so unpretentious and seemingly effortless and spontaneous that one had the impression he was just chatting and making things up as he went along. In fact, he worked on each one for hours and days, sometimes doing as many as three or four drafts, until "every comma was in the right place".

Some of these televised talks later appeared in book form as *Leonard Bernstein's Young People's Concerts for Reading and Listening* (1962) which, together with *The Joy of Music* (1959), *The Infinite Variety of Music* (1966), and *The Unanswered Question* (1969), based on six televised lectures he gave at Harvard University, constitute the literary output of Bernstein the writer.

And one shouldn't entirely leave out Bernstein the celebrity, the superstar, the friend of Broadway and Hollywood stars and producers, of writers, playwrights, presidents and chancellors, the Bernstein of "radical chic" fame ("It's a Hamlet-like torture to be truly liberal," he sighed in exasperation after the furore that his party for some Black Panthers caused at the time), the Bernstein on whom the gossip columns of publications which have little to do with music have fed for years.

All those Bernsteins in one chapter? Impossible. They could only be captured, if they could be captured at all, in a thick volume. But that, he announced à propos of a colleague's recently published biography, is something he would never allow. If he lives long enough, he will write his own. "I'll write the whole fucking thing. Tell everything." Until then, I thought it best to concentrate on the Bernstein I met during those two crazy days in Paris, and later in New York, and to let him come across in his own words, in his inimitable, unfailingly effective way.

Hotel Crillon, Paris, Friday, September 14, 1979

After his shower, he emerged in a splendid multicolour striped silk dressing gown, a present from Franco Zeffirelli, and we settled down to a short talk before leaving for the recording sessions. But first he opened the windows, savoured the view of the Place de la Concorde, sniffed the crisp autumn air and exclaimed how much he loved Paris. But, he sighed wistfully, it was sad that he had never been in love here, because "love is what gives you your best memories of a city". Still, he had enjoyed himself and been in a good mood throughout his stay. "There are days, whole periods really, when everybody becomes my friend: flower shop kids, lift boys, just about everyone I come into contact with; passers-by come and shake my hand. And times when nobody comes near me and I feel old and forgotten."

Forgotten? I had just watched a repeat of his televised "Sixtieth Birthday Tribute" from Washington on BBC TV, a glittering occasion packed with his famous friends from two continents. Yet this, he said, had been one of the saddest nights of his life. He was still in anguish and turmoil over the recent death of his wife, Felicia. About a year before her death, they had decided to separate temporarily after twenty-eight years of marriage, but were reconciled again shortly before her fatal illness. So his grief was worsened by a deep sense of guilt.

"The birthday concert was one of the worst nights of my life. One of the most touching too, because everybody came: Yehudi, Lauren Bacall, and that angel, André Previn. It was wonderful to be surrounded by so many close friends. Slava [Rostropovich] ran the whole thing like a dream, and Lillian Hellman spoke wonderfully about Felicia; there was a tribute from Bill Schuman, and Aaron Copland conducted the last movement of my 'Jeremiah' Symphony with Christa Ludwig singing. It was all unbelievable. But it was horrible too, because I had to smile and be gracious when inside, I was feeling rock bottom. At the end, I also had to conduct—one movement of Beethoven's Triple Concerto—and I can't tell you the effort it took. It seemed like I was conducting all six Tchaikovsky symphonies. That was in September 1978, and Felicia had died on June 16th.

"Exactly six months later, on December 16th, I took my children, my sister and a friend of my son's to Jamaica for Christmas and on the day after we arrived, everything changed. The sun was out, we went swimming, water-skiing, we got drunk, we had fun. I slept again, for the first night in six months. Till then, I couldn't sleep at all. Total insomnia, for six months. The kind of insomnia when you can't work, you can't read, you don't know what to do with your body, your muscles tickle and everything itches. But during the day, I slept non-stop, to avoid living. I had fantasies about Felicia, and guilt about whether I was in any way responsible.... And does science know, how does medicine *really* know that cancer can't be caused by some great agony, some great emotional stress....

"Of course, doctors said that I had to stop this, that there is no proof at all that such things exist. But then, there is also no proof that such things do *not* exist. So, I was entitled to my guilt. And I can't tell you what havoc guilt can cause. You can't know. I mean, such a deep-rooted guilt at the death of your most beloved person in the world which, for me, she was. The only person in the world, unique. The most beautiful, the most gracious, the funniest, the smartest; she could also be the most vulgar, she could be the most racée, a wonderful mother, a marvellous wife and companion. Irreplaceable.... And to feel that you may have had something to do with her dying.... I went to psychiatrists, but nothing helped. I thought I was finished. And I was wrong. Now, I feel young again. I feel so good again, after this dancing class! And it all started coming back on that day last year, December 16th.

"We arrived in Jamaica, and for the first time in six months I slept at night. I woke up in the morning to all sorts of *fabulous* smells! I can't tell you what bliss! Those herbs, those flowers, those trees and that sea.... We all rushed into the sea—wow, instant refreshment—we had banana daiquiries on the beach, we got stoned at night. It was Christmas, so we went into town to a black disco and danced all Christmas Eve—'Jingle Bells' to reggae rhythm—I don't know *what* we did! It was all fun, all the time—feeling alive again. But *why* it happened is a mystery. My friends who believe in astrology tell me that it had something to do with Saturn. No, I don't believe in astrology particularly, but I believe in everything, in anything that anybody believes in, because I believe in people. In other words, I believe in belief. I believe in faith. If someone has faith, I identify with them.

"So, June 16th—rock bottom of my life, nadir. People did say that it would take six months—the worst part of it, that is, because, basically, it will take much, much longer—and perhaps I remembered this subconsciously. But anyway, on December 16th I felt alive again. This euphoria lasted through January, February and March. And I happened to be free at the time. I wasn't conducting. I was composing, and although I didn't get much *actual* composing done, I started on a lot of projects, met many different people, went down to Mexico with President Carter and came home feeling marvellous, rested and refreshed.

"On April 1st, there was the opening of Franco Zeffirelli's film *The

Champ and, as I had helped him with the score, I went along to the opening and to a party afterwards and had a marvellous time. And on the morning of April 2nd I couldn't get out of bed. I stayed in bed all day. I thought I must have drunk too much the night before and called it a hangover. But towards the evening I got feverish and couldn't get up for dinner. So, I called my doctor—the nose, throat and ear specialist I see all the time—who found a strange virus in my throat which he said normally belongs in the intestines. So he suggested that I see the main specialist for tropical diseases, who examined me and announced that he had never seen so many bugs in his life. They were simply eating me up in there. They had been colonizing in a cyst ever since that Mexican trip in February, before breaking out.

"So, I spent the whole month of April in bed, and with a huge depression on top of it, because amoebas do have this side effect. Then, very slowly, I started trying to rejoin the human race once again. I came to London in May for that concert you heard—Haydn's *Theresien-messe* and the Shostakovich fifth—but felt very weak. I gave it everything I had, but it was painful. Then, I went to Vienna to open the Festival with the same programme, which was an enormous effort too, because the Vienna Philharmonic consider everything after Bruckner to be modern music and never play Shostakovich, whose works they call 'Soviet brutality', or any other Soviet music for that matter.

"Shortly after that, in June, I started a long tour of the United States, Hawaii and Japan with the New York Philharmonic and during the last week in Japan, little by little I began to feel better, almost human, and the concerts began to be good. Because, up to then, they had not been very good. They are a difficult orchestra, those New Yorkers. They play only as well as you can conduct or force them to play. If you let go even a wee bit, the whole thing falls apart. And that last week, I found the strength to do just that. The last concerts were really remarkable, which is just as well because the Shostakovich fifth was filmed and recorded. So, that was my year; June 16, 1978 – June 16, 1979—the worst year of my life."

By then it was time to leave for the sessions, where we arrived late. He went straight into rehearsal (Rachmaninov's Third Piano Concerto) with the Orchestre National, addressing them in perfect French and warning them that the acoustic in this hall was deceptive. Therefore, he begged them not to count on playing by ear, but to watch him as carefully as possible all the time. As always his rehearsals were friendly and informal but also very precise, to the point, and technically explicit. (Some of the time, he conducted and smoked simultaneously. He is a chain smoker—the reason, perhaps, for that sexily croaky voice of his.) After a few bars, he tapped his baton and said: "I conducted this passage very badly and you played it very badly. Let's try again."

The sessions went on till seven, when we adjourned to a nearby bistro for dinner. He badly wanted a scotch but worried that it might impair his concentration at the evening session, even though he knows the Rachmaninov Third Piano Concerto backwards and loves it "with all my adolescent heart". In the end, he settled for a Ricard and we got down to talking about conducting.

"My problem is that I cannot talk to you as a conductor. Because I am not a conductor. I'm a sometime conductor and an all-the-time musician for whom conducting, like composing, teaching, and playing the piano, is part of the same activity: sharing with people what I feel and what I know about music. And when critics talk adversely about me and say that I overdo, underline and overemphasize things too much sometimes, I have to admit that they have a point. It's true. I do this. When I listen to myself on records fairly objectively—total objectivity is impossible because you are so lost in what you're doing— I can hear me overdoing things, digging out a bass line or an inner voice more than necessary, in order to show it to the public. Because I love that inner voice and I want to share it with them. That's what it's all about, as far as I'm concerned: sharing.

"And it's the same with composing. If I had to sit in a room and compose for myself alone, compose music which I knew no one would hear and no one would like, I couldn't do it. It wouldn't interest me. And it's the same with playing the piano or watching a sunset or hearing a joke. If I'm looking at the sunset by myself, there *is* no sunset. If I hear a joke and cannot share it with somebody, it doesn't exist. Nothing exists unless I can share it. It's a disease.

"Because of this I have a certain sensibility to people and can sense when they have a problem, or read the truth between the lines, with my third ear. And I have a certain gift for psychoanalysis, too, because at times, I've had terrible depressions and various other problems as well. Mind you, I've never completed a course in analysis, because I was never in one place for long enough. But I've tried, I've begun and then had to stop or change psychiatrists, either because they were too dumb, or because they were over-impressed—you know, famous patient, etc.—or because they were determined *not* to be impressed and therefore antagonized me. Anyway, either something was always

wrong or I had to go away or something. But in the process, I learnt a
lot. And I've read a lot, too—Freud, Jung, Adler—and talked to people
about it. But the main thing is that I have a nose for it. My big Jewish
nose smells it when somebody has problems they would desperately
hide, or when everything is not what it seems.

"You may think that I am digressing again, but everything I say is
relevant. And now you can understand why I can't talk to you as a
conductor. Because the mystery of conducting is the same as all musical
mysteries—although, to me, no mystery *begins* to approach the
mystery of getting an idea—and I try to find it out for myself so that I
can share it with people. Many conductors say that it has nothing to do
with transmission, that it's all in the stick. But it's not. Or that it's in
your authority, that you have to control the musicians who have to be
your slaves. I have never used any of these methods. The musicians are
my pals and it's as though we are making chamber music on a large
scale, together, which is why there must be someone to make the final
decision.

"And the reason why I love conducting is that I love the people I
conduct, and I love the people for whom we play. It's a great love
affair, what's going on out there. But it's a mystery because, whatever
happens, it's the most potent love affair you can have in your life. And
it involves over a hundred people. It's incredible when you have over a
hundred people breathing together, pulsing together. It's almost
unbearable at times ... when they are in the mood and this special
something happens. Then, I just love it. And that's the mystery of
conducting, that's your answer: love. We love one another. Every
orchestra I conduct is a love affair. I don't choose them the way that
you would choose lovers. It can be any orchestra: the Vienna or the
New York or the Israel Philharmonic, the Boston, the Philadelphia, the
London Symphony or even a student orchestra.

"But when you get through two horrible rehearsals in the heat and
know that this will be their last concert before the summer break but
succeed in making them *long* to come on stage and play the Mahler
ninth, you earn their deepest gratitude. Because you make them forget
that they are playing in a professional orchestra, where it is so easy for
them to forget why they ever wanted to join it in the first place: because
they loved music. Often, they just sit there and stare, and think of their
union rules. So, to be able to remind them why, brings back to them
that whole gism, that whole almost sexual thing they felt at the
beginning, when they first discovered music, which is very thrilling. I

had just this kind of experience last summer, when I did a truly great performance of the Mahler ninth with the Philadelphians.

"How do I know when a performance is truly great? Obviously I know when it's bad. Everybody knows that. Or if it's just boring, because I suddenly become aware of the lights in the hall or something else in the surroundings. Or if it's just a performance which is not bad, it's fine, but without anything much happening. And then there are those performances which *I* call good, in which all the time I am conducting I feel—without being conscious of this at the time but only realizing it afterwards—that I'm composing the piece as we go along: now, we bring in F sharp, now we bring in the basses, next, the trombones, now we bring in the choir. It's an unbelievable experience, as if I were composing a piece which I know very well on the spot.

"At the end of such performances, performances which *I* call good, it takes minutes before I know where I am—in what hall, in what country—or who I am. Suddenly, I become aware that there is clapping, that I must bow. It's very difficult. But marvellous. A sort of ecstasy which is nothing more and nothing less than a loss of ego. *You* don't exist. It's exactly the same sort of ecstasy as the trance you are in when you are composing and you are inspired. You don't know what time it is or what's going by.

"When I'm composing I live a completely different life, because I'm all alone and I don't answer the telephone and sometimes don't see people for long periods of time. But, at the back of my mind, there is always the potential listener.... I suppose that being a composer makes me experience conducting differently from other conductors. It's not that I understand music better. I'm sure there are many conductors with greater powers of analysis. But my power, no, that's not the right word, my *need* to identify with the composer is so automatic, that his style becomes immediately apparent."

(This, of course, is a debatable point. Many feel that his Dionysian interpretations of the finale of the Beethoven ninth, the finale of *Fidelio* or some of the Haydn masses, are not at all suited to the style of these composers, who manage to contain the most extreme of emotions within a strictly classical propriety. But, as in all matters of interpretation, there is no proof that either he or they are right.)

"So while conductors often tend to boast about 'the' sound of their orchestras—the Boston, the Philadelphia or the Vienna sound—they are wrong to do so. For there is only one sound: the sound of each composer. And when I was Music Director of the New York

Philharmonic for eleven years [1958–69, longer than any conductor in its history], I was very proud of the fact that I turned it into a kind of chameleon: a virtuoso chameleon. As one piece changed into another, the sound and the style of the orchestra changed. And they reached such a point of virtuosity and togetherness and understanding that it was a joy to conduct them."

Back at the Salle Wagram for the evening's session, with Alexis Weissenberg as soloist, Bernstein reminisced about the times when he had played as a soloist in this very place.... The session lasted until after eleven and was followed by the usual playbacks ... only in this case they weren't *quite* the usual playbacks, because in the middle of it all Lenny got a bit bored and started dancing in the control room, repeating all the ballet steps he had learnt with Nureyev for the benefit of the recording personnel, who like the rest of us were in stitches. But he insisted that, as the next morning's session meant that he would miss his class, he had to have his exercise here and now!

Finally, well past midnight, we were ready to leave. Yet suddenly, the incorrigible, irrepressible Lenny perked up in the car and remembered a performance of *Carmen* "in drag" which he had sung in as a kid. Needless to say, this was followed by a demonstration of him singing both the parts of Carmen *and* Micaëla—perfectly in tune.

Back at his hotel, he made straight for the piano, and I asked him whether something he had said long ago was still true: that the most difficult composer to perform, both as a pianist and as a conductor, was Mozart.

"Oh, you mustn't hold me to things I say! Because sometimes, when I'm in the middle of conducting Mozart or practising one of his piano concertos I think, my God, there's nothing more difficult than Mozart. And there are times when I'm playing say, Schubert, and I think that there's nothing more difficult than Schubert. But having said this, it's true, all the same, that I practice longer for a Mozart concerto than for *anything* that I play on the piano."

After slamming the cover of his grand piano at about two a.m., he also had me listen to his début as a singer on record—in a song called 'Big Stuff' from his musical *Fancy Free*—before saying goodnight!

Saturday, September 15, 1979

We resumed our conversation in the car after the next morning's session. I remembered that Bernstein—who was born in Lawrence,

Massachusetts on August 25, 1918—went to Philadelphia at the age of twenty-one to study at the Curtis Institute with Fritz Reiner, and once said that it was then that he first started looking at scores "from a conductorial point of view", whereas until then as a Harvard student where the emphasis was on detailed analysis, he had examined them either from a composer's or from a pianist's point of view. What exactly did he mean by that?

"I meant that I had never before looked at a score with the *idea* of conducting it. Otherwise, I don't think that there is such a thing as 'a conductorial point of view.' There is just the composer's point of view, what I talked about yesterday: the identification with the composer and the effort to get to a point where you know the work so well that you feel you have composed it yourself.

"Apart from this, there are, naturally, many things to be said: I mean, how do I go about studying a new score, for instance, or even a score that isn't new, because in the *real* sense of the word, *every* score is new every time you come to study it. For example, when I took up the Beethoven ninth for the fiftieth time two weeks ago, I said to myself that I would spend one hour with it after dinner, just brushing it up and refreshing my memory before going to bed at midnight. Hah! After half an hour, I was still on page two. And I was still at it at two in the morning, and nowhere near the Finale, mind you. I was somewhere in the Adagio, lost in the stars, because I was finding so many new things. It was as though I had never seen it before. Of course, I remembered all the notes, as well as all the ideas, the formation, even the mystery of it. But there is always something new to find, and the moment you find *one* new thing, it makes other things seem new too, because it alters the relationship to everything else. And you cannot imagine how many new things there are to discover, especially in Beethoven, who was particularly close to God, and one of the most personal composers that ever lived. . . .

"But if I'm dealing with a new score for the first time, I usually go through it as I would through a thriller, a detective story, reading through to see what's going to happen. Oh boy, the suspense of what's going to happen next, what's going to happen *now*? How will the second or the third movement end, how is it all going to come out?

"Then, when I have its basic form in my mind, I start all over again, this time analysing it in detail—not memorizing the notes bar by bar or even phrase by phrase, but just analysing. The memorization comes by itself and the better the score, the easier it is to memorize. Beethoven, for instance. I never have any trouble memorizing Beethoven. Or Mozart. But I had terrible trouble with Mendelssohn's 'Scottish' Symphony. Not with all of it, but with the first and with parts of the last movement, which have spots where you feel that the music could have gone this way, but it could equally well have gone another way, i.e. spots which are arbitrary as opposed to being inevitable, unlike Beethoven's music, which is *always* inevitable: the next bit *has* to come the way it comes, and so does the next dynamic mark and so does the next chord. There is no problem in memorizing that. Therefore, studying is not a question of memorizing, but of analysing the progress, the movement of the music, the way it unfolds. And in doing this, if the score is good, you automatically memorize it at the same time.

'After analysing the structure and the relationship of each component to everything else, you go back for the details. It's endless. And the better the score the more endless it is for studying, as I always discover whenever I return to the Beethoven ninth. [He had just conducted two performances of this work in Vienna, which were recorded and televised, and was full of this work.] I can't tell you the secrets I found in it, especially in the Scherzo.

"I suppose that the easiest composer to interpret from a conductor's point of view is Mahler. And I mean easy in the sense that you can never be in any doubt about what he wanted. Because he tells you so himself in no uncertain terms. Music is very difficult to write down exactly the way you hear it in your mind. But Mahler, being a conductor himself, put in not only many marks like bowings, etc. that a conductor would normally put in, but also a lot of words and verbal instructions, like 'Anmerkung für den Dirigent', 'Nota bene' ... and long paragraphs about, say, if the contrabassoon cannot play this note pianissimo, you could substitute a tuba, and so on.

"At the beginning of the second symphony, there are those *fermate* [pauses] between the figures. And he says that the figures should be rushed and played very fast, while the pauses should be slow, in the tempo of a funeral march because the tempo of the whole movement should be 'funèbre'. But a *fermata* has no time value, so it's really up to you, the conductor. So, as a fellow conductor, he tells you, in words, that he wants those pauses to be in the slow tempo. His is the most annotated music that anyone has ever tried to write.

"Usually, after conducting his works himself, he made all sorts of retouches, but sometimes decided subsequently that he had been right in the first place and crossed out the retouches. People went crazy trying to figure out what his last wishes were. Sometimes he didn't know himself. He changed the fifth symphony thirteen times, because every time he conducted it, he found something else that displeased him: that in such and such a spot, the orchestration was not right, so you should add four oboes to double the clarinets. But the next time he did it, he decided that this was too many oboes and that nobody should double the clarinets. Of course, it all depended on which orchestra he was conducting: if it had weak clarinets, then he would stick in oboes to fortify them.

"Even the ninth, which he never lived to conduct and which is his greatest symphony, is full of wordage. He doesn't just say allegro or allegretto like everybody else, but 'nicht zu schnell, etwas täppisch und derb' ['not too fast, somewhat rustic and robust'] and, as if that weren't enough, he sticks in yet another synonym. He just couldn't stop explaining what he meant, and the ninth, which received its first performance under Bruno Walter, still contains a staggering number of words.

"Take the last page of the ninth: the greatest page he ever wrote and the page which, to my mind, comes closest among anything in all art, including poetry, literature and painting, to portraying the act of dying, the actual experience of letting go, little by little. Well, this last page is marked 'sehr langsam' ('very slow'), and in case you don't understand, he also says 'adagissimo', a word no one had used before, because 'adagio' or 'adagio molto' is the slowest possible speed. Yet between that 'adagissimo' at the top of the page and the last bars there are about seven more verbal instructions: 'zurückhalten' ['hold back'], 'immer zurückhalten' ['always holding back'] 'immer langsamer' ['even slower'] 'äusserst langsam' ['as slow as possible']. And *this* for a page which already began 'adagissimo', i.e. at the slowest possible speed!

"And nobody plays this page slowly enough. Except me. But sadly not on my record, because my recording producer and everybody else in the control room persuaded me that I couldn't do it as slow as that on disc which makes everything sound even slower anyway, whereas the atmosphere of a concert hall would allow me to get away with it. Stupidly I fell for it, and as a result I heartily dislike my record. But something much better is in the can now, because I conducted this work later with the Vienna Philharmonic at the right speed—about which I also spoke a great deal in my Harvard lectures.

"So, what I mean about the Mahler ninth being easy to conduct is the fact that you cannot possibly misunderstand Mahler's intentions.

Yet so many people *do*, because they don't *believe* his instructions, they don't believe the *extent* to which he meant the exaggerations he wrote. When he writes as slow or as fast or as loud or as soft or as powerful as possible, he always means it. But people are always saying that I exaggerate Mahler even more, which is so stupid, because you cannot exaggerate Mahler enough! To play any Mahler symphony, you have to give it your whole heart and body and soul and everything. And you have to take chances. You have to have the courage to play that last page of the ninth, where the music dies away, at a rate of speed which people judge to be impossible, at a speed so slow that you almost cannot follow it. That's the point. Disintegrating. And those silences ... I mean, 'ein Viertel Pause', how do you say in England, yes, a crotchet, can last ten seconds, it gets so slow. Then it holds on and dies away...."

Does Bernstein himself write his own compositions with conductors' possible difficulties in mind?

"As I said, being a composer makes me conduct more like a composer, more like *the* composer of each work, I hope. And being a conductor makes me compose more like a conductor, with more attention paid to problems of performance, unlike Beethoven. In this respect, I'm the exact opposite of Beethoven, who wrote in any old way and left you to bloody well do it, somehow."

His mention of Beethoven in this context reminded me of something I had heard him say at a press conference given by the London Symphony Orchestra in London in May 1979. He was enthusing about his reading of the C sharp minor Quartet, Opus 131 with full strings, because he felt "it didn't work as a quartet!" I had felt highly incensed at the time at what I took to be an unbearably arrogant statement, especially coming from a *composer*/conductor. How does he justify this inteference with Beethoven's intentions, and how would *he* react if 150 years from now some conductor came along and decided to tamper with one of *his* compositions in such a drastic way?

Having heard him conduct the work with the full strings of the Vienna Philharmonic at the Herodes Atticus theatre under the Acropolis during the 1977 Athens Festival (he remembered the occasion well: "What a night! What a moon! What acoustics! What air! I'll never forget it. And a wonderful party afterwards at Michael Cacoyannis's with Melina Mercouri and Theodorakis"), I admitted that it sounded good but that it didn't calm my misgivings.

"You have a point, I know. The Vienna Philharmonic also resisted the idea at the beginning. I have letters from them begging me not to do it. They said, look, *four* people can't do it. Four people go crazy and have to work all year to prepare this quartet, which lasts an hour and has seven movements without a stop, with no place to breathe. It's an exhausting thing to play—with all those cadenzas and recitatives to worry about—how can you expect a whole section to play it? I had letters from viola players saying please, we beg of you, cry off.

'But I insisted, and after half an hour of the first rehearsal, there were tears in their eyes. And I'll tell you something else. I used to have one enemy in the Vienna Philharmonic, that red-haired viola player who always refused to play when I conducted because I stamp about too much and he is nervous and cannot bear my stamping about because it makes dust rise up from the podium and gives him an allergy. So, he would never play for me. But he came to listen to this rehearsal because he is very keen on chamber music, even though he was sceptical and cynical about my adaptation of this quartet. Well, there were tears in his eyes too, and since then, I've never conducted the orchestra without him being there. He is at every concert I do.... And the whole violin section understood everything straight away and played like one violin. We hardly had to rehearse. The piece still sounded like a quartet, a very rich quartet, even when played by sixty strings."

Interesting and incredible though all this might be, it still didn't answer my question about the motives behind his interference with Beethoven's score, about the guidelines to be observed when changing or adapting a work, and about his own reactions to possible interference with his own scores by future conductors.

"I got the idea from Dimitri Mitropoulos. I heard him do this quartet with full strings in 1937, and was greatly impressed. He gave me a whole pile of those old steel 78 records which I played until they wore out. I was very, very moved. I felt I had never heard anything like this in my life. I loved this quartet, and had heard the Budapest String Quartet and other famous ensembles wrestle with it without making it really come off because of that skinny first violin and that skinny second violin trying to come to grips with this piece, which is enormous.

"Beethoven, who at the time was busy writing three promised quartets for money, which he badly needed, thought that he could say what he felt at the moment by writing just another quartet. Only it isn't just another quartet. It's something unbelievable. It stands alone among all the other quartets. I know what I'm talking about, because since the success of this reading, I've looked at some of the other late quartets with the idea of doing them with full strings, in the same way that other conductors did certain movements of the late quartets with full orchestra: Furtwängler conducted the *Grosse Fuge* and Mitropoulos did the Opus 132. But even though I studied all of them really hard, I decided that none of them would work. They are just quartets and shouldn't be disturbed. Only Opus 131 is not just a quartet. And what we did with it, I feel, helped realize it in the way that Beethoven must have heard it in his mind."

Yes, but if so, why didn't he write it differently himself?

"He had been deaf for over twenty years and by this time was also getting quite crazy. He was writing his last crazy music, and although some critics hated what we did, I don't think that we violated the spirit of the work. And yes, if I were old and deaf and crazy and misjudged something in one of my works—I mean, I often misjudge things, but if I were to misjudge a whole work, which should really have been a symphony—then I would be grateful if a sensitive interpreter came along and recreated it for me in a way that fulfilled it.

"And the experience we had with it was so sublime, so incomparable, that I don't know when or if I ever had another like it. It's the record I'm proudest to have made, which is something when you consider the hundreds I have made, some of which are very good and some of which are not so good. But here I am talking about peak achievements. And this record, along with one I made long ago with the Juilliard Quartet—the Schumann Piano Quintet, Opus 44, on one side and the Mozart Piano Quartet, K.478, on the other—is very special. I'm really proud of those two."

I was about to voice my astonishment that both these should be recordings of him as a pianist rather than as a conductor when a friend, the translator of *The Unanswered Question* into German, who was having a drink with us before lunch, volunteered that he would add a waltz from *Wiener Blut* to this shortlist of peak achievements, much to Bernstein's surprise.

"It's funny that you should say that, because while I was recording those waltzes and marches in Vienna, a Viennese friend who was the Assistant Manager of the New York Philharmonic came along to the sessions and was horrified, particularly at what I was doing with the *Radetzky March* and the waltz from *Wiener Blut*. He said that they were much too slow, and that they were never done this way in Vienna. But I decided to stick to my guns, and made the march very slow and very elegant, like a proper military march, because all the time I could visualize a parade with those horses from the Spanish Riding School. And I remember having many letters from people in Vienna saying that, at last, someone was playing this like a real march.

"But my greatest experience with so called Viennese tradition was when, in 1968, I was invited by the State Opera to conduct *Der Rosenkavalier*. I stared at them in disbelief and asked: '*I* should come and do this? I mean, I love it, but it is the most Viennese of operas and full of dialect and local jokes I couldn't possibly understand.' Even the taxi drivers know it better than I did then, in fact, they even *talk Rosenkavalier* dialect. But they insisted that no, I must come and do it. So, being cheeky and chutzpahdich, I agreed.

"And it proved a great experience! And the greatest part of that was the orchestra, who know it by heart and barely look at their scores. So, when I asked for ten rehearsals, they were absolutely horrified and said that they were born already knowing every note and every word of this opera. And they also have all sorts of little traditions which I didn't know about, certain spots like Annina's cadenza, for instance, where the whole orchestra sing, because the singer is usually some broken-down soprano who can't quite make it, so they help her out and it's quite fun. But I didn't know any of those traditions. All I knew was the music.

"And I knew it fairly well, because one of my first jobs as a twenty-five-year-old in New York had been a commission from Boosey and Hawkes to rework the *Rosenkavalier* Suite for Rodzinsky, then Music Director of the New York Philharmonic, who was not satisfied with the existing Suite. So I got to know the piece quite well, going through it and deciding what should follow what in the Suite, but understanding neither the words, nor the subtleties nor the implications of anything. These I learnt from that Viennese friend who was the Assistant Manager of the New York Philharmonic and who sat next to me on trains and planes whenever we went touring, and went through the score with me line by line, explaining every reference, every level of diction and nuance of pronunciation until I really got to understand it.

"And when I arrived at my first rehearsal, the orchestra were furious. But I said that we would start at the beginning and rehearse absolutely *everything*! They replied that this was ridiculous. Well, it turned out that they couldn't even play two bars correctly, the way that Strauss had written them. They were playing by heart, and what they did was so messy and sloppy that it needed a lot of cleaning up and working on details. Because it's the details that make this opera so incredible.

"For instance, I made them play the finale of the first act, the Marshallin's farewell to Quinquin—where she tells him she must now go to church ... and then proceeds to tell him her plans for the rest of the day—very, very slowly. No one had heard it this slow before. But," he added, singing the passage with tears in his eyes, "I feel that this is *the* climax of the whole act, which, like most of Strauss's music, has so many climaxes. But this softest, quietest moment is the biggest climax, the highest tension in the whole act. And little by little the orchestra understood that it was as if they were playing *Rosenkavalier* for the first time, because I made them really *be* the Marshallin and cry with her, instead of just sitting there and playing.

"Then we came to the second act, and the waltzes, particularly the *Herr Kavalier* Waltz, and during the break, one of the viola players came to see me, saying that here in Vienna they play waltzes with the second beat slightly delayed. 'Oh, I see,' I replied. Five minutes later, a second violinist knocked on my door and explained that, here in Vienna, the second beat comes in a little too soon, and is followed by a short pause. 'Ach so,' I nodded. Close on his heels came the principal clarinettist, who said something different again!

"So, basically, they have *no* idea how waltzes are played in Vienna, or rather they have not one but a hundred different ideas! Yet there is supposed to be one way, *the* way that makes a Viennese waltz sound like a Viennese waltz. I listened to everybody very carefully, and even followed around some of those quartets who play waltzes in the pubs but who also have disagreements and just do it the way they feel. So in the end I went ahead and did it my way, the way that I had done it in the first place.

"Because when you have one hundred and ten people sitting there you can't just sit back and let them play the way each of them feels like. So, for the first time in my life I was a really tyrannical and autocratic conductor. I said, 'Now everybody, shut up. I have heard much too much about Viennese waltzes, and nobody seems to agree with anybody. So, we will do it *this* way, and whatever I do, you follow.'

"And at the end of the first act, Strauss's son came backstage sobbing and saying that he had never heard it like this before, and that his Papa would have loved it, but had never dared to do it this way himself, because of all those rules and regulations about no sweating and so on which he had imposed on himself (and which I knew all about from Fritz Reiner)." The public gave him ecstatic, interminable ovations, but the critics were split down the middle—the way they have often been about many of his interpretations.

Our conversation then trailed off to more personal subjects and soon it was time to go and leave him to his translator.

A month later, in mid-October 1979, we met again at his beautiful New York apartment overlooking Central Park. The apartment, which has style, character and is very cosy and welcoming, was, he explained, "all Felicia's taste, everything is as she left it." Soon we moved to the top-floor studio where he does most of his composing and listens to tapes of his recordings and films. He had invited me to sit in while he watched a video of the Shostakovich fifth filmed during his Japanese tour with the New York Philharmonic and, with memories of his recent performance of this symphony in London still vivid in my mind, I readily accepted.

I was not disappointed, even though the London performance was hard to top, "terribly emotional, totally ruled from the heart, but with a lot of intelligence as well", as the principal oboe and Chairman of the London Symphony Orchestra, Anthony Camden, put it. "And, of course, Lenny is such a natural musician that his whole body just breathes music. Technically, he is very easy to follow, except sometimes when the emotion goes away from the baton and into the face and eyes, which is not so easy to follow, but a wonderful thing to be part of."

Bernstein loves this symphony so deeply that even while we were watching the tape, he felt as though he had composed it himself— which, as he explained, must mean that he was satisfied with the performance. And his bar-by-bar explanations were so convincing, elucidating and occasionally self-critical ("wonderful tempo here in the slow movement, slower than I normally take, but wonderful", at the beginning of the fourth movement he complained that he had "started this too fast and left no room for accelerating"), that I regretted that this session of Bernstein-watching-Bernstein was not on film, too.

The next day, I joined him again for a playback of his recording of the Shostakovich fourteenth. Along with Mahler, Shostakovich seems to be one of the composers closest to his heart. His performances certainly point to and reflect a most unusual degree of empathy and identification. While preparing this work, he felt so full of it, so obsessed with it, that he couldn't get away from it for weeks. "For years, Shostakovich had been writing junk, and then suddenly, out came this incredible piece of protest."

The haunting content of the work seemed to permeate the place and colour the mood of the day, which had begun with news that one of his best and oldest friends had died during the night. Death seemed to be all around him at the time, he felt: first, his wife, then a string of friends, now this. Next, he knew, it would be the turn of his old teacher, Nadia Boulanger.* Twice, during the symphony's most despairing moments, he broke down. He managed to pull himself together enough to listen to the rest of the playback, but in the circumstances, I didn't press him for what was to have been our last interview.

On my way home, I found myself reflecting on his career since 1969, when he resigned as Music Director of the New York Philharmonic to concentrate more on composition. On the whole, he has tended to divide up his time more or less evenly between the two: six months spent conducting or touring with a handful of the world's top orchestras, plus an occasional opera, usually in Vienna where he is lionized in that special way reserved by the Viennese only for their special darlings. Otherwise, most of his time is spent composing.

But because the transition from one to the other is always a lengthy and painful experience—for he has to empty his mind of the music of so many composers he has been living and experiencing with every fibre of his being during all these conducting months, and slowly find the voice inside himself again—he decided to put one year aside, 1980, entirely for composition. It proved a fruitful and productive time, and some of the works composed then have already had their world premières.

Halil (the Hebrew word for flute), a Nocturne for Flute Solo, String Orchestra and Percussion, was premièred on May 26, 1981 in Tel Aviv with Jean-Pierre Rampal as soloist and the Israel Philharmonic conducted by the composer; the work had its European première at the Vatican on June 12th, with Bernstein conducting the Orchestra dell'Accademia di Santa Cecilia and the principal flute of the Israel Philharmonic as soloist, and its American première at the Berkshire Music Festival at Tanglewood, with the Boston Symphony and its principal flautist, Doriot Anthony Dwyer, as soloist.

Halil is dedicated to the memory of Yadin Tanenbaum, a nineteen-

* Nadia Boulanger (1887–1979), the well known French composer and teacher, whose pupils include many distinguished contemporary composers.

year-old Israeli boy who was apparently an extraordinary flautist and who was killed in action in the Yom Kippur War. Bernstein had never met him, but his parents went backstage after one of his concerts in Tel Aviv and asked if he would be prepared to write a piece in his memory on commission. He replied that he never writes on commission but that he would bear it in mind if ever he wrote a piece for flute. He forgot the whole thing for about six years, until some time in 1980 a simple flute tune came to him. So, he "fooled around with it" and found that it led to all kinds of very symphonic things, as he explained to the American magazine *Ovation*, and so he found himself remembering this young boy and his parents. "I never knew Yadin Tanenbaum. But I know his spirit," he wrote in his programme notes.

Other recent compositions include a Divertimento for Orchestra, written for the 180th anniversary of the Boston Symphony Orchestra, and dedicated to it and to his mother; *A Musical Toast*, a tribute to the late André Kostelanetz; and *Touches* (Chorale, Variations and Coda) for piano solo, commissioned by the Van Cliburn Competition.

This should be an eloquent answer to some of his detractors—his informal approach, wide popularity and unconventional personality have always earned him enemies—who feel that in recent years he has been "drifting" and become increasingly "irrelevant" in the context of today's music world, whatever that might mean. Such views were echoed by the critic Alan Rich in an article in *New York Magazine* in which he attacked him for the fact that his compositions are firmly rooted in tonality; for not doing more to champion avant-garde contemporary works, and for the standards of his conducting which, Rich feels, are deteriorating (this last judgement based on a perform-ance of *Fidelio* with the Vienna State Opera and one concert of all-American music with the New York Philharmonic). Rich concluded that Bernstein's entire career has been a waste!

Ridiculous, of course. Yet worth mentioning here, because many are puzzled about why Bernstein chose to pursue a "split" career. What they don't realize is that in so doing he is only fulfilling himself and his many-sided talent. "Lenny has now found a magic formula," says Anthony Camden, "because every time he comes back to conducting he starts almost as a beginner and wonders whether he has gone rusty or whether his memory will hold out. And when it comes to composing, he worries about whether there is anything inside him. So he's looking over his shoulder and testing himself in two ways."

A courageous choice for someone who could have gone on reaping laurels as the celebrated Music Director of one of the world's great orchestras and "a sometime composer". Especially so for someone whose farewell words to me were: "I hope you didn't mind my not talking music all the time. But everything I said is relevant. Because I love *people* more than anything. Even more than music.... No, I love music the most. Because that's my way of sharing with people ..." and who now has to spend so much of his time in front of a white page, alone with that "potential listener at the back of my mind".

PIERRE BOULEZ
The Evangelist

"When I was very young, I was explosive," admitted Pierre Boulez—who has called opera houses mausoleums and concert halls museums—when, after witnessing one of his now rare outbursts, someone commented that he hadn't heard language like the torrent just unleashed at an obdurate Soviet piano-tuner since his days with the French army in the war! "But maybe this is the lesson conducting has taught me: that really to have force in yourself, you must not show it. I know the words. I don't use them very often."

It is ironic but perhaps not surprising that this man, possibly the most creative musical intelligence of our time, should have been accused at different times and by different people of being both too violently passionate and too cold. For his is a galvanic personality, at once impatient and controlled, fanatically, obsessively dedicated to his vision of today's and tomorrow's music and tirelessly, ceaselessly searching for the ideal conditions in which it can flourish. Such people inevitably arouse extreme reactions—vehemently pro or vehemently anti—and easily lend themselves to clichés and misunderstanding.

The feverish, sometimes vitriolic explosiveness that prompted the first accusation was much in evidence in Boulez in his twenties and early thirties in Paris when, with that mixture of missionary zeal and crusading fervour so typical of him, he was always attacking someone or something—usually in order to champion someone or something else. Shortly after the war, for example, he was the leader of a faction of booing students at an all-Stravinsky concert at the Théâtre des Champs Elysées. The motive? To draw attention to the then neglected genius of Schönberg. But by the time Schönberg died in 1951, his influence on twentieth-century music had been fully recognized and Boulez decided that he was lionized and overestimated at the expense

of Webern. So he promptly wrote an article in *The Score* entitled
"Schönberg is Dead", putting the dead composer's achievements and
failures in perspective. This piece of vintage Boulez polemic lost the
magazine's editor, Sir William Glock, many friends for several years!

The accusations of aloofness and lack of warmth began much later,
after he had become a conductor and taken over the music directorship
of the New York Philharmonic, and it's hard to pinpoint exactly why;
probably a combination of reasons: his proverbially restrained,
dispassionate manner at rehearsals, where his dogged patience sometimes bores musicians unused to such an intense level of concentration,
unpunctuated by flashes of temperament or attempts to ingratiate
them; the lack of flamboyance in his personal life which consists mostly
of work, work, and more work (Has he ever been in love? a journalist
once wanted to know. "That has happened, yes. One cannot say it has
happened often."); his disinclination to participate in the time-
consuming, draining para-musical activities—fund raising, women's
committees, etc.—that are part and parcel of life as the Music Director
of an American orchestra. ("Sixty per cent of my activity is to do with a
lot of people, so I long to have forty per cent to myself to compensate;
so whenever I can, I put myself in confinement.") But whatever the
reasons, the reputation for coldness grew and culminated in a *New
York Times Magazine* article entitled "The Iceman Conducteth".

Rubbish, of course. Boulez is a devastatingly charming man whose
intellect, enthusiasm and uncompromising personality are enough to
invigorate and stimulate anyone who comes into contact with him. In
the words of his former pupil Simon Rattle, he is "a warm-hearted,
rather traditional man, in fact, who always has time for everybody".
He also has a gift for lasting friendships, mostly with those few among
his collaborators with whom he has a true affinity. "With friends you
have a kind of immediate feeling, a mixture of feelings." And he bothers to
nurture those friendships and keep them in good repair by staying in
touch, wherever he happens to be—often with postcards written in his
tiny, microdot handwriting which can only be read with a magnifying
glass! His hospitality at his homes in Provence and Baden-Baden is warm
and constant: so much so that he gives the impression of spending as much
time and careful thought on tiny, considerate gestures for his guests, as he
does on any of his meticulously planned undertakings.

He is also blessed with a sense of humour—even about himself.
"Thank you for your telegram to celebrate my progress towards
maturity and to wish me many more steps towards this ideal end", was

his reply to birthday greetings from his friend Sir William Glock, then Controller of Music at BBC Radio and the man who first brought him to Britain. Another friend reports that having unsuccessfully tried to persuade him to go to a performance of *Il trovatore*—he *hates* Verdi, whom he calls "repetitious, rhetorical and da-di-dum"—she accused him of not even knowing it. A few days later they both attended the same dinner party and after some good food and wine, Boulez proceeded to sing the whole of Azucena's second-act aria. "You see, I *do* know it," he beamed.

Even his rehearsals are not always the dead-pan affairs they are reputed to be. I remember reading in *The Guardian* some years ago, an account of an episode that happened during rehearsals for Schönberg's *Moses und Aron*. The horns were struggling with a fast passage, high notes followed by low notes and so on, just the sort of thing they hate. A few of these notes have the letter 'U' over them, which means that they should be accented. During a pause for breath, one of the horn players called out: "Mr Boulez, could I ask you something? This thing like a horseshoe over some of the notes—does it mean good luck?" Boulez fell apart.

And while it's true that he doesn't often say thank you to musicians, there are exceptions to this rule, too. After his first concert with the BBC Symphony Orchestra in 1964, he wrote a note saying: "Before leaving London I'd like to express to you my deep gratitude for last night's concert. I enjoyed not only the way you performed but also and not least the effort you made to rehearse in such a short time a programme that was not really easy. Thank you for the music and the friendship. P.B." Years later, in 1980, he ended a rehearsal of his own work *Éclat/Multiples* with the same orchestra by asking: "Any uncertainties? No? And thank you for working so hard all those weekends. I'm very happy." What does all this prove? That all images created by rumours and by the media are almost invariably false.

Boulez's reputation for being unemotional is another misrepresentation. Unemotional people don't get so overcome by their feelings at the funerals of friends—as Boulez did at the funeral of Heinrich Strobel, head of the Südwestdeutscherrundfunk and Director of the festival at Donaueschingen—that they cannot continue with the speech they had prepared. Nor do they cry so violently that they eventually have to be taken away. Nor do they compose works like *Rituels*, a beautiful piece, obviously out of the deepest places, and dedicate them to the memory of dead friends as Boulez did to Bruno Maderna.

But while these accusations of coldness at a temperamental level can summarily be dismissed as nonsense, they are worth more serious consideration when they are directed against his conducting, as they often have been. Boulez's main characteristics as a conductor are precision, clarity and perfect intonation. His conducting is "intelligent" in the sense that it makes even the most complex scores emerge crystal clear, with their structure, instrumental details and continuity between the various sections suddenly perceivable, not only to the public at large but also to other composers who might have been baffled before. "What a refreshing change it is to hear a piece done so that you can grasp how it is written," commented Peter Maxwell Davies after a Boulez concert.

But while everyone is agreed that Boulez does this wonderfully, some complain about the lack of sumptuousness or sensuousness in his string sound, and, according to Hans Keller, BBC Radio's former Chief Assistant, New Music, his "inability to produce a well shaped phrase", in short his lack of "expression". This is fully intentional. For according to Boulez, there is no such thing as expression. To him that is merely adding the superfluous, adding your own feelings to the music.

Boulez has always conducted without a baton, because "it freezes my hands. I've always been like this. I like doing it with my hands, having open hands. And you can be just as precise without a baton. You can indicate the beat in many ways and don't always need to point at people." One of his most characteristic movements is what Glock describes as "a wave-like, undulating gesture which makes musicians instinctively play in long lines without accents. When he wants an accent, but without changing the character of the music at that point, he brings his body into it and makes a forward body movement. This reminds me of a conversation we had during one of the BBC Symphony Orchestra's foreign tours, and in which Boulez talked very interestingly about the difference between German and French rubato: one with the whole body, as it were, the other a swift movement of the arm. There is no doubt that he thinks intensely about these things."

Most of Boulez's chief characteristics are clearly observable at rehearsal: the structural clarity which results from establishing the continuity of a musical idea through the various changes of instrumentation—especially in the composers of the Second Viennese School—is achieved firstly by patient explanation of where every musician's notes came from and how they are linked with what is to follow; secondly, by his insistence on absolutely pure, perfect intonation. "His famous ear seems to connect him to each member of the orchestra by a hundred invisible threads and absorbs every detail so precisely that he is not satisfied with anything less than a hundred per cent perfect", continues Glock. "When he was rehearsing *Le Sacre du printemps* with the BBC Symphony Orchestra, the players nearly went crazy. Yet they were thrilled when it came off because they had neither heard nor played it really in tune before. It's usually about seventy-nine per cent right, because most conductors don't hear this kind of detail. I remember that soon after their entry in the Introduction, the two piccolos have a very difficult passage which I suspect is usually played more or less correctly, but that's all. Boulez asked them to play this passage alone, over and over, until it was absolutely right. Later on, there is a passage where the clarinets and the oboes have the same difficult figure one after the other and the piccolo, clarinet and the first oboe go up to a high F sharp. What Boulez did was to draw the two figures together and have them played in unison, which shows at once whether everything is in tune or not. You may ask, why bother when nobody will know the difference? There are two important answers to that. First of all, the five or six players sitting around the piccolos and oboes will know very well whether it's right or not, and when it is, there is an electric feeling of the musicians surpassing themselves, which is bound to have an effect on the performance in general and on the attitude and effort of the rest of the orchestra. Secondly, even though you may not be able to hear such details in tuttis, when everything is accurately played and not merely skated over, then the texture, the sound as a whole, is bound to be clearer. And this is what always happens with Boulez."

Many professional musicians find his insistence on one-hundred-per-cent accurate intonation annoying, because they feel that this is *their* business, something that players in major orchestras are used to working out between themselves. This is partly why, according to bassoonist John Whitfield who played *Le Sacre* under Boulez with the International Youth Orchestra, some players find his intensely analytical rehearsals boring. "Yet at the actual concert, if he wants to take off, he will. I remember him being astonished that our performance seemed to be working and that every bar was getting a bit faster in a different time beat, and feeling rather excited and carried away by this energy." Boulez admits that he gets excited during performances, but that he doesn't feel obliged to show it. Outward excitement, he feels, uses up inner excitement.

But at rehearsals, he is very much the mechanic, putting things together piece by piece. His ear makes it impossible for him to tolerate any of the traditional "ways around" instrumental difficulties. For example, in Schumann's *Manfred* Overture, there is a very difficult passage with a low E flat for the trumpet, which is usually taken up by a horn. Yet when this was attempted at a Boulez rehearsal, Glock remembers him spotting it at once and saying that while this E flat passage was difficult on the trumpet, it certainly wasn't impossible. "One is left wondering why these habits and subterfuges have become accepted practice among orchestral players and I suppose it is because most conductors don't hear what's going on precisely enough. But while these very high instrumental standards he demands sometimes result in some of the players losing their nerve, the best players are devoted to him, and elated by the extraordinary musical and instrumental discipline he produces." One can therefore understand why one of the principles in the BBC Symphony Orchestra was occasionally heard to remark: 'I think it's about time we had another Boulez servicing!' "

Boulez first took up conducting in the late fifties, mainly for two reasons. A desire to acquire a first-hand knowledge of the difficulties of performing his own works, and a determination to raise the performing standards of works by composers of the Second Viennese School and of today. His conducting career amounted to an evangelical movement on behalf of these works and eventually a crusade to bridge the gap between conventional concert life and the avant garde. Twentieth-century music was in dire need of such a champion. Standards were appallingly low and these works were usually performed in a way that made them seem totally incoherent.

Alfred Brendel, who has played Schönberg's Piano Concerto five or six times with Boulez, found it fascinating that "even with such a master of the twentieth-century repertoire as him, this piece needed time to develop. And it developed in a way that, to me, makes it far more convincing, more natural and even more matter-of-fact than before, without too much frenzy but with the necessary kind of incisive energy. I know both from the pianist who first performed the Concerto, and from Schönberg's assistant in Los Angeles, that the metronome markings as far as they are realizable should be as indicated, and I think that, by developing our performance, we've come quite close to them."

In a totally gripping book, based on several radio interviews, which no admirer of Boulez should be without—*Conversations with Célestin Deliège*—Boulez explained that he remembers hearing certain performances of, for instance, Schönberg's Chamber Symphony, not, according to him, a problematic work, or of Berg's Chamber Concerto, that were "so incoherent, so utterly inadequate, and in which the tempi were taken at such an inappropriately slow pace that I can quite see why the public had their doubts about the music. In fact, I felt the same when I heard some of those concerts. I knew the works from the scores and when I suddenly heard them performed in this way I wondered whether I was not perhaps suffering from some sort of aural squint: when I read the scores I heard the works in a certain way in my mind and found them both valid and valuable; and then suddenly at those concerts I found myself thinking that they couldn't possibly contain any musical substance of interest; I would then return to the music and finally convince myself that the score was right, after all. I could see the reasons for my disappointment, but performances of this kind discouraged a lot of people from ever again submitting themselves to similar experiences.

"What was so pitiful, both with contemporary music but above all with that of the Viennese, was the complete lack of professionalism. Perhaps this is an obsession with me, but if you have to be professional you might as well strive to be the best, and if you have any gifts, you must work sufficiently hard to be genuinely in the first rank and give really good performances. Then you are much more at ease with yourself. As long as one has not completely mastered professional standards, contemporary music will always be a kind of specialization that is always suspect. You can only get it accepted if you yourself are regarded as professionally reliable. If you have been seen working on other music in which everyone knows you cannot cheat, people—and not just the public but musicians, too—will feel confidence in you. It is in the realm of professional high standards that I have largely contributed to contemporary music." Indeed, Luciano Berio remembers that Stockhausen's *Zeitmasse* had very little impact on him until Boulez conducted it in Paris, six months after its world première (December 15, 1956), when he had thought it "a tight, coercive piece, because its elasticity had not been made apparent."

Boulez is convinced that some of Schönberg's works are still performed relatively seldom because most people don't know how to rehearse or cope with them properly. "For works like that need much more than the right gestures or mere intensity and cannot be put together without a thorough analysis of the score. From the purely *technical* point of view of conducting, they are not so very difficult. In fact very few pieces are really difficult *only* from the technical point of view and it's usually works in which there are many changes of tempo—because you are then obliged to be more demonstrative and indicate absolutely everything, otherwise people won't follow you—and pieces with a lot of rubato, because that really is like a change of tempo and again you have to exude great intensity so that everybody can follow you but without giving the impression of being under pressure.

"But as conducting does not consist merely of beating time and giving cues but also of clarifying the score for the audience—both from the point of view of physical balance and from the point of view of perception—if you don't analyse it right, you are simply not doing your job. For nobody can follow a complex work like Schönberg's *Variations for Orchestra* or Berg's *Three Orchestral Pieces* Opus 6 if you don't clarify their structure, or show how their various sections are composed, and if you don't balance them properly. And this task of analysis is the biggest difficulty in conducting. Which is why rehearsals are often more difficult, and in a way almost more important, than the performance itself. For without a good rehearsal, you cannot get a good performance. I am exaggerating of course, in the sense that there are *some* works which don't present very many problems and which, even if rehearsed quickly and not very thoroughly, still tend to come off well at the concert because the energy of the performance itself puts things together and carries them. But most works never come off properly without very long and painstaking rehearsal."

My second talk with Boulez took place after just such a series of long—eight hours a day!—and meticulously painstaking rehearsals with the Orchestre de Paris. The programme consisted of Wagner's *Faust Overture*, Mahler's *Das Klagende Lied*, Schönberg's *Five Orchestral Pieces*, Opus 16 and Webern's *Passacaglia*, Opus 1. It had been fascinating to see him put the latter two works together, strand by strand, tirelessly, with only a moderately disciplined orchestra which found the high level of concentration required a strain at times. So when, after the last rehearsal, he suggested that I go to see him half an hour before the concert, I was surprised and felt uncomfortable at the idea of intruding at such a time. But, as it turned out, he had already been doing a radio interview in his dressing room, from which he emerged sprightly, excited and more intensely communicative than I've ever known him. He was surrounded by dozens of packets and boxes of tea—mostly Chinese and Japanese—and had obviously decided to use the time before the concert for these two interviews to build up steam and energy to concert pitch, thereby saving more valuable time for more valuable things. He talked rapidly, non-stop, and seemed very much at ease. Yes, he had learnt conducting very quickly, in a couple of years, mostly by teaching himself. He was no more gifted than anybody else, and at the beginning, he found it terribly difficult:

"The first and most important thing you have to learn is communication, how to explain what you want, not always verbally, but through gestures. And you also have to start looking at scores differently—noticing all the details and figuring out how to make them work in practice. This kind of analysis came as a surprise at first. Because generally speaking if you are outside the orchestra, you tend to read scores differently. But as a conductor you have to analyse them from the point of view of performance and to find out what things are difficult, or less difficult, or downright impossible to communicate and therefore require you to become part of the communication yourself. Basically you must make a very clear transcript of your image of the work in your mind, and then transmit this to the players quickly and efficiently, without being pedantic or giving them your analysis of the whole score in detail—for they don't require from you *your* work but *theirs*—so that they produce the right sounds at the moment required. And it was interesting for me to observe at a conducting class I once taught in Basle how some students who knew the scores well and were also technically gifted, still could not get through to the orchestra because they lacked this ability to communicate.

"Yes, conducting did bring a new dimension to my work as a composer, and although I wouldn't say that it influenced my actual *way* of composing, it has certainly had an effect on my way of *thinking* about it, and on the way I orchestrate: because as a conductor, you automatically learn a great deal about balance, the weight and register of each instrument and what combinations of instruments would work best for what you have in mind. This gives you a lot of imagination, because it makes you *think* about isolated situations in a score and perceive the various possibilities you might follow from there."

The fact that Boulez is a composer—sadly the only major composer of our day to be a first-rate conductor—makes a great deal of difference to the way he approaches the scores he conducts. Simon

Rattle, who both studied and played in an orchestra under Boulez, who was a "vast influence" on him at the time, remembers that "his way of analysing scores and cutting them down to the bone was very much a composer's way of looking at things". Sir William Glock remembers a friend of his paying Boulez a supreme compliment after an unforgettable performance of *La Mer* at the Edinburgh Festival. "'How marvellous,' he exclaimed, 'to hear *La Mer* without having to think of the sea!' What he meant was that Pierre had approached the music from the *inside* without trying to evoke its title or superimpose images on it. I suppose this must be the difference that being a composer makes to conducting, for it was true of all his interpretations."

For the works of composers with whom he is in total sympathy, Boulez is a wonderful conductor. His interpretations of the Classical and Romantic repertoire are, as we have seen, controversial. (Although I must say that I have seldom heard the opening of the Beethoven ninth sound as profoundly mysterious as under Boulez at the Festival Hall in the mid-sixties.) Glock finds that Boulez's interpretations of Beethoven leave him with the impression of looking at a favourite painting that has just been cleaned and is not necessarily the better for it. "He conducts Beethoven not from the bass, the harmonic progression, but from the top, the structure. But he approaches all Classical works with exactly the same care and attention lavished on his favourites. Throughout his time with the BBC Symphony Orchestra there was never any suspicion that a Haydn symphony, for example, was being glossed over." He has always avoided composers he doesn't like: Verdi, Tchaikovsky, Britten and Shostakovich—he always refers to work of the latter two as "needlework"—and Brahms, whom he considers "petit bourgeois". (On the other hand he is very fond of Schumann.) A propos of neo-classical Stravinsky, whom he also dislikes, he told me that "for me it is difficult to conduct pieces like that because I cannot get involved, so I don't know what to do with them, even though the technical problems are not especially difficult. To put it simply, the relationship does not exist."

Does he consider himself the best conductor of his own works? "For the time being yes, because I know them much better than anybody else. But I don't think that the style of my works is so tied up with my own conducting style that they couldn't be performed by anyone else. Interestingly enough, they are easier to perform now than they were before, because the rising standards of orchestral playing have meant that many technical problems have disappeared. Musicians are now more familiar with this style of composition [serialism] and you can therefore get over technical problems much more quickly. I suppose that our way of *thinking* about this kind of music and about performing it has also changed. I myself now conduct some of my works better than I used to. Because if you return to a work two or three years after its composition there is a certain distance between you and it that gives you a better perspective and enables you to manipulate it better. Whereas works you have just composed are always full of blind spots which are difficult to place in context because you don't yet know how to handle them. But after performing them several times, you know the landscape, you know exactly where you can relax and where you should give out more intensity. Yet there is seldom quite the same bond with works I composed say twenty years ago as with those I have just finished: for while I know that what I am conducting is certainly me, it is not the same me any longer."

Is he more nervous when conducting his own works? "Oh yes, certainly. I am less secure and the whole thing is more difficult. I don't have the kind of distance that I have from other works—for however much you identify with another's work you can never identify completely, except in those very rare cases when you suddenly get a feeling of fusion. But with your own work, well you are there, you are the composer and psychologically this is something quite different. Of course, sometimes I'm also nervous when I conduct standard works which are not part of my usual repertoire; or works which I know to be especially difficult for the orchestra to play; or when I'm not totally confident about the quality of the orchestra. Whereas if I'm doing say Berg's *Three Orchestral Pieces*, Opus 6 with the BBC Symphony Orchestra with whom I have performed it dozens of times, then I'm just normally tense but perfectly comfortable because I know that nothing can go seriously wrong. But if I'm conducting something like Bartók's *The Wooden Prince* for the first time, as I did the other day— a rather difficult work from the point of view of tempo—then of course I *am* nervous because I know that I have to watch everybody very closely and conduct much more intensely than I would if I had confidence." But wouldn't that make for a more electric performance? "No. I like intensity, but I don't like anxiety. There is a big difference between the two!"

I reminded him that he once said "a composer doesn't abdicate his responsibilities when he allows a performer the freedom to choose certain ways of interpreting his work", and indeed he himself

sometimes composes such a choice of possibilities *within* his compositions. But as a composer, what guidelines would he recommend to
performers, and where is the frontier beyond which an interpreter's
freedom may not stretch?

"Generally, I conceive of a composition as a kind of canvas, created
to be respected, certainly, but also to be transformed. The limit
between transformation and distortion is crucial. Basically it rather
depends on the specific works you have to realize: some can be
modified by interpretation and others are absolutely rigid and leave no
room for changing anything whatsoever, like Stravinsky's *Les Noces*,
for instance, which is totally rigid from the rhythmical point of view.
Rhythmic accuracy is so crucial throughout this piece, that if you
changed anything whatsoever you would distort it and lose any chance
of realizing it as it was conceived. But as you point out, this rhythmic
rigidity does not stop every conductor from delivering a different
interpretation. This is because even when the frame, or part of the
frame, of a work is rigid, there are always other aspects—the quality of
sound itself, the accentuation, the kind and amount of energy the
conductor brings to the rhythmic pattern—which are less rigid and can
be emphasized more or less strongly, according to his view. So every
interpretation is bound to be personal and to vary in forcefulness.

"On the other hand there are works like Berg's which allow you a
much greater freedom of interpretation, and there are works like mine
where a certain freedom is actually composed within them and which
leave you room to move, where you know all the possibilities but are
free to choose the one you want at the last moment."

The best example of such a work is *Éclat/Multiples*, originally an
eight-minute score for piano and chamber ensemble, to which Boulez
has been adding fragments ever since! Stravinsky fell under the spell of
this work which struck him as "not only creative music but creative
conducting as well, which is unique". For the conductor's part is
composed just like any of the instrumental parts and is the most
interesting. Everything is controlled not by beating but by cueing, and
every player has to be forever alert, ready to play his group of notes
whenever and in whatever order the conductor decides on the spot. As
Boulez once explained in a talk, the inspiration behind this work was
Eastern music, where, unlike Western music, sound is simply allowed
to die, to be static, instead of being constantly moved from here to
there by gestures. There is no metre in *Éclat*. The conductor does not
beat, but leaves the sound alone. The effect is overwhelming and as the

concept behind this work—my favourite among all his compositions—is so fascinating, I was eager to know whether his own experience of conducting also influenced its conception?

"Yes, certainly. I did not want to have a fixed text, that you play from A to Z every time without stopping and without any difference. I wanted a text that would provide the conductor with the same kind of freedom that a soloist has of not doing the same thing every time. Of course, this poses a great many problems. The system of cueing is tiresome at the beginning because you have to explain to the musicians very precisely what you are doing. In a normal work, you don't have to explain very much: all the conventions are taken for granted by everybody. But here you have to explain first of all how to use the score, and the first rehearsal is always particularly tiring because you have to talk very much, something I rarely do as I normally prefer to get on with the music-making. But in this case I *have* to talk and explain the rules of the game. Once these are assimilated, the whole thing becomes a marvellous experience because each of the musicians doesn't know exactly what will happen; so he is tense. *I* am tense, too, because I cannot foresee exactly what *I* will do, but let it happen spontaneously at the last second, which brings a sort of concentrated suspense to the proceedings. But at the same time, it's a game. What makes it musically a rewarding experience is this aspect of freedom: i.e. if you are feeling flat, you will get a flat performance. Because although there is, naturally, a frame to the work, this is not strong enough to carry the performance. For that, you need something more, something extra, to pick it up: a kind of rapid exchange between the players and yourself, and plenty of adrenalin!"

These rules of the game cannot be explained verbally; they would make no sense. While they concern very simple things, they have to be explained through the score. "The most important thing is that there should be a very quick visual reaction; players should learn to react to cues instantaneously—even if they have something difficult to read—and be prepared to jump like a cat or something. When you watch a stray cat jumping you see how it first prepares its muscles and then hop, it jumps in a flash and is instantly gone. I find that kind of ... Japanese reaction very stimulating. Sumo wrestlers, for example, are quiet, motionless for a while and then suddenly, everything happens in a second! I like this kind of perception and concept of timing and this kind of music-making very much. It is very different from what we are used to and has not been used in Western music before."

Apart from this element of timing, of improvisation and freedom, which he incorporates into many of his works, Boulez's other main characteristic as a composer is his liking and infinite capacity for proliferation and elaboration. He simply cannot leave his works alone and keeps adding to them over the years. In *Conversations with Célestin Deliège*, he explained that he conceives of a musical idea "as a seed which you plant in a compost and which suddenly begins to proliferate like a weed, which you then have to thin out". *Éclat* and *Rituels* are among the many works to which he keeps returning and I sometimes can't help feeling that he is almost trying to hide his original idea, perhaps because it is too personal. It was therefore interesting to discover that this view is shared by Sir William Glock, who knows him well:

"Pierre can't seem to get rid of a work and leave it alone, but keeps returning to it and covering it up, hiding its structure in tendrils and throwing a bit of a smokescreen over it all. The fact that some people say that in his works the structure is everything, doesn't worry him at all. He *wants* to hide the essence, perhaps because he doesn't really like to be known. In fact the Barraults* who are extremely close to him have said how sensitive he is and how many of his tiger-like outbursts are due to oversensitivity."

Or perhaps the explanation may lie in something Boulez said years ago to his biographer, Joan Peyser: "If it were necessary for me to find a profound motive in such a work, it would be the search for anonymity. Perhaps I can explain it best by an old Chinese story. A painter drew a landscape so beautifully that he entered the picture and disappeared. For me that is the definition of a great work: a landscape painted so well that the artist disappears in it."

Boulez was born on March 26, 1925, in Montbrison, a town of some seven thousand inhabitants near Lyon. His father was an engineer and the family typically bourgeois. According to him, neither heredity nor environment played any part in his formation. "It was just a seed; the most important things need no explanation," he told his biographer. He first heard classical music at the age of six, when his father returned from a business trip to the States with a small radio, and his early musical education was very ordinary since, in a town of this size, the only thing a musical child could do was learn to play the piano. At the

* The celebrated French husband-and-wife actor team, Jean-Louis Barrault and his wife, Madeleine Renaud.

age of thirteen, he changed to a more sophisticated teacher in a nearby town.

He also sang in the choir of his Catholic school, where he was a good pupil, top of his class in physics and chemistry, neat, docile and outwardly obedient. Yet inside, he felt completely alienated by organized religion and "its inability to combine an existence of real meaning with formal observances which have lost all their ethical content. What struck me most was that it was all so mechanical. There was a total absence of genuine conviction behind it. It was a parody, and when you are young, you feel much more acutely because you want a way of life that bears some relation to your beliefs," he told Célestin Deliège, who gently pointed out in the book mentioned earlier that in those days there was no sign of the vigorously polemical attitude which later became so characteristic of him.

Yet he found the strength to resist his strict, authoritarian father who wished him to become an engineer and enrolled him for a year's preparatory course at Lyon University. It was at this time that he heard his first 'live' orchestra, saw his first opera, *Boris Godunov*, and met a singer who had sung with Chaliapin and who asked him to accompany her in a recital of arias from *Aida* and *La Damnation de Faust*. She joined Boulez's sister Jeanne in persuading her father to allow Pierre to apply to Lyon Conservatoire. But this establishment rejected him (will it, one wonders, be called the "Boulez Conservatoire" one day, like the Verdi Conservatoire in Milan which rejected Verdi when he applied for a place?), so he studied harmony and counterpoint privately for a year.

In 1943, aged eighteen, he moved to Paris—to rather primitive, underheated lodgings in Rue Beautreillis near the Place des Vosges where he often composed wrapped in a blanket—and enrolled at the Paris Conservatoire. Twice a week, he took lessons in counterpoint from Arthur Honegger's wife, Andrée Vaurabourg, and a year later entered the advanced harmony class under Olivier Messiaen, whose stimulating and enlightened teaching "brought music" to this otherwise stiflingly conservative Conservatoire. Messiaen remembers Boulez as the most gifted pupil ever to pass through his hands, not only in the harmony class but also at the extra-curricular seminar in score analysis held outside the Conservatoire for specially talented pupils, and where Boulez produced an analysis of *Le Sacre du printemps* which surpassed his professor's.

At the beginning, Boulez was overawed with admiration for Messiaen, who had incorporated so many exotic sounds into his compositions, and the two frequently rode together on the Métro. Messiaen remembers his young pupil often being in despair about the sterility of current musical life, worried about the "tired" musical aesthetics then prevalent and anxious lest "music itself would die, for who was there to give it birth?" "You, Pierre," was Messiaen's reply. And, despite his pupil's subsequent partial repudiation of him, Messiaen's opinion has not changed: "Pierre has surpassed us all," he told an Italian journalist a couple of years ago. "For me he is the greatest musician of his generation, perhaps of this half century. I must say that he is a genius." Boulez's cooling towards his teacher as a composer—which didn't stop him from organizing a petition to confer on him a full professorship—was caused by his discovery of serialism (the serial treatment of pitch, i.e. dodecaphony), which became the only possible musical grammar for him. Everything else was out!

Although he didn't know of the existence of serial music until one evening in 1945 when he heard Schönberg's Wind Quintet conducted by René Leibowitz, he had "felt a distinct sense of the need for something like it" when working on some of his first compositions: *Trois Psalmodies* (1945), a Sonata for Two Pianos (1948) and a Quartet for Ondes Martenot,* an electronic keyboard instrument.† He describes that concert as "a revelation. Here was the music of our time, a language of unlimited possibilities. No other language was possible. It was the most radical revolution since Monteverdi, for all the familiar patterns were now abolished. With it, music moved out of the world of Newton and into the world of Einstein. The tonal idea was based on a universe defined by gravity and attraction. The serial idea is based on a universe that finds itself in perpetual expansion." Above all, he wanted to learn how such music was composed and began having regular sessions with Leibowitz.

Throughout his Conservatoire days, he had supported himself by playing the ondes martenot at the Folies-Bergères and when he graduated—with top grades—Honegger recommended him to Jean-Louis Barrault and Madeleine Renaud who had set up their own theatre company at the Théâtre Marigny and needed someone to play ondes martenot and arrange and conduct incidental music. He was to stay for ten years and conduct "with extreme vigour and authority" according to Barrault, ten to twelve minutes' incidental music nightly, by Poulenc, Milhaud, Auric and Honegger among others; he learnt the

* Invented by Maurice Martenot (1898–1980). It became very popular and fashionable with French composers, and eventually was taught at the Paris Conservatoire.
† These three early compositions were later withdrawn by Boulez.

rudiments of conducting and toured Europe and America. He only actually composed music for one production, *Oreste*, and the cast remembers him throwing chairs and beating the rhythm so violently on an actress's back that she burst into tears. But "behind his savagery there was an extreme bashfulness, a quivering sensibility, even a secret sentimentality," says Barrault. "He had an extraordinary personality, a combination of rage and tenderness, was aggressive and possessed by music. Although he was only twenty years old, I made him Music Director straight away (1946), and my wife and I became like mother and father to him and remained that way for over twenty years."

The job was ideal for Boulez at the time: for it occupied his evenings and left him free to compose during the day. Indeed in the late forties and early fifties his output was prolific: *Le Visage nuptial*, a setting of poetry by René Char; the Sonatine for flute and piano; two piano sonatas, the first of which was dedicated to René Leibowitz. When the latter started criticizing it, suggesting changes and corrections and marking the score with red pencil, Boulez screamed, "Vous êtes merde!" and stormed out, never to be reconciled to his former mentor.

In 1953, Barrault gave him use of the Petit Marigny, a little theatre with a capacity for two hundred at the back of the main building, free of charge, so that he could launch a modest series of chamber concerts of twentieth-century music. This venture, called the Domaine Musical, was Boulez's launching pad and made a name for itself. Boulez chose the repertoire, invited the musicians of his choice, organized the concerts, handled finance and even arranged the music stands (in this he still frequently gives a hand, undeterred by considerations of 'position' or other such *folies de grandeur*). The works performed were by Stravinsky, Bartók, Debussy, the Second Viennese School—between 1954 and 1964, sixty per cent of the combined output of Schönberg, Webern and Berg was played—and contemporary works by Varèse, Messiaen, Stockhausen, Maderna, Nono, Cage and, later, Berio. But despite, or possibly because of, the fact that the Establishment was hostile to the Domaine and the programmes planned by Boulez were usually much too long, the venture took off and attracted both the avant-garde and the chic. Boulez was already becoming the leader of the avant garde all over Europe with his compositions, his polemics and crusading spirit. But at the beginning, he did very little conducting at the Domaine. This was mostly left to Hermann Scherchen and Hans Rosbaud, both specialists in contemporary music and among the few conductors capable of performing twentieth-century works in a way that did them justice. But the fact that they were both in their sixties filled Boulez with panic. So he decided to become independent of any indispensable people by taking up conducting himself.

But even though the motive behind his conducting career was evangelical, at the beginning he found himself intoxicated by his new profession. He learnt fast, partly by watching Rosbaud and Scherchen but mostly just by doing it: at the Domaine, in Cologne, at Donaueschingen, in California while on tour with the Barraults. In 1957 he decided to leave the Barrault company, which had moved to the Palais Royal and was now physically separated from the Domaine at the Salle Gaveau, judging that he couldn't spend the rest of his life conducting incidental music. The following year he was one of the three conductors in Stockhausen's *Gruppen*—along with Maderna and the composer—at Cologne; next came a concert at Donaueschingen where he substituted for Rosbaud and, despite technical shortcomings, electrified the audience with a programme consisting of Berio's *Allelujah* and Bartók's *The Miraculous Mandarin*. At the time, he had no intention of ever conducting the classical or romantic repertoire. But as the works he had chosen to champion require a great deal of rehearsal, he began having to "buy" this extra rehearsal time by agreeing to conduct some of the standard repertoire as well. Then, as he explained to his biographer, things began to snowball: "there is such a need for conductors today that if you are just a little bit gifted you are sucked into the machine."

But before this began to happen, his long-standing admirer Sir William Glock, who had first brought him to London for a concert with the Domaine, approached him with the idea of a series of concerts with the BBC Symphony Orchestra. The list of works Boulez was interested in was very short: some Stravinsky, some Schönberg, Webern and Berg, some Debussy, Haydn's Symphony No. 104 in D major ('London'), Schubert's Symphony No. 6 in C major. But he was persuaded to add a few more works. Some of the concerts took place in the studio, some at the Festival Hall and one, with Ashkenazy as soloist in Chopin's E minor Piano Concerto, in Worthing. (The idea of Boulez conducting Chopin is so unthinkable that it isn't surprising to learn that afterwards he confessed to Glock that he'd felt like a waiter who keeps dropping the plates!) At the time, he was not well known in Britain as a conductor. In fact somebody asked Glock, "Who *is* this Boulez anyway?" to which he replied: "In terms of what we are trying to do with this orchestra, he is simply the best conductor in the world."

Events proved Glock right, for the series was so successful that Boulez was promptly invited again, both to the next season's Proms and to the BBC Symphony Orchestra's tour of the Eastern American seaboard where his concerts at Carnegie Hall took New York by storm and are still talked about in some circles. Glock confirms that, as in those early London concerts, this was Boulez at his best: "I honestly don't think that things were ever better. Everything was fresh and new to him, he was fresh to the orchestra and still in love with conducting and with those pieces which, under him, sounded quite different from the way they usually did. The way he got the continuity in Webern through the constant changes of instrumentation, for example, was incredible, and the players felt the difference; for Webern usually sounds like a senseless succession of different weights which don't connect, and the players don't connect either." ("Like tennis played by too many people, without rules and without a lined court", is the way Boulez himself describes the average performance of Webern works.)

So it was not surprising that when Colin Davis announced his intention to leave the BBC to become Music Director of The Royal Opera House, the job was offered to Boulez, as from 1971. He stayed for four very happy and musically fulfilling years, during which he offered London audiences a rich, varied and always adventurous diet of concerts, some at the Festival Hall, some at St John's, Smith Square, and the most avant-garde at the Round House, as well as Proms at the Albert Hall. He aimed to give each season a distinct profile, and described the policy behind the programmes to Peter Heyworth of *The Observer* as "perspective—i.e. the cantata through the ages; prospective—i.e. an exploration of everything going on in contemporary music; and retrospective, aiming to place the works of a neglected Classical or Romantic composer, or the seldom-performed works of a famous composer, in context".

He was fortunate to have the full backing and support of Glock throughout his tenure. "Why are you sixty-three?" he sighed in despair when Glock was due to retire in 1973. The two had met in Baden Baden in 1955, four years after Glock had put his head on the block by commissioning from him the "Schönberg is Dead" article for *The Score*, and got to know and like each other during the late fifties. "I like working with people with whom I can communicate easily and on a very precise level," says Boulez, and their collaboration was warm and cordial. "We never battled or anything like that; it was more like a game of tennis," reminisces Glock. "Our goals and attitudes were harmonious, and we had complementary views about some aspects of programming: Pierre, being essentially a pedagogue, always wanted seasons of something—Haydn and Stravinsky, for example, or cantatas or something that people would remember, while I preferred mixing things up, and liked programmes that were symmetrical, like sandwiches, starting with something from the past, then a very daring work in between and then back, in a way. Pierre hated that, although he occasionally put up with it. He liked his programmes to unfold in a straight, crescendo line: once they had got to the Bartók or Stravinsky, they had to go further. They never turned in on themselves, they weren't crescents, or circles or curves or whatever you like to call them. Usually I would draw up some suggestions and take them to him for discussion or modification. I remember his shocked silence when I suggested his own *Éclat* coupled with the *Symphonie fantastique*. But after being momentarily taken aback, he thought for a minute and said, 'Ah, yes, it will be an evening of orchestral virtuosity and original writing for instruments!' So he accepted it. As long as there was a theme, a rationale or consistency behind two apparently madly chosen works, it was all right by him.

"Of course he wanted not merely to do something enterprising, but also to get good audiences. Any fool can get so outré that he gets no audience. But that wasn't his aim and we spent long, long sessions trying to guess what programmes, which combination of works, would be authoritative as well as enterprising enough to draw 5,000 instead of 2,500 at the Proms. And we often succeeded. One night, the Albert Hall was fuller for a programme consisting of *Gruppen*, *Le Sacre du printemps* and the *Drei Bruchstücke aus Wozzeck* than for *Fidelio* on the following evening. I remember writing this to Pierre, who was staying at his home in Provence at the time, and getting a charming postcard back: 'We must go on!' It was always a crusade.

"But trying to find the psychology behind reasons for attending concerts was fascinating, and we spent a long time looking for such combinations, little discoveries, that worked better than others. Once, for instance, we had a packed house at the Albert Hall for a programme consisting of Sibelius's Fourth Symphony, *Pierrot Lunaire* and *Le Sacre du printemps*. Had we had the Sibelius followed by *Erwartung*, not less good a work of Schönberg's, and *Petrushka*, not less good a work of Stravinsky's, the house would have been half-full. Can you guess why? No? Probably because both *Le Sacre* and *Pierrot Lunaire* are more myths than works, and known even to people who don't actually know them, if you know what I mean. So they *must* come. Something like that. But finding these sorts of combinations that compel people to come rather than split the audience, means all the difference between failure and success. You can't live on myths alone, and Pierre was always infallible about what wouldn't work."

Before his first concerts at the BBC, Boulez had made his operatic début when he conducted a historic production of *Wozzeck* at the Paris Opéra in 1962, at the invitation of its Director, the composer Georges Auric, who had been one of the founding members of the Domaine Musical. This had always been one of Boulez's very favourite works. When Horenstein had conducted it in the early fifties—in French because of the anti-German feelings still prevalent at the time—Boulez had written to fellow composer John Cage that he found the piece "more and more remarkable in its complexity, at times indecipherable, resembling a Labyrinth without Ariadne's thread. He will have fifteen orchestral rehearsals and I shall do my best not to miss one. It should be quite an event and I am elated beyond belief!"

When Boulez came to performing this work himself he asked for and got thirty rehearsals. The production was a triumph and at the end of the opening night, the entire orchestra rose to applaud him. (Although Boulez is not applause-crazy in any way, he does miss it when it's not there. Friends remember a concert in Warsaw with the BBC Symphony Orchestra, when there was some organized opposition in the audience and the applause at the end was not acclaim. Boulez felt this and was seldom seen as restless and unhappy after a concert as on that occasion.)

As far as his choice of the operatic repertoire is concerned, he is guided only by his own preferences. "As it's something I do very occasionally, I choose only the pieces that please me. That's all." In the late sixties, he conducted an unforgettable production of *Pelléas et Mélisande* at Covent Garden. But before that, in 1965, he accepted Wieland Wagner's invitation to conduct *Parsifal* in Bayreuth, and eventually *Tristan und Isolde* on the Festival's Japanese tour. The rapport between the two men was such that Boulez says that had Wieland lived, he would "certainly never have accepted the music directorship of a symphony orchestra, but would have concentrated on doing more operatic work with him. But life is a matter not only of choice but also of chance. After Wieland's death I was discouraged from doing further operatic work until I found Patrice Chéreau." The two collaborated on the controversial Bayreuth Centenary production of the *Ring* in 1976, and the historic Paris Opéra première of the completed three-act version of *Lulu* in 1979.*

Chance would have it that shortly after being offered the chief conductorship of the BBC Symphony Orchestra, Boulez was also invited to become Music Director of the New York Philharmonic, as from the 1971 season. Many had tipped him as Georg Szell's successor at the Cleveland Orchestra with which he had been having a close and successful association since 1967. But the offer from New York intervened and against the advice of many friends and colleagues, he accepted. The workload he was about to impose on himself was harrowing, but as he told Glock, who begged him "not to make himself an exception to the rule that conductors live to be as old as Titian", "I sleep fast!" However, this meant that henceforth he would spend four months in London and four in New York, which, as far as cities go, he loved. (After his return to Paris in 1978 to become the founding Director of the Institut de Recherche et de Coordination Acoustique/Musique (IRCAM) he bought himself a pied-à-terre in a thirty-storey modern building because it gives him the feeling of being in New York!)

This also meant less and less time for composition, much to the dismay of many of his admirers, including Otto Klemperer and Lord Harewood. Before too long, anguished phrases began to crop up in letters to friends: "finally I am struggling to compose. January, February and the early part of March were dreadful. I become more and more impatient by the fact that I have so many ideas unfulfilled and unrealized when life is passing so quickly...."

Yet he accepted the job fully aware of what it would mean in terms of hardship on all levels. First of all he had to train the New York Philharmonic and acquaint it with many facets of contemporary music. The most important things he had to emphasize were precision, pitch control and rhythm control, all of which required very long, very hard hours of work. This is perhaps why some of the musicians felt bored and depressed by his rehearsals, especially after so many years of Bernstein's more informal and extrovert manner. But he thinks that this extra precision also benefited their performances of Classical works.

His principal aim, however, was to change the musical tastes and habits of New York, just as he was trying to do in London. After very successful visits to Boston, where he gave the first US performance of Berg's *Three Orchestral Pieces*, Opus 6, fifty years after its composi-

* Act 3 was completed by Friedrich Cerha.

tion—which, he said, amounted to "mental retardation"—and Los Angeles, where he sensed a malaise concerning the stiffness of current concert life, he was convinced that "the time is ripe for deep and significant reforms. And we are here at the right time to create, with the BBC, a model of what could be a new conception." The experiment was beginning to prove quite successful in London, and he hoped to export it with equal success to New York.

"After that, anyone can do it," he told Peter Heyworth. "But if I don't, I fear that nobody will—that's what's so distressing. And that's why I've been invited by both the BBC and the New York Philharmonic. It's not because of my ability as a conductor. There are plenty of conductors as good as me and some who are much better in parts of the repertoire. But it's the ideas I want to put into practice that count. I want to create conditions in which the music of our own time can once again be an integral part of concert life. That's a creative task and that's why I accepted it."

Achieving his aim proved much harder in New York than in London. For unlike London, which has five major orchestras sharing out the repertoire between them, thus offering music-lovers a good chance of hearing the programmes of their choice, New York has only one resident orchestra, the Philharmonic, supported largely by a subscription system. In a way, this can be a great advantage for artistic independence, for it enables the management to choose its repertoire free from financial considerations, i.e. the need to fill the hall. But in the long run, if one systemmatically antagonizes the subscribers, they will simply stop subscribing. And to some extent, this happened under Boulez.

During one season, the orchestra had to advertise for subscriptions, for the first time in years. Gradually, Boulez was persuaded or pressured into conducting a much wider repertoire than he initially desired or envisaged. "What makes you think I conduct modern music?" he replied, with a touch of bitterness, when someone asked why he had put on weight despite conducting so much modern music.

But while the general view seems to be that Boulez ultimately failed to change the attitudes and tastes of the New York musical public, he feels that his work there can never be completely undone. "By the end of my eight years people were at least *staying* to listen to contemporary works rather than leaving the hall. Now, maybe it goes a little back, but it can never be quite the same again. Had I been only a conductor, I would have stayed much longer, say ten or twelve years, and then maybe things might have changed more drastically. But my main business is composing, so as soon as I had showed the way, it was time to return to my real work.

"At the beginning, I found conducting quite fulfilling because I was discovering new ways of doing things, of making works sound the way I wanted them to. Now I no longer make any discoveries of that kind. I'm not complaining. I learnt a great deal from conducting. But I certainly don't want to spend a large slice of my life doing it any more. Being a composer, dealing with creative things all the time, there comes a point, after having conducted those pieces forty, fifty times, when you have simply had enough. Which is why I won't conduct very much in the future."

Since leaving New York to become Director of IRCAM in Paris in 1978, Boulez has limited his conducting appearances to a few concerts a year, mostly with the Ensemble Inter-Contemporain, a group of IRCAM-based musicians whose performances of twentieth-century music are exemplary, and occasionally with the BBC Symphony Orchestra, and has also limited his repertoire to those works close to his heart. But before looking at the origins and aims of this institution, and what it meant to Boulez, I wondered whether, looking back on his conducting career, he could remember any of those unforgettable moments, when everything sounded even better than he had imagined?

"Yes certainly. There have been some moments of ... extra-special excitement, let's put it that way. Certain performances with orchestras—like the BBC Symphony Orchestra or the Cleveland—which I like very much, were really very exciting: a performance of *Le Sacre du printemps* in Cleveland, Bartók's *Concerto for Orchestra* with the BBC and *Daphnis et Chloé* with the New York Philharmonic still stick in my mind because through everybody's excitement, and through *my* excitement, suddenly there was a kind of experience, a fusion, which you don't often get in a concert. You try to do your best every time, of course, but sometimes—let's put it that way—it clicks better."

One day in 1970 Boulez was on holiday at his house in Provence and received a telephone call from the Elysée Palace inviting him to dine alone with President Pompidou and his wife. Since 1959, when he became resident conductor of the Südwestdeutscherrundfunk, Boulez had been based at a three-storey house in Baden-Baden, to which he is devoted and will never sell. (In fact its linear, clean, modern décor,

Mies van der Rohe chairs and fully electronic kitchen are sometimes used as ammunition by those who argue that his musical interpretations are mechanical and cerebral!) There is a part of him that feels a profound affinity for the German psyche, and a remark he made to an American interviewer in 1963 (reprinted in his biography) is interesting in this context: "For me the external shock value of music matters little. The work I find really important is the one that has a kind of metaphysical truth, a truth in harmony with its time. An artist must be able to speak for his time in language of both precision and freedom. The trouble with 'beautiful' and 'ugly' as criteria is that they are tied up with superficial pleasure. I know I'm Germanic in this respect because I find sensual pleasure only a rather limited part of music. That is quite un-French isn't it?"

Boulez had had no contact with official France since 1966 when the then Minister of Culture André Malraux dropped a plan for a thorough reform of French musical life which Boulez had drawn up at the request of his Ministry. Boulez swore that henceforth he would have nothing to do with his country's official cultural life. But since then he had become a great conductor and a universally respected figure, whose visits to Paris at the head of foreign orchestras were greeted with rapturous welcomes: BOU-LEZ-A-PA-RIS, BOU-LEZ-A-PA-RIS, shouted a large section of the audience after a BBC Symphony Orchestra concert. Outside, someone wrote on the BBC bus: "VIVE BOULEZ!" So, the President wondered whether there was any way of inducing this great Frenchman to return to France. He explained that he was planning a huge Arts Centre at the heart of Paris, in which naturally he wanted music to play a big part. Would Boulez be prepared to consider heading the musical section of such an institution?

He replied that first he would like to examine the musical plans in detail, and these were duly sent on to him in America. He summarily dismissed them and wrote down his own conception of a musical research unit in great detail. Pompidou accepted this and agreed to the unit being housed underground since there was not enough suitable space in the main Arts Centre building, even though the construction costs then amounted to £6,000,000. Boulez's other conditions—that the unit was to be entirely international and independent of the Ministry of Culture, and that it should be granted the status of an independent foundation allowed to receive outside donations on top of its £2,000,000 per annum State subsidy—were also accepted. He therefore agreed to head this institution, due to open in 1977, and relinquished his positions with the BBC Symphony Orchestra in 1975 (but continued as Principal Guest Conductor for a further two years), and in New York as from the end of the 1977/78 season.

For Boulez IRCAM was "a kind of dream which has become reality". For he is convinced that music can no longer move forward without science. The problem, as he explained to Peter Heyworth, is that today's ideas are more advanced than the materials composers are working with and therefore new materials must be developed. He compares the state of music today with that of architecture at the end of the nineteenth century, when it was at a dead end and only able to imitate the past and dish out pseudo-Gothic, pseudo-Renaissance buildings. But once concrete, glass and steel became available, they imposed new laws of construction implicit in those materials, which automatically made it impossible for one to make a Gothic capital out of them. So it is with music which is still using materials—"both scales and instruments"—that were devised between the sixteenth and eighteenth centuries. "Now there is a need for new materials. When we find them, I believe they will bring about a transformation in music as drastic as concrete, glass and steel brought to architecture." He believes that without new resources, today's composers are locked in a ghetto from which they cannot break out. In short, they need the help of scientists and researchers into the field of acoustics, audial psychology, and computers, harnessed to the service of music. This is what IRCAM is about. (Boulez likes to draw a parallel with the great revolutionary and innovator of the last century, Wagner: "he didn't only compose, he built an opera house and created the conditions in which his own music could be performed.")

The underground building houses an elaborate network of studios, laboratories, a completely sound-proof room, and a hall, the *espace de projection*, where concerts and other events take place. Everything in this hall—the floor, the panels on its walls—can be moved to create different acoustic conditions. The formidable computer section is headed by an expert called Jean-Claude Risset; Luciano Berio is in charge of electronics and the Yugoslav composer Vinko Globokar looks after the department of instruments and voices. The artistic administration is headed by a young Englishman, Nicholas Snowman. But although all these departments are more or less autonomous, a great deal of administrative work and organization falls on Boulez's shoulders. Sometimes his friends fear that he has as little time for composing as he did during his days as a music director in two cities, and occasionally one can detect a note of disenchantment with his "dream". But until he, or any other composer, produces a great work which could not have been created without the resources and facilities housed in the IRCAM, one cannot tell whether this will prove an instrument of freedom or merely another gilded cage.

But if you are made in a certain way, you must always go on. "It is even stronger than my will, it is quite unconscious." Yet is it not a terribly lonely fate to be born a visionary, a pioneer, a twenty-first-century man, to have to endure the resistance of more backward-looking people, to suffer articles like the ridiculous "The Iceman Conducteth", in which he was attacked by some of the less enlightened among his own musicians whom he nevertheless had to face and continue to make music with the next day?

"No. You don't feel lonely. You feel involved in something important, and I don't call that lonely. You are lonely if you have nothing in your head, if you are empty and without thoughts. That's awful. But this very crowded loneliness is very important. Sometimes, of course, you would like this course to be quicker and without so much effort.... But after a while you become accustomed to that and say well, you know here's where you must give your strength in order to achieve something. Nobody achieves anything without a great deal of contradiction and a great deal of resistance, and once you know this you just accept it as part of the game."

Epilogue

Boulez's major new work Répons *had its world première at the festival of contemporary music at Donaueschingen in October 1981, to universal rave reviews: David Cairns wrote in* The Sunday Times *in October that "with this new work ... Pierre Boulez ends a silence that lasted virtually with no interruption for seven years. Apart from a couple of minor pieces, there has been nothing from him since* Rituels, *composed in 1974. The task of setting up and administering IRCAM seemed to have absorbed all his energies.*

"There were those who saw the whole elaborate, expensive exercise as a cover up for the loss of his powers; and the tenor of the statements that issued from this institution (e.g. 'the problems of musical creation are no longer open to solution by individuals') seemed only to confirm his critics' fondest fears. Boulez, the quondam creative force, had sold out to the machine. Répons *puts a stop to such scepticism. It answers in*

the most decisive and luminous fashion the question whether Boulez the composer had any more to say and whether any good thing could come out of IRCAM. It makes use of the machine, but in such a way as to leave no doubt who is in command.

"One understands now why he waited. The new technology had to develop to a point where it could be really useful, and he had to learn how to write for it. In particular the invention by IRCAM's technicians of a computer of exceptional rapidity, capable of performing two hundred million operations in a second, placed in his hands a potent means of transforming sounds by enlarging them, varying their colour, pitch and rhythmic patterns, or prolonging them into an endless series of receding mirror-images—in fact what amounts to a new instrument, at once obedient and of an infinite scope—an Ariel submissive to the will of the composer-magician.

"Indeed, there is nothing 'mechanical', nothing forbiddingly futuristic about the work. It seems to me that Boulez has never written music so relaxed (though no less cogent), so genial, so—I almost said—traditional.... Répons gives the sense of an artist sure of his powers and his means and revelling in the new possibilities he has created for himself."

The twenty-minute-long work will have a second part—otherwise Boulez would no longer be Boulez!—and a performance of the complete work was announced for the 1982 Proms.

VIVE BOULEZ!!

ANDRÉ PREVIN
"A Sometime Composer"

A few years ago, a Hollywood director accompanied by a composer of film music went to hear André Previn conduct the Beethoven ninth at the Royal Festival Hall. After congratulating him, the two went out to dinner and the director remarked how much he had enjoyed the performance and how good the orchestra had been. "Yeah sure," replied the composer, "but isn't it extraordinary how André has screwed up his career? He hasn't scored a film in over fifteen years and how much money could anyone possibly make by conducting the Beethoven ninth?"

"You must agree that the point of view is almost irresistible," chuckled Previn during our first meeting, at his beautiful Surrey farmhouse.

Ironic, too. Usually, it's the other way around. It is the serious musical establishment who hurl supercilious remarks at Previn and who for years refused to accept him as anything more than a lightweight figure. After quitting Hollywood in 1960, it took a long time before he was asked to conduct anything more substantial than Gershwin or Cole Porter, and even longer before he landed a Music Directorship: Houston in 1967. Even after he moved to Britain, took over the London Symphony Orchestra and made the hugely popular BBC Television series, "André Previn's Music Night", which went on for six years and made him a household name, many still persisted in thinking of him as "The Poor Man's Leonard Bernstein".

So for a long while it seemed that he could please neither God nor Caesar. His much publicized divorce from his first wife, Dory, romance, marriage and subsequent divorce from Mia Farrow, plus his 'trendy' image and informal, unstuffy approach to orchestras and audiences alike, were ideal gossip-column material and enhanced the highbrows' misgivings towards him. A lot of it was sour grapes, of course. Yet as late as 1976, after his appointment as Music Director of the Pittsburgh Symphony Orchestra was announced, *The New York Times* acknowledged the existence of prejudice against him in the States by heading an article about him with the question "Can André Previn Succeed Despite Success?"

A great deal that happened since then has helped to dispel the lightweight image with which Previn seemed stuck. During their 1978 European tour he and the Pittsburgh Orchestra were showered with critical praise; he has since become an annual guest conductor of the Vienna Philharmonic, with whom he is also recording the complete orchestral works of Richard Strauss. His and Tom Stoppard's joint venture, a play in which the orchestra plays a vital dramatic part, *Every Good Boy Deserves Favour* (1977), enjoyed a huge success and was adapted for television. He is currently engaged in composing a piano concerto for his friend Vladimir Ashkenazy, for whom he has already composed two sets of virtuoso preludes: *The Invisible Drummer* and *Pages from a Calendar*. (Other compositions include a Guitar Concerto for John Williams (1971), a Cello Concerto (1968), some violin pieces for Itzhak Perlman, a song cycle dedicated to Dame Janet Baker as well as two musicals—*Coco* (1969) and *The Good Companions* (1974) and masses of arrangements of film music, four of which won Oscars.*) Recent compositions include *Principals* commissioned by the Pittsburgh Orchestra and *Reflections*, commissioned by the Philadelphia Orchestra.

But he stresses that he is a conductor who sometimes composes— not the other way around. "The difference is vast. There were people in musical history whose genius was so in command of them that they wrote music simply to get it out of their soul, regardless of whether anybody would ever hear it or not. I haven't even the faintest pretensions to that kind of drive. I have no ambitions for my music to be played a hundred years from now, either. I just want it played next week. I am happy to put pen to score-paper on occasion, but always with a purpose—i.e. someone has to ask me to write something specific for them."

The only exception to this rule was the song cycle which he later dedicated to Dame Janet Baker. The songs were based on some poems by Philip Larkin, which he was so mad about that he wanted to set them as soon as he read them, even though he didn't know whether

* *Gigi*, *Irma la Douce*, *My Fair Lady*, and *Porgy and Bess*.

anyone would sing them. On other occasions when he felt the urge to compose without a specific request, his instinct proved wrong: "I recently read one of John Donne's sermons to the Earl of Carlisle, and it affected me more deeply than anything I had read in a long time. So with the kind of ego that goes with sometime-composers I instantly decided that I wanted to set it. But when I examined it carefully, with an eye to that, I suddenly realized that it was already so perfect, and the cadences of its language so musical in themselves, that if anyone were capable of equating this in music, it was certainly not I.

"Because a conductor who spends ninety per cent of his time with very great music can have no delusions about approaching the level of those great composers. If immortality is what he is after, he should not have chosen conducting as a profession. Because despite recordings and video-cassettes, conducting is totally ephemeral. And once you come to grips with this fact, it's all right. I remember one of my idols, Eduard van Beinum, once saying in a lecture that twenty-five years after a conductor's death, all that is left of his life is anecdotes. Cynical but true. In some cases like Toscanini's or Furtwängler's, some of their recordings have survived as collectors' items. But the repertoire is constantly being re-recorded by the conductors of the day who interpret it with the insights of their time. And this is fine by me."

But although he is convinced that composition is not his passport to immortality, he finds it very helpful for conducting, because "the ability to fill a piece of paper with notes gives a different perspective to conducting and a more personal attitude towards the hieroglyphics of music and the mystery of music." His virtuosity as a pianist has also proved a valuable asset because the ability to make sound is a reminder of what great artists orchestral musicians are.

"It is important to remember how difficult playing an instrument is and to know what it feels like to be responsible for the fact that when your finger goes down, that note comes out. Which is why I think that when Ashkenazy or Barenboim or I conduct, the players know that many times a year we also take the gamble of playing ourselves, instead of simply standing on a podium week after month after year saying, 'No, do it this way because....' I was once on a three-week tour with the Pittsburgh Orchestra and played three Mozart concertos—nine performances in nine different cities—and during one of them I had a momentary memory loss in the middle of a cadenza. Luckily, as I had improvised it anyway, I managed to improvise my way out of it without the audience knowing. But the orchestra knew, because they had heard it before. And nothing I had done in three seasons made them as kindly disposed towards me as that moment. They realized that I, too, knew what it was to be in a cold sweat of fear. And I did, and I do, and I will, know.

"Because to put it in simplistic terms, if the conductor gets lost, the orchestra will usually put things right without anyone being aware of anything amiss. But if an oboe player gets lost or a string breaks, it's catastrophe. Which is probably why ninety per cent of all musical anecdotes are anti-conductor stories. (And I love telling them!) The point is that it is not possible to be a charlatan pianist or violinist or oboist. But it *is* possible to be a charlatan conductor, because you don't physically produce the sound."

While he accepts that there is an element of mystery in conducting, he shies away from all the "mystique" that surrounds it, because he feels that the two are often confused by people eager to make too much of something which after all is "just a profession and neither the priesthood nor a calling". But he hesitated after saying that and added that, in a way, perhaps it is.

"I don't know whether it is some kind of extra-terrestrial gift. But I do know that a conductor is ultimately as good as his orchestra. Some people can train an orchestra brilliantly well; others can just leave an orchestra alone to play well and some conductors actually interfere with good playing. But it's basically an egomaniacal profession. It has to be. Here you have a man insisting that a hundred players, each of whom has played that particular work more often than he has conducted it, do it the way *he* wants. That takes a particular kind of temperament anyway. But getting them to do it is a mystery, I suppose. Because neither threats nor cajoling will do it. They either decide in a kind of mysterious mass decision to do it his way, or they don't."

In that case, I wondered what made him want to be a conductor in the first place, and he replied that he was afraid that the answers would sound rather pompous, "but if you feel that your particular love, no, not just love—all musicians love music if they are to spend their lives practising and pursuing it and being underpaid, overworked and overtravelled—but *need* for music stretches beyond the range and repertoire of one instrument, then you have to turn to the orchestra. This, of course, involves you in a lifetime of never catching up with great works, but of simply running after them and seeing if you can get a bit closer. If that satisfies you, if that's what you want, then you ought to be a conductor. Doing it because you realize that you cannot be as good a pianist as Ashkenazy or because you think it wonderful to stand in front of a hundred men, tell them what to do and take the bow at the end—don't laugh, a lot of people do—is misguided."

He accepts that one of the drawbacks of the profession is that the orchestra is the one instrument that cannot be practised in private. Conducting can only be learnt in public, and often at the expense of the public! True, he replied, but this is never at the expense of the composer. And he disagrees with Bruno Walter who said in one of his two books that one shouldn't conduct the Mozart G minor Symphony (No. 40) until the age of fifty. "Because although an experienced orchestra may not play the Mozart G minor Symphony as transcendentally under an immature conductor as they would when guided by someone with a true vision of it, they will nevertheless not play it so that Mozart is the loser. And this is the point I'm trying to make: the endless fascination of conducting lies in the fact that the music is invariably greater than a performance, than *any* performance of it.

"I once tried to explain this to some students at Tanglewood [Summer School] using as an example the fact that every major American city has at least one amateur orchestra made up of doctors. (I don't know why, but it seems that a lot of doctors play music for relaxation.) And they give an annual concert, which is always pretty grim, yet, in a way, almost endearing. Now I said to those kids that while the Brahms fourth played by 'x' city's Doctors or Used-Car-Dealers Symphony may be devastatingly terrible, Brahms still doesn't lose out. Quite obviously he's going to win with that symphony whether it's played totally wrong or phenomenally well. *He* is still better. So being allowed to conduct pieces badly before you learn to do them well is never at the expense of the composer, which is all that matters. It's at *your* expense. But that doesn't matter."

Previn wanted to be a conductor almost as far back as he can remember. Born into a well-to-do, musical Jewish family in Berlin on April 6, 1929, at the age of five he was taken to hear Furtwängler conduct the Berlin Philharmonic, and returned home literally feverish with excitement: "I don't think that I decided on conducting there and then, but in some childish and amorphous way I knew that what I had witnessed was going to be part of my life. My father, who was a very good pianist, naturally assumed that I would be a pianist too. So for years I studied and studied and studied the piano and didn't come into conducting until much later when, after getting involved in the commercial media and starting to write music for films, I decided that I might as well conduct it as well. But between that and *real* conducting lies an enormous gulf."

Throughout his childhood there were weekly recitals and chamber-music concerts in the library of the Previn home, with André crouching under the piano and following the proceedings. In the thirties, the family saw the writing on the wall and fled to Paris leaving all their possessions behind. They stayed with relatives who had already settled there, and André continued his piano lessons. At the age of ten, he won a scholarship to the Conservatoire, but shortly after that, the family emigrated to America before the outbreak of the war, with the help of their close friend Jascha Heifetz.

His father, a lawyer qualified only in German law, was forced to earn a living as a piano teacher. Fortunately André's precocious musical talent enabled him to earn his own pocket money by doing all kinds of odd musical jobs: demonstrating pianos in department stores, accompanying silent movies in a cinema showing historical films and playing the piano at various jazz clubs where, he reminisced to his biographer, Edward Greenfield, he was driven to and collected from by his family, as he was still too young either to drive or be let out alone at night.

He says that like most exceptionally gifted children, he had an odd childhood in many ways, but especially because he didn't have to make any conscious decision about his future: his talent decided for him. When he sees the children of friends who even at the age of seventeen can't seem to make up their minds about what they want to do, which saddens him, he realizes how lucky musicians, or people with a specific talent, are: "because a person whose life is music usually knows that from early childhood. We never go through phases of wanting to be firemen or sea-captains or whatever. And we all tend to have an odd childhood, because it is directional long before most children's childhood has any sort of direction. We know what we are going to be doing at age ten, and everything we do is a half-conscious preparation. Which doesn't mean that we don't play at school or enjoy films. But it does mean that our life has a kind of nucleus and is somehow pre-disciplined. I doubt that you could find a musician, except some singers, who decided on a musical career at the age of eighteen."

Previn was barely fourteen when he started work at the film studios, orchestrating and arranging scores. This meant leaving school at three-thirty, taking three buses to the studio and returning home at seven-thirty, to do his homework and orchestrate tomorrow's film music. Gradually he earned enough money to study composition with Mario Castelnuovo Tedesco, and at the age of eighteen, he was given the task of composing a film score himself. Although he had been conducting local youth choirs at informal concerts on and off, this was his first chance to conduct a professional orchestra. "It was as though someone were holding a great sign up saying, 'Yes, this is what you should do.' A moment of both clarity and unadulterated happiness. At that moment I thought that whether I make it or not, whether I turn out to be any good at it or not, this was what I wanted to do."

Soon after that he was drafted into the US army, but posted to San Francisco where he not only had the opportunity of conducting an army band, but also the chance to have lessons with Pierre Monteux, the celebrated Music Director of the San Francisco Symphony Orchestra. His admiration of Leonard Bernstein, now one of his closest friends, dates back to those days, too, when the latter came to conduct the San Francisco Symphony. He confessed to Edward Greenfield that he was bowled over by Bernstein's mesmerizing podium presence and tried imitating him at his next lesson with Monteux. "Ah, you have been to see Mr Bernstein", nodded the old man knowingly. "Now do it again." At the end of the lesson he added: "Dear boy, before you try to impress the ladies in the mezzanine, make sure that the horns come in!"

After the army, Previn returned to Hollywood where he composed, arranged and/or conducted the music for dozens of films over a decade. At the same time, he recorded a series of best-selling LPs as a jazz pianist. And although he is defensive about his "misspent youth" in Hollywood, he also admits that he learnt the rudiments of conducting there: making sure that the right notes got played, keeping it all together and the judicious use of rehearsal time—even though the music concerned was either third- or tenth-rate.

"When I say that I am defensive about my past, I mean defensive in relation to myself. I have no regrets about having done film music. It taught me a lot. But what I'm sorry about—and like all retrospective realizations, there is nothing to be done about it—is that I did it for too long. When I finally left, both geographically and spiritually in 1960, it was pretty late in the game and I was thirty-one. I should have had the courage to do it earlier. That's what I'm sorry and defensive about. But as my colleague who thinks I have screwed up my career demonstrates,

Hollywood is a pretty insular place and once you find yourself working there, you don't believe that anything really important could be happening outside the film industry."

He spent the next seven years "bouncing around the States conducting third-rate provincial orchestras which I didn't even know existed for a pittance, to gain experience. As a late starter, he was grateful for the training and the exposure. Gradually the orchestras became less obscure, the engagements less far-between, and the pay less nominal. In 1967, after conducting the Houston Symphony Orchestra for the first time, he was asked to succeed Sir John Barbirolli as its Music Director. He liked the orchestra but loathed the city and did not get on with the Board of Directors. Eventually after being appointed Principal Conductor of the London Symphony Orchestra in 1968, and spending more and more time in Britain where his film past was not viewed with quite as much suspicion, he resigned.

The LSO appointment meant that his career finally took off. He stayed with them eleven years, during which time he toured all over the world, recorded over a hundred LPs, and became a popular television figure. Yet the orchestra's Chairman and principal oboe, Anthony Camden, remembers that his appointment was greeted with a tremendous amount of criticism from within the orchestra. "But it was an enlightened choice and in many ways he did a wonderful job for us: he pulled us right to the forefront of British musical life—there was nowhere we couldn't go with him after those television programmes. It was also a very wealthy time for us, following a period under István Kertesz when we were almost bankrupt because although he was a marvellous musician and conductor, he lacked audience appeal and couldn't fill a hall.

"Musically, Previn (who incidentally started his duties on the same day that I did) stamped us with a style of his own, but possibly a limited style: we played the Russian and English repertoires extremely well—our Prokofiev got a standing ovation at the Kennedy Center in Washington—but neglected the German Classical and Romantic repertoire. We just were not that kind of orchestra at the time. But he boosted our morale sky high and was very popular with most of the players, because he didn't go for any of that bullshitting distance. He was only happy when he was one of us, travelling on our coach and, on free evenings, sometimes playing a bit of jazz at nightclubs, incognito, in dark glasses."

Previn admits that he took over the LSO with only two years' experience as a Music Director and no experience at all of European orchestras. Therefore, his aims were partly "essentially selfish": ensuring that he acquired a repertoire wide enough for British orchestras who, unlike their American counterparts who play each concert programme four times, play two or three different programmes each week, plus recordings, which accounts for their versatility and unrivalled ability to sight-read scores. It also accounts for their tendency to get bored easily.

"Suddenly I was faced with a London concert on Thursday, one out of town on Saturday and another one on Sunday, all with a different programme, so I had to work like a dog to enlarge my repertoire. On top of this, I had no experience. So taking me on was a very generous gamble on the part of the LSO." But this inexperience may explain why he didn't spend much time improving the quality of orchestral playing or devoting more time to the Classics and the German repertoire in general.

Despite the television exposure, and the lucrative recording contracts, his detractors, both inside and outside the orchestra, accused him of popularizing classical music at the expense of quality. "I hate the word 'popularize'—an extremely Americanized word—and besides I've never ever thought of myself as doing that. I don't think that music needs it. The only thing I tried to do was to make it available and accessible to people who live in places where there are no concerts; to people simply not used to hearing music; to people who cannot afford the price of concert tickets; to people who may feel that they would be out of place in a concert hall, or who for whatever reason have no access to concerts, and can therefore only be reached through television.

"I don't know the number of people who may have turned their sets off, but I have been told of the number who left them on—a very heartening figure. And if I said something lighthearted or even surfacey that helped them listen, that's fair enough. I don't think that I've ever been guilty of performing great music with lack of sufficient care or serious intent—either in public or on TV. But if the talk on the periphery was lighthearted and didn't make people uncomfortably aware that they were being taught something, that's also fair enough."

Previn attributes part of the enormous appeal of these programmes to his enthusiasm. It pains him to think that there might be people on earth who don't respond to music and he feels a compulsive urge to help, because he thinks that like playing, "listening is a developable talent. I have been as guilty as anybody of going to a concert to hear a familiar piece and sitting in the audience, as you would in a warm bath—which is very nice and pleasurable, except that you are merely listening to the piece without really hearing it. There are many ways to help people really *hear*. The ideal way would be to teach small children to read music automatically at school, which would later lead to an extraordinary unlocking of what's in a score. They would be able to see the structure of the music and listen actively rather than passively. Until such times, though, I feel that TV programmes like ours helped raise the quality of listening. And if it takes the occasional, however clumsy, verbal imagery—and by that I don't mean saying that here Beethoven is describing a waterfall, which would be unbearably patronizing—that's perfectly all right with me."

The success of the television programmes ensured that almost all his concerts with the LSO were sold out, and attracted new audiences. Yet at the same time, a certain faction in the orchestra was unhappy because despite their recording contracts and new 'star' status, standards of orchestral playing were actually deteriorating. The Philharmonia Orchestra, then being rigorously trained under Muti, as well as other London orchestras, may not have had so much publicity, but were ahead of the LSO in terms of quality. The rumblings of discontent culminated in an ill-considered and abortive attempt to oust Previn in 1975, when the newly appointed manager, John Boyden, sacked him without first clearing it with the orchestra, which is self-governing.

Anthony Camden says that although one of Previn's few drawbacks was planning—which with him was very last-minute and therefore sometimes difficult to carry through, "in fact I have never really felt that there is a master plan for André Previn's life as a conductor—he was always extremely well liked by most of the players. And when the management decided to sack him, the orchestra rallied ninety-nine per cent behind him, turned on the management and said: 'You don't behave this way to our conductor. Either you reinstate him, or you have no orchestra.' And, having reinstated him, we sacked the Management and gave him a new contract, on the basis that he was a man of stature who had achieved a lot and who, therefore, was not to be treated like garbage.

The orchestra's Vice-Chairman, Kurt Hans Goedicke, who shared some of the musicians' misgivings about the direction in which the LSO was heading, but who nevertheless was outraged at the way Previn was treated by the management and rallied to his support along with his colleagues, explains what these fears were: "One had reached a point when one knew that Rome would fall. It had to. Because we had been going consistently in one direction and in one direction only, and, as an organization, we were beginning to become painfully aware—not just from within our own sentiments and feelings about what an orchestra like this is about, what it used to be about, what it was about now and what it *should* be about in the future—but also through outside people. For instance, we were unable to attract the services of this or that eminent conductor because there was already a 'tint' to us that had developed over the last eight or nine years. And we had also missed out on a substantial chunk of repertoire that no symphony orchestra that regards itself as truly international can do without, and cannot do without doing very *well*. So we felt that we could not neglect our long-term future for the sake of financial security. So the ideas and thoughts behind the move were perfectly sound and legitimate. But the people who were left to put it into practice were totally unsuited and ill-equipped to negotiate delicately, diplomatically and honourably, and this rallied all of us around André, who is generally very popular with the orchestra, and an extremely nice person." But inevitably, there was a lot of unpleasant publicity—the 'scandal at the LSO' even reached the gossip columns of the daily newspapers—with each faction brandishing its arguments and washing its dirty linen in public."

"The whole thing was a series of unfortunate events," Previn comments. "What was interesting was that while the management had every right in the world to get rid of me, they went about it in the wrong way. If they wanted to fire me there must have been a way to get rid of me. But not *that* way. In fact, it strengthened my relationship with the musicians. The few players [including the orchestra's Chairman, Howard Snell and others] who had tried to engineer the coup were not my favourites anyway, and most of them have now gone." What has remained is a warm and strong relationship with the orchestra, which he regularly guest-conducts every season, as their Conductor Emeritus since Abbado took over as Principal Conductor in 1979.

In 1977, Previn was appointed Music Director of the Pittsburgh Symphony Orchestra, much to both his and the orchestra's surprise, after a guest-conducting engagement. Unbeknownst to him, the Board had been looking for a successor to the ailing William Steinberg, who was about to retire, and who had lost his enthusiasm and fire for the job because of ill health and his wife's death. Previn liked the orchestra, which he considers to be the most "European" of American orchestras, a point of view shared by the European critics during their tour of 1978. (He finds it amusing that this should be so, because the LSO, on the other hand, is undeniably the most "American" of British orchestras, with a brilliant sound and sharp, incisive attacks.)

When he took over in Pittsburgh, the orchestra had neither recorded nor been to Europe for ten years. Nor had it explored any new repertoire for a long time. "So although it was basically an excellent orchestra, it was getting a bit sloppy. The musicians were demoralized, lacked pride in their orchestra and were simply doing their job, trying to maintain the status quo. I explained to them that there is no such thing, that an orchestra which tries to do that in fact gets worse. It can only stay as good as it is by constantly improving. Of course, my task was made easier by the fact that by then I had thirteen years' experience as a Music Director." (But having learnt how to operate within the framework of British self-governing orchestras, he now had to unlearn that and exercise the full authority of an American Music Director, which is considerable.)

His basic aims were to restore the orchestra's pride; to reinstate annual seasons in Washington and New York; to take them to Europe and eventually everywhere; to start recording; to put them on television. And, he points out, all this has already happened. The orchestra now has a permanent home—Heinz Hall—and as far as extending its repertoire was concerned, he did a lot of research, studying the last decade's programmes, noticing the gaps, and what had been played too much. He discovered that they had played very little French music, no English music at all, except for the odd performance of Elgar's *Enigma Variations*, and lamentably little twentieth-century music. And while they had done Beethoven and Mahler endlessly, there had been no Haydn, and Mozart had been left to the orchestra's chamber groups. He also noticed that principal players had seldom been used as soloists. So he concluded that it was "fairly easy to make up seasons that were interesting for the players and included a British Festival, a lot of Messiaen, a gradual Shostakovich cycle and several dozen Haydn symphonies".

As far as actual playing is concerned, his first goal was to teach them how to play a greater variety of dynamic shades. "It seemed to me that they had forgotten how to play a real pianissimo, and that their dynamics ranged from a kind of mezzoforte to fortissimo. I begged them and screamed and cajoled and worked on getting transparent playing so that you could hear the woodwind and all the inner voices clearly. The other thing which I have always been extremely conscious of is rhythmic accuracy—even in pieces that are not outstandingly rhythmic." Although all this required a considerable change in the orchestra's style of playing—especially in works they had played often, like the Tchaikovsky symphonies, where the strings used to indulge in masses of *portamenti,* or the Beethoven and Brahms symphonies in which the woodwinds were always doubled—it was achieved without having to replace more than eight players. The season is now fully subscribed.

Previn feels that his aims concerning orchestral playing represent the essence of his conducting style. He doesn't believe that there is, or that there should be, such a thing as a conductor's sound. That would mean doing music a great disservice. It should always be the sound of each particular composer. But having said that, he admits that it is true that every conductor has specific priorities regarding orchestral playing and these affect the results: "Karajan wants everything to sound so beautiful, and by God it does; Solti wants it to sound kind of feverish, and it does. I want everything to sound dynamically interesting, with great attention paid to the gradations of dynamic range, and I want the inner workings to be rhythmically clear. [Actually so do both Karajan and Solti.] And the end result is that it automatically sounds beautiful too, because you can suddenly hear everything. A *tutti* that gets so loud that everybody is simply playing as loud as they can, becomes a meaningless roar—except in some of the Prokofiev symphonies where you need just that."

Another of his chief characteristics as a conductor is confirmed by many soloists who have worked with him, but especially by Vladimir Ashkenazy—the meticulous preparation he puts into the orchestral accompaniments of concertos. "Indeed, I have made myself a villain with many orchestras by insisting on an inordinate amount of rehearsal time for concertos, working out the accompaniments to the solistic parts. Because things like the slow movement of the Beethoven Violin Concerto are very difficult; so is the whole Sibelius Violin Concerto— not technically, from the point of view of beating it, but making cohesive sense of it and going upwards from there. If we are playing the Tchaikovsky Violin Concerto I will find out what the soloist wants, adjust, and everything will be fine. But if we are playing a Mozart Violin Concerto, I will probably want double the time because I want everything—the phrasing, the curve of the line, the structure of a movement, to be unanimous, a co-operative effort. For no one could convince me that Mozart or Beethoven considered the orchestral parts of their concertos less important.

"From the musical, as opposed to the purely technical point of view, I would say that I have a romantic approach to conducting rather than a scholarly one. I like a certain amount of improvisatory elements at the performance and don't mind if it is different from the rehearsal. It depends on where you are and how you feel. This is the whole point of a 'live' performance. Otherwise, buy a record. But to do away with scholarliness altogether would obviously be a crime. People never used to do repeats in Mozart symphonies—which is absolutely necessary— and they played Mozart with too large an orchestra. This aspect of scholarliness is something I believe in totally."

Another thing that Previn has learnt over the years—or at least hopes that he has—is not to overconduct, and not to overcue. "There are moments, not always readily apparent to the listener, where you have to be extremely accurate and give solo players or entire sections cues for entries. But the beginning of an obvious flute solo, say in the Brahms fourth, is not one of them. The flute player doesn't want you pointing at him for Christ's sake. He knows. And you know that he is a great player who has played the piece more often than you have conducted it and all of a sudden there you are, pointing at him. What for? It's almost insulting. He knows where he is and if he doesn't you'll find out soon enough. But conversely, there are moments when everything seems to be going on swimmingly but when you have to be extremely accurate. And those things you don't learn at the Conservatoire. It just takes years of work."

Apart from the LSO and Pittsburgh, Previn also regularly conducts the Chicago Symphony and the Vienna Philharmonic, with whom he has celebrated several birthdays. He says that while all the great orchestras have the reputation of being difficult, he has never found them so—with the exception of one, which he refused to name. He had heard that the New York Philharmonic were dreadful—and they weren't. He had heard that the Chicago were as tough as old boots— and they were charming. He had heard that the LSO were conductor-killers—and he loved every minute with them. He had heard that the Vienna Philharmonic were intrigue-laden—and they couldn't have been more generous. "I love them. They make the most ravishingly elegant sound. It's not the world's most *precise* playing, if you are used to Chicago, who have this immense, ceaseless brilliance and can play absolutely anything. Nothing is technically beyond this orchestra or beyond any player in it. And this is the reason why it and the Vienna and the Berlin Philharmonic are so fabulous. Because the last stand of the second violins could be a concertmaster. And that's incredible. So, it's simple. If orchestras like you, they play well. If they don't, they are difficult."

As Anthony Camden has already pointed out, Previn is very popular with orchestras, for the simple reason that he is an extremely warm man, informal, unpretentious and natural. He lives in the Surrey countryside with his twin sons from his marriage to Mia Farrow. As he finds children on the whole "smarter, nicer, funnier, more loving, more intelligent and more interesting than most adults", he tries to be with them almost every moment of his free time. His adopted children, who are very young, live in America with Mia Farrow, and although the two are now divorced, they try to spend Christmas and vacations together so that all the children see each other.*

He did not resent his first wife Dory making public all her emotions and pain after their divorce in her long poem/song, because it was "very talented writing. If she had told it to the *Daily Mail* or some magazine, I would have sent the Mafia after her. But if it takes the form of talented writing, that's perfectly okay. She had a lot of problems which, in solving, she needed to make public, and that was perfectly all right." They agreed that she should keep a big slice of his considerable collection of mostly American paintings—a collection good enough to be lent to museums for exhibitions, because it had been her knowledge and enthusiasm for pictures that opened up his eyes to a lot of things he hadn't appreciated in painting before. (Now he has stopped collecting because of the prohibitive prices. But shortly before our second meeting, he had seen a small portrait by Derain while on tour with the LSO in Switzerland which haunted him so much that he had to have it and sold a first edition of Joyce's *Ulysses* which he had acquired thirty years previously, in order to get it!)

His basic niceness is obvious at all his rehearsals, which are informal, funny "on the periphery" but dead serious as far as the actual music-making goes. He has a very quick wit and a way of turning a joke around, even if something is his own fault. "I think that rehearsing is very much like making chamber music, but with a lot of people.

---

* Previn has since married glass-cutter Heather Hales.

Because the best way to play chamber music is with friends. Then you can argue and discuss and correct, and if you have a bad idea it doesn't do any harm. You try it, see if it works, and if it doesn't, you forget it. Whereas if you had to make chamber music with total strangers no matter how wonderful, you might still want to impress them."

In recent years Previn has matured a great deal as a conductor and finds that scores which had earlier seemed forbiddingly difficult now seem accessible, while those works which he considered easy enough to tackle become more and more problematical. "Since interpreters of any kind are always under the creative people, we conductors have the chance of growing within a lifetime into music that seemed like a mystery earlier on. Pieces which were complete anathema to me ten years ago I can now interpret with conviction. A lot of this has to do with confidence and technique: feeling sure that you can analyse and figure the work out and then make the musicians play it correctly. The Schönberg *Variations for Orchestra* are an example of what I mean. Ten years ago, I didn't do them, because I didn't think I had the technique to get the piece straightened out. Now, it doesn't bother me.

"Some works are on this level. But there are other works of which one is simply frightened. For instance, I don't think that there has ever been a work as amazing as the *St Matthew Passion*. And I've never done it. I will get to it eventually, I cannot postpone it much longer. But I've felt inadequate to cope with it because it's too immense and too incredible and too superhuman a piece, and I haven't yet felt the confidence in myself either as a musician or as a man to be responsible for it and for the length of time it takes to play it. This has nothing to do with technical difficulties. It is a question of perceiving and interpreting it right. And my fear of it gets worse and worse by the year."

Previn studies scores first by trying to learn the notes fairly well. Then he takes them to the piano and being a good pianist, can "bang his way through, approximating what's going on" even though this leaves about nine-tenths of it out. Then he has what is considered a very bad habit by teachers: he marks his scores with red pencils, blue pencils, black pencils, every manner of pencils; structural things like phrase lengths, not interpretative things like bowings. (If he has to mark a bowing, he does so in erasable pencil.) "I have found that if while studying I make a mark on the score, it helps fix it in my mind, like writing down a poem helps to memorize it. So my scores look like a crazed student's!

"Of course, if I had all the time in the world to study a complex score—say Stravinsky's *Symphony in Three Movements* which I did for the first time last year—I wouldn't need to put any marks in it. But if I'm going to learn it during a season for performance a few weeks or months later, then I need every short cut I can think of. Because the way most of us work nowadays puts an enormous pressure on our time. And it has nothing to do with that hateful word jet-setting—who on earth travels on business by boat, for goodness sake?—but has a lot to do with the fact that we all do too many concerts. There's no gainsaying it. We *all* do too many concerts; and too many recordings; and too much repertoire—on average about a hundred to a hundred and thirty concerts and about two hundred works a year."

And granted this kind of pressure, he tries to find any short cuts except listening to recordings, which he thinks is a mistake because of the danger of learning somebody else's interpretation. But he has two exceptions to this rule. One is if he is learning "a phenomenally complex and complicated contemporary score"—like a Henze symphony which he studied recently; then it's an advantage to be able to hear what it actually sounds like. "The score was wonderful, but there were a great many moments when I couldn't visualize or rather, imagine, the sound. My imagination just gave up. In that case, I borrowed a record, heard it through once, and then returned it." The second exception is large works which he may not have conducted in five or six years, but which he has recorded. He then listens to his record, to see if he still feels the same way about it. And most of the time he doesn't.

Previn, of course, is one of the most prolific recorders of the present day. He has made about a hundred and fifty LPs with the LSO alone "which is a hell of a lot of records." One of the reasons, he maintains, is that he has applied the "tried and proved true" rule of the recording industry, i.e. that if one gets through the allotted work and finishes twenty or thirty minutes early, "okay, forget it—go home. But if one finishes forty-five minutes to an hour early, one starts something else— which forces the recording company to finish it some time! So, if we were due to record a piece we had just performed and knew well, I always asked the librarian to bring along a work that I personally would like to record, so that when we finished early as I knew we would and they asked what had we got, I could say, oh, look, we just happen to have a Haydn symphony! Much better than wasting all that money it costs to set up a session, and once we started, they were committed to finishing it."

He enjoys recording, doesn't miss the audience unduly at recording sessions, likes the atmosphere of the recording studio and of getting things done, maybe because he was used to Hollywood studios. Recording companies like to use him because scheduled work always gets done, without any leftovers spilling over for future sessions. He likes recording in long, long stretches. "When I made my first digital recording for EMI I was told that at that stage they didn't like making a lot of intercuts. So I asked the producer to join me in a white lie: we told the orchestra that we couldn't make *any* cuts so that if something went wrong in the penultimate bar we would have to repeat the whole thing again. And it worked. First of all they were much more fascinated by the shape of the music and also, to be cynical, because they just didn't bloody well want to do it all again so everybody sat on the edge of his chair and we had the tension you so seldom get in the studio and which I like very much.

"I remember that when I worked on the film of *My Fair Lady*, Rex Harrison came up to me when we started recording and said: 'Listen, this is impossible, I can't do it this way, I can't stand in front of a mike and do those numbers.' I said, 'Why not?', and he replied, 'Because I need to have makeup on, I need to have my costume on, and above all, I need to be frightened!' And I understand it completely. I feel the same. I mean, I wouldn't want to have those composers angry with me...."

THE ORCHESTRA-BUILDERS

CLAUDIO ABBADO
The Man Within

"You see, I don't like to speak. I prefer to conduct," concluded Claudio Abbado, apologetically, at the end of his brief speech of thanks to the Chairman of the London Symphony Orchestra who had just welcomed him as their Principal Conductor, at a reception in his honour in September 1979. And it's true. Abbado, Music Director of La Scala, Milan, and of the European Community Youth Orchestra as well as the LSO, and Principal Guest Conductor of the Chicago Symphony, talks very little, least of all about himself. Partly because of his shy, introverted nature, partly because he really communicates mainly through music and partly because he is, has made himself, that rarest of phenomena: a conductor with no Ego.

How he did it, how long it took, or how difficult the struggle was, one doesn't know. But his words, his actions and his behaviour both in public and in private, prove that the beast is slain. Perhaps this is why he is not only one of the best conductors alive, but also the most *important* of his generation. For his aims and achievements transcend the narrow confines of personal ambition and mere career-advancement. Through his tireless, unstinting support of the ECYO—for which he receives no remuneration—he has helped create a superbly trained generation of young musicians all over Europe; he has built up the orchestra of La Scala to high symphonic standards and broadened the Theatre's accessibility to audiences who might otherwise never have been exposed to music. All this has been achieved well before the age of fifty. This passionate dedication to the future of music as much as the *depth* and quality of his musical interpretations is what makes Abbado unique among his contemporaries.

For the sake of music, "because you get better results that way", Abbado has also taught himself to control his temper, have an iron grip on his nerves and hide his worries. (In the process, he acquired three ulcers. But that, according to him, is not important!)

No one attending an Abbado rehearsal can ever hope to glimpse the fire, tension and electricity he exudes at the concert or performance itself. His rehearsals are low-key, concise and technical with a minimum of verbal explanations, not merely owing to his innate reserve, but also to his conviction that an orchestra should learn to understand his intentions through his hands and eyes—the only channels of communication available at the concert itself. This ability to communicate through the hands, eyes and facial expression is, he feels, a conductor's most essential quality. The other necessary attributes, "and I speak generally now, not of myself", are: "First of all, knowing the score really well. There are no limits to knowing enough! There is always more to learn. The conductor must know everything that can be found out about the composer, and this should include studying all his chamber and vocal works as well, to get a 'feel', a better idea of his style. He should also have studied composition; be able to play an instrument; have a good sense of rhythm and good pitch; enough psychology of people; tenacity. It's *very* important to love what he's doing, to have a passion for music, otherwise the work would become routine and that's the end, that's death. He should also understand and respect other musicians and singers who may have personalities different from his own. This is especially necessary when working on an opera where so many other people are involved, or with soloists. Because it's impossible for two or more people to have *exactly* the same conception of a given work, and great soloists are great personalities. So a conductor must understand and communicate with them at a very profound level."

Abbado attaches more importance than any other conductor in this book to the ability to co-operate with other artists, and this may explain why he has achieved rewarding and long-standing musical partnerships with so many top soloists. One of the closest is his collaboration with Maurizio Pollini, with whom he has performed almost every concerto in the piano repertoire, plus the world première of *Como una ola de fuerza y luz*, composed for them by their friend Luigi Nono in 1973.

Pollini and Abbado have known each other since their student days in the fifties and first played together in 1961, when the former was only nineteen. But although they didn't become close friends until the sixties, their *musical* rapport was instantly apparent. "Sometimes, you may admire a conductor very much only to find that, when it comes to working together, there is no rapport between you and your ways of looking at music are dissimilar," says Pollini. "This can happen even with very famous and important conductors. Sometimes you may even find yourselves in perfect agreement during your *discussion* of the work but discover that, in terms of actual music-making, your ideas are not the same after all! So, in talking about music, words are sometimes not enough.

"But the musical affinity between Claudio and myself was obvious from that very first concert. Since then, we have worked together constantly, and every year I notice a further development, an enrichment and a new maturity in his musical personality. He experiences the music he conducts very intensely, and although I agree that this should be the rule, it doesn't really happen all that often. But with him, something new and different happens at every concert and this freshness of approach to music is something which, I feel, is absolutely characteristic of him."

Of course, soloists have a clear conception of the character of every concerto which forms the basis of their interpretation. But there is an element of improvisation, or rather of natural spontaneity, in their response to the work at every performance, and a conductor who is sympathetic and on the same wavelength can sense and pick up their impulses. "Claudio does this without fail and I always feel very secure with him. He is a most sensitive accompanist and always in the right place. For example, when we did the Schönberg Piano Concerto in London in January 1980—a very complicated work which proved an extraordinary experience for both of us—we had only discussed and gone through the score together for an hour in Milan and an hour in London. Everything happened in the music-making!"

Alfred Brendel is another great pianist who has worked regularly and closely with Abbado in recent years and finds him "wonderfully co-operative". "And I have also heard him in marvellous partnerships with artists who play very differently from the way I do, so he must have this particular gift of understanding what a musician who has his own convictions is trying to do, and helping him to do it. Conductors can do an extraordinary number of things that can hinder or inhibit a soloist. And they happen quite often! I wouldn't say that most conductors don't *try* to be helpful—especially if they are under seventy!—but there is a great gap between the desire to help and the ability to do so! Because so many different factors must be present before a really fruitful conductor/soloist relationship can develop. The most important is a profound and thorough knowledge of the score combined with a certain elasticity in the solistic parts, yet one that does not leave too many blind spots. Secondly, an ability to listen plus, maybe, a genuine interest in what another musician, an experienced soloist who has played the concerto more often than *he* has conducted it, may have found out.

"But this, of course, is a human quality and one which Claudio possesses to a remarkable degree. And it ties in with the fact that he is un-egocentric, relaxed, totally sincere and genuine—one of the few conductors to give an orchestra the impression of a collaborator interested in bringing the best out of them. [Abbado indeed hates being called 'Maestro' and greatly values the fact that he is Principal Conductor of two orchestras who elect their conductors themselves.] He is also one of the few I enjoy looking at during the *tutti* sections of a concerto, because his movements are very natural, never pretentious, and beautiful, but not beautiful merely for the sake of beauty. They always serve a musical purpose and are easy for the orchestra to understand and follow."

Brendel has found that from the technical point of view there are several degrees of conductor/soloist partnership. Conductors who try to change his conception to match theirs; those who will, at least, let him play his version of a concerto even if the orchestra doesn't sound the way he thinks it should; "and conductors like Claudio, with whom everything comes together, and who also make the orchestra play transparently and teach them how to produce beautiful sound when playing pianissimi and who make all those voice-meanings in the background, usually lost in the overall noise, apparent. For example, we recently did the Beethoven G major Concerto in a series of concerts, and the wonderful thing was that I didn't have to play louder than I wanted, something which, alas, I often have to do with other conductors who don't produce the required gentleness and transparency of orchestral sound and thereby force me to upscale the whole first movement."

Everything these two artists have said, and everything I myself observed in numerous rehearsals and recording sessions, must make it clear that Abbado is not an authoritarian conductor. "Of course I, too, have my ideas and my personality. But I try to find a way of realizing music *together* with other people. It is a far more enriching way of working. In opera in particular, there is today a very great temptation for a conductor to be his own producer as well, and I think that, at least as far as *I* am concerned, this is wrong. [In some other cases, it works.] Sometimes I do catch myself thinking that I might enjoy producing some of the operas I conduct. But ultimately, you get better ideas and better results by collaborating with a great producer."

When Claudio Abbado was eight years old, he wrote in his diary that one day he would be a conductor. Earlier that evening, he had been taken to La Scala by his fifteen-year-old brother to hear Antonio Guarnieri* conduct Debussy's *Nocturnes* and "something in the unusual combination of sounds, especially in 'Fêtes', struck a chord and made a deep impression on me. I felt that I could get *inside* this music and grow with it. . . . That night, I wrote in my diary that I too would like to conduct it someday."

The home that Claudio—born in Milan on June 26, 1933—grew up in was bursting at the seams with music. His father, Michelangelo Abbado, was a violinist, musicologist, violin-teacher and Vice-Chairman of the Conservatorio Giuseppe Verdi, and later an occasional conductor of the Milan String Orchestra; his elder brother Marcello, now Director of the Verdi Conservatoire, played the piano; his Sicilian-born mother, a well known writer of children's books—*Sicilian Fairy Tales* and *Persian Fairy Tales*, among others—under her maiden name of Maria Carmela Savagnone, was also a gifted pianist. In fact, she was Claudio's first music teacher, and started giving him piano lessons when he was eight. Three years later, it was time for a professional teacher, Enzo Calace. He continued studying the piano and harmony privately until the age of sixteen.

The middle one of three brothers, Claudio was a sensitive and withdrawn child, slightly afraid of his father who was strict and demanding with the three boys but more indulgent with their younger sister, Luciana. "I was very shy and always dreaming ... almost like now," he laughs. "My early memories are vague and hazy, and when I think about those days I find it difficult to distinguish the real from the imaginary. My mother had this incredibly rich and vivid imagination and was forever telling me stories, beautiful stories, sometimes out of her books, sometimes things she would make up on the spur of the moment. I remember having an animal-patterned wallpaper in my

---

* Antonio Guarnieri (1883–1952) was Toscanini's successor at La Scala until his death, and was highly regarded by fellow musicians.

bedroom and gazing at it for a long time before falling asleep ... imagining that the characters in her stories and the little animals on the wall were my friends and playing with them. To this day, I'm not sure whether some of my early memories really happened, whether I made them up, or whether they were part of one of my mother's stories."

Although he was very close to his mother, his fondest memories are of the times he spent with his maternal grandfather, Guglielmo Savagnone, who lived to be ninety-six and who was "one of the greatest loves and influences in my life". He was Professor of Papyrology at the University of Palermo, an expert in ancient languages and the author of a book on Roman Law, and in the process of his research he discovered new information about the origins of the Emperor Constantine: that he was more humbly born than history would have us suppose, for instance. During frequent walks in the mountains around Valtourmanche he would tell little Claudio all about his researches:

"Every day, at a specific time, my grandfather had an appointment at a farmhouse where he collected two large fresh eggs for us—three when my younger brother, Gabriele, came along. On the way he talked to me about a lot of things and I loved listening to him. He always treated me man-to-man and talked about serious things: his researches, his distaste for Fascism, his reflections about the ways of the world. He was a very special and wise old man, one of the wisest men I've ever met, and I felt closer to him than to anyone else in my family. He had respect for children, something sadly very rare in adults.

"When I was about six, I started keeping the diary you asked about, and to it I confided all the things that fascinated me, things I never told anyone. Then one day, I stopped writing, because I found out that someone had read it. It had been a very private, deeply secret thing. I *liked* to keep myself very closed and very secret, it seemed important to keep some personal, intimate moments to myself alone. [He is the same today. 'Did I really tell you that? I shouldn't have. I've never talked about it before,' he grumbled whenever I referred to something particularly interesting to me that had cropped up during one of our many conversations.] I was interested to discover in La Grange's marvellous book that Mahler also felt this need for seclusion as a child and longed for moments when he could be alone and concentrate on some thought or idea. His family didn't understand this need at all, so he often disappeared, just to be by himself. I find this very beautiful. ..."

The war was not an easy time for the Abbado family. In 1944 Claudio's mother was briefly imprisoned for hiding a Jewish child, whom she managed to save. His father, who made ends meet by playing on the radio, was accused of collaboration. Abbado seldom refers to these days, but his reluctance to 'judge' others and his dislike of labels of any kind may have something to do with these traumatic experiences.

It took much determination and many financial sacrifices for him to achieve his ambition to conduct. His father had hoped that his second son would choose an easier and more lucrative career than the exacting, often ill-paid, and frustrating lot of a musician and took some convincing before he allowed him to enrol at the Verdi Conservatoire. "Who would have guessed at the time that Claudio would make such a successful career?" he exclaimed years later. Who indeed, especially as his son himself acknowledges that he was a late developer, "sleeping" until the age of sixteen. But his mother sided with him, and together they managed to persuade his father. At the Conservatoire he studied the piano (and had a 14-note stretch), conducting and composition with Bruno Bettinelli. At about the same time as he took up these studies, around his sixteenth birthday, he started playing the organ in various churches, for extra cash. "I always played Bach, the composer for whom I felt the deepest affinity at the time," he recalls, "and as I knew very little about the Mass or how long I should play for, I just went on and on playing my favourite pieces, until one day people got angry because they were longing to go home and stopped me in the middle of a Sanctus." When he was eighteen, he played and conducted a Bach concerto from the keyboard in Toscanini's house.

He got his piano diploma at the age of nineteen and two years later graduated from the conducting and composition classes. He decided to spend the following summer in Siena where that season's masterclasses at the Accademia Chigiana were taken by many distinguished artists including Alfred Cortot and Carlo Zecchi, who was in charge of the conducting class. There he met Zubin Mehta, then a conducting student in Vienna, and their encounter proved important both from the personal and the professional points of view: Mehta, who was to become a close friend, was full of enthusiastic reports about his conducting class at the Vienna Music Academy and his teacher Hans Swarowsky,* and whetted his friend's appetite for the Austrian

* Hans Swarowsky (1899–1975), Hungarian-born conductor who never reached the top rank, but was a brilliant teacher of conducting, whose pupils also include Michael Gielen.

capital's rich and varied musical life. Abbado, who had also briefly
studied the piano with Friedrich Gulda in Salzburg, felt that he had
learned as much as he could learn in Italy at the time, and decided to
give the Vienna Academy a try. But the only way he could afford to go
was by winning two scholarships for two successive years, 1956–57
and 1957–58.

At first he found Swarowsky's cold, analytical approach to music
uncongenial, although gradually he began to see its point and has, in
retrospect, found it valuable in many ways. "Swarowsky was a very
good teacher of technique and score analysis. He taught in many
different ways and showed us how to divide a score into small arcs,
musical periods and phrases; how to study instrumentation and the line
of each instrument; and how to practise technically difficult pieces by
playing the score on the piano with one hand while conducting it with
the other, to achieve independence of one hand from the other. He was
very much of a mathematician, and I found this depressing to begin
with. I hated studying a score like mathematics. But this was his way,
and gradually I realized that if you used this method as a mere basis for
learning a score, it could prove quite helpful in the first stages,
especially with modern music. Later, of course, you should forget all
about it and concentrate on the musical, interpretational problems."

When learning scores, Abbado prefers to get his mental picture of
the sound without using the piano, although he sometimes finds it a
help in getting a clearer idea of the harmony. Sometimes he listens to
records and tapes as well, because he feels that there is always
something to be learnt from others, even if it is something *not* to do. He
doesn't find that this either disturbs or influences his own sound image
of the music, because by the time he gets to the stage when he listens to
records, most of his own interpretative ideas are already formed. His
golden rule about interpretation is that the composer is always right
and the interpreter's sacred duty is to stick to what is written. But
naturally he admits that the interpreter's own personality colours his
view and understanding of the score.

"This was brought home to me most effectively by a record of Ravel
playing one of his own compositions. His playing was quite, quite
different from the way one could have interpreted his own indications!
This made it clear that you should interpret scores in your own
individual way and try to read between the lines and beyond the
conventional musical signs and indications, i.e. that there should be a
certain freedom in your interpretations. But it's very hard to decide to

what extent an interpreter should be free and how far his freedom should stretch. Only self-criticism can provide the right guidelines and prevent one from over-stepping the mark. Sometimes, I come quite close to doing so, but then I force myself to make a sharp U-turn! For it is imperative to remember that one is here only to serve the composer, and that one should approach his work with humility and respect."

It was in Vienna that Abbado became increasingly familiar with Mozart, Beethoven, Schubert, Schumann and Brahms and discovered Mahler, Bruckner, Schönberg, Webern and Berg. From the musical point of view he found—and still finds—that the most difficult to interpret were the Classics, whereas Mahler or Stravinsky are closer to us and to our time. "Which is why nowadays there are so few really good interpreters of Mozart and Beethoven." From the purely technical point of view, one of the most difficult works for him to master was the Brahms third, and only after he had conducted the other three Brahms symphonies in public did he dare give it a try. "The tempi in the third are particularly difficult, for exactly the same reasons that the first tempo of the Brahms D minor Piano Concerto is difficult. There are all these tempi in six or in three, which have to pass to one or two. But I think that musical, interpretational problems are far more important. You can always find a way around a purely technical problem. And you can solve every single technical problem in a score and still conduct it like a dog!"

Some of Abbado's best music lessons in Vienna were the rehearsals of the great conductors of the day—Walter, Klemperer, Josef Krips, Böhm and Karajan—into which he used to sneak with Mehta. Those rehearsals were usually closed and the only way they could think of around this problem was to join the bass section of the Singverein, the Choir of the Gesellschaft der Musikfreunde, which Karajan had developed from a semi-amateur group into a first-class professional choir, and they sang many of the masterpieces of the choral repertoire under these great men—watching and learning all the time. But as they only bothered to sing when the choir was working with the orchestra, they offended the chorus master who attempted to throw them out of a Karajan rehearsal in public.

Watching how these great conductors obtained their results was an invaluable experience. "Because as I said, acquiring a good technique is important, but not *that* important. I know some great conductors, great musicians, whose technique is not very good. I remember once hearing Rafael Kubelik conduct a particularly wonderful performance

of the Schumann Second Symphony; and some thrilling Haydn and
Mozart concerts conducted by Szell: both very great musicians with a
less-than-perfect technique. And so was Furtwängler who, for me, was
the greatest conductor ever, the greatest! The tension he generated was
unique and he knew the music better than anybody else. I deeply,
deeply love his Beethoven, Brahms, Schubert, Schumann, Bruckner and
Wagner—the wonderful creative imagination at work and the freedom
of his interpretations, in which every note has meaning and is given
enough time to unfold and grow in interest. Yet his technique, his beat,
was not always clear for the orchestra. This must mean that other
factors like a certain magnetism, a certain emanation and power to
transmit energy through the eyes and body play a vital part in
conducting and I understand why you feel that it is a mysterious art."

He is right, of course. Yet it is somewhat ironic that these comments
about the relative unimportance of technique should come from
Abbado, whose stick technique is considered by musicians and singers
alike to be one of the best in the business. In fact, until a few years ago,
he was sometimes accused of being a "cool" conductor, technically
brilliant but emotionally holding something back. He himself admits
that at the beginning he was "too controlled and thought about
technique too much, because I was unsure of myself and also because I
didn't want to conduct in a showy way". Nowadays, nobody could
dispute the deeply felt commitment he brings to his interpretations.

Indeed, the enormous energy and emotion that go hand in hand with
a superb technique are among Abbado's chief characteristics as a
conductor. Another is the fact that he is as good a 'staccato' as an
'espressivo, cantabile' conductor, which, according to his former
classmate at the Vienna Music Academy and now his producer at
Deutsche Grammophon, Rainer Brock, is rare. Placido Domingo
agrees and adds that his way of indicating legato to orchestras is
unique, possibly because his arm movements are so good and seem to
flow into one another.

Massimo Bogianckino, Director Designate of the Paris Opéra,
observes that Abbado's interpretations are always distinguished by "a
long line and a terrific driving force in which there is always a sense of
incessant, galloping movement towards the climax, the conclusion of
the work—but one which has nothing to do with speed as such.
Nobody could say that his readings are fast. But they are always
urgent. There is no lingering over phrases per se and indeed nothing
sweet or sentimental in his phrasing. His interpretations are always

devoid of anything superfluous and touch the neuralgic points of the score. In recent years, they have been imbued with a greater calm, a more Olympian aspect, although he will never be an Olympian conductor as such, looking at a score from a distance." "Claudio's conducting is a perfect blend of the Classic and the Romantic conducting styles," says soprano Shirley Verrett. "There are moments of great outpouring of the soul, and moments when everything is very contained and very precise—a perfect balance between the head and the heart."

"When Abbado conducts, everything functions," says a musician from La Scala. "His technique is clear, precise and concise, very much in the Toscanini mould. Like Toscanini, he concentrates on essentials and every single gesture has a point, a musical reason, which makes it very easy for us to follow and fulfil his wishes. This is particularly important when we are playing difficult music—Mahler, Schönberg, Berg or Stravinsky, for example—where it is easy for a conductor to get in our way, because we have to concentrate so hard that any superfluous, inessential gesture on his part would distract us."

The Chairman and principal oboe of the London Symphony Orchestra, Anthony Camden, confirms that Abbado's technique is "excellent, clear and easy to follow. Which means that it helps rather than hinders him, and makes us players relax because we know that he will always be there with his entry, and at the right tempo. (I have sometimes played for conductors who had the most wonderful music pouring out of them but who were held back by a technique which was unclear and hard to follow and who therefore sadly didn't get as good a performance as they could have.) And *within* his technique, Claudio has probably more flexibility than I've ever come across in a conductor. He can be flexible even in the *middle* of a beat, enough to allow for something that's coming in a little early or a little late and, with a fraction of a movement of his baton, control and synchronize everything again. This is something few conductors can do. Most people try to *drive* the whole thing together by *pushing* in the player who is early or late. But Claudio can just go 'flick' and the whole thing knits together again. And as he conducts everything from memory, he is in a position to see in his mind exactly where the fault is and choose the right moment to pull in and re-integrate the instrument who made the false entry into the whole."

The violinist Professor Alfred Altenburger, Vorstand of the Vienna Philharmonic, also appreciates the excellence of Abbado's technique but adds that it is "impossible for anyone listening to his terse, purely technical rehearsals to imagine the tension and electricity he generates at the concert itself". He has a point. All the rehearsals I attended were interesting and illuminating about Abbado as a person in funny little ways, but offered no clue as to what kind of performance he would give in the evening. "Sometimes there is a little restlessness at his rehearsals because he is so very introverted, speaks so little and concentrates just on essentials," continues Professor Altenburger. "For example, he limits himself to asking for more accentuation, or for something to be quieter or more transparent, but that's all." Carlos Kleiber remembers dropping into an Abbado rehearsal in Vienna. "Claudio made the clearest speech: at some point in a Schubert symphony when he didn't like what he heard, he stopped the orchestra and asked, 'Why?' Just that. And nothing could have been clearer!"

The Leader of the LSO, Michael Davis, thinks that this is because at rehearsals Abbado "is *outside* the music, as if standing back and listening. But his concerts are a different story altogether. He generates tremendous intensity, electricity and emotion, and you can see that he feels the music very, very deeply, that he is giving it absolutely everything he's got, and that he is *inside* it, a hundred-per-cent involved."

Abbado graduated from the Vienna Music Academy in 1958. He and Zubin Mehta had been the most promising students in their class and when they conducted the Tonkünstler Orchestra in public for their matriculation concert a well-known columnist remarked that, of all young conductors, Claudio Abbado and Zubin Mehta had been outstanding and that Viennese music circles should take note of their names because the world would be hearing of them before long. That same summer, both young men headed for Tanglewood where Claudio won first prize—the Koussevitsky Prize—of the conducting class much to his astonishment, as he had automatically assumed that the winner would be Mehta who was "already a conductor, even in our student years, whereas I knew that *I* would have to study all my life."

Despite an offer to conduct an American orchestra, he decided that he preferred life in Europe and returned to Italy where he spent five lean years, flatly refusing to conduct anything for which he did not yet feel ready, which meant that he conducted only two or three concerts a year, plus an opera in Trieste. Frustrating though this was, it left him free to study and learn a great number of scores by heart without any time pressures or limitations—the foundation of his staggering ability to conduct virtually everything in his vast repertoire from memory. This prodigious memory of his is much talked about in the music world. Yet he himself doesn't quite understand why or how it functions:

"I'm sure that there is music going on in my mind all the time. Even music I haven't conducted for years must be playing somewhere in the back of my head. Take *Wozzeck* of example. When I first studied it in 1971, I took months and months learning it, and it was really difficult to memorize. I conducted it again in 1977, and in May–June 1979, when I thought 'Oh, God, this is terrible, I can't remember a single note!' But after two or three days, it all came back and to me this is something mysterious, something I don't understand. I have no photographic memory, I don't know how everything comes back. Dimitri Mitropoulos, whose 'live' recording of *Wozzeck* is fantastic, by the way, could glance at a score and memorize it almost on sight. I can't. And I don't really know *how* it happens."

Two years after his operatic début in Trieste—Prokofiev's *Les Amours des trois oranges*—he made his début at the Piccola Scala in a concert commemorating the 300th anniversary of the birth of Alessandro Scarlatti. But as he had meanwhile got married (to Gianna Cavazzoni), and had two children, Daniele and Alessandra, he desperately needed a full-time job and accepted an invitation to teach chamber music at the Parma Conservatoire, where he remained for two years, commuting from Milan twice a week. Bruno Walter thought that the ability to perform chamber music really well was an essential attribute of a conductor. Abbado agrees and considers that his two years at Parma were vital for his future development. "I don't know how much my pupils learnt from me, but I certainly learnt a lot from them," he explained to the magazine *Opera News*. "And the most important thing was not so much how they played but how I listened, because listening to others is one of the most important things in life."

The repertoire he taught was rich and varied: quartets, quintets, octets; a lot of music for two pianos not only by the standard Classical and Romantic composers but also by Schönberg, Webern and Berg who were still virtually unknown in Italy; Hindemith's *Hin und Zurück* and several of his chamber works; Stravinsky's *L'Histoire du soldat*; Bartók's Sonata for Two Pianos and Percussion; plus Brahms and Schumann quintets. His pupils were more or less his contemporaries and he socialized with them a great deal, dining after class, playing football or attending concerts together. Five of his former pupils are now members of the orchestra of La Scala (the principal trumpet, two double bass players, a horn and a contrabassoon player), one leads the RAI Orchestra in Turin and a sixth, Cesare Alfieri, is La Scala's chief prompter. All remember their student days under him with fondness and a great deal of respect.

"He never taught just notes," says Alfieri. "He taught *music*; tempi, colours, balance. He was already a very strong person, and consequently never had to resort to distance or show of rank in order to command respect. And I have never ever heard him shout. Not in Parma and not at La Scala either. When he is angry or displeased he just purses his lips in a very special way and has a different, steely look in his eyes." (Those who know him call it his "Saracen Look"—indeed, there is some Arab blood on the Sicilian side of his family—but soprano Kiri te Kanawa goes one better: her nickname for Claudio is Abdul-Abbad!)

Luciano Cadoppi, principal trumpet in the Scala orchestra, remembers Abbado as "an outstandingly interesting and very, very patient teacher who explained and analysed scores in great depth and taught us how to surmount the technical difficulties in performing what to us was new music, like, for example, the staccato way of playing required by Stravinsky's works." But one thing Abbado never taught was conducting. "I can't. I tried to recently in Milan, because they asked me. But I found that I cannot explain any of the things I do. Or maybe I don't want to...."

By 1963, after two years as a teacher, it was time to come to some decision about his future. He stuck to his childhood dream of conducting, and entered the Dimitri Mitropoulos International Conducting Competition in New York. En route, he stopped in Montreal to guest-conduct the city's Symphony Orchestra, whose Music Director at the time was none other than his friend Zubin Mehta. The programme consisted of a contemporary Canadian piece and the Tchaikovsky fifth. He was a great success with the public, but the critics savaged him, and one even suggested that he change professions. He nearly did, for his morale was shaken to the point of wondering whether he should not give the Mitropoulos Competition a miss. In the end, he did go, reluctantly, convinced that he would be the first among the sixty-six candidates to be eliminated. Instead he ended up with the First Prize. Yet this left him with a profound contempt for competitions in any field other than sport. "Competitions are the most anti-musical thing I know. It's both unjust and impossible to decide who is best after only a few days. Never in my whole life have I conducted as badly as I did on that occasion. The jury's decision to award me the prize was wrong." But he admits that winning a competition can be useful to a young musician because it helps open a lot of doors.

His prize included an official concert, consisting of works by Brahms and Stravinsky, the latter suggested by Leonard Bernstein, who offered him a job as one of his assistants at the New York Philharmonic. In major orchestras like this, assistants seldom get a chance to conduct important concerts and can only hope and pray that some eminent conductor will cancel an appearance at very short notice. That's how Bernstein got his first big break when, after being around for years, he stood in for an indisposed Bruno Walter at a concert that proved his passport to fame.

But Abbado was not that lucky. His first big break didn't come until 1965 when, after hearing him conduct the Berlin Radio Orchestra (RIAS), Herbert von Karajan invited him to the Salzburg Festival. He had already begun to make his name in Italy, with a performance of Manzoni's *Atom Tod* earlier that year, but was as yet internationally unknown. His choice for Salzburg was the Mahler 'Resurrection' Symphony, which had apparently never been heard there before. Everybody told him he was crazy, and that nobody would come to the concert. But Abbado, who has never believed the public to be as stupid as some concert organizers seem to think, stubbornly stuck to his guns. And triumphed. Yet throughout the performance, he thought it was terrible. "I wanted to kill myself. Really. It was only at the end, and later when I heard the tapes, that I realized it had not been bad. Of course, there are many things in it which I would change, but some things in it are better than in my recording of 1976, because they are more spontaneous. It's strange, but all the so-called 'special' nights in my career have been those which, at the time, struck me as being really bad." One such occasion was a monumental performance of the same work with the LSO in London in April 1979. But at the time, he felt that the first movement was terrible, that there was not enough sound from the strings, etc.... "Maybe it's important for me to think that at the time. Maybe it makes me put something extra into it."

At the end of the Salzburg concert, an old violinist came up to him and said that he had played that symphony with Mahler—a sign, perhaps, that he had sensed Abbado's extra-close affinity and identification with this composer. Alfred Brendel, who chanced to hear a broadcast of this concert, felt "immediately aware of someone very special. Naturally, he was inexperienced, but he had enormous fire, conviction and authority, which he communicated both to the orchestra and to the audience. Of course, he has developed a great deal since then—fortunately he is one of those conductors who are constantly evolving and learning and whose development is leading to better and higher things.... But the immense talent, the extraordinary ability to communicate, and passionate commitment to the music he conducts were there, right from the start."

After Salzburg, invitations started pouring in, from Paris, London, Berlin and Budapest, and a year later, in 1966, he made his operatic début at La Scala conducting Bellini's *I Capuleti e i Montecchi*, a production which he later took to the Expo 1967 in Montreal. Massimo Bogianckino, at the time Artistic Director of the Rome Opera House (he was later to become Abbado's close collaborator at La Scala), remembers an incident from those days which provides an interesting insight into Abbado's integrity and professional ethics. After his success at La Scala with *I Capuleti e i Montecchi*, Bogianckino, who had known both him and his family for years, invited him to conduct this opera in Rome as well, with Luciano Pavarotti and Margherita Rinaldi. Because of their previous acquaintance, they had been content with a verbal agreement, and left the signing of contracts for a later date. "One morning," recalls Bogianckino, "Claudio called me and said that as La Scala had offered him several more operas and a time which would exactly coincide with our Rome dates, would I please understand and excuse him from his commitment? I replied that I understood how important this offer was for his career but that I also took note of the fact that he had ceased to be his own master, but had become part of a mechanism in which his own word counted for nothing. He was silent for a moment, then he said, 'I'll come.' And he did."

In 1968, after another triumphant appearance at the Salzburg Festival, the now famous Jean-Pierre Ponnelle production of *Il barbiere di Siviglia*, the orchestra of La Scala invited him to become its principal conductor—a difficult and very demanding job, but one that was to prove that he is not only a top-ranking conductor, but a first class orchestra-builder as well. (In 1972, after the Intendant Antonio Ghiringhelli resigned, Abbado was appointed Music Director, one of a triumvirate in which the others were Paolo Grassi, Intendant, and Massimo Bogianckino, Artistic Director. In 1977 after Grassi left for

RAI and was succeeded by Carlo Maria Badini, Abbado was named Artistic and Music Director.)

One of the Scala musicians explains that "we decided to offer Abbado the post of Principal Conductor not just because of his great and undisputed merit as a conductor, but also because of his very wide musical culture, which encompasses German culture, something we hitherto lacked and which, we felt, would enrich Milanese musical life. And this is precisely what he has done. He has developed us into an orchestra that can now handle almost any area of the symphonic repertoire. Some of this music—Mahler, Bruckner, Stravinsky, the composers of the Second Viennese School and contemporary composers like Nono, Berio, Boulez, Ligeti and Stockhausen—were initially very, very difficult for us, because our tradition had always been almost exclusively operatic and mainly Italian. But he threw himself at the task with an enthusiasm and determination absolutely typical of him!" (It is also typical of him that his policy has always been to invite only the very best conductors—Kleiber, Mehta, Ozawa, Muti, Maazel and Barenboim, as well as Solti and the late Karl Böhm—and producers, knowing full well that it is the only way to ensure the best possible standards.)

It was the brass and percussion sections that first required his most urgent attention. But over the years, he has also hired new string players, totalling about ten per cent of the whole section, including Rumanians, Bulgarians and Germans, taking advantage of a new law permitting the hiring of foreigners in subsidized theatres because of the chronic lack of instrumentalists that plagues Italian musical life. He searched far and wide for the best available players and poached a timpanist from the Bavarian State Opera, an oboist from Lugano, a trombone player from Cleveland. He also encouraged the formation of as many chamber groups within the orchestra as possible. When he first arrived, there was only one chamber group, a quartet. Now there are two full chamber orchestras, three quartets, one quintet, one brass, one wind and one percussion ensemble, "so more or less everyone is playing chamber music, which makes for real musicians who love music and don't just sit in a darkened pit night after night playing only operas and ballets." Abbado adds that one fundamental quality of the Scala orchestra—their unique ability to blend sound with words and especially so in Italian opera—had always fascinated him and has always been there, as far back as he can remember. "This ability is unique in my experience and the reason why I record Verdi only with them. And I remember seeing Karajan's marvellous *La Bohème* at La Scala and then listening to his recording of the production, with the Berlin Philharmonic. Although the latter is one of the greatest orchestras in the world and plays a hundred times better than La Scala's, there was something missing from the recording, something which had been there at the performances and which La Scala's musicians have in their blood. I was sorry that Karajan didn't record the opera with them."

What really brought home to me the extent of Abbado's achievement in training the Scala orchestra for symphonic work was an all-Berg concert in Paris in the summer of 1979. The orchestra played with such technical expertise, sense of style and "feel" for the composer, that I had to keep reminding myself that I was hearing an *operatic* and not one of the great symphony orchestras of the world.

Abbado's second significant musical contribution to La Scala has been his imaginative, adventurous and far-seeing attitude to repertoire, which he has expanded to include both rarely seen twentieth-century classics—*Wozzeck, Lulu, The Rake's Progress, Oedipus Rex, Moses und Aron, Erwartung, The Miraculous Mandarin*—and contemporary works like Ligeti's *Le Grand Macabre*, Penderecki's *Paradise Lost*, Stockhausen's *Donnerstag*, Berio's *La vera storia* and Nono's *Il gran sole carico d'amore*, especially commissioned for La Scala. When Boulez completes his long awaited first opera, it will be premièred at La Scala by Abbado, who stresses that he champions modern music not out of a sense of duty, but because he likes it. For him, the only criterion for conducting a work is that it should have "musical value": "Music should be beautiful from the aesthetic point of view, and should have a profound meaning. Superficial music, and music which is not beautiful, doesn't interest me."

But the achievements of the "Abbado era" at La Scala have not been confined to artistic matters. They have also involved the transformation of this institution into a democratic theatre, accessible to a much wider and more socially varied audience than before (much to the chagrin of many who lament that La Scala is no longer chic!). Abbado and the then Intendant, Paolo Grassi, started this policy by organizing special performances for workers and students and by taking whole productions to factories and industrial estates. During the 1972 season, when this policy was first adopted, 15,958 workers and students visited the Theatre. By 1976–77, the number had risen to 102,555. This human, social goal, so in tune with today's emotional climate and aspirations, was as important to Abbado as his purely artistic aims. He is a man of the Left, a man of high ideals about the quality of life and the vital importance of making music accessible to all. "Because it doesn't seem fair that as great, as stupendous a gift as music should reach only certain people and not others who, through no fault of their own, may never have a chance to be exposed to it."

All these achievements should be viewed in the context of running this mammoth opera house and against the background of its politics and particular problems. Being an operatic Music Director is an enormously complicated job, compared to which "running a symphony orchestra is a quarter the amount of trouble", to quote Sir Georg Solti who spent a decade as Music Director at Covent Garden. Before a season can be put before the public, countless overlapping factors must be worked out and fitted into the right places, like pieces of a jigsaw puzzle: repertoire, casting, rehearsal schedules and performance slots, all of which must take into account the availability of every artist involved *and* allow them adequate rest in between; forging binding agreements with all the different unions involved. In addition to his purely musical duties—studying, auditioning singers, rehearsing, etc.—the operatic Music Director also has to attend numerous planning meetings a week: with producers, designers, orchestral representatives, chorus master, heads of administrative departments.

But if running an opera house is a complicated enough job, running La Scala must be the marathon of all jobs in the music world. Near-chaos seems to be the order of the day and things that should function and be taken for granted quite simply do not and cannot. For a start, the subsidy is always late. In 1979, for example, La Scala had still not received its £7.6 million subsidy by the end of May, and found itself unable to pay for a production of Stravinsky's *The Rake's Progress*, borrowed from the Glyndebourne Festival. The government claimed that all grants had been frozen because of the forthcoming general elections. Finally the mayor of Milan, who is La Scala's president, saved the day by signing a cheque at the last minute. The government's chronic delay in handing out the subsidy means that the theatre has to borrow from the Milanese banks at a very high interest rate (25 per cent), and every four years, the value of the accumulated interest equals that of a year's subsidy. Although almost every major opera house complains, usually rightly, that it is inadequately subsidized, no other theatre is obliged to lead quite such a hand-to-mouth existence.

On top, or maybe because of, this appalling indifference, inefficiency and laissez-faire at government level, there are constant strikes by the technical staff and the chorus (the latter are subject to the quaintest regulations which specify that they must be paid extra when wearing armour!), and it almost always looks as though the opening nights of new productions will be cancelled or postponed—and frequently are. Usually, however, at the eleventh hour-plus-fifty-nine minutes, everything somehow manages to function. But it is a nerve-wracking way to live and work and in the circumstances Abbado's artistic achievements seem even more remarkable—and his resignations of 1976 and 1979 even more understandable. The first, in support of Grassi's resignation, was prompted by the government's asinine decision to cancel La Scala's visit to Washington for the US Bicentennial, and to instigate a policy aiming at a more even division of its subsidies between thirteen Italian opera houses, which would have resulted in the halving of La Scala's subsidy and robbed it of its special position in Italian and international cultural life. Finally, after expressions of solidarity from all Italian political parties, from prominent cultural figures and from the public, the government relented, and Abbado remained.

Three years later, Abbado, and Grassi's successor Carlo Maria Badini, were faced by similar problems which resulted in the actual cancellation of their projected American tour of autumn 1979. Abbado resigned again, and only after an overwhelming public reaction and a letter of protest signed by four hundred top artists from all over the world asking that everything possible be done to make him change his mind, did he relent. But he decided to remain only as Music Director, thus relinquishing his administrative responsibilities as Artistic Director. Henceforth, he would conduct one new production a season plus a revival or two, and tours. His strong love/hate relationship with La Scala is difficult to escape from. It is hard to imagine any artist who wouldn't hate working in such conditions. Yet as he recently explained to the Italian magazine *Musica,* "If underneath it all there weren't a great love, a link, a passion for La Scala, I would have gone years ago. This is difficult to explain. But every time I return to La Scala, walk on stage and see this enormous swimming pool of an orchestra pit which strikes terror into some and acts as a stimulus to others, this stupendous auditorium ... and this sometimes highly knowledgeable but always impassioned public ... well, you see how it is?"

A characteristic feature of Abbado's career is that it has avoided specialization. His time is more or less equally divided between opera and concerts and he is at home in every area of the repertoire. Until recently, the only great composer conspicuously absent from his programmes—apart from a concert performance of *Tristan und Isolde* in Philadelphia many years ago—was Wagner. He feels deeply drawn to Wagner, but for a very long time he felt unready to tackle his works. "Soon, I hope," he kept promising, but declined every invitation from Bayreuth and elsewhere. "You have to wait for these things to come to *you*," he explains. And he did.

Until December 1981, when he conducted *Lohengrin* as La Scala's inaugural production of the 1981–82 season (directed by Giorgio Strehler), and drew universal praise. That a conductor of Abbado's standing should have the humility and conscientiousness to wait this long before conducting Wagner may serve as an example for conductors of both his own and the younger generation who cannot refrain from tackling everything, everywhere, and often produce results totally lacking in artistic substance.

In 1971, after a series of successful concerts together, the Vienna Philharmonic named Abbado its Principal Conductor, a more or less honorary title since the orchestra is self-administering, chooses its own guest conductors and gives only nine subscription concerts in Vienna itself. The appointment involved a lot of touring, but no administrative responsibilities. "We always have big successes with him and love him very much, because he is one of the few conductors who can really relate to Bruckner, whose music he conducts in a very moving way. And his approach to Mahler and the Second Viennese School is also wonderful," says Professor Altenburger. Abbado reciprocates their feelings and finds conducting this orchestra in works of the Romantic and post-Romantic period an especially gratifying experience. "They have something particular in their string sound which is marvellous for Romantic music, but hard to describe. It's something ... dirty—this is a terrible word, but you know what I mean?—something mushy in the string sound which is unique. In a way, the Israel Philharmonic also have this kind of sound, probably because of the central European background of so many of their players. If you play Romantic works with too clean a string sound—and most German and English orchestras do—the effect is not the same." Abbado has, of course, conducted every major orchestra in the world and in 1981 was named Principal Guest Conductor of the Chicago Symphony. He has also been Principal Conductor of the London Symphony Orchestra since 1979, after eight years as their Principal Guest Conductor. He first conducted them in London in 1965–66 and later in Salzburg. There was an instant strong *simpatia* between them, and he particularly enjoys their relaxed, informal way of working, sense of humour and flexibility.*

Anthony Camden explains that the LSO had explored the French repertoire thoroughly under Monteux, and had done a lot of the Russian and English repertoire under Previn. But the Classical and Romantic repertoire was something that needed firm development. "Until Claudio became our Principal Conductor, we had not paid much attention to that part of the repertoire. We were not that kind of orchestra. But when, on the same day five years ago in Salzburg, we asked him to be our Principal Conductor and Böhm to be our President, we put the seal on a new era of music-making which would see our expansion into the Classical and Romantic repertoire, and which has resulted in our Haydn, Mozart, Beethoven, Schubert, Brahms and Mahler cycles."

I wondered about the specific technical difficulties involved in such a drastic change of direction, which would obviously require a new kind of sound, a far cry from the sharp, incisive brilliance for which the LSO was chiefly known. Was it a question of hiring new players, of buying new instruments, or simply of changing the way that people played? "A little bit of everything," explained Camden. "Apart from a change of phrasing which a new Principal Conductor automatically brings, the orchestra actually *play* differently now. We have a new leader, Michael Davis, who has had many conversations with Claudio about the quality of string sound he would like. This involves the softening of our sound which, owing to our previous emphasis on Russian music, had become too hard and too bright. The quality of the bass sound also needed strengthening, and we raised enough money and ordered a set of five double basses from Germany, which will produce a bigger, deeper sound."

While Abbado doesn't want to lose the sharp incisiveness for which the LSO became famous, he is after warmth and sonority in its sound, explains Michael Davis: "He wants a big sound, but a big, beautiful, *round* sound. Which means that even when we are playing full out, he doesn't want us to thrash and dig at our instruments. To produce his kind of sound, there are several technical things you can do, like, for

* In fact Abbado's contract as Principal Conductor of the LSO was signed in a motorway café, en route from the 1977 Edinburgh Festival to London. It was going to be signed at that evening's recording session of *Carmen*, but as both he and Camden chanced to stop at the same café for lunch, they decided not to waste any time!

instance, playing a melody on a particular string. Say you have a melody that can be played either on the 'A' string in a low position, or on the 'D' string, in a much higher position. If you want a warmer sound, you would obviously go for the 'D' string rather than the 'A' string which has a much brighter sound. Claudio has a great understanding of string instruments, possibly because his father was a violinist, and most of what he says makes technical sense. I think I can say that our style of playing has already begun to change, and will continue to do so every season, because constant exposure to a particular conductor is the best way of acquiring his sound."

The orchestra are delighted that Abbado is giving them so much of his time—more than they had dared hope for, because of his numerous international commitments. He even insists on being offered all their touring, both at home and abroad, and during his first season he managed to conduct ninety-five-per-cent of the LSO's concerts abroad. "I never cease to be amazed by his endless enthusiasm for music and by his total loyalty to those with whom he has sided. And he gets the same kind of loyalty back from us," says Anthony Camden.

One of the greatest joys and most fulfilling experiences in Abbado's life is his music directorship of the European Community Youth Orchestra, to which he devotes six full weeks every summer, as well as time for occasional spring tours. The ECYO, which grew out of the International Youth Orchestra whose Edinburgh Festival and Promenade concerts Abbado conducted in 1977, consists of young musicians from the member countries, aged from fourteen to twenty-two, who come together for a European tour every summer, at the end of the school year term. The tour is preceded by a ten-day training period under Abbado at some Convention Centre, usually Courchevel. Of course, this means that he has to turn down numerous lucrative assignments during this period. Yet nobody who has not seen him together with these young people can possibly have any conception of what this orchestra means to him or of the full extent of his commitment. A few hours after arriving at Courchevel, he seems to shed the tension, the demands made on him by an international career as a leading conductor, and emerges looking years younger. Abbado looks much, much younger than his years anyway. At Courchevel, he looks almost like a student himself—and he becomes one of them.

Mrs Joy Bryer, the orchestra's tireless and energetic organizer, remarks that "if you asked any other famous conductor to give up ten days and work from scratch with 137 young people from ten different countries, all trained differently by different teachers, and then take them around Europe, their answer would be: 'Train them for me, bring them up to standard, and then yes, Mrs Bryer, I would be delighted to take them around after a couple of rehearsals.' But of all the conductors I have met—and I have met some who have and love children deeply—Claudio is the only one who has the time, the patience, the interest and real feeling to sit down and work with them for two weeks before the tour."

When Mrs Bryer first approached him to find out whether he would be interested in taking on this group, he answered yes, but added that he wanted to be more than just a music director. And, as I had the opportunity to observe when I accompanied them for part of their 1979 tour, he is involved in just about everything: he wants to know how the young musicians are travelling, where they will be staying, what they will be eating. He even goes to the extent of checking over menus with Mrs Bryer who had "naturally expected him to be interested in his rehearsals and the arrival dates of the various soloists; but I had not expected having menu-sessions with him." ("I want them to be treated like other musicians would be," says Abbado.) "And nobody imagines what kind of hell I go through if one of them has backache or the sniffles or anything else wrong with him or her. Does he have a good doctor, and couldn't I get a better instrument for so and so because the one she has is not good enough and so on and on," continues Joy Bryer. "And until one witnesses this, it's impossible to understand how deeply, how totally, this man cares! Not just about their music-making, but their whole lives, what bothers them, what they are looking for, their hopes and aspirations. And he always notices when someone has fallen in love with someone else, or when they have personal problems.

"For example, we had a very talented German leader who became ill in Courchevel, and it was Claudio who called his parents, it was Claudio who sat with him, it was Claudio who put him on the bus when, after doing the first two concerts, he had to go home, and who kept calling him to find out how he was. And when I met him in Milan later, and La Scala was exploding, and the unions were on strike, and people were calling from New York and couldn't get him on the telephone, there he was, asking how Matthias was!" [I happened to be in Venice when another of the young players was stricken with acute appendicitis and had to be whisked to hospital. Claudio was rehearsing all day, but his second wife Gabriella went around to the hospital with fruit every day, composer Luigi Nono, their close friend, was asked to contact his own doctor, and daily visitors were organized for the days after the orchestra had to go on to Salzburg.]

"And he doesn't just leave and forget about those young people at the end of each annual tour. If there is anyone whom he could help with a scholarship, or for whom he can find a job, by writing to the right people, he will unfailingly do so. [In 1980 he hired two for La Scala.] And those who write to him, from all over the world, never fail to get a reply. I always feel that music is Claudio's religion and that this, in some way, is transferred to those 137 young people, each of whom he manages to know deeply. I'm sure that his heart, his centre, or whatever you like to call it, is very much tied up with this orchestra. There is a very spiritual side to Claudio, which has to do with music and his ideals about life and society, and which, I feel, escapes most people. Maybe you'll catch a glimpse of it at the end of our video of the performance of Strauss's *Tod und Verklärung* at the Albert Hall.

"I vividly remember that, on the day before that concert, the father of one of the girls in the orchestra died. She was shattered, and Claudio was deeply moved and had a long talk with her, explaining, through this music, his feelings about death, and he picked up a distraught, desperate young person and got her through the concert, somehow. And there was a particular moment during the performance when I saw him look straight at her and I saw something in her eyes that only the music, and that contact with Claudio through the music, could have brought."

Abbado himself acknowledges that the ECYO is one of the most beautiful and worthwhile things in his life, and not just for musical reasons. "The enthusiasm of those young kids is wonderful. And they are very mature, they believe in what they are doing and have not been spoilt by bad habits or wrong interpretations yet. And there is no routine, no unions, no limitations to our music-making. We are free to play as long as we like. I particularly love those ten days in Courchevel when we are completely cut off from the outside world in this hotel with its beautiful pool and nothing else in sight except the mountains. We start rehearsing in the morning, and sometimes work in the afternoon and evening as well. But sometimes, we cancel the morning rehearsal and go for walks in the mountains. For me, the whole experience is out of this world."

He rehearses them exactly as he would a professional orchestra and never talks more than usual. Nor does their inexperience make him alter or vary his interpretations. The only things he might spend longer on are certain details: "Wait a little longer before the third beat", he told them during rehearsals for the Bruckner seventh at the church of Santo Stefano in Venice. "The acoustics in the church make the sound linger longer, so do it as if there were a *fermata* at this point. Perhaps you might like to write in a *fermata?*" "I treat them as I would any other musicians, and they know it, which is important," he comments.

The only thing he does differently from standard orchestral practice is to rehearse them in small sections—not split rehearsals, but just the violin or cello or double bass section and so on. And each section is allotted a special teacher. The cellist of the Amadeus String Quartet for the cellos, Thomas Brandis, Leader of the Berlin Philharmonic or Michael Davis, Leader of the LSO for the violins, the principal double bass of the Orchestre de Paris for the double basses, Mike Bloom, a horn player from Paris, for the brass, LSO oboist Anthony Camden for the winds, David Searcy from La Scala for the percussion, Douglas Cummings of the LSO also for the cellos, Bruno Giuranna for the violas, are among the many outstanding players persuaded by Abbado to give their time to his young musicians.

Abbado never makes allowances for the orchestra's inexperience when choosing its repertoire. In the summer of 1978 they played the Mahler sixth, one of the greatest, most difficult, most complex and wearing of works, with a huge, elaborate orchestration, including offstage cowbells, etc., to boot. "We all thought he was crazy to choose such a gigantic work for such a young orchestra," says bassoonist John Whitfield. "But he worked us really hard, sometimes doing three rehearsals a day—punctuated by intervals of football and ping-pong—until all the details were right. He can be quite determined with players he doesn't like, by the way. But never insulting. He is too much of a gentleman for that. In fact, even though this sounds crazy, I always think of him as an Italian 'English Gentleman'.... Another very compelling thing about him is his amazingly communicative face. He is a very passionate conductor, a performance conductor. As you probably know, the Mahler sixth ends with a huge big crash, with A major dissolving into A minor, dissolving into nothing, and this is always a very moving moment. We had rehearsed it dozens of times, but the performance was more extraordinary than anyone could have anticipated. And I shall never forget Claudio's face at this point: as if his temples carried all the grief of the world...."

I vividly remember one of the ECYO's performances of the Bruckner seventh in the summer of 1979, one of the most moving and gripping readings of this work I have ever heard. Much to my shame, I had gone to the concert in a slightly condescending mood, prepared to make allowances for age and inexperience. But I still cannot think of this performance without it sending shivers down my spine. It was as if conductor and players alike had broken through the boundaries of self and were hanging in the air, like tremulous antennae, in touch with the composer's spirit....

Abbado's favourite performance of this work is Furtwängler's: "It's just wonderful. Bruckner was an Austrian from Linz and some soft passages in his symphonies and chamber works are influenced by Schubert. But he also wanted those big contrasts in his symphonies and wrote that the second movement of the seventh was influenced by Wagner, which is why the instrumentation for the strings and brass is very large. And if you visit San Florian* and play the organ or listen to someone playing Bruckner there, you hear first something very soft, almost tender, and then something echoing ... which makes you understand why he wrote those huge, big chords for the strings and brass. So Furtwängler was right. Bruno Walter's interpretation is also marvellous, but I prefer Furtwängler's. I turn to Walter for Mozart— his readings have an innocence and a tranquillity indispensible for Mozart—and Mahler. I think that his and Mitropoulos's are the best interpretations of Mahler I have heard."

Dimitri Mitropoulos died during a rehearsal of the Mahler third at La Scala in 1960, and for a long time the orchestra didn't want to play this symphony anymore, because they were afraid. The first time they did so was during their Mahler cycle with Abbado. "I could see that they were frightened during rehearsals, because they thought of this man, whom they had seen drop dead in a flash.... But he had known that he would die soon. And he wanted to. He told me so. He had already had two heart attacks and preferred to go quickly than suffer Victor de Sabata's fate, of going on and on, unable to conduct any longer. I understand this. There comes a point where living one year more or one year less is meaningless."

Abbado thinks about death often. "Everybody does. And there come

---

* The monastery of San Florian in Linz, Austria, where Bruckner was first a choirboy and subsequently an organist, and where many of his works were composed.

moments—when one is conducting Mahler, for instance—when one also thinks of taking one's own life. In fact, it would be impossible to conduct Mahler without thinking about death, because it's in the music. So *much* of his music is about death, and sometimes, about suicide. My own feelings about death are difficult to put into words. Words are earth-bound, like us. They are fixed and they have limits. I could describe what I conceive of as death—a continuity with no end, no limits—much more with music, because in music there are no limits. Absolutely none.

"I don't know why, but if I could choose the way to die, I think I would like it to be on a glacier, high up in the mountains. Perhaps because I once read a book about death on a glacier, and it stayed in my mind. Or perhaps because of other experiences, of nights when I couldn't sleep and walked out, or looked out, at this all-white world, under the moon. It seemed fantastic, and I thought that dying there, a White Death, passing through the cold and just ... not waking up anymore, could be very beautiful."

Abbado can describe his idea of infinity "much more with music" because for him, music is a mystical experience. "I can never put into words what music is to me", he told a British newspaper a couple of years ago. "But everything I do, everything I say, is about it." It's true. When he conducts, one is conscious of a man in touch not only with infinity but also with himself, his deepest, innermost self, the man within. In everyday life, only when alone in a room with him talking about last night's concert, a future production, next season's pro-grammes, colleagues he admires, or listening to a favourite recording, do I feel that, suddenly, the man within is there, for a few seconds. (You can always tell by the eyes. They change gear when "he" is there and emit an immensely powerful shaft of a look: a conductor's look, capable of drawing who-knows-what out of people.)

Away from music, I feel that he is sleepwalking, not wholly there. Despite the fact that he is a charming, generous, unfailingly hospitable host, who keeps constant open house, both in London and in Italy, with his beautiful, highly intelligent and immensely warm-hearted wife Gabriella and young son Sebastian; despite the fact that he is a good listener, genuinely interested in other people, in what's going on in the world and in the other arts; fond of sports and outdoor life; and despite the fact that he is a great giver, profoundly idealistic about friendships, and consequently frequently hurt and disillusioned by people incapable of returning even a quarter of his committed, enthusiastic and ultra-loyal friendship. He knows the world for what it is and people for what they are. Indeed, he has a deep and sharp sense of irony. But there is within him that innocence of the truly clean, which will always try again, in spite of disappointments. In short, this enigmatic, shy, elusive man of few words is difficult to get to know. As he is quoted at the beginning of this chapter, he doesn't like to talk. Which is why he reminds me of a score: to know him, one must read behind the notes, and between the lines; and as in scores, what isn't said is often more important than what is.

KARL BÖHM
A Fount of Wisdom

Karl Böhm died on August 14, 1981. Two days later, Herbert von Karajan, deeply moved and barely containing his tears, addressed the following words to the audience before dedicating a performance of Mozart's Maurerische Trauermusik *to his memory at the Salzburg Festival:*

"It is already two days since Karl Böhm departed from us, and we are still numb with grief and cannot grasp the fact that a man who gave his best to Art and to the service of this Festival for forty-three years, will now never appear here any more....

"In the Revelation *of St John it is written: 'Let them rest from their Labour; for their deeds shall follow them.' And in old age this is a ray of hope.... He leaves behind an immense treasurehouse of recordings and films of concerts and opera. Those who admired, knew and loved him will always be able to live with his music as a symbol of what I would perhaps call a musical epoch. And for those who do not yet know him, he will be an example and a challenge for the future.*

"The Festival is losing an irreplaceable contributor and most faithful supporter of its events; I, a dear colleague and a true friend.... Let us remember him with the thing he loved most in the world: music."

(My conversations with Karl Böhm took place in Salzburg in August 1979 and in London in December of the same year.)

In the autumn of 1978, Karl Böhm went to hear a concert performance of the final scene from *Salome*, sung by Montserrat Caballé and conducted by Zubin Mehta. But he left in the middle, because "he just couldn't take it," says Mehta. "He no longer has the stamina to conduct these hour-and-three-quarter operas with no interval and so he couldn't bear listening to it. He went to my dressing room and cried and cried, because even there, the music came through. And the fact is that he will never again conduct *Salome*."

Hard to imagine anything that could describe more clearly or poignantly the pain of a great musician whose mind is still one-hundred-per-cent there, whose enthusiasm and emotional responsiveness to music are still fresh and intact, but whose physical powers are declining and gradually taking away from him the possibility of conducting work after favourite work: *Elektra* (his farewell performance of which took place at the Herodes Atticus Theatre under the Parthenon at the 1977 Athens Festival, "an incredible experience, doing this work in the country where the events actually happened"); the *Ring* and *Tristan und Isolde*, the opera which, as he explained at our first meeting a few days before his eighty-fifth birthday, gave him the most profound musical fulfilment of his career and brought him to the brink of the most dangerous experience a conductor could have in the pit: losing himself in the music to an extent that would instantly result in his losing control of the orchestra.

"It happened at either the second or third performance of *Tristan* at the 1962 Bayreuth Festival. There I was in this magnificent pit where you can go in shirtsleeves which I must say is a great relief—it's so stupid for conductors to have to wear tails when in most places the men in the audience go in jeans, but that's only by the by—and during the love duet in the second act I suddenly had this feeling that we were swimming, I can't say it any other way, swimming on waves and not quite knowing where we were going. In fact, I felt that I was losing control.

"So I pulled myself together inside and reminded myself that conducting does not only consist of losing oneself in the music, 'drowning, sinking' as Isolde sings in the 'Liebestod', but also of keeping a firm grip on the orchestra and stage. There must always be this compromise, this balance between letting oneself go completely and maintaining control. But I shall never forget those two moments ... Birgit Nilsson and the late Wolfgang Windgassen, too, had sensed that something out of the ordinary had happened."

Böhm is now almost blind and, at eighty-seven, a fount of wisdom and a living link with two of the century's greatest composers—Richard Strauss and Alban Berg—and with the era that saw the emergence of the conductor as a figure of importance and power. His father was a friend of Hans Richter's; he himself was taught everything he knows about Wagner by Karl Muck* and was given his first important job by Bruno Walter, through whom he also learnt to understand and love Mozart, the composer with whom he identifies most closely and calls "the spring from which I constantly receive new strength".

"When I recorded all the Mozart symphonies with the Berlin Philharmonic, I discovered in the first symphony, which he composed at the age of eight, a four-note theme which runs throughout his creative life like a leitmotiv and reappears in his last symphony, the 'Jupiter'. To me, this perfectly demonstrates the essential point about Mozart: that he came into this world already fully mentally equipped, as a ray of light for centuries to come.

"He is also a profound mystery, one of the greatest mysteries in music. It has been calculated that if somebody sat down to copy all the 600-plus works which Mozart composed in twenty-nine years—from the age of six until his death at thirty-five—and worked eight hours a day, they just couldn't do it in twenty-nine years! And *he* not only wrote them down but conceived them as well! And amidst all the travelling, the recitals, the performances and all the tribulations of his short life."

Every artist who has worked with Böhm has been struck by his unusual degree of affinity for Mozart, and by the fact that his interpretations leave one unaware of the presence of an interpreter, an intermediary, between the music and oneself. One is convinced that one is hearing Mozart, not Böhm conducting Mozart. Whether this is due to his great love for this composer or to his uncanny gift for finding the right tempi—one of his most remarkable characteristics as a conductor—or to a combination of both is hard to tell.

The producer Otto Schenk, who has collaborated with Böhm on eight productions including two of *Così fan tutte*, says that they never had to have any discussion about the action or about the characters in each opera. "Yet the music came out of that pit so naturally and unselfconsciously that one had the impression Mozart himself was sitting there and the certainty that one was hearing natural, authentic Mozart pouring out of that magic baton without the slightest difficulty, without any problems. He made very small movements, it was as though the music was happening by itself and at the right tempo. Whether this was because some of the players were afraid to get it

* The eminent German conductor (1859–1940) who conducted at Bayreuth from 1901 to 1930 and was Generalmusikdirektor of the Berlin Royal Opera from 1908 to 1912.

wrong while others were happy to get it right, the result was sublime."

The pianist Maurizio Pollini has developed a particularly close artistic relationship with Böhm in recent years. The two have frequently played and recorded together and Pollini found each experience "fantastic". "We had an instant musical understanding and an excellent, extremely happy collaboration. He has a particular and very personal attitude to music, an attitude which, perhaps, resembles that of musicians like Wilhelm Backhaus and Annie Fischer and is natural, profound, deeply serious but at the same time very spontaneous and permeated by a kind of simplicity towards music. Or rather, an attitude which is a combination of all those things. For me, he is an absolutely extraordinary conductor with an extraordinary relationship to music and a special and very rare serenity. For instance, when we did a Mozart concerto in New York, with a minimum of gesture he succeeded in creating a totally 'Mozartian' atmosphere."

The other composer with whom Böhm is closely linked is Richard Strauss with whom he enjoyed a close artistic and personal friendship. He conducted virtually all of Strauss's operas in the composer's lifetime, often under his supervision, and was in charge of the world premières of *Die schweigsame Frau* and *Daphne*. He participated in every important Strauss anniversary, as well as celebrating his own milestone birthdays with performances of his friend's works, and was the sharer of many of this great composer's thoughts about conducting and the interpretation of music. Indeed, it was Strauss, himself a great Mozart lover and conductor, who was responsible for enhancing the love of Mozart that Bruno Walter had aroused in the young Böhm and for enlightening him with many insights into Mozart's music.

In many ways, Böhm's career has been strange and uneven. In the last twenty years he has enjoyed universal respect and acclamation. This is probably due to the unusually late flowering of his full artistic potential, which meant that he became a truly great conductor in his seventies. He began by carving out a solid, respectable career in Austria and Germany between the wars and earning the reputation of being a good, reliable Kapellmeister but not an especially exciting or inspiring conductor. His experiences at the end of the Second World War prompted him to aim at an internationally based career and, after a trough in the mid-fifties, emerged the great conductor we now know.

From the musical point of view, the main characteristics of his conducting technique can be summed up in the two points made by Otto Schenk and Maurizio Pollini: small, strictly essential movements and a remarkable feel for tempo. Slack tempi are anathema to him, "my idea of hell". Carlo Capriata, principal double bass at La Scala, remembers that when they were rehearsing the slow movement of the Beethoven ninth, Böhm kept pointing out that "the tempo should continue to pulse throughout, even in an adagio, exactly like the human blood, which never stops pulsing."

Karl Böhm was born in Graz, Austria on August 28, 1894. His father was a lawyer who acted as legal adviser to the local opera house and a passionate music lover, a frustrated musician who loved singing vocal exercises after lunch accompanied on the piano by his son. "But he was not really musical in the proper sense of the word—he had difficulty in learning new songs, for instance—whereas my mother was extremely musical as well as music-loving."

Karl was the eldest of three brothers and very close to both his parents. As a small child he was so attached to his mother that she could hardly set foot out of the house without him starting to cry. The only way the poor woman could get around this was to send a street musician to play "to the weeping little boy at the window of such and such an address", because the very first word that he had ever uttered was not Mamma or Papa but "mie", which stood for music. His parents encouraged his musical inclinations and took him to concerts and operas. The first opera he ever heard was *Fidelio*, at the age of five, and it was to prove an opera strangely linked with his destiny. It was also the first score he received as a present from his parents.

He first visited the then Vienna Court Opera at the age of ten, with his father who, seeing the boy's excitement and rapt response, bought him a season ticket for operas and Vienna Philharmonic concerts. He saw his first Mozart opera, *Die Zauberflöte*, at the age of twelve, and while still at school in Graz, he attended all the rehearsals for *Der Rosenkavalier* at the local opera house. His parents encouraged him to study music in every way—in 1913, his father sent him to Eusebius Mandyczewski, a friend of Brahms, and Guido Adler in Vienna—but insisted, gently, that he also study law as an insurance policy which would enable him to take over his father's legal practice should he prove to be anything but a first-class musician. He got his Law Degree in 1921, on the same day that he conducted his first *Der fliegende Holländer*!

The musical atmosphere at home was predominantly Wagnerian

Bernstein the composer, "alone with that listener at the back of my mind".

Bernstein "the Sometime Conductor": "In those performances which *I* call good, I feel as if I'm composing the piece as we go along.... At the end, it takes minutes before I know where—in what hall, in what country—or who I am."
CHRISTINA BURTON

Bernstein's televised sixtieth birthday tribute in Washington (with Mstislav Rostropovich conducting the National Symphony and André Previn and Yehudi Menuhin looking on), "the worst night of my life. One of the most touching, too, because everybody came, but also horrible because I had to smile and be gracious when inside, I was feeling rock bottom." CHRISTINA BURTON

Bernstein the teacher: "the best pedagogue in the world" among students at the famous Tanglewood conducting class. CHRISTINA BURTON

Right: Boulez has always conducted without a baton because "it freezes my hands". BBC

Below left: A warm-hearted and devastatingly charming man who always finds time for whoever wants to learn. CLIVE BARDA

Below right: Boulez at the IRCAM: a fruitful collaboration between artist and machine that resulted in his much acclaimed new work *Répons* in 1981. JEAN PIERRE ARMAND/IRCAM

Left: The first time André Previn conducted "it was like someone holding a banner saying 'THIS IS WHAT YOU MUST DO!'"
CLIVE BARDA

Opposite below left: For Claudio Abbado "music is a mystical experience...."
DECCA

Right: Claudio Abbado with his wife Gabriella, off for a morning's run down an Alpine slope.
CLAUDIO ABBADO

Below left: Abbado's "Saracen Look" which prompted soprano Kiri te Kanawa to christen him "Abdul-Abbad".
CLIVE BARDA

Below right: Claudio Abbado with Maurizio Pollini. The musical affinity between them was immediately apparent....
DAVID STEEN

Left: Claudio Abbado (front left) aged three, with his mother, brothers and sister in the mountains near Valtourmanche.
CLAUDIO ABBADO

Below left: Karl Böhm (left) with his father Dr Leopold Böhm and two brothers at home in Graz.
KARL BÖHM

Right: Karl Böhm visits his friend Leonard Bernstein during the break of a rehearsal for the televised concert performance of *Tristan und Isolde* in Munich in December 1980. "Bernstein and I like each other very much. I have always been nice to him and he has always been nice to me."
ROLAND FISCHER

Below: Karl Böhm with his son the famous film actor Karlheinz Böhm, who played the speaking part of the Bassa Selim in a Paris Opéra production of *Die Entführung aus dem Serail.*
J. CECCARINI/L'AURORE

Karl Böhm: "One has the feeling that one was sent to earth with a mission, a service to perform through music and that one should never think of one's work as a career but as a vocation." CLIVE BARDA
Sir Adrian Boult: "The Point of the Stick is the focus of the whole orchestra/ conductor contact." CLIVE BARDA

Left: Sir Adrian Boult's collection of famous batons, belonging to (top to bottom) Sir Henry Wood, Arthur Nikisch, Sir Adrian Boult, Arturo Toscanini. JOHN THOMSON

and, looking back, Böhm finds it astounding that "this magician, Wagner" should have succeeded in converting his father—who stemmed from a family of bakers and had previously had little to do with music—into an out-and-out Wagner fan in middle age, after only a few performances! "He was one of the first visitors to Bayreuth, and in those days, Wagner's struggling years, one needed those impassioned Wagnerites! My mother accompanied him on most of the trips or visits to the opera and I vividly remember that whenever the conversation came to Mozart, there was always the same refrain: 'Mozart is totally undramatic, with all those constant repetitions in the text.' Only many years later did the meaning of those repetitions dawn on me, with the help of Richard Strauss!"

His father befriended many singers as well as the conductor Hans Richter,* whom Karl asked one day how one set about becoming a conductor. "You go to the podium, and you can either do it immediately, or you will never learn how," was his reply. "And," adds Böhm, "with a pinch of salt, because you also need technique and experience, this is true."

Böhm himself never had a conducting lesson in his life. But through a stroke of luck, his practical experience started very early. While doing his national service during the First World War, he was kicked by a horse and suffered internal injuries which resulted in a medical downgrading and a chance, in 1917, to do the rest of his service at the local opera house—as a coach and assistant conductor—instead of at the front. Three years later, he was offered the principal conductorship.

"The whole business of conducting, around which so many people build up some kind of mystique, is none other than a job. I take the score and I study it very, very thoroughly—that's the first pre-requisite: knowing your scores, not *thinking* you know them, *really* knowing them—and become clear in my mind about the tempo I will take. And so it is that I form an ideal picture of this score in my mind. I try to achieve this ideal. Of course, I never do. If I realize, say, ninety per cent of this ideal image, I am very content, because the result then more or less matches my conception. But this depends on so many things! Less so in a concert hall where it's only a question of a hundred musicians than in the opera house where, to put it crudely, in the last instance you depend even on the man who operates the curtain. If he lets it down or up too early or too late, at a stroke he ruins a

* Hans Richter (1843–1916) who had been Wagner's secretary at the time of the composition of *Die Meistersinger* and eventually Conductor of the London Symphony Orchestra.

pianissimo! All these things are unpredictable and beyond one's control.

"From the technical point of view, it is important not to make unnecessary gestures. Personally I make very small movements, especially when I am working with the Berlin or the Vienna Philharmonic with whom I have been linked for over forty years and who understand my every glance. Because music has to come from the heart and from the mind, and *this* is the mystery in conducting: that I have the possibility, the gift of communicating my view of a score, of imposing my will on men and of understanding people. For I have to understand that a principal player in my orchestra who has a beautiful oboe or clarinet solo also has a desire to give his best. But when does he give his best? When he feels the melody more or less within the framework of my own conception, so that he can feel that *he* is producing not merely the sound but his interpretation of it, and can then give freely out of his inner feelings.

"The players should not be oppressed or constricted but given a certain degree of freedom, within the confines of one's own interpretation, of course. They should not be smothered, but allowed to participate in the music-making as partners rather than subordinates. That's when you get optimum results. Audiences also sense it when an orchestra is giving its all, giving out as much emotion as the conductor, and it is an incomparable experience! I have been lucky enough to share such experiences with all the orchestras with whom I have been closely associated: the Dresden Staatskapelle, the Berlin and the Vienna Philharmonic, and the London Symphony Orchestra."

Trumpeter Bram Gay, the Orchestra Director at Covent Garden, stressed precisely this point when discussing Böhm's conducting, using one of his recordings of the Mozart Symphony in E flat major (No. 39) as an example: "In this recording, you can hear the Vienna Philharmonic playing Mozart almost by itself, without him getting in their way! And it's wonderful when a great conductor can allow a great orchestra to give its consensus on a great composer! For, as Sir Adrian Boult said, anyone who thinks that they know more about a great composer than a great orchestra is daft!"

Yet good orchestras will only accept an interpretation from someone who knows what he is doing and takes more or less the right tempi. "If you put a conductor in front of the Vienna or the Berlin Philharmonic who takes the wrong tempo in a Mozart symphony or in *Die Zauberflöte* or in *Der Rosenkavalier*—and don't forget that some of the players will have played this music under Strauss himself—they can get very stroppy. They try to resist, sometimes even subconsciously, but resist they do", says Böhm. "And that's totally unproductive, isn't it?"

As far as *operatic* conducting is concerned, he thinks that experience is crucial and found the three years he spent as a coach and assistant conductor in Graz invaluable, because it was there that he began to understand the voice and the mechanics of singing and of accompanying singers—all of which must become second nature to someone intending to spend a part of his conducting career in an opera house. He remembers once hearing a young conductor answer a singer who had asked for more time in a certain passage that it was *he* who decided where and for how long she should breathe, "which, needless to say, is absolute rubbish!"

Böhm stressed that it is essential for a conductor to understand and accept the fact that some singers have a short breath, while others have a long, and some a very long, breath, and to develop a sixth sense about when they will hold back or rush forward. Because he will then have to make a lightning decision: whether to go along with the singer so that the audience doesn't notice anything amiss or cling to his own speed and thus expose the singer. Needless to say, this would be wrong. For while a conductor may interrupt or even rant and rave at rehearsals, on the evening itself his job is to smooth and camouflage any mishaps and preserve the flow and continuity of the performance. "And *that* can only be learnt from constant contact with singing—not from records, as many of my young colleagues seem to think."

While still an assistant in Graz, he conducted a performance of *Lohengrin* which, by chance, was attended by Karl Muck. Muck, who knew Wagner's own ideas through his widow, Cosima, was impressed by what he heard and invited Böhm to study all of Wagner's scores with him. In fact, he taught him almost everything he knew about performing Wagner: how to solve the problems of orchestral balance, in which parts the orchestra should be more prominent, how to handle the Bayreuth acoustics. Muck knew all the spots in Wagner scores where something was likely to go wrong, and Böhm remembers sitting next to him during a performance of the *Ring*, in Bayreuth: "Watch out," whispered Muck, "in the bar after next, the second horn will crack!" And sure enough, it did!

"Of course, now that I am older and wiser I, too, have learnt that horns are bound to crack. Which doesn't stop me from getting incredibly annoyed—within moderation—and finding it very hard to sleep after performances in which such things happen. Why do they crack, I still ask myself. They have to, it seems! Horn players have explained this to me hundreds of times but even now that I am so old, I still don't understand it! But they crack, they crack, sometimes less, sometimes more. In Vienna they crack more than elsewhere, because they have this crazy notion that they have to play 'F' horns, which certainly sound exquisite—especially in the middle register—but for this reason have the tendency to crack more easily. And even a layman can hear a crack. Immediately. There may have been dozens of wrong notes throughout the evening, but the one thing that will stick in his mind and which he will repeat to other people is that the horns cracked!

"When I was younger, I reacted very badly to cracks. I even stared at the player who cracked for, well, hours would be an exaggeration, but for very long. And what did I gain from it? He became even more nervous and in the next tricky passage, cracked again! Unfortunately by now I, too, know all the places where this is likely to happen. Frightful, of course. You can't enjoy it, of course. But you should discuss it with the musician later and avoid staring at him at the time. For, as Strauss used to tell me when the orchestra was too loud and swamped the singers, 'My dear Böhmerl,* you shouldn't even *look* at the winds, or they'll play too loudly!'"

But although all this wisdom lay in the future, Böhm's conducting ability was innate. In 1920, the town of Graz organized a Beethoven Festival and the Music Director of the opera house, who was given a choice between *Fidelio* and the ninth symphony, chose the latter and left Böhm in charge of *Fidelio*, which was performed three days after the concert. The most important critic in town wrote that the real event of the Festival had been *Fidelio*. (The second in a long string of coincidences linking this opera and Böhm's destiny.) The article caught the attention of a powerful and influential Frankfurt-based agent who mentioned the young Kapellmeister's name to Bruno Walter, then Music Director of the Bavarian State Opera.

One day, in the middle of a dress rehearsal for *Otello*, Böhm suddenly received a telegram from Bruno Walter stating that he was looking for a fourth Kapellmeister and that if he were willing to come to Munich and conduct a performance each of *Der Freischütz* and *Madama Butterfly*, he would be considered for the job. This put him in a serious dilemma, because he had already been offered the post of Principal Conductor in Graz, with carte blanche as far as repertoire

* an affectionate diminutive for 'Böhm'.

was concerned. "I thought to myself that if I risked going to Munich and they didn't like me, this would also cast a shadow here in Graz.... But then I thought, yes, I'll try it. I'll go."

Der Freischütz, for which he had only half a rehearsal (for the final scene of the last act), was well received, and on the day after his performance of *Madama Butterfly*, Bruno Walter called him in and asked him how he liked Munich. He replied that he liked it very much and Walter then added that Munich liked him very much, too.

"Then I told him about my dilemma, that I had the Principal Conductorship of Graz in my pocket and that the position of fourth Kapellmeister in Munich was less substantial. He replied that was a decision which nobody else could make for me. 'But,' he added, 'here is something for you to think about: every step forward that one takes in one's career has to be paid for by a hundred steps back. If you think that you know everything and that there is nothing more for you to learn, stay in Graz. But if you feel that you still have a lot to learn, come to me.' I spent a sleepless night, thinking and pondering over all the pros and cons and ended up deciding to take up Walter's offer—a decision I never regretted."

He remembers Walter as a hyper-sensitive, deep-feeling, immensely civilized Jew who reminded him a little of Mahler, about whom he spoke a great deal, and always stressed how much he owed to him as a teacher—just as Böhm will be forever grateful to Walter for broadening his own musical horizon. The two men got on well, corresponded throughout the war and remained friends until Walter's death. (Indeed, when Böhm was in financial difficulties before his de-nazification, it was Walter who came to the rescue by offering his wife a singing assignment under him.)

At the beginning of his six-year (1921–27) stay at the Bavarian State Opera, he had to conduct numerous operas which were still new to him because with only three years' experience behind him, his repertoire was limited. This meant long nights of study, just as in the days before his law examinations, except for the fact, of course, that he found scores more congenial than legal codes.

It was in Munich that he met his wife, soprano Thea Linhard, then a seventeen-year-old protégée of Bruno Walter's, who made her Munich debut as Oscar in *Un ballo in maschera*. Böhm remembers that when she sang Mimi with him, Walter was always reminding him that "Thea Linhard has a sweet but very small voice, because she is only seventeen. But the Puccini orchestra is so terribly loud! Mute them down, make them play more softly!" Böhm and Linhard were married in 1927, shortly after he left Munich to become Music Director in Darmstadt, where he stayed until 1931 and worked closely with Carl Ebert, the General Administrator, and his assistant Rudolf Bing.*

The most important event of the four-year stay in Darmstadt was a production of *Wozzeck* in 1928, under Alban Berg's supervision— barely three years after its original première in Berlin under Erich Kleiber. "Yes, in 1928 I *dared* to conduct *Wozzeck*. I use the word 'dared' deliberately, because you cannot imagine how difficult, how new, this work—with its thematic overlayings and immensely complex yet transparent orchestration—was for everybody concerned. From the rhythmic point of view, it is still extremely difficult today, and every musician must know what his colleagues are playing to a great extent, because it is impossible for the conductor to give everyone a lead. We had forty orchestral rehearsals: the first ones with wind and percussion only. The strings came in later.

"I had been studying the work for well over a year, playing it on the piano, or rather, trying to, because Berg's music is scarcely playable. *Today* it can be played, just—not very well but well enough to reconstruct the sound that Berg wanted. I read the score again and again and tried to solve the problems of orchestral balance in my mind. I was at once totally gripped by the drama in the work, something that had been absent from the operatic stage since Wagner. Berg has this incredibly strong sense of drama, unlike Schönberg who, although a phenomenal musician, was never a dramatic composer which is why, as Alban Berg told me later, when we had become friends, he worshipped Wagner.

"But before his arrival for the last twelve days' rehearsals, I trembled as never before in my life. I didn't know whether I had perceived the truth of the work even, or if I had been preparing it in the right way. But he tapped me on the shoulder and said that I had been doing it wonderfully and wrote a dedication in my score. I was so happy, of course! You go through all kinds of hell when confronted by such a challenge, believe me! Sleepless nights, the lot. I am a very bad sleeper anyway, but at the time, I seemed unable to sleep at all. I remember that Karlheinz had just been born and was three months old—and I

---

* Carl Ebert (1887–1980), the Berlin-born producer and administrator, founded the Glynde-bourne Festival with Fritz Busch in 1935 and was its Artistic Director until 1939, and from 1947 to 1959. Sir Rudolf Bing, the eminent British, Austrian-born administrator (knighted in 1971), was Artistic Director of the Glyndebourne Festival, 1947–49 and General Manager of the Metropolitan Opera, New York, 1950–72.

had my piano moved to a little cottage by a mill, and the sound of its wheel calmed me. Something in this constant, unchanging sound seemed to soothe my nerves and help me sleep."

In 1931 he left Darmstadt to become Music Director of the Hamburg State Opera for three years, and it was here that he first met Richard Strauss, but only briefly, after a performance of *Elektra*. This was the composer's favourite opera. He felt that in this work he had stretched himself musically to his furthest limits, "beyond which there was nowhere to go except come back" and considered himself the originator of atonality (in the Elektra-Klytemnestra scene), as he once shouted at someone who called him a musical renegade. Böhm remembers that during a performance of this opera, which he conducted later in Dresden, Strauss sat in a box with Mrs Böhm and immediately after Orestes' arrival, gripped her hand and didn't let go of it until the end. Then he held it to his face and exclaimed: "Did I really write this music? I had forgotten!" Strauss was most concerned that *Elektra* should not be played too loudly. Böhm once overheard him explain to an orchestra, after only a short rehearsal, because the musicians already knew the work well, "Gentlemen, you can do this piece and so can I. I have only one request for tonight. Play very quietly, for it is too loudly composed."

The two men got to know each other really well in Dresden— indeed, the Dresden State Opera house was known as the "Strauss Theatre" because most of his operas had their world premières there— where Böhm had succeeded Fritz Busch as Music Director in 1934, after the latter resigned his post in protest against Nazi policies and left the country. Böhm's nine-year period here was one of the most important in his career, and as long as he didn't resist the party line, he was provided with almost ideal working conditions. He had a good and stable ensemble, which included Maria Cebotari and Marta Fuchs, a first-class orchestra, and worked free from the demands of travel and guest conducting. He is quick to point out that such conditions have now vanished forever, what with singers flying in on the morning before the performance and over-reaching themselves by singing the wrong parts, or the right parts too soon. Only in festivals like Salzburg can comparable results be achieved.

Shortly after joining the Dresden State Opera, he conducted the two-hundredth performance of *Der Rosenkavalier* on Strauss's seventieth birthday. And while Strauss much preferred not only *Elektra*, but also *Salome*, *Ariadne auf Naxos* and *Die Frau ohne Schatten*, Böhm says that it is difficult for anyone today to imagine the extent of the popular response and enthusiasm aroused by *Der Rosenkavalier* at the time: there were special "Rosenkavalier trains" taking ticket holders from Berlin to Dresden and returning on the same night.

The following year, 1935, Böhm conducted the world première of *Die schweigsame Frau*, with a libretto by Stefan Zweig, under Strauss's supervision. The composer's behaviour at rehearsals varied greatly according to whether the work was new or a revival. At rehearsals of new works, he was always interfering. He once rushed up to Böhm after a particularly difficult rehearsal for *Die schweigsame Frau*, shouting, "Böhmerl, Böhmerl, I can't hear the words!" Böhm calmly replied that he shouldn't expect to, with an orchestration for four bassoons, four clarinets and full strings. Strauss thought about it, and that same evening reduced the bassoons and clarinets to two, with red ink, in his hotel room.

A few days before the première Strauss was playing his favourite card game, skat, with a 'star' tenor and the Director of the Opera House. Suddenly he asked to see the posters and billboards for the première. The Director, who had a bad conscience because he knew that, in compliance with Nazi regulations, the name of Stefan Zweig had been omitted as he was a Jew, tried to stall the issue by thinking up all sorts of excuses. But Strauss insisted and when his suspicions were proved right, threatened to cancel the performance.

His attitude caused great displeasure in Nazi headquarters and all hell was let loose. The Nazi leadership, which was supposed to attend the première en masse, cancelled—Goebbels was reached just as he was about to board the plane to Dresden—Strauss resigned as President of the Reichsmusikkammer, and *Die schweigsame Frau* was allowed only four performances.

Two years later, in 1938, Böhm conducted the world première of *Daphne*, which, he says, is his least favourite Strauss opera but a great favourite of the composer's wife. An interesting problem arose at one of the rehearsals which is worth mentioning first because it shows "how a conductor and a composer can sometimes be surprised by a note or a chord" and secondly because of the light it sheds on the subtleties of orchestral playing and intonation.

In the prelude, there was a particular woodwind chord which didn't sound right. Each individual note sounded all right on its own, but together they sounded wrong, and this puzzled both Strauss and Böhm, until by pure chance the latter asked the basset-horn player to try playing it a bit sharper. He did, and immediately the chord sounded right, "and this has something to do with overtones and frequencies which, of course, a composer can't be expected to take into account, otherwise he would be a mathematician. Yet it is one of the complex factors which make up the 'sound' of an orchestra.

"Because the sound of an orchestra is not the result only of its expression, but also of its tuning. Musicians can play an 'A' over and over again and it can still sound wrong, and it is only by adjusting and making concessions for each other's instruments that they can make it sound right. But only good orchestras know this. Bad orchestras will insist that they have the right 'A'. But there *is* no such thing as an absolutely right 'A'! It doesn't exist! That's a mathematical certainty. The whole process of music-making is so subtle that only when musicians are on the same wavelength can all these problems be solved.

"Every wind instrument, for instance, has its weak notes, which lie just on the break. Say that the bassoon ends with an 'E' and that the clarinet starts with an 'E', and that this 'E' is either too sharp or too flat on the bassoon. The player knows this and automatically adjusts it in a way that is hardly noticeable in the overall sound of the orchestra. But if he stubbornly insists on playing the correct 'E' according to the tuning fork, the 'E' would probably be correct according to that but sound wrong when the whole orchestra plays together. This is why, however angry the conductor might get when at a particular concert he is told that some of the best players are not there because they are giving a wind quintet chamber concert, he must remember that such chamber concerts are vital and essential for a great orchestra, because they are the best way for players to get to know each other."

In 1938, while still Music Director in Dresden, Böhm made his début at the Salzburg Festival conducting *Don Giovanni*. Among the many honorary titles he has received in his long career, none pleases him more than the Honorary Citizenship of this city—awarded him in 1964—"because it makes me a compatriot of Mozart".

He has conducted and recorded all the Mozart operas, symphonies, concerts and serenades, and his wife remarks that he is "a different man, tense and excited, when conducting Mozart". He himself once said that if he were to meet Beethoven coming up the street, he would doff his hat. But if he were to meet Mozart, he would fall to his knees!

He discussed Mozart endlessly with Richard Strauss, often during those long walks which Strauss was so fond of taking. Strauss thought that Mozart was the inventor of unending melody, and quoted Cherubino's aria 'Voi che sapete' as an example of a melody which starts with the first bar and ends with the last. He also explained to Böhm the reasons for some of those repetitions which his parents and other ardent Wagnerites had complained were undramatic. His example was the Belmonte-Constanze duet in *Die Entführung aus dem Serail*, and he reasoned that the dramatic situation in which the lovers find themselves, i.e. convinced that they will soon face certain death, causes them to reaffirm their love again and again and with increasing fanaticism.

As far as tempi are concerned, he always told Böhm that in every piece of music—even in Bach who hardly ever put any markings over his scores—there are one or two bars which invariably give a clue as to what the right tempo should be. The problem is to find them, but if one is really musical, one will do so.

"His example for that was always the quintet in the second act of *Die Zauberflöte*. 'Wie? Wie? Wie? Ihr an diese Schreckensort?', which one is always tempted to take at too fast a tempo because it is marked 'Alla breve' and 'Allegro'. But then you come to the Ladies' quavers, 'Man zischelt viel sich in die Ohren', which must determine the tempo of the whole piece because it is imperative that the words should come out clearly, which they wouldn't do if you took it at too fast a tempo."

As a Mozart *conductor*, Strauss was sometimes too fast for Böhm's taste. He remembers that in a particular performance of the G minor Symphony with the Vienna Philharmonic, the slow movement was played so fast that it sounded almost like a minuet. But he adds that this criticism does not imply that he didn't cherish and enjoy most of Strauss's performances of Mozart works.

Another of Strauss's important contributions to the understanding of Mozart was his tireless and enthusiastic championing of *Così fan tutte*, very much neglected before the Second World War because its libretto was considered too frivolous. Böhm has continued the good work by conducting this delectable score all over the world and lived to see it become firmly established in the international operatic repertoire. Yet he admits that he had to struggle before coming to a complete understanding of the work and argued about it a great deal with Bruno Walter who took a more sentimental view of it than he does. His own view is that *Così* is a 'drama giocoso' without a trace of sentimentality, and with an ambiguous ending.

"What makes it so interesting and so particularly ambiguous is that the two sisters seem to defy the universal law of attraction. Because if through all this disguise and masquerade in which the men look different and act differently, they fell for the men they were actually engaged to, then everything could still be all right. Yes, they succumbed and fell prey to a trick, but their behaviour would be in accordance with the usual law of attraction which is that one either likes somebody at first sight or never—or so I have found in my own life. There is something, a certain air, an aura, even an imperceptible odour, if you like, about a person which instantly attracts or repels another. It has been so since time immemorial.

"But in this opera everything is definitely not going to be all right, because the girls are suddenly attracted to two completely different men—Dorabella to the baritone Guglielmo and Fiordiligi to the tenor Ferrando—with different physiques and characters, and find them erotically attractive. So, one has to wonder about the eventual result. They get married under pressure, they return to the original men out of fear—rather them than no one at all—and one would be safe in assuming that the whole thing will not last long. One sees through Dorabella who gives in faster—and you can tell by the excitement in the strings before her entry that she will be the first to fall—how fast these things can happen: in one day.

"Therefore I find that the end is not at all funny. They all toast each other happily but what is bound to happen, if you really think about it more deeply, is that Dorabella in particular will fall into the arms of the first man to come her way. But, of course, the audience is no longer interested, because the action is finished."

He finds it amazing that everything, even these doubts about the future, is actually composed into the score which has been constructed in such a way that one can immediately tell the difference between true and false feelings. "When, for example, the wedding papers are found and the girls can no longer talk themselves out of the situation but have to admit what happened, they do so by screaming, 'Oh, oh,' with a *fermata* in between, 'We won't do it again', and the men scare them with their swords and the whole scene is composed in such a theatrical way because Mozart, who understood all human emotions despite his young age, wanted to convey insincerity."

Long experience of performing this work, though, has led him to conclude that it is best to cut some passages from the original in which, as he discovered when he performed it complete in Dresden in 1939, the libretto is not substantial enough and made it seem too long. Richard Strauss, with whom he often discussed this matter, agreed, and the composer's view is a particularly useful guideline for conductors faced with similar problems.

Consequently, Böhm's 1974 Salzburg production, which was recorded live for Deutsche Grammophon, does not include the arias "Tradito, schernito" and "E Amore un ladroncello" which are included in his previous studio recording for EMI. But he stresses that devotion to the composer and to the particular work is a conductor's only possible justification for making cuts to the original score, and the only guideline when trying to decide which, out of several editions of a work, he should perform.

An interesting example of the latter point is *Idomeneo*, another previously neglected Mozart opera which Böhm has championed throughout his career. He considers this work to be the high point of *opera seria*—the furthest that Mozart went in his life—and musically on the same level as *Don Giovanni* and *Le nozze di Figaro*. But the problem was to decide which existing edition was the most authentic. Mozart himself had cut some arias included in the original Munich production when he prepared the performance of the work in Vienna.

Paumgartner, "a great and profound Mozart expert who contributed a great deal towards the understanding of Mozart especially here in Salzburg", had prepared his own version, which he felt would help popularize the work. "But perhaps he went a little too far, albeit in all good faith, and added certain overtones which anyone who has had anything to do with Mozart could see straight away weren't his. After a while this came to bother me, and after I studied the Vienna edition of the work, I was convinced that this was by far the most authentic—it was after all Mozart's corrected version—and this is the one I performed at the 1973 Salzburg Festival. But these are very, very difficult decisions to make."

In 1943 Böhm left Dresden to become Music Director of the Vienna State Opera, where he conducted a performance of *Ariadne auf Naxos* for Richard Strauss's eightieth-birthday celebrations on June 11, 1944.

About a year later, the opera house was destroyed by Russian bombs. In fact the first bomb that fell on the house hit the stage, sent the safety curtain flying into the auditorium, and trapped Mrs Böhm—who was there on an errand for her husband—in débris. But miraculously a second bomb, a few minutes later, scattered the wreckage and freed her. Böhm was then lying in hospital after a car crash, but as soon as he was better, the couple left Vienna to escape the Russian advance. They went via Linz to a village on the Attersee in the Salzkammergut, which was soon to be part of the American zone.

In his autobiography, Böhm explains that his reasons for fleeing Vienna were first, that there was no artistic reason for him to stay, and secondly because his is not a heroic nature. This frank admission probably also explains why he chose to remain at his posts in Dresden and Vienna under the Nazis, although he was never a member of the Nazi party. When questioned about his unwillingness to join *any* political party, he replied that the only allegiance he felt was to music, to the "musical party". As long as he was left alone to get on with his music-making, he was content. He did not even resist the decision to allow only four performances of *Die schweigsame Frau*—a direct infringement of his artistic authority, and his willingness to bow to the powers that be has been severely criticized and was dearly paid for at the end of the war.

"This was the beginning of a horrible time for me," he confesses in his autobiography. For a while, he did not even own a piano in the cottage by the Attersee. In 1945, shortly after leaving Vienna, he was supposed to conduct a concert in Salzburg but at the very last minute the American authorities informed him that the Russians insisted on imposing a ban on him, and on Furtwängler, Knappertsbusch and Karajan. The ban lasted two years, and during this time he was not even allowed to give private lessons. As he had lost the savings he had invested in a factory in Dresden, this put him in strained financial circumstances. He had to rely on the generosity of his two brothers and on the singing lessons that his wife started giving in Graz.

This made him understand how caged animals in zoos or circuses feel, because although his physical movements were not restricted, his musical gift was "imprisoned, behind bars", and he experienced a profound artistic starvation, of a kind which only someone who has a gift which he longs to communicate to the world, could know. Bruno Walter, with characteristic generosity of spirit, tried to intervene on his behalf after his return to Vienna. But the Russian authorities were immovable, and the only way that he could help was to offer Thea Böhm a singing part in one of his concerts.

In 1947, Böhm and his three colleagues were allowed to resume their careers. The last two years had convinced him that never again should he be artistically dependent on one or two countries alone. His aim would now be an international career and he set about achieving this goal immediately. He made his début at La Scala in 1947, with *Don Giovanni*; conducted a series of operas at the Teatro di San Carlo in Naples; from 1950 to 1953, he spent several months each year at the Teatro Colón in Buenos Aires, where he conducted a season of German opera. At the same time he continued to conduct at the Vienna State Opera, which was now housed at the Theater an der Wien, pending the restoration of its bombed building.

In 1954, he was reappointed Music Director of the Vienna State Opera, and was thus in charge of planning and supervising its return to its former, restored building in November 1955, which took place amidst widespread popular rejoicing. Anyone who doesn't know Austria and Germany cannot properly grasp the importance attached to musical life in those countries, where it is a part of life, even for people who are not musical themselves—even they recognize it as a vital part of national life and heritage.

But before accepting the Music Directorship, Böhm had insisted on being allowed time to conduct abroad and had this clause written into his five-year contract. He was thus obliged to spend only seven months at the State Opera and was free to work abroad for three. He immediately set about establishing a good and stable ensemble of the kind he had known in Dresden—a task which was not as simple in post-war circumstances. Singers had also discovered the advantages of international careers and found themselves heavily in demand all over the world. Böhm considered this a very bad system which urgently needed reforming. "Leading singers would tell the Management that they were off to London, New York or Milan and would return for a few days next month, when they would sing such and such a part before going off somewhere else again. This meant that they were just using the Vienna State Opera as a shop window between lucrative trips abroad, and made it impossible for me to plan my repertoire ahead. It also led to a sad decline in overall ensemble standards."

So he put his foot down and insisted that singers should now sign three- instead of one-year contracts which stipulated that they work in Vienna five months each season, so that he could plan his repertoire a year-and-a-half ahead and allocate the right parts to the right artists. But shortly after the excitement and high quality of the inaugural Festival performances, the State Opera settled down to routine standards and Böhm, accused of making money abroad rather than doing his job at home, was held responsible. He was even vociferously hissed and booed as he entered the pit after his return from one of those visits abroad, and says in his autobiography that he can still hear the "terrible noise" in his ears!

Within a week, he resigned. But he soon regretted his decision and offered to reconsider the matter, only to be told that his resignation had already been accepted. Since then, he has never held a full-time post. Instead he has concentrated on guest conducting. In 1956 he conducted the opening performance of the newly rebuilt Deutsche Oper am Rhein in Düsseldorf (*Elektra*). But it was Rudolf Bing, then Director of the Metropolitan Opera, New York and previously Böhm's colleague in Darmstadt where he had been Carl Ebert's assistant, who came to his rescue by inviting him to conduct *Don Giovanni* at the Metropolitan Opera in 1957, the beginning of regular annual visits which culminated in his conducting *Fidelio* in 1970 during the Beethoven Bicentennial. He has also continued conducting at La Scala, the Bavarian State Opera and Salzburg regularly, and at Covent Garden, Bayreuth and Paris from time to time. Concerts with the New York, the Berlin and the Vienna Philharmonic—plus numerous tours to the United States, Japan, Russia and Europe with the latter orchestra—have occupied the rest of his time.

Having conducted all the best orchestras in the world many times over puts him in an excellent position to comment on each orchestra's individual characteristics, even though he dislikes the idea of comparisons in Art, be it of orchestras or of individual artists. Beyond a certain level both may be considered first class, and as such have nothing to fear from other outstanding people or institutions.

"How could one compare Bernstein and myself, for instance? You simply couldn't. We like each other very much. I have always been nice to him and he has always been nice to me, and we have always attended one another's concerts. But as musicians we are totally different. I like to think that I, too, have sufficient energy, even though I can't jump as high as he can! Yet I completely disagree with those who go around saying that he is superficial, because of some of those crazy movements he makes. It is not true. I can accept all this from Bernstein because I know that he experiences the music very deeply and that this is just his way of expressing himself. Therefore, although I am not generally an advocate of wide, wild gestures, I can accept them from him, because I find him totally convincing.

"In the same way, I hate comparing and categorizing orchestras. Both the Berlin and the Vienna Philharmonic are perfect, *alpha plus*, and so are some of the great American orchestras, perfect to the nth degree, unbelievable, but, of course, lack the 'soul' of the European orchestras, because they are not homogeneous, unlike the players of the Vienna Philharmonic, all of whom come from the same musical milieu, have breathed the same air all their lives, and have certain kinds of music in their blood. Schubert, for instance. There is something extra special in the way they play Schubert ... perhaps it is essential to have known the vineyards of Grinzing and the atmosphere there before one can play the third movement of the Schubert 'Great' Symphony, and re-create the melancholy inherent in the whole of this work.

"But when one is discussing orchestras at this level, one can only comment on differences of nuance, not of quality. For example, the Berlin Philharmonic, with which I have been associated all my life and which has never disappointed me, has a vast repertoire—they now play a tremendous amount of modern music under Karajan as well as the standard repertoire—a perfect collective memory, and are a perfectly disciplined group, because of the Prussian origins of many of the players. They are therefore capable of delivering good performances even under mediocre conductors, or people they do not respect. The Viennese, on the other hand, play like Gods for those they like and admire, but can get a bit slovenly under conductors who don't convince them."

The Vorstand of the Vienna Philharmonic, first violinist Professor Alfred Altenburger, says that the orchestra fully reciprocates Böhm's affection for them, and that there is a deep bond between the two which goes beyond conducting. "He has fatherly feelings towards us, and has never let us down. He has always helped, whenever somebody cancelled at short notice we have always been able to count on him and, of course, we have had tremendous successes with him all over the world. Despite his age, he is a man who can still generate very high tension, and whose every look and gesture conveys a message to us. He has never been an 'easy' conductor—indolent or satisfied with mediocre results—but always after our best. When he doesn't get it he gets very upset and nags, and even rants and raves at us."

Böhm adds that another important consideration to bear in mind when discussing orchestras is that one may have a first-class oboist, "like Koch of the Berlin Philharmonic, or the lady player at Covent Garden [the late Janet Craxton], who is unique, a fabulous musician and instrumentalist who blows unbelievable phrases", while another may have an ace clarinettist, and so on. Sometimes it may be that an entire section of a certain orchestra is of a particularly high level. "A good example of this is the Dresden Staatskapelle, a great orchestra with which I have worked regularly over the years, and which has wonderful strings, always has had, because of the Czech element there: it was the first German orchestra to be influenced by and to assimilate Czech violin playing."

In 1977, Böhm was invited to become Honorary President of the London Symphony Orchestra, which he conducted for the first time at the 1973 Salzburg Festival. Despite the fact that it is unusual for a conductor to develop a new musical partnership with a new orchestra in his eighties, he accepted with pleasure, and has since appeared with them every season.

Yet their relationship started with fear on their side, and unease on both sides, according to the orchestra's Chairman and principal oboist Anthony Camden: "When he first conducted us, at the 1973 Salzburg Festival, he was very suspicious. The programme included Mozart's 'Haffner', and Brahms's Fourth symphonies and I remember that whenever something went well at the rehearsals of the Brahms, he would say 'good' in a surprised, rather patronizing way. Whenever anything went *badly*, he got so bad-tempered that he almost spat on the floor, which was terrifying for a lot of the players.

"Then, very slowly, he began to warm to the extrovert qualities of our orchestra—which, I admit, is sometimes *too* extrovert—and to get a lot of feedback. But it was not until our third trip to Salzburg, by which time he had also conducted us in London and knew many of the players by name, that he began to feel part and parcel of us and to dispense with old-fashioned ways of demonstrating his authority.

"We were playing *Tod und Verklärung* and at the end he broke down in tears* and said, in the presence of his son, that this was the first time since Strauss's death that this piece had been completely revealed to him, that he had been able to achieve something very special with it, and that he would not record it with any other orchestras." Camden then rushed to report this to the orchestra's Board and to Claudio Abbado, its Principal Conductor, and they all decided to offer Böhm the Presidency, which he was delighted to

---

* Perhaps he was remembering his friend Richard Strauss who regained consciousness for a few minutes before his death and told his son Bubi that "everything is exactly as I described in *Tod und Verklärung*".

accept, "provided I did not have to write any letters!" But he sends the orchestra telegrams for all their special occasions, and during a visit in the summer of 1980, found the time to meet members of its club and sign autographs. He had even thought of bringing chocolates for some of the principal players' children.

He has the reputation of being unpleasant at rehearsals, as Anthony Camden's story demonstrates, and was earlier accused of ruling his orchestras through fear. Yet he is much more restrained and considerate when guest conducting. For example when some players of the orchestra of La Scala—which, like most Italian orchestras is not perfectly disciplined—were talking during the rehearsals of the Beethoven ninth, instead of the expected tirade, he just said: "Gentlemen, you can take it from me that this is the most beautiful piece of music ever written. You should be listening to it instead of talking."

Before a performance of *Così fan tutte* at Covent Garden in December 1979, he asked Bram Gay whether the usual horn players were on duty that night. He was assured that this was so. "Strange," he said, "they are playing *più forte* tonight." "Shall I ask them to be quieter?" "No," he replied, "they have probably been playing all day, they are tired, they are worried about the performance, they are playing *più forte* because they wish to be clean."

Böhm is likeable and human, despite his irascibility, his nagging and his foibles which occasionally include a certain pettiness: for example, when he was named General Musikdirektor of Austria by the Chancellor in 1964, he stipulated that the title should not be given to anyone else, i.e. Karajan, in his lifetime. In 1973, he complained to the Chancellor because another conductor, Zubin Mehta, to whom he is close, was asked to conduct *Salome* at the Vienna State Opera, and *Salome* was a work that was "his" only to conduct in that institution. He won, although he did not consider this in any way a personal attack on Mehta and the two men remained friends.

He immensely enjoys the many honours and titles he has collected throughout his life: the Honorary Citizenship of Salzburg (1964), the same city's Golden Mozart Medal (1959), the Grosses Bundesverdienstkreuz which he received from Willy Brandt, then Mayor of West Berlin in 1964; the Honorary Conductorship of the Hamburg Philharmonic (1977) and of the Bavarian State Opera (1978); the Presidency of the London Symphony Orchestra (1977); and the Honorary Citizenship of Vienna (1978). He not only revels in applause, but admits it. In a candid interview with *Die Zeit* on the occasion of his eighty-fifth birthday, he discussed his weaknesses in a forthright manner, and added that he had done many petty things, and told many lies in his life. But, he stressed, he has "always been honest in music". And indeed this is so.

During Böhm's second visit to Covent Garden, in December 1979, the orchestra noticed a marked decline in his physical powers since his previous visit two years before, and on certain evenings, it had to rely on leads from principles of the various sections—what orchestras call 'Plan Z'. Yet a few months later, he returned to London to conduct the London Symphony Orchestra in a superb concert which included the Beethoven fourth and the Dvořák 'New World' Symphony. He was in great form, totally alert. A few months before, he conducted a slack performance of *Die Entführung* at the Bavarian State Opera and a magnificent concert which included a memorable reading of the Schubert ninth—both within a week. This unpredictability has become a regular feature in his work since 1979 and obviously has a great deal to do with his failing health. He himself is well aware of it and of doing far too much for his age. But conducting is what keeps him alive, and after a good concert or performance, he feels rejuvenated. But after a bad one, he feels "very, very old".

"But sometimes this hectic life gets very tiring, and full of so many inconveniences despite the fact that people always try to be nice, helpful and do everything for me. They put me in nice hotels, but you suddenly find that there is construction work and hammering going on all the time—inconveniences against which you cannot defend yourself—and find yourself wishing you were back home."

When I met him in London in December, 1979, Böhm was looking forward to going back to his flat in Grinzing, and to conducting a Vienna Philharmonic concert with Maurizio Pollini as soloist, "who is sure to play the Brahms D minor Concerto wonderfully, just as he did in our recording, but the experience will also be very strenuous for me. Not the performance itself, but the fact that, in order to be at the Musikverein at three o'clock, I will have to give up my lunch and afternoon nap and drive in a car for three-quarters of an hour, and this is something I do with reluctance. My doctor advised me that this nap was the best thing I could do for myself, because it cuts the day in two, which is important, especially when I am working late into the night. Because when I have an evening performance I don't get to bed until midnight, and I can't eat and I can't sleep.... You will think me a grumbling, ungrateful old man, but you see, these are sacrifices which become much harder with age. So, sometimes, inevitably the thought crops up that maybe I should stop....

"But then I get some extraordinary experiences which convince me that I should go on: for instance, a man writes saying that he has bad rheumatic pains but hearing one of my concerts over the radio made him forget his pain for an hour. And the other day, during the Vienna State Opera's visit to Washington, I received a letter from a lady whose husband was dying of cancer of the lungs saying that his last wish was to shake my hand because my music-making had given him so much pleasure. He had only a few weeks to live and was not allowed out of hospital for the performance of *Figaro*, but after *Ariadne* he was there in a wheelchair—a man under forty, completely white and emaciated, with a black beard, like a living Christ. He held my hand as if in prayer and his wife said that now he could go in peace because his last wish, which he had apparently been going on about for weeks, was granted.

"This made a very deep impression on me. I shall never forget it. I knew that he was going straight back into hospital, and may even be dead by now.... At times like that one has the feeling that one was sent to earth with a mission, a service to perform though music, and that one should never think of one's work as a career but as a vocation. And one must go on for as long as one's powers allow. And the offers keep piling in and one has to make dates for a concert in '81, a recording in '82, and I think, oh, dear, how do I know whether I shall still be alive? One makes plans but ... who knows?"

SIR ADRIAN BOULT
Britain's Grand Old Man of Music

"Boult is one of the two conductors—the other is Giulini—whose readings of the Brahms symphonies I admire most. Take his recording of the First Symphony, for example. One wouldn't wish for one note to sound different from the way it does. And yet people abroad just don't know about this man!" enthused Simon Rattle, the brightest and most promising young British conductor, who had sought the help and advice of Britain's Grand Old Man of Music about some problems in the interpretation of Brahms scores which the younger generation of conductors tends to find particularly difficult.

And his remarks are an accurate pointer both to Boult's excellence as an interpreter of Classical and Romantic music—as well as British works which one automatically associates with him—and to the relative insularity of his career, which never became truly international. Yet, at ninety-three and now in retirement, he is a much-loved and revered figure in his country, a man whose contribution to British musical life can hardly be overestimated. His twenty years (1930–50) as Chief Conductor of the BBC Symphony Orchestra, for part of which he was also the Corporation's Director of Music, not only resulted in a first-rate orchestra of international standing—good enough to astonish and delight Toscanini who hardly had to rehearse the Brahms Fourth Symphony during his first encounter with it—but also helped shape British musical tastes and rendered tremendous service to contemporary music. It was Boult who conducted the first British performances of Bartók's *Concerto for Orchestra* (1946), Berg's *Wozzeck* (1934), *Three Orchestral Pieces* (1938), and countless other contemporary works (as well as, amazingly enough, Schumann's Violin Concerto), and the Viennese première of Schönberg's *Variations for Orchestra*, on tour with the BBC Symphony Orchestra in 1936. He remembers with a chuckle that the Austrian President who attended this concert bent over at the end and asked him confidentially, "Who *is* this Schönberg, anyway?!"

As a man, Boult—knighted in the first Honours List of King George VI at whose Coronation he had conducted the music, and made a Companion of Honour on his eightieth birthday in 1969—is far from insular: an excellent linguist, bilingual in German and English since childhood, a keen, tireless and open-minded traveller, an avid reader of the literature of many cultures. The fact that his career remained predominantly British-orientated was due partly to accident—his health prevented him from starting off as he had planned: as a répétiteur in a provincial German opera house, and by the time he had recovered the First World War had broken out—and partly to his self-effacing personality which lacks the kind of show-business glamour and other outward signs of an 'artistic' temperament. Boult looks what he is: an upright, decent, modest and dignified upper-middle-class English gentleman of slightly military bearing who oozes integrity and despises the cult of the conductor and all the star trappings associated with his profession. "It is an unfortunate thing that the conductor's job, even when we over-exert ourselves as most of us do, looks quite easy and, what's more, glamorous: for, like playing the organ, it gives a great sense of power," he writes in his book *Thoughts on Conducting*.

So in this sense it is, perhaps, slightly ironic that his mentor and idol should have been Arthur Nikisch (1855–1922), the legendary Hungarian conductor who spent twenty-seven years (1895–1922) at the helm of the Berlin Philharmonic (and also led the Leipzig Gewandhaus) and whose charisma and hypnotic effect on orchestras and audiences alike made him the first 'star' conductor par excellence! A good looking and magnetic man, Nikisch understood the art of audience appeal and manipulation and took infinite care of his appearance. Otto Klemperer noticed that his shirts always seemed to have extra-loose, extra-large cuffs that showed off his beautiful hands to perfection, for "there is a great deal of showmanship involved in conducting." (A statement which Boult would dismiss with a sniff.) Nikisch's colourful personality lent itself to an abundance of anecdotes, some of which were still in circulation in pre-Second-World-War Berlin. One of the funniest was recently told by Herbert von Karajan (who has inherited Nikisch's orchestra and star quality). An old Saxon couple attended a Nikisch performance at the insistence of the wife who had cultural aspirations. The husband, who was dragged to all such events somewhat reluctantly, had the unfortunate habit of dozing off for the best part of most concerts. But even *he* had heard of Nikisch's mesmerizing presence. So, not wishing to miss anything, he whispered to his wife, "I'll nod off now, but give me a nudge when he begins to fascinate!"

But as well as glamour and audience appeal, Nikisch also possessed a formidable and effective stick technique (based on an expressive stick which he held "as an elongation of his arm" and manipulated through small, flexible wrist and finger movements that freed him from the need to make frequent use of his elbow), which was, nevertheless, completely spontaneous and unconscious, so much so that he never discussed it in the conducting classes he held in Leipzig for several years. (And indeed an English violinist who once accompanied him to a photographic studio confirms that when the photographer asked the Maestro to pose with his baton, Nikisch duly picked it up but didn't know what to do with it.) But by the time Boult arrived in Leipzig, in the autumn of 1912, Nikisch had given up teaching. However, as he had already met young Boult through mutual friends in England, he granted him access to all his rehearsals, as he did to many other conducting students. Boult also sang under him in the Gewandhaus choir, which gave him an excellent opportunity to experience Nikisch's electric emanation and to study and analyse his technique minutely. What he saw impressed him so much that he subsequently practised this technique throughout his career—"everything I give you is Nikisch," he explained both in his above-mentioned book and in his handbook on the art of conducting, *The Point of the Stick*. He also taught it in the first conducting classes ever to be held in Britain, at the Royal College of Music from 1918 to 1924.

And indeed, no-one is better qualified than Boult to survey the rise of the conductor from his emergence as a figure of importance and power to his virtuoso status of today, and the development of the art of conducting throughout the last century. As he explains in his handbook, conducting is much newer than any other form of music-making, and in those days it was just in the process of forming itself into various schools such as one knows in singing, string or piano playing. "The conductors of the present day [1909] may be divided into three schools: those who beat time, like Dr Hans Richter; those who guide the orchestra like Mr [Vassily] Safonov; and those who hypnotise the orchestra, like Mr Nikisch." Of course a great deal has happened to the art of conducting since then. Toscanini, Furtwängler, and Karajan who 'modernized' it while retaining the best traditions of his predecessors;

and eventually, today's virtuoso conductors, who have excellent techniques. And among the most important things that have happened to conducting is the spectacular improvement in the standards of orchestral playing and the calibre of orchestral players, whose musicianship, skill, expert intonation and pride in their work could only be dreamed of in those days.

"A century ago, it was considered adequate for a conductor to beat time with his stick in his right hand and to give any necessary directions of expression that might not have been properly arranged at rehearsal, with his left," Boult writes in *The Point of the Stick*. "Except as regards pace, the conductor was indeed almost powerless unless he had had adequate time for rehearsal. The modern orchestra or chorus is a very different kind of instrument—it will, for instance, take a sign at rehearsal where formerly it needed a verbal explanation and possibly even a double repetition of the passage. Rehearsals are now greatly reduced in number and it is quite usual, though never satisfactory, for a difficult programme lasting two hours to be rehearsed in three sessions. The conductor must therefore learn to show his ideas on interpretation by means of the stick in his hands.

"And if the stick, which is the focus of the whole orchestra-conductor contact, is held firmly with a stiff wrist and the pivotal point back at the elbow, there can be little expressive life at its point because stick and arm then form an inflexible rod, and there is nothing but the elbow with which to direct the performance as to ensemble, pace and expression. Only when one has achieved this finger freedom and consequently eloquent use of the stick, can one possibly claim to know when to use, and when not to use, the stick. For the hand itself needs a lot more looking at before its message can get across. Therefore the left hand should be kept for any expression which is, so to speak, beyond the vocabulary of an expressive stick. It must never duplicate the point of the stick."

He explains that acquiring a good and foolproof technique frees a conductor from technical worries, allows him to concentrate his mind on the music and on encouraging and stimulating his forces. "For in conducting, there is a double mental process. There is the process of thinking ahead and preparing the orchestra and choir for what is to come, that is to say, driving them like a locomotive. There is also the process of listening and noting difficulties and points to be altered, in fact, of watching the music the way that a guard watches a train. At rehearsal, the second of these processes is the most important.

Occasionally, one must take hold and drive one's forces to the top of a climax, just as a boat's crew on the day before a race does one minute of its hardest training, but otherwise takes it pretty easy. The main thing at rehearsal is to watch results and act on them. At the performance, it's the other way round: the conductor must take the lead. It is then too late to alter things like faulty balance or wrong expression, but the structure and balance of the work as a whole and the right spirit and feeling are of paramount importance."

In fact, as he had pointed out at a lecture he gave to the Oriana Society at Oxford as a twenty-year-old, among the main guidelines on performance is "a clarity achieved through emphasis on balance and structure and a final effect of music made utterly effortlessly". But he is the first to admit that there are any number of ways of achieving this freedom and effortlessness, that every conductor has his own way of doing things, and that it is perfectly possible to be a good or great conductor without ever doing any of the things he preaches. "Take Debussy's conducting of his own works, for instance. He used a tremendous amount of energy and a tremendous amount of elbow—all the things that are anathema to me—yet that magical, ethereal sound came out.... But that was Debussy. Most people making similar gestures would produce a very rough sound. (In fact when I listen to the wireless I can often *hear* a conductor's gestures and say to my wife, 'Listen to that beggar's elbow!') But what I *am* saying is that my method will get a quicker, readier response from orchestras and choirs and produce better results faster, as many people, both professional and amateur, who have tried it over the years, testify. But it is perfectly possible to obtain your desired result without it, so please make sure you put that in."

Surely this must mean that factors other than technique play a vital part in the art of conducting. Yet Boult never refers to any of these intangible, mysterious elements in any of his books. Why?

"Yes, it is a mystery, even after all these years.... But I, being a pragmatic Englishman, don't go in for that sort of thing very much."

Boult was born in Chester on April 8, 1889, to well-to-do and very musical parents, and grew up in the outskirts of Liverpool. His mother was gifted enough to have been a professional concert pianist had she not married. So there was constant music-making in the house and by the age of two the child would sing almost everything he heard at perfect pitch and spent hours crouched under the piano listening to his mother playing. Soon, he started climbing up onto the stool, trying things out for himself and learning all about scales, pitch and bass line by trial and error, and gentle explanations from his mother, when strictly necessary. His was a happy, well-ordered Victorian home—from his mother's diaries, his parents come across as considerably more affectionate, relaxed and enlightened than one's (perhaps erroneous?) image of Victorian parenthood—well able to afford and practise the art of gracious living that the English upper classes developed to perfection. This shows in Boult's bearing, perfect manners and kind of effortless, second-nature consideration for others which he shares with Giulini and which is all the more delectable for being so very rare today.

At the age of seven, he started composing—a Romance for Violin as a present to his only sister—and, under the spell of the first concert he attended (conducted by Hans Richter and including the Tchaikovsky *Pathétique*), a Concert Sonata in C major which, along with all his childhood compositions, he burnt soon afterwards. He went to Westminster School, but as he was abnormally tall for his age (six foot by the age of fifteen) it was not considered wise for him to be a boarder. So he was a day-boy and lived in a flat his mother rented for him just across Westminster Bridge, with a housekeeper and a cousin of one of his mother's friends. His schooldays were therefore happier and more carefree than those usually enjoyed by boys of his upbringing, despite the fact that there was no time for music except at weekends, when, being the proud possessor of a season ticket to Henry Wood's concerts, he unfailingly attended them all on Sunday afternoons and the occasional Saturday.

Despite the rapid and spectacular progress he had made in his music studies, his parents resisted suggestions to turn him into a *Wunderkind*, judging that if his 'gift' was genuine, it could only profit from a normal childhood and a good education. So he went on to Oxford to read History and work for a Music degree. On arrival at Oxford, in 1908, his first task was to seek Dr Hugh Allen, whose performances with the Oxford Bach Choir in London he had enjoyed many a time, and to persuade him to accept him as a chorister. He describes his first experience of singing a great Bach work (the *B Minor Mass*) in a big choir as overwhelming. From that day, all his spare time was spent either practising with the choir or busying himself with other musical tasks—such as playing the parts of missing instruments on the piano—

delegated to him by Allen. On the latter's advice, he persuaded the Dean that a third- or fourth-class degree in History would in no way help him become a better musician and the man, astonished to hear that the young man intended to become an orchestral conductor— something almost unheard of in England at the time—agreed to let him drop History and concentrate entirely on Music.

So he spent his free time conducting local choirs, taking charge of incidental music in the theatrical productions of the OUDS (Oxford University Dramatic Society) and eventually rowing for the University. It was then that, thanks to Allen's adventurous programming, he came into contact with British music for the first time, at a concert devoted to works by Hubert Parry, who had just left his Music Professorship at Oxford to head the Royal College of Music in London. It was a revelation for, as he confessed in his autobiography *My Own Trumpet*, until then he had always thought of British music as second-rate. So he could hardly believe his ears as the choruses of *Job* followed one another, each more beautiful than the one before.

He got his Bachelor's Degree in Music in 1912, and his Doctorate in 1914, shortly before the First World War. But between the two came that monumental year in Leipzig in the proximity of Nikisch that did so much to shape him as a musician and conductor. Boult had first heard Nikisch during the latter's 1902 visit to London when he conducted the London Symphony Orchestra, took the place by storm and did more than anyone to arouse and stimulate public interest in the art of conducting as such, as Boult states in his autobiography. Until then, the conductor was looked on as part of the orchestra and people weren't really interested in how he got his results, or indeed, whether it was the players or he himself that was responsible for them. "But suddenly this man appeared and, in a perfectly familiar programme, extracted an utterly different sound from the orchestra and threw a totally different light on the music."

Boult was lucky enough to meet Nikisch through the tenor Emanuel Hedmondt and his wife, who had been neighbours in Liverpool for a while before moving to Leipzig where she was Royal Professor of Singing at the Conservatoire (her pupils there included Elena Gerhardt). Nikisch explained that he was about to give up teaching conducting, but extended an invitation to his rehearsals. So Boult set off and spent a very happy and musically invaluable year (1912–13) in Leipzig, at the end of which he planned to become a coach in one of the provincial German opera houses. But his years of rowing for Oxford had damaged his heart, which gave him trouble during that winter. His father therefore counselled him to come home, get himself in shape again and return to the Continent the following year. On his return, he was engaged as a coach at Covent Garden for both the winter and the summer seasons which was exciting because the former included the first London performance of *Parsifal*, and the latter the *Ring* conducted by Nikisch. Between the two seasons, he conducted his first public concert—on February 27, 1914, at the Town Hall in West Kirby— with an orchestra made up of musicians from the Liverpool Philharmonic.

Before he could return to the Continent, the First World War broke out. His health precluded active service in the war, and he spent the first two years drilling Lancashire miners and the latter two in various War Office departments in London. In 1916, he conducted the Liverpool Philharmonic and made his London début with the London Symphony Orchestra in February 1918. This was followed by a series of concerts spread over two months and a repertoire consisting of standard classics and a substantial number of works by British composers—Parry, Holst, Elgar, Bax, Butterworth and Vaughan Williams. The most important new works were: Vaughan Williams' 'London' Symphony (which was receiving its second—and first uninterrupted—-performance, as the first had been disturbed by a Zeppelin raid, and after which the composer wrote: "May I say how much I admired your conducting—it is *real* conducting—you get just what you want and *know* what you want and your players trust you because they know it also") and Holst's *The Planets*, which was being heard in public for the first time. Holst, who was about to be despatched to Salonica, just before the Armistice, was given a farewell present of the Queen's Hall and its orchestra for a performance of this new work and asked Boult to take charge of the proceedings. "Then followed feverish activity: I think the whole of St Paul's Girls' School, where Holst taught, helped to copy the parts; somebody trained the choir; scores were sent to me as they were released from the copyists, and the great day came. Most of the School and all his friends were there, and we had a happy party." (During that time, to try to understand the spirit behind each movement of *The Planets* better, Boult studied a little astronomy and astrology.) "When the score was engraved, Holst wrote in my copy, "This score is the property of Adrian Boult who first caused *The Planets* to shine in public and so earned the gratitude of Gustav Holst."

The concerts were judged a great success and Sir Hugh Allen, who knew that he would soon succeed Hubert Parry as Director of the Royal College of Music, asked Boult whether he would consider starting a conducting class there, run on the model of Nikisch's classes in Leipzig. These, the first conducting classes ever to be held in Britain, started in 1919 and continued until 1923–24. But Boult soon became dissatisfied with academic life alone. He was already thirty-five and judged that if his conducting career didn't take off soon, it never would. "I said to myself suddenly, 'Look here, this is a very pleasant life, dancing about in London, going to lots of concerts and lots of parties and occasionally conducting, but this is not a career' and I thought, well, I'll give myself another year here in Britain and if there's no sign of a career whatever it may be and wherever it may be, I shall take steps to find one elsewhere, which would probably have meant cutting everything out and going to Canada or America. And before the autumn when I was due to do this came an offer to become Principal Conductor of the Birmingham City Orchestra and the Birmingham Festival Choral Society, which was exactly what I wanted, because it only involved the six winter months, thus leaving me free to continue my work on the staff of Covent Garden. For I don't know whether you realize that in those days the opera season was very short and lasted only three months—May, June, July. There was also a short winter season, and the rest of the time Covent Garden was completely shut except for dances. So this suited me admirably. But had this offer from Birmingham not turned up, I would surely have gone to America and things would have been quite different. As it was, I intended to stay in Birmingham for ten years. But five years later came the invitation to become Director of Music at the BBC, so there we are. There was no question of saying 'No' to either."

He was then forty years old, and though relatively unknown in London at the time (1929), was asked to take over the Music Department of the BBC mainly for three reasons: the Corporation had tried and failed to reach agreement with Sir Thomas Beecham, whose attitude to the idea of a BBC orchestra giving public, as well as studio, concerts was ambivalent; Boult's sterling work in Birmingham had been noticed and appreciated by the right people; and, as Boult himself picturesquely put it to Nicholas Kenyon, author of the admirable, eminently readable *The BBC Symphony Orchestra, 1930–1980*, "because the best musicians in the country were quite hopeless administrators ... couldn't run a show to save their lives. My father had been in business, so I suppose it came naturally. I realized it was my job to cope." The greatest assets he brought to the job were his selflessness before the goals ahead and towards other colleagues (when he heard that Bruno Walter had been forced to leave Vienna he immediately offered to share his subsequent job as Chief Conductor of the BBC Symphony Orchestra with him, but insularity in the corridors of power prevailed); his total identification with the orchestra; his exemplary capacity to delegate authority, to trust his delegates to do their jobs without interference from him; and his absolute willingness to conduct everything and anything. "There are precious few works that I have absolutely refused to do. Precious few. Nearly always I have done what I've been told or asked to do; it's been for me to do. In the BBC days I did a pretty well all-round picture and on the whole was only given good things to do," he told me.

But during his first year at the BBC Boult was not yet Chief Conductor of its Symphony Orchestra—just Director of Music, with responsibility for planning all the public concerts and broadcast programmes. He had stipulated that he wanted to conduct the orchestra as well. Their inaugural concert—on October 22, 1930 at the Queen's Hall in Portland Place—was a great success. (The programme consisted of the overture to *Der fliegende Holländer*, the Saint-Saëns Cello Concerto, the Brahms Fourth Symphony and Ravel's *Daphnis et Chloé*.) The *Morning Post* reported on the next day that "In the very sonority of God Save the King which opened the first BBC Symphony Concert at the Queen's Hall last night we felt that London now possessed the material of a first-class orchestra. And as the evening progressed, the feeling became a certainty.... We had, from the technical point of view, the best English orchestral playing since the war ... not to mention the admirable conducting of Adrian Boult to whom must go a very considerable share of the credit for the triumphant success of the evening." The rest of the Press echoed its praise.

At the end of the orchestra's very successful first season, during which Boult's reputation grew, his stylistic awareness and care in the shaping of phrases and drawing out of the musical line were all noted by several critics as was the fact that the orchestra seemed to play better under him than under any other conductor. John Reith* asked him if he would become its Chief Conductor and did he also want to remain as Director of Music as well? He answered "yes" to both questions and

* The Powerful Head of the BBC (1889–1971) who was made a peer in 1940.

for the next fifteen years had a hectic time doing both jobs, which, he admits, was sheer madness, as it involved making every major policy decision as well as conducting a vast repertoire in a huge number of public and studio concerts. Indeed, sometimes he had to interrupt his rehearsals and make some snap decision over the studio telephone. But his capacity to delegate and trust his lieutenants stood him in good stead. One of his key delegates was Edward Clark, a brilliant musician in charge of devising programmes and a passionate advocate of contemporary music, who had excellent contacts abroad and was constantly abreast of everything that the major composers of the day were producing.

To his everlasting credit, Boult was sympathetic and receptive to Clark's suggestions and his willingness to perform new works by Berg, Schönberg, Webern, Stravinsky, Hindemith, Bartók, Busoni as well as British composers like Walton, Bax, Holst, Elgar, Vaughan Williams, Delius, Parry and Butterworth, and to start a new series of Friday evening concerts devoted to contemporary music alone, was one of his two most important and far-reaching contributions to British musical life.

The second was the very high standard to which he trained the BBC Symphony Orchestra. Right from the start, the BBC's aim had been, as stated in its concert programmes of the day, "to set a standard for English orchestral playing that would bear comparison with the finest orchestras in the world". And in those pre-war days under Boult, it did. Not only had the BBC secured the best players in the country for the principal positions, but great care had also been taken in the selection of the rank and file. As harpist Sidonie Goossens says, "Boult was an excellent trainer. He taught us everything." Under him the orchestra reached a level and acquired a reputation that it has never enjoyed since, partly because it has never been able to attract players of the calibre that Boult recruited. But in those days it was good enough for conductors like Walter, Toscanini and Koussevitsky to conduct, and all praised its excellence.*

Boult remembers that despite his reputation as a tartar, Toscanini was sweetness itself when he first came to conduct the orchestra for the London Music Festival in June 1935. "He was wonderful, wonderful! He started off with the Brahms fourth which the orchestra and I had

---

* The orchestra's European tour of 1936 was such a success that the entire Vienna Philharmonic turned up at the railway station and played "The Blue Danube" and the "Radetzky March" on the platform by way of farewell!

done ten years before at our inaugural concert when the orchestra was founded, and took it easy during the first movement, occasionally stopping to repeat certain points; the second and third movements he played right through without stopping at all; at the end of the second movement he said, "*Bene, bene*" and just bent over to check a marking in his score. He shouted only once—and he was right to do so—at the principal flute who was a dour and dictatorial Scotsman who needed it and got it. At the end Toscanini said a lot of complimentary things about the orchestra and its leader (Paul Beard) who he said was the best he had ever come across.

"In general the orchestra were a very nice, sensitive and responsive crowd, very sympathetic towards whoever confronted them from the podium; they didn't react violently even against those they didn't like. For example, there was a very eminent Dutch conductor—I won't name him but you can guess who [Mengelberg], who caused three nervous breakdowns in a fortnight ... yes, really. Three of our girl players had to give up. He was trying to do the *Enigma Variations* actually, and one of the critics said that he took such a long time undoing the usual BBC Symphony Orchestra performance of the *Variations* that he had no time to build up his own! I *am* telling you a lot of naughty things today, by the way.... But it's always the same. The greatest conductors interfere with orchestras very little, just as the greatest composers interfere very little with conductors, and simply leave them alone to do what they want.

"Of course composers *as* conductors in general or of their own works in particular, are a different story altogether. Take Richard Strauss, for instance. I don't think he could make his stick talk to the same extent that Nikisch could, but it was an expressive stick, and of course there was a great mind at work on the music—he had a very, very clear and precise picture of the music and of the sound he wanted. I remember him giving a simply monumental performance of the Mozart G minor Symphony (No. 40) in London just before the 1914 War—June I think it was—and it all seemed so easy and effortless ... the pace of the first and last movements was quite deliberate, one heard absolutely everything, he gave you time to listen to every detail, but as always, he took the slow movement fast: he wrote somewhere that all Mozart and Haydn slow movements must, if possible, be done two-in-a-bar...." Did he have the same hypnotic power over the players that Nikisch had? "Oh, I think that the moment you have a man like Strauss in front of an orchestra you have everybody thinking, 'My God, here is this great man, in front of our very eyes' and everything has already begun to happen before he even raises his baton. It was the same with Elgar, who conducted his own works extraordinarily well. Of course, the moment he walked in the whole orchestra got excited straight away; and they all loved him and he got everything he wanted out of them.... But of course it all depends on whether the composer in question is in the top rank as a conductor. Both Strauss and Elgar were top-rankers and got superb performances. Up to a point, so were Stravinsky and Schönberg."

Of course, Boult and his collaborators had not only had to overcome initial resistance—and jealousy in many quarters—to the idea of a broadcasting orchestra that also performed in public and could afford to lure the best players from other orchestras, but also to deal with occasional attacks on their choice of repertoire from the Press and the musical establishment. In those cases, Boult's behaviour was invariably calm and implacably firm.

He steered the orchestra through the difficult days of the war, which lost it several of its best players, and meant evacuation to various places outside London for long periods of time. At the end of the war, he gave up his administrative post as Director of Music to remain as Chief Conductor only. But by then many things had changed. The most serious development was the continuous loss of players and impossibility of replacing them by others of equal calibre, owing to the BBC's inability to match the salaries now offered by the other London orchestras. Morale was low and despite Boult's efforts, the orchestra never regained its pre-war level. Which must mean that a remark made by A. H. Fox-Strangeways in the *Observer* in 1931 and quoted in Nicholas Kenyon's book has a point: "What a conductor can do for an orchestra is much; what they can do for him is more. Conductors are sometimes born, but more often made; made by their orchestras—whom they make...."

But although the BBC professed undying gratitude to Boult for all he had done to build up the orchestra and assured him privately that he would not be retired when he reached sixty (in April 1949), it did 'retire' him a year later. Needless to say, the stupidity of treating creative artists like nine-to-five clerks knows no bounds! For without exception, conductors invariably get better with age, it's in the nature of their profession, and this must have made the BBC's decision all the more hurtful. "It was, well, not *very* painful, it was painful," Boult says with the dignified stoicism characteristic of him. (Yet his wife says she blames the BBC for the ill health he suffered afterwards.) "I hated being separated from the orchestra but luckily two days after the announcement the London Philharmonic asked me to be its Chief Conductor and they were very nice people and I was very happy with them so that really was all right. I was equally busy straight away."

He remained the LPO's Principal Conductor for six years and forged an excellent relationship with the players—as he invariably *has* done, throughout his career. "This orchestra has tremendous respect for this man," says its principal timpanist Alan Cumberland. "He has done an awful lot for us, particularly in hard times and it's a shame he cannot conduct us any more. We'd love to have him, even in a wheelchair. But he's too proud for that. He would never be seen like that in public. He always refused even to be helped on stage. The last time he conducted us he insisted on walking slowly by himself without anybody helping him and then sitting down, admittedly. Such an *elegant* man in every way.... He has a natural presence.

"As a conductor, well, he always looks the same, no matter what kind of music he is conducting, and we got to know his stick technique so well that every tiny movement of his wrist conveyed a message to us. Whatever it is he emanates comes through his eyes. Otherwise, apart from occasionally caressing his moustache, he stays motionless except for his wrist, which is what he conducts with. And that's all." [Perhaps this is why his was once labelled the "Up, Down, Left and Across" School of Conducting.] "Nevertheless, he always makes you sit at the edge of your seat, and not just at concerts, but at rehearsals as well. For he is one of those conductors who will pick on you if he catches you chatting while he is explaining something and ask you to demonstrate what he has just said. So you can't relax for a moment."

Double bass player Kenneth Goode adds that "something that all good conductors should have at their fingertips is psychology: knowing how far they can rehearse an orchestra and how much they should leave for the concert itself. Sir Adrian's judgement as to such matters is always excellent and he carried us to a point where we felt that, on the night itself, there was going to be just that bit more." [Indeed, never over-rehearsing is one of Boult's firm maxims, especially when working with Nordic or Anglo-Saxon orchestras.] "The intricate detail wasn't as important to him as the whole shape of the thing, the journey through a work from its beginning, through all its movements, to the end."

People have always commented on the sense of 'architecture' that

Boult's readings convey and this is indeed deliberate. In his handbook on conducting, he states quite clearly that "the main object of the interpreter of music should be to give his audience the impression that the music which has been flowing past their perception is now standing, as it were, congealed before them, so that they can contemplate it at leisure, like a picture or a building.... It is impossible to lay too much stress on the fact that it is not the detail, but the shape and structure of the work as a whole that really matter and therefore, as the time of the performance comes near, thought must be more and more directed towards structure, and the work looked at from a distance, as it were, and as broadly as possible. The audience should be made to feel the score is laid out in two gigantic pages which can be seen at a glance, without even the disturbance of turning over, and the reason that this idea must be firmly fixed in the mind during the early stages of preparation is that during the performance so much detail work inevitably arises that the issue will be obscured unless a very definite impression has been formed beforehand."

The principal oboe of the London Symphony Orchestra, Anthony Camden, whose father was principal bassoon in the BBC Symphony Orchestra under Boult, was quick to remark that this was one of the things about Boult's interpretations that first struck him at the time: "Structure was his predominant preoccupation then, i.e. that a work has a story to tell, that you start, introduce all the main characters and trace them through to the end. While many other conductors see a work as a series of different experiences and treat them as such, Sir Adrian builds, constructs, a whole edifice.... Yet I think that his truly great performances came very, very late in life when after very, very long experience of testing and testing every day, he came to this very smooth, economical, long line of phrasing. Towards the end of his career, he could conduct a symphony and see a phrase starting right at the beginning and tracing it right through to the end, which is a spectacular thing."

Indeed, Boult himself has a great deal to say about the flow, the forward movement of music, in his handbook on conducting: "It is really true to say that every bar begins with its second beat and ends with the first beat of the next bar," Boult has written. "Music leans forward and its course might be compared to a waterfall or a ball rolling downstairs; pushing forward to the edge of each step and then dropping to the step below." And later on he urges that great care must be taken that the stick never stops in the middle of a bar, as this is certain to interfere with the smooth run of the music. "Even in *ritardandi* this should be avoided; in fact a complete stoppage of the stick should only occur when the rhythm is definitely broken—in a *ritardando* it is only bent, and the curve of the bend would be spoilt if the point of the stick were allowed to stop."

And it is this ability to allow the music to flow in one unbroken line that makes his recordings of the Brahms symphonies such landmarks in the recorded history of these works. Yet those Brahms recordings happened by accident: the late fifties, which saw his seventieth birthday (in April 1959), were a low ebb in his career, a time when, as he puts it, "they thought I was finished." But he made a great comeback in the sixties, chiefly in the recording studio. (He has made forty-three recordings since then!) Christopher Bishop, now Managing Director of the Philharmonia Orchestra, who was his recording producer for several years, revealed in an eighty-fifth birthday tribute to Boult in the *Gramophone* how those recordings came about:

"During the years between 1965 and 1970, all his recordings were of Elgar and Vaughan Williams works. It was in August 1970, when we were recording the *Enigma Variations* and *Job* with the London Symphony Orchestra, that we found we had two spare sessions because Sir Adrian and the orchestra had worked so efficiently. Here was a chance to start on something different and I suggested a Brahms symphony. He decided that No. 3 was his favourite at the moment ['the one conductors hate to end concerts with, because it doesn't finish with a great racketing fortissimo,' Sir Adrian comments wryly, twitching his moustache], and that recording was so successful commercially that I was allowed to complete the set of four. One might ask why I started the Brahms symphonies in the rather hole-in-the-corner way. I am afraid there is a tendency to pigeon-hole conductors and Sir Adrian had been very busy recording the English repertoire which we all knew he could do with more authority than anyone. However, as he had 'served his time' in English music, I felt it was time to put on record his magnificent Brahms and his famous Schubert 'Great' C Major. Having tasted blood (and most gratifying sales) we embarked on the Wagner series."

Boult had loved Brahms since childhood when he had heard Hans Richter's performance, and his mother playing the symphonies on two pianos with a friend and later with himself. "Brahms's music has everything: there is an enormous range of every kind of mood in the literature of the four symphonies. I think it was Joachim who said that sometimes he felt that Brahms was a greater composer than Beethoven. I can understand that." But it was hearing Brahms's great friend Fritz Steinbach conducting the Fourth Symphony with the London Symphony Orchestra that really revealed Brahms to him. He was sixteen at the time and remembers that when he returned home from Westminster at the end of term his mother remarked: "You do seem to be playing Brahms much better than last time; you've evidently learnt some more about it." And the fact that Boult has the true Brahms sound and style in his blood and ears was why Simon Rattle sought his advice over the symphonies. Yet, as Rattle points out in the last chapter of this book, whenever he had a question about something that seemed difficult to him, all Boult would say was, "Well, of course, naturally, it goes like this." "And for him it does. But not for us. We have lost the style and the tradition."

Wagner is another composer that Boult has loved since early childhood when, at the age of seven, he first heard Hans Richter (who had been Wagner's resident secretary at the time of the composition of *Die Meistersinger* and radiated affection for his music, "so that one became very addicted to it"), conduct the Overture to *Tannhaüser*. "Wagner created a new musical language. His use of chromatics brought the language beyond Beethoven and Brahms. Strauss, of course, wouldn't be anywhere without Wagner, and Elgar too would have been a very different person without Wagner. It is interesting that although Wagner wrote a lot of nonsense about what he was doing and about the stage and a lot of poets sniff at his texts, nobody questions the power of his music."

His own interpretations were influenced by both Richter and Nikisch, whose mercurial temperament made him an ideal conductor for *Tristan* while Richter "was the personification of an opera like *Die Meistersinger* and the *Ring*. The way he directed the *Ring* made you feel that it was not just an opera that was going past but a great building that you were looking at, quite solid. I remember thinking that the moment he began the long E flat at the beginning of *Das Rheingold* you knew that nothing but an earthquake would stop the thing going on for days, until one came to the end of *Götterdämmerung*."

Sadly Boult never conducted much opera, much to the shame of the Royal Opera House. He did a few performances of *Parsifal* at the Royal College of Music in 1919 which resulted in his being invited to conduct this opera on tour with the British National Opera Company a few years later—seventeen performances all over the country. But perhaps the greatest shame was not being allowed to conduct *Wozzeck* on stage at Covent Garden, after his triumphant concert performances with the BBC Symphony Orchestra in 1934, which prompted an enthusiastic letter from Berg himself. When I asked him why, he replied, "Do you know the English word 'jealousy'? The BBC offered a complete cast, the orchestra, and myself to Covent Garden for three performances and Covent Garden said, 'No, thank you.' Who was Director at Covent Garden at the time? You can find out. Whoever it was [Sir Thomas Beecham] he wouldn't let anyone near him who was of comparable stature and education." (Perhaps there was still a residue of bitterness and resentment at the success of the BBC Symphony Orchestra, to whose concerts, Beecham had predicted, no one who was anyone would go. "They would just send their servants!") But Boult did conduct some ballet at both Sadler's Wells and Covent Garden. Margot Fonteyn wrote after a performance of Ashton's choreography based on Elgar's *Enigma Variations* that "the *Variations* were incredibly beautiful under your inspiration."

When I met Sir Adrian for our only conversation in July 1979, a few months after his ninetieth birthday, his mind and memory were in tip-top condition. He never officially retired and gave no farewell concert: a few months before his ninetieth birthday, after completing his new recording of *The Planets*, he quietly let it be known that he wouldn't be working any longer. One of the last things I asked him was whether, looking back on his long career, he had any regrets or wished that anything had been different. He replied that "of course, I would have liked a Europe without wars. And I should have liked to have done some more opera. But apart from the first four or five years which I would otherwise have spent in a German opera house, I don't think my career would necessarily have been very different. I was very lucky really and enjoyed myself a great deal."

Yet the first thing he would advise a prospective young conductor is to think about getting another job. And only if he feels that "I'd rather put my head in a gas oven if I can't conduct" should he embark on a conducting career. Otherwise, best to settle for a comfortable nine-to-five job and indulge in plenty of amateur musical activities which will give him all the pleasure and none of the headaches of professional music-making. He says that many a time has he received grateful letters from contented amateur musicians whom he thus discouraged from pursuing an active career, "because an artist's life is awfully taxing, not only for the artist himself but also for his wife and family. I mean if you read Busoni's letters to his wife, poor man, longing to be home and compose, yet having to travel, travel, travel in order to make money. And those poor wives ... they do have a miserable life. Take my wife. It's been a terrible life for her. We have been together now for fifty years and she spends her life as a servant girl, really. She organizes me, cooks every meal, looks after this house, does it all, for we have no servants, there aren't any servants nowadays.... That's why I try to advise all but the most dedicated to seek other jobs.

"And the strain is sometimes very great. You ask why I said that someone or other [Nikisch] was the only one free from the impulse to turn the other way and run before coming out onto the platform. But you can't possibly do creative artistic work without feeling awful about it beforehand. We all suffer like that." And afterwards? Did it take him long to unwind and relax and could he sleep at night? "Oh, yes. A lot of these people get frightfully het up but why? If you have control of the orchestra and have thought it all out beforehand, what is there to unwind *about*? It's like making a speech. People don't lie on their backs on the floor having to recover after making speeches. If you are giving out something you have prepared properly you know how it's going to go and that ought to be enough. Two or three minutes should do you." Can he not remember any extra-special nights, then, nights when suddenly "something" quite out of the ordinary happened to him and to the orchestra?

"I know what you mean but, well, I'm an Englishman, I don't think one can let anything get out of control. If you let yourself get as het up, as completely involved, as that, I can't believe that you are giving the work all you can. After all, if it's out of control in one way, then it may also be out of control in another way that you don't want."

Is he a religious or "politically aware" kind of person?

"Not terrifically. A little of both. I vote. I believe in doing one's job. I'm not a Catholic, I don't go to confession or anything like that, but I believe in doing the work properly and in not telling lies like everybody does nowadays."

In the speech Boult made to the Oriana Society at Oxford as a twenty-year-old, he had named "observance of the composer's every wish" as the first guideline for interpretation. And this sums up the essence of his artistic credo. It is illustrated admirably in a delightful incident that happened when he first conducted the Vienna Philharmonic, in 1933. When they were rehearsing the Mozart G minor

Symphony (No. 40), he was astonished to find that the violas, followed by the second and first violins, slurred their first two notes. (This is printed in the parts but not in the full score and he had always supposed that it was put in by some nineteenth-century editor when the parts were engraved.) So he stopped and asked their leader, Professor Rosé, if they always played it this way. "He gave a delightful Viennese shrug and replied 'We do what the conductor wants.' But it's not what the *conductor* wants that matters, but what *Mozart* wants. The autographed manuscript of this symphony is in the library in this very building [the Musikverein]—we can find out at once. We sent up and found no sign of a slur in the original." The orchestra, which was most amused that a foreigner should have questioned a point like that and known that the original was there, remembered where the manuscript was and a few days later sent Boult a copy of the relevant passage of the original, bound together nicely with a folio with all their signatures. Only with typical Viennese carelessness, they had copied the wrong passage. "But never mind. It was a charming gesture and later on I showed it to Bruno Walter who was delighted to see the signatures of all his friends and we laughed very much."

SIR COLIN DAVIS
Philosopher and Psychoanalyst

"I think you only develop if you accept responsibility," said Sir Colin Davis, knighted in the New Year's Honours of 1980, in reply to my question about whether the cumbersome administrative duties associated with his job as Music Director of The Royal Opera, Covent Garden, were not too frustrating for an artist. "There isn't any other path, really. Of course it all depends on how you define the word responsibility. Beethoven's was obviously to his own gift, and he took it very seriously. But only if you have an outstanding creative gift are you justified in doing that. We interpreters and re-creators are middle men and have quite a different task: we are here to serve the creations of other, greater men and this puts, or should put, our egos in perspective. As a conductor I'm responsible not only for my own attempt to penetrate the composer's mind, but also for all the other people taking part in this attempt: first, for creating the conditions which will enable us to engage the best possible people, and secondly, for getting them into the frame of mind in which they can do their best."

He is convinced that these responsibilities can best be carried out by occupying a full-time job rather than by guest-conducting, because "it's only when you stay with the same group of people that you get past the superficial level to what's important. Otherwise, there are all the distractions of novelty, entertainment, etc. But they wear off very quickly and then what are you going to do? You'll have to get down to what you have inside yourself and what *they* have and to how you're going to bring these two things together. You can't rely on your face being you; it has to come from down there, from your solar plexus or somewhere, anywhere you can find it. Because you have to get hold of the orchestra and the cast and expand them so that they can let out a cascade of sound; and when they do it well, it can be incredibly exciting. . . .

"But it can't be done if there is jealousy or meanness or antagonism in the air—especially inside you. All the deadly sins must go. The Devil must be banished from our rites. He has to go and he is feeling pretty miserable a lot of the time. The most difficult moments are the rehearsals where you have to talk and deal with people and their personae. Somebody said the other day that music is indecent because in the process of making it you are asking people to lay aside their persona, their outer crusts, the crusts that argue, criticize, are defensive. You have to get rid of all that. And you're inviting people to share something which is in the air; it is not theirs, not mine, not anybody's. Yet, somehow, we have to find this thing. But before we do, they have to accept me. And I must not get in their way, or my own, or come between them and what they are trying to do. And sometimes, amazingly enough, it happens. If people are musical and *want* to play, they will share this thing with you. I don't know why or how it happens."

A long time ago, Davis came to the conclusion that his job and his human responsibility is not giving the best performance of anything, because "that isn't a sane concept", but making the people he is working with relax and want to play well. "And if you can't change orchestras there are certain things about them that you have to accept; and sometimes you get it wrong because you haven't found the pulse of that particular group; sometimes you find yourself making mistakes and then, by backing off a bit, you take yourself to task and try something else. You always have to be sensitive to the situation, open to the music, to the players and to the general atmosphere, and try to manipulate it so that it goes in a positive direction. It's no use shooting yourself because you did something you despise; you just have to pick yourself up and say, well, next time I'll try not to do it. That's how one tries to live with one's wife and children—and with music.

"Music, of course, is a colossal compromise because on the one hand you have something in your head and on the other you hear something played, and the two don't necessarily coincide. You try to bring them together, but it's no use demolishing the world because they don't quite match. You have to include the things that are deviations from your ideal in the same way that you do in your dealings with human beings."

It is his nature to deal with people directly, outspokenly, and to tell them exactly what he thinks. However brutal this may sound at times, he finds it preferable to indulging in sneaky backroom intrigues and behind-the-scenes conspiracies. Basically, he acknowledges that there are as many methods of conducting and dealing with orchestras as there are conductors, and he has chosen the way that goes best with what he really is—"otherwise I'd be out of gear with everything." His way is not to insist on a performance at every rehearsal—"that would be auto-eroticism"—but to organize the technical side of things so that something can happen at the performance—if it wants to. "For, as Robert Graves says in one of his poems, the Goddess of inspiration is a bitch. It's our business to prepare ourselves technically, to put the linen out, light the candle—and not get so excited that we cannot control ourselves. Because if, after all, the bitch Goddess did come and you had spilt your seed, she wouldn't be very pleased with you. She might come—and you might miss her. Occasionally suddenly there's the rustle of a dress, and, oh boy, we're there, we've got it all.... I might write a poem about this myself one day."

Davis does, on occasion, write poetry, to overcome what he calls his intellectual inferiority and "to explore the business of creation, which, as I'm not a composer, I could only do with words." He has always felt that if ever he did anything creative, it would be with words, for which he has a passion. Literature, in fact, is one of the greatest influences on his life: he has often said that a conductor who doesn't read is depriving himself of a road to being a better musician. And when, at around thirty-five, he went through a period of intense personal and professional crisis, it was literature—Hermann Broch's *The Sleep-walkers* and *The Death of Virgil*, and *The Odyssey* by Nicos Kazantzakis in particular—that helped him put himself together again. He knows these books almost by heart, calls them his bibles and quotes from them constantly. He considers this kind of intellectual curiosity to be an essential quality for a conductor: "no use being entirely intuitive, a child of nature."

"Other necessary attributes are obviously good health, in order to cope with his strenuous job. And charm. Otherwise, how is he going to get around people? A conductor has got to be either charming or terrifying; or else have such prodigious gifts that people will put up with his eccentricities. But these days making people do things by frightening them is out. So that leaves charm. But to be charming, he has to be genuine, he has to like people. Because you can't fool musicians; their instincts are too sharp. Sometimes they're wrong, but in the end you can't fool them. And he has to have stamina, juice, voltage; and a certain shamelessness: he has to stand up there and be counted. Because all those eyes will be seeing straight through him. As Kazantzakis said, 'Let them look until the Day of Judgement: stand there and be counted—unashamed. . . .' And most important, he has to be able to handle power. In fact one of the reasons why I accepted the Music Directorship of Covent Garden was to find out whether I could cope with power and still go on being myself. That's *really* inviting the Devil to supper: 'Come on then, let's see!'"

Colin Davis was born in Weybridge, Surrey, on September 25, 1927— the fifth of seven children. His father was a bank clerk, a troubled man, to whom he often refers as "my poor father". The family, who lived above a draper's shop, were not well off and didn't possess a piano. They did, however, own a gramophone and Colin's father had a sizeable collection of classical records, to which the child started listening with intense concentration from the age of nine. He felt that his response to music was something very secret and very personal and seldom talked about it to anyone else.

When he was eleven, a great-uncle who had made good in South Africa found a place for him at a public school—Christ's Hospital— where one of the senior boys encouraged him to learn to play the clarinet. (The fact that he never learnt to play the piano at all well was later to prove a drawback at the beginning of his career.) Soon he was good enough to play the clarinet in the school band, which played the boys into the Dining Hall three times a week. He also taught himself to read scores and spent most of his spare time playing chamber music with friends and some of the masters, or listening to records. At the age of thirteen, he heard a recording of the Beethoven eighth symphony, and it proved an experience that could be described as a conversion, a calling to dedicate the rest of his life to music. "It turned my head: the power, the tenderness, the beauty, the ferocity of music. I loved it passionately!" There and then he decided that he wanted to be a musician, and particularly a conductor. His parents were sympathetic but powerless to help with money, and worried about the poor financial prospects of a musical career. Along with several of his masters at Christ's Hospital, they tried to discourage him. But he wouldn't budge, and is convinced that it's good for every musician to be tested in this way.

So off he went and won a scholarship to the Royal College of Music, where he sometimes found the fact that he was technically less good than most of his fellow students a strain. "I wasn't a professionally trained musician like someone who has learnt properly, with a real teacher. If my sons were to decide to become musicians, for example, they would at least have some background. I had nothing except this passion for music and this lustful ambition to be in it, part of it," he told his biographer, Alan Blyth. "I was drunk on this noise, this fantastic material. It was the greatest pleasure of my life and it still is."

But although his heart was set on conducting and his musical perspective wider than the confines of his, or of any other instrument, Davis was not allowed into the conducting class, because he could not play the piano. At the end of his years at the Royal College, he was drafted into the army where he was not considered "officer material", and spent his time as a bandsman in the Household Cavalry stationed at Windsor and playing at parades and banquets. But a chance to conduct finally beckoned when a group of musicians formed themselves into the Kalmar Orchestra, which met in a Bayswater basement every Wednesday. They chose Davis as their conductor. Out of this able orchestra grew the Chelsea Opera Group, which started off by performing Mozart operas at Oxford and Cambridge.

It was with them that he made his conducting début in 1950—the first of what he calls his seven years in the wilderness—with *Der Schauspieldirektor* and *Don Giovanni*, an opera which was to play an important part in his career. Mozart had already become his consuming passion among composers, and he explained the reasons for this in an interesting interview in the *New York Times*: "I loved Wagner as a child. After adolescence, however, Mozart became more and more the main thing. I suppose in order to protect myself from my own adolescent explosion, I tended to admire those things that helped keep me together. Wagner is dangerous stuff; it's better to be in some possession of your faculties before you get involved in it.... And so in my early twenties I pursued other things. And in Mozart you find a fantastic balance between the elements that make up music and make up a human being. Nobody has to die for love in *Le nozze di Figaro*; nobody is tempted over the border into irrationality. You touch one of the most dangerous buttons of the human computer, and then sheer love of life, and the sheer senselessness of destroying it, overcome the dangers at the end."

His conducting in both those operas greatly impressed the audience and those working with him, which included Robert Ponsonby (Masetto), now Controller of Music for BBC Radio, and David Cairns, writer and critic. But at the same time he played the clarinet in various orchestras including Glyndebourne (under Fritz Busch) and Alec Sherman's New London Orchestra. He had meanwhile married soprano April Cantelo, and had it not been for her earnings, his own meagre £200–300 a year would have meant living on the breadline. They had two children—now fully grown up. (Indeed Davis, who now has five younger children from his Persian-born second wife Shamsi, is himself a grandfather.) He says that he was "terribly idealistic" as a young man and couldn't reconcile the struggle to eat with all those crazy ideals. Which is why he wasn't as involved a father to his two elder children as he is to the younger five. "I was too much in the way, much too anxious, too frightened and I'm very sorry now. Looking back, I'm not too proud of the way I was then—which is not to say that I'm proud of the way I am now."

To make ends meet, he took every job that came his way: summer schools, teaching, private lessons, the odd assignment with a provincial orchestra. Unfortunately, even though he was already conducting, the fact that he did not play the piano precluded a job as a coach in provincial German opera houses, which would have been the ideal opening. Finally, in 1957, his seven years in the wilderness came to an end when, after three applications, he was appointed Assistant Conductor of the BBC Scottish Orchestra, a post which offered him the golden opportunity every conductor needs of learning his craft thoroughly. He forged a good rapport with the orchestra and learnt a great deal: "finding that you are driven by this compelling thing [music], very slowly over the years you try to acquire all the knowledge, all the other things needed by you to serve it well."

At the same time, he continued his association with the Chelsea Opera Group, and conducted *Fidelio, Falstaff, Der Freischütz* and plenty of Mozart. His big break came in 1959 when he substituted for an indisposed Otto Klemperer in a concert performance of *Don Giovanni* at the Royal Festival Hall, with Elisabeth Schwarzkopf and Joan Sutherland. The critics raved ("Best since Beecham," said the *Observer*): but he didn't feel ready for the sudden onslaught of attention and for the offers that soon started pouring in. "Frankly, success at first made my life a misery. The strain of having too much to learn while the public expected you to be marvellous all the time was immense." But it opened the doors to the kind of job he needed most:

the Music Directorship of Sadler's Wells Opera where he spent five years and learnt both how to cope with all the intricacies of operatic production and "how to behave myself". At the time, he was reportedly abrasive, often defensive and occasionally rude. But he forged a good rapport with Glen Byam Shaw, the Director of Productions, and together they instilled a team spirit right through the opera house. After he resigned in 1965 *Opera* magazine summarized his achievements by praising the improved standards of orchestral playing and the sense of corporate musicianship that permeated his performances.

After his resignation, both his professional and his private life plunged into an all-time low for the next two years; although many thought that he would be invited to become Principal Conductor of the London Symphony Orchestra with whom he enjoyed a lively relationship, the post in fact went to Istvàn Kertesz. He tried, but failed, to get the Music Directorship of the Frankfurt Opera. If a reasonable job didn't turn up by the time he was forty, he reckoned he would fall apart. But William (now Sir William) Glock, who had known him for years, saved the day by appointing him Chief Conductor of the BBC Symphony Orchestra in 1967—just in the nick of time—"the greatest challenge of my life and the completion of my education".

Before the BBC offer, he underwent what he called his crisis of middle age: "I felt very lost and troubled about why I was being a conductor, what I was doing it for. I felt I was doing it for myself and knew this to be entirely wrong. I didn't like it. This was the time I chanced upon Broch's *Death of Virgil*, in a New York bookstore, in which Virgil on his deathbed came to believe that all his attempts at writing verse were self-indulgence. 'If only,' he thought, 'I had made one useful human gesture!'" He told *The Daily Telegraph* that the book dissuaded him "from my ambition to be the greatest tiger, to be powerful and rich. This was the time when my first marriage went to pieces, because we were aiming at different things. If you are trying to live together you have to have a common aim, as you do if you're trying to play a piece of music together with other people."

Looking back, Davis feels that his ambition coupled with professional insecurity at the time contributed to this break-up. Then slowly, with the help of Broch's books, he began to put the pieces together again. "I tried to make myself all of a piece, somehow. Of course, I never made it—I still haven't completed the jigsaw, there are always bits missing—but there is an aim which goes for my private life and my attitude to music, however badly I might fail: I try to lead a positive life, which means that I wage war on vanity and greed. So what are you left with? You're left with a talent, a little talent, which you don't wish to disgrace. You never fall into the trap of thinking that you granted it to yourself—you didn't. But that's what keeps you humble; and you just have to get on with the work and accept it and do your best—there isn't really any more to be done. In the same way that narcissism is annoying in other people, so you have to watch for it in yourself—are you being narcissistic, are you being self-indulgent, are you being an idiot, are you being angry for no purpose, and so on. One is continuously criticizing oneself...."

Davis remained Principal Conductor of the BBC Symphony Orchestra for four years, during which time he worked harmoniously with Glock—an immensely charming, kindly, erudite man with a quicksilver brain and an excellent sense of humour—who chose the repertoire in consultation with him. Within a year, his relations with the orchestra became very good, as he gradually acquired more tact and checked some of the forthrightness with which he was used to dealing with the London Symphony Orchestra. An orchestra like the BBC Symphony, which has to give both public and studio concerts all over the country and tour abroad, offered a marvellous opportunity to learn a great deal of symphonic repertoire and tackle works—like the Beethoven ninth—which he had previously shied away from.

"The Ninth, particularly the slow movement, is very difficult. In fact all slow movements are technically difficult: you have to decide where to beat so as to leave the players some freedom to do something wonderful. You simply have to trust them. Twenty years ago I didn't and consequently couldn't help overconducting. Now I do trust and believe in them instead of trying to conduct every note they're playing, because I'm *not* playing it; *they* are; and a lot of them are damned good at it and so you want them to have some freedom to express themselves. They know this music terribly well and those of them who are artists have much to express. So give them the freedom to do it. It will be all the more beautiful for coming out of them rather than merely obeying your instructions.

"This goes for lots of those slow movements; like the Funeral March in *Götterdämmerung*, which is full of complexities. It is very slow and full of awkward rhythms written right across the pulse. If you have the courage to beat in four, very slowly, and persuade the musicians to do it this way, it works very much better, because you can make something of the architecture of the piece. If on the other hand you're merely beating so that the players can be together, you cannot really make music out of it. So it's usually a compromise, and a challenge for them to listen to one another, because when they have nothing to hang on to, they have to know exactly where they are.

"Another very difficult work from the technical point of view—perhaps *the* most difficult I have ever tackled, was Peter Maxwell Davies's *Worldes Blis*— a thirty-seven-minute-long piece which begins very slowly with a great white, egg-shaped note which finishes up several seconds later. In fact all the notes at the beginning are very long and very slow. So you can either beat very big beats that allow maybe too much freedom in order to get some sort of line, or you can beat small staccato beats which make it easier to control the thing. Another difficulty in this piece is that later on you get some very fast music with very complex divisions which requires a lot of arithmetic on my part. And while the arithmetic wasn't too difficult, getting the changes of pulse into your system was. Because most of these rhythms cannot really be heard at all: they are just there, in parts of the score. It's easy to mark up rhythms which are actually heard. But keeping a changing pulse of this kind going on independently of what's happening everywhere else in the orchestra, is very, very hard."

Haydn is another composer whose symphonies Davis found techni-cally challenging. (He has conducted excellent recordings of several Haydn symphonies with the Concertgebouw Orchestra of Amster-dam.) "You have to watch your step in Haydn because he's always pulling the carpet from under you. Nothing in Haydn is predictable. He was endlessly fascinated by the art of composition and there is nothing regular about the way he composes; the length of his phrases is very uneven indeed. So you have to be sure to understand the process of his thoughts, read right through the symphony first and then break it into sections so as to get the structure right; otherwise you may trip up, thinking there might be another bar. Of course, there *could* be, and then you would have another version of this symphony—although there is no reason why there should be. It just *could* have gone another way.... The possibilities of music are never exhausted just by the score in front of you. Yes, you are right that a good score should convince you that everything in it is inevitable, the *only* way the music could have gone, like Beethoven's usually do. Beethoven always worked by doing many sketches and hammering at them until they sounded right; and he expresses himself with such force that you cannot dislodge these versions any more.

"But Haydn doesn't speak in that kind of voice at all. At times, he is doing the most prodigious juggling act. Technically, the only other thing to ensure when conducting Haydn symphonies, any symphonies, any music, is that you don't get in the way, but listen to what he's trying to do and not impose anything on it. With Haydn you always feel that the *composer*, rather than the man, is to the fore, that he doesn't aim any higher than to be a good composer and that any insights into life are drawn into the actual act of composition. And sometimes he comes up with something so grave, so profound ... but sometimes he doesn't. Yet even then, the music is always very well composed, with great *joie de vivre*, dancing, singing, and perhaps too many witticisms."

Davis believes that the deepest and truest feelings of which Haydn was capable are contained in the Symphony No. 99, which is very beautiful and which he is supposed to have written on hearing of Mozart's death—his tribute to his old friend. And it seems to him that Mozart, too, felt that he had something to learn from Haydn as far as composition went. "In the string quartets dedicated to Haydn, you actually notice Mozart composing, which is something you very rarely do—you never feel him composing in *Figaro*, for instance, or in anything after the E flat Symphony (No. 39)—so you conclude that he was trying to learn something."

But technical difficulties apart, there are some works, like the Mahler sixth, which he finds hard to identify with from the emotional point of view—and others, like Beethoven's *Missa Solemnis*, which are always exhausting to do because he identifies with the music *too much*, "and this makes it difficult for me to keep control and not go under", as he is very moved by the Christian story and finds it impossible even to read the Passion without tears.

His difficulty with the Mahler sixth—in fact, in his youth he disliked all Mahler—is the first movement. He considers that Mahler, who like Haydn composed prolifically, is better in vocal pieces like *Das Lied von der Erde* and *Des Knaben Wunderhorn* than in orchestral works, because the discipline of words makes him condense and distill his ideas in a more compact and effective way. Whereas here he takes a song from *Des Knaben Wunderhorn* and stretches it out to twenty-five minutes. "The question is: Do I want to wallow in it? I'm not sure.... Yet other works, which I also couldn't have conducted twenty years ago, have come to mean a great deal to me. Take the Sibelius fourth, for instance. It meant nothing to me then. But now I find it haunting, magnificent, because of its utter loneliness. Anyone who has sat in a room and gone into his black hole and under knows...."

In 1971, after four years as Principal Conductor of the BBC Symphony Orchestra, Davis was offered the post of Music Director of The Royal Opera, Covent Garden. At the same time, the Boston Symphony Orchestra invited him to be its Music Director. But he felt that he was neither experienced enough to tackle the vast repertoire the Boston offer would require, nor "old enough to handle such an intelligent body of men". So he accepted the post at Covent Garden, fully aware of all the difficulties it involved, which he saw as an incredible opportunity for growth, after which running a symphony orchestra would seem comparatively simple.

"I also wanted to have experience of the great operatic literature, which lies behind all the symphonic music. Traditionally all music came out of opera, out of the theatre, out of song, dance, rituals and processions. So how could one honestly tackle our symphonic heritage without a theatrical background? That's what I thought then and that's what I still think. I mean, how can you understand Mozart's piano concertos if you don't know *Le nozze di Figaro*? If you don't know the meaning of an aria, how can you cope with the arias in those concertos? (For what is the slow movement of K.467 but an aria?) But this is too obvious even to talk about. And interestingly enough, colleagues who started off as symphonic conductors, like Seiji Ozawa whom I like enormously, are now trying to conduct as much opera as they can because they feel, 'My God, behind all this stuff lies all *that* and I must get my hands on it!' So I did the right thing in accepting this job, and I suppose that in a way I've had the best of all worlds. I have the gruelling, sometimes really *gruelling* task of trying to cope with this job and at the same time, delightful interludes with my old friends in Boston and Amsterdam."

So having invited the Devil to supper, Davis then got down to the job: how to plan programmes in a top quality institution which is expected to run a year-long festival, which is impossible, of course, in present day circumstances. Too many opera houses in the world are trying to do exactly the same thing, while there are only a limited number of first rate singers and conductors to go round; therefore, no single opera house will succeed in assembling the best all the time.

"You're lucky if you get thirty per cent top class, forty to fifty per cent middling and twenty to thirty per cent bad performers," he sighs. "You struggle against it, of course, but you know that, in the end, this is what is going to happen."

All decisions are made jointly by Davis, the General Director of the Royal Opera House, Sir John Tooley and, until her enforced departure through ill health in autumn 1981, the Artistic Administrator, Helga Schmidt, who had a special flair for casting. They try to build up a repertoire that includes new pieces, bearing in mind what went on during the previous seasons and trying to strike a balance between the various sections of the repertoire: German, Italian and French and British. Next they cast the new productions and decide who will conduct and direct them, all of which is extremely risky because, like most major opera houses, they have to plan up to five years ahead, and meanwhile some singers may lose their voices, the budget may be cut, or someone may quarrel with someone else. So those plans often have to be changed. In fact, about fifty per cent of their plans materialize: the rest are usually a compromise. "And when the critics say that we have bad planning, they just don't know a thing about the facts of life. They imagine that we can just snap our fingers and say, 'We'll have this, we'll have that.' Then they also criticize us for being cosy. We're not being cosy, we just don't want to waste energy for things that don't matter. It's not for me to say, but this is probably the nicest opera house in the world to work in." (He's right. It is.)

Getting the best conductors is as essential as, if not more so than, getting top singers, because "they are the dynamos that drive the machine. This means that all the little banalities of human nature, all feelings of competition and jealousy towards colleagues—and I've been as idiotic in my day as any human being—have had to go out of the window. Because if you don't get the best conductors, if you can't get Kleiber, Abbado, Mehta, Muti, Maazel, Haitink, Solti, you won't get a top class opera house. (I've probably left several out, but not intentionally.) And if you do have them, where does this leave *you?* The answer is that it leaves you right at the top. Because you have a forever-improving orchestra that loves playing."

The overall standard of orchestral playing at Covent Garden has improved consistently over the years, as was proved by the fact that during the Company's exchange visit to La Scala, the audience cheered the orchestra and Davis alone for a long time. "This was the best thing that will ever happen to me in my job," says the Orchestra Director,

Bram Gay. "This very educated opera audience standing up and cheering *us*, a tired old orchestra from London which everybody thought was very bad. (Don't forget that Solti had never recorded with us. He did all his operatic recordings with the Vienna Philharmonic.) It was very exciting, and at that point the Board realized that a good orchestra was a feasible proposition and has been very good to us ever since. Of course, Colin came to us with a recording contract and records all his operas with us, which, apart from being very nice from the financial point of view, is good for morale because it shows he trusts us.

"If as a Music Director you don't do your operatic recordings with your own people, how are they going to know that you have faith in them?" confirms Davis. "They would believe that you simply didn't think them good enough, and it would be absolutely true. It has to do with identifying with the situation you're in and goes back to what I said at the beginning about responsibility: this place, this job, this chorus, this orchestra are all your responsibility."

Perhaps this is why Gay considers his Music Director pretty well perfect for this particular house. "Everything about him is right for us, and we are grateful that he is English—even though this seems to be a handicap in his career because nobody here seems to take enough notice of him. But they do in Boston and Amsterdam and elsewhere. This is not to say that we have anything against foreign music directors. We don't. But if someone has all the right qualities of musicianship and character *and* is English as well, then it is even better because he instinctively understands our ways. We've known Colin since he was very young of course, and a bit hard and tactless. But now, he's irreplaceable."

Like Solti before him, Davis's first years at Covent Garden were difficult: he was not liked by the orchestra, or the public, or the critics. (Indeed, even now, a few of the older players told me that they would prefer a firmer, more authoritative style of leadership.) The year 1973, when he was vociferously booed on several occasions, was the nadir. By 1975, despite the severe blow of Peter Hall's resignation as Director of Productions which left Davis stranded for his two first seasons, things started looking up: some of his policies had begun to work, especially as regards repertoire. He survived, despite the attacks, and gradually began a series of productions of his favourite works: *La clemenza di Tito*, *Idomeneo*—which he adores almost more than any Mozart opera, because he feels that there is more of Mozart in it than in any of his other works—*Wozzeck*, *Der Freischütz*, *Benvenuto Cellini* (which he took to La Scala along with *Peter Grimes* and *Clemenza*), *The Rake's Progress*—a sparkling production, the first night of which was attended by the composer's widow—and the British première of the three act version of *Lulu*.

As Music Director, it naturally fell to him to tackle the Garden's productions of the big Wagner operas, the *Ring* and *Tristan und Isolde*, for the first time in his career. The *Ring* was directed by Götz Friedrich, with whom Davis seemed to have struck "an ideal relationship" at the time. He needs the stimulus of a strong producer and says that he lacks visual sense, and cannot tell whether he will like a production until he is faced by it by which time it is too late to change. The production was highly controversial, and got mixed reviews at first, although gradually, as it matured, most people liked it (a similar reaction to that accorded by audiences to Patrice Chéreau's equally controversial 1976 Bayreuth production).

"It's all very well to say go back and do what Wagner wanted, but what he wanted wasn't really practical; it couldn't be done. Wagner himself wasn't successful in staging it the way he's imagined it, because none of the machines worked, the dragon got lost and so on, and one reads of his despair about his production. So you're forced to do something else. And as the *Ring* is essentially an opera of ideas, it doesn't really depend on the physical facts of dragons or people riding horses through clouds. This is all poetic nonsense, and can be done only in one's own imagination. So do you actually try to cut across Wagner? I mean what is Valhalla? Even Wotan doesn't give a proper answer. The only important thing is what Wagner tells us in the music: he serves us the cliché of all time, with lots of cosy, beautiful notes. But what *is* it? Basically the fact that Wotan wants something for nothing. He wants his castle and doesn't want to pay for it. So it doesn't really matter if you put a corrugated iron shack on stage, or a fairytale castle, which is already gilding the lily. I think it's more effective to put something cynical, something that contradicts the music, which is plastered with all that lovely harmony and all those shiny brass instruments. Then Fricka says, 'For God's sake man, wake up, what are you talking about?' And everybody hates her because she's sensible.

"None of the characters in the *Ring* are anything to get excited about, in fact, or very attractive. Perhaps because they are not really characters, but embodiments of certain ideas. If you consider the goings on in *Rheingold*, for instance, you probably wouldn't feel inclined to go and see it at all. But the problem is that music can't really criticize. Wagner is *trying* to do so through music, but of course he can't. Because when you hear the Valhalla passage I've mentioned, you think gosh, isn't it beautiful? But it's not meant to be: it's meant to be a stupid old cliché—and yet it isn't because Wagner can't do it. And so he sets up a contradiction in the listener, who is supposed to think that Valhalla is an impermissible absurdity of people who want power without being prepared to pay for it, and yet *hears* a luscious piece of music with Wagner tubas and glittering trumpets—and falls headlong for all those loopholes. For in this respect music is like a woman: so attractive and dazzling that none of her appalling faults, hidden beneath the paint, can show."

Davis found that doing all those Wagner pieces for the first time was the greatest possible challenge, physically, intellectually and emotionally. "You really have to measure up." When they started the *Ring*—in 1974 with *Das Rheingold* and *Die Walküre*—most people felt that his interpretations and general handling of the score left a lot to be desired. This is natural, because, as Karajan says, nothing approaching an artistic result can possibly ever come out of the first time anyone tackles these gigantic works. Before the first cycle, all the old hands in the orchestra were extremely anxious and unconvinced. "'My God, this will never work. I know you've got to be loyal, but this is going to be an appalling *Ring*.' But by the last cycle in 1978, we believed in him: he had developed a feeling for it, and paced it well."

Another major challenge was tackling *Tristan und Isolde* for the first time—to great critical acclaim. Apart from grasping all the musical and technical difficulties in this immense score, he was also forced to face the problem of keeping himself under control in situations where the music moved him close to tears. "The first contact with the thing is so totally overwhelming," he explained to *The New York Times* shortly after the première. "The third act especially, I found very, very depressing. I think Tristan's final outburst where he curses the drink, 'Verflücht sei, furchtbarer Trank', is the greatest passage Wagner ever wrote: the music groans, there are fantastic complexities and the use of the leitmotive is profoundly moving because the English horn tune is one of the most powerful he ever composed. And the way it just touches G major when Tristan remembers Isolde and how he went back to Ireland to see her—when you're conducting it, it's touch and go. You're *just* holding on. Otherwise you'd rush off and disappear into the night. And that's not bloody practical. This is why this stuff is so dangerous.... The 'Liebestod' is also very difficult. I did *Tristan* recently at Covent Garden and I was doing fine. Then suddenly at the very end, I nearly broke down. And that would be ridiculous ... giving up during the last two bars.... Of course at the end of *Tristan* the music does run down—which is not to say that Wagner was tired. But compare this to the end of a Mozart opera, where the inexhaustible surges of energy in the finales make you think that he is about to start composing a new work there and then. Consider the last two minutes of *Figaro*, *Così* or *Don Giovanni*, for instance: the Don has gone to hell and hey presto, we have a big concerto followed by a moral. Crazy, demented energy bubbling underneath....'

Davis's time away from Covent Garden is mainly devoted to the London Symphony Orchestra, the Boston Symphony where he is Principal Guest Conductor, and the Concertgebouw. He has also been appointed Principal Conductor of the Bavarian Radio Orchestra as from 1983. What he most appreciates about foreign orchestras—"and I'm sure that my colleagues in London won't be offended if I say this"—is the quality of the string playing, which is invariably better than in England. He also appreciates the subscription system, now slowly filtering into British concert life, too, which enables conductors to plan a more esoteric repertoire by ensuring regular patronage. In Boston, this made it possible for him to introduce Tippett, who is currently composing a major, eighty-minute choral work specially commissioned by the BSO as part of its centenary celebrations.

Davis has been immersed in Tippett's music since his early days, when he conducted *A Child of Our Time* at the Central Hall, Westminster; later, he conducted *The Midsummer Marriage* at Covent Garden. He also conducted the world premières of *The Knot Garden* in 1970, and of *The Ice Break*, dedicated to him, in 1977, and several other major Tippett works. He is devoted to Tippett, both as a musician and as a person. "There are not enough people like him," he told Alan Blyth. "He has a very fine mind and it's of use to him because of what he does with it in his music, which is *about* something. People who write music about music are pointless. He is an entirely individual voice and his music stems from his relationship with his own psyche which, surely, is why he writes his own librettos; to use another's would allow an impossible intrusion into this relationship.... Those men who, like Tippett, have tried to express inward experiences have either had to disguise their meaning under a superficially attractive façade or lay themselves open to the charge of attempting to express the inexpressible. Tippett has borrowed from every mythology, psychology and esoteric tradition. And since all myths come from a central pool of psychological knowledge, the confusion is only apparent." Another reason for his deep attachment to this composer is his originality and unpredictability, which make each work sound quite different from the one before: for while Tippett doesn't really change his language, he is interested in new sounds, and in how to put the music together in different ways.

The two men are very much on the same wavelength as far as their perceptions of inner life and the mystical side of things are concerned, and this is probably *the* true reason for their affinity both as men and as artists, and for the deep friendship between them. "When I got to know him, I put my complete trust in him as a conductor of my music," Tippett explained to Alan Blyth in 1972. "When it came to *The Knot Garden*, I left him entirely in charge—in any case I simply will not interfere with the way someone is conducting my work and anyway I know that Colin has an instinctive understanding of what I want without our ever having discussed it. I just feel that as far as interpreting my music is concerned, he's the tops. I certainly prefer him to myself in my own works."

Davis is also well known as a conductor and champion of French music in general and of Berlioz in particular. He discussed Berlioz's genius and works at length and very interestingly in Bernard Jacobson's book *Conductors on Conducting*. He has conducted (and recorded) *Benvenuto Cellini* and *Les Troyens* at Covent Garden and took the former to La Scala during the exchange visit of 1976. He feels deeply drawn to the world of this composer, his originality, his interest and inventiveness in melody and rhythm, even though these were at the expense of harmony, which meant that Berlioz was somewhat out of date with his times. Davis feels that had Wagner not placed such an emphasis on harmony, thereby killing off a lot of what was happening in the nineteenth century and precipitating the advent of Schönberg and Stravinsky, musical language would have developed more slowly and naturally.

Apart from his regular commitments to Boston and Amsterdam, Davis also conducts more of the world's best orchestras from time to time, in order to stretch and test his own worth. Shortly after our last meeting, he was off to Berlin to conduct the Berlin Philharmonic and had just made plans for Cleveland in 1982. "It may be disastrous; we'll see." He doesn't generally thrive on what he calls a relentless succession of situations, but prefers going back to orchestras he knows, who have watched him grow and change and whom he has watched develop in a way that makes it possible for them to dispense with all the unnecessary preliminaries. "You don't have to sit on top of a wall like a couple of cats glaring at each other, waiting to see who will move first. Although the excitement of discovering a new orchestra can sometimes be electric, this seldom happens instantaneously: the first quarter of an hour everyone just watches and waits and it's an acute discomfort. But from time to time I expose myself to it and go and seek my fortune with new orchestras in order to create danger. Otherwise you tend to get too cosy. But I must say, it makes me look forward to coming back to Covent Garden!"

Davis feels that the only way an artist can survive the pressures of a busy conducting career is "by keeping his feet firmly on the ground and himself firmly grounded in his private life so that the blandishments of the world don't mark him any more". He is lucky in his family life, very happy with his wife Shamsi, whom he pursued all the way to Iran and for whose sake he learnt Persian, and their five children. In fact he revels in paternity and considers children "the most perfect beings in creation. All life is a regression to childhood. If only I could conduct like a child ... then all the music would come out directly, absolutely nakedly and unashamedly, with all the rubbish, all the sediment, cleared away."

Seven years ago he took up playing the violin as a hobby, because his sons started learning by the Suzuki method which stipulates that the best way of encouraging a child to play is for the parent to do so as well. "Now, of course, they are better than I am. I had a charming lesson yesterday from my eldest son on how to improve my playing. We have now started on Mozart duets for violin and viola and it's great fun because not only does it help keep me close to the children, but it also enables me to enjoy music free from the responsibility of having to be good."

The Davises live in London, and have a house in Suffolk where they retreat as often as his career permits. It has a pond with ducklings and birds and moorhens and there he indulges in one of his favourite pastimes: planting trees. He has already planted pines, spruces, firs and azaleas, and finds manual labour and doing something with the earth wonderfully relaxing. His is a household in which "there are no Rolls Royces and nobody living in it but us: me, my wife and all those kids— three boys and two small girls—and nobody coming between us. Damned hard work. My wife, especially, works very hard. So do I, I'm very keen about that because we both know that we don't want anybody else around. That would only mean more people to be responsible for, and more people getting in the way. So we decided to stick to our values. It's extraordinary how my wife and I, coming from such different backgrounds, have moved together and have a common aim. In fact a good wife is the greatest blessing in the world. Although I suppose it's true that good wives and good husbands are created by each other."

In the house in Suffolk Davis also has the time to read (but never newspapers, which are banned from the house because according to his wife they stop people from living, from looking at the women they sleep with or at their children) and to study. Although he tries to do most of his studying when abroad on guest conducting assignments, because doing it quietly means doing it more efficiently, he says that he has nevertheless learnt plenty of scores surrounded by kitchen noises. "I try not to let the studying interrupt the normal running of my life, because that would mean making a special case of myself, sort of locking myself up in the top room and making a point of not being disturbed. Everyone's got to be disturbed sometime. And it took me a long time to learn that, to make music and study just a part of life and not get too excited about it. It's back to Kazantzakis and *The Odyssey* again, where Odysseus is in a village, his last port of call, and they are having a religious procession, parading statues of local gods in the streets; and among them he sees them carrying his own statue: they've turned him into a God. And you mustn't do this to yourself."

On the day of a performance, Davis tends to have a normal day, with a big lunch cooked by his wife—some rice dish plus a little wine— and then an afternoon sleep. Then he washes his hair and has a bath, sometimes with his two daughters. He finds that this kind of normality calms him and takes him out of himself; again he wants to ensure that he doesn't cut himself away from life by over-protecting himself. "And if somebody asked how on earth can you have children with you in the bath just before you go to conduct my answer would be: because they're life, because they are there, because they are fantastic creatures and the best part of me responds to them." He arrives at the opera house about thirty mintues before the performance and has a cup of tea with honey, goes to see the singers and generally tries to relax as much as possible—something which, fifteen years ago, he used not to be able to do, although he realized that feeling tense was counter-productive. And afterwards? Can he switch off and leave it all behind straight away?

"No, I can't. It doesn't seem to be in my nature to be able to keep cool during a performance. [Both orchestral players and Vladimir Ashkenazy have commented on the 'crashing intensity and overwhelming love for the score' he exudes throughout.] If I could, I'm sure I wouldn't be any good at it. One's heart goes on pounding until two or three in the morning. I go home and have some soup and some wine and gossip for a bit, because if I get tired enough I can sleep. I'm better at that now. When I was younger, I used to be pursued by the music all night long. But it's hard to sleep when you've done the Beethoven ninth, or the 'Jupiter' Symphony or *The Seasons* or anything, what difference does it make? And the next day, I'm finished. Spent. Salmon die when they return to their native pool and lay their eggs. Then they just float sideways up. I must say, I feel just the same."

CARLO MARIA GIULINI
"Conductor, Gentleman, Mystic"

My earliest impression of Carlo Maria Giulini dates back to 1963, when he conducted a deeply moving and unforgettable performance of the Verdi Requiem at the Royal Festival Hall in London. I was still in my teens and, although I knew the work from recordings, I had never heard it 'live' before. Overwhelmed, I made my way backstage to ask him for an autograph.* There was a long queue, and the late Sydney Edwards (Arts Editor of the London *Evening Standard*) was in front of me, congratulating the maestro and saying how delighted he was to know that he would soon be recording "his" Requiem for posterity. Giulini thanked him in his unfailingly courteous manner, but tapped him on the shoulder and gently admonished him: "*Verdi's* Requiem, not mine!"

His answer was completely spontaneous, almost a reflex reaction, and stated something ridiculously obvious—yet something seldom, very seldom, to be heard from a conductor, especially when addressing an adulatory admirer. It implanted itself so vividly in my mind that, sixteen years later, I could clearly visualize the incident as I walked to his Milan apartment for our first meeting. The apartment was in a bit of a mess as his younger son was in the process of moving in. This meant that his parents, who wanted to help him settle in, would miss their annual holiday to the Aegean island of Lemnos for the first time in years. Instead, Giulini planned to spend most of the summer exploring the little towns of Tuscany and Umbria, "with their treasures of architecture and painting".

He has always liked a lot of time off conducting: time to relax and

---

* Gillian Eastwood, the Philharmonia Orchestra's principal second violin, well remembers that concert, "when the applause went on for over half an hour, and I didn't sleep all night. I still get goose pimples when I remember those trumpets in the Dies Irae!".

replenish the well, to read widely—whereas after a long day's work he only feels up to a detective story or maybe a cowboy film—to study, but especially to think, reflect on, and rethink about scores until they are soaked into his system and he feels at one with them. One of his characteristics as a conductor is his single-minded, almost religious dedication and his equally single-minded determination to work only in the right conditions—a courageous stand, considering the tempting offers he has been inundated with throughout his career.

He feels that an artist should "defend himself against too much work" and considers that one of the major problems of our time is the fact that we do not allow ourselves enough time to think. Action is the byword today, and jet travel relatively easy and comfortable, but a little bit too quick for him! "When I was younger, I needed time to study. Now, I need time to think." He accepts the fact that every human being has his own rhythm of doing things, has never been in a hurry, preferring to risk being "five years too late rather than five minutes too early", and is the first to admit that his repertoire is not vast.

"After so many years as a conductor I am, of course, able to look at a score and conduct it. But this is not enough. I need to be one-hundred-per-cent involved, to feel that this work now belongs to me, to my life, heart and body as well as to my mind. This is why there is some music which I cannot conduct. It doesn't belong to my nature, and I don't want to conduct it just because I can read the score and learn it."

Surprisingly for a conductor who can produce exquisite lyrical sound, he does not conduct Puccini, because he feels that he sometimes wrote music purely for melodic reasons, unlike Verdi, whose every note emerges out of the text and dramatic necessity. He also shuns most contemporary music, mainly because he thinks that it fails to involve the listener emotionally. "You come away from hearing a work and say '*molto interessante*': there is no emotional response." He cannot identify with Schönberg or late Stravinsky either, although he loves the latter's Russian period. The works of Richard Strauss have been conspicuously absent from his repertoire, possibly because he had a surfeit of them as a young man when playing the viola in the Augusteo Orchestra in Rome. "But maybe I'll come back to them one day." Up to now he has not conducted any Wagner, although he feels ready, inside himself, for *Tristan* and *Die Meistersinger*, if and when the right circumstances should arise. (The *Ring*, on the other hand, with its world of "superhuman and subhuman beings", does not interest him.)

When Giulini conducted Beethoven's *Eroica* in Chicago in 1977—a work he subsequently recorded with his own orchestra, the Los Angeles Philharmonic—it was the first time he had tackled this symphony in seventeen years. Before that, he had left it alone for fifteen years, because he was dissatisfied with his interpretation. Finally, he became deeply convinced that "the strange and very dangerous word 'Eroica' has nothing to do with the usual sense of the word 'heroic' or with the still more dangerous connection with Napoleon, but is linked with the classical Greek concept of the Hero as a man with high ideals about life, man and freedom, ideals for which he is willing to sacrifice himself. [Heroes in ancient Greece were somewhat akin to Christian saints and were admitted to the heroic state—the Heroon—by a unanimous decision of all the Gods after a noble life of self-sacrifice.] The real protagonist of the *Eroica* is the human being, and Beethoven later wrote a line dedicating the symphony to Napoleon, thinking that here was a man who embodied these ideals. But you should see the page of the original manuscript in Vienna where he cancelled the dedication; obviously this was done with such rage that the paper is torn!"

Despite the fact that music seldom needs verbal explanations, it was interesting to hear his thoughts about the *Eroica* just after listening to his very personal, noble and profoundly affecting interpretation, with its uncommonly slow first movement—a reading devoid of any hint of bombast or military triumph.

Among the many honours that Giulini has received over the years is the Gold Medal of the Bruckner Society. Yet as late as 1967, he confided to a British critic in *The Times* that he found it hard to identify with Bruckner and Mahler (except for *Das Lied von der Erde* and the first and fourth symphonies), and felt that in those two composers, the structure of the symphony has got out of proportion, with the thematic material going to pieces in the development sections, unlike Beethoven symphonies where everything is essential. Yet he recorded the Mahler first in 1971, the ninth in 1979, and the Bruckner second in 1975, and I was curious to know how this change of heart had come about and how he decides when he is ready to perform a certain work.

"The problem is always in myself and, as I said before, in my inability to conduct works that have not yet become part of me. But there comes a moment when something, a certain score, seems to be knocking at the door. Then, I open it. It's a little bit like a love affair: suddenly, who knows why, something happens. The same is true of conducting, which is a very mysterious art. We, alone among musicians, have no physical contact with sound. We have our mental picture of what a composer wanted to say, and we try to communicate it, first to our hands, and through our hands, to the hundred-plus musicians in the orchestra—a spiritual and technical connection.

"Music itself is mysterious. In a way, you could say it is mathematical, because we know that two is the double sum of one. But we don't know what one is.... Sound is mysterious, too. Take the string chords of a violin. There is no sound until they start to vibrate, and when the sound comes, it is always different and varies according to acoustic conditions.

"Musical language, notation, is also mysterious. It is not concrete, unlike poetry which uses words meaning something exact. But a note? What is a note? A note is nothing. A few notes produce a line, a melody, a harmony. A composer can write down on paper only a part of his thought, because some things are impossible to write—and sometimes these things are the most important—and because the music isn't *there*. We have to *make* it, and every time we try, something new, something different happens.

"So we have to deal with mysteries all the time. Our problem is not just how to study the score and learn the notes, but how to read behind the notes and between the lines, and *understand* what a genius wanted to say. We conductors are small men. But because of our activity, we have to deal with geniuses all the time, great geniuses who created something out of nothing, out of the air. We are servants, but servants who serve with love, not because we have to, and we must join with these giants' minds and try to feel what they wanted to say. And for this, we need time. At least, *I* do."

Carlo Maria Giulini was born on May 9, 1914 in the town of Barletta on the Apulian coast, but both his parents came from the North, and one of his grandmothers was Austrian. In 1915 the family moved back to the North, to a village farm where Giulini and his two brothers spent their very happy early childhood, reared by warm, affectionate parents in a loving atmosphere. To this day, he considers this to be one of the two great blessings in his life—the other is his extremely happy marriage and close relationship with his own three sons. It was in this village that he had his first musical experience: a gipsy violinist with a puppy, playing for money in the street.

When he was five, his father, who was a timber merchant, moved his family to Bolzano. They were the first Italian family to settle there after the area became part of Italy, and this put the boys in contact with the Central European musical heritage—waltzes, ländlers, Hungarian and Czech folk songs—from an early age. That first Christmas in Bolzano Giulini decided that he wanted a violin as a present, and his parents managed to find one, three-quarter size. He was first taught by a nun in the local kindergarten, but after a few months it was time for a proper teacher.

During the next nine years he had to get up at dawn to have his violin lessons at eight in the morning before going to school. When he was fourteen, a new, more advanced teacher was found, and one day, two years later, this teacher's old Professor from the Santa Cecilia Academy came to Bolzano from Rome to give a recital. Giulini turned the pages and later had the benefit of a private audition at the request of his teacher. The Professor at once suggested that the boy join him at the Academy in Rome. Until then Giulini had also toyed with the idea of joining the Italian navy, largely, he suspects, because of its brass bands. But on that day his parents summoned him and told him that the moment had come for him to choose.

He chose music and went to the Academy in Rome, where he became the youngest student in the composition class and where he took up playing the viola instead of the violin. Two years later, when he was still only eighteen, he applied for and won the position of twelfth viola player in the Augusteo Orchestra, after a national competition. He found his years as an orchestral player "the greatest, most absolute joy" of his life. Until then he had only played in string quartets and watched the full orchestra from afar from where it looked "like something abstract", he told *The Sunday Times Magazine*. But now his perspective changed: he was an insider, part of a group of people making music together under some of the greatest conductors of the day: Richard Strauss, Bruno Walter, Wilhelm Furtwängler, Otto Klemperer, Erich Kleiber, Victor de Sabata, Willem Mengelberg.

He remembers being particularly impressed by Bruno Walter, who conducted "a marvellous, thrilling, unforgettable" performance of the Brahms First Symphony, because of his sheer joy in music-making and his ability to involve each player as a partner in his effort to realize a work. "Nobody felt he was being 'conducted'. Even I had the impression of playing the Brahms first as though it were written for orchestra and twelfth viola solo!"

At the age of twenty, he conducted an orchestra consisting mainly of friends and instantly decided that this was what he wanted to, what he *had* to, do. His mother later reminded him that at the time he wrote to her that if he couldn't conduct, he would die.

"Conducting was the only thing that came to me naturally and easily. Everything else was difficult. There are violinists, cellists or pianists who simply pick up or sit down at their instrument and just know what to do. Sadly, I am not one of them. I had to study and practise the violin and the viola really hard, and composition was even harder. For example, writing a fugue counterpoint in eight voices was never easy. I was just not a composer—I didn't have enough to say. And I couldn't just glance at a score and memorize it, either. I had to, and still have to, work really hard at my scores. But I never had to practise conducting. I simply got up and did it."

Giulini is completely unaware of technique or of his particular conducting style. "I have no idea what I do up there, as I have never practised specific movements for indicating specific things. I hope that I can express what I want the orchestra to understand through my hands and that they will play it." He has often said that if there is anything wrong in his hands, it is because it is wrong in his mind, and considers eye contact one of the most vital ways of communicating with an orchestra. Before his first rehearsal as Music Director of the Los Angeles Philharmonic, he told the orchestra: "I will not remember your names for a little while. But I shall know your eyes!"

Orchestral players appreciate this and find his stick technique clear and easy to follow. "I loved him, there's no other word," says Jeremy White, principal viola at Covent Garden, where Giulini has conducted *Don Carlos*, *Il barbiere di Siviglia*, *Falstaff*, *Il trovatore* and *La traviata*. "His technique? I don't even remember it. I remember his eyes, that very concentrated urgency about everything, but especially his eyes! That's how he conducts."

"Giulini was fantastic," adds the first trombone in the same orchestra, Harold Nash. "He produced the traditional Italian sound all the time, a beautiful but contrasting sound: sometimes it was a sort of brash Italian sound and sometimes a broad, beautiful, lyrical Italian sound, and he could switch from one to the other very quickly. His technique was very clear, and I particularly remember a marvellous trick of his which I have never seen anybody else do so successfully. You know how most Verdi arias start with a rhythmic figure in the second violins? Well, he would turn to the second violins—which he had seated opposite the first violins—with a most intense look and make them play this rhythm absolutely regimentally, like a military band for the first bar or two. Then he would leave them to it, turn around to the first violins and conduct the melody in a completely different, lyrical way, and keep both going at the same time. He said very little, possibly because his English was poor at the time. He sang the way he wanted things to sound and expressed his ideas through the beat and through his eyes."

"Giulini gives incredible performances that drain you of all emotion," says John Wallace, principal trumpet of the Philharmonia Orchestra. "He belongs to the old school of conductors for whom technique mattered less. He doesn't arrive at his performances through technique but through a profound and intense emotional contact with us. He is direct, tense and draws a wonderful, refined sound from the orchestra—but sometimes at the expense of ensemble." The assistant leader, Martin Jones, confirms that "it is sometimes difficult to play very precisely for Giulini—but it's never difficult to play very beautifully!".

After deciding that he wanted to become a conductor, Giulini went to the Accademia Chigiana in Siena, where the composer Alfredo Casella, who was also a remarkable pianist and a promoter of contemporary music, was holding what was partly a postgraduate seminar and partly a master class. There was no prescribed course, but a number of musical personalities were around, and Casella himself took a master class for pianists which Giulini, although not a pianist, attended because of the exceptional interest of what Casella had to say about composers. (An interesting aside about those master classes is that they triggered off the revival and eventual explosion of interest in Vivaldi.) After Siena, he did masterclasses at the Accademia di Santa Cecilia for three years and, as a prize for the very tough last examination, was invited to conduct a concert there. But because of his dislike of Fascism, he had disappeared and gone into hiding.

Earlier he had been an officer in the King's army and sent to fight the partisans in Yugoslavia as a second lieutenant. As a convinced pacifist and deeply religious man, he found war an agonizing experience, "a terrible thing which I fear more than anything else in life and hope never to see again. I don't want to speak about the war. But one thing I *can* tell you: I never killed a human being, and neither did my two brothers. All three of us were on the front and, thank God, all three of us survived."

When the regiment was recalled to Rome to fight the Allied Invasion,

Giulini and three companions deserted and went into hiding for nine months. There were posters with their names and faces all over Rome, and the commanding officer of the regiment—an exceptionally handsome, exquisitely courteous and fiendishly cruel man who made Giulini understand exactly how Iago should be portrayed in Verdi's *Otello*, "as an artist of Evil"—had sworn that if the three men were captured they would be shot in front of their houses. They nearly were, when the Fascist police and the Gestapo raided the house where they were hiding. Fortunately, they never thought of looking in the attic.

When Rome was finally liberated, in June 1944, the Americans were eager to restore normal life as soon as possible. Giulini's impeccable Anti-Fascist credentials meant that he was invited to conduct the concert at the Augusteo that would have been his prize before the war—the first post-Liberation concert there. The programme he chose was the Introduction, Passacaglia and Finale by the young Italian composer Salviucci (one of the brightest talents on the Italian music scene, who died in 1937 at the age of twenty-eight), a Mozart violin concerto and the Brahms fourth. He has always felt an instinctive, spontaneous and irresistible attraction to Brahms's music—not just the symphonic works, but his chamber music and Lieder as well.[*]

The same year, 1944, Giulini was appointed deputy to Fernando Previtali at the Rome Radio Orchestra, where two years later he succeeded him as Music Director. He was thirty and on the road that was to bring him to the pinnacle of his profession—although he deeply believes that in the world of music there is no such thing as success, no such thing as "a good performance". Everything should always be "better", or at least the best that he and the musicians can do at the moment.

While on leave from the front, Giulini had married Marcella de Girolami, the good-looking, elegant and highly intelligent daughter of an industrialist who lived opposite the Verdi Conservatoire. Marcella was eighteen at the time and, with her excellent head for business and organization, was helping her father run his business so successfully that he felt chagrined she was not born a boy! She and Giulini saw a lot of each other at the time, but he didn't want to get married: he felt that an artist should be free and thought that they should therefore remain just good friends. "But I tricked him," she explained with a chuckle. "I rang him up and said that, in that case, my parents objected to our

---

[*] There is an excellent, thoroughly absorbing chapter, in which Giulini talks extensively and exclusively about Brahms, in Bernard Jacobson's book *Conductors on Conducting*.

seeing each other. That did it."

Although only twenty at the time, Marcella proved an invaluable and altogether exceptional life partner, totally and passionately dedicated to him and his career, willing and able to rid him of all the burdens of organization and finance, which he hates and is no good at. And that without ever playing the martyr.

"Little by little, I realized the responsibility of being married to an artist like him. During our first years together I desperately tried to hide my ignorance. He was preparing for his composition exams, and I understood nothing! He is a superb, devoted husband who gives a tremendous amount emotionally, and a very, very tender father. When I was ill for a whole year, he was incredibly supportive. That's why I'm so dedicated to him and have coped with what is, at times, a very difficult life for a woman. For example, when our three boys were growing up, I had asked not to travel, which was very hard for me, because my role as a mother seemed to be in conflict with my role as a wife. But, believe it or not, he deliberately slowed down his career so that he, too, would have to travel less."

To have such a strong and happy marriage, especially in a musician's peripatetic life which involves a lot of time away from home and myriad opportunities to fight loneliness by forming new ties, is rare. In the case of a man as handsome and attractive as Giulini, very, very rare indeed. "Yes, but what is the meaning of love?" he replied to this suggestion. "When you really love somebody, who knows who gives and who receives? I have this great, this very great good fortune of having found a woman who has, and who has given me, everything I want. And I have also been extremely lucky in my three sons, to whom I'm very close. I would never do anything to endanger this. I would defend it against anything. Even against my career. In fact I did do just that, when I was younger."*

He is "an absolute catastrophe" at anything practical, and while he likes to look nice, it is Marcella who orders all his superbly cut clothes from his tailor as and when he needs them. He claims to know nothing about money, nor the financial side of contracts. She does it all and he has "no idea what she agrees to". In fact, Giulini is one of the world's best-paid conductors, along with Karajan, Solti and Bernstein. "He is absolutely straightforward in his business dealings," says Peter Andry, Head of the International Classical Division at EMI. "He has this

---

* In December 1980, Marcella Giulini suffered a near-fatal stroke which left her bedridden for many months and as a result of which Giulini cancelled all his engagements for six months.

wonderful quality of deflecting any talk about money! Of course, he knows exactly what is going on, but he always manages to create an atmosphere of having absolutely nothing to do with it, in the nicest possible way. And he always avoids signing contracts. I remember once having a very nice lunch with him with a lot of wine and good conversation. At the end, Marcella went out shopping and left us to have coffee and more wine. Now I had this contract with me, to which his signature was long overdue, so I suddenly said: 'Come on, Carlo, why don't you sign this contract?' And he did. Then Marcella came in and said, 'Oh, what have you boys been doing?' and I said that Carlo had finally signed the contract. She was absolutely furious!"

"You see, when I was young, I never believed that it was possible to make money through music, that anyone would want to *pay* me for making music," explains Giulini. "In fact, this was partly the reason why I didn't want to get married. [Massimo Bogianckino, the Director Designate, Paris Opéra, who has known him well since those days, remembers him as an exceptionally otherworldly, chaste young man.] At the very beginning, while I was an orchestral player, I had my salary, of course. But when I started conducting and people asked me how much money I wanted, I found it impossible, I couldn't bring myself to speak about money. It felt dirty and I felt ashamed. Then my wife said that it was all very well, but we now had a child for whom I should make provision. I accepted that but made a resolution (one of the very few times in my life when I have actually made a resolution) never to speak about money again. Somebody else would have to do it."

In 1950 Giulini was appointed Music Director of the newly founded Milan Radio Orchestra, where among other things he conducted numerous operas, including Haydn's *Il mondo della luna*. Toscanini, who happened to hear a broadcast of the latter, was so impressed that he invited the young man to his house and told him that, although he didn't know this work, he felt that his tempi had been just right! It was the start of a discipleship and friendship that was to last until Toscanini's death in 1957.

Although this orchestra was not comparable to the ones Giulini was to conduct later in his career, he rejoiced at the experience of human contact and warm rapport with the musicians, which has been a characteristic feature of his relationships with all the orchestras he has worked with. He does not consider that a conductor's function is to "tell the musicians what to do, but to make music together with them, to serve together this great thing that is music, because I feel and think that if somebody does something because he is convinced, he does it better than if he were just obliged to do it. A conductor, if he is a real conductor, needs a week at most to put his stamp on an orchestra, and I suppose I am lucky, because orchestras everywhere have always played as I wanted them to.

"To make music you need two fundamental things: technical expertise—an orchestra capable of responding to every necessity of expression, phrasing and dynamics; and you also need that spiritual thing, love. There are, of course, many different levels of orchestras, and with some it is possible to arrive at a high point. But even with a bad orchestra, it's possible to make music. This means that the performance will have many technical flaws. But, if there is great love and enthusiasm from everyone, it is still possible to make music."

Giulini's orchestra-training methods have never been authoritarian and he particularly dislikes both the word and the concept of discipline because "it smacks of the army, of colonels and majors, and is totally alien to our world of music. All that is needed is the knowledge that we are all here to make the best music we possibly can. It's tiring, it's difficult, it takes a lot of concentration, because I realize that I ask a lot of the musicians and that rehearsals with me are tiring." Anyone who has watched the intensity and urgency he exudes at rehearsals would agree that Giulini also asks a great deal of himself. He prefers short, concentrated sessions and feels that once everybody knows what to do, it is preferable to finish early and let everyone have a rest, rather than just repeat what they have already grasped.

"I like to leave something extra, an 'x' factor, for the concert. While the orchestra must be as well prepared as possible, there is a mysterious plus, which is hard to define but which makes all the difference. I am convinced that the audience plays an important part. It is not just a passive factor in a performance. It gives out so much emotion, and this is reflected back at us. Orchestral players have souls, usually sensitive souls, and feel the concentration focused on them. In the end, who knows who gives and who receives? It is, and I keep coming back to the same word, like love. Like ideal love, the ideal performance would happen if these two energies were to blend together perfectly."

After a performance, Giulini finds it impossible to sleep at night, and I asked him whether this inner anguish and tension that musicians experience almost all the time was the reason why he once said he feels thankful that none of his sons are musicians. He replied that although he realized this would sound melodramatic, it was nevertheless true; and it was also true that composers often wrote their works because of and out of their sufferings, which are transmitted to any sensitive interpreter who experiences their works deeply. But he was quick to add that music is also a blessing and a rare privilege which gives back rich spiritual rewards in return for the effort and energy put into it. "If you accept the principle that everyone in life has to work and that some people have to do so in terrible conditions, then you realize how lucky we musicians are. We sit in comfortable chairs in nice halls, and we have Mozart!"

A year after his appointment as Music Director of the Milan Radio Orchestra, Giulini conducted his first opera on stage: *La Traviata* at the Bergamo Festival, with Renata Tebaldi in the title role. Soon after that, he was invited to become de Sabata's assistant at La Scala, where he made his début conducting Manuel de Falla's *La vida breve* in 1952. The following year, following de Sabata's death, he was appointed Music Director of La Scala, where he remained for three historic years during which he was responsible for some of the great operatic triumphs of the postwar era—in collaboration with Luchino Visconti and Franco Zeffirelli—and earned his reputation as one of today's greatest operatic conductors. Among the most acclaimed productions were Rossini's *L'Italiana in Algeri*, *La Cenerentola* (with Giulietta Simionato) and *Il barbiere di Siviglia* (with Callas), all directed by Zeffirelli; Gluck's *Alceste* and Verdi's *La traviata* (both with Callas), directed by Visconti.

(Shortly before this and before even hearing him conduct, Peter Diamand, the former Artistic Director of the Holland and Edinburgh Festivals, remembers first meeting Giulini at the office of a Milan concert agent in 1951. "We started talking and went on doing so for a couple of hours. I enjoyed this meeting more than I can say and returned to Holland, where I was working for the Festival, and said that we must engage this man Giulini for next year's Festival. They asked, 'But who is this Mr Giulini, what has he done and what have *you* heard him do?' I said, 'Nothing, absolutely nothing. I met him, I talked to him', and they answered, 'But this is no reason to engage a conductor!' to which I replied, 'Yes, in this case it is!' So he came for the first time in 1952, and every year until 1965 when I left. Then, when I started in Edinburgh in 1966, he came there every season until my retirement in 1978. There are very few people in the world for whom I have such admiration, respect and affection.")

During the years 1953 to 1956, La Scala made it possible for Giulini to work in almost ideal conditions, with total control over every aspect of the production and seemingly unlimited time for him to work on every musical, dramatic and scenic detail with his producer and cast. Before their legendary production of *La Traviata*, for instance, he, Visconti and Callas worked together for three weeks *before* beginning official rehearsals. He admits that this period spoilt him as far as opera is concerned, and when in 1956 it looked as if this happy state of affairs would not last much longer, he resigned.

He continued to conduct opera from time to time over the next twelve years, mostly at the Holland and Edinburgh Festivals, at Covent Garden and in Rome. There were plans for him to conduct *Tannhäuser* in Bayreuth, with Wieland Wagner as producer, but when he learnt that the cast chosen by him could not be engaged, he withdrew. He also cancelled his planned comeback at La Scala in 1963. It was to have been a new production of *Don Giovanni*, but the management felt that the designs by the Spanish painter Burgos were too expensive and decided to borrow a production from Vienna or Salzburg instead. Both these cancellations are interesting, because they demonstrate Giulini's artistic integrity and unwillingness to compromise where artistic standards are concerned—a characteristic he shares with Carlos Kleiber, as singers and orchestral players are quick to point out.

The last opera he conducted—before his return to opera in 1982 with a production of *Falstaff* in Los Angeles and Covent Garden— was a Visconti production of *Le nozze di Figaro*, which he took from Rome to the Metropolitan Opera, New York in 1968. He explained his decision to withdraw from opera by comparing it to the end of a love affair, when "suddenly, without one knowing precisely why, things start going wrong." All the same, his reasons for quitting the opera house were sound enough:

"The interpretation of opera does not involve merely its musical interpretation plus, perhaps, a handsome set and pretty costumes, but the realization of every aspect of its dramatic content, making psychological sense of every character. It is difficult enough for a soloist's conception of a concerto to be absolutely identical to one's own. Imagine how much more difficult this is in opera, where so many people are involved and where we are not only dealing with musical conceptions, but also with interpretations of a written text.

"For something really worthwhile to happen, for everybody's ideas to come together and blend into a harmonious whole, you need time, a lot of time, for all of us to go into the score and the libretto *together* and as deeply as possible. And time is something which nobody seems able to afford these days. Singers jet from place to place, which makes it difficult for their voices to be in top form, and you just cannot book them for long enough periods."

Generally, he is not sympathetic towards the new breed of producers either, because he feels that often they aim at something different, "different rather than new" at all costs, and think that Mozart's or Verdi's music is simply not enough, but requires help from them. He passionately believes that the real director of an opera is the composer, and that if one listens carefully, one can see the characters and the logic of their actions emerging out of the music and find that every direction, every movement, every psychological explanation is indicated in the score. A singer remembers that Giulini once caught a producer giving stage directions to a Donna Anna while Don Ottavio was singing during rehearsals for *Don Giovanni*, "because nothing is happening here, Maestro!" "No," he replied coldly. "Only Mozart's music is happening here!"

Visconti and Zeffirelli fully understood this. Indeed when the former was asked, shortly before his death, whether he would like to direct an opera again, he replied, "Yes, but with Giulini!" The two were close friends and Giulini found that their collaboration enriched both his artistic and his "human" life, as he calls it. "Ours was like a marriage of spirits. Luchino had a deep awareness of this unity and balance between music and action which is essential to opera. I'm not sure whether he could actually read music, but he certainly was musically knowledgeable. His parents had had a subscription to La Scala throughout his childhood, and he grew up steeped in music and culture and with theatre in his blood. At home they used to put on plays and he, with his excellent taste and vivid imagination for scenery and costumes, always helped.

"He brought something new to the theatre, and you could sense it just as well in the first play he directed, Chekhov's *Uncle Vanya*, and his first film, *Senso*, as in his operatic productions. But he was not an easy man. There was this deep conflict inside him between the *gran signore* that he was and some of his attitudes: his communism and the sensitivity with which he responded to the social, political and spiritual changes of our times. The conflict arose because he couldn't cancel in a flash something that was also part of him, habits that originated four hundred years ago."

Franco Zeffirelli is the only other producer to have worked often and closely with Giulini, whom he found "wonderfully sensitive to beauty". "He works very intensely, gets along very well with singers, and only interferes with stage directions when asked. Then he gives invariably sound answers to any questions. During performances, he gets genuinely excited and seems capable of enjoying the production. And he very, very seldom gets angry. But when he does, it's war. There's nothing you can do about it. He doesn't say much, but you can feel it all right! It's solid, cold anger, and I have seen it both in his private and in his professional life. But he is almost always extremely nice, polite and very much a gentleman in the old-fashioned sense of the word, who would never say a bad word. Never! Only once did I hear him say 'stupido' to a singer, and even then, he went back on stage and apologized to him in public. He hadn't changed his mind, he still thought that the man was stupid. But he felt that he should never have allowed himself to say so."

Zeffirelli and Giulini also collaborated on *La Cenerentola* and on *Falstaff*. In fact Giulini subsequently conducted *Falstaff* also at Covent Garden and the Holland and Edinburgh Festivals*. In 1982 he chose this opera for his long-awaited return to the operatic stage, first at the Los Angeles Music Center and then at Covent Garden. I was puzzled about his choosing this, an opera he has often conducted before, rather than *Otello*, a long-cherished dream of his, or *Rigoletto*, which he recently recorded.

He explained that soon after becoming Music Director of the Los Angeles Philharmonic Orchestra, he was asked whether, granted the right conditions and the right cast, he would be prepared to consider conducting an opera. He replied that he would be, and opted for *Falstaff* firstly because it is a symphonic opera, marvellous for an orchestra to play, and secondly because it is also an ensemble opera for which you need excellent singers but not necessarily "the" tenor, "the" soprano or even "the" baritone. Thirdly, because he loves it most particularly and considers it one of the few *great* operas in which the three elements of music, action and drama are on the highest level— probably because Boito could draw from three Shakespeare plays.

"But one thing about *Falstaff* moves me above all else: the fact that Verdi, at that advanced age of eighty, after all the experience of his life,

* This production was by the late Carl Ebert.

after having composed music for so many terrible, tortured characters like Iago and Rigoletto, could find in himself the purity and poetry to write music for these two ... birds ... [Fenton and Nannetta] who are in a dream of love, not in love but in a dream of love, on the moon. And he gave them the most beautiful, innocent music. Think of it! A very, very old man, after such a tense and turbulent life, could find the freshness and purity of the love of love!"

While still at La Scala, Giulini had begun to devote considerable time to concert work. He had a long and happy association with the Philharmonia Orchestra in London,* distinguished by some outstanding performances of choral works: the Bach *B minor Mass*, Cherubini's *Requiem*, Beethoven's *Missa Solemnis*, Verdi's *Four Sacred Pieces* and *Requiem*. Peter Andry of EMI remembers that Giulini had a wonderful relationship with this orchestra: "He gave it what he was good at, that wonderful *legato*, *bel canto*, 'operatic' sound if you like, that singing quality, which was particularly wonderful for choral works. The orchestra always enjoyed him and he remained absolutely loyal to them when the late Walter Legge decided to disband it. Of course, he expected Giulini to pull out, too. But he said no, and supported the orchestra instead. Then Walter and he never saw each other again for many years. Until then, he was very much under the influence of Walter, who was a very dominant personality. Of course, it was Giulini who decided what he wanted to conduct. But once he had made up his mind, it was Walter who took over, organized and managed everything. Giulini never seemed to mind that; in fact, he rather enjoyed it, and the two got on well until the disbanding of the orchestra. Giulini has always paid homage and acknowledged his debt to Walter."

Elisabeth Schwarzkopf, who sang in a great number of performances and recordings with him—all produced by her husband, Walter Legge—remembers him as "a marvellous orchestral trainer for a certain kind of sound. He had an incredible intensity—in fact, I would say that what mattered most to him in a performance is dramatic intensity and rhythm, and all his performances had swing, Italian emotion and a marvellous palette of colours. But musically he never appeared to relax. There was no, how shall I put it, no ebb and flow, in the music. As a singer it didn't bother one at all, but I always felt that it was an ingredient that was missing from his performances...."

* Under the management of the late Walter Legge.

In 1960, Giulini went on a world tour with the Israel Philharmonic Orchestra, and has frequently and regularly conducted the Concert-gebouw, the Philadelphia Orchestra, the Vienna, the Berlin, and the New York Philharmonic, which stood up and applauded him *en masse* after a performance of the Mahler ninth. But one such guest-conducting engagement proved particularly important for his future: an invitation from Fritz Reiner to conduct the Chicago Symphony. It came in 1954, while Giulini was still Music Director at La Scala, and led to a "twenty-four-year love affair" with this great American orchestra.

He never discovered what had prompted the invitation, because as far as he knew Reiner had never heard him conduct, although he might possibly have heard a record or a broadcast, and the two men never actually met, except once, many years later in a Viennese hotel lobby. Giulini spotted Reiner, walked over, introduced himself and thanked him for everything. It was over in a minute and a half. But the invitations kept coming in, season after season, always leaving the choice of programme to him.

He developed a strong artistic and human bond with the orchestra, who after Reiner's death in 1963 offered him the music directorship. But family reasons compelled him to turn it down: his sons didn't speak English well enough to attend an American school, his wife didn't want to leave them behind in Italy to be cared for by relatives, and he himself would not consider living away from his family. Instead, he continued guest conducting it every season and was named its Principal Guest Conductor from 1969 to 1973—an appointment involving a purely musical association.

His association with this orchestra also resulted in several much-acclaimed recordings for his new recording company, Deutsche Grammophon, with which he has had an exclusive contract since 1978, including the Mahler ninth, the Dvořák eighth and 'New World' symphonies and the Schubert 'Tragic', 'Unfinished' and C major symphonies.

Schubert was much on Giulini's mind at the time. He feels that at last Schubert's place in the history of music has improved, and is deeply drawn to this composer's world: "In all great composers, you find the whole range of human emotions and feelings: love, hate, passion, jealousy, joy, tragedy, laughter. But in Schubert, you also find tenderness, this very, very intimate and special sentiment which you also find in some of Bruckner's music and which requires great tenderness from the performer. In our times especially, we need Schubert very much. Perhaps this is why his greatness is finally recognized in the way it deserves. He was a very, very humble person, sandwiched between these two giants, Beethoven, whom he venerated, and Brahms, and this probably blinded people to his own greatness. But now, it is coming out, blossoming like a marvellous flower."

Giulini has studied the original manuscripts of both the 'Unfinished' and the C major symphonies at the Musikverein in Vienna. Generally he finds looking at facsimiles and originals a particularly moving experience "because you can see the very first moment when a genius's thought was written down. You are in contact with the hands that wrote the music." A few days before we met for our third conversation he had received a facsimile of Mozart's 'Jupiter' Symphony which he was then conducting during his first European tour as Music Director of the LAPO and was thoroughly absorbed and enthralled to see it, "written by this marvellous man who wrote music almost like writing a letter, because he had no time to do sketches—the exact opposite of Beethoven, who did lots of sketches. But Mozart had no time. He had so much to say in such a short life."

He thinks that one should be prudent and cautious about the way in which one approaches original manuscripts, though, because they don't always necessarily represent the composer's last will. It is therefore important to investigate each case on its merits, because sometimes the composers themselves changed or cut certain things after the first performance of their works. But even in such cases, Giulini finds it rewarding to study original sketches as well, and compare them to the final version, and to make sure that any cuts or changes are the composer's own and not just "tradition", which sometimes amounts to little more than an accumulation of bad habits. In Schubert's case, the manuscripts of the 'Unfinished' and the C major symphonies do represent his last will, because these two works were never played in his lifetime. As he explained to the KUSC Radio Station, Los Angeles when asked about the distinction in pace between the introduction and the exposition in the first movement of the C major Symphony:

"After Schubert's death, Schumann found the manuscript and brought it to Vienna, where he published it. I thought it must still be there, somewhere, and found it in the Musikverein. This original score makes it hard to understand why people introduce the accelerando between the *Andante* of the introduction and the *Allegro ma non troppo* of the exposition. Schubert, who wrote very precisely, could easily have indicated a change of pace himself. But no, in all parts it is written 'Andante alla breve'. Then, in the exposition, he had first written 'Allegro vivace' and then cancelled the 'vivace' and substituted 'ma non troppo'. So he really wanted the pulse of the whole movement to be 'Andante' and 'Allegro ma non troppo'. This is one of the cases where the only truth is in the original manuscript, and everything else is apocryphal."

In the same radio talk he was then asked whether, after conducting the 'Unfinished' Symphony, he is left with a sense that something has been left unsaid, or whether it feels "whole" to him. He answered that to him the work feels complete, and that although it is a mystery why Schubert did not go on with it, the answer might be that the symphony was really finished, like some paintings and sculptures—Michelangelo's *Pietà* is an obvious example—which are not actually finished, yet are.

"What matters is Schubert's need to express himself, to say something, at a certain moment. It doesn't matter that the 'Unfinished' symphony is not written in four movements. Because in those two very contrasting movements, Schubert said everything that he had to say at that moment. And although I have, on the whole, great regard for musicologists, I disagree with those who place Schubert back in Haydn's world. Schubert breathed the air of his contemporaries, not of Haydn, and in any case, geniuses tend to look forward rather than backward. If one absolutely *had* to associate Schubert's world with another composer's, it should be Bruckner's rather than Haydn's, because there are moments in Schubert when one can breathe a new world—the same feeling that one gets with Mahler, who was composing in pre-first-world-war Vienna, and in whose music one senses all the dramatic changes that lay ahead."

A lot of Giulini's research into Schubert was done in Vienna while he was Principal Conductor of the Vienna Symphony from 1973 to 1976. Roughly at the same time that Giulini left the Vienna Symphony, Ernest Fleischmann, Executive Director of the Los Angeles Philharmonic, was beginning to look for a successor to Zubin Mehta, who was leaving to become Music Director of the New York Philharmonic. He offered the post to Giulini, who turned it down straight away. About a year later Fleischmann wrote again, inviting him for a series of guest appearances.

Giulini replied explaining the reasons why he had turned down the

Music Directorship in the first place: because of his dislike of conducting too much; his loathing of and ineptitude at administration; and the social, fund-raising obligations that go hand in hand with the music directorship of American orchestras. Fleischmann then decided to work out an offer which would not involve any of those things and jumped on the first plane to Chicago to see Giulini. The two negotiated for several days in a hotel room and reached agreement on everything: Giulini would only conduct eight or nine programmes a season, and he would not have any non-musical obligations.

The eventual announcement of the appointment in 1978 literally stunned the music world. Indeed, it was hard to imagine a more unlikely match. Rumours and speculation began to circulate with alarming speed: and everyone predicted that the association would be brief. It was felt that Giulini was bound to be disillusioned within a few weeks of working in 'Tinseltown', a place of facile, materialistic values, surely a different planet from Giulini's world of music, contemplation, artistic and human integrity, quiet-living habits and unplumbable depth.

So far, everyone has been proved wrong. In 1980, Giulini renewed his contract for a further five years. His original contract stipulated, at his request, that he would not conduct any other American orchestras (e.g. Chicago), "because I want to give myself to my orchestra completely", and that he wouldn't conduct at the Hollywood Bowl, with its picnic-like atmosphere, hardly conducive to a high level of musical receptivity. Yet as he has often admitted, he is not a man who can love coldly or give only half of himself. It is therefore typical of him and his satisfaction with his new orchestra that, after his first season in Los Angeles, unprompted, he volunteered to conduct a few concerts at the Bowl.

After only one season, he already felt that his acquaintance with the LAPO musicians was developing into a feeling of belonging to a family, "with all the human, personal, psychological and emotional involvement that this means, and a sense of building something together: not just preparing interesting concert programmes, but getting to know each other, improving every day and trying to reach the highest point we can. Because while conductors are transient, the life of an orchestra is long and should be viewed in a different dimension: seventy-eight-year-old orchestras like the LAPO are quite young. And when you look at it this way, it becomes even more vital for each of us to keep improving and make his contribution to the orchestra so that it is better every year and every decade.

"In any case, I greatly dislike the concept of the conductor. I would be much happier sitting in a chair among the musicians were it not for the sheer physical necessity of having a podium so that they see the beat. But the podium is a dangerous thing.... It can so easily become a mental podium, a place which the conductor can come to consider the rightful place from which to survey the whole world and human life. In this sense, conducting can be a dangerous profession. We conductors should therefore be humble in everything, especially in our attitude to the composer, his score and our colleagues who actually produce the sound.

"And yet from the moment we step on the podium, it is no longer permitted to be humble. I know this sounds contradictory, but you see at that moment we must have the feeling that this work we are about to conduct now belongs to us, that we are at one with it and experiencing it with every fibre of our being. But once the rehearsal or performance is over, we should instantly become humble again. Because the podium is not the base of a statue or monument to ourselves. It is merely a physical necessity."

Giulini's first rehearsal with the LAPO sums up the man even more clearly than his own words, typical though these are of his spiritual integrity. He urged the players always to ask him questions and voice any doubts they might have in their minds about interpretational or technical points: "I stand here with a baton, and have opinions that I can air, too. But if you think that I am doing something wrong, then you must correct me. And even though I stand up here with a baton and call myself a conductor, we are all one: you in the last chairs are as important as anyone in the first chairs, because unless we are all equal, we are not an orchestra."

Then, remembers Mrs Olive Behrendt, a long-standing member of the LAPO Executive Committee, he started to conduct and one could have gone away thinking that this was a wonderful theoretical statement. But suddenly he stopped rehearsing and said: "Excuse me, but I see an expression in somebody's face that wants to ask me something. Now, please don't be shy and don't be silly. If you are questioning something, I can see and sense it anyway, so go right ahead and ask!"

No wonder then that his musicians seem enthralled with him and that he has never had problems of discipline at his rehearsals—in fact he has never had to say "Quiet!" at a single rehearsal. As the principal cellist, Ronald Leonard, puts it, "he is a very inspirational person. It is as if he comes to music as to religion. If you are at all sensitive, there is no way you can go through a rehearsal with him, to say nothing of a performance, and not be enveloped by it." Violinist Michael Nutt adds that "Giulini does not conduct for the audience, but for music. I've been playing those symphonies for twenty-five years, but with him I hear new tones."

In fact, the orchestra-conductor rapport is such that Giulini does not feel especially physically tired at the end of a rehearsal or a concert. "I am away, but I'm not tired. I feel physically recharged. There is something about conducting that enables you to get back some of the energy you are giving out, and if you get back even half, it's always new fuel for you. What is really terrible is to make music with an orchestra that takes everything but gives back almost nothing. You are giving out a hundred per cent and only getting back thirty per cent. At the end you feel absolutely exhausted and totally drained. But when you are making music with a great orchestra and getting the sound you want, it's a complete regeneration for you."

Giulini's professional life and what he calls his "human" life are closely interwoven. As he explained to a Washington newspaper, "I couldn't come here to conduct and then go home and say, '*This* is my life, *that* is my work'." In fact he consciously relates his human experiences to music—a friend remembers seeing him link a personal problem to one in a Beethoven symphony, for instance—and understands full well that "music without the human aspect which is what makes it possible to communicate" would not be music, and this is what makes him one of the most advanced conductors of our times.

He has few close friends, most of whom are not musicians, and all of them comment on his exceptional loyalty, concern and interest in other people, and the fact that he never seems too busy or too harassed to *really* listen or to be bothered with their problems. He says that he knows he is somebody's friend "if when I'm shaving in the morning I think, 'oh isn't it wonderful that such and such a thing should be happening to so and so', and feel happy for them. This sharing and experiencing another person's joy and feeling that it also belongs to you is what friendship is about. Commiserating with their misfortunes is not enough. Any kindly person would do that."

Zeffirelli, for instance, was amazed to find that he had found the time to see his latest film *The Champ* twice and then to spend hours discussing it with him. "Giulini is a strange man, very, very relaxed and at the same time very tense: always creating, reflecting or appreciating—always doing something constructive: *un uomo per bene* in the nineteenth-century northern-Italian concept of the word, and a charming, interesting person to have around. But sometimes I find him a little frightening. There is a point beyond which he won't loosen up and let go, and beyond which you cannot probe—possibly because of his innate sense of dignity."

The only things that totally relax him are the sea and solitude. It disturbs him that nowadays we seem "incapable of living with ourselves, in silence". He used to sail his boat alone in the Tyrrhenian Sea for many years. But when his sons were old enough to water-ski, they persuaded him to sell it and replace it with a criss-craft. He also loves reading, but conducting consumes so much time, mental and emotional energy, that there are still a lot of unread books in his library, and what he calls his "lack of culture" bothers him a little.

"You remember asking me what I would like to change in myself?" I did, and I also remembered him saying that he was wary of answering that question because he has noticed that in interviews, even faults are sometimes made to sound like qualities. "Well, first I would like to do everything I do a little better—that goes without saying.

"Secondly, on a lighter level, I would love to be able to play jazz piano! Many negro jazz pianists can't read music and know nothing about notes but have this amazing natural ability and gift for improvization, plus an incredible contact with sound and sense of melody and rhythm. Once, when I went to Chicago, a friend invited me to various jazz clubs—the kind of places where you go to listen, not to dance—and I remember a trio consisting of a piano, double bass and percussion who, when informed by a friend that there was an Italian musician present, proceeded to play a variation on a theme of Gershwin for me. And what they did, especially what the percussion did, with melodies was unbelievable! I shall never forget it. But, sadly, jazz is not in my blood. After the war, I was asked to do an all-Gershwin concert in Palermo, and accepted with alacrity. But afterwards, I decided never again to conduct this music, because it doesn't really belong to me. It's something you have to have in your pulse. You have to feel it racing through your blood.

"I would also like to be less hopeless at mechanical and scientific things, and to be able to do something with my hands, because I greatly admire people who can. As it is, if my car stops, I gaze at it helplessly and walk away. At home, if something goes wrong, I call my son who goes 'bang, bang' and the thing works again.

"But these are lighthearted, superficial wishes. What really bothers me is my lack of culture. Because throughout my life, I have had the good fortune of being friends with people who had a true and profound comprehension of the whole mainstream of human thought and experience, and who could link the flow of history, art, literature and philosophy with the political and spiritual development of mankind through the ages. You know the painter De Chirico? Well, his brother was an astounding example of what I mean. He was a writer, a painter, a musician and a mathematician and seemed to know everything! He would pick up his pen and write not only articles for the *Corriere* but also an important book; he would pick up his brush and paint, seemingly just like that; he would sit down at the piano and play like a virtuoso; he could talk to doctors about medicine and to mathematicians about mathematics; he completed an important commission from RAI [Italian Radio], the opera *Cristoforo Colombo*, while at the same time painting a portrait of my mother. Surely the next step up from this must be Leonardo da Vinci. This many-sided brilliance—the Homo Universalis—is something I deeply admire."

The single human quality Giulini most admires and likes is goodness, because he feels that at its peak, goodness contains all other human qualities. "You cannot be good if you have no courage; you cannot be good without also being intelligent; you cannot be good if you are not generous and altruistic." He therefore accepts that it is impossible for any human being to be truly good, in the same sense that music-making can never be truly good. Only better, a little bit better, all the time.

Everything he told me, and everything one was able to observe while watching him at work or to learn from friends and colleagues, must make it obvious that, apart from being a gentleman through and through, Giulini is also a deeply religious man and a committed Christian for whom consideration for other people has become second nature. He stems from a religious family but does not consider this to be the reason for his own faith, because he feels that faith, belief, is something that one either has or one hasn't, "as there is no proof either way". His own faith does not embrace reincarnation or other Eastern mystical concepts and philosophies. He doesn't dismiss them in any way, but just finds that he doesn't need them.

"When I was in Israel, I went to Mount Thabor, a small hill in the desert, in the middle of nowhere, completely isolated and quiet, and you could easily imagine yourself two thousand years back, standing in that very place where one poor man said to other poor men things that changed the world. ... Because from the moment when men were told to love and forgive one another, which went against the grain of all past and contemporary thought, the seed of change was sown. ... And in this teaching, I can find everything I need for my spiritual, social and material problems."

I felt that this was the right moment to ask whether he has never experienced the sort of ecstasy that comes when 'something extra' happens at a performance, and he can abandon himself to his inspiration and perhaps reach other dimensions of experience. It was my only question that he felt unable to answer completely, for "this question touches the eternal mystery of the interpreter. A performer has to reconcile two opposites: technical perfection and total freedom of inspiration. As always in life, the ideal would be to have both control and freedom. But thank God, ideal performances never happen! If a performance ever comes *near* to being ideal, it's almost dangerous, because while performing, the concentration is such that you often don't know who or where you are. You exist in a different dimension. If the ideal should happen and these two opposite forces came close to fusion, you would probably lose control.

"There were two instances in my career when I was almost afraid. No, I don't think I can tell you when or where, because it is very, very difficult to speak about these things. What happens at such moments during a performance is something very secret. Because while performing, we have to expose all of ourselves. Nothing can be held back. We are not musical geniuses, we are not composers. We are merely performers and therefore our only truth is the moment we perform. At that moment, we give all of ourselves, and if it's good, it's good and if it's bad, it's bad and you tell yourself that maybe you'll do better next time. But it's difficult ... impossible to talk about it ... about those things."

BERNARD HAITINK, KBE
A Musicianly Conductor

"One of the most important things a conductor must learn is how to live with himself off the podium," said Bernard Haitink, Artistic Director and Principal Conductor of the Concertgebouw Orchestra of Amsterdam and of the Glyndebourne Festival Opera. As he makes it so remarkably easy for *others* to get on with him, one assumes that Haitink discovered the secret of living with himself long ago. It probably explains why, even in a world as bitchy as the music circuit, where unscrupulous sycophants and behind-the-scenes intriguers abound and jostle for power, often using the artists as pawns, one tends to hear only nice things about Haitink: that he is a *musicianly*, profound and utterly professional conductor and a gentle, unassuming man, genuinely humble towards music and fellow musicians.

But lest this give an impression of him as the male equivalent of a "milk-and-water miss", one should hasten to add that he is very determined, knows his own mind, and once it is made up about, or against, something, that's it. He won't budge. For instance, no amount of persuasion, cajoling or flattery could convince him that he was ready to record the *Missa Solemnis* when he knew otherwise. In short, he has integrity and a great deal of inner strength. A hint of it can be glimpsed in the joking reply he tossed at someone who told him how surprised they were at his apparently genuine modesty. "Modest? *Of course* I'm not modest! If I were, I wouldn't be a conductor!"

"I meant," he explained, "that inside every conductor there is this power thing, something that wants to dominate. But it is, or should be, only a small part of the story. Because essentially, the whole business of conducting and of music-making is a maturing process; which is why I don't really resent getting older: I get a secret satisfaction from the fact that, with time, I'm acquiring more natural authority, more experience and the ability to dive deeper into works which, like all masterpieces, reveal their mysteries only very gradually, in layers, as you keep returning to them again and again. And for *that*, it's well worth losing one's youth."

He cites his recordings of the Mahler and Bruckner symphonies, all done in his late thirties, as an example. He felt particularly dissatisfied with his interpretations of the Mahler first and the Bruckner seventh and re-recorded them twelve years later. By coincidence, he had been listening to both versions of those symphonies shortly before our first meeting and found the differences between the old and new versions "incredible". The first recording of the Bruckner seventh, he feels, was typical of a young man "rushing his way through Bruckner", while the second is that of a man who has "well, grown more into it, shall we say".

Haitink admits to being a late developer, a "slow grower" who needs time to assimilate scores, whose last performances in an operatic run are invariably better than the first, who re-reads favourite books three or four times. Perhaps this is why, in his earlier years, before his remarkable musicianship grew to full fruition, this slow rhythm of growth plus the absence of flamboyance or any of the obvious signs of audience appeal from his temperament, sometimes caused him to be labelled "dull". Occasionally it seemed as though he himself subscribed to this view: "God, I was dull in my young days," he confessed to a recording executive; or, "Was I *too* Dutch tonight?", he still asks a well-known pianist after performances. But there is nothing dull about the music he makes. "Dull? Oh, no! We *never* found him dull," say a group of players in the London Philharmonic with whom Haitink has been associated for fifteen years. "Not this man! His music-making is much too interesting. You could say that in earlier years he was a little slow, perhaps, at times. But dull, never!"

The absence of pyrotechnics extends to his conducting style which is very economical and unobtrusive to a degree. But the eyes, as those members of the audience who have sat in seats facing the podium will know, do it all and go a long way towards explaining his unusually warm and deep rapport with orchestral players. "He has a very clear stick technique and a very economic beat. We always know which part of the bar we are in, which with many other eminent conductors we often don't," confirms Kenneth Goode, double bass player in the London Philharmonic. "And his whole personality comes across in his conducting. There is a quietness of demeanour and, as a man, he is inclined to be a little receding, not too forthcoming. This is reflected in his conducting style which is smooth, gentle, urging, and coaxing, rather than beating or thrashing about."

Haitink acknowledges that there are as many styles of conducting as there are conductors, and therefore, it is very difficult to make any sort of sweeping generalizations about an art as mysterious as this. For while one side of it is simply a job, a profession that one can learn to do well, there is another side that cannot easily be explained in words: "First and foremost, inside every conductor, there should be a musician. This is so obvious that it must be taken for granted. Next, one should discover whether this musician is fair, good or outstanding. And from this point on, all sorts of peculiar things can happen: in some cases a fair musician may have some kind of magic inside him which an outstanding musician lacks and this question of personality, plus the ability to draw things out of orchestras and audiences through his personality, is a very strange and mysterious thing. But this is a dangerous topic, because the moment you start to 'think' about it you are already on the wrong track and it doesn't work any longer.

"For the only source that this 'it' can come from is the music itself. Furtwängler, who still has an enormous following everywhere, always talked about the innocence of music, which in turn requires a childlike innocence in the performer's approach to it. What I think he meant was that you shouldn't lose your spontaneity, but keep a freshness in your approach to things and not get too hard-boiled or self-conscious about things like 'How do I come over' or 'What effect am I having on the orchestra and the audience'. Much more important to keep your integrity as a musician and maybe also as a human being, so that what comes across is more or less pure. Maybe this is not the right word ... what I really mean is that you should be a clear channel through which all the things contained in music and which make music the marvellous thing it is, can flow: tenderness, power, sense of form and beauty, everything. Because everything, all human emotions, are there, in music. This is why you can talk about music as long as you like, but there comes a point where you can't talk any further, because music is a different language, itself a mystery. It is the most subjective and least tangible of all the arts. You cannot see it; and when the last chord is played, it is finished; it exists only as a memory."

Another mysterious thing about it, for Haitink, is that every time it is made, it sounds different. A painting, once painted, stays the same, even though the person responding to it may perceive different layers each time. So does a book. But a musical composition does not exist, it's not there until you come to make it, and it never sounds the same twice. Although Haitink always tries to get the technical side of things on as high a level as possible, sometimes there is "a special chemistry" that suddenly makes everything come together and lifts the proceedings out of the realm of the ordinary. "You always hope that something will happen, at every concert. But don't count on it, for this could be dangerous. Don't wait for it, for then it won't come; don't work for it, because then it won't come, either. It will only come when it will come."

But it cannot come unless both conductor and orchestra are meticulously well prepared. This doesn't mean only careful, pains-taking rehearsal, but also a profound knowledge of the score, which usually comes only after a long period of study and a thorough assimilation of all its layers. Being a slow learner makes studying more difficult for Haitink than for many of his colleagues who can read and "hear" a score almost simultaneously. He can't, and he first has to leaf through it once or twice, "as if it were a novel". At that stage, it doesn't say *that* much to him. Then he starts examining it movement by movement, examining the technical side—the structure, the harmonies, etc.—breaking it down into small musical periods and seeing how everything is related to everything else. "Then I put it all together again and begin to translate what I'm reading into sound."

Yet the first rehearsal, especially of works he has not conducted before, is always a surprise, because he calls himself "a man who is ignited by sound", like Nikisch, who started to create the image of the conductor as we now know him and whose interpretations really took shape only after the first rehearsal, after he had heard the actual sound of the orchestra playing. "In this respect we are alike, for I, too, find that my interpretation becomes complete only after I have heard what the work sounds like." (He has often said that even the sound of an orchestra tuning is so stimulating that it banishes all traces of nerves and stage fright, and sets his adrenalin flowing.)

This means that his interpretations are never so rigid that they cannot accommodate or be modified by the particular qualities of individual orchestras. "I always listen very carefully to the orchestras I work with. It's not that I'm not prepared: I do have a pattern, ninety-nine per cent of my interpretation, in my mind. But you must always leave something to orchestras. For example, I'm about to conduct the Mahler sixth in Paris [this was in autumn 1979] with the Orchestre de

Paris which has different qualities, a different chemistry, and whose approach to Mahler is different from that of the Dutch. So the outcome will be totally different—probably not as good as with the Concertgebouw who have played it so often, but possibly very interesting, because people who play something only rarely may have a fresher attitude. I don't know. We shall see."

Orchestral players greatly appreciate the room that Haitink allows for them in his interpretations: Kenneth Goode says that "with him we feel that there is a chance of expansion, of *personal* expansion. His interpretations are never uncompromisingly rigorous. He wants a fusion of the whole, but with more of a presence of our own will than most other conductors. He is prepared to lead gently, and this, again, is wrapped up with the personality of the man."

Haitink seldom interferes with soloists' interpretations either, because if they are not good it doesn't help, and if they are, it isn't necessary. "I am in a very privileged position in that I can always work with people I like, even though I am not one of those conductors who say: 'I want only him or her', but open to suggestions from people I trust. And I am always happy to get new ideas from soloists—eighty per cent of them are invariably good ideas. When you are dealing with an artist like Sir Clifford Curzon, for instance [with whom he had just performed the Mozart C minor Concerto, K.491], who is such a marvellous musician, you must give him all the room in the world, the best possible conditions to work in. You give him two rehearsals because he is an artist and not a machine, a man so totally involved in what he is doing and so self-critical, that you must give him all the nourishment and attention he needs. When you do and when the chemistry is right, something ... wonderful comes out." (It did on that occasion, with the London Philharmonic, and the second the last bar was over, Haitink turned to him and uttered a spontaneous "wonderful!")

This explains why so many great artists find working with him an especially rewarding experience. Vladimir Ashkenazy, who has played all the Beethoven piano concertos with him in Amsterdam, New York and Washington, is an unqualified admirer and often seeks advice about conducting problems of his own. "I love him; he is one of my greatest favourites among conductors. And his 'Pastoral' is simply the best I have ever heard. I heard it twice and both times I just couldn't believe it!" Dame Janet Baker told *The Observer* some years ago that Haitink "is one of the easiest people to work with from the personality point of view. He maintains a superb control over the total piece. Yet an artist never feels in a straitjacket with him. Sometimes you work with a conductor so four-square you wonder why you are doing it, because you are left no room for manoeuvring. But Haitink gives an artist freedom; he understands."

Prior to conducting the Mahler sixth in Paris, Haitink had "spent the weekend with it", refreshing his memory and listening to various recordings. He often does this with works he knows well, for then his own interpretation is firmly implanted in his mind and in no danger of being influenced. So, hearing all sorts of different versions is "fascinating for me. I would hate to live in a world with only one recording of every work. What makes life so fascinating is the variety of personalities. And I can only hope that people building a record library don't stick to one recording but listen to several versions of the same work, because then you approach music with a much more open mind. It is very dangerous to stick only to the performance on your single recording, bought with your own money, so to speak. If you can afford the luxury of two or three different recordings of a certain work, then I would be delighted. When people tell me that they have all my Bruckner or Mahler records, I always think, although I don't actually *say* it very often, that I hope that they also listen to other people's so that they know the difference! So now you know how modest I am not!

"But what I don't like about recordings is the fact that music is a living thing, and when the last bar is over it is finished; and when you start again, it is a completely new experience. But a recording is a frozen experience of a certain period and, as I said, I hate to be judged now by what I did twenty years ago, or even what I did a year ago. You develop, you change, not always for the better, but that's human life, and all human life is reflected in music. But a record is a frozen reflection and this makes me a little doubtful."

In recent years, he has begun to listen to his own recordings more than he used to. He still has not listened to all his Mahler symphonies—except in the playback room, of course—but only to bits and pieces, the beginning or end of a movement, whenever he is about to perform them, just to see if he still feels the same about specific interpretational points. But he listens to the entire recordings of other colleagues whenever he returns to works he knows well. Every time he finds that, even if he has conducted them dozens of times, they seem new:

"You start off by learning the piece and conducting it several times, say five or six a season; you leave it alone for a couple of years and then return to it. This is just what I'm doing with the Mahler sixth. I started yesterday by listening to Karajan's new recording, his first, which is marvellous. I like Karajan's Mahler very much. The fact that he came to Mahler so late in his career gives him a totally fresh approach which I find very, very interesting. I spent a really gripping time with his recording yesterday before returning to the score and finding that, to my surprise, it still felt new to me."

Mahler is a composer with whom Haitink is closely associated; his interpretations of all nine symphonies, both 'live' and on disc, have won high praise. But he tries to space out his performances of Mahler works, not only because he wishes to avoid being labelled a Mahler and Bruckner specialist, but also "because Mahler's world is a sick world in a way ... not *really* sick, but hysterical ... perhaps not even hysterical, but certainly illogical and neurotic. And while all of us have neurotic strains in us, too large a dose of Mahler—especially of the sixth and the ninth which are so depressing—affects me deeply. I have to be very careful because I get so emotionally involved that it spills over and colours my whole life. Then I have to force myself to remember that I'm a professional and that this state comes from the music and not from inside myself.... But this is why I could never contemplate a whole season of Mahler and am grateful for the chances to conduct so many different composers and styles of music.

"Bruckner, for instance, who always gives me the feeling that I'm high up in the mountains, above the trees in this sort of immense, rocky landscape and very clear, clean atmosphere; or things like Debussy's *La Mer*—I must say that every time I conduct it I can almost smell the salt of the ocean; or Haydn, the perfect antidote to Mahler: his symphonies are so healthy, so full of rhythm and vitality and always convey a feeling of the countryside and of a sunny day. It never rains in Haydn! Like Schubert's chamber and piano works, Haydn is a real mental relaxation for me; a return to sanity and normality."

Haitink was born in Amsterdam on March 9, 1929. His father was the Director of the city's Gas and Electricity Board, and the family, who were not musical but music-loving, had never produced a musician before. At the age of nine, for no particular reason, Bernard asked for violin lessons. Family folklore has it that it was because he envied the violin case carried by another little boy. His parents acquiesced, decided that he might as well have a really good teacher and sought out one of the violinists in the Concertgebouw. Both his teacher and parents encouraged the little boy to attend concerts—alone since the family home was only five hundred yards from the Hall. The first performance he heard, at the age of nine, was of the *St Matthew Passion*, about which he remembers little besides the contralto solo 'Erbarme Dich, mein Gott' and the woman sitting next to him crying. But the next concert, conducted by Mengelberg and including Tchaikovsky's 'Pathétique' Symphony, made a deep impression and possibly laid the foundation for his eventual decision to be a conductor.

By this time, Amsterdam was occupied by the Germans, which made it dangerous for any male between the ages of sixteen and sixty to roam the streets, lest they were taken hostage as a reprisal against the Dutch Resistance. (Haitink was then only eleven, so this didn't apply to him. But it meant that the audience in the concerts he attended consisted largely of Wehrmacht officers.) Indeed, his father had been picked up at the beginning of the Occupation and spent three months in a concentration camp, from where he returned in such an appalling state of health and having lost so much weight that his son had trouble recognizing him. He returned to his job where he had to face the difficult task of working both with the Germans and with the Resistance. One day he was tipped off that the Gestapo were about to pick him up again, and thought it best to spend the day at home. But in the end he decided to go to the hospital for a check up, and took his son along. As they turned into their street on their way back, they saw two German officers leaving their home. Of course, had they been really determined, they would have returned. But, as he explained to the *Gramophone*, this was part of the uncertainty of the times and left a deep mark on him: to this day he hates loud noises, is allergic to uniforms and ambivalent about all things German, despite the fact that, thanks to an inspiring teacher, German was his best subject at school, and his favourite music and literature are German.

After the war, he enrolled at the Amsterdam Music Academy where he studied the violin and conducting. Yet the conducting class was far from what he had expected, and run by a professor who was a marvellous pianist and man of the theatre but not a professional conductor. The only conducting he ever did was at those classes, during one of which he beckoned to Haitink and asked him to conduct—bits of the Tchaikovsky Violin Concerto—in his place. "Fine!" he pronounced at the end, "but where's your instrument?" Haitink stared at him in disbelief. "My instrument? What do I need my instrument for in a conducting class?" "Next time you come to this class, bring along your violin," replied the professor, "because conducting is music-making, not something divorced from it." And he proceeded to show his pupil the meaning of a musical phrase: how to shape and play a long phrase, how to colour it, etc. This went on and on, until Haitink wondered whether this was a conducting class or simply an extension of his violin lessons. But undeterred, the professor continued asking him to learn new scores on the piano and then allowing him to conduct a bit, not too much, just long enough. Then, "Back to your violin," he commanded, "play this phrase and let me see how you feel it." He never taught much about stick technique. This Haitink had to learn later, through trial and error.

Towards the end of his studies at the Academy, he felt at a loss about what to do next. So he applied for a place in a six-week conductors' seminar organized by The Netherlands Radio, even though he knew that, not having yet passed his examinations, he was, strictly speaking, not eligible. But he pleaded with the judges to hear him conduct before rejecting him outright. They agreed. Yet this caused quite a hullaballoo, because it turned out that the two had opposite opinions about his potential. The first maintained that he was mad, no good at all. The second, Ferdinand Leitner, Music Director of the Württemberg State Theatre in Stuttgart at the time, disagreed and felt that there was something there, something worth trying out, despite the apparent disorder.

"And for the next six weeks he kept an eye on me, helped me develop some sort of rudimentary stick technique, showed me what to do and what not, and at the end of the course, suggested that I also enroll in the next one, for another six weeks. By the end of that, I still felt a little out of my depth, so Leitner suggested that I apply for a job as a musician in The Netherlands Radio Orchestra, to gain experience of the orchestra and learn by watching other conductors." So he spent the year 1954–55 as a back-desk violinist (he says that his potential as a player would never have stretched beyond an average position in an average orchestra), an excellent vantage point from where to observe some of the famous men of the day, and the various styles of conducting.

"It takes all kinds. I don't know whether you remember Hans Rosbaud? He was a very gentle, scholarly sort of man, and as he approached the podium you thought, surely *that* can't be the conductor? But he was such a highly educated man with so much to offer that the moment he lifted his baton or started to talk about music, even the most hard-boiled musicians fell under his spell. Mengelberg, on the other hand, was quite different and always talked a great deal. [Even, as Giulini who played the viola in the Augusteo Orchestra remembers, to orchestras who couldn't understand a word of what he was saying!] There are masses of anecdotes about him but the one I like best is about the time he went to Paris to conduct the Lamoureux Orchestra and spent most of a rehearsal for the 'Pastoral' talking about nature, and God and the moon and everything, until finally one of the woodwind players stood up and said: 'Maestro, please, piano or pianissimo?'

"And this is the gist of the art of conducting. Don't use five words when two will do. And a wide vocabulary isn't necessary, either: just things like 'too loud', or 'this is not quite together', etc. The rest, the phrasing, you can indicate with your hands. In fact the amount you can show with your hands is amazing and conductors who tend to talk a lot should remember that at the concert itself they cannot talk at all. The stream of music has to flow through their arms, and maybe also through their eyes, to the orchestra. But there are no rules about this, because Karajan, for example, always conducts with his eyes closed. So, every conductor is a different personality and does it his way."

At the end of his year as an orchestral player, Leitner suggested that he either accompany him to Stuttgart or seek an assistant conductorship at The Netherlands Radio Orchestra. He applied, was engaged, and many years later a player confessed to him that the orchestra had felt that he was a conductor from the very first moment he walked onto the podium. Before long, he became their Principal Conductor and remained for five years (1956–61), which were beset by difficulties because he had to learn an enormous amount of repertoire with inadequate time for study, with an inadequate technique—as he lacked formal schooling—both of which meant that there was little chance of anything better than surface readings.

He told *The Times* some years ago that a conductor needs ten years to learn his job thoroughly: how to use rehearsal time, plan a programme, react to audience and critical response, work with the management and, not least, learn to live with himself off the platform. In fact it was mastery of the latter point that proved most helpful in coping with these challenging circumstances: "I think that my habit of withdrawing from everything and into myself stems from these days.

As I had no real schooling, I can never be sure of what I'm doing unless I retire inside myself, *think*, question everything and examine what I'm about."

During those five years with The Netherlands Radio he got his first break when, in 1956, Giulini fell ill before a performance of the Cherubini *Requiem* with the Concertgebouw. The orchestra's Artistic Director, Eduard van Beinum, rang Haitink, who happened to be the only conductor in The Netherlands who knew the work (and had performed it with the same chorus that the Concertgebouw were using). But he felt unready and took a great deal of convincing before finally agreeing. The rest is Dutch musical history: the concert was a triumph, the orchestra liked him, started inviting him to guest-conduct them regularly, and after van Beinum's sudden death in 1959, appointed him Co-Chief Conductor along with Eugen Jochum. Three years later, they named him their Artistic Director and Principal Conductor.

As the Concertgebouw is one of the best orchestras in the world, there was little orchestra-training as such to do, and Haitink says that he had no specific aim except "to grow into it and with it". Indeed, defending the standard repertoire there felt "like being a museum director who has to hang famous paintings in a certain light", he confessed to a British newspaper many years later. "It was not an easy job." Apart from "defending the standard repertoire" as he puts it, he also had to expand his own considerably. He remembers that among the most difficult pieces for him to master were Debussy's 'Ibéria' from *Images*. He loves Debussy and Ravel—"a world apart from Beethoven, Brahms, Bruckner and Mahler, but one in which I feel very much at home and derive a great deal of satisfaction from"—but found this work fiendishly difficult to rehearse, because it is so elusive, both from the musical and from the technical point of view. "I particularly remember struggling with the rubato in 'Ibéria', and tried to put so much into it that, of course, nothing came out. But as you get to know it, you improvise a little bit, and try to lead the orchestra around all the different sections, and all of a sudden, it comes out right. Till then, any problems you might have should be worked out inside yourself, without ever letting the fact that they are difficult to conduct, show. *You* may know they are. But no one else should."

But such wisdom does not come to conductors when they are still young: it can only be acquired slowly, by experience, or passed on by older, wiser maestri. Indeed, Haitink has often been approached by students who would like to take lessons from him. But at the moment, the pressures of his career preclude any such thoughts. In the future, maybe. But meanwhile he always answers such requests by inviting the students to come to his rehearsals and recommending that they also attend other conductors' rehearsals, to see all the different ways of doing things. "That's how you learn. And I also tell them that if, after the end of a rehearsal, they have any questions, I'll be happy to try to answer them."

And if one of these students were to ask about the essential qualities a conductor needs, what would his answer be? "Discipline (you have to be on time; when you arrive on the podium in the morning you must not look sleepy; you must be fresh, in order to overcome the drowsiness of the orchestra). A good ear and eye for psychology, so that you know how much you should rehearse and how much you should leave for the concert. And on top of all your musical baggage, you should have a tremendously open mind as a human being. For heaven's sake don't display any signs of egomania, because orchestras hate it. Of course, you must have the ability to communicate and maybe also the gift of inspiring the players. But this should only be done spontaneously, through being your normal self, for the only authority you need is a natural authority. You shouldn't spoil this by showing off, because orchestral players have a terrific instinct for what is real and what isn't. I know this from my own experience, and also remember my old violin teacher, a very simple man, telling me that just by the way a man picks up his stick and turns the pages, the orchestra can feel whether he has personality—yes or no."

Haitink's repertoire starts with Haydn and Mozart—Bach and Handel he does not conduct because he feels that, with so many specialists around, he has nothing of value to contribute to the interpretation of these composers—and stretches through Beethoven, Brahms, Bruckner, Mahler, Wagner, Richard Strauss and the French school to Shostakovich, whose symphonies he is in the process of recording for Decca. In fact the whole project started as a surprise. He had just performed the fourth symphony in London and New York and the tenth in Chicago when Decca approached him and suggested that he might record the entire cycle.

"At the beginning I didn't say yes, and I didn't say no, for the very simple reason that I didn't know the rest of the symphonies. I had to look at them first and find my way around them very gradually. For it is imperative that you believe in a score before you conduct it. This is even more true of works like Shostakovich's which are sometimes confused and take a long time to unfold; you have to guide the orchestra and the audience so that they know what's happening and where you are going. You have to control the balance in the enormous orchestras he demands very carefully, and bring out the wildness and savagery in the works without any hint of disorganization. Everything should sound absolutely clear. I always liken those symphonies to a long and often difficult mountain climb, for which you need a guide who knows the proper places to rest and take a look at the beautiful scenery, and the places where you should push on. In short you must clarify these works so that people can follow them.

"The first symphony of his I ever learnt was the tenth, which fascinated me, because it was instantly obvious that here was a tremendously talented symphonic composer with a great deal to say in human terms. I know that many people talk about his banalities in the same way that they talk about Mahler's banalities, but I'm not impressed, because I know that whatever is there *belongs* to the work, to the style and spirit of these composers, and is relevant to what they are trying to say. Of course you cannot deny that a lot of Mahler's and Shostakovich's music is not all that well composed from the technical point of view. The seventh symphony, the 'Leningrad', for example, has some awful moments: there is a terrible second movement, like a machine, but the whole symphony is very human and obviously written by a very accomplished composer who knew exactly what he was doing. And the more I dug my heels into this work, the more I discovered the extent of this man's grip and the range of his extremes. His wit, his cynical wit, is sometimes terrible and very much a part of him. But he also wrote some very tender and moving moments: endless bassoon solos in total contrast to his noisy climaxes – very much a Russian soul, I feel.

"And I am fascinated by the whole controversy of his book* at the moment. I hate ideologies and dictatorial systems and was totally gripped by his struggle to remain himself in such gruelling circumstances. And although he was awkward at times, he still wanted to write music that people could understand and respond to. And who can blame him? Nowadays composers who try to do this, like Ligeti

* *Testimony: The Memoirs of Dmitri Shostakovich*, as related to and edited by Solomon Volkov (1979).

and Penderecki, are condemned by their more avant-garde colleagues. Maybe these people's time will also come—like Mahler's has, the way he said it would—but they have to accept that now people cannot respond to their works and not blame other composers whose works strike a more immediate chord."

Haitink does not conduct what he calls very avant-garde music, first because he doesn't understand it and secondly because some of the technical facilities and skills it demands cannot be met by normal conductors in charge of normal symphony orchestras, but only by specialist ensembles who don't tackle the standard repertoire. He finds this "ivory tower of specialized art" a very disquieting development. "Nowadays, there is a vast gap between performers and composers and audience and composers, which I don't like at all and which results in a ghetto-like attitude: on the one hand you have special series devoted to new music and on the other the normal repertoire. The two never seem to converge."

But he feels if anyone is to blame it is the composers themselves who write music far beyond the comprehension of most of the audience. But as far as he is concerned, he tries to keep an open mind and confront himself with as much new music as possible, first, in order to see whether it's for him or not—"for example I feel that I could and should tackle Berio, for whose works I think I have the necessary technical ability; but people like Stockhausen are a closed book to me"—and secondly, in order to differentiate between good music and not-so-good music. He is struck by the fact that a composer/conductor of Boulez's stature, for instance, does not always make this differentiation when it comes to new music. (Boulez believes that one's motive in exploring contemporary works should not be a search for the masterpieces of the future but curiosity about what is going on today.) "He just performs it and communicates almost without trying."

Haitink thinks that the reason behind this unprecedented alienation of the public from the music of its own time could be that we live in an age whose technical developments we cannot possibly keep abreast of. "It is frightening to see what the human brain has done and how it has developed. No wonder that art in general, and music in particular, is in such disorder. When you think that when Mozart was a young boy he couldn't even stand the sound of a trumpet. What would he think if he heard the noises around us and some of the noises we hear in music now? He would probably die if he heard the 'Leningrad' Symphony. Yet Mozart is one of the most difficult composers to conduct—far, far more difficult than Shostakovich whose style is so much more obvious—because of his very delicate equilibrium between the human heart and mind."

In 1967, Haitink also became Principal Conductor of the London Philharmonic Orchestra. This meant that for thirteen years, until he was succeeded by Solti in 1980, he held this post simultaneously with that of Artistic Director of the Concertgebouw—a stimulating but burdensome task, leaving him very little free time indeed, what with touring, recording and guest-conducting appearances with a few of the world's top orchestras (Vienna, Berlin, Chicago, New York). Yet he developed the London Philharmonic to a considerably higher level and forged a warm and rewarding relationship with its players.

Although he basically "looked for the same things" in both his orchestras, he tried, as he explained, to capitalize on their specific individual qualities: with the Concertgebouw, famous for its strings but now possessing equally strong wind and brass sections, he spends longer on getting a good ensemble and gives the players longer to learn a piece. In London, on the other hand, with the musicians' ability to sightread and their team spirit making it easier for them to be together, he has to work harder at obtaining certain shades of sound and warmth from the strings. "Mr Haitink is always concerned about the quality of sound, about being as true as possible to the note on the printed paper, and keen to avoid interposing his own personality between the music and us," says the LPO's principal viola, Anthony Byrne. "We have a very special relationship with him," adds the principal timpanist, Alan Cumberland. "He is a great friend to the Orchestra and now he has relinquished his association with the Orchestra as far as concert work is concerned, we are lucky to have him as Music Director at Glyndebourne." (Where the LPO is the resident orchestra.)

Haitink, who was knighted in 1977, but cannot be addressed as 'Sir' as he is not a British citizen, became Music Director of the Glyndebourne Festival Opera in 1980, after happy and regular appearances that stretched back to his operatic début in 1972 (*Die Entführung aus dem Serail*). He had conducted *Don Carlos* and *Der fliegende Holländer* in Holland in his early youth, but prefers to forget about those performances. Since then, his operatic appearances have been confined to Britain (a superb *Lohengrin* and *Un ballo in maschera* at

Covent Garden; *Die Zauberflöte, Don Giovanni, The Rake's Progress, Fidelio, Der Rosenkavalier, La fedeltà premiata* and *A Midsummer Night's Dream* at Glyndebourne), but made his début at the Metropolitan Opera in the 1981–2 season with *Don Giovanni* and *Fidelio*.

He says that the reasons why he came to opera so late in his career were accidental: The Netherlands possesses neither a strong operatic tradition nor many opportunities for operatic conductors. So, while he has always loved opera and feels very much at home in the theatre, the right offers never seemed to come at the right time. Being a slow learner and an artist who has to grow into things gradually—which explains why the last performances in an operatic run are always the best, unlike some conductors who put their all into the première—he finds the working conditions at Glyndebourne ideal: "Reasonable time to rehearse, a peaceful setting and a very well-run opera house with an extremely able staff who know their jobs and do them well, which suits me perfectly because I'm not an operator. Just a performer. And as long as I do my stuff well, things should stay as good as they are. It's one of the happiest things in my life, and I hope to stay there a long time."

But however accomplished a symphonic conductor might be, operatic conducting is not something that can be learnt overnight: it is much more difficult, requires even quicker reflexes in emergencies which are infinitely more frequent than in concert halls, and the ability to blend stage and pit. "Haitink brings symphonic thinking into the opera house," says Alan Cumberland. "He seems so concerned about orchestral detail that he brings a new life to operatic scores by bringing out a lot of detail which operatic conductors sometimes tend to miss. But he tends to panic in emergencies! At rehearsal, he's on the telephone straight away, asking, 'My goodness, what's wrong?' His mind is so totally on the score that the slightest distraction unnerves him. He can't help it. He laughs about it himself afterwards." Most conductors usually prefer to start off at an opera house and learn the difficult things first. A few, like Haitink and Ozawa, did it the other way around, which is much harder, and this might explain why in the beginning Haitink's operatic performances were praised more for their musicality than for their dramatic impact. But he learnt fast and his interpretations of works like *Lohengrin* or *Die Zauberflöte*, which he is really in tune with, are unforgettable.

He says that his main reason for accepting the job at Glyndebourne was the fact that Mozart is the centre of this Festival's repertoire, which is partly limited by the size of its theatre (indeed, this also affects interpretations up to a point: Verdi could easily sound overblown and overwhelming in such a small house, for example) and partly by the stark fact that, as the Company receives no state subsidy, and has to survive on full houses, mistakes could be fatal.

But Glyndebourne possesses another enormous asset: the quality of its producers, Peter Hall, a regular Guest Producer, and John Cox, both of whom are prepared to listen to what the music is telling them—sadly a comparative rarity among today's producers.

"Peter knows the music backwards and has a marvellous way of getting things out of artists by first asking them questions and exchanging views. I shall never forget his announcing, during our first talk together, that this week, *he* would be the one to ask me questions. In this way he gets a terrific amount of adrenalin out of the artists who think that here is a man who wants to know their opinions and views of the work." "Another remarkable quality of Hall's," as Haitink explained to *Opera* magazine, "is his ability to put his finger on the gist of things, and make remarks that immediately clarify situations: 'Remember that Mozart was in love with two women but only married one,' he said at the first rehearsal of *Così.*"

John Cox, Glyndebourne's former Resident Producer, who has since become General Manager of Scottish Opera, has a marvellous wit, "especially with Strauss and he brings out those tongue-in-cheek situations superbly". Haitink also appreciates his knack of making people feel involved in a project and getting them on his side. He, too, always asks whether they agree with what he is doing and gives them the impression that he will never intrude on their territory. In all, Haitink's collaboration with Hall and Cox and the almost ideal working conditions of Glyndebourne have spoilt him for other opera houses.

But he regards the Covent Garden production of *Lohengrin* as one of the highlights of his operatic career: the producer was Elijah Moshinsky, who worked miracles with an extremely tight budget in the midst of all sorts of industrial disputes, and produced one of the most poetic, "medieval" productions ever mounted. He and Haitink brought out all the mystical content of the work, in a simple setting, exquisitely lit mostly with a misty, silvery-blue light. Wagner is Haitink's "secret love", and judging by his treatment of *Lohengrin*, one has every reason to look forward to his interpretations hopefully of all the Wagner operas. His other secret love is Verdi and we met some months before he conducted his first Verdi opera, *Un ballo in maschera*, at Covent Garden. He was in a very Italian mood and getting into the Italian idiom, and trying at least to understand the Italian language, which he doesn't speak, so as to get not just the meaning of the words, but the inflections—crucial in Verdi who took such trouble over the blending of words and sound.

He began his preparation by reading the libretto first, before the score, because he was trying to retrace the composer's steps, and Verdi read the libretto before composing the score. Then he listened to the music with the libretto in hand, which he found very interesting. As yet he had no idea whether he is a Verdi conductor. "We shall see." After the opening night the critics were favourable.

But although Haitink is in love with opera at the moment and is learning all the intricacies of operatic conducting, he never listens to opera for relaxation, "because it's too demanding when you're tired", but goes rather to symphonic works he doesn't know yet, like the Sibelius symphonies or unknown pieces by Szymanowski, and especially to chamber music: Beethoven string quartets, Beethoven piano music, Schubert's chamber and piano works, which he finds "a marvellous consolation against professional and commercial pressures".

His life is so well organized and under such constant pressure, that when he has a little free time, he likes to really flop, forget all about discipline, switch off, become absent-minded and feel free for a change. A shy, solitary man who hates the idea of facing a restaurant on his own, he loves to stay at home on the Dutch coastline or his sunny top-floor flat in Belgravia. He has five children, all grown up. He had married young but the peripatetic and workaholic existence that conductors have to lead took its toll: he and his wife split up after many years of marriage, much to the shock of Amsterdam's more conservative citizens, and he remarried in September 1980.

In London he loves going to performances of colleagues he admires—he'd been to hear Carlos Kleiber conduct *La Bohème* the night before we talked—and his favourite way of spending his free time is reading in bed: literature is "one of the happiest things in my life". He reads all sorts of things: Thomas Mann, his favourite writer whose works he has read about three or four times each; when we met he was trying to improve his French, which he had neglected, so he was "dipping into French literature and even reading Dostoyevsky in French". He also reads a lot of poetry "because good verse—for example Shakespeare when read by someone like Gielgud—is almost like music.... But music goes a stage further, a stage beyond words. It says things that cannot be said in any other way...."

HERBERT VON KARAJAN
The Master

"The Master no longer seeks, but finds. As an artist, he is the hieratic man. As a man, the artist into whose heart, in all his doing and not-doing, working and waiting, being and not-being, the Buddha gazes. The man, the art, the work—it is all one. The art of the inner work, which unlike the outer, does not forsake the artist, which he does not 'do' but can only 'be', springs from depths, of which the day knows nothing."

(*Eugen Herrigel*: ZEN IN THE ART OF ARCHERY)*

1: THE MAN

If there is on this planet another human being as misunderstood and misrepresented as Herbert von Karajan, I have yet to meet one. Nobody disputes the quality of his work, which has consistently ranged from very good to superlative. Yet many resent and envy the fact that, in his case, top quality goes hand in hand with 'best Box Office', immense power and total artistic independence—the latter two unique in the history of conducting.

At the same time, his great personal charisma, style and passion for the newest in contemporary technology, machines and gadgets, have captured and held the imagination not only of the music-loving public, but also of the public-at-large. To both publics, Karajan is a superstar: lionized everywhere he goes, selling more records than any other conductor, endlessly written up and photographed at the controls of his private jet, the wheel of his fast cars, the helm of his racing yacht. (His toys. No more, no less.)

But at a price! Throughout his long career he has been hounded by a plethora of inane clichés, rumours and half-truths which have little to do with reality—*his* reality as an artist and as a man. In earlier years, this bothered him a great deal and once "almost put me into a state of shock", he confessed in an interview on Austrian television. But he has

* Translated by R. F. C. Hall, Routledge and Kegan Paul.

learnt to ignore it—mostly by withdrawing deeper into himself.

As an artist, he is, of course, one of the greatest conductors ever to step onto a podium, and one of the very few whose musical achievement transcends the confines of their own individual interpretations. For the importance of Karajan's contribution to music does not consist merely of the excellence of most of his performances but also of the crucial and lasting way in which he has changed and improved the art of conducting. His combination of a remarkable imagination of sound with aesthetic and technical perfectionism has resulted in a new approach to this elusive art and has influenced every conductor of the younger generation, a prominent member of which pointed out to me some years ago that conducting can easily be divided into two distinct eras: B.K. and A.K., i.e. before and after Karajan.

The only other conductor to have had such a profound and far-reaching effect on the interpretation of music was Toscanini who, incidentally, is Karajan's musical idol. But *his* contribution consisted of changing people's approach to *scores* by insisting on absolute fidelity to the composer's intentions and sweeping away all the bad habits that had accumulated over the years under the guise of 'tradition'. Karajan's contribution, on the other hand, directly affects the art of conducting as such. I won't try to explain the nature of this influence here, because he does so himself in section two of this chapter.

A fundamental characteristic of Karajan's, both as an artist and as a man, is his ferocious independence and inability to compromise or bend his will to other mens'. Indeed, the overriding motive and goal behind the so-called 'Karajan Empire'*—which comprises the Berlin Philharmonic, the Salzburg Easter, Whitsun and Summer Festivals, films, video-cassettes, the Karajan Foundation and recordings, over every aspect of which he is in total control—was, and is, not power or greed, but the desire and need for total independence from people and from institutions: an independence which he won for himself inch by inch after suffering for a long time under both people and institutions, and starting with far fewer advantages than most of the young conductors of today.

As a man I found him immensely and instantly likeable, dramatically different, infinitely more complex than his public image suggests and

---

* I use the expression 'so-called' deliberately: for the essence of Karajan's power lies neither in ownership nor in direct financial control of the institutions he is associated with. He 'rules' solely and entirely through—and because of—the respect he inspires by the quality of his work, his personality and by the love of his public.

full of the contradictions of a temperament which, despite his prodigious managerial gifts and financial acumen, remains totally and quintessentially artistic. A man who, like Goethe's Werther, is prized for his talent and understanding whereas it is his heart—which nobody ever mentions—that is the true source of his greatness. Instead of someone ice-cold, remote, steely and typically Germanic, to quote some of the adjectives used to describe him over the years, I found a warm, very spontaneous, rather shy, solitary man who has few friends and is himself an exceptionally loyal friend; who hardly ever goes to parties or even social functions associated with his job—so much for that 'jet-set maestro' cliché—but likes discussions with one or two people and is invariably rivetting in conversation; who is often absent-minded, hopeless about dates and figures—friends doubt that he remembers even his own telephone numbers—and always slightly unpunctual; who has a good sense of humour, loves to laugh, is very sensitive to atmosphere and likes working with people who can create a relaxed and friendly environment that eases him out of the tension and concentration of the podium.

As one would expect from someone of Greek/Austrian/Slovenian ancestry, he is quick, resourceful, versatile and very much an individualist. He once joked that "the Balkans begin in Salzburg and I was born in Salzburg" and, joking apart, his ancestry probably has something to do with the daring, rebellious originality and tenacity with which he set about achieving his goals by bending the system to his will instead of changing his goals to suit the system. In fact, the only remotely 'Germanic' trait in Karajan is the remarkable discipline and regularity that now govern his personal daily habits.

He usually gets up at six, does yoga exercises for about an hour or so and has a swim—there are pools in his houses at St Moritz, St Tropez and Salzburg, and in the hotels he frequents—followed by a copious breakfast. Then he works at rehearsals, recording sessions—where he often complains that he is already hungry halfway through—or at his scores until lunchtime, after which he has a siesta before resuming work until the evening. At the end of a working day he likes a walk, preferably in the country as he is no city-dweller or -lover. He eats and drinks sparingly—mostly good plain food and a little wine—and smokes a very occasional cigarette.

Yet this self-imposed discipline is as hard-earned as his artistic independence and was sought in the first place as a much-needed antidote against his extremely restless, highly-strung, many-sided nature which, in his youth, lacked mental discipline. His now proverbial self-control and enviable capacity for total concentration were achieved after a long battle with himself. In this he was greatly helped by his discovery of yoga while still a Kapellmeister at Aachen, and eventually of Zen Buddhism to which he has now adhered for nearly forty years and which has had a profound effect not only on his approach to conducting and to orchestras, but also on his ultimate aims as an interpreter of music: the fusion, through loss of Self, of composer, conductor and orchestra into One and a passionate belief in the healing power of music.

Needless to say, no one could attain such heights, either externally in terms of worldly success or internally in terms of artistic fulfilment and self-mastery, without possessing a strong, indomitable will. Karajan's will, which is coupled with a burning, obsessional and rather touching enthusiasm for everything he does or wants, is indeed relentless and hard to resist: hard and useless! Firstly because it is impossible to stop him from getting his way—if he doesn't get it with the barrel he is certain to get it with the butt—and secondly because he wants things so intensely, chooses such logical, convincing arguments, and his charm, when he wants to use it, is so magical that rather than disappoint so singular a being, one chooses to go along with him most of the time. After meeting and watching Karajan at work for a while, I understood something that José Carreras had said months before and which at the time I considered to be just plain feeble. When asked why he had accepted the role of Radames, usually sung by much bigger voices, he replied: "Because Karajan asked me. And he is so persuasive that if tomorrow he turned around and suggested that I sing Micaëla, I probably would!" Yet despite his iron will and determination, Karajan is also prone to indecision and procrastination—but only over decisions not directly linked with anything he desperately or immediately wants—and tries to put off chores for tomorrow ... and tomorrow ... and tomorrow.

Another characteristic quality of this demonically intelligent and widely cultured man is his insatiable curiosity. Learning something new is as essential to him as oxygen and music. He has often explained that his motive in learning how to fly was not a need for luxury or speed—the amount of travelling he has been doing in the last decade could easily be covered by commercial flights—but the exhilaration of controlling and planning something minutely and preparing for every eventuality. He sometimes spends evenings mapping out the next day's flight, i.e. what height to fly, which corridors to avoid, etc. "I hate to be overpowered by things I'm unprepared for or don't understand," he told *The Sunday Times* a few years ago. Yet—a reminder, perhaps, that one cannot imprison great minds in their own words—he also recently told French *Vogue*, albeit in a different context: "I am waiting for astonishments.... Let us dream of everything we cannot foresee."

His curiosity has taken him far and wide: to a hospital in China, during a tour of that country with the Berlin Philharmonic, to watch an operation in which analgesia was achieved by having two people press and massage specific points in the patient's feet; to electronic factories in search of the newest, most advanced film cameras; to having himself wired up with electrodes while conducting *Siegfried* in order to measure the changes in his pulse rate and blood pressure during various stages in the music; and to innumerable other adventures over the years. No wonder that he never bothers to read fiction, "because that is for people with no imagination; I have already lived everything in fiction more vividly", but avidly devours books that reflect the scientific, philosophical and artistic development of the human brain (plus technical manuals by the dozen that enable him to keep abreast of the latest developments in all fields that interest him).

A big ego? Yes. He has no false modesty and is fully aware of what he has achieved. Yet an ego which he has consciously and willingly subjugated to his life's work: the interpretation of music. "Created not to be commanded, I also render myself obedient." The vanity and narcissism he is sometimes acused of are limited to his very personal, natty but casual style of dress, perfectly suited to his slim good looks and innate elegance, which once caused him to be voted the Best Dressed Man in Vienna. (The "Karajan style" is epitomized by polo neck sweaters, an additional sweater casually knotted over the shoulders, masses of colourful socks, and watch worn facing inwards.) Otherwise, he despises flattery and only when he sees, or senses, that a performance of his has moved or affected one is there a very momentary pleasure on his face. In private life, he is genuinely unaware of "who he is" and often seems surprised and apprehensive that people should stare at him in public places.

Unlike every other conductor in my experience, he never waits backstage after concerts for the handshakes and the compliments, true or false. Before the clapping even stops, his chauffeur is waiting with the Maestro's coat in hand, and by the time the audience start leaving their seats, Karajan is already on his way home or to his hotel. Chic, that. In fact, everything about this man is chic. In life as in music, he is incapable of anything vulgar.

Which is one of the reasons why one has hardly ever heard him complain about his two desperately serious illnesses—to do with displaced discs which dig into the spinal chord and nerve roots—or about the almost constant physical pain that he had to live with for over a decade. For many years, he sometimes had to have pain-killing injections even during the intervals of concerts. His first operation, in 1975, lasted eight hours, was just in time to save him from complete paralysis, and required a seven-week stay in hospital, during which he took stock of his life. But not only did he make himself fully active again within a few months, despite a lingering pain and discomfort, but also emerged from the experience "a new man", able to savour the simplest pleasures of life with a new awareness and enjoyment.

In 1978, he collapsed on the podium of the Philharmonie in Berlin, crushed some nerves and had to re-learn how to walk straight. He can no longer ski, play the piano properly or do many of the things—like skin-diving and mountaineering—which he used to love and be so good at that he could have earned a living teaching any of them. Yet, apart from a passing remark to *Der Spiegel* about now understanding the book of 'Job', there has been no complaining. Just continuous music-making which, amazingly enough, remained unaffected by all the suffering and sleepless nights. His pride and dedication would not have it otherwise. But not surprisingly, these experiences have brought a new depth, new insights and a new kind of intensity—almost a thirst for music, one could say—to his work.

Inevitably, a man as successful, powerful and at the same time as direct and generous as Karajan—who has never used his power to harm or hinder let alone destroy anyone—has frequently been let down, disillusioned and sometimes betrayed by people. And like many people basically ahead of their time, he has often been criticized first and imitated later. Throughout it all, and throughout the malicious or merely silly personal attacks against him in the press and elsewhere, he has remained silent—and continued working. He firmly believes that the only weapon against malice and animosity is the quality of one's work. But perhaps this is why, although he is simple and devoid of any trace of snobbery, he does not encourage easy contacts (only very few, very close friends are on first name terms with him), why he has not bothered to dispel or discourage the cool, controlled, super-efficient and impregnable image built around him and why he has withdrawn deeper and further into himself and into music which, he rightly feels, protects and revitalizes him.

He recently replied to the French television interviewer Jacques Chancel, who asked him whether he suffers at not being able to do everything he would like, that: "Admitting it would amount to acknowledging that it hurts, and one must defend oneself against any form of complaining. One must jealously guard one's secret gardens and give the impression of being untouchable. I hope to give more than has been asked of me and if I happened to get hurt, I would have the boat for falling into rhythm with the sea and welcoming the celebration of the first rite: silence."

2: THE ART

"Do 'I' hit the goal, or does the goal hit me? Is 'It' spiritual when seen by the eyes of the body and corporeal when seen by the eyes of the spirit—or both or neither? Bow, arrow, goal and ego all melt into one another so that I can no longer separate them. And even the need to separate has gone. For as soon as I take the bow and shoot, everything becomes so clear and straightforward and so ridiculously simple."

(*Eugen Herrigel*: ZEN IN THE ART OF ARCHERY)

In January 1981 I met Herbert von Karajan in Berlin and had the opportunity to watch him at work for a week that included recording sessions (the Bruckner first and second symphonies and Holst's *The Planets*); rehearsals for a concert consisting of *Verklärte Nacht* and the Beethoven seventh and the first rehearsal—the Shostakovich tenth—for a future concert.

It was the reading of the latter symphony, which immediately followed the Bruckner recordings, that brought home to me the fact that after twenty-five years' association, Karajan and the Berlin Philharmonic simply begin where others end: this complicated and difficult work, which they had not played since their Russian tour of 1969 in the composer's presence, was rehearsed without interruption and only one whispered instruction from him: "tempo, tempo", in a sharply rhythmic passage. No wonder that even he was moved to say "bravo" to the players at the end.

The next day they rehearsed *Verklärte Nacht*, a particular favourite of Karajan's and a work that he and the orchestra have recorded and played dozens of times. But he spent a very long time on it, perfecting details even further and refining, refining, refining the already transparent sound the orchestra were producing—at least transparent to *my*, and I dare say to most people's, ears. But he turned to the first violins and asked them please not to give him this thick soup, and just before the cello pizzicati near the end, please to play without expression—until the sound became completely ethereal and insubstantial. At the end of the rehearsal, the orchestra clapped *him*. On the morning itself, the performance was followed by a minute-long hush before the audience recovered its breath—the highest compliment to a musician. After the interval came one of the most searingly intense and electric readings of the Beethoven seventh I have ever heard him do, either alive or on disc. The last movement especially, which he took very, very fast but with every note perfectly articulated, "otherwise quick music becomes dull", will remain forever in my memory.

Later on that day we met for our first interview, after his afternoon sleep. He had "slept very strongly, because it was very tiring. It *is* very tiring, the Beethoven seventh, it's a terrible piece. You can't get away from it." Because of the exceptional interest of what he has to say, not only for music-lovers but for other conductors as well, and because a long conversation with Karajan is a rare privilege, I decided that this interview should be included here in full, with only very minor editing, and followed by a third section dealing with biographical matters and aspects of his work and achievements as opposed to the art of conducting as such.

Our second talk, two days later, exactly picked up where we had left off, and in order not to interrupt the flow, I have not indicated where the break was. For the same reason, my own questions are included only where they precede a change of subject or direction, and because Karajan is very quick on the uptake, his answers often anticipated my next questions and came almost before I had finished asking them. He talks fast and eloquently—exactly as he conducts, in one long line, uninterrupted by full stops—and occasionally jumps from subject to subject leaving sentences unfinished when he sees that one has grasped the essence of his reply.

When we met briefly to discuss the book and arrange an appointment shortly after my arrival in Berlin, Karajan made only one request: that as he is at present writing his own book about the origins and interpretation of music, the art of conducting and the psychology of the orchestra, would I please try to refrain from asking direct questions about these subjects! But as it turned out, he was generous in this as in everything else: both time and unlimited access to rehearsals, recording sessions including the playback room, and eventually all the rehearsals of the 1981 Salzburg Easter Festival.

The following is a transcript of our taped conversations in Berlin, on January 25 and 27, 1981:

HM   I remember you saying once that for a very long time you preferred listening to what was in your mind while conducting rather than to what was actually being played. Why was this, and when did the two sounds begin to converge and reach a point where, as at today's concert, one could be sure that one was hearing your own mental image of the sound being played?

HvK   It began when I first started conducting. Because I had my lessons like everybody [at the Vienna Music Academy], but very early on I started work in a small theatre, Ulm, where everything was ... [an expressive grunt meaning that everything was pretty grim] and of course at that time I was used to the sound of the Vienna Philharmonic and the State Opera and Chorus and suddenly I was confronted by this sound which was ... well, quite different. So as a sort of self-defence, I made an ideal picture of the music for myself in my mind and tried to put it into synchronization with what I heard. Because if I had believed what I heard I would have got so depressed that I think I would probably have given up.

And gradually, knowing exactly what I wanted, I waited to see what I could do, how much I could improve an orchestra which in itself could never be of a quality comparable to what I was used to, by employing all the means at my disposal—explaining and singing to them in order to show the expression I wanted—and get them to a point where they were at least making a decent sound, some kind of approximation to what I heard in my mind. Of course it's a torture to hear these two different sounds simultaneously. But I have a strong imagination. I can hear anything, anytime I want to, as it should sound, as it sounds....

And through a long, a *very* long pilgrimage, we've reached the point where a concert like the one you heard today surpasses anything I had imagined. Yes, really. It goes *beyond* what I had thought, and this is what makes this orchestra, and also the Vienna Philharmonic, so great: the fact that they give you what you want, but they also give you something more, and this completely revitalizes you. Otherwise you would have a situation where everything is sounding just right and no more. It happened once in my career: things were sounding just right and they said, 'we do our best' and they did, but it left me with no imagination. And then I had to stop it because I feared that I would get dried out.

And this is part of the mystery of orchestras. When does an orchestra by itself become, from a mass of a hundred-plus people, one person with very strong characteristics? Where is this sort of amalgamation, what actually happens, and how? In nature, out in the fields, a flight of birds suddenly comes up and they make movements so controlled and so harmonious that nobody wonders who incites them. They do it by a sort of mass feeling, and this will always be a mystery. It can't be explained, but it's there.

The same is true of orchestras. When they are in the right mood, something unexpected suddenly comes. Maybe it comes because you have been working on the details and the letter of the score with so much careful preparation, and I believe, as so many schools of yoga and Zen Buddhism believe, that once a thought which is really concentrated and well-conceived in the brain of man gets in a sort of wheel motion, it will always remain there. And by carefully approaching the thing, it springs into life again.... And these are some of the great moments we experience. And we wait for them, and we prepare for them, but we cannot summon them the way that one can summon a waiter. This ... something just comes, and it's the grace of the moment.

HM   One of the many mysteries in conducting, which is a profoundly mysterious art, don't you think? Especially this fusion, this merging together of identities: you, the orchestra, the composer's imagination ...

HvK   Yes it *is* a mystery and nearly unexplainable.... But of course, first you must ensure that you are completely free. That's why for a long time I conducted everything and anything I could lay my hands on. I wasn't ashamed of doing operettas or light operas for example, because I said to myself that what you need first of all is that your hands do everything automatically and without thinking, that you have the whole thing in hand. *Then* you can be free, your mind can be free to concentrate on the music instead of doing what I feel so many people are doing: conducting not music but notes and bar lines, chiefly bar lines.

HM   When was the first time you experienced something 'extra' with this orchestra and when did you first hear your own mental picture of the sound being played?

HvK   A long time ago, when I first conducted them in 1938 following my appearance at the Staatsoper.* I knew from the very first moment, from the first rehearsal, that this was what I really wanted in life, what I should have and what I would spend the next fifteen years dreaming of. And when I was named its conductor for life in 1955, it was as if a solid wall had been built behind me, on which I could lean. I *felt* it. That's why I told them that I couldn't discuss two, three, five or 'x' years' contract. I was sure to give this orchestra everything I had and so I couldn't depend on someone coming along and deciding that they didn't like my nose and so on. It should be like a *real* marriage: for life.

But even though I was immediately aware of the orchestra's possibilities, which are well illustrated in our first recordings, made during the American tour of 1955, it has been a long way from there to what you heard today. You see, one of the fascinations of our profession is that at the beginning you are trying to find your way into how the music evolves, without being really sure of what will come out. But after doing those symphonies sixty, seventy times, you *know* that the music is there, that you don't have to bother about whether it will come out like this or not. And this spares you an immense amount of force which would otherwise be expended, how shall I put it into words, in the effort of getting from what you actually have to what you had imagined. You find this difference, this disparity, between the two not just in conducting, but also in other forms of art. And it is normally expressed by the conductor as a certain effort. Toscanini, for example, used to sing the whole thing, but one note deeper, as I myself witnessed at his rehearsals. And he did so because he felt that in those passages he was not supported in the way that he would have liked, supported in the sense that an aeroplane is supported by its wings. Furtwängler was always breathing very heavily, while other conductors get cramps in their arms. But it all happens because of the desire to have more than one is getting.

One of my main concerns was how to get rid of this effort, this unnecessary waste of energy. And the *only* way to get rid of it is by rehearsing your orchestra to the point where you see that they are at one with you. They carry *you* instead of you carrying them. The beat, the technique, bah, I don't give a damn about those things! The important thing to know is that you don't carry the orchestra. And what brought this home to me was a parallel experience I had many

* Here he made a mistake: this was on April 8, 1938 *before* his appearances at the Staatsoper which were in October and December 1938.

years ago, when I took up horse-riding in Aachen. One day they said that today, we were going to jump over a fence for the first time. I was well, not afraid, but astonished and asked how on earth was one supposed to carry that enormous thing over a fence? They laughed and answered: "You won't carry the horse, the horse will carry you! You will put it in the right position so that it can do it naturally and it will go by itself, you won't even feel it!"

It's much the same with orchestras. Let them go! There is a Latin phrase which is particularly apt: *Quieta non movere.* Why should you? Orchestras, like aeroplanes, do it by themselves. And until you learn this, there is always something in you which prompts you always to *do* something, which in itself is nonsense! The *real* art in conducting is to realize that music comes implicitly, by itself. But it takes a long time to know and accept this and you become quite old before you do. You cannot as a young man. You are trying too hard, you always want to be in and don't allow yourself the luxury of interfering *only* when you are needed, in places where there is resistance.

Because basically, before you can make music you have to move something. You have to start it from rest. And of course, it has resistance against you, quite clearly, in the same way that a car has, when you try to push it. Gieseking* once told me how he experienced this resistance as inertia in his fingers, and we also know that Michelangelo approached the marble almost with hatred because he felt that it resisted the unveiling of the thoughts inside his head. *My* partner is the orchestra and every time I come to make music I hurt myself on its inertia in exactly the same way. And only after playing the same works often do you get a feeling of what is needed from you in order to overcome this resistance.

Otherwise, you just move it from being quiet, and as you move it, an expected piano already gets to be a mezzopiano, and a mezzopiano gets to be a forte, because motion gives it that extra impetus. This is one of the reasons why, when I sometimes need a certain kind of sound, especially a piano sound, I have the orchestra play one note and long. This way they get the volume of sound that I expect from them in their ear. And it always works, because then they know where they are, have the right feeling and play into this sound. If I didn't do this, I would get another, a different sound. [I watched him doing this again and again in certain pianissimo passages of *Verklärte Nacht* and in parts of *The Planets*, especially in 'Mercury, the Winged Messenger'. It worked

* Walter Gieseking, the distinguished German pianist (1895–1956).

every time!]

HM   This, knowing exactly where the resistance lies in each work, explains why you interfere with the orchestra so little and only in such places. You once said that these spots were the same with orchestras all over the world, good or bad.

HvK   Every time! Usually they are places where there is some sort of change or transition. Like a crescendo, for example. Now I am against *conducting* a crescendo. It has nothing to do with me. They must know that a crescendo is coming and where they are *within* that crescendo. But you see, this is more or less guesswork, because in no crescendo is it written that it starts here with so many decibels and that in three bars, it moves to so many decibels. So you can play a crescendo in many different ways and be, let's say, faithful to the composer's will in making a crescendo. But what is a forte and what is a piano? No one can tell you by way of phons. There are crescendi which start very slowly and come up right at the end, while others start faster and even out later. Then there are crescendi right at the end, where the orchestra feel that they are conforming with you in the force. But orchestras all over the world will always start too early and give out their forces so that, maybe eight bars before the real climax, they are already climaxing. I always tell them that when they reach the end—*that* must be the strongest point of any crescendo.

Other such trouble spots are places with changes in tempo. Say you have to start something slowly and take it into another tempo. There are pieces in which the whole thing takes a long time. In the first movement of the Sibelius fifth, for instance, there is a spot where you are nearly adagio and then comes an accelerando which goes right to the end of the movement and takes about six minutes. The art of it lies in the fact that there is not one bar slower than, or even at the same tempo as, the last. It must always be quicker, but to achieve this you need an enormous sense of economy. You can't get it right the first time of course, because the orchestra will always try to slow down at the most difficult places. It can only come with experience of the work, because you can't say when it should have this beat or this beat or that.

Another example of what I mean is Bartók who wrote in some of his works that getting from letter *A* to letter *B* should take sixteen seconds and from *B* to *C* twelve seconds and so on, so that you could measure everything absolutely, with a metronome. But I once played one of them for my pupils on the piano in five different ways! I was exactly there, on the stations, but *how* I came from *A* to *B* was different! First I remained longer on the previous station and accelerated more, then I started off faster and evened out. And so on and on. But, and this is the point I'm making, there can be no proof that you are right. Only long experience of a given work can give you a feeling for what is too fast or not fast enough.

And this can take years. You see, there are still mysteries in the great Classical and Romantic literature which are sometimes revealed to you suddenly, in a flash, like lightning. Suddenly you *know* what is right, and of course this makes you very happy. But it only happens with works you know very, very well and have done many, many times. And then you see how deep these compositions are and that there is no possible hope ever of coming to the bottom of their content. This is what is so fascinating: the more you get into them, the more you see what there is still to do.

HM   Is this why you spend such a long time studying and preparing works—much longer than most of your young colleagues would ever dream of devoting even to the most difficult and complex works? I remember one of them telling me that they were going to learn the whole of *Die Meistersinger* on holiday, in a month! But you spent eighteen months-two years on each of the Mahler symphonies....

HvK   Yes, and it isn't as if I didn't know them! In post-first-world-war Vienna where I studied, we were virtually fed on Mahler, who was very much part of the repertoire thanks to Bruno Walter. And everybody thought that by playing Mahler they could be friends with the critics. But try to imagine these post-war orchestras which had undergone so many changes owing to political reasons, retirements, etc., and were so new that most of their members had never before played Mahler. And suddenly a Mahler Festival was organized, in which all the symphonies were played under different conductors with two or three rehearsals, and it was just ridiculous! They were fighting the notes! The same thing happened at the premiere of the Beethoven ninth. Imagine that the musicians who had to play the ninth for the first time at a noble household first came together on that same morning, at ten o'clock, with the new material. Now, don't tell me that they could possibly have played this work, after six or seven hours' rehearsal, with no faults. There must have been hundreds of faults!

Personally I wouldn't *dare* to perform this symphony with fewer then four complete rehearsals, even with this orchestra who have played it seventy times and recorded it three times. Otherwise I wouldn't even have a *chance* of arriving at some sort of artistic result. It would be impossible. So when for years people kept asking me why I wasn't doing Mahler, I replied that I would do Mahler only when I felt that *my* time for it had come, and let the whole Mahler boom pass me by. Because Mahler's music is full of dangers and traps, and one of them, which many fell into, is oversensualizing the thing until it becomes sort of ... kitsch.

HM   Or vulgar?

HvK   Yes. And since you mentioned the word vulgar, I should tell you that as part of my development, I always tried to understand why it is that certain music can sometimes become vulgar. And it's nearly always a question of holding the notes too long, or not long enough, or letting them jump away from you—at any rate it's always to do with something that *can* be changed and this has always been a particular obsession of mine, which dates back to the first time I heard Toscanini conduct *Lucia*, when he came to Vienna with La Scala.

I was still a student, and all of us knew that he was coming and prepared ourselves for the event by getting the score, playing it on the piano, discussing it and so on. And after looking at the score, we all decided that we couldn't understand why he should bother with a work as banal as this. But it took just two minutes of the overture as conducted by Toscanini, to convince us that we were wrong. It was indeed the same score we had studied, but it was played by him with the same devotion and meticulousness that he might lavish on *Parsifal*! And this completely changed my attitude: *no* music is vulgar, unless it is played in a way that makes it so.* It's the same with all forms of aesthetics, including the way a woman dresses: a little bit too much of this or that, and it's terrible!

Since then, I have made a point of both performing and recording operettas or other works which, like the Barcarolle in *Les Contes d'Hoffmann*—which we recently recorded and which I consider to be one of the best things I have ever done, but only now, after so many years—are abused in a way you can't believe. Yet for me, this is one of the most tragic moments in all opera, because what happens is that in the course of the evening, a man comes from life to death, but the waters of the canal flow past as though nothing had happened and it's all forgotten.... And to get this feeling in the sound I told the orchestra. "Here you have the accompaniment of the flute and harps, and they fix

---

* The Berlin Philharmonic were slightly supercilious about recording *The Planets*, but when they saw what Karajan made of 'Mercury: The Winged Messenger', they admitted that there was more to the work than they had imagined.

the tempo. Now, try to be together with them, but at the same time try *not* to be together with them, so that you are never *really* together." So they let themselves drag a little bit behind and suddenly the whole thing flowed so naturally, like a tiger walking on something which is so heated by the sun that it has to drag its steps....

When later I came to conduct *Lucia* myself, around the middle of my career, I noticed at the first rehearsal that the orchestra were very eager but also a little bit frightened and sort of wondering what I would do and thinking that I probably wouldn't bother a great deal but just let them get on with it. But I had asked a good friend of mine who owned the second original score to lend it to me for the rehearsals. So we started the overture which begins with the timpani accompanied by the *gran cassa* [bass drum] beats, but there was no *gran cassa* in sight. I asked why this was so and they replied that there wasn't one and that anyway, Maestro Toscanini had never used one. So I said, "Just a moment. Here is the original score, you can see for yourselves." And from that moment on, everything went smoothly and with a minimum of explanation, because they realized that I was really serious about the work.

I had also had long talks with people who are well aware of and understand the Italian mentality. One of them, a friend of mine working for the *Corriere della Sera*, had pointed out to me that Italians look at things in a different way. "Think of Edgardo's death," he said. "The Germans would have written a funeral march, of course. But Donizetti simply wrote: *Cade e muore* [he drops dead], and the music makes a joyous D major with trumpets and fanfares. Because we Italians look at death in a completely different way."

And this man knew what he was talking about! Because among other things, he was responsible for supervising the *Domenica dell' Corriere*, the paper's colour supplement, which specialized in all things dreadful and fearful, like pictures of a man falling under a train and such-like which the Italians simply *love*. I once witnessed a tram accident and sure enough, people were still flocking to the scene days later, gesticulating and going over all the sordid details. They have no feeling of sorrow, none at all, and this comes out in their music. But they have no feeling of triviality, either, and their music is *not* trivial unless it is played in a way that implies that one expects it to be different. Only we, foreign conductors, often transform it into something *really* trivial, maybe because of a certain attitude of contempt.

But first of all, the formation of an Italian as a musician is very much influenced by the *banda* on Sunday at noon, where instead of violins they play little clarinets, etc. Now, when you hear the *Semiramide* overture, which can be fascinating, you can hear a certain sound which is in the ears of an Italian when he thinks of fast movement. It was also in Toscanini's ears. And he never had the slightest difficulty with things like *L'Italiana in Algeri*, for instance. He knew exactly the kind of sound he wanted. But he never fought so much or had so many scenes as with the Beethoven ninth. Something always went wrong. And he threw his score in the air or his watch to the floor, and walked out. Actually, one day, the Vienna Philharmonic got so fed up with his walking out that they locked the doors. And he tried one door, and he tried another, to no avail. When he realized what had happened, he put himself in a corner like a little child and shamed himself. Now, in Austria we have an institution called Lotto—a kind of lottery where you place a bet on two numbers—and this is something that all Austrians do. And the Vienna Philharmonic took the two figures—bar numbers—in the score where he had walked out, put it in the lottery and won quite a respectable sum. When Toscanini heard about it, he gave them double this sum out of his own pocket. This is an incident not generally known, but it's a nice story, isn't it?

HM   Yes! But you, of course, worshipped him and once bicycled all the way from Ulm to Bayreuth to hear his *Tannhäuser* and said that your greatest reward was being allowed into his rehearsals.

HvK   Yes, I was really under the spell of this man! Because first of all he was a *professional* conductor: the orchestra was together, the chorus were together, the orchestra was together with the chorus— something which, believe me, was not all that usual in those days. Standards were mostly very bad. I remember that one of the first things he said when the singers started shouting in the way they often think they must when singing Wagner, was: "No, no, no, nix Bayreuth, Café Chantant!" And he trained them to sing piano, which produced marvellous results, especially in *Tannhäuser* which has so many big ensembles. I came away from this unique experience, went on holiday and when I returned to Ulm in September, the orchestra was transformed right from the first rehearsal. Because *I* was transformed, I had a completely new picture of sound in my head. And this is one of those magical things. Nobody can say *why* they happen, but one knows that they do.

This is also the reason why I so greatly admire good artisans, people who do their work with special skill and expertise. There was a wonderful man, a carpenter who specialized in old wood and who worked on my house in St Moritz. You could tell by the way he touched and felt each piece of wood that his attitude was different from a normal man's. You could see that he was deeply in love with the thing. And this, being in love with the thing, is a necessity for every artist. When he does it purely for scientific or experimental reasons, it doesn't work.

HM   A minute ago you were talking about Toscanini and how he raised the standard of conducting in those days. Now everybody knows that you have done just that yourself, in our time. In fact, the way that you transformed the art of conducting has influenced the approach of most conductors. Are you aware of this and, if so, how would you describe your influence?

HvK   Yes, I can tell you exactly how, and why. Because first of all, as far as playing is concerned, I admired two sounds: one was the whiplike sound that Toscanini could produce, with utmost clarity and flexibility. But he was very direct. Finesse was not his cup of tea. And he always lacked that line, that in-between thing, that elasticity, that Furtwängler had and which I also admired enormously. Yet Furtwängler was sometimes afraid to take the lead in some places, not because he didn't want to, but because he seemed afraid to move forward. In fact when I first came to the Berlin Philharmonic we had a concertmaster who had played with him and who told me that in some passages, he could see a sort of pleading expression in his eyes, please help me, and then he would start the change himself with a slight bow and could then see the relief and gratitude in Furtwängler's eyes. And in some places, his beat was not clear or precise. He didn't *want* it to be, being always between two things was part of the man's ambiguity, part of his personality and of his genius. In fact people say that he never said *ya* or *nein* but *yein*. And this ambiguity was what he expressed in his conducting. Like all mysteries, it happened automatically and unconsciously. Yet sometimes, it lost him some orchestral flexibility.

Now I said to myself that it must be possible to combine these two things: precision and elasticity. I don't think that one excludes the other, only that in some music you need more of one, while other music may require more of the other. And as soon as I acquired an orchestra that I could mould, I set about putting this into practice. And this is the essence of what I think I have achieved, to some extent. If I want precision, I try to get it, but not to the point where the orchestra feel driven by a man with a whip. I also allow them to be themselves and to have the flexibility of changing their colour and mood....

But only in the last eight years or so have I felt that we now have a sort of palette of different string sounds which they didn't even know, and which *I* didn't even know existed, not being a fiddler or cellist. But I knew that there were possibilities in the strings which each single soloist would say make no difference to the way each player sounds individually, but which make a great deal of difference to the collective sound. So, we tried various things and when I was sufficiently sure that we had this sort of palette, we started on the Mahler symphonies. And we took considerable pains with each one of them.* Because, you see, there are two different layers in one's preparation of a work: there is the inner preparation and the outer preparation. I might have a work inside me but wait six, seven years before I conduct it. Then, when the necessary technical possibilities are there, I say "Now, I must do it." This is true of both operas and symphonic works, and it was so with Mahler.

Now we have finished our recording of the ninth, which will come out any moment [it was released in March 1981] and in a year's time [in January 1982] we will play this symphony in concert, as I usually like to give myself a year between the two. But this work is an obsession with me. It's terrible. From the conducting point of view it's easy, it's nothing. But the content ... this constant seeking of a relief which cannot come ... and this *brutal* scherzo. Mahler of course knew that he was going to die. Right at the time, those very days when he was writing this symphony, his doctor had told him that there was no hope. And how the first movement suddenly breaks down, there is in one place a cadenza with only a few instruments and the double basses.... This is music the like of which has never been written. It says things that have never been said before. This longing for beauty and harmony with which the first movement ends.... But of course it is a beauty and a harmony with death already in it. Wonderful work.... As I said, we have finished the recording.† I only have some corrections to do, and of course, the mixing.

HM   Talking of which, I would like you to tell me your views about

* When they first prepared the fifth, they made a trial recording, then worked on it again, then recorded it properly—sixty hours' work before they first gave it to the public.
† The record won the *Gramophone* magazine's 'Best Orchestral Recording of the Year' Award and the Deutscher Schallplattenpreis for 1981, and his first public performance of this symphony in Berlin, on January 31, 1982, was possibly the greatest concert of his career; one of those very rare, unrepeatable moments of music-making that seem to reveal a work in all its truth, and cannot be described. Only remembered.

an accusation which has been hurled at you from time to time and which personally I have always found imbecilic: that all this mixing and balancing of tapes in the studio amounts to 'manipulation' of music, although it seems clear to me that music should be adapted to and make use of each different medium, be it disc, television or film in the same way that a play does.

HvK   But of course! And anyway, if you were going to look at it this way, you could say that music begins to be 'manipulated' the moment it is interpreted by a conductor or a soloist and played by an orchestra in a hall with a specific acoustic. All these factors 'manipulate' music and so does the fact that I ask the oboe please to play more piano. And you are manipulating the orchestra for one reason only: to get the sound you want. In the recording studio you are using the equipment at hand for exactly the same reason. Today we have this marvellous digital multi-track machine which can produce such wonderful results! And there are some works like Schönberg's *Variations for Orchestra* which is one of the greatest works ever written, but which I would no longer dare to perform in public, because in a live performance it is impossible to achieve the result we did in our recording, i.e. the exact sound Schönberg asked for in certain passages.

For example, there is an English horn solo during which the whole woodwind section goes on playing complicated rhythms in three pianissimi at the highest pitch. It never works, you cannot hear the man. But for the recording, we put them twenty yards to his right, mixed the two sounds and got it right. One does sometimes come across spots like that in Schönberg, and it could be because, as we know, he often composed with his pupils and wrote difficult passages out with chalk on a blackboard, and had them all experimenting with solutions which are sometimes too rich and obscure the original idea. And I think that it is quite legitimate to use the means of electronics for clarifying the music in such spots. You could play this piece live and never achieve a comparable result. I had conducted it several times before our recording, but since then I vowed that I would never do so again because it could never sound as good....

And at today's concert I thought again about this man who wrote *Verklärte Nacht*, the greatest romantic work ever written. Yet he realized that now he could go no further. And I often wonder when conducting it: was it frustration, was it some new thing that wiped out his sense of the romantic, which was fantastic—it is still there in *Pelléas* but after that it's finished—and how could he come to ignore it? I don't know if he ever spoke about it, but it is a question I often ask myself. What *was* it that made him turn his back on it? Maybe a man doesn't like to say when something is finished. Maybe. But then, to speak in such a contemptuous way about everything that he had done before.... But of course we all hate what we have done in the past. Sometimes, when I listen to some of my old recordings, I envy painters who can simply burn the pictures they don't like. I cannot.

HM What a different attitude Schönberg's was from Richard Strauss's who immediately after composing *Elektra*, his most advanced work, took a step back and composed *Der Rosenkavalier*, a much more conservative work.

HvK Yes, he was different in a way. In his youth he sought an outlet in the tragedy that he saw in the story of *Elektra*. And he knew that, for his lifetime, this was enough. I have good proof of this, because he came to Berlin for the performance we mounted for his seventy-fifth birthday and afterwards I was presented to him and he said what he always said to every conductor, no matter who, that it was a wonderful performance, the best performance of the work that he had heard in his life. I said, 'Doctor, I don't want to hear this, I want to hear what's *wrong*!' So he looked at me very closely and said, 'Come to lunch tomorrow.' I went and we talked and he gave me some small hints like, 'You see I've written *piano* here in this or that spot because I was anxious that the singers should be heard, but you have followed it too closely. Don't do it. It disturbs the line. But there is a much more important thing: I know that you have studied, rehearsed, conducted and lived with this work for more than two months now. Don't you think that you are closer to it than I am, after so many years? Go ahead and conduct it exactly as you did last night.' And after a few seconds' silence, he added: 'And anyhow, in five years' time you will do it differently.' Wonderful wisdom from an old man. It touched me very much.

And as we are talking about Strauss, Deutsche Grammophon recently asked if I would consider recording the *Alpensinfonie*. I replied that if they took it for granted that I would need eight rehearsals instead of the usual three—because I knew how difficult the piece is— it would give me great pleasure. It needs an enormous orchestra, and I said that I didn't want to put the company to such great expense, but they insisted that it is really needed. And we did it, indeed at great cost, but with enormous joy. The orchestra loved it, because we really had time to prepare it properly. We played it, rehearsed it, I explained all the details, etc. [The record was released in the autumn of 1981 and shortly after that I heard him give two stupendous performances in Berlin, following one in Leipzig, which the orchestra consider one of the best performances of anything it has ever given in the players' memory.]

You see, technical problems can always be overcome by careful preparation, by doing it slower or faster or softer or louder and so on. The acoustical problems are naturally much more difficult, inasmuch as people must be able to hear each other. This is why I try to have different sections listening to each other so that they get each others' sound in their ear. And gradually, we come to it. Because unless they make music in this way and forget the notes—and orchestral musicians are attached to their scores not with strings but with chains—nothing worthwhile can happen. But of course, it takes a long time. In this sense, our profession is one of the few that go against the tide of our times. Until recently, and especially in ancient civilizations like China, a man was always trying to get old, old, old, because he was then regarded as a sage and everyone had to be silent when he spoke. But now, our times have reversed everything, whether for good or ill we don't yet know, but the whole evolution of our world demands that it be so. Yet certain things, like our profession, are an exception to the rule, because they cannot be learnt quickly.

We know that for a serious operatic conductor, anything less than fifteen years' preparation will not do. I don't mean preparation *before* you do it but preparation *while* you're doing it: you form yourself by doing it. It is impossible for anything worthwhile to come out of the first time anyone conducts *Tristan* or *Die Meistersinger*. You have to start somewhere, of course, but it should not be at the Metropolitan! We, in this profession, have the advantage of having time on our side and if our health is good, the possibility of getting things right as we go along. Which always reminds me of Wagner and *Die Meistersinger*. When, in the third act, Stolzing asks Hans Sachs how one can become a Master, he replies: 'You see, when you are young it comes by itself, because Spring sings for you'.... But then comes maturity, illnesses, broken marriages, divorces, operations, difficulties in your marriage and so on, and he who, after all this, is still able to sing a beautiful song, that is a Master. And nothing is so well said, or, in our language, more beautifully....

HM   One of your many achievements has been the founding of the Salzburg Easter Festival, in 1967. At this festival you always use the

Berlin Philharmonic which, unlike the Vienna Philharmonic, was not an operatic orchestra. Was it hard to train them for operatic work?

HvK   No, it was very, very easy. First of all I,decided always to record the operas in question before, so that by the time we come to perform it, the orchestra is thoroughly familiar with it. And I clearly remember our very first rehearsal at the Festspielhaus. They were sitting in the pit which is very high, and I showed them how I could lower it by as much as three metres, and said that every time I couldn't hear the singers, I would lower it by ten centimetres and that maybe by the end of the first act we would find ourselves in a cave. Or maybe we would stay right where we were, and this would mean that the singers were audible throughout. The choice was theirs. And I never had to touch the button.

Mind you, as far as 'killing' the singers is concerned, you could never kill a singer with trombones. It's a completely different kind of sound and the singers will always come through. What you *can* kill a singer with is the dense sound that comes from senseless, heavy down-bowing in the strings. And the same goes for instrumental solos. When there is an oboe solo, I *do* want to hear it! (That's why I insisted on the orchestra sitting as they do for concerts—which is quite different from the way operatic orchestras normally sit—and this way I have all the key men near me. It does mean that the last violin desk is rather far away, but he has the bridge of the other violins, so it is all right.) Hearing every solo is crucial, especially in Wagner. And I remember that when we started with the *Ring*, there were such silly remarks to the effect that I made chamber music out of Wagner! I didn't make chamber music, I made the music as it is written. If I read that there is an oboe solo but cannot hear it, it's completely senseless. And for me to hear it, the rest of the orchestra must necessarily play down. It has nothing to do with chamber music. I can play with my seventy strings a pianissimo which is much, much more subtle than a chamber orchestra's. What I did do, though, was to enlarge the *scale* between a pianissimo and a fortissimo, to a great extent. And the fact that this orchestra could play opera was spoken of as a wonder, but in fact, it happened so naturally that I didn't even feel it.*

HM   Last year's production at the Easter Festival was *Parsifal* (which you will be repeating again this year and have also recorded), a work which I know to be particularly close to your heart.† Yet you waited a

---

* Pierre Boulez has said that the only time he has heard Wagner as he should be played was when he heard Karajan's interpretation of *Die Walküre*.

† This production is considered to be among his greatest.

long time before recording it and before tackling it in Salzburg. Why?
HvK   It was not because of lack of time but because of the imminent
dangers inherent in staging such a complex work. I realized that it
could not be done on a normal stage in a way that could do it justice. It
needed all the complex technical facilities that we have in Salzburg. I
had done it many years ago in Aachen and again in Vienna in 1961.
And one thing always failed to please me: the changes of scenery in the
first and third acts where, for fear of something going wrong, you were
apt to accelerate in a way which is wrong, and always made me feel
uneasy. So my first preoccupation was that the scenery should be
conceived and arranged in a way that would free me from this worry.
Because the passages that accompany the changes of scenery are
wonderful music, but if you have to rush them because something is
not in place on stage, the whole thing is finished. For me this was the
major test. And when I saw our finished sets, I knew that I could drag
those passages as long as I wanted.

But I confess that this production was a labour of love for all of us.
Personally I spent two years under the spell of this work, and put
everything else aside so that I could concentrate on it fully and get to its
truth. Then I had all the problems with which I had been burned before
put before my technicians, and we spent a long time discussing them. I
felt that we must solve them in a way that enables you to see the magic
of the work right from the first scene. And I think that we found a
solution which is creative and conforms so well with the music that you
are hardly aware that those changes are actually taking place. It's really
like magic with film, with something going up and something else
going down, and of course the bells! And here we could use our special
facilities with acoustics: we did them half electronically and half with
real instruments and then put the whole thing into a synthesizer and
evolved a plan which enabled us to control them for volume. It was a
long and painstaking process but one which, I think, makes an
overwhelming impression and helps to create a feeling of great space,
which is what I like in music, theatres and concert halls. (My
experience in Ulm, where the theatre was tiny with a six metre stage,
has left me with a lasting shock or complex of narrow places—yes,
claustrophobia—and I only feel well in a hall with some air above and
around me.)

Once we had solved the scenic problems, the music was no problem.
It came by itself. Of course a great deal depends on how *Parsifal* is
sung: the pronunciation of the words, how you mould them, how they

blend into the sound—because the text is crucial and especially so in the part of Gurnemanz. But granted the artist we had—Kurt Moll— the rehearsals were more of a joy than work. He had already proved that he was the man to do it in the recording. And you see when you have recorded the opera before, the singers can hear their own voices on tape during the rehearsals, concentrate on their acting and synchronize their singing with their movements, i.e. that they should not sing a ritardando if they have to climb up steps, because after you have climbed up six steps, you *cannot* sing a ritardando.

And I always warn them not to look for me, because they won't see me cueing in their every entrance. They have to sing as they want, as they have done before. In fact, by then the whole thing is so much a part of them that they won't even be able to do the contrary. And when they know exactly what to do, *then* I can accompany them. Because they have been prepared in such a way that they think they are free. And the moment they think they are free, they will sing well.

Take Dunja Vejzovic for instance. She was completely new—but I prefer that to somebody who has already been spoilt by bad habits— and responded wonderfully to the challenge of the part of Kundry. We worked on it together for a year, which meant that she came back again and again when she had absorbed all she had learnt before, and we went on further. When she eventually came to the recording sessions, I had her sitting in the orchestra for five days, without singing a single note. I always do this, so that singers can hear what is being played. Then, one evening, I asked if she now felt like singing a scene. And she was so 'in' it by then, that she didn't have the slightest fear and we did forty minutes' recording there and then.

HM   The recording (which won the *Gramophone*'s 'Record of the Year' and 'Best Operatic Recording of the Year' Awards and the Grand Prix du Disque) stands out for its wonderfully lyrical approach and the clear articulation on the part of the singers—a far cry from the big, meaty, wobbly sound so often mistaken for Wagnerian style.

HvK   Oh, I can't *stand* that! If people start to shout when they should be singing piano, or speaking piano because so many things are spoken on the notes, they lose their reserves of dynamic scale. It's an odd thing, but if you start with almost nothing, people concentrate much more on hearing you. Then when the outbreak comes, it makes a far greater impact. This applies to most roles, with the possible exception of Ortrud who is in a fury all the time, and to Italian roles as well. Take *Turandot*. [This recording was released in summer 1982.] I have never understood why this part should be sung by a 'vocione'. She is not a nice woman, she is holding herself back and so on, but if she were screeching all the time, no man would have any interest in getting her! So Katia Ricciarelli will sing it with the same Italian style with which she sang Tosca. It's enough.

But of course, as far as singing is concerned, preparation is everything. Singers must have the note already in their mind before they sing it. Normally they just sing it and then adjust it if it's too low or too high. But I don't call that singing. I always tell them that one bar before, they must already be so full of it that it seems to come because they cannot hold it back. They must be in a sort of ecstasy so that they cannot speak but *must* sing. Otherwise everybody will wonder why they are not saying it instead. But enormous emotions can only express themselves in singing.

HM　After *Turandot*, you will start re-recording the Beethoven symphonies for the fourth time. Why?

HvK　Because once you have heard any music reproduced on the new digital multi-track machine, the beauty of sound is so overwhelming that we just *have* to do it. We will re-record about fifty or sixty works.

HM　Last time you recorded the Beethoven symphonies, somebody asked you how your interpretations had changed over the years. You replied that they had naturally mellowed with maturity—for instance that you no longer made the mistake of taking the finale of the seventh slower than you felt it should be—but that the greatest difficulty, the thing you still spent most time on, was the first movement of the first symphony. What makes this so especially difficult?

HvK　Everything! The introduction is very complex as far as intonation is concerned. It's not written so that it plays itself, and has to be very carefully prepared. Apart from intonation, there are those chords that dissolve themselves, those pauses.... It will always be a problem, and only very rarely can you get it more or less where you want it. It seems so easy, but to me it's full of mysteries. First of all, there are those changes in the harmonies, then comes the scale and then there is that Allegro which, for me, is a whole world. I spent a lot of time working on it with the orchestra. I know exactly where the difficulties are: in those chords which are composed so that instruments stick out. You see, there are things in music which sound by themselves and others which have to be worked on. This movement is definitely one of the latter.

HM　What about the difficulties in Bruckner? A few days ago at the sessions you said that only comparatively recently have you been able to get one pulse running through a symphony....

HvK   Yes, and again this is something that comes with experience and a complete overall knowledge of each work, so that you can see it all stretched before you from the beginning. As far as tempo is concerned, you can nearly bring those symphonies up to the one universal tempo he describes. Normally the second subjects are not marked, but it was very much a habit—even in Beethoven works—to take the second tempo a little slower. But the old school of conductors used to drop 30–50 per cent of the tempo and the work would lose its coherence, especially in the last movement of the eighth, which seemed to be in ten pieces. Only lately, after doing it for forty years or so, have I come to a solution that makes me feel as if the whole movement goes in two minutes. Not because I'm playing it fast, but because it now feels coherent. In the original scores, the tempi were much simpler than they became in later editions, but this is something which, like the tempi in a Viennese waltz, you must know by feeling. (No one has ever tried to edit a Viennese waltz: all those subtle inflections of tempo would come out terribly exaggerated if written down.)

In many cases the orchestration in the original scores was different, too. Bruckner, who started composing quite late, had a small group of devoted friends, including Franz Schalk, the Director of the Vienna Opera, who also indirectly influenced my own career, and who was a great believer in Bruckner. But he was also a practical musician, and when he saw that these scores were full of traps for the orchestra, he and the other friends persuaded Bruckner to make some changes and modifications. For example, they realized that there might come a time when a difficult passage for the third horn would be played in a way that would do it justice. But in those days, the third horn was sure to be a very modest player who could never get it right the first time, so why not double it with violas to make sure that nothing went wrong. And they made the whole thing lighter, and those later editions were full of errors because they were trying to make it easier. But now we have got so much into the spirit of Bruckner and standards of orchestral playing are so high, we can play the original scores.

HM   A moment ago, we were talking about how you manage to have one pulse running through a Bruckner symphony. Another characteristic of your interpretations is that you always manage to find the one true climax in each work. How do you arrive at your conclusions about this?

HvK   There are no real, concrete guidelines. It just comes with experience. Now, after such long experience, I know what was wrong with my interpretations of twenty or thirty years ago—because naturally you cannot know what is right unless you have some judgement of what you have done before. Indeed, sometimes I feel that my best ideas are not inventions but an effort to avoid previous mistakes! There are cases when even then I knew that I was wrong, wrong about the whole thing, the whole layout of the work, and didn't dare take it up again for a very long time. *La Bohème* was one of them. The production I did at La Scala with Zeffirelli in 1963 was my first in thirty years, although I was always going to any performances within my reach. Eventually I worked out all the problems, mostly scenic and casting problems, in my mind: the second act was one of them. As you know it's Christmas and everybody is gay, joyful and so on. Now if, in your scenery, the Café Momus is right in front and you have all the chorus walking up and down as usual, you cannot hear a word that the principal singers are singing, and I told Zeffirelli that the only way to do it would be on two levels. As I said before à propos of *Parsifal*, until you find a believable scenic solution, you always have musical problems. But when the basic concept is right, everything falls into place and every detail comes out right.

HM   On the symphonic side, you only recorded all the Schubert symphonies fairly recently, about five years ago. Was that because you felt that something was wrong with your interpretations or because you just don't like them?

HvK   My favourite Schubert symphony is the Unfinished. Even the ninth, I never want to do again. I don't know what it is about it.... I really wanted to do it and I did it often, and every single time I felt, not that I couldn't get close to it, I was always full of it, but that, maybe, I had the wrong ideas. So I think it much better to leave it alone. I'm waiting to hear it played by somebody in a way that will convince me that it's a great work. Everybody does it but for me so far it has never come alive. Toscanini, too, had a fight with this work all the time. And he never stopped doing it, and he knew he couldn't do it—the same problem that he had with *La Mer*, which he also kept conducting without ever reaching the point where he felt that he could really *see* the work.

HM   While looking at a score—say a new score like Penderecki's *Polymorphia* which you are doing again next week—at what point do you begin to 'see' a work and acquire your mental picture of the sound? And what is your method of learning scores?

HvK   In the case of *Polymorphia*, I happened to hear a tape and found the work interesting because there are colours in it that nobody else seems to have. But the mental picture of sound that you form while studying a new work can sometimes be quite different from what eventually comes out. It is impossible to look at the score and hear exactly what it will sound like. And this is true not only of us, conductors, but of composers as well. They, too, are sometimes shocked by what they hear and say that they imagined something completely different from what actually came out—I mean different in the substance of sound, not different from any individual interpreta-tion—and I never know how to explain this. Occasionally I can tell them from experience why something sounds wrong: maybe it's just a single instrument, or the way it's blended into the orchestration which makes for a sound they didn't want. (Richard Strauss, on the other hand, was a master at instrumentation and usually knew exactly how his scores would sound.)

If I'm studying a standard repertoire work, I make a first reading with the orchestra, so that I can have a tape to study and see what is really in the notes, and whether I can hear anything in my reading which I cannot find in the score. This helps very much. Sometimes you don't know why something sounds wrong or what to do to make it sound right, while sometimes the right idea or solution jumps out at you.... I often listen to my old records as well, and try to forget the notes and get a feeling of the music and *see* it in my mind. And then it becomes an obsession, like the Mahler ninth, which we have already discussed.

HM   When conducting a work as intensely tragic as that, does it take you longer to unwind and be yourself again afterwards?

HvK   No, no. Once I'm away from it, it's over. I want to be quiet of course, I want to enjoy it in retrospect, but it no longer wears me. I'm rid of it, you see. But the time before can be very trying....

[When I saw him a few hours after his first performance of this work and asked if he had finally "got rid of it", having been obsessively and almost painfully possessed by it for weeks and months, to say nothing of the days preceding the performance when he could think of nothing else and was acutely nervous, he replied that his solution had been to plunge into something else immediately; "it's the only way."]

HM   How did your search for yoga and Zen Buddhism begin?

HvK   They were a necessity. I had a lack of mental discipline, difficulties in communication, I couldn't express myself and was looking for something that could help me. One day I was walking past a bookshop in Berlin and there was a book about yoga in the window, called *Is Yoga for You?* There are books which when you look at them, seem to say, "Buy me, read me". So I bought it, read it on the plane en route to Aachen, and started doing yoga exercises the next morning. I got into it as a necessity for conducting and for concentration.

HM   And the fact that you have adhered to Zen Buddhism for nearly forty years now is evident in a lot of what you have said today, especially in connection with the mystery of conducting and of orchestras and your way of conserving energy and releasing it at moments when it's really needed....

HvK   Yes, it has made a great deal of difference. When I first conducted *Tristan und Isolde*, for example, I practically needed an ambulance to take me home. Now, I don't feel especially exhausted.... But when one is young one sees dangers where there are none and is liable to think that every second the whole thing will break down, which makes it very, very tiring. But every big operatic scene, once started, can only go on. Take the love duet in Act Two of *Tristan*. Once it has started, nothing can possibly happen. It *has* to go on. But you only learn this from experience. Yet, as in *La Bohème*, there are six bars followed by a ritardando, for which you must be very much there. You ask how one is able to maintain a hold on oneself during the second act of *Tristan*. But in most operas so much is happening at the same time, both in the orchestra and on stage, so much starting and stopping, that you are required to concentrate on the work to be done.

HM   Were you ever in danger of losing control during a performance?

HvK   Yes, once during *Die Meistersinger* in Bayreuth, but it was more or less a joke! In the spot leading from the first to the second part of the third act, the music is more or less a memory of the prelude and written in a very simple way: first come the woodwinds followed by the rest, and this is a moment where everybody relaxes, one cleans his glasses, another wipes his head, etc. Well, all evening, there had been a fly in this hot stand where the score lies, and I felt that now, at last, I could hit it. And I hit it in the middle of a bar where half the orchestra were on one. And they thought I had made a mistake. After two years of doing this together, they were quite relaxed, but suddenly they jumped up thinking, "Oh, we're on one": and half of them jumped forward while the other half jumped backward, and suddenly *Die Meistersinger* sounded like Schönberg, all mixed up and on the point of breakdown. But I summoned my technique, put the orchestra down and then beat one, so that it all came together again. Unforeseen emergencies like this do happen sometimes, and this is why I sometimes ask for a solo to come in two bars early at rehearsal and then say to the orchestra, "Hey, what do you do now?" This way they get used to coping with emergencies and into the habit of not merely looking at the notes but also listening to what's being played. Because, in theory, anything could happen in the performance. You never know.

HM Which requires quicksilver reflexes on the part of the conductor. And, by the way, apart from musicianship, what qualities do you consider essential for a conductor?

HvK That he feels what he does—that's the most important thing—and that he has the ability to transmit it. Everything else, he can learn. Those two things, he cannot. And every time someone steps onto a podium, I can immediately tell whether or not he has them.... You could be a very bad musician, but if you have the power to transmit your thought and make the orchestra play it, you can still be a conductor.

HM One last question: why do you conduct with your eyes shut?

HvK Because I don't want to see the trombone making his entry! Or any other thing that would distract me. I want to see the music stretched out before me. And I am much more *with* the musicians if I have my eyes shut. I *feel* it if someone is nervous about their entry or someone is short of breath in a long passage, and I can help them—my hand which is trained by long experience, will respond and accelerate. I never know what my hands do at the time, but the next day, a player will come and say: 'How did you know that I was nervous or short of breath at that particular passage?' I can never answer that.... I just *feel* it.

3: THE WORK

"Tomorrow I would like to be the companion of him who will know how to propose opera, music and poetry to the most remote and least privileged of beings on this earth. We are at zero point of a new adventure, at the stammering beginnings of a grandiose audio-visual machinery. We have not yet left harbour, and the great beyond is fantastic. Will I do what heaven commands me or will I need another life in order to continue the march?" (HERBERT VON KARAJAN)

To say that work is the cornerstone of Herbert von Karajan's being is to utter an understatement. For no one who hasn't witnessed how hard, with what total dedication, indeed self-abnegation, this man works—through illnesses, through pain and discomfort of a degree that would cause many a colleague to cancel a concert or tour at any cost or inconvenience to orchestras or organizers—can have any conception of his almost religious attitude to his mission in life, which he conceives of as constant service not only to the composers whose works he tries to realize more and more truthfully all the time, but also to mankind.

"I can only see it from my point of view that I have a duty to do," he said in an interview with Austrian television in 1977, reprinted in *Opera* magazine, "something for which my destiny or creator or call it what you like, put into my hands extravagantly abundant means, and I have to put them to best use. I alone am responsible to myself for this and it is, I believe, one of my deepest satisfactions.... I find that the supreme aim is that one sees one's profession as a vocation. And, thank God, this is a principle I will never relax until ... [quasi-aside, half-laughing ...] until I can no longer hold a baton."

Almost the attitude of a priest. Or a *true* doctor. Which in Karajan's case is particularly relevant, because he says that this attitude towards his work was transmitted to him by his father, Dr Ernst von Karajan, who was chief surgeon at the main hospital of Salzburg and whose exceptional devotion to duty and human contact with his patients are still talked about in that institution. He once told his son that "what matters ultimately is what you give as a human being", and the boy never forgot these words.

Although Dr von Karajan had settled in Salzburg—where his second son, Herbert, was born on April 5, 1908 at eleven o'clock at night—his paternal ancestors were Macedonian Greeks from Kozani who had emigrated first to Saxony, where they established such a successful yarn and textile industry in Chemnitz that the Elector dubbed Herbert's great-great grandfather, Georg Johannes Karajannis, a Knight of the Holy Roman Empire. A few years later Georg Johannes settled in Vienna, having dropped the suffix from his name: henceforth the family were to be known as 'von Karajan'.

His son Theodore became Professor of German Literature at the University of Vienna, President of the Antiquarian Society, Director of the Imperial Library and a passionate music lover who frequently hosted chamber music concerts at home. But after being passed over for the deanship of the University because of his Greek Orthodox faith, he resigned from all his posts in disgust. Herbert's grandfather Max saw the writing on the wall and converted to Roman Catholicism. Originally he was professor of classical literature at the University of Graz and eventually Director of all Austria's public health institutions. (As a mark of recognition of his services, Emperor Franz Joseph confirmed the family's German title.)

Had Herbert's father been left to his own devices, he would have opted for a career as an actor. But he bowed to his father's wish that he follow a more secure profession, became a doctor and moved to Salzburg. Still, he remained a keen amateur actor all his life, as well as a clarinettist with the Salzburg Chamber Society which gave weekly concerts in the von Karajan home by the Salzach, next to the Österreichischer Hof Hotel. Herbert's Slovenian-born mother Martha—whom he says he resembles in many ways—was also very musical but had a distinct predilection for romantic music, especially Wagner.

Their parents' musical activities meant that Herbert and his elder brother Wolfgang were exposed to music from a very early age. Wolfgang, now a well known organ-builder and player, started piano lessons at the age of five, and it was not long before his younger brother followed suit. But not until his talent and persistence—for Herbert von Karajan at three-and-a-half was essentially the same Herbert von Karajan one knows today—convinced his reluctant parents who had initially thought him too young. "I was always being told I was too young—or too small or too weak—to do this or that or the other", he said on French television when surveying his life for a programme in honour of his seventieth birthday, "whereas my brother was older, bigger, stronger. It made my first twenty years very hard, but taught me how to fight in life."

At the time, however, he was very attached to, and rather

competitive towards, his elder brother and wanted to do everything he did: eat the same food, play the same games and learn the same things. So whenever Wolfgang had a piano lesson, Herbert hid under the piano or behind the curtains and listened intently to everything his brother was taught. At the end, the moment Wolfgang and his teacher left the room, he would come out of hiding, climb up on to the stool and try to play it. And succeeded in doing so from memory and at perfect pitch, week after week. In the face of such natural talent, his parents gave in and henceforth encouraged him in every possible way. So he got his lessons and within a few months surpassed his brother. A year later he started studying with Franz Ledwinka, a well known Czech piano teacher, and made such rapid progress that he was judged good enough to play a Mozart Rondo at a charity concert. Although at five he was too young to reach down to the pedals, he was as yet untouched by stage fright and totally unaware of the audience: "neither nervous, nor excited—just indifferent", he remembers.

Three years later, he joined Professor Ledwinka's classes at the Mozarteum where, at the age of nine, he also gave his first public concert as a child prodigy and where he was to continue studying until 1926. At the time, he and his brother often sang as choirboys at the Cathedral, in local choirs and, after 1920, at the newly founded Salzburg Festival. One of his professors at the Mozarteum was the distinguished scholar Bernard Paumgartner who took a keen interest in him and became a lifelong friend. In those days he lent the restless, adventurous boy his motorcycle to roam the countryside, took him on trips to Italy where he introduced him to Italian art, and was the first to spot that his temperament was better suited to conducting than to the piano.

Throughout his teens, Karajan continued giving concerts from time to time, but fortunately neither he nor his parents were inclined to push him into a fully fledged career as a child prodigy. As he was a very quick learner at school—he had only to hear something once in order to remember it forever—he had plenty of time for sports and outdoor life which he adores and which to this day is what, more than anything else, helps him relax and unwind.

At the age of eighteen, it was time to decide on a future career. His father wanted him to study science at the Vienna Polytechnic, but was prepared to allow him to continue his musical education, too, by paying for further piano lessons with the eminent Professor Hofmann. For a while, his son acquiesced, and stayed at the Polytechnic for three semesters. But like Bernard Paumgartner, Professor Hofmann also felt that this pupil's particular talent and temperament were better suited to conducting: "After three months, he said: 'Look here, now I think I know you; you will never get any real satisfaction out of the piano because you think in terms of a tonal volume that could only be satisfied by ten hands. The only thing I can advise you is to become a conductor: otherwise you will always be frustrated.' It was the best lesson I had in my life", Karajan reminisced in a radio programme. This advice, plus the fact that he developed an inflammation in the tendons of his left hand, led him to drop the piano, give up his science course, and enroll at the conducting class of the Vienna Music Academy. At the time he had no specific plans or ambitions. But he knew that he could choose nothing but music as a way of life.

Work in the conducting class consisted mainly of playing orchestral scores on the piano, "which gives you a distorted perspective" (yet maybe explains why Karajan can still play the entire orchestral score of *Elektra* at a stroke), or beating time while someone else was playing them. There was no practical experience of conducting at all, because Clemens Krauss, then Director of the Vienna State Opera, had given up his post of Professor of Conducting at the Academy, and his place had been taken by Alexander Wunderer, first oboist of the Vienna Philharmonic, a man with no practical experience of conducting—in fact, he wanted to *become* a conductor and seemed keener on conducting the student orchestra himself than on letting his pupils do so, much to their disgust and despair. "All we could do was stand and watch and we really got very frustrated; so we formed a working group and every day we would spend about eight hours on the opera which was due to be performed at the State Opera on that evening: one conducted, four played the score on the piano, two or three others sang the chorus and solo parts, etc. When we finished, we went to the Opera and watched it performed—from the fourth gallery—and afterwards went out and discussed the whole thing over a glass of beer. We certainly acquired a thorough knowledge of the repertoire, if nothing else: seventy operas or so by the time I left."

His summers were spent back home in Salzburg working as a coach at the Festival where he learnt the whole of *Falstaff* by heart without even glancing at the score: just by listening to all Toscanini's rehearsals hidden behind the organ. (Needless to say, the rehearsals were closed. But then as now, stopping Karajan from doing anything he has set his heart and mind to was well nigh impossible!) But he never met

Toscanini at the time because, he explains, "in those days these people were as remote as gods", and a young, inexperienced conductor, especially if he were as shy as Karajan, would never dare approach them. He was already in his forties when he eventually met Toscanini and remembers that "he attacked me for doing *Carmen* in French at La Scala, adding that he could see the day when *Il trovatore* would be done in German! We both laughed, of course!"

Yet perhaps the remoteness of the great conductors of his day lies at the root of his own subsequent determination to be as accessible as possible to both colleagues and students in search of help and guidance. Both Mehta and Ozawa have commented on his readiness to go over scores with them whenever they ask for his advice. But his willingness to answer any student's musical questions, even at the busiest of times, surprised me a great deal when I first got to know him. Karajan is almost always in a hurry and hates wasting time; yet I have never seen him turn away anyone wishing to ask a musical question worth serious consideration: he may keep cars, planes, orchestral and recording personnel, entourage and friends waiting, but answer it he will, with maximum attentiveness and concentration. Although we have never discussed this particular issue, I have seen enough examples to be convinced that this master-disciple aspect of "the passing of the flame" is a part of his work that he takes particularly seriously.

Karajan's first chance to conduct—Rossini's *Guillaume Tell* Overture—was at a concert given at the Academy by students of Alexander Wunderer's class in December 1928. His performance dazzled the entire institution and convinced him that truly "I had it in my hands". The next step was to try himself out with a professional orchestra: on January 22, 1929, he made his official public début in Salzburg—the programme included Strauss's *Don Juan* and the Tchaikovsky fifth— having hired the Mozarteum orchestra "with my last money". The concert was a great success, and the Intendant of the Ulm State Theatre, who was in the audience, offered Karajan the job of First Kapellmeister in this small Bavarian town at a monthly salary of about £10! Karajan replied that to be perfectly honest, he had never conducted an opera before in his life, but that didn't seem to deter the man. "Fine," he replied, "come and learn how."

This was precisely what he did, in the five years (1929–34) he was to remain there. He has already described his shock at being confronted by this Theatre with its tiny, six-metre stage and small, 24-member orchestra with its four first violins. Yet this is where he learnt his craft from scratch, familiarized himself with all the intricacies of operatic production and realized that if you cannot find the right people for the right jobs, it is infinitely preferable to do them yourself: accordingly, he often carried the orchestra's instruments in a wheelbarrow from the theatre to the restaurant where they rehearsed; helped shift the scenery; occasionally even raised and lowered the curtain; and personally went to fetch the reluctant townsfolk who sang as extras in the chorus from their shops. This experience shows, and anyone watching Karajan rehearse operas can instantly sense a man of the *palcoscenico*, with theatre in his blood.

Within two months of his Salzburg concert, he made his operatic début in Ulm—on March 2, 1929—with *Le nozze di Figaro*. Although the only music that an orchestra of this paltry size was fit for was Mozart and Verdi, Karajan managed to mount productions of *Salome*, *Lohengrin*, *Fidelio* and *Die Meistersinger von Nürnberg*. His usual quota of performances was a new opera a fortnight, plus an operetta once a week. He still spent his summers in Salzburg as a rehearsal coach and teacher of conducting at the summer courses of the Mozarteum International Foundation, already displaying his amazing ability for constant hard work and for doing several things at the same time. "I *can* sometimes be lazy," he protests when one points out that he is exactly the same today, "but lazy with a purpose: to recharge my batteries." But he admits that he gets irritated when, faced with a couple of days in which there is nothing to do, he cannot justify the fact to his conscience by calling them a holiday.

At the time, his way of recharging his batteries and escaping from the stiflingly provincial atmosphere of Ulm, which imbued him with a lasting allergy for anything that smacks of provincialism, was to visit Milan, Florence, Venice and Vienna to keep abreast of what the great conductors and producers of the day were doing. Soon, in 1933, he was to work with one of them when, after conducting the Vienna Symphony Orchestra for the first time, he made his first appearance at the Salzburg Festival, arranging and conducting the music for the 'Walpurgisnacht' in Max Reinhardt's production of *Faust*. His career was slowly beginning to get off the ground. But suddenly, in 1934, his boss at Ulm summoned him to his office and announced that he was going to fire him, while at the same time admitting that he liked both him and his work. Only later did Karajan discover that his real reason was anxiety lest this prodigiously gifted Kapellmeister got stuck in Ulm forever, completely out of the public eye; for no one ever came to Ulm; he laboured in total obscurity. (Indeed, when Max Reinhardt enquired after "that interesting young man" who had conducted the music for his *Faust* and was told that for the past five years he had worked at Ulm, he sighed: "*Five years* in Ulm? Then he will never make it!")

Although Karajan managed to convince his boss to give him one extra season, he spent an agonizing year, with many, many sleepless nights, travelling all over Germany by train looking for a job. To this day, he hates the sight of a railway station, because it reminds him of that dreadful time. He ended up in Berlin where for three months he lived in extremely difficult conditions, doing odd jobs and sometimes having barely enough to eat. He knew that if by the end of the season he had not found a job, it might mean the end of his career. The combined strain of overwork and anxiety brought about nervous exhaustion. There was no help from anybody and, again, this has a lot to do with his own subsequent determination to do all he can to help young colleagues. "I know there is a theory that great qualities will always reveal themselves in the end. But you could spare *very* much trouble."

At last, an opportunity did come up. The Intendant of the Aachen State Theatre came to Berlin to hold auditions for a First Kapellmeister, and Karajan went to see him. "I saw that he was not very strong willed so I proceeded to hypnotize him. I was desperate because I knew full well that this was my last and only chance. So, while hypnotizing him, I told him that I needed to conduct a rehearsal (of an operatic production). But the season was over and this could not be arranged, so I conducted a trial concert instead." This took place on June 8, 1934 and involved his conducting the overture from *Oberon*, the first movement of Mozart's 'Haffner' symphony and the Prelude from Act III of *Die Meistersinger*, "with great vigour and conviction", according to a member of the Aachen State Orchestra, violinist Willy Wesemann, who remembers being "bewitched by the young conductor's élan". Two months later, Karajan was officially notified that he had got the job, despite objections from some of the players who were somewhat frightened by his spontaneous and intense way of working and would have preferred a "more comfortable, more experienced personality".

He made his début at Aachen at the start of the 1934–35 season, conducting *Fidelio*—a "sensation" according to Wesemann, despite the fact that at the beginning the orchestra had found him difficult to play for, because he always asked for too much. Indeed, Karajan says that in those days he had difficulties in communication—as he has already explained, this was his main reason for taking up yoga—and sometimes felt as if there were a glass wall between him and the orchestra. But his time at Aachen reads like a continuous success story and at the end of his first season he was named Generalmusikdirektor—at 27, still the youngest in Germany.

He has been much criticized for accepting the job at Aachen, as this automatically involved the acquisition of a Nazi party card. Yet after a year without a job, with no money, no prospects and not the remotest chance of finding a job abroad at that stage of his career, should he have felt inclined to emigrate, it is hard to see what else he could have done; one can easily understand why, as he explained to an American magazine, he "would have committed any crime to get that job"!

After the war, he was accused of collaboration, along with other famous colleagues. Yet his honesty about his motives impressed even the Occupation authorities. Lieutenant H.C. Alter of the US army later told Karajan's biographer, Ernst Haeusserman: "My impression of Karajan was that of all the artists with whom I was in constant contact, he was the only one who discussed his connection with the Nazi party and the Nazi era in general, quietly and clearly without the usual constant attempts to present himself in a better light. He said simply that he had never been politically minded, that he has little respect for governments and political institutions and that by no means could he now promise to become a convert to American democracy or to respect the Occupation authorities. The whole thing simply did not interest him, had never interested him and never would interest him. He was first and foremost a musician and nothing else really interested him in the last resort."

Yet he has not been allowed to forget his tacit acquiescence. He was barred from conducting in public for nearly two years at the end of the war, and ten years later, his first American tour with the Berlin Philharmonic was marred by violent demonstrations; certain Jewish musicians will still not play with him. Throughout it all, rightly I think, he has kept quiet and proudly refused either to excuse or to explain himself. "Then, I suffered. But today I'm happy about it because through it I learnt how to withstand such things. The negative also has a part to play. One has to accept it and learn to understand it...."

Karajan remained at Aachen for seven years, during which his career really took off. During his first few seasons, he conducted a staggering number of performances—no less than one hundred and fifty evenings—one of the reasons why his future achievements stood on such firm foundations. Aachen possessed not only a large, seventy-strong orchestra, but also a good chorus of three hundred under the direction of Wilhelm Pitz, with whom Karajan worked very closely. (And later brought to London to found the Philharmonia Chorus.) He seized the opportunity to explore the choral repertoire with great relish and his first choral concert in the autumn of 1935—the Verdi *Requiem*—was enthusiastically received.

His reputation grew and in June 1937 he was invited by Bruno Walter to conduct *Tristan und Isolde* at the Vienna State Opera, with no rehearsal, as it turned out. It was one of the greatest triumphs of his pre-war career and he remembers the experience vividly: "I had said that naturally I needed a certain number of rehearsals, three with the orchestra and three normal ensemble rehearsals with the singers," he told Austrian television. "He conceded me three orchestral rehearsals. So I arrived and was met at the station by some functionary who said: 'Yes, please, the Direction wishes to apologize but you can only have two out of the three rehearsals promised because there has been a change of programme'—apparently *Lohengrin* was being put on instead of *Il barbiere di Siviglia*, so the orchestra would not be free—in any case, now there were to be two. Three days later, after starting our piano rehearsals, another official came along and said: 'Please, we must unfortunately take away another rehearsal, because now a Philharmonic concert needs an extra rehearsal and there is no way around it.' Oh well, naturally, as a young Kapellmeister I didn't want to make difficulties, so I let them take that away, too. Then a day before what was to have been my only rehearsal, old Professor Rosé* came along and said: 'Look, you have only one rehearsal, in which you cannot get anywhere at all. Give it up and we will play for you as if it were for Mahler!' So there it was—without rehearsal." (An example of how managements all over the world treat young artists—as long as they can afford to.)

Yet the twenty-nine-year-old Karajan scored such a success that he was offered the post of First Kapellmeister under Bruno Walter straight away. But his glimpse of working conditions in Vienna left him unimpressed and prompted him to decline the offer. He realized full well that "in Vienna one doesn't *become*, in Vienna one *is*" and preferred to remain at Aachen for the time being, where working

* The famous leader of the VPO, Arnold Rosé.

conditions were more conducive to artistic growth. For similar reasons, he also declined the first invitation to conduct the Berlin Philharmonic, in June 1937: instead of proper rehearsal time, he was offered one 'run-through' and replied: "Please call me when you can offer me the usual four rehearsals. I can wait."

He didn't have to wait long. After his triumph in Vienna, the Berlin Philharmonic were back with an invitation for next season—this time with proper rehearsal time. His début, on April 8, 1938, was enthusiastically received by public and critics alike. He was hailed as "a thoroughly modern conductor who sought to clarify the structure of a work while passionately identifying himself with its content". The programme he had chosen was Mozart's 'Haffner' symphony, Ravel's *Daphnis et Chloé* and the Brahms fourth, and, much to the orchestra's astonishment, he asked for split rehearsals—strings first, then wood-wind, then brass, etc. This, they grumbled, had never happened to them before. They were the Berlin Philharmonic, they had played these works hundreds of times and knew them backwards. Who did this young Kapellmeister from Aachen think he was? But undeterred, Karajan went on to make the violas play difficult passages at a slower tempo, to get the right sound in their ear (as he has explained in the previous section of this chapter), and although they were disgruntled, they admired and respected him for it. For him, this first concert with the orchestra that was later to become his, boiled down to love on sight. And what, in retrospect, is so significant about this encounter is that it reveals that Karajan had already begun to synthesize the two elements that constitute his "modern" approach to conducting and that his distinct orchestra-training methods were already in evidence.

In September of the same year, he made his début at the Berlin State Opera with *Fidelio* which was extremely favourably reviewed and was followed within a month by rapturously received performances of *Tristan und Isolde*. After hearing the Prelude, Victor de Sabata rushed out of his box to Heinz Tietjen, the powerful Intendant of the State Opera, and told him: "You see that young man who's conducting *Tristan*? Listen to me: starting from today, he will lead the world's musical thought for half a century!" (Later de Sabata was instrumental in bringing Karajan to La Scala after the war, and helping smooth any problems in his way.) One of Berlin's most important papers headed its review with the now famous headline *"Das Wunder Karajan"* ("I was no wonder", is Karajan's dismissive reaction today), in which it was also hinted that some older conductors had something to learn from him. Furtwängler took this as a personal insult and protested to the authorities.

Yet characteristically enough, Karajan had again risked having to let this chance pass him by. Heinz Tietjen had first approached him with an offer to conduct a new opera by Wagner-Régeny*, *Die Burgher von Calais*, and enclosed a score for him to peruse. Karajan replied that he would be happy to conduct this work provided he could also conduct *Fidelio*, *Tristan* and *Die Meistersinger*—with enough rehearsal. Tietjen replied through a secretary that this was impossible but that they might consider offering him *Carmen*. In that case, Karajan wrote back, regretfully he had to decline the invitation. This prompted a handwritten letter from Tietjen offering him *Tannhäuser* instead. "There must be some mistake," replied Karajan. "I don't wish to conduct *Tannhäuser*, but *Fidelio*, *Tristan* and *Meistersinger!*" Tietjen finally gave in—the first in a series of managers and functionaries to discover over the years that the only way to work with Karajan is on his own terms. He shrewdly assessed exactly when he was in a position to insist on what, but never risked a confrontation over a mere bagatelle; only about issues which could seriously affect his career or compromise the quality of his work.

Soon after *Fidelio* and *Tristan*, he was invited back to the State Opera for *Die Zauberflöte* at the specific request of the famous producer Gustaf Gründgens. (This remains to this day the best *Zauberflöte* in living memory according to Professor W. E. Schaefer, the former Intendant of the Württemberg State Theatre and for a brief spell Karajan's collaborator at the Vienna State Opera.) He also returned for the production of *Elektra* mounted for Strauss's seventieth birthday. (*Elektra* is in fact one of the three works which he finds "devastating" to conduct. "You may be under the spell of the thing for three or four days and still not get rid of it. Along with Berg's *Three Orchestral Pieces*, Opus 6 and the Sibelius fourth, which is a complete breakdown, it puts a very heavy weight on you....")

But that "Das Wunder Karajan" review had earned him the undying and increasingly obsessional enmity of Furtwängler, then in disgrace with Nazi circles over his protection of Jewish musicians and his stand over Nazi interference with artistic policy, as a result of which he had resigned from all his posts. But as soon as he was reinstated in 1941, he

---

* Rudolf Wagner-Régeny (1903–1969), Hungarian composer of German descent whose operas included *Der Günstling*, *Mary Tudor* (after Hugo), *Der näckte König* (after Andersen's *The Emperor's New Clothes*), and *Der zerbrochene Krug* (after Kleist).

barred Karajan from both the Berlin Philharmonic and the State Opera and, after the war, also from the Vienna Philharmonic and the Salzburg Festival until his death in 1954. (There were two exceptions: Karajan conducted two concerts with the Vienna Philharmonic in 1946, before Furtwängler was de-Nazified.) This amounted to attempted artistic strangulation, and it is hard for any admirer of Furtwängler's genius to understand how a man of such stature could stoop to such mean, petty, spiteful and downright evil behaviour. As the following incident shows, his fear and jealousy of the younger man sometimes reached absurd proportions:

Karajan has always conducted without a score and with his eyes shut, for reasons which he has already explained, plus the fact that he considers musical notation to be inadequate and bars the stupidest things ever invented. At the time, there was a rumour that this was because he was blind! But evidently the rumour had not reached Goebbels who attended a Karajan performance with Furtwängler and was surprised to find that the young man conducted without a score. Was such a thing possible, he wanted to know? "No," replied Furtwängler, and Karajan was ordered to use a score in the future. He did, but turned it upside down, cover side conspicuously up!

He admits that in his youth he suffered terribly from this competitive antagonism, with every colleague doing his best to harm and hinder another's career. But now he has forgotten it, and all that remains is his admiration for Furtwängler's genius. He explains that he trained himself early in life to ignore negative human reactions. "Emotionally one could react in three ways: with love, with indifference, or with the opposite of love. But in this profession one *may* not hate—otherwise, one is finished. The moment one feels jealousy or envy, one becomes hateful—and then one can no longer make music."

In 1941 while on a visit to Rome with the Berlin State Opera, Karajan heard that he had been dismissed from his post at Aachen. Since his successes in Berlin, he had been spending less and less time there and blamed himself for not having had the strength to admit to himself that that stage of his life was over. But he liked the place, was very happy in his little house in the woods, and so he let the situation drag on. In 1938, he had married the Aachen Theatre's leading operetta singer, Elmy Holgerloef—according to her, they had a great deal of fun together—but the marriage did not survive his constant comings and goings. After two years they were divorced and in 1940 Karajan married Anita Gütermann who was a quarter Jewish.

This marriage, which was soon followed by Furtwängler's reinstatement at the Opera, deprived Karajan of any support against the latter's enmity which he might otherwise have had from the authorities, especially from Göring who had special responsibility for the State Opera and had hitherto been favourably disposed towards him. (Partly because Furtwängler was greatly favoured by Goebbels.) Tietjen, who had sworn that Furtwängler would only set foot at the State Opera again over his dead body, apologized profusely and tried to explain that it was nothing personal, that it was all politics, etc, etc. But the realization that until one has power one is merely a pawn in other people's games must have been a painful and bitter pill to swallow.... After 1942, Karajan's only engagements in Berlin were six concerts a year with the Staatskapelle. Towards the end of the war, he decided to leave Germany, using an invitation from the Milan Radio Orchestra as a pretext and with the help of a friendly air force general, escaped to Italy with his wife. The two years he was to spend there were possibly the leanest and most difficult in his life: he had to spend the closing days of the war hiding in the house of friends, and the rest of the time in a primitive rented room near Lake Como, with no engagements, no music and very little food. But even in such depressing circumstances, he managed to do something positive: as he feared that doing nothing might result in another nervous breakdown, he decided to learn Italian, sometimes forcing himself to concentrate by diminishing his meagre rations of food whenever he failed to work for his prescribed number of hours.

By 1946, he managed to get to Trieste, where he conducted a few concerts, and he vividly remembers the exhilaration of being in front of an orchestra again after such a long period of musical starvation—to say nothing of once again having enough to eat and drink and cigarettes to smoke. Shortly after that, he made his way home to Austria—with difficulty—and on a bitterly cold afternoon, conducted the Vienna Philharmonic in an unheated hall for an audience clad in overcoats who responded to his readings of *Don Juan* and the Brahms first with wild enthusiasm. Soon after that, he was also invited to conduct the Philharmonic in his native Salzburg, and was asked to take charge of *Der Rosenkavalier* and *Le nozze di Figaro* at the following summer's Festival. But alas, this was not to be, because the Russians insisted on imposing a two-year ban on his public performances. (Along with

Böhm's, Furtwängler's and Knappertsbusch's! One fails to grasp what possible criteria they used for judging such different nuances and gradations of behaviour. As a former American officer confessed when I tried to find out, "the whole de-Nazification process in the arts was a shambles, ridiculous, really.") As the ban on Karajan was announced only very shortly before he was due to conduct *Der Rosenkavalier*, which he had already prepared and rehearsed, he agreed to conduct it from the prompter's box—thus letting his official replacement have all the credit and glory—so that the show could go on.

He spent the rest of this time in a simple rented room in St Anton, studying and reading (while his wife, who spoke four languages fluently, worked as an interpreter for the occupying forces). "I said to myself that soon the time would come when I would have a great deal to do, so I wanted to make the most of this period of inaction for a concentrated revision of the works I would later have to perform. It was a good and, in retrospect, a decisive time," he told his biographer. "Each day I spent six hours outdoors in the fresh air, and six to seven hours working, re-studying all the important works and thinking about problems of interpretation; what were the various possible ways of looking at each work? How had one looked at it earlier as compared to now?"

He was rescued from this period of inaction by Walter Legge, the Head of Classical Artists and Repertoire at EMI, London, who had heard a pre-war recording of the overture from *Die Fledermaus* and decided to seek him out as a conductor for his newly-formed Philharmonia Orchestra, founded principally for recording and moulded along the lines of Toscanini's NBC Orchestra in America. The American occupation forces in charge of the Salzkammergut area would have liked to block those recordings, too. But the British authorities intervened and pointed out that Karajan was banned only from public performances, and that they had no right to interfere with anything he did in a private studio.

So in 1948, he made the first of his vintage recordings with the Philharmonia: the Schumann Piano Concerto with Dinu Lipatti. He trained it to a very high standard, which was appreciated by both Furtwängler and Toscanini when they came to conduct it and prompted Legge to call him the best orchestra-trainer he knew, "a natural teacher". "He had a wonderful stick technique and wonderful discipline at rehearsals," remembers second violinist Gillian Eastwood. "He also had good contact with the orchestra, and the sound he used to draw out of us was exceptionally beautiful, possibly because of his arm movements which were so different from everybody else's: he always held his stick in the first finger so that he could sweep it across in a wonderfully flowing way, and this gave the *music* a terrifically flowing quality which was always characteristic of his interpretations. (The famous 'Karajan line'.) Perhaps this is what made him seem a very relaxed conductor although he could build up great tension when he needed it."

After the Allies officially lifted the ban against him, he also conducted an annual series of live concerts with this orchestra as well as a string of excellent operatic recordings: *Il trovatore* and *Madama Butterfly* from La Scala with Maria Callas; *Hänsel und Gretel, Così fan tutte, Le nozze di Figaro, Die Zauberflöte, Die Fledermaus, Ariadne auf Naxos, Der Rosenkavalier, Falstaff, Die Meistersinger von Nürnberg* and Act Three of *Die Walküre*, the last two live from Bayreuth, and all, apart from the last and *Die Zauberflöte*, with Elisabeth Schwarzkopf, who says that she learnt more from Karajan than from any conductor she worked with: "If he likes a singer, he is the best accompanist in the world. You feel you are swimming in salt water. I don't think I could have sung many of the roles that I did sing if it were not for him being in the pit and keeping the orchestra down so that I could paint with a very fine brush, as if I were singing a recital", she told an American magazine a few years ago. "But although you never felt 'hemmed in', you were on fairly tight reins, nevertheless. Yet you trusted him enough to know that this was for the good of the whole performance."

In 1949, Karajan started conducting regularly at La Scala where he was to make his name anew as a top operatic conductor and where, with his looks and magnetism, he became something of a matinée idol. "Women went *crazy* about him," remembers a friend. "So much so that a lot of men were infuriated and were stupid enough to ask what made him so extra-special. What a question! For a start, you don't have to go much further than those eyes, do you?" As a matter of fact she is right. Karajan's mesmerizing eyes—brilliant blue (unless he is bored or angry when they visibly recede and turn a slushy greeny-grey), capable of emitting just about anything he wants them to with extraordinary power, and of X-raying anyone he meets in a matter of seconds—are a chapter in themselves.

Which makes it easy to understand why orchestral players' opinions about his conducting with his eyes shut, are divided. Professor Alfred

Altenburger, violinist in and Vorstand of the Vienna Philharmonic, regrets that Karajan closes his eyes at concerts, "because at rehearsals and when he conducts opera you can see how intense, powerful and fascinating his eyes are." But he stressed that this was his own personal opinion and not the general consensus of the orchestra. Professor Thomas Brandis, one of the three Concertmasters of the Berlin Philharmonic, is of the opposite view: "It doesn't bother us in the least. On the contrary. It relaxes us. Because you know that if something goes wrong you won't have him glaring at you like most conductors do; and when you have to play a solo, his having his eyes closed is so calming and relaxing. No, it makes no difference at all to the amount of tension he exudes, which is tremendously exciting. The electricity is there all right."

In 1951 and 1952 Karajan also conducted memorable productions of the *Ring*, *Tristan* and *Die Meistersinger* at Bayreuth in collaboration with Wieland Wagner. But he disagreed with some of the latter's ideas, especially his automatic rejection of anything that had been done before and, as he was not allowed to present his own stagings there, he never returned to Bayreuth.

Karajan's need to be his own producer stems from his desire for complete visual and musical unity: he can only make "the right music" acoustically when visually he sees what he wants to see. As he explained to Haeusserman many years later, after the first Salzburg Easter Festival, he never found anyone who could stage the music he conducted in a way that could convince him. "He has an exact, complete vision of a work both in his ears and his eyes," says Michel Glotz, Karajan's recording supervisor and friend. "When we record operas which he will eventually stage in Salzburg and I look at the maquettes, I can tell in advance what kind of sound he will produce. And if we record before I have a chance to see any maquettes, I can visualize more or less exactly how it's going to look."

Some of Karajan's stagings have been criticized over the years for being too dimly lit, but all have been visually spectacular and given the impression of emerging out of the musical content of each work. Indeed, when asked where he places the emphasis in his stagings of the *Ring*, he replied that he places it in the music, which is where it *is*.

During the late forties and early fifties most of his symphonic work was done with the Philharmonia in London and with the Vienna

Symphony which he had first conducted in the early thirties and which he now proceeded to build up to a standard that could compete with that of the Vienna Philharmonic. He was also appointed Artistic Director of the Gesellschaft der Musikfreunde and developed its choir, the Singverein, from a disorganized, amateurish group to one of the great choirs of the world, according to H.C. Robbins Landon, the Vienna-based Haydn scholar.

Of course, Karajan was barred from the Philharmonic by Furtwängler, who tried to retaliate against all his successes with the Symphony by attempting to top them! If, for example, Karajan conducted the Tchaikovsky fifth, then next week Furtwängler would do the 'Pathétique', and so on and on. The result was one of the best musical seasons Vienna had had in years! In fact this competitive rivalry had reached such proportions by then that it was reported in *Time*.

After Furtwängler's death, Walter Legge explained to *The Musical Courier* that "It was my misfortune to be the principal buffer between Furtwängler and von Karajan from 1946 until the former's death. Von Karajan's stoical fortitude in those years was a model of long-suffering patience; not even his closest friends ever heard a word of complaint from him. His only comment was, 'the old man is making his own life hell. But he is teaching me that the only way to enjoy eminence is to encourage and help one's colleagues.' That is what von Karajan is doing now." (And has continued to do ever since.)

Soon after Furtwängler's death, the Vienna Philharmonic dispatched its Vorstand to Rome to see if he could woo Karajan into becoming the orchestra's Principal Conductor. But it was too late. The Berlin Philharmonic had got there first. In fact the Berliners, whom he had not conducted since 1938, had invited him to conduct some concerts in 1953, when Furtwängler fell seriously ill. He immediately felt that same rapport that had so overwhelmed him fifteen years before. "I knew that this orchestra was all I wanted in the world." Soon after that, the orchestra's Intendant, Dr von Westermann, approached him saying although he didn't wish to be disloyal to his chief, it was, nevertheless, his responsibility to look after the future. As a major American tour had been planned for the coming 1954–55 season, and Furtwängler's health was fast deteriorating, would Karajan be prepared to take it over? Karajan replied that nothing could give him greater pleasure. But only as Furtwängler's official successor. And for life.

A few months later, Karajan was in Rome and received an

anonymous telegram: "Le Roi est mort, vive le Roi!" He sent his secretary out to get a paper and its headline read: "FURTWÄNGLER IS DEAD." The Berlin Philharmonic got in touch straight away and once again Karajan confirmed that he was willing to take over on his terms. The only obstacle was his planned production of *Die Walküre* at La Scala which would clash with the dates of the Philharmonic's American tour. Karajan explained the situation to the Director, Antonio Ghiringhelli, and added that although this offer meant everything to him, if the latter felt that he could not release him from his contract, he would honour it and forget the Berliners. Ghiringhelli readily released him, and he started his preparatory work for the tour straight away.

At long last he had a "wall on which I could lean", indeed *the* wall he had always longed for. Over the past twenty-seven years his relationship with this orchestra has blossomed into one of the most mutually enriching and fulfilling musical partnerships of all time.

Their first six years were a period of transition, with many players reaching retirement age. But within six years the orchestra was almost completely new, and this partly took care of some of the deficiencies that Karajan was aware of at the time. Otherwise, he was clever and tactful enough not to attempt to overhaul everything that had been done before at a stroke. According to principal cellist Professor Finke, who has been with the Berlin Philharmonic since Furtwängler's day, Karajan set about acquiring his own sound very, very gradually and never gave the orchestra the impression of wanting to change specific things.

At first his commitments elsewhere—especially at the Vienna State Opera where he was named Artistic Director in 1956, a year after his Berlin appointment—meant that he couldn't spend as much time with the orchestra as he has in the last fifteen years or so. But since the mid-sixties, his symphonic work has been done almost exclusively with them. And it is easy to understand why: the combination of these first-rate musicians and this first-rate, relentlessly perfectionist conductor has resulted in an orchestra which, despite its initial top level status, is nevertheless still forever developing, forever growing and forever refining its interpretations: a group to whom the concept and practice of routine is unknown and whose artistic pride in their work is unique.

"From the first, I asked that every member of the orchestra have within himself great musicianship, great culture", Karajan explained to Richard Osborne in a fascinating and exceptionally well-conducted and reported interview in the *Gramophone* in 1977. "At first, I could not devote so much time to the orchestra; but now after twenty-five years, I can say that I don't leave them for more than two weeks at a time, apart from the summer holidays. We work on concerts, films and of course records, for eight to ten days at a time. This way we can work seriously, patiently, and always with great joy.... In recent years I strengthened the volume and tone of the bass section but of course, after you have reached a certain level, progress must necessarily become slower. It's like going on a race track. You can go from four minutes to three quite quickly, but to improve from there, that's a struggle for life. We look for better players and greater knowledge all the time. But it's difficult to maintain standards. It was my realization of this that led me to found the school in Berlin [of which more later].... Some things we have played two or three hundred times together; and yet we work and experiment and discover new things and remember old ones, all the time. All this is a constant joy. Also I tell them that the audience must *see* that we enjoy playing well! Perhaps this is all to do with my interest in Zen Buddhism which I have followed for nearly forty years now: always do a thing as well as you can and never, ever think of falling into routine."

But the special bond between him and the orchestra extends beyond the quality of orchestral playing to a sort of unity immediately obvious to anyone watching them at work. "Today the orchestra is almost a family. I am interested in educating them from the musical point of view, but there must also be human contact. So, if they are ill and do not have good doctors, I can help. If there is a divorce...." He has also helped make them one of the richest orchestras, not only through their numerous recordings together, but also by his constant solicitude on their behalf, which has occasionally prompted him to pester the Senate for overdue raises in salary and increased pensions. "And this, I think, has very much to do with the kind of music-making they give me in return. But, my goodness, it makes it difficult for me to go away from them and conduct other orchestras!"

In W. E. Schäfer's book *Bühne eines Lebens Erinnerungen* there is a touching story that well illustrates Karajan's deep love and attachment to his Berliners, who, he feels, are "the best thing that life has given me" and whom he has come to think of as extensions of his fingers:

"I once asked him: 'Herr von Karajan, between friends, would you say in good conscience that the Berliners are the best orchestra in the world?' 'Yes,' he replied after a short pause. 'Some time ago, I conducted one of the great American orchestras. It was excellent, and suddenly I asked myself in fear: can my Berlin Philharmonic do it as well—or better? I had butterflies in my stomach throughout the flight from New York to Amsterdam, where I was to meet them. And I still had butterflies in my stomach when I stood on the podium and reluctantly picked up my baton. And, Herr Schäfer, they were better!"

A year after his appointment in Berlin, Karajan was also named Artistic Director of the Vienna State Opera and remained at its helm for eight stormy, often frustrating, but sometimes artistically interesting years (1956–64). Running an institution like the Vienna Opera is an extremely difficult task for many complex reasons, some of which are connected with the unique, peculiar character of the city itself and of its inhabitants. In Vienna, intrigue, gossip, rumours, smiles and backstabbing, treacherous unreliability and fanatical, inflated factions and cliques are endemic and exist side by side with a deeply ingrained love of music and culture in general. It would be hard to imagine anyone less suited to the Viennese mentality, bureaucracy and laissez-faire than this direct, energetic and impatient man who 'tells it like it is', prefers radical remedies for all artistic wrongs and despises bourgeois convention. Yet Vienna was mesmerized by Karajan and everything he said and did—most of which was misquoted—and fed on him for years.

It still does, up to a point, and whenever he is there on one of his annual visits in the spring, he is again hounded by absurd, inaccurate and often ridiculous rumours. "I try to understand it but cannot really see what it's all about," he told Austrian Television. "Why don't they just leave things as they are and say, 'He comes here, he conducts and then he's off again and we don't see him for a year.' Why must it all be so inflated—one lot for, the other against?... Obviously here it is impossible to love two things at the same time: the person who likes cucumber salad *must* hate whipped cream.... And if you prefer lean beef to fatty foods they will say you have cancer; they are incapable of saying simply: he likes it that way—let him have his pleasures.... But that is what Vienna is like in its whole structure. It was always like that."

Nevertheless, he enjoyed many artistic triumphs during his years in Vienna. But some of his administrative aims were thwarted, either at conception or at execution level. His first radical step was to abolish the old system established by Böhm, based on a permanent ensemble of singers on long-term contracts who were supposed to tackle all areas of the repertoire, and which was now out of date, and to try and replace it by a stagione system, in which the best singers in the world for each part were hired for limited runs of specific productions.

His second fundamental aim, which could have proved crucial and possibly salutary for the future of opera, was a scheme whereby all major opera houses would stage two new productions a year and then exchange them between them, so that all major operatic centres would see the best principal productions of the other houses with the best possible casts. The plan is logical, economical and the only way around today's grievous casting problems which mean that for every work there is, if there is, one ideal cast for which every opera house competes. Yet the scheme was taken up only by La Scala and the Salzburg Festival, with both of which Karajan had close and cordial connections. The other houses shied away, frightened lest they should end up being dominated by Karajan who, they feared, now wanted to reign supreme over the musical life of the whole planet! Yet the exchange with La Scala, which was judged to be a great success, proved that, granted good will on all sides, this scheme *could* work.

One of Karajan's main problems in Vienna was that his other commitments meant frequent absences, and the moment he was gone, standards dropped to a disastrous low—the very thing he had hoped to remedy. He tried to solve it by appointing a co-Director—originally W.E. Schäfer, the Intendant of the Württemberg State Theatre, who was reluctant to relinquish his post in Stuttgart, and eventually Egon Hilbert, with whom he could not get along.

On top of all this there were constant disputes with the unions over rehearsal time, strikes, disagreements with the bureaucracy and the ministries—in short, all the things that are guaranteed anathema to an artist. His health suffered several setbacks during those years, and in 1962 he attempted to resign in disgust. Yet the overwhelming support both from the public and from the opera personnel persuaded him to change his mind. But as nothing changed, two years later, after a round of disagreements and intrigues too confusing and sickening to merit mention, he resigned for good, vowing never again to conduct in Austria. Fortunately, the Directors of the Salzburg Festival which had begun to go downhill after his resignation in 1960 after three years' association, wooed him back by appointing him its Artistic Director and giving him virtually complete artistic freedom.

Karajan's appointments to Berlin and Vienna in the mid-fifties had meant the end of his struggling years. He was now in charge of top class institutions and could henceforth pick and choose his guest-conducting engagements. Since then, his career can be divided into two distinct and very different phases: a decade of expansion and intense international activity up to the late sixties, followed by a period of eclecticism and concentration on the few things that really matter to him: the Berlin Philharmonic, the Salzburg Festivals, films and his foundations. This latter period is also marked by his increasing concern about the future of music and its role within the whole context of human experience, and reflects his deepest, innermost spiritual beliefs and aspirations—which he very seldom, almost never, airs around.

During his decade of expansion, he seemed to be just about everywhere: apart from Berlin and Vienna, he was also to be found in Salzburg, with the Philharmonia in London, at La Scala, the Metropolitan, the New York Philharmonic. It was this period that gave rise to all the clichés of the 'Karajan here, Karajan there' and 'Generalmusik-direktor der Welt' variety and the now famous New York cabbie anecdote (Karajan gets into a cab in New York and when the driver asks where to, he replies: 'Oh, it doesn't matter, they want me everywhere!'), which amused him at the time, but exasperates him now, when people still consider it typical of him despite the fact that his pattern of activity has been so drastically different in the last fifteen years.*

He admits that in those days he did too much—and deliberately so. He was already in his late forties and early fifties and, after the artistically claustrophobic time in Ulm, the ups and downs of the period of purely national prominence in Aachen and Berlin and the lean war and post-war years, he suddenly wanted to get around, discover what his "real worth" was and find out which were the things that mattered most to him. He says that he is glad he did it all because if he hadn't, he might regret it now. "This way made it so much easier for me to liberate myself and now the things remain which are closest to my heart." (But in his case doing too much never implied a debasement of standards; his career had begun too slowly and stood on too firm foundations for that.) This was also the first time in his life when he was totally free from both financial and professional worries and could therefore, at last, relax a little and begin to enjoy some of the good

---

* A still better story of those days was told by Karajan himself recently. In Vienna it is customary not to applaud after Requiems or other religious works except for the Verdi *Requiem*, which is considered operatic. An American couple, unaware of this tradition, once attended a Karajan performance and, surprised at the lack of applause at the end, asked another member of the audience why this was so. "Oh, it's Herr von Karajan, you see. He has no *time* for applause!" was the answer.

things of life. The period coincided with his third marriage, to twenty-six-year-old French model Eliette Mouret, the mother of his two grown up daughters, Isabel and Arabel.

The second phase, which covers, roughly, the last fifteen years, is a time from which everything superfluous like guest conducting—apart from a brief, loose association with the Orchestre de Paris from 1969 to 1971—has been eliminated. His symphonic work is now limited to about sixty concerts a year, almost all with the Berlin Philharmonic (fourteen–sixteen in Berlin itself, eight at the Salzburg Easter Festival, three at Whitsun, two at the Summer Festival plus two annual tours of about ten concerts each) and one or two with the Vienna Philharmonic. His operatic work is done exclusively at Salzburg: about half a dozen performances at the Summer Festival, plus two at the Easter Festival, which he founded in 1967 basically in order to realize his conceptions of Wagner operas, although it also consists of a choral and two symphonic concerts, all of which are performed twice.

The idea for this festival came to him in a flash, in the middle of a performance of *Boris Godunov* at the Summer Festival: he realized that all the technical means necessary were there at his disposal, and all that remained was to think of the right way to organize it. He remembers feeling so overwhelmingly elated that after driving home he went walking for two hours in pouring rain in the middle of the night. And by the time he returned, everything was there, crystal clear in his mind.

That the Easter Festival has been a financial as well as an artistic success is a tribute to his financial acumen and managerial skills. The first year, they just broke even: the surplus, i.e. Karajan's fee, was the princely sum of £9! But by 1974, it was recouping 79 per cent of its costs from ticket sales, as opposed to 57 per cent for the Summer Festival. (Although in fairness it must be pointed out that the latter lasts much longer and has to finance many more events.)

Artistically, Salzburg is the place where Karajan can work in ideal conditions, spending a great deal of time on preparation and a great deal of money both on casts and technical personnel and equipment, and where he has realized his superb and very personal interpretations of the *Ring, Tristan, Die Meistersinger, Lohengrin* and *Parsifal*,* all distinguished by his lyrical, delicate approach to Wagner scores, both in terms of singing and orchestral playing, in which one can hear myriad hitherto unnoticed details. As the doyen of German critics, the

---

* As this book went to press, Karajan was preparing his 1982 Easter Festival Production of *Der fliegende Holländer*.

late K. H. Ruppel wrote in the *Süddeutsche Zeitung* after the Festival's inaugural performance of *Die Walküre*: "Karajan paved the way for a new conception of Wagnerian sound—and triumphed. Never before had one heard the second piece of the Tetralogy so transparent, so 'solistic', so unendingly rich in gradations of dynamic and with such sensitive phrasing, which allowed the character of each individual instrument to be clearly profiled while ensuring that everything merged and blended together in one grandiose concert." (Indeed, anyone sitting near the orchestral pit can observe Karajan frequently pointing at the flute or oboe, thus reminding the orchestra that this must be heard above the overall noise—one of the secrets of the amazingly transparent sound he achieves in his Wagner interpretations.)

He feels that the standards achieved in his Salzburg productions have spoilt him to a degree that makes it impossible for him ever to work in other opera houses: "I have created this place for myself where I have a staff that knows me and where I can project my conceptions as I want—and that is artistic fulfilment for me. We have all the equipment, but more important, we have the people. This is now a place where a man who cares for his craft—lighting and stage work—comes to show what he can really do," says Karajan with justifiable pride. "And the way we work is different from the way they do in other theatres where you have to put the toys out and then put the toys in again, and where you have to finish rehearsing just when you are getting in the right mood. We can just work on, eight hours a day, Saturdays and Sundays included—there are no restrictions—and if I shift singers I don't tire anybody and can get the best results out of everyone."

He and his designers—Gunther Schneider-Siemssen (whom he discovered when the latter worked at the Salzburg Marionette Theatre) for the sets, and George Wakhevitch for the costumes—start planning and discussing a new production years ahead. First they do sketches from which small and eventually large maquettes are made. Then there is a special rehearsal for marking the height, distance and proportions of everything because once the sets are constructed it is difficult to discard anything. Then come lighting rehearsals and eventually the full stage rehearsals he has described in the previous section of this chapter. His way of rehearsing seems so extraordinarily logical and energy-saving that one wonders why nobody thought of it before and why more people are not emulating it.

And unlike current practice at most opera houses where the costumes are often not ready even in the rehearsal before the Dress, in

Salzburg, for example, the costumes for the Karajan 1981 production of *Falstaff* for which rehearsals were due to start in July, were already finished by the end of the previous January. All this means that singers have time to get used to and feel comfortable in their costumes and helps them to achieve the extraordinary degree of visual-musical unity which caused a regular visitor to the Easter Festival to remark that "here I sometimes listen with my eyes and see with my ears"—surely the highest tribute possible to any operatic conductor-producer.

But of course such a degree of artistic independence and quality requires a great deal of money, and Karajan explained his attitude to the role of money in art to Spanish writer José Luis Perez de Artéaga: "From the beginning of my career I told myself, among other things, that I didn't want to take orders from anybody. I have now reached a position where I can do what I choose to do and from the financial point of view this amounts to freedom in choosing the best artistic material available without being concerned about the cost. To me, money in itself has no attraction. But insofar as it allows me to achieve my artistic aims, money is important.

"For example, at the Salzburg Easter Festival we have set a standard and we never question its cost. If an artist tells us, 'I need that much', nobody disputes his 'cachet'. But accordingly, on completing his work and from the very beginning of it, everything in the world that can be given to him as far as artistic material is concerned has been made available to him, and there are therefore no grounds for making excuses and saying 'If I had this or that, I could have done better.' I say, 'You have it, and you take full responsibility!'

"Think of all the advantages there are, as regards preparation and the much more important aspect of having time available for a smaller output of music, which means that we can spend a whole year perfecting nine days of music! Consider the three hundred days of music in repertory opera houses: it is obvious that the results cannot be good. To sum up, I am content with what I present, which is executed in a comparatively short period of time but after exhaustive preparation. Therefore, to produce performances of this kind, the financial aspect is of the greatest importance. The paramount consideration is the perfection of the final product, and not the money involved. And this is as it should be."

In 1973, Karajan also founded the Salzburg Whitsun Festival, which consists of three concerts with the Berlin Philharmonic—usually before or after their summer tour. Ticket prices at all these festivals and tours are very high and this has caused Karajan to be labelled an 'establishment conductor'. Karajan, who has not a trace of snobbery in his make-up and who dislikes and despises the powers that be, is fully aware of the validity of this accusation and this is partly why, at this stage of his career, he has placed such emphasis on films and televised relays of opera and concerts. He passionately believes in the accessibility of music to anyone willing to listen—yet will never compromise on the quality of the artistic product itself. His solution is to use the financial resources of the well-heeled, 'privileged' audiences who can afford to attend his live performances in order to create top quality productions and then make them accessible to mass audiences through television and films. (Indeed he waived his fee for the televised relay of his Salzburg production of *Il trovatore* from the Vienna State Opera which borrowed it, so as to make the transmission possible.) "We must break through the gates of privilege," he said after his remarks at the head of this section.

Indeed Karajan was the first and in many ways the only conductor fully to grasp the significance of this century's technological advances for music and to utilize them both for purely creative purposes in his productions, and for his social aim of reaching the greatest possible number of people. What brought about his whole-hearted conversion to the mass media, of which initially he had been suspicious, was an experience during his third visit to Japan with the Berlin Philharmonic when, on the morning after his arrival in Fukuoka, he was mobbed by a crowd of two thousand who had watched the televised transmission of his concert from Tokyo the night before. "In my young days, a concert in Salzburg was attended by, say, two or three hundred people at most; but today through records and films you can get an audience of a hundred million for a single concert." And when a series of his best-known films—including *Otello*, *Madama Butterfly*, *La Bohème*, *Carmen* and *Der Rosenkavalier*—was shown on America's cultural Channel Thirteen, sponsored by the Exxon Company, and rose from fifteenth to first place in the ratings, which means that they were watched by forty–fifty million people, he felt understandably happy and vindicated.

His first five films were directed by Henri Georges Clouzot whom he watched like an apprentice and from whom he learnt a great deal about technique, charging behind every camera, ordering new equipment, asking questions about everything, his enthusiasm barely containable. Yet the film company he eventually formed, Cosmotel, was the only

Karajan's mesmerising eyes—brilliant blue, capable of emitting just about everything he wants them to with extraordinary power, and of X-raying anyone he meets in a matter of seconds—a chapter in themselves.
SIEGFRIED LAUTERWASSER

Karajan's extraordinary hands—immensely strong, immensely sensitive—mirror the range of extremes of his life and character. SIEGFRIED LAUTERWASSER

An enviable capacity for total concentration, achieved through Yoga and an adherence to Zen principles.
G. MACDOMNIC

"Sometimes something unexpected suddenly comes . . . and it's the grace of the moment."
SIEGFRIED
LAUTERWASSER/EMI

Karajan in rehearsal: "You must rehearse your orchestra to the point where you see that they are at One with you. *They* carry *you* instead of you carrying them." SIEGFRIED LAUTERWASSER

Left: Karajan at Oxford shortly before receiving the degree of D. Mus. Honoris Causa on June 21, 1978. "... originality grounded in tradition, vitality continuously renewed." PETER SOMOGYI

Top: Karajan with Victor de Sabata who, after hearing his *Tristan* at the Berlin Staatsoper before the war, foresaw that "the young man will lead the world's musical thought for the next half century."
TEATRO ALLA SCALA

Above: Trying out the drums at La Scala. TEATRO ALLA SCALA

Right: With Renata Tebaldi at La Scala, where his looks and magnetism turned him into a matinée idol.
TEATRO ALLA SCALA

bove: Karajan felt justifiably proud and vindicated when a series of his opera films shown in America's cultural Channel Thirteen rose to first place in the ratings, i.e. were seen by forty-to-fifty million people, and would "like to be the companion of him who will know how to propose music, opera and poetry to the most remote and least privileged of beings on this earth." SIEGFRIED LAUTERWASSER

bove right: Karajan was the first conductor fully to grasp the importance of twentieth century technology for music, and insists on controlling every stage of his recordings of which he has made more than eight hundred. ROGER HAUERT

ight: Karajan during the filming of the Beethoven Ninth in 1968, charging behind every camera, asking a thousand questions, his enthusiasm barely containable. SIEGFRIED LAUTERWASSER

Karajan on tour with the Berlin Philharmonic:

With the US Immigration authorities during his first tour with the Berlin Philharmonic in March 1955, shortly after he was named its conductor for life.
BERLIN PHILHARMONIC

... heading for the US Customs Department during his 1955 tour: the last time anyone has seen him carry his own bags!
BERLIN PHILHARMONIC

... with Dmitri Shostakovich after a performance of his tenth symphony in Moscow during the Berlin Philharmonic's tour of 1969. REINHARD FRIEDRICH

financial failure of his career and was later absorbed into the larger German film and television company, Unitel. (As this book was going to press, Karajan was starting a new film company.)

His latest and most advanced film project to date is *Das Rheingold*, the sound track for which was recorded in Salzburg by EMI, with the cast he used for his Easter Festival production (the film was released in Germany in 1982). All cinematic devices were used to create visual credibility, so that the truth of the work comes through, because Karajan believes that as far as the *Ring* is concerned, a film can reveal more than a live performance: "I spent a lifetime trying to understand the *Ring*. The nucleus of this vast work is in the spoken word, and it is nearly impossible to make all of it understood in the opera house," he told *Der Spiegel*. "But if the viewer can really see the singer in close-up in an important moment and really understand every word, the whole work suddenly appears in a completely new light." As far as the visual effects were concerned, he even went so far as to hire Dick Parker, the technician responsible for many of the acquatic sequences in the Hollywood film *The White Shark*, who used his expertise to create an impression that the Rhinemaidens really were swimming in the Rhine.

No chapter on Karajan would be complete without some mention of recordings, of which I am told that he has made more than eight hundred!

His boxed set of the Beethoven symphonies, released in 1977, sold over eight million sets; his album of music by Schönberg, Berg and Webern, which Deutsche Grammophon were reluctant to record because they doubted its commercial potential, and for which he waived his fee, just to make it happen, sold in numbers that surpassed even *his* hopes. The fact is that the public will buy any record with his name on its sleeve, because over the years they have learnt that anything connected with Karajan is an automatic guarantee of quality; at worst, very good; at best, incomparable. Oddly enough, the man who first alerted me to this, several years ago, was Decca engineer James Lock, who was leased by his Company to EMI in order to work with Karajan on his recording of *Salome*, because Karajan wanted it recorded in the Sofiensaal in Vienna, which is equipped as a Decca studio. As he is a disinterested observer with no vested interest either way, his observations of Karajan are unbiased and therefore more noteworthy than those of recording personnel constantly associated with him.

"He is, without question, the best conductor in the world—a true conductor, not a specialist in this or that. He studied his art very, very hard, has stuck to it over the years, and has become the best at it. Unlike some other famous conductors, who dabble at this and that, and are marvellous when they conduct well and awful when they conduct badly, Karajan never does this sort of thing and never goes below a certain standard: everything he does is either good or superb, it's always very well rehearsed, it's always a polished performance, and this is what I adore. His professionalism, conscientiousness and dedication should be an example to anyone who presumes to hold a baton in his hand.

"You would have thought that a man of his age and experience could now relax and make things easier for himself by cutting on rehearsal time. But no: never have I seen or heard of him ever giving a performance even of works he had conducted three hundred times without a rehearsal, even in places like the Musikverein, where the acoustics are familiar both to him and to the orchestra. [He told me that he once calculated that he could, really, play about fifty to sixty programmes without rehearsal—but that this would miss the point of the exercise, the new insights and constant perfecting of detail that come with regular repetition of familar works. And it takes him roughly three years to really learn works that are new to him and to complete both 'the inner and the outer preparation'.]

"He never has a precise recording schedule. He wants all the cast assembled there and on call at every session, and usually seated in the orchestra. Then he comes in and says, right, today we shall do such and such a scene, which produces an incredible tension. Now, I had learnt *Salome* backwards, because I was so excited by the challenge of working with him, and had decided that there were certain scenes, like the scene with the Jews, which, if recorded without prior notice, would result in disaster. So I explained this to Michel Glotz who, as you know, supervises all his recordings and who in turn explained it to him. He saw the point at once. I found him very easy to work with, relaxed, co-operative and with a good sense of humour. But obviously, he neither likes nor suffers fools gladly, or people who don't know their jobs.

"And he does not, rightly I think, allow singers to use music stands, because he feels that if they don't know their parts, they shouldn't be there in the first place. Because this is what we have come to, you know. Singers come, accept these enormous fees, but arrive without knowing their parts and thinking they will get by just sight-reading."

Karajan likes to record in long sustained takes, and then return to the studio for any necessary corrections. He never listens to a completed recording immediately after the sessions, because he likes to approach it from a certain distance—say six to eight weeks—that enables him to judge its merits and demerits in a detached and dispassionate way. Then, if he feels that something is not quite right, he may ask for one or two more sessions. Finally, there is a second, and maybe a third "mixing" and balancing, which he considers crucial because of the possibilities it offers for clarifying certain aspects of the music better than he could in a 'live' performance. For this reason, he has always insisted on being in total control of every aspect of his recordings.

In the studio, "we do a first take, and if it is very good, which sometimes happens, we just do corrections and that's it", explains Michel Glotz. "If, on the other hand, it is not exactly as we would like it, we do another, and sometimes more than one, take. Then we do corrections on the master tape. But Karajan hates corrections, you know! He realizes that they are necessary, but he doesn't like them." ("An artist is not a factory of perfection!", he protested during the recording of the Bruckner first, when Glotz was quibbling about one single note that could, perhaps, be done better.) "And he postpones and postpones and procrastinates, and tomorrow is another day, and the day after tomorrow is the ideal weather for doing something else, until finally I get to the point where I have to say, NOW, I need my corrections! And he looks at me as if he could positively hit or bite me or something, so I remind him of something he said several years ago, when there was a difficult decision to make: 'I am a modest conductor paid for doing his job!' Well, as you can imagine, the phrase stayed in my memory and so [roaring with laughter in his typical way that makes Karajan fear he may have a stroke in the process], when I come to the stage when corrections can no longer be put off, I tell him: 'Now, remember that you are a modest conductor paid for doing your job— and this is your job!'

"Then he gets impatient because he wants to finish, rings up on the podium telephone and asks if I think that we have everything. And that is the moment of truth. Because you have only one split second in which to say 'yes' or 'no'. And there can be no shenanigans. No 'maybes' would work with him. This is when you have to tell him that at bar 95, for instance, the clarinet is not together with the bassoon, or that the intonation of the oboe is slightly flat, and you have to tell him quickly, so that he knows exactly why you want to repeat a certain passage. And watch out! If you tell him something nonsensical, he will never trust you again. Basically, you have to have a very precise, very concentrated idea of every detail of the score, and form a judgment on what is happening as compared to what you know he hears in his mind. Because that's what you are there for: to reproduce *his* way of thinking, *his* sound—not yours. [Karajan says that he and Glotz 'have the same ears'.]

"Karajan has a very special and personal concept of sound: in his mind, the music is like a tapestry—he has a complete and precise idea of every detail, there is no ad-libbing—and he makes it unfold in a great, seamless line, the famous 'Karajan line', which is so characteristic of all his interpretations. And the sound is always beautiful and shaped, as if by a sculptor, in a way that rounds off and smooths all its edges and blurs even the harshest accents."

Karajan agrees that this sinuous, legato quality in his sound is indeed typical of him, and eight years ago explained some of the reasons why he goes for a great long unbroken line to *The New York Times*: "You see, I keep telling the orchestra that the bar line is not a door which is closed. Notes have to be written down after the bar line, so necessarily they come in too late. And when printers compress more bars than usual into a line, invariably all orchestras will play the music in a way that sounds compressed. We try to play *through* the bar lines and, for legato melodies, have already done away with all even bowings and phrasings."

But apart from perfecting his own interpretations, be they live, recorded or filmed, some of Karajan's main preoccupations during the last fifteen years involve areas which have nothing to do with his own personal career.

His desire to ensure continuing high standards in orchestral playing prompted him to found the Academy affiliated to the Berlin Philharmonic, and the Berlin-based branch of the Herbert von Karajan Foundation, which organizes a Young Conductors' Competition and an International Festival of Youth Orchestras in alternate years.

The Academy was founded in 1968—the year of his sixtieth birthday, which also saw the establishment of his Foundation, "because towards the end of my life, I felt that I wanted to give back some of the things I have so lavishly received through the years: the joy, the pleasure in music"—with an annual grant of DM 250,000 from the Dresdner Bank, whose late head, Jürgen Ponto, who was so tragically killed (kidnapped and murdered by terrorists), was a great music lover and wanted his company to make a contribution to cultural life. The Academy is open to young players from all over the world, who are offered scholarships to study under the principal soloists of the Berlin Philharmonic, and ensures that Karajan's eventual successor, whoever he might be, will have players of superlative calibre at his disposal.

"The idea is quite clear," he explained to the *Gramophone* at the time. "Our soloists in the orchestra are the professors, the upper age limit for the pupils is 25, and we have no lower age limit. Race, religion, nationality, Prix de Rome—we take no notice of any of these. Only quality. Someone asked me recently: 'Surely, you are not founding an élitist system?' 'No,' I replied, 'I am founding a *super*-elitist system!' All I can say is that if someone cannot play in rhythm and has not got music within him, then we cannot admit him. ... And sometimes the pupils are called on to play in the orchestra with us— sitting in with the principals, who give advice and show them what to do. It's like the pilot and the co-pilot. Of course, we cannot always employ them straight away. But other orchestras will take them—often without auditioning them—because if they come from us they need no references. But we know that one day they will return. They never forget the atmosphere of this orchestra. They know the disciplines and how special they are."

The Conductors' Competition organized by the Karajan Foun- dation—which was endowed by £20,000 of his own money and is constantly funded and maintained by him—can count several bright young conductors among its prize winners: Okko Kamu (first prize, 1959), now Principal Conductor of the Oslo Philharmonic; Dmitri Kitayenko (second prize, 1969), now Principal Conductor of the Moscow Philharmonic; Gabriel Chmura (first prize, 1971), now Music Director at Aachen; Daniel Oren (first prize, 1975), now in Rome. This understandably makes Karajan very proud and happy: "I always say to my juries that we don't want proficient Kapellmeisters. You have got to take somebody, even if he is still unformed, who has a really compulsive and penetrating temperament. Because in the last resort that's what a real conductor must have, otherwise he'll never achieve the conviction within himself, and the power to display it to the orchestra, and finally to the audience."

In addition, and prior to this Competition, Karajan also taught several prominent young conductors, including Seiji Ozawa, and discovered and nurtured many a singer and soloist. He has a special tenderness for young people and is a born teacher, patient and encouraging but never indulgent, as one of his latest discoveries, the prodigiously gifted young violinist Anne-Sophie Mutter—whom he discovered when she was only thirteen—points out:

"Every rehearsal with him is a music lesson," she told me when I interviewed her for *The Sunday Times Colour Magazine* in January 1980, "and I hope that I shall be lucky enough to play with him for many years to come. He is a terribly *nice* teacher and accompanist. At the beginning I found this surprising, because so many people seem to be scared of him, although I cannot understand why. He is amazingly patient and not at all authoritarian. He never seems to want to *impose* an interpretation on you, but is more concerned with helping you acquire the insights and technical expertise that will enable you to realize your *own* view of the work. He has an unbelievable imagination of sound and can make just the sort of technical suggestions that help you play what is in your head. For instance, he taught me to play really long, broad lines. Our concerts together have been my most fulfilling musical experiences."

In the summer of 1982, Karajan was due to start an annual Singers' Symposium in Salzburg, something he has wanted to do for some time, but which only became possible when a lady patron of the Festivals made a sizeable donation. The project will consist of seminars, master classes and a competition; the contestants will be asked first to submit tapes, which will be evaluated by a panel of specialists; then, those selected will be invited to Salzburg for three weeks at Easter, two weeks at Whitsun and four or five weeks in the Summer, to attend master classes given by singers like Elisabeth Schwarzkopf and Nicolai Gedda, among others, and have lessons with expert coaches—Italians for Italian opera, French for the French repertoire and so on. Karajan will attend all the recitals and work with the young singers himself before the final competition.

He hopes that this project will help alleviate today's tragic shortage of well trained singers. For he doesn't think that it is talent and vocal equipment that are missing, but expert guidance that will enable it to develop to its full potential in the way that the old Italian conductors helped shape and nurture an entire generation of singers. Today's conductors are generally much too preoccupied with the furtherance of their own careers.

Of course, few conductors have done so much for singing or discovered and trained more singers than Karajan himself. Nicolai Gedda, Helga Dernesch, Gundula Janowitz, Hildegard Behrens, Mirella Freni and Agnes Baltsa, to name just a few, all owe their international careers to him, and it was he who first brought Leontyne Price to Europe. He has spies in opera houses great and small who feed him with tapes and information about any exceptional talents that emerge. If he thinks they are really outstanding, he sets to work with them himself, and anyone who remembers the difference that a few comments and instructions from him made to the singing of the young artists auditioning for his *Zauberflöte* recording, in Jeremy Marre's documentary for London Weekend Television's *South Bank Show*, will have a clear picture of the value of such training.

In fact, Karajan's influence has transformed operatic singing as profoundly and significantly as it has the art of conducting. Quite apart from "sweeping those fat people off the stage", as he proudly admits, all the singers who have passed through his hands are distinguished for their delicate handling of their voices, their clear articulation, their ability to project maximum excitement in quiet, hushed moments, and the subtlety of their overall singing style. His influence on them can be seen even when they sing under other conductors.

Karajan has always been passionately interested in medicine, and is deeply convinced about the healing, revitalizing potential of music. Indeed, the only aspects of his work that he finds truly tiring are the interviews he gives from time to time and the organization of the Easter Festival, which he runs himself, so that everything can be got absolutely right. "But the moment I get into a pullover and walk onto the podium to rehearse, I don't feel tired anymore; there is something in the thing that completely revitalizes me." A year after setting up his Foundation in Berlin he endowed a special Research Institute for Experimental Psychology in Music affiliated to the University of Salzburg. The Institute, which has now moved to Vienna, holds an annual seminar immediately after the Easter Festival and has carried out many exhaustive experiments into the physical, mental and emotional effects of different kinds of music on both healthy and sick people and on the formation of children's personalities.

It was in relation to one of these that Karajan had himself wired up with electrodes—"the same measuring equipment as the astronauts!" he adds excitedly—to determine the difference in his bodily reactions during a dress rehearsal of the finale of the third act of *Siegfried*. His heartbeat, blood pressure and the static electricity on his skin were all monitored. "Now one would be justified in thinking that as there was no public, why should I be nervous? And anyway, the passage begins very softly, and involves no risk at all. Yet the moment before it started, my heart beat went up from its normal very low 67 or 68 to 170 for about three seconds, and then went down again. It is the tension inside you which you are not actually conscious of that makes it do this. And we also discovered that the passages which we call energetic are not at all tiring for your body. The most difficult are those very slow passages with intermittent pauses where you have to wait—which is an enormous strain on your body ... and in the latter part of my life I've developed a habit I didn't have before: whenever I feel tension, I start to breathe very freely. Breathing, as I keep pointing out to young conductors, is very important for conserving your strength.

"Basically we at the Institute want to find out how people are affected by different interpretations, different rhythms, different kinds of music. A man who breeds cows in the hills above Baalbeck once told me that they produce more and better milk to the music of Bach. And I know that *I* immediately feel at ease with music that goes with the tempo of my heartbeat. I know what my heartbeat is: I feel it in every part of me, possibly because of my long experience of yoga. And if I fall into the pulse at the beginning of a piece of music, it is a physical joy. This way, your whole body makes music.... And of course, different conductors have different pulse rates and their tempi are often mathematical proportions of this."

Yet another mystery in the art of conducting that cannot be explained in concrete terms ... like the healing effect of music both on those who listen and on those who make it and are constantly renewed by the hidden force inherent in and emanating from it—responsible, perhaps, for the longevity of most musicians in general and conductors in particular. This is one of the many subjects that Karajan is unshakably convinced and continuously curious about, in that typically enthusiastic way of his that keeps him perpetually youthful.

Now that one has briefly surveyed some of the quests, goals, achievements and aspirations in the life of this adventurous, restless, forward-looking and generous spirit—which have caused him to be honoured with doctorates from the Universities of Oxford, Tokyo,

Salzburg and Parma—the question must inevitably crop up: Would a man choose to devote so much of his time, energy and private resources to activities that have nothing to do with his own career when he could be amassing extra millions by guest conducting anywhere, anytime and filling any concert hall or opera house many times over (as he does in Tokyo, for instance, where the annexe of a sectarian temple had to be converted to a 4,500-capacity concert hall at a cost of £75,000 expressly for his Beethoven cycle, which despite this extra cost, recouped all the expenses of the two-week tour for his sponsors), if he were as greedy, power-hungry or megalomaniac as his detractors claim?

The answer is obvious. And the public, who have always flocked to his concerts and bought his records in millions, sense it. Which must mean that, along with his musicians, they are the people who know him best; and which perhaps explains why he is so fond of quoting the saying of Paracelsus: "Emperors and Kings have not liked me, the powerful, those in authority, the Lord Mayors have not liked me, the magistracy has not liked me—but my patients have liked me!"

JAMES LEVINE
The Met's Maestro

"When I was a small child, I had a speech impediment," grinned James Levine, Music Director of the Metropolitan Opera, New York, halfway through the last of four talks in which he had proved brilliantly articulate and hardly ever stopped to fumble for a word or to wonder how best to express an idea. "I know it's hard to believe," he added, noticing and rather enjoying my incredulity, "because I have since made up for it by becoming a marathon talker!"

He was born, on June 23, 1943, in Cincinnati, Ohio, to artistic parents. His father had been a violinist and dance-band leader before becoming president of a dress-manufacturing firm; his mother was a former actress, and his maternal grandfather had written liturgical music for the synagogue. The family owned a piano, a gramophone and a large collection of records, which meant that sooner or later, Jimmy's own musical talent was bound to be discovered. But what speeded up the discovery, and prompted his starting piano lessons at the age of four, was this slight speech impediment.

It happened when Jimmy (nobody seems to call him James) was suffering from some standard childhood illness and his mother asked their wise old family doctor if anything could be done about his stuttering. The doctor wanted to know what kind of things the child was most interested in. "Well," replied his mother, "every time he passes the piano, he stops, reaches up and starts banging on it until he drives us all crazy!" "Give him piano lessons," prescribed the doctor. They did, and sure enough, he soon stopped stuttering.

He learnt easily and quickly and says that, as far back as he can remember, he always wanted to be a musician, and loved being taken to concerts and the opera, where he would sit with a score in his lap and conduct with a knitting needle! By the age of nine, he was producing operas at home, singing, conducting and directing with the aid of a gramophone and a miniature puppet theatre. When he was ten, he made his professional début as a pianist, with the Cincinnati Symphony Orchestra.

Yet neither he nor his parents seemed anxious to push him into a career as a child prodigy. He went to a normal school but, thanks to an enlightened superintendent of schools who was willing to count his musical studies as a scholastic credit, he was allowed to leave school two hours early every day—at 1 instead of 3 p.m., in order to have a full afternoon's music lessons and practice.

He and his younger brother and sister had a happy home life, with parents who never gave him a sense of having to *succeed* in anything— only of the importance of making himself happy. The only disciplining they ever resorted to was to cancel his piano lessons whenever he didn't practise. Like most children, he hated practising, and they said that this was fine by them, as long as they weren't expected to pay for lessons for which he was not prepared. But any time he felt like practising, he could have a lesson. "So I missed a few lessons from time to time, but learnt a valuable one in the process: that some things in life you can have right away, while other things require patience and discipline, and if you want those things that require discipline, then you must have the discipline, too."

When he was thirteen, he went to the Marlboro Music Festival to study with Rudolf Serkin. Marlboro didn't yet have its modern hall, but consisted of an old farm building and a community of about sixty people who performed chamber, choral and symphonic music and had a small opera workshop, which was preparing a production of *Così fan tutte*. They had only one opera coach who, they realized, was going to have to play the cembalo recitatives in the pit, so they desperately needed someone else to conduct the offstage chorus, and asked Jimmy, who had attended all the rehearsals. He accepted with alacrity and enjoyed himself so much that he realized that he was not cut out for a solitary life of travelling around the world alone playing solo piano, but felt more drawn to music which involved combinations of people. It was during this summer at Marlboro that he began to think of his future in terms of conducting.

In fact, he was ready to give up the piano altogether and it took all his father's eloquence and two sound arguments to persuade him not to. "My father said that although I now felt that I would be happier trying to get results out of other people, there might be times in my life when I would be tired of other people's shortcomings despite my own and wish that I could just sit down and make music by myself, with my own ten fingers. He also pointed out that the piano would prove a very useful tool in conducting, which involves coaching singers—something I had been too naïve to think about at that stage. So I agreed. And needless to say, I have never regretted it."

He also spent some summers at the Aspen Festival, where he studied chamber music, orchestral repertoire, style, theory, score reading and interpretation with Walter Levin, first violin of the La Salle Quartet. After high school, he went to the Juilliard School of Music in New York where, because of all his private studies in Cincinnati and his experience of practical work at Aspen and Marlboro, he was put straight into the post-graduate division and studied the piano with the great Russian teacher Rosina Lhevinne (1880–1976), and conducting with Jean Morel.

When he was twenty, he auditioned for a project for American conductors sponsored by the Ford Foundation. The late Georg Szell, Music Director of the Cleveland Orchestra, was on the jury and asked Jimmy, one of the finalists, to become his Assistant. He accepted at once, because the Cleveland Orchestra had been developed by Szell into the best orchestra in America for Classical styles, and he was "anxious to learn *how* he had developed it and to be in contact with his perceptions of Classical music". He was also aware that at the time there was no other Music Director in America whose quality, culture and experience could match Szell's.

The apprenticeship lasted six years (1964–70), during which Levine attended all Szell's rehearsals, concerts and recording sessions; conducted rehearsals and concerts himself while Szell—who said that he had never before encountered a young American conductor with such a wide repertoire and cultural background—watched and criticized; and spent many sessions alone with him at the piano, analysing symphonic and operatic scores. Even though he didn't wholly agree with Szell's approach, he learnt so much from him about Classical style, Classical structure, Classical discipline and Classical training, that he will "feel forever grateful" for those years in Cleveland.

"The good things about my response and relationship to Szell as a musician were *very* significant. He knew those Classical works in a way that could produce amazing results. But he had disciplined the orchestra to a point where they were almost overdisciplined, almost too dry, almost without breath. Yet suddenly, there would be those incredible concerts, maybe on tour, when he would conduct the Brahms fourth or the Schumann second or Mozart's 'Posthorn Serenade' as if he had the chains off him, and then you could see where that discipline could go, how much flexibility and fluctuation were possible within that discipline, and those performances were *fabulous*!"

Gradually, he began to discover the differences in their personalities and musical temperaments. After a time, Szell's music-making didn't seem *vocal* enough for him, i.e. not firmly enough based on the human voice, on singing and those characteristics of singing that composers expected one to apply to instrumental music and were forever insisting on. "He was also a rather vertical conductor, very concerned with the vertical balance within the chord, but less concerned with the line, so that his performances often lacked breath, breadth, physical pulse and that breathing and tension in the extreme registers that comes from singing—the sustained legato and vitality of singing, which is why they often struck me as rhythmically awkward. They were rhythmically abstract rather than rhythmically pulsating."

"All this is terribly hard to describe in words," continues Levine, "but these were the basic differences in our personalities and our approach. Of course, I, too, want performances to be disciplined, but not in a way that takes some of the vitality out of them but rather in a way that injects vitality. And by vitality I don't mean that everything should be frenetic all the time, but that there should be vitality to the sound and the shape of the phrases as well as the appropriate dramatic character to everything. We also differed in our attitude towards orchestras. I could never relate to them in the cold, distant way that he did. That's just not me. But on the other hand, maybe my performances of Classical scores aren't as good as his."

The two men also had different methods of studying scores. Szell always used the piano as a learning tool and worked out structural and interpretational details in this way, whereas Levine has always found this to be a limitation, even in the studying of piano music. He prefers first to learn a score thoroughly before taking it to the piano, because he is concerned lest the physical limitations of the instrument prejudice his knowledge of the piece, and aware of his own technical idiosyncrasies and limitations. "If I sight-read a piece I will play it at a certain tempo and this will make an impression on me and I would later be adjusting to this impression rather than to a judgement made directly from the score." Of course, studying works he knows but has not yet conducted is different from learning new music.

As far as interpretation is concerned, Levine's golden rule, established back in his Cleveland days, is never to conduct music which he
has only just learnt, because it hasn't had sufficient absorption time. He
likes to live with a score for a long time, "a long period of gestation and
gradual digestion" before he feels ready to tackle it in public. In every
score, there are some elements of stylistic perception which can be
mastered only by a sort of "cultural absorption", which involves
knowing a lot more than the score itself: some history, philosophy and
languages, all of which help acquire a clearer picture of each period.

Although his method of learning scores varies according to their style
and period, the first step is always to try and establish "a direct
relationship to them. I look at all the lines independently; I look at
them together; sometimes, I listen to recordings, to hear other people's
solutions to certain problems and decide which ones work and which
ones don't. And as I turn the pages and study more and more deeply, I
hear a certain amount, and I see a certain amount, and I find myself
drawn to certain elements in the content, certain elements in the
structure and in the proportion, so that when I eventually take it to the
piano or start coaching singers, I have some undistorted impressions.

"But actually learning a score, even knowing its practicalities well
enough to conduct or play it, is only fifty-per-cent of my work. I then
start reflecting on it, relating it to other works by the same composer,
trying to feel what this particular piece meant to the composer, and
trying to get *inside* his work and understand his excitement with it, his
purpose, his expressive and communicative feelings. And I try to use
every bit of energy, every bit of talent, every bit of perception, every bit
of technical skill and volatility I possess to make the audience feel them,
too. This, conveying to any receptive listener all the levels—or as many
as I can—of the impulses, feelings and ideas which the composer has
expressed in musical terms, is my responsibility as a conductor.

"But what are my means? On every page of a score there are
countless questions of tempo, tempo relationships, sonority, balance,
dramatic character, textual character if it has words, which means not
only pronunciation but also inflection and expression of those words
and the way they relate to each other and to the instrumental sound.
"And my answers to these questions, which, I hope, are what the
composer meant, are not necessarily the same as those given by my
colleagues, some of whom are also convinced that they are fulfilling the
composer's intentions! We all claim to be doing the same thing, yet

what comes out is not the same thing! This is one of the most fascinating aspects of conducting. But what really matters is not whether we are all doing the same thing, but whether we have the same attitude: serving the composer rather than putting our own stamp *consciously* on his work."

A conductor may sometimes arrive at a point in a score where he does not agree with what is written and thinks that this is not as effective as something that he could substitute in its place. What is he to do? He could, for example, re-orchestrate it, he could change the tempo, he could say that this ritardando is no good, that there shouldn't be a ritardando there. In Levine's opinion, his point of departure should be that the composer is right and that his own feeling is wrong, because the composer was the genius. "Therefore, if somebody, for example a producer, tells me that performing a certain cabaletta in a Verdi opera is undramatic, my answer should be that Verdi was a man of the theatre par excellence and knew more about the theatre than a hundred of you. Your job is not to change it, but to make it work!"

But if he were dealing with an early Verdi score—and we know that Verdi himself revised some of his early operas but never got around to this particular score because he was busy composing another and this didn't urgently need that much revision—does he then take a gamble and adjust the odd thing here and there? He may feel sure that Verdi would have *wanted* those changes, that he, as a conductor who has lived and conducted the work often, knows that it would then work better, and he thinks he is on Verdi's wavelength, but ... what does he do?

"This is a legitimate point, but ... and the extent of this 'but' is the crux of the question. Some people carry fidelity to the composer to an absurd degree and in the process imprison some of his creative genius. Our purpose as performers is to present as truthful a representation as possible of a composer's work for *now*. Of course the composer understood that every singer, every instrumentalist would make a different sound—that all performances would be different from another. The point is the *degree* of difference, the subtlety of the difference. Some fundamentals are crystal clear and can be *right* or *wrong*, but many details will change within certain boundaries. For instance, what good would it do for us to use Bach's original instruments when we play in 2,000 seat halls? The point is worth pursuing because people are forever arguing about what instruments

Bach should be played on.

"Yet one of the things we know that Bach cared the least about in some cases was what instruments his music was played on! But a man whose top priority is actual instrumentation could never take a Vivaldi concerto for four violins and transcribe it for four harpsichords! What do the violin and the harpsichord have in common?"

Therefore, he considers it perfectly legitimate to play Bach on the piano, "even though many people" will cry "treason". Bach was living at a time when instruments were constantly changing, and what mattered most to him were the dramatic points, the character and clarity of the counterpoint, the tempo—but the instrumentation, only relatively, that is, the blending and contrasting sonorities of, say, oboes and flutes—but not in an *absolute* sense. This, of course, would be unthinkable when one is dealing with scores by Mahler or Berlioz, both of whom cared passionately about instruments—in fact they even cared about the *make* of instruments, the construction of timpani sticks, etc! A conductor must therefore adjust to each composer's priorities and always bear them in mind when he comes up against a problem.

Levine considers that each conductor's individual conception of what a composer would want him to do, and the formation of his mental image of the sound, is a very 'chemical', and therefore, mysterious, part of conducting. The conductor then goes in front of the orchestra to rehearse this conception, in which some things are very clear-cut and can be rehearsed directly, either through technique or facial expressions, aided by verbal explanations and repetition. "Yet come the performance, and more mysterious things happen, because something in the sound, something in the rubato, some of the nuances and subtleties are communicated by your chemical rapport with the orchestra, in the same way that they are in personal relationships.

"In relationships between people, you can describe the tangible aspects of their communication only up to a point. Beyond that, it's in the air, it has vibrations, and there is no way that this element can be controlled! It either happens or it doesn't and sometimes it does and sometimes it doesn't. My philosophy is that in our work, we should try to have all the tangible elements as much under control as possible. Then there is a better chance of getting the Gods involved and having them smile on us...."

By 1970, after six years' apprenticeship with Szell, Levine was beginning to receive invitations to conduct both operas and concerts at home and abroad. In 1971, he conducted *Tosca* and *Luisa Miller* at the Metropolitan Opera, with such success that the late Göran Gentele, the General Administrator, appointed him Principal Conductor—a post created specially for him—at the same time that Rafael Kubelik was appointed Music Director.

The public, the critics, the orchestra and the Board liked him right from the start. The Concertmaster, Raymond Gniewek, who had held that position for seventeen years, said that he considered Levine "the greatest conductor since Karajan, which to me is the epitome of compliments, since Karajan is my ideal." The personnel manager, John di Janni, confirmed that "they are all crazy about him. He is one of the few conductors who really know opera. He makes his decisions and as an intelligent man would do, if there is a mistake, he listens. There is no 'I am the maestro' feeling. He is the same on the podium or in your office. A great talent and a regular guy."

When Kubelik resigned in 1974, Levine was offered the Music Directorship of the Met, as from 1976, much to the delight of the orchestra. He was only thirty-three, and took six months to decide, because he was fully aware of the gargantuan task ahead of him and wanted to be sure that he was doing "the right thing for me and for the Company". Despite the fact the Met was going through one of the greatest financial and artistic crises of its history, he accepted. He chafes under all the non-musical, administrative aspects of the job, but sees no way of avoiding them, "if you want to achieve the results you envisage and get the people you want.

"It's a question of accepting artistic responsibility in order to have artistic freedom. There is no way I could exert the same consistent control over artistic results as a guest conductor. This is why some of the greatest music-making in the last fifty years was made in situations where the orchestra, the singers and the conductor had developed subtleties of rapport over many weeks, months and years together. Don't misunderstand me, I have had many happy and fulfilling experiences as a guest conductor. But basically, I'm a builder, a nester, and find that the situation here at the Met is very happy for me."

He became Music Director at a time when the Met was emerging from a long period of artistic instability and required nothing less than a complete artistic upgrading. "We needed the orchestra and the chorus to be functioning at their full capacity; a complete development of the visual side—lighting, costuming, scenery—plus an eye for the development of the production side as a whole; a sharp increase in the consistent international quality of the casting; and a much, much broader repertoire.

"At the same time that we were trying to accomplish these artistic goals, Mr Bliss and his Board had to produce financial stability, and the fact that he succeeded in doing so was a miracle, because the quality of what we had to offer was not very high, the box office was not very good, the financial report was at a disastrous low, and how do you set about improving financial support without a better product? The problem was that we had to do both simultaneously."

The measures taken by Anthony Bliss, the Met's Executive Director, involved a tighter budgeting, keeping a close watch on expenses, and a more adventurous approach to fund-raising, which covers about a third of a season's costs. The rest is provided by the box office, interest on investments, profits from certain outside presentations and the Met gift shop.

Within three years, Levine's primary artistic goals had been achieved to a great extent, and achieved much more quickly than was originally anticipated, largely because of "the incredible dedication, effort, commitment, discipline and pride of the entire house, from top to bottom." The orchestra and chorus are now on a much higher level than at any time during the last thirty years. The late Karl Böhm and Erich Leinsdorf both remarked that, by the 1978 season, the orchestra was in better shape than ever before in their experience, which meant a lot to Levine. The casting, including small-role casting, has also improved considerably.

Bernard Haitink, Music Director of Glyndebourne Festival Opera and so "spoilt" by the marvellous working conditions there that he very rarely accepts invitations to conduct opera elsewhere, agreed to make his début at the Met in 1982 with *Fidelio* and *Don Giovanni*, because "the Met is a very good house at the moment, very well run. Jimmy Levine is doing marvellous work and is really there eight months a year, which is exceptional—apart from Sawallisch in Munich, I cannot think of another music director who spends so much time in his house—and so the house is well cared for, which is very, very important. You have to sacrifice a lot when you are music director of an opera house."

As far as the repertoire was concerned, although there had of course been some exciting and unusual works, like *Wozzeck*, *Werther* and *Peter Grimes*, during the Bing régime the repertoire was nevertheless overwhelmingly middle-Italian and could stand a great deal of expansion. Levine's specific goals were: to include more twentieth-century classics, like *Lulu, The Rise and Fall of the City of Mahagonny, Les dialogues des Carmelites, Billy Budd* which had never before been seen at the Met; to include works which had been done very little and not for a long time: *Lohengrin, Tannhäuser, Der fliegende Holländer, The Bartered Bride*, for example; to begin a Mozart cycle which would include not only *Don Giovanni, Così fan tutte, Le nozze di Figaro* and *Die Zauberflöte* but also *Idomeneo* and *La clemenza di Tito*, which incredibly had never been part of the Met's repertoire; to begin performing uncut versions of works which had previously been seen in severely truncated editions, which resulted in the first uncut *Parsifal, Die Meistersinger von Nürnberg*, and *La forza del Destino*, and the first five-act *Don Carlos*, judging that America's big international opera house should be a place where one could see works in authentic versions and for the most part in their original language. (There are obviously some exceptions to the last rule: some of the comedies, contemporary works or operas not written in one of the standard operatic languages—like Janáček's—are done in English.)

The responsibility for the repertoire is shared between Levine, John Dexter the Productions Advisor, and Joan Ingpen, the Artistic Administrator. Dexter and Levine have done most of the producing and conducting during the past four years, because their aim was to raise and maintain consistently high standards. "For years and years the Met had been a kind of showcase for lots and lots of producers and conductors and this had made for a very uneven standard: not because of the quality of any individual producer or conductor, but the fact that with a different team for every opera you could not develop any depth of rapport or consistent attention to detail that would result in the raising of the House standards.

"One of the great advantages of having a Production Advisor is that John—who has built up and developed a first-rate, independently run technical department—is able to see, improve and develop every production he does, because he can watch it a dozen times each season—something which a producer who comes, does his job and goes away after the première could never do. We do ask our guest producers—Schenk, Ponnelle, Everding, Zeffirelli, Hall—to come back and supervise the revivals of their productions and sometimes, when their schedule allows it, they do."

Guest producers are chosen either because Dexter finds their work interesting, or because Levine, and sometimes a guest conductor, would like to work with a specific director. The same applies to designers who also have to be able to produce the goods exactly within the confines of the budget allocated to specific productions. As far as guest conductors are concerned, there is a long list of people whom Levine would like to have but as yet does not, for reasons which usually boil down to time, how much time they would be prepared to give to a new production and its eventual revivals, and to their commitments elsewhere analogous to his own at the Met.

He has strong views about production and the controversial role of the producer during the past decade. "A producer's job is to follow George Bernard Shaw's definition of the purpose of a theatrical enterprise, which was 'to make the audience feel that real things are happening to real people'. Yet Shaw was talking in 1881 and here we are in 1981 with nearly a century of cinema and half a century of television behind us, which has radically changed our expectations and assessment of what is believable on stage. If we had gone to the 1876 Bayreuth Festival, we might have accepted a degree of unconvincing stage illusion, which we would now find comic. But is this a justification for coming up with some kind of random abstraction that has nothing to do with the composer or superimposing ideas onto his music?

"As I said when we were discussing fidelity to the score from the conductorial point of view, one must again find a way of staging a work that serves the composer, and producers can be divided into two groups: those who serve the composer and those who serve themselves. I even know some who are sometimes one and sometimes the other, depending on their relationship to a particular opera! I also know producers who direct an opera as though it had no music—as if they were directing a straight play—which is fine, until the music gets in the way. For example, how could one present the ball in the Duke's palace in Mantua in the first act of *Rigoletto* as an orgy while the orchestra plays a minuet? Our modern orgies are not danced to minuets so we obviously would have trouble accepting it!"

There is, he thinks, a certain type of opera-goer who wants to see a cinematic kind of production: if the action is meant to be taking place on a beach in Algiers, they want to see the floor looking like a beach and a blue backcloth. Not Levine. He would spot the wrinkles in the backcloth and the divisions in the floorboards and have no illusions at all. "My imagination would go 'click' and everything would be finished. I would just sit there and watch the whole thing like an old school play."

He only wants to see this cinematic approach in an opera in which the specific culture of a certain place is intrinsic to the drama. For example, he only wants to see *Cavalleria rusticana* the way Franco Zeffirelli did it, i.e. Sicilian to the core, because Sicily is the sort of place with specific concepts about personal relationships, religion and sexuality and should therefore be omnipresent in every production of *Cavalleria*, because it's part of the essence of the work. "Of course, a producer can always come up with a few varieties, like Jean Pierre Ponnelle's idea of making Santuzza's pregnancy obvious—brilliant, because it made the contemporary audience understand why the old Sicilian community were treating her with such hostility."

Levine says that sixty-per-cent of his own artistic temperament is theatrical and vocal. To him, working with voices means working with dramatic situations, with poetry, with text, with that link between abstract musical substance and human experience. At some point in his life, he would like to perform *all* the operatic repertoire, but only sixty-per-cent of the symphonic and forty-per-cent of the piano and chamber music repertoire. "It's that kind of balance," he says, and adds that he wishes that all instrumentalists had some of the volatility, variety and unpredictability of the voice!

"For me, music falls into three clear categories: first, music to which I have some emotional, inspirational and practical relationship and which I conduct because I feel that there is some honesty to the possibility that I might re-create it faithfully. (But sometimes I've been wrong and wished that I had just sat in the audience and listened to someone else doing it! On other, but rare, occasions, the opposite has happened, and I have been surprised by works which only began to excite me after I started rehearsing them.) Secondly, music which may be wonderful, but which I recognize that it's not for me to conduct, even though I can listen to someone else's performance with great pleasure. Thirdly, music which I just don't like, cannot get inside and become at one with, and which I would never conduct! Examples? Some Shostakovich and Prokofiev, some Vaughan Williams and Walton, and some Sibelius and Bruckner. But this list is by no means fixed, rigid or final. It has gradually continued to change."

Individual performances also fall into three categories. Those which he experiences as bad, nights when *he* is not good, or the orchestra is not good, when the whole thing is downright bad and doesn't work, either because of bad chemistry, or because the piece was inadequately rehearsed, or maybe just because it's one of those evenings that seem cursed. Then there are performances which are okay, they are a good representation of the work, they cannot be objectively faulted, yet they lack magic, that miraculous fusion of all the different elements into something special. And lastly, those evenings when something *extra-*special happens, when the Gods smile on it, and he feels that this can only be because they are getting close to the composer's intentions, his inspiration, vision and challenge. On those nights, he doesn't necess-arily feel that everything is right—not at all! Many things could go wrong: there might be an ensemble slip here, bad intonation or a mistake there, but it doesn't seem to matter, because there is such truth in this performance, such depth of communication and fidelity to the essence of the work, that those technicalities become unimportant, "whereas in a mediocre performance, technicalities become *very* important!"

He accepts that there can be no such thing as total, utopian perfection in an operatic performance. With a hundred people in the orchestra, a hundred people in the chorus, with twenty solo singers, with all the acting and staging details, there will always be things that go wrong. He is not looking for, and is not interested in "a technically perfect performance" and neither were the composers themselves.

"If you read the letters and prose works of composers, you will not find a single instance where they are complaining about technical inadequacies. Only about the character of their work being wrongly understood and presented. Only when the truth of what they were trying to say was not obeyed or perceptively communicated did they get upset. But the fact that the horns made a crack or that some chord was not together—*that* didn't bother them much, they expected that! What they were looking for was conviction in the communication of their work and, needless to say, they wanted this communication to be of *their* work and not of somebody else's distortion!"

Despite his insistence that absolute perfection is not his goal, Levine works and reworks at details of operas, which he conducts over a number of seasons, both in Salzburg and at the Metropolitan—improving and polishing things, always insisting that this passage was not really as good as it could be and should therefore be approached in a different way, or that this balance here and that pacing there were not quite right. He explains that continued exposure to a work always leads to new insights, and that a lot of things may need modification even after he has conducted it dozens of times.

This doesn't mean that his original conception of the work has changed, but that it is being modified by all the other human beings involved, "by the fact that when you sit down to work with a cast, they have ideas, too, they are human beings, too, they are artists, too. Occasionally, you might have a conflict and when you work through that, you may sometimes end up with something that is better for this circumstance than what you originally envisaged."

However detailed a conductor's conception of a work might be, he maintains it should never be too rigid, because every time he comes to conduct it he will be dealing with different orchestras, different halls, different acoustics and different singers, and while certain things in his conception can be fairly clear—tempo-range, the quality of sound, character intentions—these are subtleties, nuances and details which cannot be objectively fixed but have to be worked out together with the other artists.

"A certain degree of flexibility is therefore essential to an operatic conductor. Say I am performing an aria with a singer who can make every conceivable expressive point at a tempo just one-split-hair slower than I originally wanted. Would I not be an idiot to force him? All that would happen is that we would lose all those expressive points and not get what I wanted either! That doesn't mean that I would take any deviation from my mental image of the work lying down. Not at all. But one must work at it and shape it, exactly as if one were working in clay, and try to bring out the singers' best assets and diffuse their liabilities. And every singer, every conductor, every human being has liabilities!"

Singers are quick to respond to his deep and rare understanding of the voice. "Jimmy can really talk a singer's language," says Sherill Milnes. "He has incredible insight into the range, potential and problems of each individual voice and often comes up with amazingly *technical* suggestions related to the shaping of a phrase. Believe me, this is very rare indeed! Very few conductors can talk about the voice and really know where it's coming from!" Placido Domingo agrees and considers Levine one of those conductors whom he most enjoys working with. Apart from his understanding and empathy for singers and singing, "it is marvellous to see his cheery face in the pit during a performance, and realize that he is the first to enjoy everything that you do well!"

Levine finds his terrifyingly responsible and taxing job immensely gratifying, "and more so every year, because I am working on some of the greatest musical masterpieces with the greatest artists and with a company in which the chemistry, the rapport, is constantly growing. The pride and enthusiasm here is tremendous and everybody seems to be giving more every year." An essential part of his job as Music Director is to develop house talents—Neil Shicoff, Maria Ewing and Kathleen Battle are Met products—and not a week goes by without his having a coaching session with singers not currently singing with him or working with others on operas they are doing with different conductors, because this is the best way to fight the sad decline in vocal standards that has plagued opera in the last couple of decades, and which is now beginning to improve.

"All sorts of factors contributed to this decline: first, too much singing; secondly, too much travelling; thirdly, a dearth of good teachers; fourthly, the need for people to exploit singers beyond their capacities at a time when opera was proliferating, with more and more opera houses springing up all over the place. But I think that now a number of conductors in my generation have started influencing things in a constructive way. By staying in one place for longer periods ourselves, we are helping things to balance again, and a greater awareness of this problem on the part of music teachers, managers and the opera houses themselves can help improve the situation even further.

"We now find ourselves going into a period when operatic productions are displaying an unprecedented level of musical/theatrical totality. Originally we had a period when vocal development triumphed, but opera was often dramatically ridiculous. This was followed by a time when there were great dramatic strides, but opera was vocally inadequate. Now, the pendulum has begun to balance somewhere in the middle, and this balance is essential to the medium, because if the composers themselves hadn't wanted this musical-dramatic unity, they could easily have written oratorios.

"Voice teachers in particular can do a great deal to help shape and develop the singers of the future. In general, the aim of a voice teacher should be to maximize a singer's assets, minimize his or her defects, and balance them in such a way that when the singer is fully trained, no one can tell any more what was easy and what was hard to master. If, for example, a young singer appears with a wonderful expressive gift and no vocal technique, you should work on technique; if another has a wonderfully trained but dull voice, you should work on expression; if a third one has both but no flair for languages, you should obviously concentrate on that, and so on."

Levine tries to apply these principles when working with singers and cites *Otello*, which he prepared twice in 1979—once with Jon Vickers and once with Placido Domingo in the title role—as an example. Each time, he had to change the tempi in certain parts, and pace some things differently, to suit each of the two artists. "I couldn't imagine two more different artists or two more different interpretations of the same role! Placido is an incredible musician, has a beautiful Italianate voice, is very comfortable with the language and sings the part with impeccable style. Vickers is a towering, skilled dramatic lion who sings the role with an overwhelming intensity and has a voice with tremendous pulling power. You couldn't say that one is better than the other without first defining your priorities. I try to support, encourage and merge with the assets of each artist."

He stresses the fact that composers were looking for artists who were empathetic with their creations, and you don't help achieve this empathy by putting square plugs into round holes or by working in a high-handed, dictatorial way. "You do it by establishing good communication and rapport with your fellow artists and by being flexible, as long as the basic conception of the work and the spirit of the particular production are not interfered with. If the artist in question is capable of changing whatever I think is not quite right, I insist that he does so. But there are times when to insist would ruin the psychological underpinning of the artist to the extent of making him unable to communicate his assets, so one must exercise a lot of judgement. And of course, one is not always right!"

Although Levine devotes most of his time to the Met, he is an annual visitor to the Salzburg Festival, where he has conducted *Die Zauber-flöte*, *La clemenza di Tito* and *Les Contes d'Hoffmann*. Even though he would love to accept invitations from La Scala, the Vienna State Opera and Covent Garden, he does not at present conduct staged opera anywhere else, but does a limited number of guest appearances with a handful of the world's top orchestras, like the Vienna, the Berlin and the Philadelphia Orchestra, and the Chicago Symphony. He is also Music Director of the Ravinia Summer Festival (the summer home of the Chicago Symphony).

"I don't rush around trying to be everywhere, every year. First of all I can't, because the Met is my top priority and consumes most of my time, and secondly because I can't see how that could be good for my artistic growth. One has to choose and pace everything, and right now I'm doing a selective number of things at great density. In ten years' time, things might be totally different. I might be working full time with an orchestra and doing three operatic productions a year, plus a month at a festival. Eight years after that, I might be spending six months with an orchestra and the other six travelling about and doing productions of the same opera with the same director in four different opera houses, and playing some recitals with a couple of singers with whom I would develop a strong artistic relationship over a long period of time."

He seems to have no limitations in repertoire or style, and attributes this to the good fortune of having been born a naturally very talented person, "which means that it is very easy for me to do bad work. I have perfect pitch, I am able to play almost anything on the keyboard and learn scores superficially easily. This is why I try double-hard and give myself a lot of time to go through all their levels. My definition of talent has always been that it is the ability to get results *if you work hard*. Because everything, all music, is difficult. It's only a matter of degree."

While his own immense talent ensures that he experiences no fundamental difficulties in mastering scores, there are two kinds of music which he finds particularly difficult at the time of performance. "The most difficult is the kind of music that is overwhelmingly emotionally draining and which demands a considerable degree of control: you can't give everything all the time, otherwise you wouldn't make it through, yet you can't withhold anything, or you wouldn't get an even flow. You've got to pace the give-and-take and guide the music carefully to its climaxes. I am referring to works like *Tristan und Isolde*, *Pelléas et Mélisande*, *Parsifal* and the big Mahler symphonies, works which wear out your nerves and your psyche and demand that you learn to give everything but be able to spread, control and pace it through the piece, which is excruciatingly difficult! Take *Otello*, for instance. If the tenor rants at every climax, the audience will start to yawn! It has to be *so* carefully shaped, yet the audience must experience it as spontaneous combustion all the time. And the second act of *Tristan* has to be very cannily paced, too, and yet unfold as if its flow were inevitable, the only way that the music could go.

"The other thing that's also very, very hard to conduct is music which requires an unremitting level of intensity with an unremitting level of discipline. The best example is Beethoven, who demands that you play technically very difficult, very sharply contrasted, very rhythmically disciplined music at a level of focused intensity that does not permit the ebb and flow of force and relaxation that you can use in a lot of nineteenth-century music.

"Music which *has* an ebb and flow of intensity and relaxation, and music which is not the ultimate in nervous, psychological and emotional drain, is somewhat less difficult to conduct. In operatic terms, this means that melodramas, like *Tosca* and *Il tabarro*, and works of a straightforward dramatic thrust, like *Il trovatore* and *Un ballo in maschera*, are a little easier to do than the works I just mentioned. But some of the classical works, especially Mozart's, are also very difficult because they have so many more elements to balance in the psychological and dramatic areas, but with fewer notes and a greater demand for the right atmosphere, transparency and rhythmic discipline."

He finds that difficulties stemming from purely technical problems are far less interesting. Because, while there are considerable technical difficulties in Debussy's *Ibéria*, in the third movement of the Schumann 'Spring' Symphony, for example, and in a lot of the standard nineteenth- and early twentieth-century Italian operas of Mascagni, Leoncavallo and Puccini, for example, a conductor "can solve all of them and still not give a good performance of these works".

After conducting a performance of *Tristan* or *Pelléas*, he can seldom go to sleep until four or five in the morning, because he is still too much in the world of the piece to let it go, and often goes over the whole performance again in his head. But sometimes he also finds it hard to unwind after the première of a very happy piece, because he's too excited, and on such occasions he prefers to go out to dinner with friends. But most often, he goes straight back to his flat, has something light to eat, reads a little or goes over the score he has just conducted once more, then straight to bed.

He prefers to work up to a performance by having as normal a day as possible until four o'clock in the afternoon, but avoiding any unnecessary expenditure of energy. "I don't like an idle day. I find that I don't conduct well after an idle day. I haven't got my body going, I haven't got sufficient energy. Trying to make my concentration and my muscles work at top capacity after lying flat all day is too much of a shock. So, I try to do something that gets me out of the house and walking and moving and awake, and at about four in the afternoon, I drop everything, lie down for a couple of hours, then have something light to eat and go. I don't in the least mind having a rehearsal in the morning, even a dress rehearsal. The only thing I find a problem is having to conduct a Friday-evening performance followed by a Saturday matinée of a long opera."

He finds that the "least pleasurable" part of his work is studio recording, first because it is under such financial pressure that one can't have a moment's relaxation or contemplation. A tape is made, then everybody has to rush to the control room, listen with full concentration and see what is there and what isn't, then rush back and make another take, or patch this one up. "No one could say this is fun. Once I've given everything I have to the last movement of a Mahler symphony, the last thing I want or need is to have to listen to it on the spot then turn around and do it again."

Secondly, he feels that the standard studio result has become completely divorced from what 'live' music really is. He is a great lover of live recordings—most of the ones he listens to are 'live' or 'pirate' tapes!—and hopes that one day the majority of his own recordings will also be "live", because for him the only purpose in recording is documentation: preserving the work of certain singers, conductors and soloists of each era, and he thinks that the ideal way to record would be to tape three 'live' performances and take any given scene from one of the three.

"My only objection to recording is when it becomes a medium in itself, divorced from 'live' human performance. 'Live' human performances have technical flaws, composers *expected* them to have technical flaws, as we already discussed, because *people* have technical flaws. Composers only complained about *conceptual* flaws, and I would like recordings to reflect that. I would like them to be recordings of some of the great music-making that goes on at every point in time, and not something produced in a can for a can!"

He is aware of a contradiction in himself, for he is one of those rare birds who don't actually mind about the absence of a 'live' audience in the recording studio, because he is aware and conscious of his relationship to the score and to his colleagues and can therefore conduct a hyper-emotional performance of the piece for the composer and for himself; he does, nevertheless, acknowledge that the presence of a 'live', excited and responsive audience can make him give out more vitality and take more gambles.

"You always get something from the audience which is, perhaps, on a metaphysical level. You feel it, you smell it, your sixth sense gives it to you. And instead of playing safe, you try to give them every possible excitement. This is also true of singers. Take a tenor who may have a very difficult high note, which he usually saves himself for. When an audience is giving him an enormously warm feedback, he may try to make it on that evening *without* saving himself, knowing that if he doesn't quite make it, the audience will understand and still be excited! But for a dull, drab, or hostile audience who react as if they were listening to the radio or watching TV, he will play safe and make damn sure he gets that top note!"

Levine is "obsessional" about music and cannot imagine even a day without it. Even when he goes on vacation, even when he is away from rehearsals and performances for a few days, even on a boat trip, he still studies his scores, and says that this is part of his breathing. Yet if he lives long enough, he would like to reach a point when he would work a maximum of nine months a year and leave the rest free for "doing spontaneous things, like learning another language, playing a recital tour for a singer, spending four months in my holiday home in upstate New York.... Once in a while, I find myself getting up in the morning and spending the day walking in the mountains and the woods, or lying in the sun, taking a nap in the afternoon, then playing a little game of bridge in the evening, or studying a score or reading a book, and thinking Mmmm... I could easily imagine myself drifting into a pattern like this and feeling a deep sense of peace, contentment and gratification.... But would it compare with the excitement of my present life? Of course not. But life goes in phases.

"Which brings us to my big, basic, internal conflict: much as I love people and working with people, I sometimes feel that, psychologically, I would have been better cut out as a composer. Don't misunderstand me. I am happy that my 'career' is 'a success', mainly because it enables me to work with the best artists in the best conditions. But I have never made a single decision in my life solely for the furtherance of my career. I don't believe in doing that. If anything, it takes away from what you do. You have to be who you are and do what you *want*, what seems right for your artistic growth at each particular moment."

Apart from walking, what relaxes him most is swimming and reading—about sixty-to-seventy-per-cent fiction, and thirty-per-cent social criticism and philosophical essays—and re-reading because he doesn't like "in one ear and out the other". He avoids periodical literature, which he finds "awful, because everything is so watered down and so full of inaccuracies, as I have observed when reading about things I know something about, that it would amount to a waste of time. And I never, literally never, read the daily papers, I just can't. They all look alike to me. I used to try, but after a while, I found that one day's papers said pretty much the same thing as the next day's. The worst thing about the so-called media explosion is that it enables people to pretend they are interested in what they have not experienced first hand. They sit around and dish out pre-digested opinions.... I find this so frightening that I sometimes have a surrealistic image of human beings evolving into people with very tiny, semi-adequate eyes and ears but very huge mouths!"

He is fascinated by words and precision of communication. "I am sick to death of generalities, of vague, foggy ideas and words. I am fascinated by detail. I find that my ability to feel pleasure, delight and fulfilment in relation to myself, another person or a work of art, depends upon their specific individuality, and I have come to value two human qualities above all others: character, intelligence, and the ability to think. By character I mean people who, in any moment of truth, will be who they are; and by intelligence and ability to think I mean people who understand the difference between fretting, worrying, debating, and *thinking*. I want to see people who know how to think about a specific point and why it is different from, and in what ways it is similar to, another point, people who can think in the way that the ancient Greeks understood the word, and are not such a mass of defence mechanisms, reaction patterns, habits, religious conditioning or nerves, that they cannot think.

"Because we don't communicate only in metaphysical, i.e. vibrational and chemical ways. (This very important kind of communication is often debased, though, by people always remarking that they know what one means. But do they really?) We also communicate in specifics, and the more accurate this communication of words and ideas, the stronger and more all-pervasive our general perceptions will become.

"And one of the greatest mysteries on this planet is the universal communication of music, its ability to communicate moods and feelings with a density and immediacy that amounts to an electric charge. A good example of this is a poem which one might have known since childhood. If one learns a musical setting for it—say Schubert's settings of Goethe poems or Britten's *Serenade* [for tenor, horn and strings]—one can never again think of the poem without its musical setting, can one? It communicates the essence, the deepest meanings of the poem far more deeply than the words it was written in.

"In fact I doubt that I, or that any of us musicians, fully understand the mystery of the communication of music, of how notation, those black ink spots, manage to transcend the obstacle of language barriers, which is why people all over the world are listening in full concert halls and opera houses to *St Matthew Passion*s, to *Eroica* symphonies, to *Figaro*s and *Otello*s. And I always wonder whether all the great composers, Bach and Beethoven, Mozart and Verdi had any idea that one, two hundred years after their death, the music they left behind them would have lost none of its power to communicate with all the peoples of the world...."

LORIN MAAZEL
Master Technician

Sounds of Mozart's A major Violin Concerto wafted out of Lorin Maazel's dressing room at the Royal Albert Hall, London, where we were to meet for our first interview. He was due to play this work in France in a few days' time and had seized this short gap in an otherwise frenetic schedule for putting in some extra practice. Not surprisingly, I lingered on for a few minutes before knocking, enjoying the exquisite sound and regretting the fact that we in Britain never had a chance to hear his record of two Mozart violin concertos which in the seventies had outsold all his other records in Germany by ten to one. Of course, I knew his recording of *Thaïs*, in which he plays the violin solo in the 'Meditation' 'for fun', having borrowed the Vieuxtemps Guarneri for the purpose. But I had not realized that from time to time he still played the violin in public.

"Oh, yes!" he replied. "I love it. As a matter of fact, I have recently been trying to do a bit more violin playing than usual. Because a violinist's best years are over by the age of fifty-five, and I am now forty-nine. After that, there begins a gradual, a very gradual, decline which has to do with muscle flexibility and which, in very great virtuosos, might remain imperceptible for many years. Before each appearance, I like practising all day long, on and off, to keep my hands warm and supple. Because stiffness spells death to a virtuoso. If you're stiff when you go on stage, a certain roughness comes into your playing, because your hands just aren't ready for it. To do what you've prepared yourself to do they need to be loose and supple. Practising the violin requires a very high degree of concentration. So many things— control, focusing your energy, making your blows tell—have to be practised with extreme precision." Which is why, before such a concert, Maazel likes to be quiet and avoids giving out any unnecessary nervous or physical energy.

"Because when you're out there playing and giving it your all, every muscle in your body aches. You may sometimes touch beautiful phrasing, and you're thrilled by it, you're happy and not unmoved.... Yet all the time you're controlling everything, knowing just what you want to do and saying to yourself: 'Now, I'm going to communicate. I'm going to get it out from within me and across in sound. I'm going to make it happen so that anyone listening will know what I'm feeling.' So off you go and obviously the effort of it all might produce a stance, a violin stance. You may have noticed that when I stand out there I don't move, I don't grimace, I don't do anything. My hands and fingers alone must do the work and communicate what is in my mind. Acting is not necessary. My profession is communication, not self-indulgence."

This attitude of controlled concentration applies as much to Maazel the conductor as to Maazel the violinist, and is one of the reasons why the (now) fifty-two-year-old Music Director of the Orchestre National de France and General Director of the Vienna State Opera has the reputation of being as cool as a cucumber—on and off the podium.

He sees his function as the obligation not just to communicate, but "to communicate honestly" what he thinks and feels about a composition not through words, verbal explanations and podium mannerisms, "but through the various techniques that one uses as a conductor". He stresses that by technique he doesn't mean merely the ability to beat time and execute the letter of a score. A conductor, he maintains, has to use his cultural knowledge to place a particular score in the right context, both within the composer's overall development and within the period of its composition.

"But bringing a lot of unfocused energy on stage, like some kind of raging sea lion, is completely superfluous and redundant. What you are trying to do is communicate what it is you have to say about the work—if you have something to say, and the assumption is that you do—and produce a result that is technically acceptable and spiritually meaningful. Now, in order to reach that stage, you must obviously be talented for the profession." The attributes which, in his opinion, constitute "a talent for the profession" are good pitch, as near to perfect pitch as possible; an excellent memory, both visual and aural; a knowledge of instruments and of the orchestra, preferably based on some experience as an orchestral player; a thorough knowledge of the repertoire; plus a manual gift for conducting.

For many years, he ran a Conductors' Symposium in Cleveland, at which applicants were first given a list of works to memorize. Next, they were asked to open one of them at some random page and explain exactly where this was within the context of the whole work. Then they were told to write down a page from one of the prescribed scores from memory. Lastly, they had to write a fugue to a prescribed theme. If they managed to get through this tough first stage, they went on to phase two, which consisted of a fifteen-minute exposure to the orchestra—with eight minutes to rehearse in, and seven for the performance—during which they had to conduct a five-minute work. This was to show whether, despite nerves and inexperience, there was any communication. "And I don't mean a ballet, but functional conducting," says Maazel. "What I was looking for was that inner fire."

The current debasement of standards which afflicts his profession saddens him and he deplores the fact that inexperienced, inadequately trained musicians are nowadays being hailed as conductors. This, he bemoaned to *The New York Times* a couple of years ago, sometimes includes world-famous soloists who expect to become conductors at the drop of a hat and who, because of their virtuosity as instrumentalists, demand to be taken seriously as conductors despite their total lack of experience. Conducting is an art which requires long, long training and constant polishing, constant reviewing of everything that a conductor has done in the past. It also implies "access to the true flow of the piece and a sense of the time elapsed from the first note to the last". And he is quoted as having told *The New York Times* on February 17, 1978 that only three conductors today have this ability of cohesion and generally maintain the necessary standards in "the profession" (the way he always refers to conducting): Herbert von Karajan, Georg Solti—and Lorin Maazel.

Many would argue that this statement is a pointer to a certain arrogance which is considered to be a characteristic of both Maazel the conductor and Maazel the man, and which seems to enter into his dealings with orchestras and musicians, who almost invariably admire but seldom like him. In fact he has the distinction of having had a rehearsal break down at the Royal Opera House, Covent Garden during the preparation of Verdi's *Luisa Miller*. Anyone connected with the music business knows that Covent Garden is one of the cosiest, most relaxed and friendly places to work in and that its musicians are generally very well-disciplined, hard-working and good-tempered people, whose relations with guest conductors are seldom strained.

"The second rehearsal for *Luisa Miller* was after the dress rehearsal for *Tristan und Isolde*, from six to nine-thirty in the evening," remembers one of the violinists. "Needless to say, the orchestra were exhausted. Maazel said that he would therefore take this rehearsal reasonably easily. Well, he didn't. He didn't finish until one minute before nine-thirty, and as if this weren't enough, he proceeded to tell people how to play the violin. Of course he *is* a very accomplished violinist, but he should have known that after playing a whole dress rehearsal of *Tristan*, which is both physically and emotionally draining, they just would not take this kind of onslaught." The next few days, things went from bad to worse, with comments like: "Please, ladies and gentlemen, this is completely unacceptable. It's nasal, metallic, unpleasant and everything we don't want Verdi to be. Let's try it again, shall we?" Finally, one rehearsal broke down and was resumed only after the tactful intervention of Sir Colin Davis.

I observed a tendency to sarcasm in most of his rehearsals that I attended. All were extremely precise, concise and concentrated, slightly didactic in manner, and usually lacked humour, or any sort of human contact with the players. I suspect that he is aware of this problem in himself, even though he defends it by saying that "in this profession, modesty is stupid".

"It's a question of having to do the job that one has been given and that one has decided that, for one reason or another, one can fulfil. If you don't fulfil it, you will be replaced, whether you like it or not. Nobody's ever re-engaged who doesn't deliver the goods. So, obviously, they re-engage you because they think that you can still fill the bill, or do the job, as the saying goes. And if you *can* do the job, there is no point in hesitating, no point in saying well, what am I doing here, somebody else could do it better. That's not modesty. It's false modesty. And in my experience, it often means disguised egotism." To me, it didn't seem like a problem of modesty true or false—in any case the number of modest conductors around is nearly zero—but of warmth, charm and the quality of creating not merely an efficient but also a pleasant working atmosphere around him—a quality which he seems to lack. Perhaps this is why, to everybody's surprise, he is the only conductor who employs a firm of public relations consultants full time.

But perhaps the explanation for this sharp contrast between his public persona, which is cool, distant and supercilious, and his very pleasant, courteous and sensitive manner in private, is to be found in his unusual, and perhaps difficult, childhood. An American of Russian extraction, Maazel was born at Neuilly-sur-Seine, just outside Paris on March 6, 1930. His parents soon moved back to the United States and when Lorin was four, his father noticed that he had perfect pitch. A year later, he was encouraged to learn how to play the piano and the violin. A couple of years later he also started studying conducting in Pittsburgh, and made such rapid progress that he was launched into a career as a prodigy conductor.

At the age of nine, he conducted the Interlochen Orchestra at the New York World Fair, and the Los Angeles Philharmonic at the Hollywood Bowl, sharing the podium with Leopold Stokowski. Two years later, Toscanini invited him to conduct the NBC Orchestra, and this was followed by an invitation to conduct the New York Philharmonic in a summer concert at Lewisohn Stadium. At the age of thirteen, he first conducted the Cleveland Orchestra, whose Music Director he was destined to become many years later, to very favourable notices.

Yet he did not enjoy life as a prodigy and would have infinitely preferred a normal childhood. "Children don't really like performing. I was not exactly pushed, but certainly encouraged to do it and while I didn't like it, I didn't resist it, either. I did enjoy the music, but I didn't enjoy anything else. I hated those rehearsals, I hated walking on stage, standing in front of all those people and trying to impose the authority of a ten-year-old mind on all those forty-year-old-plus minds. But I took my music-making very seriously, had a lot of poise and was very self-assured. But it was probably all a sham because otherwise I could see no point in standing there, on the podium, in short trousers, somewhat overweight and with hair a trifle too long...."

Even though his professional appearances were limited to about ten a year and confined to the school holidays, he was made acutely aware of being somehow "different" by the other children at school who, on the whole, tended to be beastly. "But I was a tough little kid who could hold my own physically. I was by no means a fragile little boy. I boxed pretty well, I was a pretty good wrestler, I played football, and was therefore able to survive reasonably well, which gave me self-confidence." Although he would rather have led a normal life, he does not blame his parents for pushing him into an early career, which in any case enabled him to "absorb the professional world of music at a very receptive age". They were certainly not motivated by greed. Misguided ambition is the term he would use.

"But I decided long ago that one has no time in life to waste worrying about what one's parents did, right or wrong, when one was two-and-a-half. Forget it and get on with life—that's my motto. That's why I have never been psychoanalysed or anything like that. I've never seen any reason for it. I don't want to spend an hour on a couch, I want to get on with things: work, read a good book, get a suntan, make love to a girl, *do* something."

Maazel's years as a prodigy conductor were succeeded by a phase in his teens during which, having shed his "market value as a child monstrosity", he suddenly found himself a nobody. He spent those years, before re-emerging as a fully-fledged adult conductor, studying mathematics, languages and philosophy at Pittsburgh University. At the same time, he played the violin in the Pittsburgh Symphony, where he graduated to the position of leader and, during his junior year, served as apprentice conductor. He also organized the Fine Arts String Quartet of Pittsburgh, in which he played the violin.

To this day, chamber music is what he most enjoys listening to for relaxation—symphonic music seems too much like a busman's holiday. He also loves folk music, particularly the Portuguese *fado*, and Indian classical music, which he discovered during a visit to the subcontinent, inspired by his father's keen interest in Buddhism (which meant that he had begun reading Upanishads at the age of eight). He learnt a lot about it while in Madras, has since acquired a large collection of records and considers this to be "the music of future, the nearest thing to the music of the spheres".

In 1951 he was invited by Serge Koussevitsky to the Berkshire Music Center at Tanglewood for two consecutive summers. At the same time he won a Fulbright Scholarship to study baroque music in Italy, an experience which he found fascinating and enriching. Indeed, he would counsel every aspiring young conductor to spend some time in Europe, "the best possible finishing school", because of the opportunity it offers to absorb many different kinds of idiomatic playing. In any case, he considers a knowledge of several languages and of the culture of many places to be essential for a conductor.

His European career started in 1953, when he substituted for a sick colleague in Catania. This was followed by a slow build-up until four years later, he conducted the opening concert at the Vienna Festival. In 1960, a few months after his thirtieth birthday, he made his Bayreuth début, with *Lohengrin*. Three years later came his début at the Salzburg Festival with *Le nozze di Figaro*. He was the first of the new wave of young conductors who were to make their names in the sixties and seventies. "Early on I decided that a mediocre career in the Arts is a very boring life. So, I resolved to be in the first class."

In 1965, he was appointed Music Director of the Deutsche Oper, Berlin, where he was to remain for six years, and Chief Conductor of the Berlin Radio Orchestra, where he was to stay for a further four years, until 1975. This meant the simultaneous tenure of both an operatic and a symphonic full-time post, something which, because of the enormous pressures that running a major opera house entails, is very rare indeed. Yet the opportunities that such a combination offers for a broad, overall musical development are colossal. And Maazel made good use of them, emerging from his Berlin years as one of the most impressive conductors on the music circuit.

At the Deutsche Oper, he changed a great many things that needed to be changed, often after considerable struggle: he ensured that the same musicians played in the pit at every performance of a particular production; insisted that even the casts of repertory evenings have at least one full stage rehearsal, something unheard of in German repertory houses; provided a double cast for every new production and specified that it, too, should have equal rehearsal time with the conductor, thus achieving almost a *stagione* system within a repertory house; made drastic changes to the repertoire, which had hitherto included no *Ring*, no baroque opera and no Italian opera sung in the original language! (During his tenure, all new productions of Italian operas were sung in Italian.)

Unlike most operatic Music Directors who emerge from their posts vowing never again to head an opera house—once in a lifetime is definitely enough, it seems—Maazel, after an interval of ten years as an exclusively symphonic Music Director, found himself longing for total involvement with opera again. Our interviews took place before his appointment as General Director of the Vienna State Opera had been decided. At the time, he was conducting and recording the very successful production of *Luisa Miller* at the Royal Opera House, Covent Garden, and was so elated at the experience of working with a first-class cast, a first-class producer in a first-class opera house that he felt an impulse to go and buy a sweatshirt and stamp it with "I LOVE OPERA!"*

"I really do. Enjoy it enormously. I like it well done and get terribly upset over performances when, for some reason or another, it is not

---

* He has a vast selection of colourful shirts and ties, which he seems to collect, and for which he is famous throughout the music world.

well done. And I try to make my contribution, for what it is worth, to ensure that at least the musical part of the undertaking is really at an acceptable level. Which is why I have always refused to conduct opera unless conditions are absolutely right. I do it for love. No other reason. I'm not here to earn a living. I'm here for purely selfish reasons: to enjoy myself. Opera takes up a great deal of time and requires a lot of very hard work. Therefore I want nothing but the best conditions available today, in order to make the experience a happy one."

Naturally, Maazel has strong views about the controversial role of the stage director in opera today, and about the much-publicized conflict between conductors and stage directors. In view of the fact that he is now starting to run one of the great opera houses of the world, his thoughts on the subject are of particular importance.

"To direct an opera, one obviously needs a visual and dramatic sense as developed as the aural sense of the conductor. Because conductors don't necessarily have a visual sense. In fact, a great number of musicians have no visual sense at all and are therefore incapable of staging an opera except in an oratorio-like way of placing the singers at an advantageous position and wrapping the whole thing from there. And when I talk about visual sense I mean the ability to translate sounds into motion. Because stage direction is not merely a question of where you make people stand—after all there are only so many places on stage where they *can* stand—but of the interaction of scenery, lighting, costumes and the music.

"All this requires a great deal of expertise and very, very few conductors have the talent, or the time, to develop themselves as seriously as one must in order to direct opera successfully. I know exactly what I am talking about, having once directed an opera myself—*Eugene Onegin* in Rome. I took it very, very seriously and devoted a great deal of time to the task and collaborated really closely with the designers. I happened to be in Moscow shortly before going to Rome, so I had a chance to see the photographs of the very first production of the work at the Moscow Conservatoire. Then I checked up every production of this opera that had ever been done, anywhere.

"Then I read the Pushkin story and asked myself: What images do you visualize when listening to Tchaikovsky's music? What do you believe *he* was visualizing while writing this music? And the ideas came to me instantly and spontaneously, sort of springing out of the music. I made detailed notes of everything as I saw it then: positions on stage, movements, coordination of movements with text and music, everything down to the last detail. And only about two per cent of these had to be changed during the course of the production.

"I mention all of this because it is not the case with so many so-called great stage directors who in fact haven't the vaguest idea of what they are doing. They will call a cast rehearsal, everybody will be on stage, and our hero will be pacing up and down somewhere in the fourteenth row of the stalls, surrounded by assistants, his head in his hands, or better still, his chin in his chest, and hands behind his back, waiting for inspiration!

"And finally, about ten minutes later, he'll say, 'I have it: you, you, you, move to the left, no, not quite that far, just a little bit, yes, that's it. We'll have a tableau there for Act Three . . .' and the assistant will then point out that, sir, these people are not in Act Three but in Act Two. In any case, after three-quarters of an hour, he decides that the tableau that struck him as being so spectacular really wasn't quite what he was looking for, and the singers are moved back to where they were standing in the first place, an hour ago.

"Now, this sort of thing drives everybody insane and the pretentiousness of these untalented and unprepared stage directors knows no bounds and goes in inverse proportion to their talent: the less talented, the more pretentious they are. And this creates an atmosphere where unnecessary conflicts arise and you get a prototypical profile of those relationships, i.e. the historic clash between conductor and stage director. And everybody says, look, they are running true to form. Needless to say this is nonsense, because such clashes only arise out of desperation.

"But assuming that you are not dealing with a charlatan but with somebody who *is* intelligent and well prepared, who *has* a visual and a dramatic sense, who knows the theatre and the text, then the next question is, is he musical? Can he respond to what the score implies? Not insofar as the thrust of the story is concerned, but to the way that the composer chose to treat the story from the interpretative point of view. Because a composer responds to the dramatic events of a given story in a subjective way and writes a certain kind of music. Another composer may write a very different kind of music to the same story— Massenet's *Manon* and Puccini's *Manon Lescaut* are a good example of what I mean.

"The stage direction should therefore reflect not the stage director's interpretation of the story, but his reflection of the *composer's* interpretation of the story, which is quite a different thing. In short, one is asking of a stage director to be sensitive to the medium, the art form, he has chosen to work in. And I can't think of more than two stage directors who combine all those qualities. One of them is Joseph Losey, with whom I collaborated on our film of *Don Giovanni*, in which he did a magnificent job." (The other is Filippo Sanjust, whom he considers to be "a minor genius. And if *I* say *that*, it means he is pretty close to God!")

Like all responsible operatic conductors, Maazel is concerned not only about the problem of unmusical stage directors, but also about the grievous dearth of good singers that afflicts opera today, and most especially about the number of good voices that are prematurely ruined by overwork and unintelligent over-extension. He has seen this happen to no less than four gifted young singers whom he had personally cautioned against doing too much too soon.

"Because the voice is an instrument which grows stronger over the years—in fact it is at its peak condition sometime between thirty-three and forty-three—and a young voice can be torn apart by a schedule that an older voice would think nothing of sustaining. But as soon as a promising youngster appears, he or she is grabbed by jackal managers and eager heads of opera houses, stretched in the wrong direction until nothing of their initial vocal bloom is left. This is such a serious danger that before too long there will be no singers for certain operas."

A problem with which the future General Director of the Vienna State Opera has very good reason to be concerned. Although he officially assumed this post on September 1, 1982, he was already actively involved in the planning of the 1982–83, '83–84 and '84–85 seasons from 1980, and has changed the repertory system into what he calls "a block system": i.e. five operas every fortnight, performed with the same cast, the same conductor and the same musicians in the pit. When each series is over, they move on to the next block of five. He has also reduced the number of operas played during each season from about twenty-eight to thirteen so that, when he takes over the house will already operate on a system that is half way towards a stagione system.

But he would still like to change the rotation system in the orchestra and the chorus and reach some compromise whereby the same musicians and choristers will be playing and singing the same repertoire within a given period. He also wants to reform the ballet, their hours of work, the way they work, the quality of the dancing and the quality of the choreography. Naturally he is very keen to develop young singers, and to expand the repertoire to include works which have so far been neglected.

"So far, apart from *Carmen*, there has been very little French repertoire: no Gounod, no Massenet, no Saint-Saëns, very little Berlioz. At the moment we are considering a production of *Benvenuto Cellini*, plus an expansion into the Slavic repertoire, which has also been neglected. I would like to see more Mussorgsky, Prokofiev, Shostakovich and some Szymanowski. But my main concern will be to maintain consistent high standards of performance, so that most evenings are on an even keel and you don't get sharp fluctuations between performances that are part of a new production and those which are odd repertory evenings." He is planning four to five new productions a season, and has committed himself to conducting about twenty-five to thirty performances each year out of about 320, i.e. ten per cent, which is a good deal but not as many as some house conductors have been conducting over the years.

Maazel is very excited about this job, particularly because it unites both the artistic and the administrative functions and gives him the clout with which to carry out his artistic policies, and does not seem put out at the prospect of having to cope with Viennese intrigue and the Viennese bureaucracy. "For a start, I *am* the bureaucracy. The Director *is* the bureaucracy, and if he chooses to exercise his full authority—and I shall—which is very great, there is no one to interfere. And I don't know why it is always called a snake pit. It is a great opera house, combining the finest imaginable ingredients in any category. There is no orchestra in any opera pit that can hold a candle to the Vienna Philharmonic,* the chorus is great, the stage is superb and very modern, and some of the great singers of the world belong to its ensemble. It's a marvellous place to work in and I think that its reputation as a nest of vipers has been fostered by other opera houses who are jealous."

As far as conductors are concerned, he believes that a great opera house needs to have the highest artistic forces united under its roof: "I hope to have the best stage directors, the best stage designers, the best singers and naturally the best conductors. And I don't believe that between 1982 and 1986 there will be any conductor of importance, fame or established reputation who will not appear in Vienna, which is a claim that no other opera house can equal."

From the purely technical point of view, he has found operatic

---

* With the exception of the Berlin Philharmonic and the Salzburg Easter Festival!

conducting a great help in acquiring an adaptable stick technique and a quickness of response to emergencies: "Because you must vary your technique from singer to singer and tailor it to each individual artist's way of responding: some singers tend to sing after the beat, while others are always ahead of it; some know the whole score, while others learn only their own parts, and in those cases you must be even more alert, make more allowances and expect more things to go wrong."

In fact, Maazel has the reputation of being one of the quickest conductors to notice and remedy any on-the-spot emergencies during a performance. The musicians of the Philharmonia Orchestra told me about a recent incident in which a well-known cellist skipped a bar at the end of the slow movement of the Dvořák Cello Concerto. "But Maazel knew straight away, went right with him, and nobody noticed anything amiss."

His association with the Philharmonia began in 1971, when he became its Associate Conductor, alongside Otto Klemperer. Later, when Muti took over as its Music Director, he was named Principal Guest Conductor until 1981. His remarkable capacity for obtaining precision of ensemble and his stupendous stick technique are greatly admired by the Philharmonia players: "Maazel is probably the greatest technician I have ever played with," says the Leader, Christopher Warren-Green. "And probably the cleverest man that one has ever seen," adds the Assistant Leader, Martin Jones. "You sit there thinking, what a *clever* man this is. And being a very good violin player, he has his own ideas about bowing, about what you should play in what position, about 'D' strings and 'G' strings. Certainly a great conductor. Yet not one to arouse a great enthusiasm in British audiences who find him too analytical and not emotional enough in his response to music. Only in the last two years has he begun to have a bigger following here in London. Until then, even concerts with what would appear to be a very popular programme would not be all that well attended. There is this lack of ... whatever it is, which communicates itself to audiences."

The orchestra's principal trumpet, John Wallace, agrees that there is "a cerebral quality to Maazel's talent—for instance even his rubati are worked out in a completely computer-like fashion, with an incredible sub-divided beat—to which French audiences would be much more attuned, because of the mental, analytical qualities of their own temperament, but which is alien to the British, who prefer a more instinctive, more emotional response to music."

In 1972, a year after he began his term as Associate Conductor of the

Philharmonia, Maazel was appointed Music Director of the Cleveland Orchestra, which had had no chief conductor since Georg Szell's death in 1970, and was in a pretty grim position with only twenty-three-per-cent subscriptions, a sizeable deficit and no recording contracts. Within a few seasons under Maazel, it became fully subscribed again, and began recording with both Decca and CBS. Indeed, two of their recordings for Decca—*Porgy and Bess* and Prokofiev's *Romeo and Juliet*—won the Grand Prix du Disque Mondiale. (These recordings are remarkable not only for the staggering precision so characteristic of Maazel's conducting, but also for the commitment one senses on his part, which is what distinguishes his truly great performances from the merely technically dazzling ones.) His first task on arrival in Cleveland was to restore the orchestra to its former status and then maintain it at that level throughout his tenure. Another principal aim was to expand its repertoire to include many more contemporary works.

The British composer Gerard Schurmann, whose works Maazel has introduced in the USA through performances with the Cleveland Orchestra, says, "As a composer, I am enormously impressed by the warm and positive commitment of his musicianship. It seems to me quite extraordinary and ironic that the liberating qualities of his polished conducting technique and craftsmanship could by some people be regarded as an emotionally inhibiting factor, unless emotion is somehow misguidedly equated with a kind of idiosyncratic self-indulgence. In Maazel's case, the technique is anyway so innate that it has simply become an extension of his personality. I once said something to him about that phenomenal ability of his to conduct even a brand new work almost from memory. He explained that he tries to approach a piece in the earliest stages of study with as fresh an ear for content and detail as possible, going so far as to improvise his own version by adding and elaborating alternative phrases here and there. After these initial notions, he returns to the true text and tries to understand why the composer has done it his way. In the course of this process he usually feels that he has come to know the work pretty well. It seems a strangely laborious method, until one appreciates the astonishing fluency with which he is able to grasp a work from the written page."

When Maazel conducted Sir Michael Tippett's oratorio *A Child of our Time*, naturally he had his own views about how it should be done. The composer, who makes a point of never interfering with the way conductors interpret his compositions, found that Maazel "was totally inside the work and did it magnificently". But needless to say, before a conductor can do any composer's work justice he needs an orchestra capable of responding to any challenge in virtually any score. And this requires long and painstaking work.

"Orchestra building," says Maazel, "is a very slow and subtle process, which forms part of your daily work with an orchestra. It means achieving a certain kind of imaginative sound, a certain kind of imaginative phrasing, good intonation. And if you are dealing with an orchestra which has been trained to within an inch of its life in those very areas, you obviously find a lot there."

When he took over the Cleveland Orchestra it had not had a stable conductor for over two years and although it certainly was not floundering, it was, nevertheless, getting older. It took him a while to find out exactly what needed to be done, and he ended up by hiring eighteen new players, all in their mid-twenties, a new generation, and this brought down the average age by about fifteen years. "I think I can say that the orchestra is now [we were talking in 1979] completely different from what it was ten years ago, with a different sound and a much wider repertoire. Its activities must now be administratively widened, bolstered by using television and video recordings and by setting up its own summer festival, like the other great American orchestras. [Boston have Tanglewood, Chicago have Ravinia, Los Angeles have the Hollywood Bowl, Philadelphia have Robin Hood Dell, and New York have their summer season at Lewisohn Stadium.] And it must find a new home. Our hall, Severance Hall, is lovely and has great acoustics, but is a little bit too small.

"The point is that the eighties will require something more from an orchestra, and we're not going to be able to meet this challenge if we don't have proper recording and video facilities. For every orchestra should be able to record in its own home, which should be fully equipped as a film studio, like the Musikverein in Vienna and the Philharmonie in Berlin, with adequate rehearsal area and stage facilities for recording operas, which requires a large enough pit to take at least sixty musicians. Our pit at Severance Hall only has a capacity for twenty which makes it suitable only for chamber operas."

He is very excited by the prospect of televised concerts in the future, and, as far back as the early seventies, had made several experimental television programmes, and felt that televised concerts should stand on their own as living experiences and not merely as documentation. Like Karajan (who was the first to realize the potential of filmed and televised music for the future and to champion it whole-heartedly, sometimes to the sneers of his short-sighted contemporaries) he was eagerly awaiting the advent of quadraphonic sound. Meanwhile, he thought that viewers' awareness of music during televised transmissions can be increased "only by stimulating our fantasy, possibly by the use and projection of different kinds and colours of laser beams. At the moment we're at a stage when it's neither fish nor fowl", as he told the *Gramophone* in 1973. "But elements of television together with music can help create a new art form."

He has in fact made a short thirteen minute satirical film for French television, called *A Week in the Life of a Conductor*, to a musical background in which he played the violin solos himself. "It describes people's ideas and prejudices about what a conductor is and what he does, and was great fun to make! We go through a conductor's week: Monday, he meditates; Tuesday, he spends a day at the office; Wednesday, he's the Renaissance man, able to perform all kinds of sport, something of a superman; Thursday, the rehearsal; Friday, the concert; Saturday, the great lover and Sunday is Mother's Day", is how he described it at the time. The film won Third Prize at the Chicago Film Festival in the category of Comic Television Entertainment. (And no, he doesn't think that conductors make great lovers, by the way. "We are serious-minded people. Music is our profession and we care a great deal about it," he replied to a curious journalist from the London *Evening Standard* at the time!)

But, to return to 'serious' things, he is convinced that those facilities for recording and filming should be available to every great orchestra in the eighties. And none of them exists in Cleveland, as yet. "I know that they would cost a lot of money. But the longer they wait, the more they will cost, and dollars will get even more scarce. I have made my point to them quite clearly and it's really up to them to decide whether or not they wish to meet this challenge. If they don't, I will obviously reduce my commitment to the orchestra. Because up to now, this has been the basis of my activities and I have put an enormous amount and proportion of my time into it.

"And I don't feel that, nowadays, we're there merely to satisfy the justifiable yearnings of the townsfolk to have a good orchestra to play for them in their local hall. I used the word justifiable because every town ought to have its orchestra. But the Cleveland Orchestra is a world-class group which belongs not only to its city but to the world and must also satisfy other needs which have now been specified. The outcome is up to them."

These words summed up his frame of mind, i.e. ripe for a new challenge, shortly before his Vienna appointment was announced. Since then, he has resigned as Music Director of the Cleveland Orchestra, but will continue to conduct there for six weeks a season. He will also retain his very close and happy association with the Orchestre National de France, whose Principal Conductor he was named in 1977. Much to the universal admiration of the French, he has developed this group to a level which was unthinkable when he took over, and has scored spectacular successes with them. And, bearing in mind that French orchestras tend to be considerably less well disciplined, infinitely cheekier and require twice as much effort to train than their German or Anglo-Saxon counterparts, this admiration is well earned.

His popularity in France is largely due to the considerable television exposure guaranteed by this orchestra, which made him all the more aware of the lack of such a factor in Cleveland. In fact, their much-acclaimed televised cycle of the Beethoven symphonies attracted a higher number of viewers than the cup final! Naturally, he was pleased.

He hates discussing his musical interpretations—of the Beethoven symphonies or of any other works—because he is totally against the "superimposition of philosophical or intellectual ideas on the music". He feels that these should grow solely and entirely out of the music, which the conductor must know so well that "it is fixed in his brain as though it were a minidot, one of those magically all-wise dots of a computer". This gives him access to the whole flow of the work, and enables him to shape and pace it in the right way. Pacing he considers to be particularly important, and he wishes that the public would realize that this does not mean robbing the performance of spontaneity, or imply coldness, but merely doing the scientific work which is essential in all art.

"Take Brahms, for example, who is somebody to whom we look for passion, emotion or whatever. Well, he went on long country walks and worked out those symphonies note-by-note in his mind. And he wouldn't sit before the manuscript paper until he had the symphony or whatever completely worked out. The process of refinement and sheer focusing of energy involved is absolutely stupefying." And he feels that, as a conductor, he, too, must go through a similar process of analytical familiarization with every aspect of the work in hand before he can presume to abandon himself to inspiration or the grace of the moment, or whatever one likes to call it.

Obviously, maturity has a great deal to do with the evolution and refinement of a conductor's interpretations. Yet, paradoxically, although some of the details are now done differently and "the perspective is deeper", most of his interpretations remain essentially the same, even after long gaps. What does change, though, is the ability to respond to yet more composers and works that felt "foreign" during his salad days. "This is very curious, and very sudden. Out of the blue, you develop certain reactions to certain music which you used not to have, probably because you have meanwhile had some experience, you've grown older, you've matured. And you suddenly find yourself open to some works that escaped you before when in the words of I forget who, you didn't have enough life experience."

Good examples of what he means are Mahler and Sibelius, both of whom he rejected in his youth, but who are now an important part of his repertoire. Yet he came to them very late, as he explained to *Records and Recording* in the early seventies, shortly after completing his recordings of all the Sibelius symphonies. As an adolescent, he had studied Sibelius's first symphony and judged it to be "second-class Tchaikovsky". So he decided to leave Sibelius alone until a performance of the seventh symphony by the Berlin Philharmonic under Barbirolli "knocked me out" in the early sixties. He realized how silly and puerile his dismissal of this unique, totally individualistic composer had been, started studying each symphony in turn, and "grudgingly" became a lover of Sibelius.

As far as Mahler is concerned, he had always loved the second symphony, the 'Resurrection', and the ninth, but shared the conventional objections towards the rest, i.e. that they were too long-winded and repetitious. Now, having overcome what he rightly recognized to be a "fault in myself", he has grown close to all of them.

"Now, I've got to the point where everything seems equally difficult and equally easy. At a certain level, I assume that an orchestra and a conductor are highly professional, can handle almost everything from the technical point of view and make it work. But to make it work and come together *just in the way you want* is very difficult, and a task that can never really be completely fulfilled to anybody's satisfaction. But you try. You try to make it come out just right. And some succeed more than others and the very best succeed more often than others.

"Assuming that you are a highly technically competent professional, trying to make a Mozart symphony come out right is just as difficult or just as easy as coping with Schönberg's *Variations for Orchestra*. At this point in my career, I feel precisely the same, emotionally, towards the entire repertoire. I don't fear any area more than another. My only concern is to make it come out exactly the way I hear it in my mind.

"Besides, I recently began to wonder whether, at a certain level, one can say that some works are greater than others. Is anything greater than something else which is perfect of its kind? Is a perfect lullaby less great than a Beethoven symphony, if it is functioning perfectly within its realm? Not really. Once you are on a certain level, every work is as important as another." We were talking after a sizzling all-Gershwin concert he gave at the Royal Festival Hall, which he looked as if he had enjoyed enormously. "It's brilliant music, and, until another all-Gershwin evening I gave two years ago, I hadn't touched it in twenty-five or thirty years."

But the composer he turns to when he gets "all twisted out of shape" with too much work, too little sleep or whatever, is Bach. He will listen, or preferably play, an hour of Bach and feel that everything is all right again. The music will have restored his stability and equilibrium. "Because too little sleep can make raving maniacs of us all. And what does stability basically mean? It means that you've equalized what you have in your cupboard, that you're able to function as a human being, and that you see a reason for equalizing the balance. What drives people into asylums and such like is lack of motivation. They see no reason for bothering, so they go to extremes. Whereas if you want to be creative and constructive in some way, you have to try to protect your body and mind. You have to rest them."

His favourite way of resting is to sail his "Hobiecat", a pontoon sailing boat which is great fun to sail. As often as he can, he takes off for the Cayman Islands, gets up at dawn and goes out to sea alone. He feels perfectly at ease with the elements and capable of coping with any gust of wind that may come along, despite some pretty narrow escapes.

He also loves reading and goes through great bursts of reading everything of a particular author: Graham Greene (he has a secret desire to write a musical based on *Travels With My Aunt*), John Updike, John Fowles and John Cheevers, and also plays. At the time of our interview, he was very intrigued and very irritated by Samuel Beckett. "And maybe I'm very naïve and old-fashioned in my tastes, but I love to pick up something good by de Maupassant, and sit by the pool or under a shady tree and just gorge myself with beautiful language, this marvellous, extraordinary flow of words which is almost music.... And the balance between the action and the words used to describe it is perfect."

If and when his hectic schedule permits it, he goes to art galleries and to the theatre, as often as he can. And now we are on the subject of time or rather lack of time, how does he cope with pressures which the pace of a conductor's life exerts on his personal life and relationships?

"I don't think that the strain is all due to the lifestyle that goes with the profession. It's true that my first marriage broke up. But then, so do most first marriages. Statistics are generally against them. But to call them a failure for that reason is a gross misinterpretation. Younger people have certain needs which are satisfied on a certain level at a certain time and which are then outgrown. People outgrow each other and instead of calling this a failure, we should consider it simply the end of stage one, and move on to stage two.

"But we have such old-fashioned ideas about relationships and this idea of holding fast to the same person from the moment you are sexually mature at the age of thirteen or so until you are a hundred and four is grotesque! I'm stretching the years, of course, but I fail to see why if you marry at twenty-two and are divorced and married to someone else by thirty-five, this should be considered a failure. To my mind, it would be a failure if you felt the need to, but didn't. Because this evolution, this sort of metamorphosis that human beings undergo is very natural and makes it hard for me to understand the claims of ownership that people have on each other. Or the conviction that the more time you put into a relationship, the more Brownie points you earn. People can only give each other their lives if they want to. The day may come, after a week, or after a year or after a decade when they have to go on to other relationships, to other things.

"Yet the people who have these things clear in their minds are at a great disadvantage, because they realize only too well that the people they are dealing with do *not* have these things clear in their minds. You're clear and they are not. Therefore, you will accommodate them, because it's so much easier for you to play yet another role. And so, the stronger person gives in and becomes a loser out of compassion, which is why it was said that the meek will inherit the earth, and why neurotics rule the world, feeding on the strong like leeches, like the spiritual and physical parasites they are. And you give them your strength and not once does the neurotic person recognize from whom he is deriving his strength. And when you have no more strength to feed him with, he deserts you and moves on to the next source ... and survives everything, whereas the strong people are finally sucked dry. They are the endangered species in our world, the true under-privileged minority."

Maazel is now married to Israeli pianist Israela Margalit, and has two children, a boy and a girl, as well as two teenage daughters by his first marriage. He remarked to *Records and Recording* some years ago that men always love having boys and I asked him to explain why this is such a satisfying and rewarding experience. "I'm old enough to have grown up as part of a generation of men who still entertained romantic illusions about women being delicate, divine, strange creatures who have to be protected. And I've never met with anything less than extraordinary levels of toughness in women who are very, very strong and totally *un*romantic. All notions of romance come from the males. So I'm rather intrigued to see this little boy grow up with what I recognize to be all those traditional male images and expectations, and saddened to know how inevitably and how cruelly disillusioned he is bound to be.... Whereas my girls are tough-minded, down-to-earth, practical human beings. I don't like them any the less for it, and love all my children differently but equally.

"Basically the whole man—woman relationship is crazy. We have a situation where each sex is fed by images of what the other sex is supposed to be like, but is not. So both are disappointed and disillusioned. Sometimes I can't help feeling that the Almighty should have created more than just two sexes. As it is, and here I can only speak of men, the greatest lovers—Don Juan, for example—are always the ones more sharply disillusioned, because they never take woman off the pedestal.

"But perhaps women should make an effort to throw off the yoke of feeling that they have to be liberated. It's not they who need liberation. It's men. And women should band together to free men of their problems. Women never had these problems in the first place. They always ruled the world, they never had to go out and sweat, they just stayed at home, had smelling salts, and talked.... Men went out hunting, but women stayed at home, and talked.... They talked, reflected on life and on the world, got it all together and then learnt to guide their men very subtly and with no effort whatsoever.

"Now women are working almost as much as men and, generally speaking, have less time to reflect. And I think that this is a great loss. Because here we had a super-race which, through this foolish self-deception, has decided to commit a slow, voluntary suicide in an effort to equalize not themselves, as they imagine, but the inferior being called man."

At this point his family arrived to fetch him and his son, an intelligent, scientifically inclined little boy who had been spending his morning playing chess with a computer given to him by his father—sadly the computer beat him, just—announced to me that when he grew up he would like to be a space scientist.

"That's what I, too, always wanted to be," said his father enthusiastically. "It's something I was seriously considering in those years between the two careers and would have enjoyed it enormously. But now, I wouldn't exchange lives with anyone at Houston, Texas, shooting rockets off to the moon. Not a chance. I much prefer *my* life!"

SIR CHARLES MACKERRAS
Musician and Musicologist

American-born Australian conductor Sir Charles Mackerras was knighted in the New Year Honours of 1979, at the conclusion of his indisputably successful eight-year term as Music Director of the English National Opera. Despite the fact that during this period he proved his remarkable versatility by tackling almost every area of the repertoire, Mackerras is best known as an authority on baroque music and as the foremost champion in the West of that idiosyncratic Czech genius, Leoš Janáček. He has introduced nearly all the Janáček operas to the British public, has subsequently conducted them all over the world, and is currently completing his much-acclaimed Janáček cycle on record for Decca. In fact, so famous has he become as a Janáček specialist that he could fill his diary for the next five years with Janáček assignments alone. But to avoid "the sort of narrow specialization that seems to have overtaken our age", two out of three such offers are turned down. Mackerras resents being pigeon-holed and does not call himself a specialist in this or that, although he does try "to hit the happy medium between being a musician and a musicologist".

"Generally I prefer conducting works by unusual composers or unusual works by famous composers. I'm always interested in something new, and I don't think that the public are particularly interested in hearing *my* new interpretation of a Beethoven or Brahms symphony when all the virtuoso conductors are doing them all the time. Of course, choosing a career of this kind means that I have to work much harder, that I must constantly learn new things and be engaged in research. But the reward is that I tend to know more about some areas of the repertoire than the average symphony or opera conductor and am so familiar with certain works that I can conduct them anywhere more or less at the drop of a hat."

An accurate, if a trifle over-modest appraisal of a career which, apart from the eight-year spell as Music Director of the ENO, has also included three years as First Conductor of the Hamburg State Opera, an experience partly responsible for the breadth of Mackerras's repertoire and one which has caused him to reflect a great deal on the mysterious nature of the art of conducting, "mysterious even for those who practise it".

"In German repertory theatres, a conductor has to tackle different operas all the time with no orchestral or stage rehearsals, as these are limited to new productions only, with a new cast for every performance, and is tied to beating the score exactly as always practised in that particular house. Now you would think that these circumstances would fetter him so much that he couldn't bring any sort of 'interpretation' to the performance. But it is amazing how *many* different interpretations you get, even under such conditions, simply because of the conductor's emanation, the unconscious projection of his personality, and the effect this has on the players. Basically the difference between a good conductor and a bad one is not only the quality of his musicianship, but his ability to make the players play the music the way he imagines it. And the difference between a good orchestra and a bad one lies not merely in the calibre of its playing, but also in its ability to accept and absorb all these different projections— in other words in its receptivity."

Mackerras stresses that in the art of conducting, technique and interpretation are so inextricably bound together that the conductor cannot analyse whether one or the other predominates at any given moment. "In every work there are passages where you are acutely aware of technique and technical problems and parts where you think more of the spiritual or philosophical content of the music, in exactly the same way that a singer singing a difficult coloratura has to concentrate on technique, but in a beautiful largo, is free to think more about interpretation." He also points out that although a good stick technique is supposed to consist of a clear beat and an expressive left hand, many great conductors disobey these rules yet never leave the players in any doubt as to what they want from them. "What matters is getting your results and not *how* you get them."

Mackerras's own stick technique, which is coupled with a dynamic approach and contagious enthusiasm for the music—his performances are never dull—is much appreciated by musicians and singers alike. This is how Dame Janet Baker, who has collaborated with Mackerras in productions of *Werther*, *La Damnation de Faust*, *Maria Stuarda*, *Giulio Cesare*,* *Dido and Aeneas* and *Alceste*, describes it:

"We performers call him 'Chuck-'em-up-Charlie' because of his ability to control the situation on stage, and not just in emergencies but at all times. As the machinery of the performance is working, Charlie is always using his hands in the most extraordinarily helpful way to us singers. He always knows the score so exceptionally well, that in the normal way of giving a lead he is free to control his musicians in the pit and yet manage to give an abnormal amount of attention, through his hands, to what is happening on stage. And I use the word 'abnormal' because I've never come across this to the same degree in anybody else that I've worked with in opera. There is a clarity of beat, a clarity of signal and a particularly strong sixth sense for any mishaps, which gives you the impression that he is completely divided between stage and pit. And the rapport! Sometimes you stand up there and on a really good night, you feel as if the two of you are composing the music together there and then. Wonderful.... But I suppose that this can happen because he is not only a very brilliant man, but also a *tremendous* worker, and this is rather rare. Usually it is the lesser talents, rather than the really gifted people, who have this ability for extra hard work. But allied together, brilliance and extreme industriousness are an incredible combination to find in a conductor, because you get the security, the clarity of the hands and concern with what's happening onstage *plus* the amazing preparation and grasp of the score. And suddenly, you can fly!"

Mackerras is extremely knowledgeable about the gradual emergence of the conductor and his rise to prominence. "Until the late nineteenth century, the conductor's job was just keeping the performance together. In the eighteenth and earlier part of the nineteenth century, there were always two conductors, the Konzertmeister and the Kapellmeister, and thus the violin and keyboard helped keep things together. When it later became necessary to have only one conductor, his job was confined to time-keeping and involved nothing in the nature of expression or 'interpretation'. Wagner was probably the first to think of the conductor as an interpreter and of the art of conducting in terms of emanation, and I believe that certain things that we now take for granted as far as orchestral sound is concerned, were first thought of by Furtwängler. Richter and Mahler were two great musicians who developed the art of the conductor as an interpreter

* These productions were in English, as always at the ENO.

and, although one can hear the same qualities in early recordings by great conductors like Weingartner and Leo Blech, it seems to me that none of them had this intense imagination for sound quality and colour possessed by Furtwängler. Those incredibly soft, deathly, ghostly sounds in some passages in the Beethoven symphonies which make his performances sound different from everybody else's were undoubtedly Furtwängler's invention. Every orchestra produced this sound when Furtwängler conducted. So this sound must have been *his*, and the same orchestras never produced it for anybody else. Just listen to that drum beat at the end of the Scherzo in the Fifth Symphony; it brings a completely different dimension to Beethoven."

Of course, the interpretation of music composed *before* the emergence of the conductor as we now know him is a subject on its own, and one in which Mackerras is an authority. Yet he is the first to point out that the realization of baroque music is plagued by numerous pitfalls and difficulties. "For a start 'interpreting' early music too much is a mistake, and so is taking strange tempi—either exceptionally slow or fast—which are apt to give the music too uneven or too hectic a quality. Nowadays, there is a strong wave of purism towards old music and many specialist ensembles have taken to using original, or copies of, old instruments. Some have even taken to performing this music without a conductor. Personally I prefer trying to achieve authentic stylistic conditions with modern orchestras and their modern instruments—something which presents far greater problems than conducting specialist groups who have the baroque style at their fingertips. But 'normal' symphony orchestras—like the Suisse Romande, a superb orchestra that managed to produce a very good approximation of baroque style when we did *Judas Maccabaeus* in Geneva—have to be prepared in a different way. For a start, I always give them my own material, marked exactly as I want it to be played. Today's orchestral players are trained to notice every marking regarding dynamics, rhythm and phrasing. My orchestral material contains markings of expression and rhythm designed to imitate the more restricted dynamic range of baroque instruments and the sharper rhythms of that period.

"Some of the *notes* are marked to be played shorter than they appear on paper. Simply because the sound of a note on an old violin with an old bow decays much faster than that of a modern player with his modern bow. In early music, even the most beautiful legato passages should be played shorter, as you can hear when baroque specialists like Harnoncourt play early music. The question of how far to go in achieving authentic baroque style is still open to a wide variety of answers. If you were going to be totally faithful to the eighteenth century, then you should dispense with the conductor altogether. For as we saw, his presence is an anachronism!"

Yet Mackerras concedes that the quality of the result when performing such music with modern orchestras depends not only on rehearsal time, but also on the players' receptivity to the idea. His favourite orchestra in this respect is the English Chamber Orchestra, which in spite of its name contains players of many nationalities. German orchestras he finds over-conservative in any new approach to eighteenth-century music. They are apt to say, "But why are you changing Mozart?" When he did *Die Zauberflöte* in Berlin and changed all the semi-quavers into demi-semi-quavers in order to make them play short upbeats, it was hard to convince the orchestra that what he was doing was not changing Mozart but striving after a more authentic result. However, this problem of rhythmic values is only one of several:

"There is the problem of playing trills in the style of the period. In the eighteenth century trills were played upside down as compared with how they are played nowadays. If a baroque musician saw a trill over a 'C', for instance, he would automatically begin on the note 'D' and play 'D-C', 'D-C' and so on, so that the accent is on the upper note all the time. A modern player seeing a trill over a 'C', on the other hand, would equally automatically play 'C-D', 'C-D', and has to be specially requested to play the trill in the baroque style, starting on the upper note. Even so, he often finds it very difficult to remember.

"Another question that requires careful treatment is that of the *notes inégales*, i.e. a row of notes written as if they should be played evenly but which were in fact played *un*evenly, almost as if they were dotted. This is a particularly acute problem in Handel who composed so fast that he wrote some notes dotted and others undotted, seemingly carelessly. But sometimes he intended even undotted notes to be played as if they were dotted, while at other times he left them undotted because he genuinely wanted them that way. Trying to guess his true wishes is very, very hard. The same is true of slurs, which both Bach and Handel sprawled mostly carelessly over three or more notes, without indicating *precisely* how many notes should be played legato and how many staccato. Maybe they did this because they merely wanted to indicate that a particular passage be played smoothly. When it *really* mattered that only so many notes should be smooth, they took good care to write very precisely.

"But perhaps the most complicated problem in realizing older music is the question of ornamentation. We know that especially vocal music was embellished quite a lot, but we don't know exactly how much. Consequently, any attempt by the modern interpreter to re-establish ornamentation can represent only the individual's taste, feeling and understanding of the style of the period. Eighteenth-century composers tailored their scores to suit the gifts of their performers. Handel was particularly known for this. For example, the reason why Cleopatra's arias in *Giulo Cesare* are written in E major is said to be that the first singer of the role had the most beautiful note 'E' ever heard by man, although I'm not sure *which* 'E' it was and presume it to have been the one at the top of the treble stave and not the one an octave higher! And the reason the role of Caesar was written so low was because its original performer was a castrato as famous for his low notes as for his acting ability."

Anyone wanting to realize a baroque work nowadays, faced with the vocal gifts and limitations of his performers, should adapt and adjust the roles accordingly. Mackerras, who is exceptionally good at this, tailored the part of Cleopatra to suit Valerie Masterson, and retouched and transposed the role of Caesar higher, to suit Dame Janet Baker, around whose appearance the ENO's production of *Giulio Cesare* was conceived.

Dame Janet explains that the reasons for this transposition were that "the Coliseum is a very big place and I felt that sitting on the lower part of my voice would make it dramatically difficult to portray and project a male role without having the best part of my voice behind me. And this is the reason why I feel that my work with Charlie has been some of the most important work of my career: because the fact that he will bother to think of how a role would work for me as a person is extremely valuable. While working on an adaptation, he keeps in constant touch with us singers, and sends pages and pages of suggestions, asking if we would try this and that in such and such a key. I try each suggestion out on the piano and sometimes it works straight away, while at other times it does not quite come off, in which case we meet again and I ask whether it could be put up or down a semitone, and he decides whether this would fit in with the production as a whole."

The two have sometimes disagreed at rehearsals over the years, in a perfectly friendly way, mostly about basic tempi. As Mackerras is not a man who likes to dictate, he usually listens to what Dame Janet has to say and lets her sing the passage in question the way she wants to until, at a certain stage during rehearsals, it suddenly dawns on her that it might be a good idea to try what he suggested in the first place. "And in every single case when we have had a disagreement about tempo, after experiencing the role on stage, physically moving about, I found that he was always proved right. But he never asks me to try it his way. It's always a question of me finding out, by my own experience of the role in action, that he knows what he's doing after all. In fact, this is one of the marvellous things about conductors: they see a work as a whole, whereas we performers don't. We are too involved in our own parts, which is crucial and exactly as it should be, as we must plumb the depths of the role before we play it. But the conductor's mentality is always to see the whole picture and to fit the parts into the whole. And the fact that he gives me a free rein to explore the possibilities of a role is a mark of his confidence in our working relationship, because he obviously *knows* that I'm going to find out that he's right in the end! For all these reasons, our collaboration has stretched me further than I would otherwise have gone and I think that, together, we have created some marvellous moments on stage."

Mackerras was born in Schenectady, New York, on November 17, 1925, of Australian parents. His father was an electrical engineer and his mother kept quite a lively musical and theatrical salon at home in Sydney, where the family returned when Charles was still a toddler. The only other professional musician in the family was his great-great grandfather, one Isaac Nathan, who earned himself a reputation as composer and teacher in nineteenth-century Sydney. The eldest of seven children, Charles started studying the violin at his convent school and later also learnt to play the piano and the flute. When his musical talent became evident during his schooldays, he was enrolled at the New South Wales Conservatoire, in 1941, where he studied composition, piano and the oboe, which was henceforth to become his instrument. But with characteristic candour, he admits that the reason for changing to the oboe was an advertisement in the local morning paper stating that there was a shortage of oboe, horn and bassoon players in the city, and so he found a quick way of getting into an orchestra.

At the time of entering the Conservatoire, he was equally interested in conducting and composition. He had been composing chamber music from an early age. He successfully persuaded some friends of his piano teacher's to come to his house and play his works. In his early teens he wrote an opera based on the legend of Marsyas, using his mother, a strong personality with considerable theatrical flair, as librettist. Soon, however, he realized that he possessed no real creative talent—"my compositions were all right, but heavily derivative of other people's styles and distinctly old-fashioned"—and that his mission in life was interpreting other people's music. But his ability to compose and 'workshop' knowledge of the structure of scores have proved invaluable to him as a conductor, editor and arranger.

After graduating from the Conservatoire, he earned his living by playing the oboe in the orchestra of the Theatre Royal, Sydney, which specialized in the works of Gilbert and Sullivan. At the age of nineteen he became principal oboist of the Sydney Symphony Orchestra. After the war he decided to come to Britain to study conducting. But, being of a practical nature, he also brought along his oboe and was soon engaged by the Sadler's Wells Opera, where his duties occasionally involved conducting offstage bands, and where he met his wife, the orchestra's principal clarinettist Judith Wilkins. (They were married in 1947 and have two married daughters and grandchildren.)

One day he struck up a conversation in a café with a Czech, and it proved an encounter crucial to the future shaping of his career, for it led to a British Council scholarship to study conducting for a year in Prague, under Vaclav Talich. Soon after his arrival there, he heard Talich conduct a performance of *Kát'a Kabanova* and was completely bowled over. "It was a revelation, because here was music unlike any other." He spent his remaining time in Prague—which saw the Communist coup of 1948—learning Czech and familiarizing himself with all Janáček's works, examining the different editions of his scores, meeting some of his pupils and others who had known him, and paying frequent visits to his home town of Brno.

The Mackerrases returned to Britain towards the end of 1948, and Charles spent the next six years as a coach and assistant conductor at Sadler's Wells, which in those days housed both an opera and ballet company which also toured the provinces. Those constructive six years, during which he learned a great deal of repertoire, also provided him with an opportunity to make excursions into ballet; he arranged the music for two ballets—*Pineapple Poll* based on a Gilbert subject, 'The Bumboat Woman's Story' and using Sullivan's music and *The*

Lady and the Fool, for which he used snippets from early Verdi operas. Both ballets were choreographed by the brilliant young South African John Cranko and have become standard works in the ballet repertoire. As early as 1951, he conducted the British stage première of *Kát'a Kabanova* at Sadler's Wells, the first step towards an aim that was to remain crucial throughout his career: presenting all of Janáček's operatic output to the British public.

In 1954, he left Sadler's Wells Opera to become Conductor of the BBC Concert Orchestra which specialized in light music as well as "popular classics", opera and ballet music. After two years, offers to conduct in many parts of the world started to come in, and he spent the next ten years freelancing with the English Opera Group—where he conducted the world premières of Lennox Berkeley's *Ruth* and Britten's *Noye's Fludde*—the Welsh National Opera and the [East] Berlin State Opera. Although he was offered the General Music Directorship of the latter, he declined, preferring to keep Britain as his base. During this period, he also conducted at least one opera a season at Covent Garden, as well as several operas for BBC Television. He visited Canada, South Africa and his native Australia for both concert and opera tours.

He returned to Sadler's Wells Opera as a frequent guest conductor in the mid-sixties where, among other works, he conducted the British première of Janáček's *The Makropoulos Affair*, a revival of *Peter Grimes* and a famous production of *Le nozze di Figaro*, performed in the style of the period with grace notes and ornamentation. This *Figaro* made a huge impact, but Mackerras remains disappointed that this style of performance was not taken up outside the English-speaking world. Mozart is another composer for whom he has special affinity and into whose style he has done a great deal of research. He points out that paradoxically enough, conductors never tend to do both the great composers of the early eighteenth century—Bach and Handel—and of the late eighteenth century—Haydn and Mozart—equally well, but tend to be "either Handel and Mozart men, or Bach and Haydn men. I'm definitely the former. My Bach has still a long way to go." I must confess that, being averse to hearing well-known operas in translation, I have not seen any of his Mozart performances. But the editor of *Opera* magazine wrote that "there is no conductor whom I would rather hear conduct *Figaro* and that includes Karl Böhm", and the critic of *The Times* hailed his production of *Così fan tutte* as the best he had ever heard.

During Sadler's Wells' tour of Germany in 1966, Rolf Liebermann, the then powerful and resourceful Intendant of the Hamburg State Opera, invited Mackerras to become First Kapellmeister after hearing him conduct *Peter Grimes*. "I would have preferred to do some guesting, but he replied that he was only interested in my going on the staff and would I come and conduct a few operas as a trial? So I did *Il trovatore* in German, for which I had one piano rehearsal with the principal singers on the day before the performance, and was told the way in which I must beat the choruses. And I did it. They seemed pleased and asked if I would also conduct *Fidelio* and *Così fan tutte*, obviously to see how I reacted in emergencies, so I did those, too, under the same conditions. Thereupon they gave me a contract. My time there was good experience because I did a vast amount of repertoire with very little rehearsal."

Mackerras remained in Hamburg for three years until, in 1970, he was asked to become Music Director of Sadler's Wells Opera, which had just moved to the London Coliseum in the West End. The eight monumental years of his Directorship saw the merging of the touring company with the London-based one, the changing of its name to English National Opera, and a spectacular rise in the standards of its productions and in attendance figures. Two years after his appointment, Lord Harewood joined the ENO as Managing Director and his flair and adventurous, imaginative leadership provided firm support and help for his Music Director. Together they conjured up unusual and exciting programmes—which have included not only most of the Janácek operas, but also rarities like Martinů's *Julietta*, Handel's *Semele*, Bartók's *Duke Bluebeard's Castle*, Donizetti's *Maria Stuarda* with Dame Janet Baker in the title role, *La Belle Hélène* in Offenbach's original orchestration, and Smetana's *Dalibor*, spliced between what *Opera* magazine called "bread and butter repertoire to balance the caviar". Mackerras describes his years at the Coliseum as "a marvellous experience. It was wonderful to see the ENO improving in quality and in reputation just at the time I was Music Director, though it's hard to tell how much effect I had on it and how much it on me. All I know is that both it and I improved together."

His greatest responsibility was choosing the repertoire and deciding who would be members of the company and who would be guests, all of which had a great deal to do with the planning of the budget. After eight years he resigned, as he found the time-consuming responsibilities of co-ordinating programming with singers' availabilities and coping with union rules frustrating. He remained Principal Guest Conductor for some years and is now an Associate Artist. The 1981–82 season saw a revival of *Maria Stuarda* and a new Covent Garden production of *Alceste*, both with Dame Janet Baker in the title roles. Historic occasions, because, along with the Glyndebourne Festival production of *Orfeo*, they marked this great singer's farewell to opera.

Since he relinquished his Music Directorship of the ENO, Mackerras has been busy recording Janáček operas with the Vienna Philharmonic for Decca in the original language. *Kát'a Kabanova* won the *Gramophone*'s 'Record of the Year' Award in 1978, and the same prize was given to *From The House of the Dead*, which also won the Edison Award and the Deutscher Schallplatten-Preis in 1980. *The Cunning Little Vixen* was not yet released when this book went to press: *Jenůfa* was to be recorded later in 1982, leaving only *The Excursions of Mr Brouček* to come. Those recordings have been among the most satisfying experiences of his career, and partly because the recording engineers' skill and the excellence of the Sofiensaal (Decca's Vienna studio) meant that he was able to dispense with many of the retouchings traditionally adopted when performing Janáček's works on stage.

"The main problem when performing Janáček in the theatre is balance. This is largely because he worked more by feeling than by knowledge. His unique treatment of the orchestra very often drowns the voices. He didn't seem to bother about the fact that a brass instrument is naturally louder than a string instrument. In fact a typical Janáček sound is violins screaming up at the top of their register and trombones growling away in the depths, with nothing in between. Exciting as all this is, singing through it is extremely difficult. So when it comes to a theatre performance you are forced to do something about it. Often it suffices to make the orchestra play piano instead of forte, but sometimes one has to resort to retouching. Fortunately when recording one can improve the balance by technical means and therefore keep absolutely to Janáček's original orchestration."

When *Jenůfa* was first performed in 1904 in Brno, people found Janáček's orchestration so impractical that this great dramatic masterpiece was not a success. Years later Karel Kovařovic* finally persuaded Janáček to let him re-orchestrate the work (rather like Rimsky-

---

* Karel Kovařovic (1862–1920), Czech composer and conductor who became Director of the State Theatre in Prague in 1900; revised and re-orchestrated *Jenůfa*, which he premièred with great success on May 26, 1916.

Korsakov's version of Mussorgsky's *Boris Godunov*) and Janáček, anxious to see the work performed, reluctantly accepted these changes. However, he later complained bitterly about them and tore up his original score, thus leaving behind only the copy with Kovařovic's changes which, fortunately, are written in red ink and are therefore easy to detect. The main problem is the end of the opera which Kovařovic changed so much that the score had to be written out again. Not only did he smooth out eccentricities in the orchestration and improve the balance, but also went as far as to substitute a robust and grandiose ending for Janáček's original, rather simple one. Mackerras has reconstructed the original orchestration of *Jenůfa*—the first person to do so, because nobody, not even in Czechoslovakia, has heard the original. The difficulty of deciding which changes Janáček really approved of and which he accepted merely because he was forced to, makes the task even more daunting. I wondered what guidelines Mackerras observes when reconstructing Janáček scores and what are the specific difficulties confronting him.

"The basic problem is recognizing Janáček's handwriting, because he wrote everything down in his peculiar style and then got some copyist who knew all his idiosyncrasies to have it copied out properly. As he grew older, he became more and more eccentric in his way of writing things down. The worst and most difficult Janáček score to read is *From the House of the Dead*, because by that stage he was so frightened of over-orchestrating, being tempted to fill all those blank staves, that he drew his own manuscript paper, using only the number of lines he thought he needed. The lines are all crooked, and so are the notes, so half the time you wonder whether the notes are on a line or in the space. How these copyists managed to decipher it I don't know. But decipher it they did. At least they had Janáček himself around to be consulted in cases of doubt. But the problem doesn't end here. Janáček would go through the neatly-copied score, cross, rub and scratch things out, insert new things and generally revise it. But he often failed to notice mistakes made by his copyists, which is a major headache for every Janáček scholar. Sometimes the original autograph provides the answer by proving that it was the copyist who had got it wrong in the first place. Not surprising when you consider the atrociously badly-written originals.

"A good example of this is his *Sinfonietta*, which is full of copyists' mistakes which Janáček failed to notice. In fact he sanctioned this error-ridden copy as the only authorized edition of the work! So every

Janáček conductor has corrected the mistakes. But our corrections are not necessarily the same, because I suppose that, again, it is a question of how each individual interprets Janáček's peculiar squiggles and hieroglyphics. But perhaps the worst case of all is again *From the House of the Dead*, because Janáček never finished revising the copy made from his frightful autograph. He only got half-way through, and so the whole thing looks like a sketch, which was later revised by two of his pupils, the conductor Bakala and the composer Chlubna, who filled in the orchestration and made it sound less eccentric: they also changed the vocal parts considerably in some cases and even went so far as to substitute an alternative, more optimistic ending. Since then, every Janáček specialist has rejected those additions and tried to find out what the original was, and so we have no fewer than four different versions: three made by Czechs—Kubelik, Gregor, the conductor from Prague, and Nosek, the conductor from Brno—and one made by myself with the help of a Janáček specialist from Nottingham, the musicologist John Tyrrel.

"I find it rather strange that three Czechs should have such differing views about their greatest modern national composer. But this seems to have been Janáček's fate, in a way. When he started composing, everyone felt that his work was highly original and that he had marvellous ideas, but simply did not know how to orchestrate. His orchestration was considered primitive, even by my teacher, Vaclav Talich, who re-orchestrated *Kát'a Kabanova* before performing it. But I feel that this primitive quality is what makes Janáček unique. Despite the difficulties it presents when performing it on stage, it is part of his style. Orchestration is as basic a part of a composer's style as his melodies and other inventive ideas.

"Take Brahms, for instance. Without his orchestration, he just doesn't sound like Brahms. What proves this beyond doubt is the Brahms Piano Quartet which was orchestrated by Schönberg and which has been referred to as the Brahms Fifth Symphony. Well, to my mind it doesn't sound the least bit like Brahms. [For an opposite view, see the chapter on Seiji Ozawa.] This is only one out of dozens of examples I could cite: Webern's arrangement of a Bach fugue, which sounds utterly Webern; or Mozart's arrangement of *Messiah*: beautiful, but absolutely un-Handelian. But here I am talking of a complete orchestration of a work by another composer. It *is*, of course, possible to make small adjustments to the existing orchestration of a work that enhance rather than change its basic character. This is exactly what

Wagner did to the Beethoven symphonies.

"Wagner suggested, with uncharacteristic modesty, that certain parts of the Beethoven symphonies should be re-orchestrated, so that the important melodies could be heard clearly. Although Wagner's suggestions have been taken up by many conductors in the past, the present tendency is to stick to Beethoven's original orchestration."

Even though I was expecting to be fascinated by the depth and breadth of Mackerras's musical knowledge and scholarship—his musicological side—our meetings impressed me even more than I was prepared for and so did the rehearsals I managed to attend. The high technical competence which everyone who works with him, or watches him work, readily acknowledges, is coupled with a terrific energy and enthusiasm at the performance. Yet he is not a 'star' or in his own word, a 'virtuoso' conductor, but rather a musician's musician, enormously esteemed and appreciated by his own kind and by the genuinely knowledgeable public.

Dame Janet Baker thinks that this might have something to do with his Australian *persona*, with the fact that he is an ordinary man who lacks 'star appeal' in the obvious sense. "And he's not easy. He's very friendly but he's detached, because he's thinking so much about the score that personalities don't really come into it. You don't get close to him in a personal way quickly. But over the years I have, and I found that the detachment disguises a terrifically lovable human being, and an exceptionally fair one, too, which is invaluable when you have to run an opera with so many people to look after and so many different strands to pull together. He's really very special and I *like* him immensely. Maybe he is not as dazzling to look at as some of the glamour boys, but we performers are not looking for that. We're looking for the hands, arms and sense of security. You see, in our profession, you have 'musicians' musicians' and you have the 'stars' for the public at large. Some people, very few, combine the qualities that attract both. But the ultimate, for a musician, is to be appreciated by one's own kind. Charlie is. In my opinion, he is one of the very best."

ZUBIN MEHTA
The Meteor with Good 'Sitzfleisch'

Zubin Mehta is indirectly responsible for this book, or at least, for making me think about the various aspects of conducting in a more profound and realistic way. When I interviewed him for the London *Evening News* in January 1978—just after the opening night of *Die Fledermaus*, which was relayed by satellite all over the world from the Royal Opera House, Covent Garden—he told me, among other things, that he felt conducting was a very misunderstood art. I replied that I had always considered it a very *mysterious*, but not necessarily misunderstood, art and asked him to explain exactly what he meant. This is what he said:

"Some people elevate conducting far above what it is, while others underestimate it. Pianists, violinists and other instrumentalists need only to be good musicians and technicians, but conductors need a terrific combination of both musical and non-musical qualities, especially if they want to be orchestra-builders as well.

"From the musical point of view, the conductor is often the only person aware of the entire expanse of a given work—orchestral players usually learn only their own parts—and must know exactly where he is going, so that he can guide the music and plan its climaxes accordingly; he must also have a knowledge of style, every composer's style, plus total conviction that what he is doing is right, even if it sometimes isn't, in order to suggest it to a hundred people and expect them to follow him.

"From the human point of view, he must be good at handling people, which calls for some psychology, diplomacy and tact, plus considerable organizing skills: for he has to plan, not only his own career but all the orchestra's tours, recordings, the auditioning and hiring of players and the choice of guest conductors as well. *And* find time for private study, which is absolutely crucial."

Later, when I decided to write a book about conductors and was discussing the idea with an agent who wanted to know why I found conducting so interesting in the first place, I caught myself quoting this clear and succinct summary of some of the aspects of a conductor's work, as well as explaining my own chronic fascination and curiosity about this mysterious art. So I thought it both fair and appropriate to give credit where it's due.

One of the things I'd found most surprising about Zubin Mehta was his extreme articulateness and the immense love for his work and for music which was evident in everything he said. I remember thinking that he himself is a little bit misunderstood, especially in the United States, where his seriousness and dedication as a musician are often overlooked by a press eager to dwell on his undeniable sex appeal and colourful personal life.

Mehta was born in Bombay on April 29, 1936—a Parsee, i.e. a descendant of those Zoroastrians who fled from Iran in the seventh century AD to escape Islam. (Zubin means 'powerful sword' in ancient Persian.) His father, the violinist Mehli Mehta, founded the Bombay Symphony Orchestra, thus ensuring that, although Western music was, and is, a rarity in India, Zubin would grow up in a home where it was played all day long, since most of the rehearsals for the orchestra and for his father's chamber group took place in the family drawing room.

He learnt to play the piano at an early age, and in his teens he became the orchestra's assistant manager and librarian, whose duties involved copying scores and transposing parts as well as arranging the players' chairs and music stands. He also started taking violin and theory-of-music lessons once a week from his father's former teacher, an Italian called Oddone Savinni, who lived in nearby Poona. But despite his obvious enjoyment of his duties with the orchestra, Zubin did not take music very seriously at the time and had to be prodded into practising the piano and the violin. He much preferred sneaking out and playing cricket with his friends! (He is still an ardent cricket fan who seldom misses a Test Match at Lord's when in London during the cricket season.)

The family, who never imagined that he wouldn't live in India all his life and who had already spent a lot of their private money on Mehli's music-making, decided that he should become a doctor and enrolled him for a preparatory course at St Xavier's College, a Jesuit establishment in Bombay. There Zubin was fortunate enough to find a Spanish physics master who had been a music student with Granados before taking his vows and who not only encouraged his pupil's interest in music, but was also willing to give him lessons in counterpoint after class.

One day, at the age of sixteen, Zubin was allowed to conduct the Bombay Symphony Orchestra in rehearsal. It happened because Yehudi Menuhin had offered to play in some charity concerts for the victims of the 1952 famine and Mehli, who wanted to save him as much rehearsal time as possible, had to play the violin solos himself, thus leaving the orchestra without a conductor. So Zubin stepped onto the podium for the first time and experienced that thrill and exhilaration which flood him whenever he finds himself on stage with an orchestra and which he calls "my reward, the place where I know peace. Conducting an orchestra is a fantastic experience. Me and a magnificent one-hundred-and-five-horse carriage working together. I can rein them in or release them to go with the music."

From then on, he found it increasingly difficult to concentrate on his medical studies and kept hearing Brahms symphonies in his head during the anatomy classes! When, one day, a professor asked why he was day-dreaming rather than cutting up a dogfish, he flung it back at him shouting "Cut it up yourself", and walked out. Back home, he interrupted his father's "quiet time" (a time of day set aside by Parsees for prayer and meditation), told him that he couldn't go on with medicine because he felt himself a musician and begged him to let him go to Vienna and join a cousin who was already studying music at the Music Academy. His parents—both exceptional, unusually enlightened people—decided to let him go, using half the money from an $8,000 trust fund set up by his grandfather. Zubin, eighteen at the time, embarked on the long sea voyage to Italy and thence by train to Vienna, leaving behind his native country which he loves with an intense, passionate loyalty. He retains his Indian passport to this day and says that living away from India makes him feel even closer to it.

In October 1954 he enrolled at the Vienna Music Academy, where he soon became known as "der Inder" and proved very popular with teachers and fellow students alike, because of that mixture of charm, warmth, candour, self-confidence and innate authority which is characteristic of him, while at the same time absorbing and adapting to Western culture and learning German.

During the first two semesters, he had to study score analysis, counterpoint and harmony, the one weakness in this otherwise brilliant student who was well ahead of his class in everything else. At the end of the year, he passed the examinations for admittance to the conducting school, where he proved even more popular with the Professor of conducting, Hans Swarowsky—a mediocre conductor but a brilliant teacher—who became the second most influential man in his life, after his father, and who was crucial in guiding and shaping the natural talent he immediately recognized in this pupil. "Your son is a born conductor," he told Zubin's father after the boy had spent only a few months in his class. "There is not much I can teach him, because he knows everything already. But I will do what I can."

"Swarowsky taught me how to look at a score, how to go into a composer's mind," says Mehta. "Of course, it is impossible to learn the entire repertoire in four years, but he concentrated on certain basic styles, mostly the Classical and Romantic periods: Haydn, Mozart, Beethoven, Brahms, Bruckner and Strauss, and left us to explore the rest of the repertoire by ourselves. He never mentioned the words inspiration or intuition, but based his whole approach on knowledge of style, and was convinced that once we knew a composer's basic style, everything else would come naturally. As he was a great art historian who knew as much about painting as about music, he would always compare the different styles in music to the different schools of painting: in the Florentine school, you look at the design, while in the Venetian school you concentrate more on colour; when you look at a Raphael, you examine the geometry, the placement of the people, first of all, not the colour or shape of the folds of a dress! The same, he said, is true of music. Haydn, for instance, wrote one hundred and four symphonies, all similar in a certain sense, but all possessing little variations, and you cannot learn them without first learning Haydn's basic tools, i.e. his first theme, his second theme, and how he develops them. He thought that, having grasped a composer's basic style, we would then perceive the inevitability in each of his compositions, the impossibility of a work being other than it is.

"Of course, he exaggerated his theories a little, as great teachers often do, and claimed that he got his unemotional, analytical approach to conducting from Richard Strauss, who once wrote in his 'Ten Golden Rules' for young conductors* that as soon as you start

---

* They are:

1. Remember that you are making music not to amuse yourself but to delight your audience.

2. You should not perspire when conducting: only the audience should get warm.

sweating, it means that you are doing too much! Swarowsky was very proud of the fact that he could conduct the Mahler third without sweating ('Look, no sweat!' he would say, and make each of us feel his shirt!). His attitude to rubato was typical of this approach: to him, rubato was an organized rubato, never left to momentary inspiration, and every performance had to be the same, with exact, identical timings. There was no question of it varying from evening to evening."

Despite some of these exaggerations, which he says that both he and his fellow students were aware of at the time, though some found them less congenial than others (Claudio Abbado, for instance, who joined the class two years after Mehta, was very depressed during the first few months because he felt alien to this cold, mathematical approach to music), Mehta considers that this was good, basic, Classical training, especially for someone with his fiery temperament, because it provided a sound grounding from which he could develop and because it taught him never to lose control, even in his most exuberant moments. (Yet a player in the Los Angeles Philharmonic commented a couple of years ago that Mehta's immense and wholehearted responsiveness to music can sometimes lead to trouble, because "he lets his instincts take over and loses his cool and if we followed him, the sound would get forced, rough, louder than anybody could possibly play.")

Swarowsky sometimes made him conduct with his left hand in his pocket and the right arm tied to the stand, or with both of *his* hands stuck into Mehta's sleeves, in order to teach him flexibility and freedom of wrist movements, a great asset for a conductor, as the timpanist of the Los Angeles Philharmonic, William Kraft, was quick to register: "I've learnt a good deal about conducting from watching him. Even the way he holds his baton makes it easier for us to follow him. He turns his wrist a little outward and holds his baton up in such a way that the

---

3. Conduct *Salome* and *Elektra* as if they were by Mendelssohn: Fairy Music.

4. Never look encouragingly at the brass, except with a short glance to give an important cue.

5. But never let the horns and woodwind out of your sight: if you can hear them at all they are still too strong.

6. If you think that the brass is now blowing hard enough, tone it down another shade or two.

7. It is not enough that you yourself should hear every word the soloist sings—you know it off by heart anyway: the audience must be able to follow without effort. If they do not understand the words they will go to sleep.

8. Always accompany a singer in such a way that he can sing without effort.

9. When you think you have reached the limits of prestissimo, double the pace.

10. If you follow these rules carefully you will, with your fine gifts and your great accomplishments, always be the darling of your listeners.

(*ca.* 1922)

players don't see the tip as an extension of his hand, but see the whole baton, which helps us play cleanly and expressively."

The first time Mehta conducted in public—a Mozart piano concerto—he came off the stage with eyes ablaze, hair all over the place, and dripping with sweat. Swarowsky took one look at him and said: "If you allow yourself to get into this state during a Mozart *accompaniment*, what will happen to you when you conduct *Tristan und Isolde*? You'll go crazy!" "And you know," adds Mehta, "these words were very prophetic! At the beginning of my career, I used to give one hundred and fifty per cent of myself. Now, I give only one hundred per cent and make better music!"

Swarowsky's analytical approach has proved particularly valuable for understanding and conducting the works of Richard Strauss and Stravinsky. The only Stravinsky music his pupils were taught was the first movement of *Le Sacre du printemps*, which they could then use as a springboard from which to analyse and learn the rest of his works.

"Stravinsky's music is very well constructed. When you look at his scores, you don't find that asymmetry you feel when listening to them. Everything is figured out and mapped out on the writing table and therefore learning his works is easier for those of us who were trained in the Classical tradition. Swarowsky showed us the basic construction of this movement and how to beat it, because how to beat is crucial in Stravinsky's music. (You wouldn't show somebody how to beat the *Eroica*, for instance. In the first place, this is not the crunch of the *Eroica*, and anyway, the whole first movement goes in three.)

"But in Stravinsky, you have to communicate this great technical clarity to the orchestra, without disturbing them or getting in their way, because they are reading scores where, in some parts, every measure is in a different time beat. There are certain passages which will invariably come out more clearly if the players are left to themselves, undisturbed by the conductor who must know where, in which particular places, he can give a little accent or a little jerk to put things right. If the orchestra feel that he is in control, they just sit back and play. But if they feel that he doesn't know his score or is prone to making mistakes, they are on guard and are playing *in spite of* that obstacle standing in front of them!"

They were taught to analyse the works of Richard Strauss in the same way. Swarowsky chose to teach, not *Ein Heldenleben*, which might seem like the obvious choice as it contains references to all the symphonic poems, but *Till Eulenspiegel*, one of Strauss's most complicated and ingenious scores. "The whole of *Till* is in one tempo, one beat going right through, with very occasional little accelerandi and ritardandi, but you hardly feel this when you hear the work. In fact, Strauss was very proud of the fact that he had composed a piece that gives the impression of great variety, but really has one beat and very little thematic material. But he exposed, expounded and worked on the little he had in a way that makes you feel that you are listening to a piece with fifteen different themes, while in fact, you are hearing the same notes all the time. He always said that the first four bars are from God, and the rest is hard work. Nobody knows why a certain melody, a certain theme, comes into his mind. But composition is what you do with it. In *Salome*, for instance, you find him expanding and playing with his thematic material in a similar way, and it was wonderful to learn, in one's youth, what can be done and *was* done, by craftsmen like Strauss and Stravinsky, with a few notes: that they retained these same notes of the basic melody, but changed the rhythm, the tonalities, the harmony and make you feel you are listening to a new theme, until you analyse the score."

When Mehta first heard a concert with the Vienna Philharmonic playing the Brahms first under Karl Böhm—the first 'live' concert of his life apart from the Bombay Symphony Orchestra—he was so overwhelmed by the sheer beauty of the sound and especially the beauty of the bass line, that he decided to give up the violin (which he was studying as well as the piano) and switch to the double bass. His double bass Professor at the Academy was Otto Rühm, from whom he learnt "the meaning of beautiful sound, something you can never learn from books, only from somebody who has it in his ears".

When he was compelled to spend the first summer vacation alone in Vienna because he couldn't afford the fare back to Bombay, he joined the Singverein, the choir of the Gesellschaft der Musikfreunde, as a bass and made his recording début, as a chorister, in a performance of the Beethoven ninth conducted by Karajan. His immense admiration and respect for Karajan dates back to this time. "After learning all the technicalities of conducting in class, it was wonderful to experience a great conductor's electric emanation [*Ausstrahlung*], and to watch the tension he experienced and exuded." (He still occasionally seeks Karajan's advice about operatic scores—*Tristan, Otello, Parsifal*—and always finds him most generous with his time and thoughts.)

As a member of the Singverein, Zubin sang under—and watched—many of the great conductors of the day: Josef Krips in Haydn's *Die*

Schöpfung, "a really great orchestra trainer who breathed with the musicians and cajoled them into polished, sparkling performances"; Bruno Walter, whom he got to know later in Los Angeles, in Mozart's *Requiem*; Erich Kleiber in the Verdi *Requiem*, "one of the greatest teachers of all time, who taught every single player and whose every comment made sense. Funnily enough, he was almost better at rehearsals than at the concert itself, when, having prepared the orchestra superbly, he would just stand back and let it happen. ('Gentlemen, you just sit back and make music, I will not disturb you,' he would say to them.) His son Carlos, on the other hand, is a performance conductor, very electric, although he, too, prepares everything meticulously."

He also started playing the double bass in various orchestras—the Jeunesses Musicales and the Tonkünstler—for extra cash and for the chance to experience the conductor from the other side of the fence. He learnt a great deal about the orchestra-conductor psychological relationship, and remembers being mean only to one, the late Hermann Scherchen, who was vehemently opposed to everything Swarowsky taught at the Academy, thus sinning against Mehta's firm loyalty to his teacher!

"So when we were playing *La Valse*, which starts with the double basses, I gave him a hard time: I asked silly questions, I pretended I didn't know where his beat was, I came in early, I came in late, I said I didn't know where I should place a certain note, maestro!" (To the comment that this was an explicit résumé of what a player can do to annoy and frustrate a conductor, he replied that one could write an entire book about that alone!)

After graduating from the Academy in spring 1958, he won second prize at the conducting class of the Berkshire Summer Festival at Tanglewood, and first prize at the Liverpool Philharmonic Orchestra's International Conductors' Competition—a prize which entailed the 1958–59 season's Assistant Conductorship at a salary of £800 (approximately US$1,600) a year, money which he desperately needed, because before leaving Vienna he had married a Canadian voice student, Carmen Lasky, and she was expecting their first child.

He spent a miserable season in Liverpool, conducting what seemed to him like an unresponsive and unsympathetic orchestra, mostly on tour, with minimal rehearsal time, needing more assistance from the Music Director, John Pritchard. Yet he admits that he was unprepared for the job and that he "learnt at their expense. But I learnt!" (The only ray in his otherwise bleak horizon at the time was the birth of his daughter, Zarina, and the proximity of his parents, who had now moved to nearby Manchester, where his father was a violinist in the Hallé Orchestra, under Barbirolli.)

But during his summer at Tanglewood, Mehta had impressed a number of people, including Charles Münch and the composer Lukas Foss, who recommended him to his New York agent, Siegfried Hearst. The latter took him on because he had "a hunch that this guy was going to make it", and arranged for his Canadian début in March 1959, conducting the orchestra of the Canadian Broadcasting Corporation in Toronto, where he was well received. The following year, summer 1960, Hearst organized his début in the United States, conducting two of the greatest orchestras in the country: the Philadelphia Orchestra at Robin Hood Dell, for a fee of $500 and to enthusiastic reviews, and the New York Philharmonic at Lewisohn Stadium, also for a pittance but, this time, to rather hostile reviews. (Interestingly enough, it was the Indian government that paid Mehta's fare to the States on both occasions. Otherwise, he couldn't have gone, and he has never forgotten this gesture.) Undaunted by the New York reviews, Hearst asked him to look up his friend, Pierre Beique, the Managing Director of the Montreal Symphony Orchestra, on his way back.

He did, and made such a good impression that when, later in the year, the Montreal Symphony needed a replacement for Igor Markevich, its Music Director, who was too ill to conduct the 1960–61 season's six inaugural concerts, Beique offered them to Mehta. He and the orchestra took to each other from the first rehearsal, and his début was a triumph. "Mehta creates sensation," ran the title of a eulogizing article in the December 1960 issue of *Musical America*, and the Canadian press and audience, who gave him a tremendous ovation, concurred. So did the orchestra: "Where did you find that guy? Keep him here!" Beique was told by enthusiastic musicians. He decided to do just that. He consulted his Board, and offered the Music Directorship to Mehta as from the 1961–62 season; he held the post until 1967. (He says that he sometimes feels as though his whole career was built on the illnesses of older conductors, which again and again provided him with the right opportunities at the right time. "But while you must be quick and ready to seize any opportunity that comes your way, you must also make sure you are good enough to be asked again!")

"When a comet passes through your life, you don't have to be a genius to realize it!" Beique told Mehta's biographers. "I was immediately impressed by this young man who was personable, who was willing to work and who needed an orchestra.... Maybe in the beginning the diamond was rough, but it was still a diamond, and I could see that later on it would become more and more polished. The talent was unlimited."

Soon after accepting the post in Montreal, Mehta was asked to audition for Georg Solti, then Music Director of the Los Angeles Philharmonic, who was looking for an Assistant. He felt that as he was already under contract in Montreal, it would be both wrong and unethical to go. But, having been persuaded by his agent that there was nothing to lose, he went and was promptly offered the job. As his disappointing experience as an assistant in Liverpool was still fresh in his mind, he declined.

Yet the trip turned out to be crucial for his future. He had so impressed the orchestra and its Board that when Fritz Reiner fell ill and cancelled four concerts in January 1961, they immediately invited him back. Even though this meant that he had to learn several difficult works for the first time, and very quickly, too (*Don Quixote*, the Schumann fourth and Beethoven seventh, among others), the concerts were so successful, and the public and press so enthusiastic, that the Board decided to offer him the Associate Directorship there and then, assuming that Solti, who had wanted him as his assistant anyway, would agree. But he objected to such decisions being taken behind his back and resigned. The music directorship was then offered to Mehta, starting with the 1962–63 season. After consultations with the Montreal Symphony—his contract did not require him to spend more than twelve weeks a season there—he accepted.

"What Mrs Chandler, the Chairman of our Board, saw, and what I saw in this unknown young man of twenty-five, was the kind of magic that separates the merely talented artists from the exceptionally, exceedingly talented," says Mrs Olive Behrendt, a long-standing member of the orchestra's Executive Committee. "The second that Zubin appeared, the moment we first talked to him about his work and his whole approach to music, we knew that here was not only a musical intelligence of almost genius comprehension, but also an exceptional human being radiating such vitality, honesty and charisma that we couldn't help but be drawn to him. We have watched him develop from a young man of twenty-five to a mature man of forty-five, and nothing has disappointed us. I think that, with time, he is going to be a giant."

Mehta remained Music Director of the Los Angeles Philharmonic for sixteen years, until 1978. He has, in his own words, "pretty good *Sitzfleisch*", preferring to work with one or two orchestras full time, building them up to reflect his musical ideals, and limiting his guest conducting to only a handful of the world's top orchestras and opera houses.

"I need to be inspired by an orchestra as much as they need to be convinced by me. This can happen more easily with an orchestra I know well, and only when everyone concerned knows his stuff and is in complete control of what he is doing. Then you develop such empathy that all the hidden meanings, the little things between the lines of a score, can be brought out and music-making becomes a joy. This is why, when I am conducting an orchestra I don't know well, I sometimes feel lonely on the podium." (He was quick to point out that this never happens with orchestras like the Philadelphia Orchestra or the Vienna and the Berlin Philharmonic, which are "pure pleasure" to conduct and where he always feels that he is learning something which he can later, maybe, transmit to his own orchestras.)

Mehta developed the Los Angeles Philharmonic from an orchestra which, at the beginning of his tenure, few top-ranking conductors were willing to guest-conduct, into one of America's top six—good enough for Carlo Maria Giulini to take over in 1978—which established his reputation as a first-rate orchestra *builder*. He believes that a music director should sit down and work with his orchestra, and not limit himself to showcase concerts and flashy tours.

He systematically set to work with every section—especially the strings, which he calls the proletariat of an orchestra because they do most of the work—persuaded the Board to buy new, darker-toned German trumpets with special mouthpieces, capable of producing the kind of pianissimi he required from the brass section, changed the sound of some of the players—he actually fired only ten during those sixteen years, and even that cost him some of his popularity for a while—expanded the repertoire to include much more Bruckner and Mahler, and went on tour with them fourteen times in sixteen years.

"Tours are very important for orchestras, because every night they have to play in different climatic and acoustic conditions, sometimes with no rehearsals and always in circumstances which demand that they put their best foot forward. The temperature in a hall affects the quality of sound, and so does humidity: as soon as it gets very hot, the strings tend to go down, while the woodwinds tend to go up, but the master contracts of American orchestras permit only one rehearsal a week while touring, so I have to find a place where we really need it, like the Philharmonie in Berlin, where no orchestra that doesn't know the Hall could possibly play without a rehearsal."

In 1961, shortly after his appointment to the Montreal Symphony, Mehta received a cable from an obscure telegraphic address, "Palphilorc", and gazed at it in bewilderment, wondering whom and where it might be from. It turned out to be from the Israel Philharmonic, who had not changed its address since the days when it was still the Palestine Philharmonic—it still hasn't—inviting him to replace an indisposed Eugene Ormandy.

He accepted the invitation and fell in love "at first sight" with Israel, its people and its orchestra, which was only twenty-five years old—exactly the same age as he himself. The concert marked not only the beginning of his long association with the Philharmonic (although, until he left Los Angeles, contractual reasons compelled him to be called a Musical Adviser, even though he carried out the duties of a Music Director), but also with the country and destiny of Israel, where he feels completely at home. (He says that he would convert to Judaism if the operation didn't hurt so much!) Every time the country went to war, he cancelled all his engagements and flew, often under dangerous conditions, to make music throughout the hostilities; he is convinced that one day he will conduct the Israel Philharmonic in a peace concert in Cairo!

The IPO are a cheeky, ill-disciplined and erratic orchestra, but at their best and when they feel like it, they can play like gods. Their rehearsals are hilarious, and resemble a classroom of unruly children, often reducing the conductor to the level of a schoolmaster. Mehta's rehearsals are usually concise, matter-of-fact, albeit pleasant and friendly affairs, but with the Israelis, before he can get down to making music he has to deal with matters like: "Sit down, X, I told you to stay in one place and stop fidgeting!", or "Y, move your stand a little so that I can see Z." Y doesn't move until even his colleagues get impatient and force him to do as he is told! Before a concert, he repeats his instructions to them as they come out to take their seats. But the moment the music begins, everything changes, and that extraordinary rapport that existed between them even at their first rehearsal, takes over.*

Their European tour in 1979 was "one of the most incredible musical experiences" of Mehta's life. "We played the Mahler fifth at least fifteen times, and they really surpassed themselves. Like the Beethoven seventh, this symphony is an abstract, geometrical work, with no plot, no story, unlike Mahler's second and third symphonies where every movement is dedicated to a particular subject. The fifth is pure music, and to play it night after night with this orchestra who know it so well, and whom I know so well, made it possible for me to just stand back and let it unfold—one of the deepest, greatest pleasures I have ever experienced. When you have reached this stage with an orchestra, you realize that guest-conducting can never provide a comparable sensation."

Mahler is one of the composers closest to Mehta's heart and has been since he followed all of Bruno Walter's rehearsals for a performance of the Fourth Symphony in Vienna during the Mahler centenary in 1960. Until then, he shared the puerile criticisms of Mahler voiced by his fellow students, who considered him a thief who borrowed not only from other composers, but also from his own earlier works. But these rehearsals opened up Mahler for him, and to this day he cannot forget the sight of Walter, nearly ninety at the time, sitting on a bench alone throughout the rehearsal break, head bent and thoughts obviously far away. Two years later, they met in Los Angeles, and Mehta took along some scores—including the Mahler first—to discuss with him; he still remembers the things Walter told him every time he conducts it.

"Mahler is one of those composers whose everyday life greatly affected the content of their work, and about whom it's vital to know a great deal. I have just read this magnificent book by La Grange, from which I learnt a great deal of previously unpublished information. It was deeply moving to know that while he was composing the Third

---

* In 1981, Mehta, with the consent of most of the IPO musicians, tried to perform Wagner for the first time in Israel and scheduled the Prelude and Liebestod from *Tristan und Isolde* as an encore to one of their concerts. This provoked a major furore, with fist-fights breaking out in the auditorium between pro and anti factions (the latter chiefly made up of survivors from Hitler's concentration camps who protested against being reminded of the music they were forced to hear when victims were marched to their deaths). This emotive issue was taken up by the press and the Prime Minister himself. The orchestra, who decided to postpone the programming of Wagner music for a later date, named Mehta its Music Director for life as a gesture of support.

Symphony, he would bicycle to the neighbouring village and visit Brahms! Can you imagine? Two of my most favourite composers talking to each other in one spot! I find the thought quite overwhelming! And Bruno Walter, who visited him at the little village in the Totesgebirge in the summer, remembered that when he commented on the remarkable beauty of the mountains, Mahler replied, 'Oh, don't worry, they are all composed into my score!'"

It was while conducting this symphony—which he finds "draining, so intense"—in February 1978 in Los Angeles, that something quite out of the ordinary happened to him during the last movement, a feeling that he was out of his body, no longer on earth, possibly, he thinks, because on the next day he would be recording it and this would be his last recording with this orchestra, "after so many notes that had flown through our fingers over the years." This is how he described it, in his biography:

"Often you feel that a performance is good, but there are many levels of good, and at the top there is a level at which you feel that you are no longer on a podium, but standing on air, the sort of feeling that people who take drugs talk about. But you don't need drugs. Only the music. You don't work at it. All of a sudden it's there. It started in the first movement, I could see Pan dancing before me, and in the background, the dark mountain landscape outside Salzburg becoming a *cosmic* landscape. It's not something I was responsible for. That night, I was in extreme danger of losing control. But every single member of the orchestra was so tuned in, that somehow, it never fell apart. Those moments are very rare; they cannot be rehearsed. And even as it is happening, you can never afford to forget that yes, it is a cosmic landscape—but it is also a trombone solo!" The next day, they recorded all of the huge Adagio in one take—apart from four bars of a violin solo which were slightly out of tune—because "you can't make a replica of this kind of music-making by pushing a button. But, since approving the tapes, I have never listened to this recording. I'm afraid of hearing it again."

He has recorded the first five Mahler symphonies for Decca, but won't as yet touch the last four because he doesn't feel that he completely understands them. For a start, he has seldom performed them, and he never likes to record a work before performing it several times, "because every time you find new insights, new ways of looking at it, some little detail you didn't notice before, and even the dozenth time you have by no means unravelled everything. I'm nowhere near that stage with the last Mahler symphonies. In a way, the Eighth is the easiest to conduct and simplest to interpret, and the most difficult is definitely the Seventh! I have only conducted it once, in Los Angeles, and could never have done it without the score and analysis that Swarowsky gave me, which was, in fact, Webern's score and analysis, given to him as a memento. But I am still afraid of this symphony, the most difficult work I have ever conducted."

I wondered to what extent a composer's world transmits itself to him, whether while conducting Mahler, for instance, who was obsessed by death, he finds himself thinking of death and if so, whether he would like to die on the podium, like Dimitri Mitropoulos, a conductor he greatly admired and loved, who died during a rehearsal of the Mahler third at La Scala: "Oh, I will!" he replied. "Either on the podium or on a plane! Those seem to be the only two possibilities! And as I became a conductor because of Brahms, who during my teens in India was my communication with what I felt to be the most beautiful music I had ever heard, I suppose that if I am lucky enough to die on the podium, I would like it to be during a Brahms symphony."

Both Mitropoulos and Walter were among a group of much revered artists, which also includes Karajan, the late Karl Böhm and Arthur Rubinstein, to whom Mehta has gone for advice whenever he has had a musical problem. (Personal problems he seldom discusses, even with his closest friends.) He feels that after his theoretical studies at the Academy, after playing in orchestras and seeing the conductor from the other side of the fence, and after his teething years as a young conductor learning the repertoire, "watching and playing with a master is the final polishing, the crowning of one's perception of what music is about."

"Standing behind the piano and hearing Rubinstein playing the second movement of a Chopin concerto or listening to his advice about the orchestral parts of a Brahms concerto, that's when you really learn, and I only realized how *much* I had learnt from him when he retired. That was a great master passing on knowledge to a disciple. And as I go along, I believe with all my heart that the master-to-disciple relationship is the only way of passing on knowledge. But only a disciple who has reached a certain level, technically, intellectually, emotionally and spiritually, is capable of receiving and absorbing knowledge in this way. There is no book, no formula that can pass on knowledge beyond that level, except a master, doing it intuitively."

Mehta made his operatic début in 1964, in Montreal, conducting *Tosca*, to such rave notices that the late Rudolf Bing flew up from New York to see and hear for himself, and promptly invited him to the Metropolitan Opera for ten performances of *Aida* during the following season. "There were many mistakes and he was totally inexperienced," Bing told *Time* magazine at the time. "But it was all overshadowed by his personality and talent. Experience, anyone can get." The Press, which had been lukewarm-to-hostile about his symphonic début back in 1960, was now uniformly enthusiastic and he was invited back regularly for *Otello*, *Carmen*, *Il trovatore*, *Turandot*, the world première of Levy's *Mourning becomes Elektra* directed by Michael Cacoyannis, and *Salome*. (He remembers that during a rehearsal of the latter he came to the point where the Jews on stage had finished their bit, and as he didn't plan to repeat the passage that day, he dismissed them saying, "'All the Jews can go home!' And you know, I looked at my pit, and there wasn't a first violinist in it!")

He chose *Salome* also for his début at La Scala in 1964, and has since returned almost every season. One of his most moving and unforgettable experiences there was conducting *Turandot* on the fiftieth anniversary of its first performance. "We stopped in the middle of a *cantabile* bar in Act Three, exactly the spot where Puccini died.* There was no applause, the lights went off, and everyone went home."

In 1965 he conducted *Die Entführung aus dem Serail* in Salzburg—one of the greatest triumphs of his career. Although most people have come to associate Mehta with the Romantic and post-Romantic repertoire, he loves and "grew up with" Mozart's music in Vienna, and considers Mozart himself one of the greatest mysteries in music. "You could conduct Mozart's music without knowing anything about his private life, because it contains no trace of the suffering and privation he went through. This wonderful, celestial sound keeps pouring out of each composition regardless of what was happening to him.... From the technical point of view, if you really know Mozart's style, you will always find a certain passage which indicates the right tempo for an aria or a symphony. Anyone really familiar with all of Mozart's work, especially his chamber music, knows that there are certain clichés, typical of the composer's handwriting. This is why it is vital to know as much of a composer's output, and to be as steeped in his style as possible. Because in chamber works you often come across a few bars

---

* The opera was completed by his pupil Franco Alfano (1876–1954), who himself composed several operas.

similar to a symphonic or operatic passage and composed at a certain tempo; and these few bars tell you what the right tempo for that aria or movement should be."

At the time, Mehta was concentrating his operatic activities on Wagner. He had already conducted *Lohengrin* at the Vienna State Opera in 1973, with considerable success. In February 1979 came his first *Das Rheingold* at the Maggio Musicale in Florence, which was followed by *Die Walküre* a year later. (He and the orchestra got excellent reviews, but Ronconi's production was severely criticized.)

"*Rheingold* is the longest piece of music I have ever conducted—two and a half hours without a break, and there isn't one spot where I can relax, even for a few bars. Even in *Walküre*, there are a few instances when Brünnhilde sings alone with a bass clarinettist accompanying her, so I can relax and wait for a few bars. But in *Rheingold*, there is no waiting, just constant conversation. Musically, it's not a very melodic opera. It's conversation and politics all the time.

"In Wagner operas, however well you might have prepared yourself or think you know the score and content, there are certain things which can only be found out at rehearsal: the fact that certain singers can't take a given passage at a tempo I originally thought they should— Wagner never used metronome marks, as he said that nobody observed them—because they are not German-speaking, and in Wagner the tempo really changes from singer to singer depending on just that. Characters like Alberich and Mime have very fast dialogue, and German-speaking singers can put it across faster. (Unlike Mozart's Italian operas where, at the right tempo, the Italian comes out quite naturally, regardless of the singer's nationality.)

"Then there are certain details of orchestral balance which, again, can only be settled at rehearsal: some of the odd instruments he uses, like the bass trumpet or the Wagner tuba, have certain passages which may look easy enough on paper, but often prove impossible for a particular bass trumpeter to play at a tempo as slow as that indicated in the score. So, you *have* to take it a little faster.

"This is why operatic conducting is so much harder. It's a bit like driving a car in Israel! You have to be ready for anything, and have very rapid reflexes, so that you can react to and mend anything that might go wrong, like a singer running out of breath, or jumping a few bars. And you have to be practical about accepting and adapting to all the limitations—and there are bound to be many, with so many people involved—and seeing how they can be fitted into your original conception of a score, without ruining it completely."

Bram Gay, the Orchestra Director at Covent Garden, remembers that when Mehta first went there to conduct *Otello*, he didn't much care for the seating arrangement and asked "if we always sat in this crazy way! I said that we did and asked him if he wanted to change it. He said 'No, because *they* won't like it and there are eighty-five of them and only one of me!' That's Zubin for you. Immensely practical and very human, too, eager to ensure that everyone is comfortable and to have a good atmosphere."

As well as *Tristan und Isolde* and *Otello*, Mehta has also conducted *Salome* and new productions of *Die Fledermaus* and *La fanciulla del West* at Covent Garden. *Die Fledermaus* was a sparkling production with many innovations and a few departures from tradition. Orlofsky was a tenor, "because women look like women however you dress them", which displeased a few critics, and Rosalinde, sung by Kiri te Kanawa, was portrayed as a New Zealand woman married to a Viennese. "We were all having a difficult time with the producer, Leopold Lindtberg," says te Kanawa, "then Zubin arrived, the whole place sort of lit up; he has this fantastic and immensely reassuring aura, an effortless authority, and we knew that, at last, everything would be all right. He always listens to what you think and want to do and then adds his own comments and little adjustments here and there. A very exciting, wonderful man to work with. A real *man*." The orchestra liked him, too. "Mehta has this appearance of being a whizzkid, but nothing could be further from the truth," says the principal viola, Jeremy White. "He is a very serious musician, very well prepared and very popular. Sometimes, though, he seems to go down slightly after the first night, as though he were not quite as interested or tense as before."

His only drawback as an opera conductor, according to some, is that he seems to make a kind of sound that is difficult for singers to sing through. "It's the *quality* of sound, nothing to do with decibels," explains Bram Gay. "All conductors have a sound of their own—a particular kind of noise which comes out of the orchestra no matter what music they are playing—and Zubin's sound is full, rich, lush, fleshy and luminous, but I don't think it's *transparent*, and I think that this will be the only problem he'll ever have in the opera house. I always suspect that he likes his music and his orchestra more than the voice."

Mehta himself told me that one of the problems in conducting

Wagner is remembering that you are conducting a drama. There is so much going on in the orchestra that it is easy to abandon yourself to just that, which would, of course, be a mistake. He immerses himself more deeply into an operatic score, especially a Wagner score, than in symphonic music and takes longer, much longer, to unwind afterwards.

"The second act of *Tristan*, for example, must be the most involving piece of music ever written, totally immersible [into] with three climaxes, one on top of the other: after that magical love music, you have King Marke's *Weltschmerz* and after that, Tristan's own outburst. I suppose that the secret is—and believe me, it's very, very hard—to conduct it as though you had lost control, so that the love coming out of the music is there, but without actually losing control even for one beat! I really look forward to conducting it in Vienna [in June 1980]. To have the Vienna Philharmonic in the pit is the greatest luxury a conductor could ask for!" They, in turn, consider him a conductor "who has music in his blood, is very convincing with his gestures and a brisk, sure musician who can electrify the players. There is never a dull moment with Zubin Mehta," says the orchestra's Vorstand, Professor Alfred Altenburger.

In September 1978, Mehta became Music Director of the New York Philharmonic. Much has been written about the circumstances of his hiring and about the fact that eleven years before he had insulted the orchestra in public by boasting that it was not as good as his own Los Angeles Philharmonic, and that it had such a habit of stepping over conductors that he and his colleagues felt that if you had an enemy, the best thing would be to dispatch him to the New York Philharmonic, who would promptly finish him off!

This careless speech caused a furore at the time—a delegation was sent to demand an explanation—and cost him a five-year absence from the orchestra's list of guest conductors. Even though he had made a very dignified and manly apology from the podium when he was finally re-invited in 1974, everybody was slightly nervous about how things would go and how the orchestra would react to him. Fortunately, everything clicked right from the first rehearsal. "I could feel it in my stick!"

"Mehta has created a good atmosphere and invariably commands marvellous discipline," says flautist Julius Baker, "and he has a way of relaxing tension at rehearsal by suddenly coming out with a Yiddish phrase, which warms the cockles of my Jewish heart!" (Mehta's own view is that if orchestral contracts weren't as they are, he'd be "a real son-of-a-bitch!") The leader, Rodney Friend, who has now left the Philharmonic to return to England, says that he has never come across anyone with a stronger stick technique in fifteen years as a Concert-master on both sides of the Atlantic.

One of the first questions that Mehta asked himself on his appointment was whether he could unearth any piece in the repertoire that would be new to the New York Philharmonic, whose repertoire is even vaster than his! This orchestra has one of the longest seasons in the business—mid-September to mid-May—and plays under so many guest conductors that it's really hard to find anything they don't know. ("You could take any obscure piece by Varèse or Stockhausen or Stravinsky and find that, sure enough, they have already played it with Pierre Boulez!") But he rejoices in the fact that the musical repertoire is *so* vast that, although he conducts ninety concerts and twenty-two programmes a year, there is hardly a concert without something new to *him*.

He decided that a gargantuan season like this would be more interesting if they had mini-cycles devoted to particular composers, rather than just odd concerts "like mushrooms". The theme of his inaugural 1978–79 season was Schubert, plus the beginning of a Haydn cycle that will go on throughout his tenure—which, because of the enthusiastic response of orchestra, press and public, was extended until 1986, after only one season. ("I feel as though I have signed half my life away," he sighs.)

"I know that we won't be able to do all the one hundred and four Haydn symphonies, but we will do about six or eight a season, which adds up to a total of forty or fifty, and this is good for the orchestra, because although every orchestra knows some standard Haydn symphonies, *no* orchestra knows them *all*!* The 1980–81 season will also include all the Stravinsky orchestral works, and in 1981–82, which is Bartók's anniversary, we shall try to do as many of his works as possible. In 1982–83 will come a Schönberg retrospective, starting with *Verklärte Nacht* and ending with the *Variations for Orchestra*, which will be interesting because it will take us on a long musical journey through the tonal, atonal and twelve-tone periods." As well as choosing a repertoire that offers opportunities to play contrasting

* Apart from the Philharmonia Ungarica who recorded them all for Decca with Antal Dorati.

styles, one of Mehta's other aims at the Philharmonic is to get the best possible guest conductors, which is proving much easier in New York than it was during his first few seasons in Los Angeles. Every now and then, he likes to invite a composer and dedicate the week to his work.

He is happy and pleased with the way things are going at the Philharmonic, not because he is considered "a success" with this difficult and temperamental orchestra ("Difficult? Compared to the Israelis, they are like pussy cats!" he told a television interviewer), and in any case he will only consider *himself* a success when all his aims have been fulfilled—but because this gradual build-up of communion, of osmosis, between himself and the orchestra, which is so essential to him, has begun: "I now feel confident enough in most of my players to loosen the rein and let them take over. Sometimes, it's nice to let the *whole* orchestra take over, when you see that things are going at a steady pace. It's like driving a six-horse carriage: if all the horses are perfectly co-ordinated, what are you going to whip them for? But if you see that one is a little out of step, you pull the rein in a fraction. (Sometimes, of course, you *have* to come in, the music demands it!) But getting to this stage is a great comfort for a conductor, and that's why I feel that with my own orchestras, I'm sitting in an easy chair."

But he feels that music directors and guest conductors alike have one problem, and "it should be the first sentence in your book": not enough rehearsal time! "We are never given enough rehearsal time. We get three or sometimes four rehearsals when we could do with twice as many. The only reason why you hear reasonably good and sometimes *very* good music, is that nowadays players are very good indeed. We may all take this for granted now, but Casals told me that in-tune playing only came in at the turn of the century; and that his teacher was one of the very first people to play in tune on the cello!

"As there are no recordings from that period, this is something we could only learn from somebody like Casals, who was alive at the time. But can you imagine what the late Beethoven quartets—which are harmonically so advanced—would have sounded like if played basically out of tune? Cacophony! No wonder people were appalled and blamed them on Beethoven's deafness.

"I don't want to go on too long about intonation, well-tempered intonation, because this is a book in itself! But, basically, in the purest sense of the word, all wind and brass instruments are out of tune, and it is only because players are so good that they manage to play what today we call in tune: certain notes on the oboe are flat, certain notes on the flute are sharp, but players, of course, know these things and compensate for them. But sometimes a musician doesn't think or isn't sensitive enough to a certain chord—say a clarinettist who has to place a note in a certain chord either wasn't attentive enough or didn't anticipate his note—and you hear out-of-tune playing. That's why rehearsals are so vital: for players to find out *exactly* where to place each note."

Mehta is not a fanatic, uncompromising personality and his eagerness to solve problems and strong practical streak are much appreciated by managements and soloists alike. According to Sir Claus Moser, Chairman of the Board at Covent Garden, their production of *Die Fledermaus* ran into so many problems that it was only Mehta's ingenuity, flexibility and determination to go on that saved the situation. Massimo Bogianckino, the Director Designate of the Paris Opéra and formerly of the Maggio Musicale finds him "one of the most human and humane conductors, genuinely concerned about everybody's comfort and always able to skirt around obstacles and solve problems so that the show can go on. A real trouper!"

Soloists find him a sympathetic and intuitive accompanist. The violinist Itzhak Perlman, another member of the "kosher nostra", the group of artistic and personal friends which includes Daniel Barenboim and Pinchas Zukerman, finds that their empathy is such that they can experiment with unrehearsed, spontaneous ideas on the spur of the moment, which is "exhilarating". Dame Janet Baker is deeply impressed by his sensitivity and respect for the soloist, and so is the soprano Shirley Verrett. "I love Zubin. He's such a natural musician, very instinctive, very quick, a perfect animal. He can respond to anything. You can rehearse something, and he follows everything you do just like that. But if at the performance you feel like trying something else on the spur of the moment, he picks it up straight away."

"I am as professional a musician as any," he shrugs, "and if I don't agree with soloists, I will at least do nothing that gets in their way. If we really don't see eye to eye, I will change or modify my own thinking, because it's *his* performance, he has spent many more hours on the concerto or Lieder than I have, and it would be much more difficult for him, who is actually producing the sound, to change his interpretation than for me to adjust mine."

The only criticism of him that I have heard concerns the fact that he simply does too much. He works non-stop, jetting from a concert in New York straight into a rehearsal in Vienna or Tel Aviv after a few hours sleep on the plane, and this sometimes results in polished, highly proficient but "skin-deep" interpretations. After all, he can hardly get any higher, in terms of jobs and honours, but can and should go deeper and deeper into the spirit behind a score. So why does he keep rushing so? Why does he not say "no" more often?

"Oh, I say 'no' more often than you imagine," he snapped. "I just don't *want* to do less. I love what I do so much that my work is my holiday. This is the crux of the matter. Before I got married for the second time [to ex-Hollywood actress Nancy Kovack] I never ever took a holiday. Now, at her insistence, I take a month, which I always see as a God-sent gap for learning another score, much to her annoyance, although, of course, she understands. I feel I am thriving at my present rhythm of doing things, and don't find the pressure as tight as people imagine, I really don't!"

He is a passionately loyal and devoted friend with a wide and not exclusively musical circle of friends and this, the fact that he can also appeal to people who are not musicians or even music lovers, might explain why the American press filled their gossip columns with items about his glamorous image for years. (Admittedly, the fact that he posed naked for *Paris Match* and upside-down for *Time* didn't help much. But he dismisses all that as the exuberant high spirits of a lively young man.)

Mehta is a practising Parsee, and neither drinks nor smokes. "Parsees are supposed to say prayers for an hour each day, but I can't quite do that. I pray in my own way. In the middle of a Bruckner symphony, I feel closer to God than any church-goer. Music is something I can touch, something beautiful and perfect, and what is God, if not perfection?"

But although he doesn't drink, he loves his food, is a good cook who never travels without a supply of chilli peppers in his pockets, who has a very sweet tooth and thinks nothing of emptying a box of chocolates in half an hour or of ordering no less than three *petits pôts au chocolat* topped with generous dollops of cream! A friend reports that once, when he was about twenty-seven, he decided to find out what the appeal of alcohol was all about, and downed enough vodkas to flatten a seasoned drinker. But it had no effect whatsoever, on his head, or his legs or his stomach.

In the little spare time he has, he likes to swim, play tennis or backgammon, or snatch a few days off and fly off with his grown up son for walks in the Himalayas. (Both children are from his first marriage to Carmen Lasky, who subsequently married his younger brother.) A sport addict, he sometimes goes over a score while watching a match on television.

The quality he likes best and looks for in human beings is warmth. "I know I should say honesty, but it has to be warmth. I just can't deal with cold people. I have nothing to say to them. So, hopefully, among the warm people, I shall find the honest ones! What I absolutely detest, in either sex, is neutrality. And there seem to be an awful lot of neutral people in the world."

Zubin Mehta is not one of them. He is well known for his fearless, whole-hearted commitment to causes and countries, and doesn't believe that an artist can, or should, isolate himself in the ivory tower of his Art and abdicate from his responsibilities as a human being. "More, many more artists should have spoken out against the Nazis and while not belittling Richard Strauss and Furtwängler as musicians, it is, nevertheless, significant that Toscanini and Erich Kleiber were not only purists in the musical sense, but acted in the same uncompromising way as human beings."

Not only has he travelled in Israel during all its wars, but will also not visit Russia until it changes its attitudes towards Jewish immigrants, did not play in Greece after the King's exile, refused to accompany the Israel Philharmonic to South Africa in protest against its racial policies—and was more conspicuous by his absence because the story got into all the papers, thereby highlighting the issue, which is "all we can do"—and will now not conduct *any* orchestra in India, where the Israelis are not welcome, which caused a debate in Parliament.

"Conducting Beethoven is not enough. People like us must make a stand some time in our lives. You can't live in today's world—a very small world because communications make ignorance of what is going on, say in Somalia, impossible—and divorce yourself from its problems by saying that for you, the most important thing in the world is the tempo of the 'Eroica'! That's rubbish! It's cowardice and escapism. Of course, we can't change governments or directly affect their decisions. But we can use the fact that we are well known to publicize our views and cause them embarrassment."

Mehta's very first public concert, at the age of twenty, was a political gesture. It was given in a Hungarian refugee camp on the Austrian border, in 1956. He was still a student at the Academy, and managed to put together a student orchestra to play Schubert and one of Liszt's *Hungarian Rhapsodies* for them. At the end, amidst the cheering and emotional scenes in the audience, a priest came up to the podium, made the sign of the cross and blessed him. "I couldn't understand a word he said, but it seems to have worked."

RICCARDO MUTI
A Normal Person Living a Far-From-Normal Life

Neapolitan-born Riccardo Muti, Music Director of the Philadelphia Orchestra* and Laureate Conductor of the Philharmonia, is a highly intelligent, well-balanced man ("simple—no eccentricities"), who intensely dislikes both the social and the musical implications of today's "cult of the conductor".

"A conductor is only a bridge between music and the public. He should serve only music and the composition at hand—never himself. If he draws too much attention to himself by what he is doing technically, externally, rather than trying to communicate the inner musical content of the work, he fails the music."

But he admits that the art of conducting is a mystery "that cannot be explained. Of course, there is such a thing as a conducting technique which everybody understands: the orchestra understand it, the singers understand it, and those members of the public who are musically knowledgeable understand it. For example, how to give an upbeat, how to beat in four, or in five or in seven, all those are technical things that can be learnt and understood. But *why* a certain conductor can obtain a certain kind of sound, a certain kind of forte, a certain kind of piano or pianissimo and *how* he succeeds in holding a hundred and twenty people together—which does not involve merely the technical ability to hold them together but also the inner will to do so—these are factors which transcend the confines of technique and are profoundly mysterious. Perhaps they have something to do with the kind and degree of electricity which we conductors have inside us and which we transmit to the orchestra. And it goes without saying that the more electricity we have inside, the more we transmit.

* Until 1982, he was Music Director of the Philharmonia and Principal Conductor of the Maggio Musicale Fiorentino.

"For nowadays a conductor can do no more than transmit his mental image of a work to the players. He can no longer *impose* his will, because the days of dictatorial conductors are over. Nor can he fool or cheat the orchestra, who must submit to his fascination or magnetism—call it what you like—voluntarily. And they either do or don't. The quality that compels them to do so is leadership, and it cannot be learnt. It must be innate. And the ways in which it is transmitted are sometimes extremely subtle. Take an orchestra waiting for a conductor it doesn't know to step onto the podium for the first time. From the moment he stands up there, before he even gives the first downbeat, the orchestra *feels* whether or not he has personality. The feeling will, of course, be confirmed by his conducting ability and musical preparation. But the *way* he walks in, steps onto the podium and addresses the orchestra already creates a certain situation, a certain tension—or it creates nothing. And this phenomenon cannot be explained in concrete terms but is part of a spiritual sphere of things which we cannot fully understand or explain. In the future, it will perhaps be possible to perceive and explain more clearly those electric, magnetic forces and the personal magnetism of a person. Today we cannot, because we know very little about the mystery of the human brain."

Muti is himself a very electric performer who creates strong excitement and whose orchestra-training ability has changed the sound of two famous orchestras—or rather, has enabled him to stamp them with *his* sound—in a relatively short space of time. The "Muti sound", a chief characteristic of which is the clarity and incredible agility of the string playing he draws out, is easily recognizable, and can now be heard in both London and Philadelphia. "Muti can't stand the high spiccato—the spiccato that rattles, while other conductors like and ask for it," says the Assistant Leader of the Philharmonia Orchestra, Martin Jones. "He is always asking for a lot of vibrato, and this makes for a tremendously voluptuous but very *slim* sound. A lot of American orchestras make a voluptuous sound, but it's aggressive and hard-edged. The 'Muti sound' never is."

After only a few seasons, the Philharmonia, demoralized by Klemperer's long illness and gradual decay and steeped in a rather heavy, almost exclusively Germanic and by then distinctly old-fashioned tradition, was changed into a modern, versatile, virtuoso orchestra, capable of distinguishing itself in every style from Haydn to Penderecki. Similarly, the full, turgid sound of the Philadelphia

Orchestra has already been refined into something lighter, more transparent and more agile.

Muti explains that an orchestra always reflects the style of its Principal Conductor. Naturally, this doesn't happen from one day to the next. But if an orchestra wants to change, it changes. And of course, the quality of orchestral sound is greatly affected by a conductor's gestures—the power, intensity, decisiveness, hardness or softness in the arm, wrist or elbow, which is partly why different conductors obtain a different sound from the same orchestra.

"For a conductor, the orchestra is a human instrument—an instrument consisting of one hundred and twenty people, but nevertheless an instrument—which must be moulded according to his will. If he does not succeed in shaping it to reflect his own style and has to resort to compromise, he is not a good conductor." ("The symphony orchestra is the greatest musical instrument, and the conductor is the most privileged musician, because he is the man who plays it. And Muti is one of the few conductors who can do this. He actually *plays* his instrument," confirms the Leader of the Philharmonia Orchestra, Christopher Warren-Green.) "This," says Muti, "is especially true when he is dealing with orchestras who have had one permanent conductor for a long, long time and are therefore used to playing the standard works in the repertoire in one particular way, which has become routine. The newly arrived conductor is then faced with the problem of eradicating this deeply implanted interpretation and substituting his own."

Muti considers that a new Music Director's main task is to give his orchestra one direction, one idea and one style of playing, an easily recognizable style, which will become "the" style of this particular orchestra, and a residue of which will remain even when guest conductors superimpose their own personalities and interpretations on it. "He must also strive to make this human instrument as technically valid and as technically perfect as possible—even though perfection is inconceivable in musical interpretation. Above all, he must work hard to ensure that the players learn to listen to each other while playing, in the same way that a string quartet listen to one another. Because, in one respect, an orchestra is like a string quartet: one hundred and twenty people who should sound like four. When the different sections— strings, woodwind, brass and percussion—all listen to each other, it makes for a better, more precise ensemble.

"He should also endeavour to develop the same kind of playing for all the strings: the same way of using the bow, the same type of spiccato, possibly even the same kind of vibrato, which is very difficult indeed. And, of course, he should also work on intonation, and on the balance between the various sections. In short, the sound of the orchestra should come across as a perfectly rounded circle in which one can distinguish all the details, the mechanism of its different parts, but without ever losing track of its 'wholeness'. Hearing only the details, only the different parts, would be disastrous. But obtaining a round yet transparent sound in which all details are discernible, is a slow, extremely difficult and delicate task.

"Yet at that crucial moment when a conductor first comes into contact with an orchestra, it is not only the orchestra who judges the conductor: he, too, instantly forms an opinion of its capacities and potential, and understands what kind of sound it has—a dry, a round, or a full, turgid sound; whether the balance between the instrument groups is right or whether one group predominates and swamps the others; whether the orchestra has good intonation. And this is partly why this first moment in which the two forces judge each other is so full of suspense: each studies the other and tries to guess what kettle of fish he will shortly be dealing with. And a great number of things are decided at that first contact. Sometimes, it determines whether a concert will be good or not."

Muti was born in Naples on July 28, 1941, and spent part of his early childhood in Apulia. By the time he was six, his father, a doctor with a good tenor voice and a great love of music, moved his family of five sons back to the city, to ensure that they had the benefit of a good education and a wide choice of outside interests. All the boys studied music, but Riccardo is the only one to have become a musician. The other four opted for careers in medicine, economics and engineering.

He started taking violin lessons at the age of eight, prompted by his father, who had noticed that this particular son had perfect pitch, but four years later, he switched to the piano. (Yet his first-hand knowledge of the violin must contribute a lot to Muti's distinctive sound, so dependent on the quality of the string playing.) His piano teacher at the Conservatoire was Vincenzo Vitale, an old pupil of Alfred Cortot's, who was quick to spot and encourage young Muti's exceptional musical gift. Until then, the boy had studied music merely for the pleasure of it. When "it was seen that I had talent", he gradually began to think in terms of a career as a pianist. Even though this meant going to school every morning and the Conservatoire every afternoon, he says that he had a happy childhood and a "healthy Mediterranean adolescence with plenty of outside interests".

He cannot single out any specific "mentor" figure among his teachers, but feels deeply marked by the Neapolitan roots of his early education. Naples was steeped in a rich and lively musical tradition dating back to the eighteenth century, when the two main schools of music in Italy were the Venetian and the Neapolitan, which produced composers like Cimarosa, Paisiello, Durante and Piccinni. It also boasts the famous Teatro di San Carlo which saw the premières of so many of the operas of Cimarosa, Alessandro Scarlatti, Pergolesi, Rossini, Donizetti and Bellini. Indeed, Donizetti had been the Director of, and Bellini had studied at, the very same Conservatoire where Muti spent his formative years—a fact which never failed to thrill him. In fact, rumour around the school had it that anyone working there late at night was apt to hear an organ being played in the distance— supposedly by Bellini's ghost!

"The fact that my education was so deeply rooted in the Neapolitan school has left a lasting imprint on me as a conductor. Had I gone to Vienna or Berlin or London to study, I would surely have developed into a different musician," he explained to a French magazine. "As it is, I consider myself a thoroughly, one hundred per cent Italian conductor. Yet music is universal, and here I am, Music Director of an English and an American orchestra. For while every conductor is educated in a certain way, it is then up to him to develop his own ideas about musical interpretation. All this is very hard to explain! But take for example Toscanini, a typically Italian conductor, and Furtwängler, a typically German conductor. This doesn't mean that the former shouldn't have tackled the German and the latter the Italian repertoire; nor did it stop them from doing so. One cannot reason this way.

"So, what I am trying to say is simply that I studied in Italy, with all that this implies, but this raw material has been enriched by my experiences in foreign countries. If I was born a Neapolitan, I did not remain simply a Neapolitan. My work in foreign countries has made me what I am now. For example, one of the greatest triumphs of my career was an all-Mozart concert at the Salzburg Festival. On paper, it sounded rather strange: a southern Italian conducting Mozart in the temple of the Mozartian tradition! Yet both the public and the critics pronounced it a great success. So one must conclude that, for an artist,

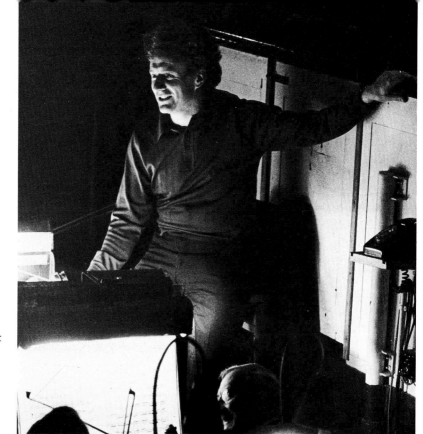

Sir Colin Davis: "Let them look at you until the Day of Judgement! Stand there and be counted. Unashamed!" CLIVE BARDA

Bernard Haitink: forever delving deeper into works which "like all masterpieces reveal their mysteries only very gradually, in layers, as you keep returning to them again and again. And for *that* it's well worth losing one's youth!" CLIVE BARDA

Top: Carlo Maria Giulini: "What happens at moments of performance is something very secret."
G. MACDOMNIC

Above: Giulini is always impeccably, immaculately dressed, in suits which used always to be chosen and ordered for him by his wife. CHRISTIAN STEINER

Giulini at rehearsal: he doesn't see the conductor's function as "telling the musicians what to do, but making music together, serving together this great thing that is music...."
CLIVE BARDA

Lorin Maazel:
. . . "And if you can do the job, there is no point in hesitating or saying well, what am I doing here, somebody else could do it better. That's not modesty, that's false modesty." CLIVE BARDA

Below: The violin virtuoso: "Practising the violin requires a very high degree of concentration." CLIVE BARDA

Bottom: Master Technician.
CHRISTINA BURTON

Sir Charles Mackerras with the eminent Czech conductor Vaclav Talich with whom he studied in Prague.
SIR CHARLES MACKERRAS

"Chuck 'em up Charlie" with Dame Janet Baker, during the recording of *Judas Maccabaeus* for Archive in 1977: a joyous and fruitful collaboration which has resulted in "some marvellous moments on stage and has stretched me further than I would otherwise have gone" (Dame Janet Baker).
SIR CHARLES MACKERRAS

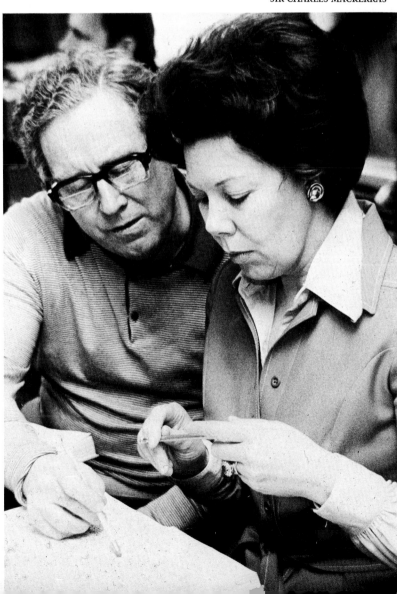

Zubin Mehta: *Left:* Warmth is
the quality he likes best in human
beings—and possesses in abundance.
VIVIANNE PURDOM

Right: Mehta is a teetotaller, whose
only drink, apart from orange juice, is
water. ELFRIEDE HANAK

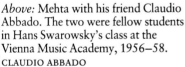

Above: Mehta with his friend Claudio
Abbado. The two were fellow students
in Hans Swarowsky's class at the
Vienna Music Academy, 1956–58.
CLAUDIO ABBADO

Right: Master and disciple: Mehta
with one of his mentors, the pianist
Arthur Rubinstein, whose advice and
guidance he has found invaluable.
DECCA

Riccardo Muti:
Right: Relaxing yet "my mind is never completely free like other people's and that's the most tiring part of our lives. We always carry our work inside us." CLIVE BARDA

Below: "*Why* a certain conductor can obtain a certain kind of sound, a certain kind of forte, a certain kind of piano or pianissimo, and *how* he succeeds in holding a hundred people together—these are factors which transcend the confines of technique and are profoundly mysterious." CLIVE BARDA

there is no such thing as national frontiers. Yet each of us carries inside him his birth, his formation, his studies, his experience. They are the components which make up our personality as conductors."

Conducting didn't in fact come into Muti's life until 1960 when, by chance, the Director at the Conservatoire asked him to try conducting a student orchestra. First, he studied the full orchestral score on the piano, and remembers the sensation of seeing the music taking shape in his mind in a way that never happened when studying piano scores. When he stepped onto the podium and "saw the results I could obtain and felt the excitement of the musicians responding to my instructions and rhythmic indications, which could not have been very sophisticated, I understood that I must have the necessary qualities for conducting and allowed myself to be seduced by the idea. It was a little bit like the apple and Adam and Eve. And once smitten inside, it became like a drug. I couldn't do without it."

That same evening he told his father that he wanted to become a professional conductor. Until then, he had bowed to the parental will and enrolled at Naples University where he studied Philosophy for three semesters, while preparing for his piano finals at the Conservatoire. Now the dilemma was how to set about becoming a conductor and where to continue his musical studies. Spurred on by reading some of Mozart's letters, he opted for the Giuseppe Verdi Conservatoire in Milan (to which Verdi himself had failed his entrance exams), where he studied conducting with Antonino Votto, a former assistant of Toscanini's and a great expert on the voice, and composition with Bruno Bettinelli, who also taught Claudio Abbado.

As soon as he decided to become a conductor, he developed a "strong need" to study composition and acquire a thorough technical training without which he would have felt "unprepared, unready". It was a brave decision because in Italy the composition course takes ten years and consists of four years of harmony, three years of counterpoint—covering all the Flemish, Italian and German contrapuntalists, with their respective styles and counterpoints in twelve, thirteen or fifteen parts, double choirs, etc.—and three years of orchestration. The aim is to provide a thorough knowledge of all forms of composition from sonatas to symphonies, plus an intimate understanding of instrumentation and the possibilities of each instrument—the latter particularly significant for prospective conductors who might otherwise find themselves tempted to ask of various instruments things which they cannot actually do.

Muti considers such a knowledge of composition, plus the ability to play one instrument really well, to be indispensable to a conductor, "because the study of composition enables him to look at a score and understand its technical structure and, through this, to arrive at an understanding of its musical and spiritual content. Take one of the more complex fugues in eight voices, for example. A conductor who has not studied counterpoint wouldn't fully understand their technical mechanism. Certainly, he could conduct them. But he couldn't *interpret* them well. Because really to understand the method by which a score is composed, one should be in a position to compose it oneself—technically that is. I'm not implying that one could also conceive the musical content, that would be sacrilegious!"

Muti completed this course which, he stresses, was a study of composition *for conducting*, in five years, and remembers with amusement his final examinations which have remained the same since the days when Mozart went to Bologna to study with Padre Martini. Part of them is a thirty-six-hour ordeal during which the pupils are given a certain theme by their Professors, and are then locked in a room with a window, a bed, a piano, plus pencil and paper. There is a small red light they can press if they are dying! In those hours they have to compose the first part of a sonata in the style of Brahms or another important composer. Now times have changed and the pupils are free to compose, according to their own inclination, a contrapuntal, a twelve-tone or an atonal quartet. A few years ago, the pupils in Milan rebelled against this "inhuman" examination—unsuccessfully, much to Muti's satisfaction, "because this test tells you a lot about yourself".

During this second year in Milan, he won a scholarship which stipulated that he had to act as piano accompanist in one of the Conservatoire's singing classes—possibly the foundation of his extra-ordinarily deep understanding of the voice, which singers who now work with him invariably comment on and praise. "The teacher was Maria Carbone, who had been a famous singer schooled in the Neapolitan tradition and possessing an astounding vocal technique. I learnt many secrets about the voice while accompanying her pupils. Nowadays, conductors seem suddenly to break into opera just like that, with only symphonic experience behind them and knowing nothing about singers or singing. In fact, singers never cease to complain about the total lack of guidance they come up against. Many conductors limit themselves to asking them to sing louder, softer, more or less legato."

After graduating from the Verdi Conservatoire in 1966—where, in Maria Carbone's singing class, he had met a pretty, vivacious mezzo-soprano from Ravenna called Cristina Mazzavillani who three years later was to become his wife—Muti entered and won first prize at the Guido Cantelli Conductors' Competition, in 1967. There, he caught the attention of Vittorio Gui, another of Toscanini's former chief assistants and Founder of the Maggio Musicale Fiorentino annual Festival, who invited him to conduct a concert at the city's Teatro Communale, with Sviatoslav Richter as soloist.

The concert proved crucial in more ways than one. Firstly, it prompted the orchestra and administrators of the Maggio Musicale to ask him to become their Principal Conductor, starting with the 1969 season. Secondly, Eugene Ormandy heard a rehearsal of his during the Philadelphia Orchestra's European tour and invited him to conduct in Philadelphia, thus triggering off a chain of events that led to his Music Directorship there. One understands why he says that he himself never sought any of the things he has. "They just happened, somehow. Yet I have always been aware of an invisible hand pushing me in the direction it wants me to go: destiny, perhaps."

Florence was the first plum that destiny dropped into his lap, and for many years (until 1981) remained the place where he did the bulk of his operatic work—two new productions a year, usually one for the Teatro Comunale's winter season and one for the Maggio Musicale— and where he established his reputation as one of today's most brilliant conductors of Italian and French opera. He thinks of Florence as "his" opera house, where he can work in conditions hardly realizable elsewhere.

"The orchestra, the chorus, the technical staff are all united and really supportive. We are a good team, and it shows in the work. For instance, a few years ago, we mounted a production of the uncut version of Rossini's *Guglielmo Tell* which lasted six hours—from eight p.m. to two a.m., and nobody demurred about the very long hours."

To date, his Florence productions include *Aida, Un ballo in maschera, Macbeth, Nabucco, I masnadieri, Il trovatore, I vespri Siciliani, La forza del destino, Orfeo ed Euridice, L'Africaine, Guglielmo Tell, Norma, I Puritani, Cavalleria rusticana, I pagliacci, Otello, Le nozze di Figaro* and *Iphigénie en Tauride*. He limits himself to three operatic productions a year—two in Florence and one elsewhere, because he admits to being extremely difficult as far as producers, designers and casts are concerned. When preparing a new opera, he is in the theatre from morning till night, and even attends lighting rehearsals. It's very difficult to obtain such conditions—and he insists on them in every theatre he works at. This is why he did two out of his three annual productions in Florence. His operatic appearances elsewhere have included a triumphant début at the 1971 Salzburg Festival with *Don Pasquale*; *Aida*, *La forza del destino* and *Norma* at the Vienna State Opera; *Aida* at the Bavarian State Opera in Munich; *Aida* and a new production of *Macbeth* at Covent Garden.

Like Karajan and Kleiber, he insists on taking all piano rehearsals himself. This he finds essential because it enables the conductor to transmit his ideas directly to the singers, without an intermediary, and to know exactly where they are going to breathe; and he can work on every word, every meaning, every phrase, until a total textual and musical unity is achieved.

"This is particularly vital in Verdi. The singers must be in total control of every word, and of the meaning of every word, because Verdi's music is born out of the words. His libretti do not consist of words casually superimposed on the music. He always studied his texts in depth and was perpetually unhappy with his librettists. And when the meaning was not profound enough, or the imagery not poetic enough, he insisted that it be changed or improved. In fact, he always made his librettists' lives terrible and miserable, because nothing was ever good enough for him.

"And only after he finally had a satisfactory libretto did he start composing his music. This is why the recitatives are so perfect and so crucial in Verdi. In fact, his true greatness as a composer lies in the unsurpassed perfection of his recitatives where every note exactly corresponds to the dramatic meaning of each word. Of course, the arias are marvellous and we all know them—in fact, the majority of the public goes to the opera to hear the famous arias and sleep in between—but the recitatives are a capital lesson, and a test for singers, even in his early operas. In works like *I masnadieri*, *Giovanna d'Arco*, *Macbeth* and *Attila*, you will find that if a singer succeeds in mastering the recitatives, he or she will realize that they become exactly like speaking, only at a higher level, because they are written in such a natural way as to sound like talking. But if they are not done with absolute precision—and I'm not talking about something as pedestrian as a purely rhythmical precision, but of the effort to penetrate, through the written signs, to the inner dramatic essence—one totally misses the point in Verdi.

"A good example of what I mean is the Nile scene in the third act of *Aida*, in which Aida is trying to learn from Radamès the name of the route to be taken by the Egyptian forces for their invasion of Ethiopia: Radamès says: 'Il sentiero scelto dai nostri a piombar sul nemico fia deserto fino a domani' ('The path chosen by us for our attack on the enemy will be deserted till tomorrow'), and Aida, who wants to know *which* route it is, answers 'E, quel sentier?' ('And, the path is?'). She knows that she is betraying him by asking this question, and this is why she doesn't just ask 'E quel sentier' but 'E', *comma*, 'quel sentier?' There is a slight hesitation, a pause, written in the music. And the tenor replies 'Le gole di Nàpata', thus betraying his country. And he, too, has a momentary hesitation before doing so. It's all a psychological game between the characters.

"So, when I hear a singer sing this phrase without this imperceptible pause, I know that she has understood nothing, and that everything is distorted, because she has missed the essence of this character, the drama of this woman torn between her lover and her father, her country and love. You see, I am not interested in singers who can sing 'La donna è mobile' spectacularly. But if a singer sings 'E', *comma*, 'quel sentier?' having understood the reason for this tiny pause, I know that she is a great singer. Because to a second-rate singer the recitatives are simply a quick way to the aria. But to a great singer, they are often the most active and intense parts of the score.

"In fact, there are very, very few great singers today. The situation is tragic and staging operas has become a real problem. To be a good singer you need a beautiful voice, a good appearance, musical intelligence plus a good technique, and it's very difficult to find all these in one person. Yet I don't really know why there should be fewer great voices now than in the past decades. It might have something to do with the way singers are taught, because there are no more good teachers.

"Then there is the time factor: to obtain really good results from singers, you need a lot of time, which is always lacking from our contemporary musical life. Toscanini, for example, had a group of assistants like Votto and Gui who worked with the singers for over two months, according to his specifications, and then he himself would arrive and polish everything to perfection. One of the problems now is that even when you do ask for a lot of preparation time—and I invariably do—you find that it is seldom long enough for you to change the bad habits that even basically good singers may have acquired over the years, habits which have the knack of reappearing during the performance, what with tension, nerves, etc."

Brigitte Fassbänder, who sang Amneris under him in the Bavarian State Opera's production of *Aida*, found him wonderful to work with. "Like Kleiber, he was there from the very first rehearsal, and worked very intensely on every word, the meaning and the inflection of every word, and knew how to explain all the moods and emotional nuances of the character. It was the first time I was tackling this role, which is not really my type of thing, and he knew this and was incredibly understanding and sympathetic. I trusted him straight away and asked how come he knew such a lot about the voice and he said that during his conservatoire days, he had accompanied singers in class, so you can imagine how fantastic this is for us who now have to work with him. I had never before met a conductor who understood so much about the voice and the technical problems of vocal production and control. He helped me mould really long phrases and gave me plenty of time to breathe. I shall never forget the experience. And at the performance he is like an animal, a lion or a tiger or something, because he has such energy ... but strangely enough although he is powerful and fiery, the fire is all underground, firmly under control and very, very disciplined. And he looks so beautiful in the pit. Wonderful man, like a young Toscanini, that kind of person, like a Caesar...."

"I think he is a fantastic man, a fantastic musician," says Agnes Baltsa who has sung several performances of the Verdi *Requiem* and recorded Gluck's *Orfeo ed Euridice* with him. "He knows exactly what he wants and explains it in great detail. His conception of *Orfeo* was very pure, classical, virginal and very interesting. And he made all those recitatives, which can often sound so boring, very, very, dramatic."

Muti's intense involvement with every aspect of production stops short of a desire to be his own producer, though, because he doesn't want a high musical level to be offset by a low dramatic one. He is basically in sympathy with the young, more controversial breed of producer provided that their scenic innovations don't kill or smother the music, and provided that they do not consider themselves masters of the situation. "They must work on and *with* the music, and in perfect agreement with the conductor."

The producer with whom he has worked most closely throughout his operatic career is Luca Ronconi, one of today's most intelligent and controversial, "a very great artist with very advanced ideas", with whom he collaborates so harmoniously that he often feels there is "something missing" when he comes to work with other producers.

"Ronconi has great respect for opera and the work in hand, and is one of the directors who best realize my musical imagination in scenic and dramatic terms—or, at least, make it possible for it to unfold without being confronted by contradictory situations onstage. He and I have endless discussions together. First of all, I explain the opera to him from the musical point of view. Then he goes away to think. Later on, he returns with some of his ideas. I tell him what I like and what I dislike, and he seems willing to modify his positions accordingly. From there on, we work together constantly. He feels a genuine need to be guided by the conductor and his interpretation."

Ronconi confirms this and adds that "while the functions of the conductor and the director are distinct—because there are two laws that govern opera, one purely musical and the other scenic, and the two are completely independent—there is great affinity and general agreement between Muti and myself, because my choices are always linked to the requirements of his musical interpretations. And this must always be so in opera: the conductor's interpretation must be the point of reference for the visual and dramatic aspects."

Many of their joint productions have made operatic history—notably *Orfeo ed Euridice*, *Nabucco*, *Norma* and *Il trovatore*—and all have been widely discussed. Muti's own favourite is *Orfeo*, "a magical, miraculous production in which Orfeo and Euridice were dressed to look alike, so that when he finds her in Hades, it is a case of meeting himself, because in life you must seek out someone who completes yourself."

Many of their productions attracted wide interest not merely because of the high quality of their musical and scenic interpretations, but also because they were invariably of the original, authentic versions of the works, stripped of all latter-day additions or distortions piled on by so-called tradition. This passionate attachment to the composer's intentions and insistence on absolute textual precision is a main characteristic of Muti as a musician, and has earned him the reputation of being a purist. He gladly admits to being one: "Conductors should never lay a finger on the score. They shouldn't change a single note. They must believe in a work in order to give it to the public. If they don't, they shouldn't do it at all. Imagine going to a museum and saying that some of the paintings are very beautiful, but need touching up at the corners, or could do with more paint here and there.

Unthinkable in painting, but, sadly, common when it comes to music.*

"It is easier, in a way, to tamper with operatic scores and add embellishments here and there to suit individual singers, or even to change things in order to accommodate their vanity. Some of these changes have unfortunately become 'traditional'—so much so that the public have come to expect them as a matter of course. But singers are not *always* to blame. They are often under great pressure from the public, who accuse them of having no voice if they avoid the usual pyrotechnics, instead of demanding of them that they sing not only as beautifully, but also as truthfully, as they can.

"Because the only 'star' of an opera is the composer. Conductors should always look for the inner dramatic meaning of a work in his notes, instructions and specifications alone. If anything sounds unusual and puzzles them, they shouldn't just assume that it is wrong, but ask themselves why this is so and seek the reasons for it. They certainly have no right to change the score."

True to his word, he used the original *Il trovatore* score—minus the high 'C' in 'Di quella pira'—for his Florence production; the uncut, six-hour version of Rossini's *Guglielmo Tell*; and the Paris version of Verdi's *Otello*, for which the composer himself wrote an alternative finale for the third act which gives much greater prominence to Iago, who is brought forward onstage and dominates the chorus whose part is lengthened and made more distant. But he knows that there are no hard-and-fast rules or guidelines for a conductor trying to decide between different editions of the same work. He should seek to inform himself about the circumstances in which each version was composed, and about the composer's motives for returning to his original score.

"The basic problem is to decide which version the composer himself considered to be his last word on the subject. Because the very fact that there is more than one version means that the composer was not satisfied with his original score and returned to it again. Therefore, as far as performing the work is concerned, the last should be considered the most valid, the definitive edition, even though any other versions might also be interesting from the musicological, academic point of view.

* The principal trumpet of the Philharmonia Orchestra, John Wallace, who is also a composer with several works to his credit, paid Muti one of the greatest compliments a composer could pay a conductor. When asked which of the conductors he had worked with would best serve him as a composer, he answered that Muti would be the one most scrupulously fair to his score. He added: "He would give it everything he has. He can make a silk purse out of a sow's ear. So, if I'd written a bad piece, he'd dress it up and interpret it in such a way that it would seem much better than it is. It is incredible what he can do even to the most mediocre of works."

"A good example of this is *Macbeth*, to which Verdi himself made some significant changes. The second edition can therefore definitely be said to represent his final wish, and this is the one I always perform. It is also the version I used in my recording. But at the end of the record, as an item of curiosity, I included the three arias from the original score, which Verdi later replaced with the ones we now know."

But the choice is not always this simple, because there are cases where the composer has left several different editions of a work, without intending the later ones to cancel the original, and trying to decide the merits and demerits of each one can be very problematic. Gluck's *Orfeo* is a good example of such a case. Gluck wrote the original version, which is in Italian and based on Calzabigi's text, in Vienna. Later he wrote a second version, in French and specifically tailored to French theatrical taste, for Paris, for which he added some musical ornamentations which are typically French in style, plus other things like ballets, etc. Muti feels that this is a case where one would be justified in performing either edition, because they are totally different and represent two totally different moments in the composer's working life.

"I performed the first version, because I feel that this is more characteristic of Gluck's intentions: extremely concise, with nothing superfluous, and the fruit of his collaboration with Ranieri de Calzabigi, with whom he reformed melodrama—his famous reform of melodrama—and in those original words lies all the dramatic essence of his response to the story of Orfeo and Euridice. The French version, on the other hand, while also authentic, represents a compromise conceived merely for practical reasons. Those *fioriture*, for instance, go completely against the vein of his original ideas." (Again, this original version is the one Muti recorded for EMI in June 1981.)

He takes the same amount of trouble in trying to establish the authenticity of orchestral scores. In one of his early appearances with the Philadelphia Orchestra, he surprised the players by insisting on their correcting their parts of a Mozart symphony at rehearsal from the recent critical edition by Bärenreiter, which involved removing the encrustations and mistakes. A year later, he performed the 'Jupiter' Symphony with all its repeats, which added twelve full minutes to it. This was the foundation of his reputation as a purist in the United States. But the orchestra respect him for it, and are excited by the experience of rediscovering works they thought they knew inside out.

Muti's gradual involvement with the Philadelphians began in 1972, after Eugene Ormandy spotted him in Florence during one of the orchestra's European tours. His first series of concerts was so successful that Ormandy and the orchestra asked him to become Principal Guest Conductor. For several years before Ormandy's eventual retirement in 1980, Muti was tipped as his obvious successor, with the latter's approval. "When I saw Mr Muti conduct the orchestra, I thought it would be wonderful if he could take over when my time came," Ormandy told *People* magazine after the announcement naming him as his successor was made. "He has excellent ears and studied with the same kind of teachers in Italy as I did in Hungary: the classicists—very brilliant, very first class."

Muti particularly appreciates the "brilliant, immediate" qualities of this orchestra, and those sharp attacks for which it, and most of the other great American orchestras, are famous and which, he points out, are so well suited to the works of Tchaikovsky, Prokofiev, Stravinsky, Bartók, Hindemith, Scriabin and contemporary composers such as Penderecki. For Vivaldi, Haydn, Mozart and Schubert, on the other hand, he explained the style of eighteenth-century string playing, quoting Mozart's letters about the quality of sound he wanted. The orchestra much enjoyed playing in this new way. So although the players are still the same, the difference in the sound of the orchestra is clearly noticeable.

Apart from his purely musical duties of working on the quality of orchestral playing, Muti's tasks as Music Director also involve the choice of programmes, soloists and guest conductors—the latter with a view to those who can complement and fill gaps in his own repertoire, so that the orchestra and public have "a full panorama" of the entire repertoire from the seventeenth century to the twentieth. He doesn't find these duties particularly arduous, nor does he expect any complications in carrying them out. "This orchestra is already perfect and has a long tradition of virtuosity established by Stokowski and Ormandy. Besides, both they and I decided on this marriage after a long, seven-year love affair."

As far as programming is concerned, one of his chief and fondest aims is to present concert performances of opera at regular intervals, something which Solti invariably does in Chicago with great success, but which has never as yet been done in Philadelphia. "It would be fantastic to hear Italian opera—especially works like *Otello* and *Falstaff*—played by an orchestra like the Philadelphia. It would help the public, who to date have only seen operas performed by a local company, to realize that opera does not consist simply of a curtain, some scenery and the odd pretty costume, plus booming voices, but also requires top-class orchestral playing of a kind that reveals all the details and subtleties of the score."

In fact, devising adventurous, imaginative programmes that do not simply consist of Brahms's symphonies, etc., but are peppered with contemporary compositions and little-known works by famous composers, like Prokofiev's *Ivan the Terrible*, Scriabin's First Symphony, Ligeti's *Ramifications for Orchestra* and Penderecki's Second Symphony, is one of Muti's main preoccupations both in Philadelphia and in London. "The public, left to its own devices, will always want to hear the same works *ad nauseam*—at least the majority of them will. This is always a problem, when one is making up programmes, because music is more than just a pleasure. It's a very potent civilizing force and, like the other Arts, an integral part of a people's education. And a people's education has to be paid for. It's not a gift from heaven. Therefore, the Government—governments everywhere, in fact— should concern themselves with their people's education, and increase grants to orchestras and other cultural institutions. It is their moral obligation to assist all the Arts, because they improve and civilize their citizens."

Muti feels that increased grants would make for far more adventurous programming, because they would free orchestras from the need to depend so substantially on the box office, and also enable the musicians to lead less anguished and harassed lives. ("In England, orchestral musicians are heroes. I admire them more than I can say.") But he wouldn't like to see orchestras become totally dependent on government subsidies, because that would smack of totalitarianism and perhaps pave the way for government interference. The best solution, he feels, would be bigger government grants coupled with support from the private sector and fund-raising activities. The Philharmonia Orchestra adopted the American subscription system as from its 1980–81 season, and have been impressed and satisfied with the results. (The Du Maurier Sponsorship Campaign, too, has been marvellous.)

Muti first conducted the Philharmonia in 1972—the same year that he first went to Philadelphia—when he was asked to stand in for an indisposed Otto Klemperer. The concert, consisting of Beethoven's overture *The Consecration of the House*, Brahms's Second Piano

Concerto and Mussorgsky's *Pictures at an Exhibition*, was a great success and the orchestra, impressed by his dynamism and incisive leadership, at once decided to ask him to become its Principal Conductor, starting in 1973. Six years later, he became its Music Director, which broadened his responsibilities and influence on artistic policy. In July 1982 he gave up the post of Music Director and Principal Conductor, and from September of that year assumed the title of Conductor Laureate.

"When I first took over, seven years ago, the orchestra had a solid Germanic tradition, after such a long time under Klemperer. My aim was not to demolish that tradition—indeed, you still hear a residue of that sound when we play the German repertoire—but to add to it a virtuosity that would make it sound modern. I think I can say that it is now a more versatile and valid orchestra, with a vast repertoire and some extraordinary solo players—the first horn, the first oboe, the first clarinet and the first trumpet, for instance."

"I think that he is very perceptive about his players, particularly about the principals in the woodwind and brass sections," says Gillian Eastwood, the Philharmonia's principal second violin. "He has confidence in them, knows what they can do and lets them play without getting in their way." "So that you feel you can phrase something in the way you want to, provided of course that it is not totally opposed to what he wants," confirms the principal oboe, Gordon Hunt. "You feel free to phrase *your* music, knowing that all the other elements will automatically be there, with you, without your having to stop and think about it."

The leader, Christopher Warren-Green, finds that Muti has the knack of making everyone play better than they possibly thought they could. And his excellent stick technique makes it easier for the players to give him their best: "Take rubati, for instance. With Muti, no matter what the rubato is, there is always rhythm in it. Every beat has some sort of rhythm in motion, which makes us play particularly well. For rubato has got to have rhythm. Otherwise it would be totally disorganized."

But he has developed and mellowed alongside his orchestra, too. "His stick technique has always been very, very clear," says Gillian Eastwood, who has been with the Philharmonia since the days when it was trained by Karajan. "But I think that he now goes more deeply into the musical meaning of the scores. Perhaps he has more humility toward the scores as well! And he can now get the most hushed pianissimi and the most enormous fortissimi of almost anyone we have worked with—with a tremendous range of colours within the two extremes—something that we have seen develop over the years. It wasn't there at the beginning."

Interestingly enough, Muti found it impossible to describe or define his own sound, but was eager and pleased to hear it described for him and agreed that the quality of string playing, now so characteristic of "his" orchestras, was a main and constant preoccupation of his. "A conductor and his orchestra are a little bit like lovers. There is a lot of give and take between them. I have received something from this orchestra which has been good for my artistic equilibrium and I think that they, too, have benefited from me. Fortunately, the mixture of English and Italian worked well."

There were rumours of teething troubles at the beginning of their association, though. It was a very taxing and trying time for him, because so much had to be changed. Some players resented what they called his dictatorial methods and insistence on artistic discipline. But players are always quick to respond to exceptional musicianship and dedication, and his relations with the orchestra soon became and have remained very good. "The reason for some initial resentment against him was that he demands a hundred per cent concentration and commitment," says Martin Jones. "Now a lot of people look upon hard work as some sort of punishment, or as something undesirable, whereas the proper reaction would be relief at having someone prepared to insist on it. But at first, an orchestra not used to it resents a hard task master, for all the wrong reasons. He is viewed as a tyrant, while all he is doing is demanding a hundred per cent concentration and effort. But after a while, everyone ceases to think of this as something objectionable." "After all, it's not only for the conductor's glorification, but for *our* glorification as well," adds Gillian Eastwood.

He admits that at the beginning of his career he was sometimes very hard on orchestras, because he was younger, more impulsive and more impatient. "But while I dislike diplomacy—both the concept and the word—and will always remain very direct, I think that I have now become more patient."

This general relaxation in his temperament and his dealing with orchestras was also immediately noticed by the players of the orchestra of the Royal Opera House, Covent Garden, when he returned for a triumphant new production of *Macbeth* in the spring of 1981, after four years' absence. The opening performance was one of the most rapturously received, searingly electric readings of any Verdi opera to be heard in London in the past decade—on a par with Kleiber's *Otello*, and the musicians played their hearts and guts out for him.

"He has certainly mellowed, and his attitude to the orchestra was quite different this time around," says Orchestra Director Bram Gay. "He began to smile at them and there were lots of laughs during rehearsals. When he was last here, four years ago, he was much more austere, hard and unrelenting, and hardly ever smiled—in public that is. In private, I enjoyed him very much indeed, even then, because he was a completely different person away from the pit—relaxed and charming. His iron mask was probably a defence mechanism, because he knows he is something of a boy, with a knack for smiling and laughing easily—he is a splendid mimic, too—and probably felt that this made him seem vulnerable."

Apart from his full-time commitments in Philadelphia, and his three operatic productions in Florence and elsewhere, Muti also guest-conducts the world's top orchestras: the Berlin and the Vienna Philharmonic and the Concertgebouw. He is acutely aware of the time factor and of the problem of doing too much, and is currently trying to cut down all guest assignments—apart from Berlin and Vienna; he gave one concert in Amsterdam and one in Paris during the 1980–81 season. He feels a deep need to keep abreast of developments in the other arts, and to keep on enriching his "cultura"—"otherwise the music-making will suffer."

"One thing is certain: all of us conductors of this generation are very brilliant, all of us want to do everything. But I'm sometimes afraid that we do too much and that we are not able to work in depth, or reach the essence of the musical content of the works we conduct. Then there is this unsettling way of life ... today it's Paris, tomorrow it's New York.... In the old days conductors were much more tied to their orchestras, they moved around less and their careers progressed much more slowly. But our accelerated rhythm today is not accompanied by a mellowing in our musical interpretations which can only come with age and experience—and this worries me a little." Yet few conductors can resist "the pattern": seeking a top orchestra, guest-conducting among the other great ensembles, lucrative recording contracts. Certainly guest-conducting a great orchestra is a highly enriching experience and, hopefully, the foundation for future maturity....

Obviously, the particular characteristics of each orchestra influence the choice of programmes and Muti has very definite ideas of what he prefers to perform and where. "In Berlin, any part of the German repertoire from the Classics to the Romantics. And their Beethoven sound is incomparable: really virile, with a masculinity which, I think, is typical of them; Vienna, on the other hand, have a simply unique sound in Mozart. It has to do with something in the air or their blood, and while they change their sound according to who is conducting them, a reservoir, a repository of *their* Mozart sound always remains, and this is quite unexplainable.... For twentieth-century composers I prefer the brilliance and immediacy of the great American orchestras, with their incisive, razor-sharp attacks; and the Philharmonia is the most versatile of the lot."

In fact, Muti has done all his operatic recordings—*Aida*, *Macbeth*, *Nabucco*, *Un ballo in maschera*, *I pagliacci*, *Cavalleria rusticana*, *La traviata*, *Norma* and *Orfeo ed Euridice*—with the Philharmonia. He would one day like to record all of Verdi's operas, from *Oberto* to *Falstaff*, and some of them more than once, at different stages of his musical development. He rightly feels that Verdi dominates all the Italian composers, not only because he was a genius, but also because he lived for almost a century, from 1813 to 1901, and thus participated in the development of Italian musical life from *bel canto* to *verismo*. "And he was constantly growing and developing—a continuous crescendo from beginning to end, with every work already containing the seed of the next one. Naturally some of the operas are more beautiful than others, but all of Verdi is extremely important. So, if asked to record the entire output of Bellini or Donizetti, I would refuse. But the whole of Verdi—yes, straight away!

"This is not to say that I don't love the other two composers. I do, but it is extremely hard to find singers capable of doing them justice. This requires a very special culture, a knowledge of their particular style, especially where Bellini is concerned. Many divas specializing in *bel canto* seem to feel free to transpose his operas to suit their voices, and add trills at will. To my mind, this is disgusting. To be sure, this sort of ornamentation was very much the habit in the past, but it was improvised on the spot and always done in the style of the period, with a lot of caution and a lot of taste—hardly the case today."

Muti has also recorded all the Schumann, Mendelssohn and Tchaikovsky symphonies with the Philharmonia, and numerous other orchestral works with the Philadelphia Orchestra, for EMI, with whom he has an exclusive contract. He likes to perform a work several times before recording it, because this enables him to learn it in much greater depth than he would just from studying the score and coming straight to the recording studio.

His method of studying scores is very personal, and he responds to them very spontaneously. For example, he found the score of Scriabin's First Symphony, which he has performed both in London and Philadelphia, in a shop in Vienna which specializes in unusual Russian scores, and which he always makes a point of visiting whenever he finds himself in that city. On previous visits, he had found some strange works by Prokofiev and Glinka, some unknown Russian operas and other scores little known in the West. And there, among the collected works of Scriabin, he suddenly came across this symphony, which he had never seen before and which immediately aroused his curiosity: "I opened it and was instantly struck by those murmurs in the strings with which the work begins, the unusual string colours and that marvellous clarinet theme which comes through. I didn't need to read any further. The magic of the score captured me from the very first page and I bought it at once. Then I returned home and left it lying around, while I studied other works. I always do this.

"First comes the idea of learning a certain score, which implants itself in my mind well before I start looking at it. Then, at a certain moment, I go to my library, take it out and leave it on my piano for a few more days, while I'm still working on other scores, as a kind of reminder that before too long I shall have to come to grips with it. I know that this might sound funny, crazy and ridiculous. But it's a bit like courting a woman, or rather like the way one *used* to court a woman, because now everything has changed. But in my early youth you used to do something like send a flower or a letter, and then leave her alone for a while. Well, I call this stage in my studying a ritual 'courting' of the score. I don't violate or assault it out of the blue, but approach it *piano, piano.* . . .

"Then I actually take it to the piano and play it through once, to get a general idea, and after this begins the real, in-depth study during which I begin to hear how it sounds and analyse its structure, and which takes much, much longer. *How* long depends on how difficult the work is. It can be three weeks or six months or six years. But you keep coming back to this particular score constantly. You take it, leave it, and pick it up again. Finally, having learnt it more or less by heart and got its structure and all its instrumental timbres clear in my mind, the phase of mental analysis is over and I return to the piano with a complete idea of its sound in my head, to experiment with various timbres, or try out a range of different intensity levels in the winds or brass parts. Yes, I know that the piano has only one timbre. You have to imagine the different timbres in your mind while playing it. I find that this last phase seals my mental picture of the score's line, and of its ebb and flow."

But when he actually comes to rehearse the work, he may have to correct or adjust some of the tempi which may have seemed right while studying, but do not work in practice. Or there might be spots where greater speed and intensity are needed. In short, this is where his mental image of the work may have to be modified by the realities of orchestral playing, the acoustics of a specific hall, or, if it is a concerto, by the soloist's views and idiosyncrasies.

"Music is beautiful because, unlike a statue, it is not static. It's more like the sea, constantly changing. A statue never changes, although your eyes do: you certainly see a different 'Moses' by Michelangelo at fifty from the one you saw at twenty. Yet music never stays the same. *It* changes, not just you. It changes with the times, for instance. Listen to Nikisch's Beethoven fifth. Is it valid today? No. And one's own interpretations are not what they were two years ago. Everything is in a state of flux, constant change and transformation. Even death is but a change of consciousness. 'Ta Panta Rei', as your great compatriot, the philosopher Heraclitus said. And nothing reflects this more clearly than music."

Most of Muti's studying and quiet, meditative moments happen during the summer break or at odd, quiet, ten-day stretches during the season, when he invariably returns home to a seventeenth-century, two-storey house in Ravenna, "a human-size house in a human-size town", where he lives with his wife Cristina and their three young children, plus a dog and eight hundred antique puppets inherited from Cristina's dentist father. (She and the children often stage puppet shows.) He flatly refuses to buy another house anywhere else and, for the time being at least, prefers to spend his time in London and Philadelphia in hotels or rented flats, because he needs to feel that he has *one* real home.

"I am like the birds. Migratory birds travel all over the world but always come back to *one* nest, one place that is waiting for them. Maybe this will change in the future. But, right now, I like this feeling of one place where I can return to be simply myself. Of course, I am also myself here while working. But in our work, or in anybody's work for that matter, there are always problems, complications, emergencies and aggravations. Whereas any problems one might come face to face with at home are problems to do with oneself as a man and as a human being.

"Cristina and the children travel with me whenever possible. But this is a very difficult and complicated aspect of a conductor's life, especially for someone like me, who was born a normal person without an 'artistic temperament' in the eccentric sense of the word. I am therefore a normal person who has to live a life which is far from normal. And the only thing that enables me to preserve this inner normality and equilibrium is the fact that, as often as possible, I return to this ... this ... bath that cleanses me. And I hope that this will always be so.

"I see my future as a challenge to keep on mellowing and maturing as a man, and consequently as an artist, too. Because spiritually, you have only two possibilities in life: either to enrich or to impoverish yourself, and this depends on you alone. I have in hand all the instruments which career, luck and destiny have given me. I couldn't ask for more. Now it's up to me. Somebody once rightly said that at thirty you have the face you deserve, which means that, if you are lucky enough to have the right means at your disposal, you are responsible for your life. Of course, this wouldn't be so if you were born destitute in a slum or in an underdeveloped country. But if you are born in a civilized society which offers you the means to enrich yourself and you impoverish yourself instead, that is your own responsibility.

"And in this life I consider myself responsible for two things: myself and the family which I have created. I have three children, who are not simply objects waiting for me to return home. My problem will be to involve them and let them participate in their father's strange life while trying to ensure that their own life remains as normal as possible, and to convince them that they are as important to me as music. Not an easy problem...."

The children have a good ear and sense of rhythm but, for the moment, do not seem very interested in music, "possibly because they know that it is what keeps their father away so much of the time". He would not discourage them if they did feel the desire to learn an instrument or to become musicians, because he considers freedom "a sacred thing, perhaps the most important thing in life". But he would be happier if they didn't.

"A musician's life is lived mostly for others, and very little for yourself—a life of service, if you like. A musician is always beset by problems, both outer and inner. Even when on holiday, I realize that I'm not free like other people, like my friends who are not musicians. There is always something, a kind of woodworm, which eats away at my mind. My mind is never completely free, except perhaps for a moment or two. This is probably the most tiring part of our lives. We always carry our work inside us. Now that you have embarked on this book, you will find out what I mean. Until you have written the last word, you will be continuously possessed and continuously tortured. Our lives are constantly like that. And, ideally, I would like my children to be spared this anguish. For them I would like something more peaceful...."

SEIJI OZAWA
The Fantastic *Japanese*

"Chorus, don't worry, one mistake! One mistake won't matter. Sing it with *feeling*! I know this passage is technically difficult, but Bach has orchestrated it with *so* much feeling! So, one mistake tonight, no matter. Tomorrow, no mistake!"

In his colourful, idiosyncratic English from which articles are nearly always omitted, Japanese-born Seiji Ozawa, Music Director of the Boston Symphony Orchestra, was trying to explain to the famous St Hedwig's Cathedral Choir that he wanted a more emotionally committed, less coolly precise response to Bach's *Magnificat*, which he was to conduct in three pre-Christmas concerts at the Philharmonie in Berlin—the first of his annual appearances with the Berlin Philharmonic.

His remarks are an accurate pointer to one of his chief characteristics as a conductor: the searing intensity and electricity which, combined with brilliant, perfectly articulated sound, never fail to grip audiences and musicians alike: "He is a virtuoso conductor, one of the best in the world," confirms Professor Thomas Brandis, Concertmaster of the Berlin Philharmonic. "So exciting and at the same time so economic in his mind and in what he says and does, which is always perfectly clear."

Although extremely happy with his own orchestra in Boston and its relaxed, "big family" atmosphere, its excellent, exceptionally *nice* musicians and its particular sound quality, Ozawa treasures his visits to Berlin, because he feels that there is always something to be learnt from working with this incomparable orchestra with its special tradition of approaching "notes and sound", which he considers unique.

"Everyone here *wants* to make music. The orchestra has big, high pride, and this is great! Because orchestral life is very tiring: many repertoire pieces pass through their ears; many conductors come and go. But whenever I come, they are always great. They *know* they are great and feel that they cannot perform at a lower level—even when playing French and American music which they don't really like."

Before the *Magnificat*, Ozawa had also rehearsed Bach's Organ Prelude in E flat major orchestrated by Schönberg, and the Ricercare from *The Musical Offering*, orchestrated by Webern, works which he had never conducted before; he found that studying them was "like discovering a new Bach".

"These works are seldom performed, because many people feel that if they are going to hear Bach, they want to hear Bach and not somebody else's view of Bach. They have a point, of course. But, for me, it was fascinating to see what a great composer like Schönberg understood of Bach. And he understood him inside out and analysed his music incredibly well, almost like taking a beautiful car to pieces, finding out which pieces should go where, and putting them back together again. For instance, it is amazing how he managed to imitate the sound of an organ. I don't think that he consciously set out to do this, but nevertheless, some spots come across absolutely like an 'organ sound'. His ears found a way of reproducing this sound orchestrally.

"And what is particularly remarkable is that he didn't try to insert his own personality into the works. He wanted Bach to emerge as Bach, unlike Ravel, who, when orchestrating Mussorgsky's *Pictures at an Exhibition*, imbued it with his own mind and sense of colour. Schönberg was not like that. He had an unusual capacity for entering another composer's world. Take that Brahms Piano Quartet [Opus 25 in G minor] which he also orchestrated: it is often called 'the Brahms Fifth Symphony', because of the unbelievable, fantastic way in which he managed to recreate the 'Brahms sound'. And the only time when you could, perhaps, sense his presence in those Bach pieces, are those spots where funny instruments like cymbals, harp or timpani stick out.

"Yet these arrangements are very hard on the performer, because the precision they demand is exhausting. If one player comes in a fraction too early or too late, or too loudly or too softly, it doesn't work. They require very patient rehearsing, even though the notes themselves are played in exactly the same way as in straight Bach. But in Bach, one instrument carries one melody, and it carries all of this melody, while in Schönberg's orchestration there are all sorts of cuts: one instrument plays one-tenth of a melody, and after a pause lasting several bars, another instrument picks it up, and this is repeated again and again. It's a bit like a jigsaw puzzle and requires enormous concentration in your ears. In addition, you must keep the same mood, the same feeling, running throughout the piece."

At the end of the rehearsal, he felt totally drained. But he added that this was nothing compared to what he feels like after a concert, especially after a *good* concert: "Empty. Like cotton. I know it should be otherwise, but a good performance takes more out of you. So I drink more!

"Because conducting is very heavy work. We use body so much to balance nerve. If you use only nerve, you go crazy. You must use arms, legs, whatever, so that it balances. And both Maestro Münch and Maestro von Karajan taught me the importance of *souplesse*. If you are physically stiff or tense, then your ears are not really open. Before your ears can open, you must relax and, funny thing, this also makes for better beating. It's a bit like swimming. You can't be stiff, or you sink. But for conducting, you must be more than just *physically* relaxed. The nerves and muscles in your head, all those nerves around the ears must also be relaxed, so that your ears can open up to the sound. And one of the hardest things to learn is how not to close your ears while moving your hands. For you must keep listening all the time and, at the beginning, it is not easy to do both simultaneously."

He feels that the reason why conductors are so much in the spotlight at the moment is that orchestras have now become so good that they could play by themselves. Which means that they need the conductor all the more, to give the musical interpretation and guide the orchestra towards the composer's spirit and intentions. And this with only three or four rehearsals. Watching an orchestra play a Mahler symphony, for example, after only a few rehearsals, always strikes him as a miracle. But, thanks to their technical expertise and the conductor's musical insights, the miracle actually happens.

"In this sense, you could say that conducting is mysterious. Kind of a magical thing. For there is no *one* way, no *one* method that every conductor must follow, possibly because music is a very personal and direct art: straight from the performer to the listener. And not just to the listener's ears, but also to his heart and feelings. For example: three thousand people, including a couple holding hands, go to concert. Couple sit together, listen together, but do not necessarily hear the same music. Each may have completely different reactions.

"The same is true of conductors and their response to a composer's score. Even though Western music is written in a very logical, organized way—every note, every rhythm, every dynamic mark is there and can be got right, unlike Eastern music which cannot be written down but goes from ear to ear and from generation to generation—there are many, many different ways of reacting to those marks and indications.

"Every maestro sees the same keys, the same notes, the same tempi, the same dynamic marks—piano, mezzoforte—but he interprets them differently, makes the orchestra play differently, and the music comes out sounding different. And this very personal quality is a fundamental characteristic of music as an art form. To appreciate poetry, you have to know the language it is written in and understand the vocabulary. But with music, all you have to do is listen, and it immediately touches your heart and your emotions."

His belief in the universal character of music and its power to reach anyone regardless of age, race or creed is so strong that he was deeply shocked when, a few years ago, a German critic asked him how it was possible for him, a Japanese, to understand the spirit and style of Mozart, Beethoven or Brahms. He realized that he was viewed as an Oriental, with no 'tradition' of Western music and only his spontaneous, natural responses to draw on.

"I had no satisfactory answer to give him," he told *The New York Times*, "except that music is international, like a beautiful sunset. You can see it from Paris or from Tokyo. But some people enjoy and appreciate it more. In poor country, where people are working for everyday bread, their eyes catch it but their mind doesn't catch it. Same with music. Everybody could enjoy Mozart. But not everybody pays attention."

Ozawa has been familiar with Western music and notation since early childhood. He was born in Manchuria on September 1, 1935, during the Japanese occupation of China, to a Buddhist father and a Christian mother determined to bring up her four sons in her own faith. So, after moving to Peking, the children went to church and Sunday school every week, sang in the "baby choir" and learnt to play several Western instruments: the accordion, the harmonica, the organ and the piano. His father, who had originally come to China as a dentist and had eventually switched to a firm publishing government magazines, had to flee back to Japan with his family as soon as war broke out, leaving everything they owned behind. This sudden displacement was a great shock for Seiji:

"It was very difficult. I was okay, but my Japanese was not as good as other people's. So, when we had fight in kindergarten, I couldn't manage without some Chinese words, which didn't go down very well. And my older brother, who had already started school in Peking, had even greater difficulties, because the educational system was different. These experiences later made me decide to move my own children back to Japan when I saw that they were undergoing similar traumas at their school in Boston."

On top of this culture shock, there was his first experience of poverty. His father was on General MacArthur's list specifying those forbidden any form of government employment, ranging from official posts to teaching at schools, which meant a sharp decline in the family's living standards: "We had nothing. Often, no food to eat. Very poor," he confessed to *The Christian Science Monitor* a few years ago. "And naturally, to learn music, to take lessons, cost money. So, my father really suffer about it. But he really helped me. When I really wanted to become musician and conductor, I saw there was no guarantee you could eat or gain money. Many people wanted to be conductors, ended up nothing, right? But my father was marvellous. He said: 'Life is only one time. You want to do something? Do it'. But he also made clear that he couldn't help me with money."

Shortly after the move to Japan, Seiji had started taking piano lessons and his father already did everything in his power to encourage his son, to whom he was, and remained, extremely close until his death in 1971. When, for example, he heard that there was a piano for sale in Yokohama at a price he could just afford, although Yokohama was twenty-five miles away, he hired a pushcart, bought it and brought it home with the help of his eldest son, "by leg". It took two days.

By the time Seiji was twelve, his teacher felt that he was ready for better things and recommended him to Professor Toyomasu, a renowned Bach piano and cembalo specialist, with whom he studied for ten years, right up to the time he left Japan. When, after a football accident at the age of fifteen, he broke two fingers, Professor Toyomasu suggested that he also study composition. But for that, Ozawa would have ended up a pianist.

Instead he enrolled at the Toho School of Music in Tokyo, where he studied with Professor Hideo Saito, who had trained in Germany and was steeped in the German tradition. Perhaps he noticed a performer's streak lurking somewhere inside his new pupil, who seemed eager to play all his compositions on the piano straight away. In any case, he suggested that he also study conducting, while at the same time pointing out that the prospects of a future as a conductor in Japan were not good, because Japanese music lovers expected their conductors to come out of Europe. But he felt that this should change and that there should, one day, also be Japanese conductors. Seiji agreed, but without really knowing what conducting was, because up to then he had only studied the piano and gone to recitals.

"But suddenly, I started going to symphony concerts, and thought that was fantastic! The orchestral sound, the chorus, fantastic! My hectic lifestyle started right away. I was busy, busy, busy, because for the first four years, I was the only conducting student in the school. One teacher, one pupil! So, I was in charge of everything that had to do with student orchestra or with accompaniments. Any orchestration that had to be done, was done by me. And great thing was, that everything I composed or orchestrated one week, was played by student orchestra the next."

But he could not afford the tuition fees at Toho, where he stayed for seven years (1951–58), so he became Professor Saito's assistant and dogsbody, looking after his house, cutting the grass, fetching and carrying, as well as lunching with him every day and studying great numbers of scores, fixing the music stands for the orchestra, setting up the stage, making corrections and additions to scores, writing bowing instructions for the strings, and playing the timpani "after studying for half year with professional. It was very hard. I am not that strong. I learn much, but I pay big price, too."

The first performance he ever conducted was of the Bach *Chaconne* orchestrated by Saito. "It was very moving. Funny to say so myself, as I was the one conducting. But I was very moved by the music and what we did. I think I was also, how you say, like owner of orchestra, with all my classmates playing. We rehearsed for six months and went on tour. And I felt I was doing fantastically important thing," he told *The Christian Science Monitor* in the interview mentioned above.

Soon after graduating from Toho, Saito suggested that he should come to Europe, to gain experience. After persuading a firm to sponsor him by providing a motor-scooter, Ozawa arrived in Paris, where his girlfriend, a former student pianist from Toho, was studying at the Conservatoire. She was soon to become his wife, but the marriage was of short duration. "Two musicians, didn't work." However it was she who triggered off his career by noticing a poster advertising the Besançon Conductors' Competition and suggesting that he take part.

His application arrived just in time, and he scootered down to

Besançon, where he won first prize by conducting Mendelssohn's overture *Ruy Blas*, Debussy's *Prélude à l'après-midi d'un faune*, *Dolly Suite* by Fauré, sections of the New World Symphony and a new composition especially commissioned for the Competition, with the local radio orchestra: "I was very nervous and very serious. I did it mainly because I never thought I'd win. But I knew that if I managed to be among the finalists, I would, at least, get a chance of conducting a professional orchestra for a few days."

Luck would have it that Charles Münch, the Music Director of the Boston Symphony, was on the jury, and he immediately invited the young prizewinner to participate in the Conductors' Competition at Tanglewood, the Boston Symphony's summer home in the Berkshire Hills, where talents like Abbado, Mehta and Maazel first came to be noticed. After conducting a variety of works—the finale from *La Mer*, the finale of the Tchaikovsky fifth, Mozart's Sinfonia Concertante for violin, viola and orchestra, plus a contemporary piece—he won the Koussevitsky Prize and caught the attention of Leonard Bernstein, who asked to meet him for an interview in Berlin during the New York Philharmonic's 1959 European tour.

He went to Berlin especially for the meeting from Paris, where he was then living, and remembers being taken to "some terrible bar" after the concert by Bernstein and the orchestral committee. "Lenny, with a bottle of scotch in front of him, asked me some questions about how I learnt scores plus some musical questions. I guess I must have passed the test, because two months later, I received letter from American Embassy in Paris informing me that I had been appointed Assistant Conductor of the New York Philharmonic and asking me to go and pick up some papers. I went and there was big envelope waiting with letter of appointment, visa, ticket and some money."

He was told that his appointment was to start on January 1, 1960. But meanwhile he had won a scholarship to Herbert von Karajan's conducting classes in Berlin, which were due to start very shortly, in September, and which he naturally didn't want to miss. So he telephoned New York explaining the situation and asking whether he could begin his duties there a few months later. They replied that they could let him off until April, but no later, because of the New York Philharmonic's forthcoming tour of Japan. So he went to Berlin and had the benefit of eight months' experience as Karajan's student before leaving for the United States.

"I learnt a lot during those months. It was very exciting! There were four of us, all there under a scholarship scheme, and as well as attending every rehearsal, we had a lesson a month. First, we would go over a score with the Maestro in his room, and he would pinpoint all potential problems and danger spots in it, explain what could be done to avoid them, and sometimes play the score on the piano himself. Then we would go out and conduct it, with him sitting in the orchestra, watching. He never said, 'Do this, do that.' He just watched, and at the end, he would ask what went wrong at this or that point. Sometimes we didn't know, so he would have us conduct it again and then ask: 'Don't you think that maybe this is wrong or that the line is missing?'

"He could see I was stiff. Back in Japan, I had been taught in a very stiff way, in a sort of pattern. But Maestro von Karajan taught me that there is no 'one way' with all music, and that I should be flexible. He also taught me that inside all music, there is a great line, a natural line running right through, and that one should never kill that line because one has to beat. (In fact he is still telling me this.) For instance, towards the end of the Sibelius fifth, I always used to give a great big whacking beat. But he showed me that this was not necessary, that the energy should keep flowing evenly, not jerking in fits and starts. The same is true of the part in *Das Lied von der Erde* where the singer comes in and where there are lots of ups and downs in the orchestra. Naturally, when I first saw the score, I assumed that I should have to take care of all those, without realizing that this might disturb the main line."

Ozawa always refers to his teachers with special reverence and veneration as *Professor* Saito, *Maestro* von Karajan and *Maestro* Münch, possibly because the master-disciple and teacher-pupil relationship plays a very important role in Japanese culture. The exception to the rule is Leonard Bernstein, from whom he also learnt a lot but whom he always refers to as Lenny. He explains this by pointing out that Bernstein didn't really teach him in the proper sense of the word, but treated him more as a colleague. "That's his approach. But I learnt a lot from him, too. He is a genius, and many of the things he did were interesting for me to watch."

He was particularly impressed by Bernstein's famous Children's Concerts, which were his brainchild from start to finish: every word, every idea, as well as the presentation were his and he put a great deal of effort into preparing them in a way that would ensure that they appeared effortless and spontaneous, which was partly the reason for their enormously wide appeal. "He is a great educator, who can take a subject, any subject, and explain it simply, naturally, truthfully, convincingly and with great passion."

At the New York Philharmonic, Ozawa was one of three Assistants whose functions included attending every rehearsal. His limited English prevented him from getting involved in many active duties, so he spent most of his time "just learning". But although all the complicated work like cueing for the TV programmes was done by the other two, Bernstein insisted on having him as his assistant for these shows. The two worked very closely together and Ozawa says that his own half-hourly music programmes on Japanese television are directly inspired by Bernstein's Children's Concerts, although they are aimed at an adult audience.

"I had a very happy time in New York. Lenny was always sweet and kind to me, to all three of us. And the way he worked with the orchestra was amazing. He just loved the orchestra, the contact with the musicians, and never seemed to fire anybody.

"My only problem was—and I can say it now—that New York without money is tough. An Assistant's job is very badly paid: one hundred dollars a season, i.e. two dollars a week for the first year, and one hundred and fifty for the second year. Out of that I had to find apartment, buy my beer to drink every night, and pay my union fees. I owned nothing when I arrived in New York, and finally I managed to find a semi-basement flat. But I was never lonely, because I had great relations with the musicians. For the first time in my life I was really part of the musicians' life, an insider. And sometimes they were terrible, they said terrible things about conductors! I had never experienced all this before, so I had quite a lot of fun. The only problem was money. *O là là!* I faced very much real life there, I guess."

At the end of his term in New York, he was taken on as Principal Conductor of the NHK, the Japanese Broadcasting Corporation Orchestra, for a brief and unsuccessful time: his ideas of style were not compatible with current Japanese taste, his 'foreign, modern' ways were resented, his suggestion that some of the renderings of the Classics by this largely German-trained orchestra were old-fashioned made him many enemies. On top of which the public, plus a sizeable proportion of influential critics, disapproved of a repertoire that wasn't centred around a staple diet of Beethoven symphonies. Before too long, Ozawa was fired.

He returned to the United States where Bernstein introduced him to Ronald Wilford of Columbia Artists, one of the most powerful agents and 'powers-behind-the-scenes' of the American musical establishment. Wilford arranged for his début with the San Francisco Symphony in 1962, and used his influence and persuasiveness to secure him the post of Music Director of the Ravinia Festival, the summer home of the Chicago Symphony. "I couldn't believe it. I thought it was a joke. They didn't want funny Japanese, but they couldn't find Caucasian," he told *The Observer* years later.

A year later came his first appointment as Music Director of a symphony orchestra: the Toronto Symphony, where he was to remain for six years, 1964–70, and where he was to form himself by actually doing the work he had prepared for all these years. It was a new world to him. Everything was so new that he confesses that he often didn't know what to do. He had learnt how to conduct an orchestra, he had been an Assistant in New York, but he had no idea about the intricacies, duties and responsibilities of a Music Director. Luckily, he had an experienced Managing Director at his side, Walter Homburger, who had been an impresario all his life and had preceded him at the Toronto Symphony for two years. The two worked very closely and, according to Ozawa, fought like cats and dogs.

"Whenever I wanted to do something, he would say it was impossible. I said 'No, it must be done.' Now, of course, I have learnt that if something is impossible, it's impossible. But then I pushed and pushed and pushed, like one push car. At the end of the first season, he even thought of firing me! But we gradually got to know each other and now we are like brothers." So much so, that when, six years later, Ozawa was invited to become Music Director at San Francisco, he had a hard time trying to decide whether to accept or not, because he was happy in Toronto and worked hard and seriously towards building up the orchestra.

And he was conducting virtually all the repertoire for the first time ever: all the Brahms, all the Mendelssohn and most of the Beethoven symphonies, some Bruckner and Mahler as well as Dvořák, Berlioz and Stravinsky. "And that must have been crazy!" Fortunately he was not guest-conducting at the time and so could spend all his spare time studying scores. This meant that he never got as far as developing a distinct style of playing or a specific 'sound' in Toronto. He was just too busy learning music.

San Francisco was a different story: much more like a conventional Music Directorship, because he had, by then, acquired a good repertoire and could therefore concentrate much more on improving the orchestra and stamping it with his own sound. He proved very popular, and by his second season, was already scoring spectacular box office successes: ninety-three-per-cent attendance throughout the season. He was also in a position to think about guest-conducting, touring (two European and one Japanese tour), and recording, even though this orchestra had not had a reputation as a recording orchestra since the days of Pierre Monteux. But, he explains, he was still basically an "immature" conductor.

"I remember first conducting the Beethoven ninth there. It was very different from the way I would do it now! Even my rehearsing technique was different. I was too busy getting the various sections together into an ensemble. But with experience, your hand learns to tell them more and you, yourself, learn to say less. You learn to stop them only when you have to make essential interpretational points. Because basically, unless you are conducting some crazy piece, orchestra tends to be together by nature, by instinct. But sometimes the ensemble *is* disturbed, and always because of some specific reason. And if conductor knows the reason, he, or rather, his hand, should work towards removing this problem.

"But this is something you can only learn from experience. Because unlike instrumental players who can take their instrument home and practise there, conductors can only find out what kind of problems may lead to this unnatural result, at rehearsal. And I use the word unnatural because the players in good orchestras are musicians of a high level. And at that level, they should be able to play together. But in practice, this is not always so.

"In this sense, conducting is a bit like driving car. When highway is straight you think that you don't have to move wheel. But this is wrong. You never see a driver absolutely still. His hands are always moving slightly. Because although in theory a car on a straight road should go straight, driver knows that he must be ready for everything and prevent car from swerving or bumping into something. And the only way to learn this is by sitting in the driver's seat.

"Orchestras are the same. And a conductor's job, a *good* conductor's job, is to feel when the orchestra will go wrong, to smell it before it happens, and to help put it right. This is the secret of a conductor's work. If he is good at this, the orchestra feels very comfortable. They don't feel that he is imposing anything on them but feel free to play what they want to play, what is in front of them, *their* music. And they are comfortable because they know that the person standing there waving stick will help when something goes wrong.

"Maestro von Karajan, whom I recently watched conduct *Apollon musagète* and the *Symphonie fantastique*, is a genius at that. He trusts his musicians and they trust him, so that when they need him, he is always there, and when they don't need him, he never disturbs them. This rapport, this give-and-take between them is so unbelievable, that orchestra and conductor are like one.... But he says that it took twenty-five years. So, I have a long way to go!"

Since 1968, Ozawa has also been Musical Adviser to the New Japan Philharmonic Orchestra, which consists of very young musicians, all under forty. This job means a great deal to him, first because it enables him to work in his own country, and secondly because he finds the task of helping form and develop this basically inexperienced group very rewarding. The orchestra has no tradition, no style of playing as yet, knows very little repertoire, and consequently the players have to work very, very hard. They learn from him like students, and although this means longer and more painstaking rehearsals than elsewhere, he enjoys working with them. "Their tone is not deep as in Berlin, or beautiful, as in Boston. But I try to find the quality, depth, the tone colours, that whole thing which can be summed up as the 'style' of each composer."

His work with this orchestra is much appreciated in Japan, where an important critic remarked that he consistently provides some of the most interesting programming and some of the best performances in the country. He says that, as can sometimes happen with imperfect or inexperienced orchestras, he is occasionally aware of "something in the air", of "the pure music of a composition coming out. And that's another fascinating thing about music: mysterious thing, part two. You can succeed in capturing the essence of a work with a mediocre but enthusiastic orchestra, while a great orchestra approaching the music purely technically, clinically, can fail to reach the audience."

The same year, 1970, that Ozawa was appointed Music Director of the San Francisco Symphony, he was also invited to become Joint Music Director of the Tanglewood Music Festival, which had played such an important part in launching his career. This brought him into close and regular contact with the Boston Symphony, one of America's "big five", which he started to guest-conduct for two weeks a season.

Three years later, he was offered its Music Directorship—an appointment which astonished many people, because this orchestra had a
reputation as one of America's most traditional, and Boston is one of
the country's most conservative cities.

"I, too, was amazed they engaged me," he confesses. "I don't have
tradition in this music, although it's true that sometimes bad tradition
can disturb good thing. I enjoy some of the good New England
traditions, but I don't wear clothes like Boston people or speak good
English !" (In fact, he wears a very colourful and very personal
assortment of garments—white smocks, mandarin jackets, sneakers,
yellow moccasins, enormous padded coats, funny hats and beads. The
latter always worry TV crews, because they jump up and down so
much while he is conducting that it is feared that they will snap and
scatter all over the orchestra. Still worse, that they might hit the baton
in the middle of a pianissimo! But his style of dress, encouraged by his
dress-designer wife, suits him and goes well with his glossy mop of
black hair, worn page-boy style.)

But although he had regularly guest-conducted the BSO for three
years before his appointment, he says that he got to know the orchestra
and its specific attributes only after his first few years as its Music
Director. "You can only really know an orchestra through constant
contact. Hearing it play, for instance, is not enough for you to know its
special quality. I can smell it, but until I come to work with them, I
can't touch it. It's funny, but both the BSO and I have grown up
together. They always had a great tradition of beautiful, polished
sound and had given superb performances under Münch. So, quality
and beauty are there, in their blood. What I have tried to do is to put a
little more meat in it, to have more beauty and more meat. Because
both are necessary. And this subtle process of an orchestra acquiring
certain characteristics of its principal conductor is mysterious and hard
to explain. You don't learn it from teachers or schools, although great
teachers can teach you some things. You learn it by working with an
orchestra day after day."

Ozawa has now been Music Director in Boston for ten years, and
finds the players an exceptionally nice bunch of people, very relaxed,
and especially so about union rules which never seem to interfere with
music-making. "And everybody knows me now, they know my good
points, my weak points, so we help each other." The top quality of
some of the BSO solo players is a constant source of joy to him and he
cites the Concertmaster, Joseph Silverstein, as an example of someone

who has moved all the way up from the back desk and has chosen to stay with the orchestra when he could be having an international career as a virtuoso.

Another factor which greatly contributes to the high quality of the BSO's collective sound is the fact that most of its principal players play and record chamber music—as the Boston Symphony Players—while the rest of the orchestra is playing as the Boston Pops. This gives the other players a chance to lead their sections—invaluable training for good ensemble. In fact both Ozawa and most other good conductors consider chamber music to be the foundation of good orchestral playing.

One of his principal aims, apart from inserting more "meat" into their sound, has been to stamp some of his "own thinking style" on their performances of the Classics and Romantics, and to include a large number of Russian works in their repertoire. It is particularly rewarding to listen to these works played by the BSO, because while it combines the brilliant, sharp, incisive attacks so characteristic of American orchestras, they are combined with a deep, round sound reminiscent of some of the great European orchestras, and this results in marvellous readings—as its Tchaikovsky recordings eloquently demonstrate.

Ozawa remarks that constant contact and a growing knowledge of each other make rehearsals much easier. He now instinctively knows when he should stop and correct something. And trivial though this might sound, it is always a crucial moment for a conductor: "Decision: should I stop them now or will they automatically play this passage okay next time? And I guess that this judgement is instinctive. Only experience and a good knowledge of the orchestra can help. Now I know this orchestra, many times I don't stop because I know they will do better next time. But when I do stop, they know that this is because they have to practise a little at that point. Yet I sometimes make the mistake of not stopping them when I should, and they say: 'Seiji, will you repeat this passage for us please?' But now, I make fewer mistakes!"

"Ozawa is our conductor, but he is also our friend. We've known him for a long time now. We trust him. I guess we love him," comments one of the violin players. "He just lets us play," adds its principal flautist, Doriot Anthony Dwyer. "You don't feel you're stifled all the time. Some conductors are over-controlling: they have to interpret every little thing you do or they're very insecure. Others are not concerned at all. There's no problem with Seiji. He's not too lenient nor too over-restrictive. That's why the orchestra is in such good shape, such a wonderful orchestra: it's a reflection of its conductor."

Yet some years ago, there were some murmurs of discontent, mainly from people who felt that the orchestra was playing too much French and Russian repertoire at which Ozawa excels, and not enough German music, especially not enough Classical works, which, some feel, are not his forte. But these voices of discontent were soon silenced by the majority in the orchestra, the Board and the public, who rightly pointed out that, apart from Karajan, no living conductor is good in *all* areas of the repertoire, and that guest conductors are chosen with the specific view of complementing the Music Director's special musical affinities, and filling gaps in his repertoire.

Ozawa's duties in Boston involve conducting half of the twenty-two subscription concerts a season, and all the orchestra's tours. He has already led them on two European visits, and a triumphant tour of Japan in 1978 which, according to *The New York Times*, took the country by storm, and during which Ozawa took over one of the country's most famous hot springs resorts for an all-night party for the BSO, which included saunas, massage, geishas, sampling endless varieties of Japanese food and quantities of potent drinks. A year later, immediately after the fall of the Gang of Four, they paid a historic visit to China. The tour was given the prominence and publicity of a state visit, and Ozawa and the orchestra were rapturously received by a country starved of music after many years of cultural oppression. The visit culminated in open masterclasses, to which musicians from all over China flocked, eager to lap up knowledge and technical expertise. But perhaps the most moving occasion for him was being allowed to visit his old family home in Peking, along with his mother who accompanied him on the tour.

Apart from subscription concerts and tours, the Music Directorship also involves conducting nine to twelve programmes at the Tanglewood Summer Festival, where he takes time to teach at its famous conducting class. But he believes that only a few basic things about conducting can actually be taught: ear training, score analysis, playing scores on the piano, and beating technique. "But what is so interesting about conducting is that even what is known as technique is the sum total of many things: how to beat, how to communicate feelings and ideas to the players. When a conductor studies a score at home, either on the piano or just reading it, he tries to get a clear picture of the sound in his ears and his mind. Then, at the first rehearsal, when he hears it actually being played, he may discover that there is a little difference between what *he* has in his ears and what *they* play, and those two sounds must be brought together. And this requires technique, which is really a combination of the conductor's musical knowledge, his depth of understanding of the particular score, his quickness in sensing that something is wrong, and the players' trust in him. All this is contained in what is called conducting technique. And all of it cannot be taught. But some parts of it can be."

One of the things that Ozawa never fails to point out to the student conductors is that they should correct anything they feel is wrong on the spot, *now*, not five minutes or half an hour later, and certainly not tomorrow. Sometimes, he can spot a born conductor right away. But sometimes they fool him: he may have thought them good when they auditioned only to find that, on the podium, they are not imaginative; or he may acknowledge that one of them has a good beating technique but fails to inspire the orchestra which soon becomes bored and boring; very occasionally, he may find substantial technical faults in a candidate, but discover that he makes the orchestra go wild because he has so much to say. "So there are no rules and regulations at all about conducting," he sums up.

He has no specific rules or methods of learning scores, either, nor any general guidelines about deciding between several editions of a given work. Coming from Japan, he is not influenced by so-called "traditions" good or bad, but tries to approach each score absolutely naturally, and to open his mind and ears to it, as he puts it. This is easy to say, but not so easy to do. "For I like to concentrate on one score alone for a few days. I cannot stop and go to chorus rehearsal or performance or planning meeting or look at another score at the same time. But because of my Music Director's duties, and because I like to do a little guest-conducting in Berlin and Paris, plus one operatic production a year, the schedule becomes very tight and there is no time to spend on all those various scores. So, I started training myself to put aside three or four hours early in the morning, block everything else out and concentrate purely on score study."

This is made easier by the fact that a few years ago, he made the very important decision of moving the family—his second, half-Japanese, half-Russian ex-model wife Vera and two young children, Seira and Yukiyoshi—back to Japan. The children, and especially his daughter, were becoming disorientated by the fact that they spoke English at school and Japanese at home, which meant that they weren't really good at either, and Seira reached the point where she wouldn't go to school without one of her parents being there, too. Memories of the culture shock he himself experienced at that age influenced him to make this very difficult decision. The family now live in Seijo, a suburb of Tokyo, and although his wife is sometimes lonely, the children, who go to his old school, are "fantastic happy". But this means that he commutes to Tokyo whenever there is even the slightest gap in his schedule. Surely, a great and painful sacrifice to have to make for the sake of his career?

"Yes. This is very serious thing, so I don't want to be misunderstood or misquoted. I believe that it's impossible, right from the beginning, to combine a career in music-making with a family life. But while I am a musician, I am also a normal person. I enjoy family life, my mother, my brothers, my wife and children. I got married twice and somewhere along the line I found a way of doing things right: being a good musician and having a normal family life. And when I found this, about ten years ago, I became a happy person. And I believe I found it because I lost my father. He died very suddenly, ten years ago, at the age of seventy-one, and I think that changed me. We had been very close, even though he knew nothing about music. In fact, he came to my concerts and slept! But we loved each other deeply and his absence made big difference to all my relationships and to my marriage. My daughter was born a year later, and I decided that I wanted to be the best father and the best musician that I could be.

"My biggest problem is that because of my career and my nationality, I have to move between three continents and distances are very great, so it gets tiring. But whenever I'm away, I call the family every day, and know exactly what they are doing all the time. Yet the sad part is that they miss me and that I miss them." When he is home in Japan, he concentrates entirely on them, gets up even earlier in the mornings so that he can do his score reading before they wake up, and then spend the time before they go to school playing with them. He takes them to school himself on most days, and meets all their friends on the way—a fifteen minute walk. Then he goes to his rehearsals, takes an afternoon nap (always, everywhere), and plays with them again in the evenings. Once a year, the whole family takes a skiing holiday near Lake Tahoe in California. He has had a passion for skiing all his life, insisted that his wife—who hated being out in the cold—learn when they got married, and even managed to take a skiing trip when a penniless student by joining cheap groups. He also loves baseball, roller-skating, jogging—"this is why I wear funny shoes! This way I can run whenever I want"—and tennis. In fact he always plays with a team of Philharmonic players when in Berlin. "For conducting, you must be fit." But he found that life alone in Boston was hard to adjust to at first.

"When I first began to think about moving the family back to Japan, I thought I'd go crazy. I didn't believe that I could live without them. But I told myself that this was something I *had* to do, and now I'm okay. It's not so difficult anymore. I've discovered that this one-man living is good, in a way. One goes more deeply into oneself. But you can sometimes get too closed in, and start not wanting to go out anywhere. When my wife is in Boston, we might occasionally go out to dinner with friends. But when I'm alone, I don't want to go. So I stay at home, which is not very good, but. . . .

"And I dislike going to restaurants alone, too, so, for the first time since my student days, I have started cooking for myself again. I have very nice Greek driver who has been with the BSO for over fifty years and who buys my food. So, when I get home, I start to cook and I start to drink. By the time the food is ready, I am already in nice mood!" He loves pasta and French food, but his staples are still rice and fish. He claims to *need* rice every day. *And* fish. "I am really fish-crazed! Most Japanese are, because our country is island."

This one-man-living, as he calls it, means that he can concentrate on music totally for long periods. He can study early in the morning, he can study late at night, he can play something on the piano at four in the morning, if he feels like it, without disturbing anyone. And he can read more, too—mostly Japanese literature and history, because reading English takes him too long.

At the moment, he is learning new scores all the time, and his studying routine varies according to the work. Sometimes he might listen to recordings with a score in his hand. Well known pieces like Mahler symphonies he studies in great detail, while new works have to be assimilated first and, perhaps, played on the piano so that he can hear how they actually sound. (If he can't play all the notes, he may play all the sections separately.) And he doesn't necessarily memorize *every* score: very complicated works like Janáček's *Sinfonietta* which has so many repeats that even the players get confused, he conducts from the score. "But when you learn very, very deeply, sometimes you feel as if you wrote the notes yourself. Every note seems somehow inevitable.

"But every score, everything, all music, is difficult to penetrate. Music I really love is always easier. When I have a problem to love, it's more difficult. For example, until recently, I didn't like Shostakovich. When I was young, I felt that I should force myself to learn some of the symphonies, for the sake of experience—never a good reason for learning anything. So I started learning the Third and the Fifth, in Toronto. But I didn't like them. In fact, as soon as I learnt them, I dropped them from the programme, because I just couldn't identify with them. And I never conducted any Shostakovich—except for the Cello Concerto with Rostropovich and the Violin Concerto with Kogan—until 1980, when I did the Tenth, after studying it for over a year. And I loved it! Now, I'd like to learn all his other symphonies. But it took me fifteen years to come to this composer. Maybe I needed age.

"But sometimes pieces I love—like *Così fan tutte*, which I conducted at the Salzburg Festival in 1969, or Mozart's 'Linz' and G minor symphonies—and which sound so natural and effortless are, nevertheless, musically very difficult to pace and conduct. Mahler symphonies, on the other hand, present different problems, because Mahler's music is shocking music, sometimes even crazy music, because he was consciously trying *not* to be natural. And when conducting it, you can never relax, not even between climaxes, because often those in-between spots are the most tense and dangerous.

"Purely technical difficulties are a different story. Oratorios, for instance, I always find hard to put together. The chorus is so far *away*, and sometimes I really don't know what to do to bring everything together. Then the Pastoral Symphony is difficult, especially the slow movement—but this is the case with most slow movements: they are always the most difficult. Debussy's *Jeux* is difficult, too, because it's so delicate. Most of Stravinsky is technically hard, especially *Le Sacre* with its constant changes of rhythm which lend themselves to mistakes and need controlling. And I found Bartók's *Music for Strings, Percussion and Celesta*, which I also recorded, very difficult. So is all of Bach, because you have to be so honest in the music-making. Everything must be absolutely straight, and you can change nothing."

Ozawa knows most of the symphonic repertoire, of course. Now he is concentrating on acquiring an operatic repertoire and tries to conduct one opera a year—either in Paris or at La Scala. Again, he has a special affinity for the Russian repertoire and has already conducted *Eugène Onegin* at Covent Garden, with great success, and was due to conduct a new production of *Boris Godunov* at the Paris Opéra in 1980, but fell ill and had to cancel at the last minute. He found that the greatest difficulty when studying those works was to penetrate the Russian spirit and to get the sound of the language in his ear. (He kept pointing out to the cast at Covent Garden that they should emphasize consonants as much as possible, use sharp accents and bite into their diction.) He feels a strong nostalgic affinity for the Russia of Tchaikovsky's time—he would love to conduct *Pique Dame* one day— and relishes the "Russian atmosphere" he absorbs through his wife's family who still speak the language to each other.

The Italian repertoire also fascinates him and has absorbed most of his energies during the past few years. He prefers Puccini to Verdi, because he wrote no choral works and no overtures suitable to be played as first items at concerts, and so the only way to taste Puccini is to conduct his operas. In 1980, he conducted *Tosca* at La Scala, and the following year, *Turandot* at the Paris Opéra.

"I am crazy about Italian opera! I love it. There is something in me that responds to Italy, Italians and Italian atmosphere very strongly. Yet it was difficult for me to learn the 'Italian style'. But wonderful to learn it there, at La Scala, where they have it in their blood, and where you can smell it in the air. All of Puccini's operas are very difficult: *Madama Butterfly* is very difficult, in fact, almost dangerous for conductors, and so is *La Bohème*. But the most difficult of them all is *Tosca*—yes, I found it harder to do than *Boris*. Not only must it be steeped in the Italian tradition, but the drama and the emotion in the work run so high that it's almost dangerous, because if I get too carried away, the whole thing will collapse. I must remain totally technically-clear throughout, and this is very hard. Again, I need experience. Because this is not something you could learn by looking at the score. You have to learn by doing it. And—terrible thing to say—if I really want to learn both it and the Italian tradition, there is no better place to do so than La Scala."

Of course, he had studied and knew the music very well, especially so because he regarded La Scala as such a challenge. At the beginning, both the orchestra and the press gave him a hard time. But the last few performances worked very well, and he was happy. "In those performances, I really tasted what it should be like, and felt fantastic!" (The following year, his conducting of *Turandot* at the Paris Opéra won rave notices.)

He recognizes that the time problem facing all contemporary

conductors is so great, and everything happens at such an accelerated pace, that quantity often substitutes for quality and that, faced with the choice of sticking to a limited repertoire or expanding, conductors usually opt for the latter. Everyone seems afraid that they will be overtaken by other people if they slow down. Consequently nobody does. It is a difficult and seemingly insoluble problem.

"I want to be more flexible and do a wide and mixed repertoire every year," explains Ozawa. "I am Japanese and grew up partly in China and partly in Japan, where there is no tradition of Western music. I learnt the German repertoire from my teacher Professor Saito, who had studied in Germany, and the French repertoire from Charles Münch. Now, I'm learning Italian opera. So, I want to be wide. But I also want to be deep. Yet this takes time. Many more years.

"And I want to learn only the good traditions, not the bad, which is not easy. I'm sure I'd be happier with more time. Maybe I should cut down on work and put aside three weeks a year exclusively for study. Then I think I would become better conductor and better musician. As it is, I have to fight, to push myself into finding time amidst all this hectic schedule. I don't know how other people manage."

The answer to this is that they don't, even though almost all of them acknowledge the need to do so. Ozawa is among the most conscientious and least self-satisfied of his generation. He says that he has never been absolutely, one-hundred-per-cent satisfied by any of his performances, and means it.

"I am not always happy to conduct. I am more of a craftsman. You know, work, work, work, to get all the details right. I believe that music is something we get from God and should therefore try our maximum to get it right, to get all the details perfect: pitch a little higher, no good. Next, the key. Then, the tempo. So many details to be worked out. One has to work very hard.

"Now I understand what Maestro von Karajan means when he says that it took twenty-five years to achieve this unity, this one-ness between his orchestra, himself and the music. I am happy to have this example in front of my eyes and in front of my ears, because this way I can look to the future and hope that, one day, this will also happen to me."

SIR GEORG SOLTI
The Hungarian Dynamo

"As soon as Solti walks through the door, there is an electric atmosphere all over the Theatre: the place gets charged and I can't help feeling that if one could devise a way of plugging him into the general circuit one could turn off the mains and find that the whole house could be lit with his own electricity," mused a player in the orchestra of The Royal Opera House, Covent Garden, where Solti spent a historic decade as Music Director.

This comment applies as much to Solti's music making and presence in general as to his conversation. Even at his most relaxed and genial he exudes energy, talks in short, staccato sentences punctuated by frequent exclamation marks and comes straight to the point. We were talking in the study of his London home—a sunny, airy room opening on to a large garden—and trying to pinpoint the tangible and intangible aspects of the art of conducting:

"Conducting is a mysterium consisting of the mixing together of some sort of spiritual, inspirational, and interpretational guidance with mental control, which is something you can never leave out. The right mixture is like an alchemist's secret. Too much control, and you lose intensity; too little control, and you become too rhapsodic and abandoned. It's always a question of this mixture of emotion and control, and every conductor must have it. Control you can learn up to a point. But the most difficult thing is to decide how much you are in and how much you are out, and where you should be both inside and outside at the same time."

At rehearsals, Solti aims for a high degree of control, with very little emotion. Then at the performance itself, he tries to forget all the interpretational and technical points he has taught the musicians and tries to get inside the music, together with them. In this he is greatly helped by the actual sound of the orchestra playing, which inspires him greatly, because he is "a sound fanatic, a sound maniac". Which is why he so particularly loves working with the Chicago Symphony, an unbelievably inspiring group who respond with a quality of sound that in itself becomes an inspiration. When working with them, the only limit is his own imagination. They can play anything, "but they enjoy the challenge because they like being stretched, and for the sake of the sheer joy of working with them I submit to the horrors of long tours and the double torture of jet-lag and fright!" For although Solti loves fast cars, he is simply *petrified* of flying. He has had some nasty flights and "once you get frightened, you stay frightened. I'm a nervous passenger."

Fortunately he doesn't have to do all that much flying nowadays because he works chiefly in two blocks: for the Chicago Symphony and the London Philharmonic. (As this book was going to press, it was announced that he will relinquish his Principal Conductorship of the latter in 1983 but will remain as Conductor Emeritus.) Occasionally, he conducts a new operatic production at either the Vienna State Opera, Covent Garden or elsewhere, as well as a few concerts with some of the world's top orchestras. He explains that by doing most of his work with one or two orchestras, a conductor can, at least, do something he believes in as far as balance and texture are concerned, and aim at a certain sound image. For an orchestra-conductor relationship is like a marriage and the more the two get to know each other the more results they get, either in love or in frustration. "Both can happen. But here I'm thinking only of good marriages. Bad ones one should abandon; good orchestra-conductor marriages have always been few, are highly desirable, and should start as a love affair; preferably love at first sight."

He revels in the fact that his own extremely happy bond with the Chicago Symphony started as a love affair and has now grown into "a love-filled marriage". With them, there are never any technical problems; no question of his not liking the way someone is bowing or blowing. All that is automatically right, and this enables him to concentrate entirely on interpretational points and abandon himself to his own inspiration. The players, who respect him as a musician, know that he is not faking but only trying to follow his inner ear and imagination. "But only up to a point. Because conductors should be flexible."

In fact he considers flexibility an essential quality for conducting. Of course, every conductor comes to rehearsals with a clearly formed musical opinion of each work. But while it is being played, he is certain to hear things that don't match his preformed opinion. "Then his natural musical intelligence should say to him: 'Is this better or worse than what I wanted and heard in my mind? Should I change it or let it be? To what extent will it fit in and how does it differ from my own concept?' Because dealing as he is with an orchestra of very fine musicians, the fact that each one of them may have a slightly different view of the same work could be very interesting for him."

Apart from flexibility, he thinks that everyone who tries to train an orchestra needs a teacher's qualities and a doctor's qualities—a children's doctor's qualities, to be precise. Musical qualities are not enough. Because the conductor is working with grown up and very sensitive children all the time. "So apart from musical talent, he needs a pediatrician's gift for psychoanalysis. And he must also be a good educator. Exactly this mixture and combination. Yet it is possible to be a good conductor without being an educator, because there are orchestra-building conductors and guest conductors—in fact there are *born* orchestra-builders and born guest conductors and I am definitely one of the former: a born Music Director who always tries to form and shape an orchestra. I think of myself as a sculpturing kind of musician and of guest conductors as painters who come, improvise something, and then go. I like to put my stamp on orchestras and therefore hate short engagements; in fact I hardly accept them anymore."

But having recently conducted Bartók's *Concerto for Orchestra* in Chicago, Berlin and Boston within three weeks, he found it fascinating to observe three different reactions to him and to his conception of the work, all from musicians of a very high calibre, and greatly enjoyed seeing to what extent he succeeded in putting his own ingredient into their performances. Chicago was naturally closest to his preformed conception, but the Berliners and the Bostonians also came very, very close to it and produced an excellent result.

Solti stresses that this ability to transmit his will to orchestras is a conductor's most essential gift. Shortly before our first talk, he had held some masterclasses in Chicago, for which two hundred applicants had to be reduced first to eighty, then to twelve and lastly to six finalists. "And it was instantly apparent who was conductor material. For while a conductor can acquire experience and perfect his interpretations, without this gift, communication is impossible. And it doesn't matter if it's in good taste or not. It doesn't even matter whether he is a good musician or not, although it helps if he is. But the martinet must be there right from the start. So, personality, talent and industry—that's the conductor's Bible."

Solti was born in Budapest on October 21, 1912. His family were Jewish and very loving but poor in a country where to be middle class but poor was considered shameful. So, although he never lacked affection, there was always the struggle not just to make ends meet, but also to keep up appearances, and he found this an awful strain. He started playing the piano at the age of five-and-a-half, and four years later was already accompanying his elder sister who was a professional singer. When he was twelve he started giving piano lessons to older, richer children, for extra money. He says that these difficult circumstances not only taught him the value of survival, but also make it impossible for him ever to become blasé about anything: a new car or gadget invariably arouses a childlike enthusiasm in him. And his experience of deprivation now makes him rejoice at being able to give so much more to his own two daughters.

At the age of thirteen he entered the piano class of the Budapest Conservatoire. A year later he happened to hear Erich Kleiber conduct a performance of the Beethoven fifth and this instantly changed his mind about his future career: instead of a pianist he decided to become a conductor and enrolled in the conducting and composition classes where he studied under Kodály, Dohnányi and Leo Weiner. Musical education at this establishment was limited almost entirely to the German repertoire—students were taught no French and very little Italian music—and his natural affinity at the time was for Bach, Mozart, Beethoven, Schubert and Schumann. Although he was later to become one of the best known Wagnerian conductors of our time, Wagner did not come to him early. He heard *Das Rheingold* and *Die Walküre* in Budapest—in Hungarian!—"but there was no strong, instant passion."

Two years after enrolling at the Conservatoire, he became a coach at the Budapest Opera, where he eventually graduated to conducting a single performance of *Le nozze di Figaro*—"I think I was the first Jewish conductor to appear there since Mahler in the 1880s." Apart from this single performance, he gained all his practical experience of conducting from watching other people and, later on, from analysing and criticizing his own performances. He spent the summer of 1937 at the Salzburg Festival and by chance ended up as Toscanini's assistant in his production of *Die Zauberflöte*. He remembers Toscanini as an incredibly electric man whose vitality was still enormous at the age of seventy-four. "He was a marvellous, volcanic talent, a non-intellectual conductor with music bursting out of him, who always came to rehearsals meticulously well prepared and knowing his scores thoroughly, which immediately created confidence and authority. He was a dictator and could never understand how it was possible for anyone to make a mistake in something which, to him, looked so absolutely natural. Otherwise he never said anything positive and never explained anything. All he said was 'più forte' or 'piano' or exclaimed that something was awful!

"For a young musician of twenty-four who was a lazy Hungarian and for whom everything was easy—for I was very talented, played everything with great ease and had no problems whatsoever—and everything, till then, had worked out too quickly and too smoothly, coming across someone like Toscanini made a fantastic impression! The man did nothing but work, rehearse, study and re-study, with very little sleep in between. For the first time in my life I realized that talent is only part of the profession. The rest is industriousness, endurance, hard work and constant study."

Soon after conducting that single performance of *Le nozze di Figaro* at the Budapest Opera, he was sacked during one of Admiral Horthy's anti-semitic purges, which directed that all unmarried non-Aryans should be sacked from government-paid jobs, which unfortunately included the opera house. This was in 1939, and although it was a severe blow, it proved a blessing in disguise, because it prompted him to leave Hungary while the going was still good. He went to Switzerland, where he met and married his first wife, Hedi. Wartime Switzerland was brimming with Swiss conductors and naturally it was not easy for a foreigner, especially someone young and inexperienced like Solti, to compete for jobs in such a small country. For the time being, he returned to the piano, won the 1942 Geneva Piano Competition and spent the rest of the war giving recitals either solo or accompanying singers and other instrumentalists. In fact, he made his recording début at the time—accompanying the violinist Georg Kulenkampff in five Brahms sonatas, one Mozart sonata and Beethoven's 'Kreutzer' Sonata for the Decca Record Company to which he has remained faithful to this day.

At the end of the war, he started looking around for opportunities to resume his conducting career. "I was already thirty-three, and this is much too late to start. If nowadays a man of thirty-three were to come up to me and say he wanted to be a conductor, I would probably tell him to go away, because he couldn't possibly learn enough in the time left to him. Like bicycling and skiing—which I find impossible!— conducting should be learnt at an early age. But even in my darkest moments I was sure I would make it. Conducting was where my talent was, where I could best make music."

With so many prominent conductors temporarily banned from conducting by the Allies, and limitless power placed in the hands of quite junior officers in the occupied zones, he felt that there must be an opportunity for him somewhere and wrote to the Music Officer of the Allied Armed Forces in Bavaria, a man called Kilenyi, a former pupil of Dohnányi's, asking whether there were any possibilities in Munich. "Sure," he answered, "come up." So he crossed over the mountains from Switzerland in an army jeep, freezing all the way.

The Intendant of the Bavarian State Opera rejected him at first, so Kilenyi took him up to Stuttgart where he conducted a successful performance of *Fidelio*; when they heard about this in Munich they relented and invited him to appear there as well. Naturally, Solti kept quiet about the fact that his operatic conducting experience to date consisted of that single performance of *Figaro* in Budapest, two performances of *Werther* in Geneva in 1941, plus that recent *Fidelio*. He acquitted himself well and was offered the post of Principal Conductor of the Bavarian State Opera; two months later, he was named its Music Director, a successor to Bruno Walter, Hans Knappertsbusch and Clemens Krauss. It was a fantastic opportunity, and he says that he took it being fully aware of his inexperience. "I jumped into deep water and tried to survive." And it speaks well for his talent that it was three years before anyone in Munich realized that he was conducting everything—including works like *Salome* and *Die Walküre*—for the first time. As nobody was allowed to travel in those days he had a wonderful, stable ensemble in his hands and learnt the rudiments of his trade in almost ideal conditions. He considers himself basically self-taught.

He remained in Munich for six years (1946–52), and as he was to spend the next twenty-five years of his life as an operatic Music Director, this training stood him in very good stead. He believes that even exclusively symphonic conductors should have *some* basic training in an opera house, because it's better to learn the difficult things first and then graduate to easier ones. "An operatic conductor must be forever on the watch—much more so than a symphonic conductor who is dealing with less volatile elements and is fairly sure of hearing pretty much what he rehearsed. But in opera, you can never be sure of that. Anything can happen, anytime! Therefore control is a doubly essential quality for operatic conducting, for which you also need very rapid reflexes, like a boxer's. Otherwise you would get lost and everything would happen without you.

"There are many other things, like a basic feeling for drama and the balance between stage and pit, also essential to operatic conducting, which cannot be learnt properly if you come to opera too late. But perhaps the most crucial is the fact that an operatic conductor has to breathe with his singers and this ability to breathe is musically essential for symphonic conducting and for orchestral playing as well. The principal oboe of the Philharmonia Orchestra, Gordon Hunt, agrees and explains this need admirably: "It's important for any instrumentalist, but especially for a wind player, to listen to singers. Because I always feel that the way we ought to play is the way that a voice could interpret each phrase. This is not to say that we ought to breathe as often as singers, because certainly on the oboe you can play a very long phrase without breathing. But the way that *I* would like to hear music played is the way it would be sung. Then you could perhaps capitalize on the advantages of your individual instrument to do things which singers would find hard. But the *shape* of a phrase should be based on how it would be sung, and most great conductors agree." Solti is glad that his career worked out so that he could start as a coach in an opera house and he says that if he had a son, he could advise him to do it this way, too.

One day in 1952, he was walking in front of the Prinzregenten-theater in Munich and ran into a man called Buckwitz who had just been appointed Intendant of the Frankfurt Opera and who wanted to know whether Solti was interested in becoming Music Director there. He replied "yes" straight away. So, with the experience he had acquired in Munich, he started again in a new theatre where he was to remain for nine professionally satisfying years (1952–61). But towards the end, he began to find the job frustrating, because by then "all the excitement seemed to be going out of opera", what with the singers' comings and goings which made it impossible either to have a stable ensemble or to cast properly any longer. He also decided that the repertory system, then as now prevailing in most German houses, was finished. Fed up, he decided to concentrate on concert life.

Two important things helped him change his mind. First the failure of the Board of the Los Angeles Philharmonic, whose Music Director he had been appointed in 1961, to consult him before naming Zubin Mehta as his Associate. Although Solti himself had earlier asked Mehta to become his assistant, not unnaturally he objected to such decisions being taken behind his back and resigned. Secondly, after guest-conducting some enthusiastically received performances of *Der Rosen-kavalier* at Covent Garden in December 1959, he was offered the Music Directorship by Sir David Webster. Although he was on the brink of breaking with operatic conducting, he replied that he would think it over and consulted Bruno Walter, who had become a fatherly influence and whose "statesmanlike point of view" he much appreciated.

"I have Bruno Walter to thank for my whole British existence! He must have been some kind of angel looking after my destiny, because I myself didn't want to do it. But he said that I absolutely must, because now that the older generation of conductors was dead, we younger men should preserve the link with operatic conducting. He added that I would like England and the English, but that I would hate the climate! At the time, I attributed this last remark to his age. Now I know exactly what he meant. The sun makes everything different. It makes *you* different."

The 'Solti Era' at Covent Garden began in September 1961 and it became a glorious decade that transformed the Royal Opera House from a charming, semi-amateur, semi-provincial theatre to a fully professional, major international house that Britain could be proud of. The knighthood conferred on him by the Queen at the end of his tenure was Britain's way of saying 'thank you' to this dynamo of a man who slowly came to be regarded as a British institution. Yet his first years at Covent Garden were far from being either smooth or easy. He was used to the autocratic, continental 'Musikdirektor' tradition and found it hard to acclimatize to the relaxed, easy-going English way of doing things and the English liking for teamwork. He drove everybody hard and had little respect for union rules.

Initially, many of his performances came under critical attack, too, which depressed him a great deal. Once or twice, he was on the brink of resigning. But the constant and unstinting support of Lord Drogheda, Chairman of Covent Garden's Board of Directors, and of Sir David Webster, the General Administrator, gave him the courage to go on. "People don't realize how difficult it is to transplant yourself to another country with a completely different mentality," he says.

Gradually, the critics, the public, and his colleagues at the opera house came to appreciate the brilliant results achieved by his energetic methods and to perceive the kindness and insecurity lurking behind his relentless energy and drive. Producer John Copley, who as a junior resident producer did his first production of *Così fan tutte* with Solti in the 1967–68 season, remembers that "he started off on the wrong foot, and we used to tease him terribly! Apart from anything else, his English was not very good and he said such funny things! His picturesque remarks came to be known as Solti-isms and could fill a book. But after a couple of years he came around to our British way of doing things, was tremendously happy here and all of us were tremendously happy with him. He is a very, very kind and dear man. When we first came together for that production of *Così*, I was very frightened of him. But he tried very hard not to make me feel insecure and spent a great deal of time explaining all the different chordings and the structural details in the music that must be got right before one can conduct it. Until then, I had never realized all the levels of preparation that conductors go through. I remember that while rehearsing *Così* he was also studying *Die Meistersinger* and spent hours and hours on it, longer than I would have believed possible. And it shows in the results; it is one of the reasons why I call his conducting '*haute couture*': it consists of a gleaming, polished, bright kind of sound, but with layers and layers of underpinning—the most luxurious lining, the best buttons and trimmings—i.e. all the structural details minutely worked out." This is confirmed by Sir Michael Tippett, whose Symphony No. 4 was premièred by Solti in Chicago. After Solti had studied the score for a certain period of time, a meeting was arranged between the two, at which Solti arrived armed with a list of precise and highly professional questions. "He must be the most completely professional conductor I have ever come across," says Sir Michael.

Solti took over officially in September 1961, on the assumption that Covent Garden was to be a *stagione* house, i.e. showing a select number of productions a season, each with its own cast and having a rehearsal period of several weeks. Then he started devising the most exciting programming, which consisted of established masterpieces performed with the best possible international casts, punctuated by brilliantly staged contemporary operas including many British works. In fact nothing was ever dull in the Solti Era. Controversial, sometimes. Dull, never! The place seemed charged with enthusiasm and the exhilaration that one was participating in or witnessing moments of operatic history. Hard to single out the highlights among so many outstanding occasions: the Solti-Hotter *Ring*; the Solti-Everding *Salome*; his *Arabella* with Lisa della Casa and Dietrich Fischer-Dieskau; the adventurously chosen triptych consisting of Schönberg's *Erwartung*, Puccini's *Gianni Schicchi* and Ravel's *L'Heure Espagnole*, all directed by Peter Ustinov; his historic, controversial production of Schönberg's *Moses und Aaron*, directed by Peter Hall; Russian works like *Boris Godunov*, *Khovanshchina*, *Eugène Onegin* and *Le Coq D'or*; the Zeffirelli *Tosca* with Callas and Gobbi, the Bavarian State Opera's production of *Die schweigsame Frau* conducted by the late Rudolf Kempe, and, and...

But of course, none of these productions could have reached the level that they did without a good orchestra in the pit, and developing orchestral standards was one of Solti's main preoccupations. Again, his sometimes high-handed methods when dealing with unions caused some resentment, and the orchestra was divided into fanatically pro and anti factions. But even the anti faction recognized the high standards he was trying to achieve and respected his musicianship and authority.

"Solti rehearses everything very thoroughly, and leaves nothing to chance. He overhauls everything, and although he jumps about a lot, makes a lot of funny noises and we often laugh at his English, he manages to cover absolutely everything in the time he has. I found this particularly impressive when we did a concert performance of *Das Rheingold* where he coped marvellously and covered all the ground in the limited time available to him," says Kenneth Goode, double bass player in the London Philharmonic Orchestra. "Solti can get you to play *exactly* as he wants," adds the orchestra's principal timpanist, Alan Cumberland. "I don't think there are very many conductors who do that. But he insists on it and gets it. And his electricity and dynamism are such that you can actually *see* him channel everything from us to him, and through him, to the audience. From the musical point of view, rhythm is what matters most to him, I would say."

Solti wasted no time in pursuing another of his main goals: establishing a link between British opera and the British theatre, which he rightly considers to be the best in the world. The first production he conducted after his appointment—Britten's *A Midsummer Night's Dream*—was directed by Sir John Gielgud. He later also conducted productions staged by Peter Ustinov. But his most fruitful collaboration has been with Sir Peter Hall, then Director of the Royal Shakespeare Company, who remembers being summoned to Solti's office shortly after he became Music Director.

"He gave me a drink and said I must come and do some productions at the Garden. This was in the fairly early days of the RSC and I was so busy at the time that I told him I couldn't manage anything in the foreseeable future. I remember that he then threw a wonderful Hungarian fit and said 'how the bloody hell am I going to run this place if people like you and Peter Brook are too busy to come and help British opera?' I remember being terribly impressed by his rage, which I knew was acted.

"Then he asked me again several times, and finally we got together in 1965 for *Moses und Aaron,* which was a turning point in my career, because it involved really *serious* work on an opera, partly because it was so difficult and everybody was so frightened that they actually *worked.* Because usually opera is a very lazy business. Really lazy. But they couldn't be lazy about this because nobody knew it, so we worked for seven weeks and had about three hundred and twenty people on stage. (This would be impossible now, because the cost would be prohibitive.) I remember losing about twenty pounds just from moving the chorus around. It was a wonderful experience, exactly what a collaboration should be: creating something together.

"Few conductors could ever be as open and receptive to ideas as Georg was over this production, which was really brutally difficult to do. And what I was doing with it was morally and metaphysically dangerous as far as this country's mentality went at the time. There was a lot of nonsense in the press—in fact we even got into the *News of the World*—but throughout it all Georg kept wonderfully calm—especially when one considers that this is not at all the way he is made! Probably he was worried, but he believed in what I was doing and supported me throughout."

In fact, Solti felt that this production was the most difficult and rewarding task he had undertaken in his life. It caused him "tears and sweat, but it was worth it". The Hall innovations that interested the press were the naked Soho strippers engaged for the Bacchanalia scene, which included blood and carcasses all over the place, a burning bush that hissed and steamed *et al.* But the production was sold out— remarkable for a work that would normally draw only small audiences of aficionados. It was also repeated as a Promenade Concert at the Royal Albert Hall. Solti felt particularly gratified, because he thinks

that an opera house supported by public funds *should* undertake to
show works like *Moses und Aaron*, which he considers to be one of the
greatest operas of this century.

Throughout Solti's decade at Covent Garden, the most difficult and
burdensome parts of his duties were neither the training of the
orchestra nor any of his other purely artistic tasks. The greatest burden
was administration, and the most difficult part of that was arranging
dates. For singers have to be booked three or sometimes five years
ahead, which can be tricky because by the time they finally appear in
the production in question, they may no longer be in good voice. "This
long-term planning, without which you cannot fix your repertoire, is a
Music Director's biggest headache. On top of this there is the short-
term planning, all those emergencies that so often crop up in opera
houses, "as the vocal chords are such a delicate instrument, which is
what makes singing such a terrifying profession. Waking up in the
morning and worrying about the merest hint of a croak must make you
a nervous wreck, which is why singers are often volatile and highly-
strung. But I like them. My sister was a singer so I can sympathize with
their problems—in fact some of my best friends are singers."

Kiri te Kanawa, who adores Solti—"he has the naughtiest, wickedest eyes I've ever seen!"—was touched and grateful when, after she had
sung Micaëla in his recording of *Carmen* less well than she could, he
rang her up much later to say that, to give her a chance to have another
go, he had managed to put aside two days on such and such a date so
that they could re-record her arias. "I assure you that this is something
that very few conductors would ever volunteer to do, on their own
initiative." Lucia Popp also greatly enjoys working with him. "He is
one of my two most favourite conductors. (The other is Carlos
Kleiber.) They are totally different, but both utterly marvellous, and
have given me the greatest 'Sternstunden' of my career. The performance of Richard Strauss's *Four Last Songs* that we did with Georg in
Chicago is something I shall never forget. At the end, we were both in
tears." Solti comments that "anyone who likes the human voice, and I
do, must be ready to help singers as much as possible".

As we continued our discussion of his duties as Music Director of
Covent Garden, he pointed out that apart from long and short-term
planning, these also included working with producers and designers,
looking after the orchestra and chorus, negotiating with the unions,
overseeing the budgeting for every production—all very time consuming. It is therefore imperative for a Music Director to spend at least six

months of the year at his opera house. "And this is the absolute *minimum*, otherwise he couldn't participate in any emergency decisions."

Apart from the rapid rise of the Royal Opera to international status, the very high musical and scenic standards achieved under his Music Directorship and the exciting, adventurous programming mentioned earlier, the 'Solti Era' also saw the emergence of a group of British and Commonwealth singers, including Gwyneth Jones, Yvonne Minton, Kiri te Kanawa and Donald MacIntyre, who, nurtured and encouraged by Solti, subsequently went on to make great careers abroad.

Yet, at the end of this brilliantly successful decade, Solti decided it was time to leave Covent Garden and realize his dream of leading a great symphony orchestra. He had completed twenty-five years as an operatic Music Director and he felt that it was "now or never!" He left at the end of the 1971 season, amidst ecstatic ovations, to become Music Director of the Chicago Symphony, America's best and, along with the Berlin and the Vienna Philharmonic, one of the world's top three orchestras. But he kept his strong emotional links with London by becoming first Principal Guest Conductor and subsequently Music Director of the London Philharmonic Orchestra until 1983. A brief association with the Orchestre de Paris as Music Director from 1972 to 1975 ended with his resignation, basically for the same reasons that Karajan's had: neither man could devote more than a token number of weeks a season to it.

After ten years as a Music Director of a symphony orchestra, he would qualify his statement that "running a symphony orchestra is a quarter the amount of trouble of running an opera house" to "half the amount of trouble. But it is still much easier!" For a start, there are no limitations in planning a repertoire, because concert soloists work on much shorter schedules than opera singers. Whereas even for the single annual concert performance of an opera in Chicago he has to plan years ahead. Apart from the basic qualities needed by a conductor, he thinks that a Music Director of a symphony orchestra needs three additional attributes:

"First, musical respect, the confidence of the players in your musicianship which is crucial. Otherwise you would have a palace revolution on your hands. They must trust you. I also find, more and more, that it is essential to have a human relationship, too—that they should trust you as a human being as well as a musician and feel free to come to you with their problems, knowing that, up to a point, you will understand. That you will, of course, oppose any dangerous tendencies—e.g. their neglecting their jobs in the orchestra and doing outside jobs for an extra fifty dollars, which is no secret, it's in the nature of the beast—but that about everything else, you will take it easy. Once they know that you won't put up with neglect but that you care about their financial position—i.e. that you are a caring boss—you can ask a lot more of them. But the essential point is that you be good at your job and that they respect you for it.

"The second necessary quality is not being afraid to invite the very best guest conductors, because this helps keep the standards of the orchestra high and stamps it with an aura of excellence. Lastly, a good all-round musicianship is also essential for any conductor wishing to be a Music Director. Of course, nobody conducts everything equally well. But a high level of competence in as many areas of the repertoire as possible is what differentiates a Music Director from guest conductors. Because Music Directors, especially in America, have to conduct twelve to sixteen programmes out of a total of about thirty-five programmes a season.

"But while there are works one conducts better than others, if you have critical sense, you should perform the pieces that don't come naturally to you more often than those that do. I did this all my life. I punished myself, so to speak, by doing pieces that did not come easily and which I had to conquer. And I think that forcing yourself to fight and conquer is very important." Examples of works that did not come easily and which Solti had to conquer are the Beethoven symphonies, especially the first movement of the Fifth and the 'Pastoral'. Until recently, he found them an enormous problem, especially because they had been part of his staple diet in his early conducting days and having learnt them in a certain way, he found it difficult to get away from those interpretations despite the fact that he knew them to be wrong. So he decided to leave them alone for a while. The 'Pastoral' in particular took him twenty years to come to terms with and only now does he feel that he has a valid image of it in his mind and in his ear.

"This was the only symphony to which I did not apply my rule of forcing myself to do it. Until three years ago, I felt it was better not to do it at all. Now, I feel quite confident about it. Another such example is the Mozart G minor Symphony (No. 40) (which Bruno Walter did not touch until he was fifty-one), which I conducted over fifty times in my youth. Well, it took a very long time for me to perceive another G minor Symphony from the one I was conducting. Again, now I feel that finally I have. But I had difficulty in ejecting from my mind the photostat of my earlier sound-image of this symphony.

"I went through similar problems as a pianist. Things which I had learnt early, with a stiffer technique, I kept on playing in the same way even though my technique had developed by then, because body and head movements are inter-related and muscles form certain habits that seem to last for ever. To a large extent the same applies to conducting: today I conduct the pieces I learnt early, back in the late forties, differently—but only with great difficulty. I find that I tend to make the same mistakes in the same places. I realize I'm doing it; I say to myself 'watch out, beat properly, don't swim, *beat*' and this awareness helps to some extent. But pieces I learnt in the last fifteen years or so present no problems. Automatically I do them differently, and, I hope, in the right way."

Of course, from the purely technical point of view, things like *Le Sacre du Printemps*, which had seemed difficult twenty years ago, today seem easier. When he first tackled it, he found it incredibly difficult, not merely to conduct, but also to learn. He spent hours and hours—over six months in fact—analysing it bar by bar and still couldn't figure out how he was supposed to beat it or what to do with it. And although he wouldn't say that it's exactly easy now, he finds that, having conducted it over fifty times, it is now manageable, because he knows all the problem spots. All he need do is spend a day going over the score before his first rehearsal, and experience does the rest. And should he make a mistake in a precision point, he is no longer ashamed of admitting it to the orchestra. "Yet you have to arrive at this silly point where you can afford to say that something is your fault. A young conductor couldn't do that. If he did, the orchestra would reply, 'Yes, yes, YES, so why don't you go away and learn it?'

"Because an orchestra-conductor relationship is also similar to that between a lion and its tamer. As long as the tamer is firm, the lion doesn't eat him up. But if he shows even the slightest signs of weakness, the lion will eat him up. It's always a question of that, particularly between strong conductors and strong orchestras. There is no real problem between a good conductor and a mediocre orchestra. But when they are equals—at whatever level, high or low—one always wants to eat up the other. And it's very natural, a classic question of subordination. A human being is easy to subordinate as long as he sees the reason for it and as long as he thinks you are right. But the moment he thinks that maybe he can do the job better, all discipline is gone."

All this, Solti stressed, concerns the technical difficulties facing a conductor when trying to convey his image of a work to an orchestra. Musical, interpretational difficulties are a much more complex question, and generally, works which seemed easy to interpret in his youth, like *Fidelio*, *Le nozze di Figaro* or *Così*—for which at the time, he thought he had found a solution that seemed like the final solution— now seem infinitely more problematic. But he points out that every talented musician goes through this phase of beginning to perceive, with maturity, that everything is not easy and that the solutions are much more complex.

"Now, for instance, every Classical or Romantic symphony is a new headache that you have to work at again and again, going over the score many, many times and *thinking*. So, after a time, every serious musician begins to realize how difficult Classical and Romantic music is from the interpretational point of view—much more difficult than the Stravinskys and the Bartóks. Again, it's partly a question of experience and partly one of modesty. And by modesty I don't mean shyness, but your own self-critical sense. I mean going home after a performance and knowing exactly what the unanswered questions are, and working on those questions the next time you come to conduct this work."

Solti's duties as Music Director in Chicago involve performing a great many contemporary works, including new American compositions; during his decade at Covent Garden he also learnt several British operas. I wondered how he studies and learns scores, especially so after hearing Sir Michael Tippett's comments. "I learn very, very slowly, in a mosaic sort of way," he replied. "First I read the score note by note. Nothing more than that, not yet forming any sort of mental image of it. Just reading. I have to be very methodical because I am a lazy man and if I know that I have two hundred pages to learn, I will never even start! But if I know that I must learn twenty pages a day for ten days, then, I can do it. So I cheat myself a little. After I have gone through the score once, I start re-reading and trying to form a bit of a tempo-image, plus a feel for its texture and balance. And slowly, out of all this, comes the music. But it takes about four or five solo readings before I form some idea of its profile, of how it should sound—right or wrong.

"I never use the piano, because it has quite a different sound and volume range. Only when I first started conducting did I use the piano a little, as a help for learning scores. But I soon stopped. So, this is my method. I learn slowly, from micro to macro, and slowly put all the pieces together. I do not have a photographic memory and envy enormously people who do, because this makes life much easier and helps you learn much more quickly. But I learn tone by tone, not by picture, which makes life very hard, because I have to learn scores all the time. This is done mostly on holiday, in Italy."

No chapter on Sir Georg could be valid without discussing one of the major achievements of his career: his long association with Wagner's *Ring* which he conducted at Covent Garden with Hans Hotter as producer (and as Wotan and Wanderer), and also recorded for Decca, with the Vienna Philharmonic Orchestra: a mammoth undertaking which took about ten years and won the Grand Prix du Disque Mondiale and many other awards. He is due to conduct it again, at Bayreuth in 1983, during the centenary of Wagner's death, with Sir Peter Hall as producer. I therefore asked him to trace his journey through this work and his various experiences of it through different productions.

"My Covent Garden *Ring*, which started in 1962 with *Die Walküre*, was designed by Gunther Schneider-Siemssen, after an abortive experience with another designer who had been Hotter's choice. I still feel that it had great merits from the staging point of view. When we first started, the public rather disliked the visual aspect. I didn't dislike it. By the time we finished the whole cycle, everybody liked it immensely. But by then, *I* disliked it! I could no longer bear to look at it because it was rigid. The scenic solution—with that ring which remained a ring whichever way you turned it—made Wagner smaller and narrowed him down for the sake of an idea which was a literary idea and which had basically nothing to do with the music.

"Then Rolf Liebermann became the Director of the Paris Opéra and proceeded to seduce me—with great aplomb and great suaveness—into doing a *Ring* for him, which, he said, would be a historic occasion because the whole tetralogy had never been done in France before. And he found a very good and very talented German producer called Peter Stein. We had a meeting at which I told him that after the mechanical *Ring* I had done at Covent Garden, I wanted a romantic production without a machine in sight! The result was an even *more* mechanical *Ring*, with many more machines and steel constructions! But then, I took the consequences and bowed out. I just did *Rheingold* and *Walküre* and that was it.

"It was the greatest, most absolute disaster of my career. Not merely because everybody disliked it, which was all right, but because *I* disliked it so immensely that I was almost sick and could not bear either the look or the sound of it—and this with the most marvellous, brilliant cast imaginable, which Liebermann, Joan Ingpen and I had got together with a great deal of effort, care and money. And it was all sacrificed to that awful, political production. . . .

"So, I said to myself: Okay. Never again. That's it, as far as the *Ring* is concerned. I shall never again do a staged production, because nobody tries to do what Wagner wrote, in such enormous and precise detail, which I felt that people should take the trouble to read. Of course, it is much more difficult to try to do this. Much easier to say, 'ho, it's all rubbish, let's have a steel mill or a political *Ring* or something *pour épater le bourgeois*'; something very clever, maybe even intellectually brilliant, but which has nothing to do with Wagner. Because some of the Wagner productions of recent years have been so unspeakably horrible that one could hardly bear looking at the stage. This expelled me from the idea of Wagner in the opera house; I vowed that I would now concentrate only on concert performances which have a certain validity, especially for Wagner exiles like me."

Solti has already conducted enthusiastically received concert performances of *Das Rheingold* in Chicago, New York and London, and Act III of *Siegfried* and *Götterdämmerung* in Chicago and on tour in New York. He found that they worked beautifully, although the musical interpretations had to be adjusted to the fact that the orchestral balance is obviously affected by the absence of distance between stage and pit. The orchestra does not have to be kept down so much, because the singers are standing in front and are in no danger of being swamped however loud they play. So, 'Bayreuth conditions' can be achieved without keeping the orchestra down. "Either you do Wagner in concert performance, or in Bayreuth where you have this wonderful, perfect balance between stage and pit."

Just as he had resigned himself to a future of doing Wagner only in concert performances, he was approached by Wolfgang Wagner who asked if he were interested in undertaking the centenary production of the *Ring*, in 1983: "I replied that nothing would give me greater pleasure, that this was what I had been waiting for all my life, but explained that I had burnt my fingers so badly twice before—not too badly in London but desperately in Paris—and that although this was the time of the Chéreau *Ring*, I could only accept if I could be sure of doing something very different.

"I would only do it if I found a producer and a designer willing to do a romantic *Ring* without abstractions, without steel constructions, without huge machines moving all over the place, but a production which is romantically conceived and in which things are what they are meant to be: fire is fire, a forest is a forest, a sword is a sword, a spear is a spear and a horse is a horse! Not something from which everything is taken away, symbolizing nothing!

"Wolfgang Wagner said fine, but whom shall we ask? I replied that I didn't know but that I would think about it. I hesitated to approach Peter Hall straight away, because I was afraid that the combination of *Sir* Georg Solti and *Sir* Peter Hall might look very phoney in Bayreuth! Before even seeing the production, people would say, oh, first we had a French *Ring*—Chéreau-Boulez—and now it's the turn of the British *Ring*!

"After trying and failing to find a German producer, I finally resolved to ask Peter Hall. As soon as I returned to London I rang him, went to see him at his office and asked him point blank. He enthusiatically said 'yes' straight away. But I added that there was a condition: that this would have to be a romantic *Ring* and nothing else, and that if he didn't see it in this way, then I was not interested. He replied that he, too, was tired of the other way, even though both of us were well aware of how difficult the task before us would be.

"Because producing a naturalistic *Ring* in 1983 will be very, very hard. We are now spoilt by films and television, which have lowered the threshold of credibility. The problem, the crux of the whole thing, will be to combine the technology of 1983 with the big, romantic pictures of 1883. For no one would wish to go back to nineteenth-century technology. We want to use today's technology to create yesterday's look."

"In a way, I would like not to have been asked," mused Sir Peter Hall. "Because then, I wouldn't have to face these problems. But having been asked, I just couldn't say 'no!' I think that it will be interesting to try and do what Wagner wrote, which so far no one has succeeded in doing. Wagner himself didn't succeed, either, because the necessary technology wasn't there. After the first *Ring* production in Bayreuth, he was in despair over the staging side of it and told Cosima that he wished he were dead. So, whatever machines there might be in our production will certainly not *look* like machines: they will just make certain things work in a way that they couldn't have before.

"I have always thought that if anybody's stage instructions merited attention—and not every composer's or playwright's necessarily do—it is Wagner's. He sees the stage as something on which a metaphysical, or sometimes an emotional, debate can go on for thirty-five minutes and then the world can turn upside down in thirty seconds flat. So *how* these images are put across forms an essential part of his concept of theatre. And it would be nice to try to do them; and it would also be nice to try to contain the fact that Wagner was a nineteenth-century Romantic composer.

"And I have always believed myself to be a romantic director who has tried all his life not to be, partly as an intellectual discipline and partly because of the current of the times. My early work was extremely romantic and now I feel that I would, once again, like to become what I am. And I think that Georg is a highly romantic conductor who has, at times, also been a highly nervous and neurotic one! I mean, when I first worked with him fifteen or sixteen years ago, he was very driven and made music in a febrile way. So, maybe we are coming together again for this project at the right moment for both of us."

Solti says that the musical conception will be very different from his interpretation of twenty years ago. Twenty years is a long time in the life of a musician, and everything will be different—not necessarily better or worse, he stresses, just different. But although his musical conception is not rigidly predetermined I think that one can expect a more relaxed approach to the score and in his conducting style which has, in recent years, grown "more *espressivo*, from Toscanini to Furtwängler", to quote himself, i.e. mellower, more elastic and paying more attention to the melody than he used to in earlier years, when rhythmic clarity and precision were his main preoccupations and the chief characteristics of his conducting style.

Of course he will now be dealing with an entirely new generation of singers. And while he will not change his basic musical approach, he will, of course, adapt it to the particular acoustic conditions of Bayreuth, where the low, sunken pit makes it possible to work with smaller voices.

"The basic problem of the Wagnerian orchestra *outside* Bayreuth is that you are compelled to combine it with big voices that cannot be killed by the volume of orchestral sound. But because Bayreuth is a happy realization of Wagner's idea that a big orchestra can be used in a way that does not swamp the singers, this fact alone will dictate a slightly different style; certain things will need broadening up, other things will need speeding up, etc. A musical conception should never be sterile, but adapt itself to different orchestras, theatres, singers, acoustics and directors."

And, according to Peter Hall, this flexibility and knack of being open to ideas is one of Solti's remarkable qualities as a collaborator. "Georg likes living dangerously, and so do I. He doesn't feel that everything should fit into his detailed, preformed idea of the music. In fact, I never feel that his musical conception is rigid. He is always prepared to allow it to grow out of the combustion of all of us working together. Of course, he gets terribly anxious, terribly worried and terribly nervous and is always on the watch in case it's going to be a *disaster*!!! [The imitation was so good I couldn't stop laughing]. But he is very reckless. He'll have a go at things. He tries."

Solti feels that one of the greatest difficulties in conducting the *Ring* is the stamina it requires to get through the sheer number of hours: at least four for each opera except *Das Rheingold*, which is shorter but has no interval. "And the problem in all Wagner operas is that he tends to emphasize the most important and essential things at the end, after you have already been conducting for four hours. In a way, *Siegfried* is the most demanding because there is hardly any relaxation, except for a brief spell in the second act. And in *Götterdämmerung*, there are those long, long stretches demanding utmost concentration and, just as you are getting very tired, the music gets fundamentally more important in the third act, just as it does in *Die Walküre*. So from the stamina point of view, all Wagner operas are extremely demanding."

Obviously, this makes it imperative for him to make adjustments to the rest of his schedule and take things easy when he is involved in a production of any parts of the *Ring*. When it comes to the Bayreuth cycles, he will stop doing anything else in April of each of the three years involved prior to the rehearsals, which will start in May and last nine weeks. He will also take at least one month off afterwards. If after the first year he finds that this just isn't enough, he will take more time off in the following two years. Having never conducted at Bayreuth before, he is interested to find out whether the hour-long interval between each act will help. At Covent Garden, they started off with twenty-minute intervals, and he had to fight to get them extended first to twenty-five minutes and eventually to half an hour. He therefore feels that an hour might help restore some of his energy. "But of course, one should remember that the performances will start at five and go on until eleven at night, and there will be three *Ring* cycles, i.e. twelve performances, in less than five weeks. There is no getting around the fact that physically this will be a great hardship."

"If we succeed in this undertaking," sighs Solti, "we will have accomplished a historic deed, because we will have produced exactly what Wagner wrote. If we don't, then we will, at least, have tried and will have to admit that it is no longer possible to do a romantic *Ring* in the way that he wrote it. So, it will be back to the machines, and I will be out! I'll concentrate only on concert performances. So, that's the whole *Ring* story," he beamed, flashing his sudden, brilliant smile. "Biography, volume two!"

Twenty-five years ago, Solti thought of producing the *Ring* and some other operas himself, because he has an eye for production, design and colour and has always been very active in all the productions he has been involved with—either liking or disliking the producers' work and always trying to influence them into respecting musical points which producers simply are not aware of. But he never actually dared to take the fatal step, which would have both advantages and disadvantages. The obvious advantage would be that he could synchronize and express musical points in scenic movements, and the main disadvantage would centre around the fact that, as a conductor, he couldn't be everywhere all the time, so that either the musical or the scenic side would suffer, in the same way that either the solistic or the orchestral part suffers when a soloist conducts from the keyboard.

"It's a similar problem: on the one hand, you achieve unity— because however good the conductor and the pianist and however close their musical conceptions may be, you always hear two Mozarts, never *quite* the same Mozart. But, on the other hand, by doing both yourself you lose some of the finer points of balance and ensemble because when you have to concentrate on playing you cannot also concentrate on every single orchestral detail.

"The best solution to the problem would be to have your own chamber orchestra. I've often flirted with the idea! If I could find a King Ludwig II to give me a small chamber orchestra, say thirty people, to play just Mozart concertos and nothing else, I would be in seventh heaven! One would work and work endlessly until one achieved the perfect blend, the same style for both the orchestra and the piano. But needless to say, this would take a great deal of time!"

Meanwhile, he does not believe in doing what some colleagues are doing: dividing their time between conducting and playing their instrument. He believes that you are either a soloist or a conductor, because in the end, something is bound to suffer. Apart from anything else, there is the basic question of muscle control, which players need to such extreme degree. For example, five years ago, he decided to have a well-earned sabbatical which was supposed to last a year. Then it shrank to six months. In the end, he managed only three. During that time, he had intended to go back to the piano with a view to playing and conducting a Mozart concerto from the keyboard. "But in the end, I chickened out. Although I practised two hours a day, it was not enough. I would have needed more than three months to go back to the level of piano playing I was used to."

Although a confirmed workaholic who uses even part of his holidays as a period of study, he is now a much more relaxed man than before. He enjoys his family life and his cosy houses in London and Italy where he lives with his second wife, BBC presenter and interviewer Valerie Pitts—whom he met when she went to interview him in 1963—and their two daughters. He dotes on the children, and adjusts his schedules to tie in with their school holidays. "I am the old-fashioned kind of adoring Papa who loves spoiling children. I am always being told that I shouldn't, but this is my way. I can't help it and I can't do it any other way."

His main hobbies are playing bridge with a small group of close friends, tennis, avidly watching sport on TV, reading widely and going to the theatre. One of his most endearing characteristics, on the light-hearted side, is his utter hopelessness with machines and everything mechanical.

As a human being, Solti is an immensely kind-hearted, sensitive and emotional man. But, as is often the case with dynamic, energetic personalities, his warmth and deep compassion are not always immediately apparent to everybody. He cares passionately about humanitarian issues, and I vividly remember having lunch with him, his family and mutual friends on the day when Britain had refused entry to a boatload of Vietnamese refugees. He was profoundly disturbed and agitated and wondered what he could do, whom he should write to, where he should send money to, and couldn't stop thinking about it. He is the same about personal friends and their problems.

A mellowed and contented man these days, he is happy with his lot both professionally and personally and, not surprisingly, this is reflected in his music-making. "I have no unfulfilled ambitions to bite me or to make me restless anymore; I relish my freedom to insist on the right working conditions and I am free of envy. For a very long time, I was wracked with jealousy and envy because I was a late starter and everyone seemed so far ahead of me. Now, I envy no one. Anyway, the music field is so vast: all the way from Anchorage to Cape Town for what I call the 'Club of Ten', i.e. *really* good conductors, to work in. But although I'm happy with my lot, I'm far from contented with my work, about which I seem to be getting more and more critical. I can hardly bear listening to my old records, because I hear only the mistakes, not the merits, and it's *agony*! [And this from a man who has won over twenty Grand Prix du Disque Mondiale and eighteen Grammy Awards.] So, you could say that my only remaining ambition is to go on doing what I'm doing now—but to do it better all the time."

KLAUS TENNSTEDT
Late Starter with a Vengeance

"In my whole career as an orchestral player, two performances stand out as truly unforgettable," says Alan Cumberland, principal timpanist of the London Philharmonic Orchestra. "And oddly enough, they happen to be of the same work: the Schubert ninth. The performance we did with Sir Adrian Boult—which we also recorded—was unbelievable and I didn't think that anybody could ever do it any better. Until Tennstedt."

Double bass player Kenneth Goode is another admirer of Sir Adrian's reading of the Schubert ninth—"especially its geniality and the way it allowed the work to unfold"—even though personally he is unmoved by this symphony. "Yet under Tennstedt I found myself responding to it for the first time in my life. He had such unusual insight into this work that at the end I felt compelled to go up to him and say: 'Maestro, I can honestly say that tonight I was able to enjoy the Schubert ninth for the first time in my life!' And if anyone can make me do that, that's my man! I was so consumed by his interpretation that I can no longer accept any other."

Yet I must confess that when this book was first conceived, in 1978, Klaus Tennstedt—who took over as Music Director of the London Philharmonic in the autumn of 1982 after three years as the orchestra's Principal Guest Conductor—was not on my original list of conductors to be included. His star was just beginning to rise and he was relatively unknown in Britain at the time, having conducted only two concerts in London; one with the London Symphony Orchestra in 1976 and one with the London Philharmonic in 1977, neither of which I had heard. So, despite a couple of excellent reviews and some ecstatic comments from the other side of the Atlantic, it seemed better to wait until I could judge for myself.

A rehearsal and subsequent performance of the Bruckner seventh with the London Philharmonic was all I needed to convince me that here was a conductor of immense stature, with a great deal to say and a compelling way of saying it. Therefore, it was imperative that he be included in the book. Yet for a long time this was easier said than done. His own schedule was packed, of course—so was mine. Finally we did manage to meet—much too near the eleventh hour for my liking and only for a short conversation. Therefore the fact that this chapter is shorter than the rest is due to lack of time alone. Yet granted Tennstedt's brilliance, a short chapter seemed better than no chapter at all.

Since 1979, of course, his career has soared. Apart from being Music Director of the London Philharmonic, he has the distinction of being one of three conductors (the others were Mehta and Ozawa) named by Herbert von Karajan in a widely read interview in *Der Spiegel* as his possible successors at the Berlin Philharmonic, which Tennstedt regularly guest-conducts and which he has the rare privilege to record with; he also makes frequent appearances with the New York and the Los Angeles Philharmonic, the Cleveland and the Philadelphia Orchestra, the Chicago and the Boston Symphony; in 1983–84 he makes his début at the Metropolitan Opera conducting *Fidelio*; a year later, this will be followed by *Elektra* which he will also record for EMI with whom he has an exclusive contract.

Yet ten years ago, nobody in the so-called musical establishment had even heard of Klaus Tennstedt, a tall, bespectacled, *simpatico* man with a mercurial, highly-strung and intense temperament. For until 1971 he lived and laboured in obscurity as Music Director at the State Opera at Schwerin in his native East Germany. Although he had held the post for nine years, had guest-conducted all the major East German orchestras like the Dresden Staatskapelle and the Leipzig Gewandhaus, and toured the Soviet Union and other Eastern bloc countries, he felt that his native country offered no further opportunities for artistic growth. So, at the age of forty-five, he decided to escape to the West, in circumstances which he still prefers not to discuss.

It was a brave decision in many ways. For heady though the leap to freedom must have been for someone used to the stifling cultural climate of Communist countries, it meant that he would have to start his career all over again at an age by which most of his contemporaries in the West are usually entrenched in important positions, if not always at the peak of their artistic powers. But despite the fact that Tennstedt's first three years in the West were spent out of the limelight at the Stora Theatre in Gothenburg, the Swedish Radio Orchestra and eventually as Music Director at the Kiel Opera, his gamble paid off. In 1974 came what *Der Spiegel* picturesquely called his "lift-off from obscurity".

He was invited to conduct the Boston Symphony after some very successful performances in Toronto. He arrived totally unknown and in an almost classic case of 'a star is born', aroused players, audience and critics alike to such a frenzy of enthusiasm that virtually overnight he found himself famous. Next morning, almost every major American orchestra was on the line, clamouring for his services. "You know what America is like," he shrugs modestly. "A musical village where everyone knows the morning after everything that happened in all major musical centres the night before." He himself dismisses the 'star system' in serious music as irrelevant and misleading. "Naturally, it can be useful to write about musicians in the papers, provided it is done seriously. Sensationalism is useless," he told a French magazine. "When I'm not rehearsing, I'm studying scores; when I rehearse, I work extremely hard with the orchestra; in the evening, there is the concert. A normal life."

But sudden and unexpected though fame was, it stood on firm foundations: twenty years' experience with various East German orchestras and opera houses had equipped him with a thorough knowledge of his craft and an extensive repertoire. Yet in recent years his greatest successes have been as an interpreter of Mahler and Bruckner. As he explained to *The Daily Telegraph*, "Bruckner and Mahler had in common the restless search for meaning and truth, but they approached it differently. Mahler had the greater intellect, but Bruckner had this firm concept of form, almost from the start of his symphonic writing. That's what makes some silly people say that he wrote the same symphony nine times over. What I find amazing is that he could keep to the same form and yet write such varied and arresting works. Many books have been written about it, but no-one can properly explain this phenomenon.... I suppose I like the Sixth, the Seventh and the Eighth best, but listen to the slow movement of the Second—marvellous!"

Tennstedt was born in Merseburg on June 6, 1926. His father was a violinist and the first musical talent in the family—*his* father had been a carpenter. Klaus started playing the piano at the age of six and, four years later, his father guided him towards the violin, which he found quite fun at first but less so later, when his playmates started playing football. Instead of practising the violin, he wanted to play football. But his father wouldn't hear of his neglecting his lessons, so he took to sneaking out for half an hour's game whenever he saw a chance, "but alas, this trick didn't work for very long." When he was sixteen he decided he wanted to become a professional musician and enrolled at the Leipzig Conservatoire, where he studied piano, violin and theory. His ambition at the time was to be good enough to become a concertmaster, and he achieved his aim by 1948 when at the age of twenty-two he was named First Concertmaster at the Municipal Theatre in Halle, Handel's birthplace.

This proved not only fulfilling at the time, but also valuable experience for his future conducting career, "because good concertmasters must always have a good relationship with conductors—and how! So it was very interesting to work closely with all of them and watch their different ways of doing things and how they got their results." And yet, he had never thought of conducting himself. But a hand injury made it difficult for him to play the violin and so, being a competent pianist, he switched to coaching singers. This was to prove his passport to conducting. For one day the conductor in charge of *Der Günstling*, an opera by Wagner-Regèny, fell ill and the only person able to replace him was Tennstedt who had rehearsed the score thoroughly with the cast. He remembers entering the pit a nervous wreck and that the first ten minutes were "fairly chaotic, with the orchestra rushing away from me. But I gradually slowed them down and within about ten minutes it all came together." Having now experienced the exhilaration of conducting, he was smitten for life. In 1958, he joined the conducting staff of the Dresden State Opera and four years later, was named Music Director at Schwerin, where he stayed for nine years, up to his escape to the West.

After his 1974 triumph in Boston—the real launch of his career in the West—he was invited to appear at the Tanglewood Festival, where he was greatly impressed by both the public and the American standards of musical education. "The American public is simply fantastic," he told *Le Monde de la Musique*. "I saw people come with their families by car from very far, just to listen to the Bruckner eighth, and knowing that it would take them over an hour to get to their car afterwards, as the audience consists of no less than fourteen to fifteen thousand people. One could never see a comparable sight in Western

Europe nor in Prague, nor in Moscow nor Warsaw either. It's an incredible atmosphere and so unlike the Salzburg Festival where one sometimes has the impression that a lot of grand ladies are there only to show off their diamonds.... America also wins hands down as far as musical education is concerned. Music schools and the Faculties of Music at American Universities are extraordinary. And some of their student orchestras—like the New England Conservatoire's, which could easily be mistaken for a professional orchestra, as anyone who has heard their recordings of *Le Sacre du printemps* and *Ein Heldenleben* can testify—are of a level simply inconceivable in Europe."

A year after his appearances at Tanglewood, Tennstedt made his British début with the London Symphony Orchestra in September 1977; a year later he conducted the London Philharmonic for the first time in a programme that included the Mahler first and prompted the critic of *The Times* to write that "it could not have taken anyone long to realize how completely Tennstedt was under this composer's skin, sharing his hypersensitive, even neurotically highly-strung reactions." The orchestra invited him back for several weeks every subsequent season before naming him its Principal Guest Conductor in 1980. A year later, Solti's resignation as Music Director and the termination of Tennstedt's own contract as Principal Conductor of the North German Radio Orchestra meant that he was free to accept the LPO's offer to become Principal Conductor and Music Director, "with great joy".

The players are plainly electrified by him, as their enthusiastic comments, made well before the announcement of Tennstedt's Music Directorship, show. Kenneth Goode feels that "Tennstedt combines the best qualities of both our previous Music Directors: Solti's vitality and Haitink's more relaxed phrasing and feeling for line. He is a very intense man who experiences the music he conducts with every fibre of his being, and has an excellent, down-to-earth technique. Yet his rehearsals are quite analytical and different from his performances, where you get all the magic. At rehearsal you never get the full sound, because he has a very keen eye for detail, and seems to spend most time working on expression, or rather, the different expression required from the various sections and instrument groups; his main concern is how to bring out all the inner voices—to which everything else must be subordinate, especially in the big Mahler and Bruckner symphonies—at the right time. But he is also deeply concerned with the relentless, forward-motion of the work to its conclusion."

Tennstedt himself finds it hard to analyse or describe his own conducting style and to explain how he gets his results. "I try to arouse enthusiasm in the players and work them very hard from the first moment. They like that. Yet apart from a certain electric spark, a conductor also needs a gift for psychology: he must know how to be severe and uncompromising but without making the musicians resent him. In the past I didn't have this gift.... Because the problem with orchestras is always the same: they consist of a hundred people each of whom has his own opinion about tempo and dynamics—for there is no *objective* guidance as to what a forte or a piano is; opinions must necessarily be totally subjective. So you have one hundred different minds responding to these indications and your job is to bring them together into one single conception. Basically good conductors and good orchestras have a lot to learn from each other. Now I know most of the great orchestras of the world and have a good working relationship with most of them; I know what to expect from each one. Because every orchestra has different qualities; some sections may be good while others may leave something to be desired and make it necessary for you to work them harder."

Visually, Tennstedt's conducting style is intense, vigorous and has often been described as 'balletic'. He uses his body a great deal, deliberately. "For," he explained to *Le Monde de la Musique* in the interview mentioned earlier, "it is human beings who are making music. The fact that a violinist's movements are different from those of an oboist is important; for the public should be able to observe the interplay of sound and motion. I express something with my movements—whether they are visually pleasing to the public doesn't bother me in the least—which draws a certain response from the orchestra. And what I express and the way they respond to it become one and the same thing. It's vital that the public should see this union between conductor and orchestra—otherwise, it's death. Both the orchestra and the public should feel that what I'm doing is sincere. I am what I am and my interpretation should express this—i.e. it should be truthful. It's very simple and at the same time very difficult."

Although most of Tennstedt's career behind the Iron Curtain was spent in opera houses, he has conducted very little opera in the West to date. (*Die Walküre* and Henze's *Boulevard Solitude* plus a handful of others at the Bavarian State Opera.) Yet like most of his experienced colleagues, he agrees that this is the best possible way for a conductor to learn his craft, "learn how to let the orchestra breathe, how to bring out the line in the music, how to shape a phrase". Yet interestingly enough, he thinks that while conducting an opera may be *technically* more difficult than a symphony because of the different elements that have to be kept under control, it is easier from the musical, interpretational point of view because "you have the plot, the text, to help you form an interpretation; whereas in a Bruckner symphony, for instance, you are alone. There is nothing to help you but your own inner resources as a musician and a human being. Everything must come from inside *you*."

He finds that the most difficult works in the operatic repertoire to interpret are the Mozart operas. "And it is not only Mozart *operas* that are difficult to interpret but Mozart himself. *He* is difficult. Because Mozart the composer and Mozart the man are not one and the same; his music is totally different from his character and his life, unlike Mahler whose music *is* his life, *is* his character."

Tennstedt came to Mahler "late, but very intensely" at the age of forty-three, and feels that a certain mellowness is necessary before anyone is ready to tackle this most personal of composers. "For how could an immature man with no life-experience come to grips with a composer whose every mood and reaction is composed into his scores; a composer so infinitely many-sided: ironic, even grotesque at times, morbid, flashily dramatic, but never banal—that is a word I will simply not tolerate in relation to Mahler; a composer so relentlessly 'honest' in his tireless search for the truth and whose range of extremes encompasses unbelievable ups and downs: from the pessimism of the Sixth to the optimism of the Seventh; from the resignation of the Ninth to the extraordinarily interesting unfinished Tenth, with its mystic sound pattern at certain moments, which seems to point to a new direction in Mahler as a composer and paves the way for what others would do in the future.... And the fact that he is so acutely relevant today, to our times, is proved by his vast popularity! The Mahler 'boom' was much more than a passing fashion."

The first Mahler score Tennstedt ever saw was the First "which is, and yet is not, Mahler." It aroused his curiosity sufficiently for him to go out and buy Alma Mahler's Memoirs, which he devoured almost like a thriller and found interesting because of the mixture of intellect and naïveté—the very reason why many people look down on them. Then he bought more scores—and got completely hooked.

"It's impossible to explain, or even to know, exactly why one is suddenly ready for a particular composer. It's a mystery. But obviously it must have something to do with one's own experiences and maturing process both as an artist and as a man." When he came to study a Mahler score with a view to *conducting* it, it took him a very long time, more than six months, to form a conception, "like reading a complex book—*Joseph* by Thomas Mann, for instance, which you cannot read and absorb all at once, but read, then put it down, then pick it up again, the first time quite fast and superficially from beginning to end, to get a general picture; then comes the detail. Scores [which Tennstedt prefers to study in bed] are just the same."

He agrees with Karajan, who took over two years to prepare the Fifth, that Mahler scores need a particularly long time to prepare. And like Karajan and Abbado, he thinks that from the technical point of view of rehearsing, it is important to develop a special string sound for Mahler, a typical Viennese-Hungarian sound, "slightly ... dirty if you know what I mean. Having been a string player myself I know exactly how to work for this. No, I don't think that playing Mahler in Vienna is easier or better than elsewhere. Any major orchestra that is flexible enough can achieve this sound."

A conductor's inner preparation also takes a long time, "for you must allow Mahler to seep through until you identify with him completely. You have to perform Mahler with all your heart and mind and soul. Other composers don't require this to the same extent. Sometimes you might get away with only partial identification. But this would never work with Mahler. You have to believe in him one hundred per cent." Tennstedt's passionate attitude towards this composer explains why the critic of *The Sunday Times* felt, after a sizzling performance of the 'Resurrection' Symphony at the Royal Festival Hall, that "never have I heard a Mahler score leap out at me so ferociously, with such blazing commitment from the whole orchestra sustained at white heat over the whole ninety minutes."

Yet, as Tennstedt explained to the *Gramophone* a few years ago, his wholehearted commitment does not extend to a feeling of *becoming* the composer at the time of performance in the sense that Leonard Bernstein describes. Tennstedt feels that achieving identification with the composer is essential while absorbing the score and forming his interpretation; but at the moment of performance, a certain distance is essential for maintaining control. "A conductor needs a good balance between emotion and control, between heart and intellect. Only when he achieves this balance can his performances be good; if he is too cool and precise, they won't be good; if he is too self-indulgent, they will not be good, either. There must always be this balance between the two, and this is very, very difficult, something you cannot actually 'learn' but only acquire by experience."

Tennstedt's favourite Mahler symphony is the Seventh—"Not all of it but certainly the first movement, perhaps the greatest movement Mahler ever wrote, and the *Nachtmusiken*. The last movement is okay but much more conventional, not nearly as good as the others. Yet both from the musical and from the technical point of view, it is the most difficult Mahler score to conduct: the whole work poses tremendous technical problems. For a start, it's very difficult to hold the orchestra together and to get the balance right. And from the interpretational point of view, those unbelievable long lines in the first movement and the second Nachtmusik are not easy ... but Mahler is never easy. He stays with you for a long time after the concert. ... You just cannot get away from him. ... But this is also true of all good composers; you cannot get rid of their music, you keep hearing it again and again and are unable to sleep for a long, long time after a concert. But with bad composers, forget it! You are out of it at once!"

Tennstedt's favourite way to unwind after concerts is with a good beer and a chat with friends or associates, but preferably not about music. He hates all the travelling, hotel life and hotel food he has to put up with but accepts it as an inevitable part of a conductor's life. His wife, a former contralto, usually travels with him; and they have a grown-up son. The little free time he has is spent at home on the Baltic coast, sailing, playing tennis, learning to fly a small Cessna plane and indulging in his favourite hobby: astronomy. He owns a telescope and finds that a few hours spent observing the heavens are a wonderful way to relax and regain the right perspective about things: "It is good for us to remember how small and unimportant we are."

A statement undoubtedly true, but all the more unexpected coming from a conductor!

INDEPENDENT SPIRIT

CARLOS KLEIBER
A Law unto Himself

I first met Carlos Kleiber in his dressing room at the Vienna State Opera. It was during an interval of *Carmen* and he was in a very good mood. He had just received a letter from a member of the public who had watched the televised relay of the opening night and wanted to congratulate him because he thought that, for a man of eighty-eight, he didn't look his age. "Obviously they took me for my father," said Carlos, shaking with laughter and finding this quite hilarious!

The incident is an instant clue to two important factors in his life and character. For this superb conductor, whom many musicians, including numerous colleagues, consider to be among the finest of our time, is the son of the great conductor Erich Kleiber, who would indeed have been eighty-eight in December 1978, had he not died suddenly on Mozart's birthday [January 27], in 1956, aged only sixty-six. Kleiber is the only instance of a top-ranking conductor following in the footsteps of his father, and it is not too difficult to imagine how frustrating this must have been at the beginning of his career.

Secondly, it shows the man's delicious sense of humour, which I had heard a lot about from friends and colleagues, who all assured me that he is not only funny, witty, quick—expert at inventing appropriate nicknames for people with lightning speed—but also able to respond to even the most English of English humour. Rare in a foreigner. Even rarer in a German.

But in fact, Carlos Kleiber is half American. (Even though his father was born in Vienna, and he, himself, has recently become an Austrian citizen, the other half is Saxon-German.) His mother, born Ruth Goodrich, was working at the American Embassy in Buenos Aires when she met and fell in love with Erich Kleiber, in 1927. A few months later, they were married in Berlin, where he was Generalmusikdirektor of the State Opera, after what must have been a quaint courtship, as she spoke no German and he virtually no English at the time.

Carlos was born on July 3, 1930—a Cancerian. (The fact is worth mentioning because he is quite interested in astrology, has read a number of books about it, and knows that his ascendant is Scorpio.) Five years later, in 1935, Erich Kleiber resigned from his post at the State Opera in protest against Nazi interference with artistic policy, and his resignation had far-reaching consequences for Carlos's life and that of his elder sister, Veronica. It meant the beginning of a long period of travelling, changes of residence, different boarding schools and inevitable separations from their parents. In 1940, after five peripatetic years, the family finally settled in South America until 1948, and Carlos went to an English boarding school in Chile.

This unsettled and lonely childhood accounts for his polyglot brilliance (he is fluent in French, Italian, Spanish, Slovenian and, of course, German and English), and may partly explain his shyness and nervousness of meeting new people, his dislike of being alone and that lack of self-confidence which is characteristic of him but puzzles all who fall under the spell of his electrifying personality when they hear and see him conduct. It takes a long time to get a Kleiber performance out of one's system; even longer to feel ready or willing to absorb somebody else's view of the same work.

This is not only true of the audience. Orchestral players also find themselves so extraordinarily overstimulated at the end of his performances that, according to John Brown, Leader of the Orchestra of the Royal Opera House, Covent Garden, "I have to go to the pub with some of the lads and steam off by going over the performance again verbally, over a pint! It would be impossible to go straight home to bed." Walter Probst, second violinist at the Bavarian State Opera, agrees and adds that "we play Kleiber's *Rosenkavalier*, Kleiber's *Traviata*, Kleiber's *Fledermaus* and Kleiber's *Otello*—Kleiber's interpretation of every work he has conducted here—no matter who is waving the stick! We cannot, and will not, have them exorcized from our minds."

As both these musicians so rightly point out, every Kleiber performance is 'an event'. A relatively rare event, however, because Kleiber conducts very little (and is even more spare with his recordings). He is a fanatic and a perfectionist who only agrees to appear when he feels that conditions are right and offer him a chance, at least, of realizing his vision of a work. This means that he turns down most of the invitations which come his way—and they come from everywhere—seemingly with total disregard for career or financial considerations. This, plus his reluctance to sign contracts, his frequent cancellations and his refusal to give interviews, has earned him the reputation of being 'difficult'.

Yet it is significant that this 'difficult' conductor has an impassioned following, that his rare appearances are eagerly awaited and enthusiastically received, that musicians respond to him with unusual warmth as well as whole-hearted admiration, and that he is becoming one of the most important conductors of our day precisely *because* he manages to ignore the temptations which the jet age and contemporary musical practice have inflicted on his profession.

From the musical point of view, however hard one might try to pinpoint and define some of the main characteristics of his conducting, there is still something more, something extra, which eludes definition: a Dionysian element, a 'divine madness' called a state of 'enthusiasm' by the ancient Greeks, which in their language meant a human being not merely inspired, but temporarily taken over, possessed, by the Gods. In our vocabulary, the nearest appropriate word is genius.

He, of course, would not agree. He is much too self-deprecating, too much of a perfectionist ever to be satisfied with his own performances, and always afraid that he doesn't know enough, that he has not understood the score completely or that he has not conveyed his mental image of the work properly to the musicians or singers. ("Forgive me, it was my fault, I didn't beat this passage clearly enough, I'll have another look at it," I have heard him say to an orchestra.) This insecurity and sense of inadequacy are generally supposed to be attributable to his father, who tried to discourage him from becoming a conductor, or indeed, a musician at all.

Yet the child's talent was apparent very early on. By the age of nine, he was already composing, as his mother reported in a letter to his father, who was then staying at the Hotel Bolivar in Lima, waiting for his family to join him. In his reply, dated December 1, 1939, Erich Kleiber exclaimed: "I long to hear one of my son's compositions. What a pity he is 'musical'." A week later, he wrote, "That he *both* sings and composes is suspicious! He'll want to be a musician next!" When, later, Carlos was studying chemistry at the Technische Hochschule in Zurich, and decided that he wanted to be a musician, his father gave him one year to work at music, with the promise to return to chemistry if there were no sign of talent—possibly because he wanted to be sure of the boy's sincerity and talent before exposing him to the hardships and ardours of a musician's life.

But whatever the reasons, it can't have been easy or pleasant for someone as intensely sensitive and as fiercely proud as Carlos to grow up in such circumstances. He never admits or refers to any feelings of resentment at having to stifle his true nature to please his family. But a letter which his father wrote to him for his nineteenth birthday, when he was still at the Zurich Polytechnic, is a clue to his frustration and uncertainty about his future. "When I was nineteen," wrote Erich Kleiber obviously in reply to a previous letter from his son, "I didn't know what was going to happen to me, either. I only knew that I didn't have enough to eat and that music was indispensible to me. Now, I hope that you *do* have enough to eat, and there is still plenty of time to find out whether music will prove indispensible to you, too."

Meanwhile, Carlos found an outlet for his artistic impulses in writing—in the style of Hemingway or of Scott Fitzgerald or of any other writer who gripped his imagination. Perhaps he inherits his literary bent from his paternal grandfather and great-grandfather, both of whom were Greek and Latin scholars as well as musical. Words seem to come to him almost as naturally as music, and he is one of the few conductors who can explain sound in words and talk a great deal at rehearsal without boring the musicians.

"He is a very, very clever and well-read gentleman. Really super-intelligent," says John Brown. "We were absolutely knocked out, not only by his conducting technique, but also by his intellect. He was never at a loss for the right words that explained exactly the kind of sound he wanted, and this was a tremendous help to us. Examples? Oh, there are hundreds! In *La Bohème*, for instance, he wanted a certain passage to sound transparent, but with the woodwinds slightly prominent, so he said, 'Imagine trying to look through a nightie, and that the woodwinds are the interesting bits!' or 'Musetta is definitely a feminist! Listen to all those fascist-sounding notes!' Tiny things like that, which helped us see what was in his mind, and what a staggeringly original mind it is!"

"Maestro Kleiber is a romantic," adds Carlo Capriata, principal double bass and manager of the Orchestra of La Scala. "I vividly remember a beautiful example of his word pictures of sound, from *Otello*. In Act I, just before the love duet, he asked for a totally weightless, transparent sound, 'like spraying snowdust on a Christmas tree', which is so beautiful to visualize that it stays in your mind forever."

Professor Alfred Altenburger, Vorstand of the Vienna Philharmonic Orchestra, recalls that when Kleiber was rehearsing the Brahms fourth, he wanted a certain passage to sound "'very, very strong but quiet, like a Rolls-Royce—a twelve-cylinder motor, but you can't hear it!' He often came up with examples like that, apparent contradictions so pronounced that they are in a state of unity, and it made me think of the Zen Buddhist concept of One, which comprises such contrasts, and where yes and no are one."

In 1950, Carlos was allowed to study music for a year in Buenos Aires. Until then, he recently told Leonard Bernstein, he couldn't even read music. Bernstein, who greatly admires him and considers his interpretation of *La Bohème* one of the most beautiful things he has heard in his life, marvelled that, at such a late stage, he started at all!

"You know how children often enjoy playing firemen and going whoosh, whoosh, whoosh with a hose?" replied Carlos, skirting around the issue as he often does when he doesn't want to give a direct answer. "Well, one of *my* favourite games was pretending to give cues and entries to an imaginary orchestra, but without knowing whom I was cueing, who was supposed to be coming in next. Then, one day, I said to myself that if I were to continue with my game, I had better find out what instruments I was pretending to cue."

"Then," continues Bernstein, "it got serious, because he is so exceptionally gifted, and suddenly he had to cope with the seriousness of a game that was no longer a game. I'm not saying that this is the truth, but it's *his* truth, it's what he tells himself."

But despite the fact that he began his formal musical studies late and in addition to his enormous talent which immediately took over, Carlos had the advantage of occasional access to some of his father's rehearsals and remembers that: "On the one hand he always wanted to demonstrate that [conducting] was mostly something based on hard work and a craftsman's skill, but on the other hand, he did not deny inspiration. He never talked about it much, but I often observed, especially once, during an *Elektra* rehearsal in Munich, that towards the middle of the performance, he seemed so visibly moved by the work, that his arms seemed to get longer and longer and there was a very strange, mysterious, unique gesture, which is impossible to describe...."

Another thing that he remembers was the degree of his father's concentration while studying scores. Erich Kleiber would go for long walks with a score in his hand and his children walking in front, immerse himself completely in whatever work he was preparing, but at the same time remain aware of everything going on around him. Once, he stopped his perusal long enough to save Carlos from an accident, and then calmly returned to his score. (Carlos's own concentration is no less amazing: when he made his début at La Scala in the 1974–75 season with *Der Rosenkavalier*, he continued to conduct throughout the Friuli earthquake, which shook the place, rocked the chandeliers and emptied the gallery. "I didn't notice!" he said later, when he was told what had happened after complaining that the orchestra had seemed restless!)

In 1952, he returned to Europe and volunteered as a répétiteur and stage assistant at the Gärtnerplatztheater in Munich. Two years later, he made his conducting debut in Potsdam, a place carefully chosen so as to avoid possible embarrassment to either father or son, according to the late K. H. Ruppel, the eminent German critic who was a close family friend. The work was *Gasparone*, an operetta by Karl Millöcker, and Carlos conducted not under his own name, but as 'Karl Keller'. Erich Kleiber sent his son a telegram: "Good luck—the old Keller!" and later told Ruppel, "You'll laugh, but the lad *is* gifted!" This must have been a turning point in their relationship, because from then on, Erich accepted his son's vocation and tried to help with both advice and introductions.

Professor Salmhofer, the Director of the Wiener Volksoper, took Carlos on as an unpaid coach, with the promise not to let him conduct until he was really ready for it. After his father's sudden death, in 1956, Dr Hermann Juch, who was then appointed Intendant of the Deutsche Oper am Rhein in Düsseldorf, took Carlos with him, first as a répétiteur. "I didn't want to let him conduct until he could emerge as 'Carlos Kleiber' not as 'Erich Kleiber's son'," says Dr Juch. After 1958, Carlos was allowed to conduct in Düsseldorf, having first conducted *The Bartered Bride* and *La Bohème* at the Salzburg Landestheater without rehearsal.

Richard Trimborn, Studienleiter of the Deutsche Oper am Rhein, was a fellow répétiteur at the time and remembers Carlos with much affection: "He was not a good pianist, even though he had a good sense of rhythm, but quite a brilliant coach. His instinct for music was always sure and his imagination and intuition helped him to understand and interpret it accurately. He was very friendly, honest, direct and natural, already sharply sarcastic on occasion, but generally well liked and very hard working: he always studied not only the piano parts, but also the whole orchestral score very thoroughly.

"Then, when he started conducting, he began to acquire this reputation of being 'difficult', which I always considered unfair because he is *not* difficult—I never found him so—provided you understand what he wants, which is the Absolute! He was, and I believe he still is, an idealist, who always tried not to compromise.

"Yet because he insisted that this or that detail should be done differently, better, all the time, I believe that he stretched the artists beyond their normal talents and often succeeded in getting more out of them than one would have thought possible. Of course, his perfectionism did sometimes cause some friction. But never on a personal level: any disagreements he had concerned factual, objective things which he considered an obstacle to the realization of a work." (I recently attended a rehearsal of his at the Bavarian State Opera and could see how upset he was when a musician whom he quite rightly corrected twice should have taken this as a personal insult. "It's nothing personal," he kept repeating to him, and when the player contradicted him, although visibly distressed, he just said, "All right, we'll forget about it.")

In Düsseldorf he conducted a great number of works with virtually no rehearsal, as is customary in repertory theatres: *La Bohème, Madama Butterfly, La traviata, I due Foscari, Rigoletto, Die Lustige Witwe, L'Heure Espagnole, Hänsel und Gretel,* Lortzing's *Der Waffenschmied,* Millöcker's *Der Bettelstudent,* Werner Egk's *Der Revisor,* Leoncavallo's *Edipo Ré,* plus Strauss's *Daphne* and *Der Rosenkavalier,* as well as ballets like *Undine, Coppélia, Abraxas* and three new choreographic realizations based on Ravel's *Boléro, Le Tombeau de Couperin* and *Alborada del Gracioso.* (The last three were performed on the same evening as a new production of *L'Heure Espagnole.*)

By 1962, the Opera's Music Director, Alberto Erede, felt that he was ready to tackle more new productions. In June 1962, he conducted an Offenbach triptych consisting of *Die Kleine Zauberflöte, Die Verlobung bei der Laterne* and *Die Insel Tulipatan.* (After which, the critic of the magazine *Opernwelt* commented on his exceptional conducting, as the local press had done after numerous repertory evenings, and noted the "dry, witty, flowing and flexible" interpretation of these scores.) This was followed by very well-received productions of *Les Contes d'Hoffmann* and *La Belle Hélène* in 1963.

It was surprising to discover that his repertoire is much wider than generally supposed. In recent years, he has concentrated on a handful of works—*La traviata, La Bohème, Otello, Carmen, Der Rosen-kavalier, Der Freischütz, Elektra, Wozzeck, Die Fledermaus, Tristan und Isolde*—and those who can find nothing to criticize in his performances are always going on about the smallness of his repertoire. I haven't had a chance to ask him but feel fairly sure that this is because, now that he is in a position to choose, he sees no point in conducting works he doesn't like or for which the right cast is either not available, or does not exist. ("Find me a Salome," he told someone who, years ago, asked him why he wouldn't conduct this opera.)

The seven-year period in Düsseldorf was crucial to his musical development. The baritone Carlos Alexander who sang Iago and Sharpless under him, remembers that he was "amazingly eager to learn, always asking questions and absorbing everything like a sponge. He attended as many rehearsals of Erede's as he could"—he still enjoys going to colleagues' rehearsals, sometimes with, sometimes without a score—"and was always discussing tempi, tempi, tempi, even in the car on our way to the Deutsche Oper's second house in Duisburg. Even though one was aware of a very special presence in the pit, I had the impression that he was still trying out tempi and ideas at this time. Two years later, when I met him again in Stuttgart, he seemed to have it all worked out, he was dead sure, and was much more concerned with characterization."

In short, Düsseldorf was where he learnt the repertoire and the intricacies of operatic production and where he perfected his stick technique—all the groundwork without which no conductor, however gifted, can hope to fulfil his own talent. Karajan, who went through a similar five-year period as Kapellmeister at Ulm, confirms that this is the best way for a conductor to really learn his craft—a training which many present-day conductors sadly lack. Kleiber doesn't, and his stick technique draws high praise from orchestral players:

"Kleiber has a masterly conducting technique," says Professor Alfred Altenburger. "It is precise, but also relaxed and elegant to a degree seldom seen in our profession. His gestures look attractive and although his conducting is very stimulating, there is no hint of brutality in it. He is impassioned and intense, but very aesthetic—a marvellous and rare combination."

"Kleiber's stick technique? It's very good, very clear, quite unmistakable," says Harold Nash, the first trombone at Covent Garden. "In *Otello*, he wanted a short, precise chord from us brass, together, which is technically very difficult to do. Normally he conducts with his right hand, of course, but for that big chord his left hand would come sweeping down very precisely, like a guillotine, spot on, and you could be in no doubt whatsoever about what he wanted.... He also loves taking chances, big chances, which is fine because his chances always come off! What kind of chances? Tremendous rubati, and in *Otello* there are several instances where everything is jogging along quite cheerfully in two-in-the-bar and suddenly, he would stop for maybe two beats, and then continue at the speed he'd just left. This is very clever indeed, because it keeps you on your toes, you have to keep watching him all the time and wondering when and where it will happen next! This is why I call his conducting 'impromptu', despite the fact that it is exceedingly well rehearsed to the *nth* degree. There is this wonderful sense of freedom about it."

The Leader, John Brown, agrees but explains that Kleiber always knows, or senses, just how long he can hold back, and obviously a lot depends on who has to come in next. "If it's a string passage it's me, and if he feels I'm lost, that downbeat is instantly there again. He has never let me down, so far.... Another characteristic of his is that he never overconducts. He can stand back and relax for a few seconds, but without losing concentration or any of his hyper-alertness to what's happening on stage, so that he can repair any mishaps almost instantaneously, with his stick. For instance, if in a sharply rhythmic passage things start rocking slightly, he is immediately galvanized and snaps us back into place with a fraction of an upbeat."

Cellist Friedrich Kleinknecht, Vorstand of the Bavarian State Orchestra, confirms that there are certain passages where Kleiber considers it unnecessary to conduct. In *Der Rosenkavalier*, for example, there is a particular spot where he just lets the clarinet play, "which means that he wants to get the characteristics of chamber music and to force the orchestra to listen to each other. This is why we, in this orchestra, always say that Kleiber is a conductor for advanced people. He doesn't feel that he has to indicate every pizzicato, but uses his gestures, which are very beautiful, to clarify the music. He is much more concerned about a musician disturbing the character of the sound by too much sforzando, by bowing too heavily, blowing too loudly, or by just not listening.... As a string player, I was particularly fascinated by something he did during our second run of *Otello*, in 1978: he had two groups of strings bowing against each other, thereby succeeding in maintaining an even level of sound and a wider legato."

"Yet great conducting is not just a matter of stick technique, but also of an overwhelming personality in the pit," adds John Brown. "I don't find Kleiber all that overwhelming in private, because despite his erudition, he is friendly, approachable and has great charm." (He hates pomposity: "I am *not* a Professor," he kept pointing out to the Stage Manager in Munich who kept on Herr-Professoring him!) "But," continues John Brown, "in the pit I find him utterly spellbinding! For him, music is not just bar-lines. He takes what is written in the score and makes poetry out of it. He studies his scores very, very hard and knows them more deeply than anyone I've ever come across, but he is prepared to let the devil in, just a wee bit, by introducing the element of chance. This unpredictability is an essential feature of his art, the reason why every Kleiber performance is a new and different happening."

"His conducting is of the spontaneous, inventive kind," sums up Oliver Bannister, the principal flute at Covent Garden. "One feels that he is quite at ease during the performance, when he is recreating the work, being creative with his hands and gestures to a most remarkable degree. One feels that the thing is now going along with a life of its own and that he is just moulding and guiding it with his gestures. He has a most uncanny insight and sensitivity about the work which is conveyed to us. If he were a creative artist, I would call him a genius. That's how highly I rate him."

In 1964, Kleiber moved to Zürich, where he remained until 1966 and conducted *The Bartered Bride*, *Wiener Blut*, *Don Carlos*, *Oberon*, *Der Vogelhändler* and *Falstaff*, plus a number of ballets. (His Yugoslav-born wife, ballet dancer Stanislava Brezovar (Stanka), whom he had met and married in Düsseldorf, was also engaged as a dancer and frequently appeared in performances conducted by him until the birth of their son, Marko, after which she gave up her career.)

These performances were well received by audience and critics alike, and Kleiber's reputation as an outstanding young conductor was growing. When Dr Walter Schäfer, Intendant of the Württemberg State Theatre in Stuttgart, started looking around for a First Kapellmeister, he despatched his deputy Dr Franz Willnauer to Zürich to see if Kleiber could be lured away, and gave him carte blanche to negotiate the necessary terms.

Dr Willnauer, who was already an ardent Kleiber fan, remembers arriving in Zürich on a Saturday afternoon and going straight into a matinée of *Swan Lake*: "I must be one of the very few people who have heard *Swan Lake* conducted by Kleiber, and it was an experience I shall never forget! I walked out of the theatre in a state of total intoxication, wrapped in what seemed like the perfect Tchaikovsky perfume: soft, svelte, fragrant but not at all sentimental. I also heard his *Falstaff*, which to this day remains the driest, wittiest, sharpest and juiciest Verdi I have ever heard!"

Later that evening, over dinner, Kleiber was persuaded to sign the contract—at 3.45 a.m. after hesitating, changing his mind and procrastinating in his usual way throughout the evening! His salary was very high: DM 3,000 a month, which corresponds to about DM 9,000 (£2,500) now, which was the salary of a Music Director. "But both my superior and I knew that he deserved it."

"I don't think I have ever come across a conductor with a greater musical imagination," says Dr Willnauer. "To me, he represents the rebirth of the Mahlerian ideal. Without being a composer, he has a composer's gift of visualizing sound. After conceiving his image of a work, he organized his rehearsals like a general who plans his tactics after deciding on basic strategy, and proceeded to put every element in its place, piece by piece.

"He always started off by reading all available literature about the composer and listening to all the recordings he could find, to see how the different conductors had interpreted the same score. Then, having decided which edition he would use, he marked the musicians' parts personally: every note was checked, every entry marked and the bowings entered.

"There were some people who, out of jealousy for the special regard which Dr Schäfer and I had for him, complained that he got away with conducting less than other people. But I don't think that anybody had any idea of the thoroughness and time he devotes to this preparatory, pre-rehearsal work. Then, when it came to rehearsals, he always insisted on having the same orchestra from the first rehearsal to the last performance. This is sometimes impossible to arrange in a German opera house—but in his mind, it is perfectly logical and consistent. But Kleiber's greatness, his genius, begins at the moment of performance, when all those carefully, analytically prepared results seem to happen spontaneously, as though improvised, and the music comes out alive and free."

Dr Schäfer wholeheartedly agrees and adds that he was lucky enough to have two geniuses pass through his Theatre: John Cranko and Carlos Kleiber, whom he grew to love like a son—not at first, but certainly at second, sight! "The first time he came, while he was still in Düsseldorf, he was meant to conduct *La traviata*, which he chose himself and for which he asked for two rehearsals. But he left without conducting, because the singer who was to be Violetta failed to turn up at the rehearsal! I can tell you that it took a long time before Franz Willnauer was allowed to mention the name Kleiber again!"

While in Stuttgart, he began to attract a great deal of attention, with his inspired interpretations of *Elektra*, *Wozzeck*, *Carmen*, *Der Rosenkavalier*, *Tristan und Isolde* and *Der Freischütz*. The latter was directed by the late Walter Felsenstein whose stormy relationship with Kleiber is almost a book in itself. The two quarrelled every single day. Carlos Alexander, who sang Otakar, was completely confused by their contradictory instructions—"Don't take any notice of that Kleiber," Felsenstein would whisper, and the next moment Carlos would come up and ask me to "ignore that man!"—until one day, he blew up and asked the two to get together and agree on what should be done *before* the rehearsal.

The evening was a triumph for Kleiber, and not an out-and-out success for Felsenstein. Still, when the latter left to return to Berlin, Kleiber went to Dr Schäfer and said: "I miss that Felsenstein so much! Do you think that, maybe, I should write him a postcard?" "I *admired* Felsenstein," he confirms.

Since 1968, Kleiber has had a guest contract with the Bavarian State Opera in Munich, but he also continued to conduct in Stuttgart from time to time until 1972. He has never accepted a full-time post since then, judging that he was by then in a position to insist on his own conditions and eschew routine, which he detests! His long and fruitful association with the Bavarian State Opera resulted in a series of much-acclaimed productions—*Otello*, *La traviata*, *Die Fledermaus*, *La Bohème*, *Der Rosenkavalier* and *Wozzeck*, after which Alban Berg's widow gave him the late composer's coat and ring—and owed much of its success, or the fact that it happened at all, to his good working relationship with the late Günther Rennert, the distinguished producer who was then Intendant in Munich.

The two had already worked together in Stuttgart, and Rennert understood and appreciated the magnitude and unique qualities of Kleiber's idiosyncratic genius, for whose sake he was prepared to put up with any of his demands ("Only some," says Carlos) and occasional explosions, exactly as Dr Schäfer had done in Stuttgart. This resulted in a 'golden age' (1968–78) for the Bavarian State Opera, according to several well-known singers.

Rennert's successor, August Everding, has been less successful in persuading Kleiber to conduct in Munich. Project after project has been cancelled—*Der Freischütz, Tristan*—for a variety of reasons which the administration always claims to be Kleiber's fault. But having a genius on your doorstep and letting him slip through your fingers to other, more accommodating opera houses, is something that cannot be done with impunity. In 1978, a substantial group of frustrated and enraged Kleiber fans besieged the opera house, armed with banners saying KLEIBER MUST RETURN TO THE PIT OF THE STAATSOPER, and delivered a petition signed by hundreds of his admirers to the administration.

The orchestra clearly miss him very much. At the rehearsal for his 1980 performances of *Der Rosenkavalier*, which took place a few days after his fiftieth birthday, they presented him with his portrait, set against a background of the moon and lake of *Wozzeck* and painted by one of the first violinists, Erich Gargele. "We have missed him very much these last two seasons," says Friedrich Kleinknecht. "The orchestra was transformed when he conducted here regularly. We became much more sensitive to nuances of sound and other conductors noticed it too, and were always asking how Kleiber did this or that. I would say that it is worth while to meet *any* of his conditions if this means performances of such a standard as he manages to draw out of us. The orchestra as a whole loves him very much, and some of our members are almost in love with him." ("Please come *back*," I heard violinist Marilyn Knüppel beg him after the performance—the best and most relaxed *Rosenkavalier* I had heard even him do. "We had fun," he admitted.)

"I admire his refusing to be pushed around into doing things he doesn't want," says Erich Gargele. "The important thing for him is not making money, but fulfilling his vision of a work, and in technical terms what matters most to him is not just precision of rhythm or intonation, but the realization of the musical idea. His genius lies in the fact that he works to an extent that he can read even what is not written—because in music only very few things can be written, a note, a half note, and these can be interpreted in dozens, hundreds of ways. But he *knows*, he hears in his mind, what kind of sound the *composer* was hearing. And, unlike most other conductors, he is incapable of producing 'grey' sound. The music he makes is always 'blue', 'red', 'green', never 'grey', and when it *has* to be grey because the text says so, there is always a trace, a soupçon of 'blue', or 'pink', something that brings life and movement even to greyness. And I also think that, like Furtwängler, he has a knowledge of the intangibles—dreams, love, death—the mysteries. I don't really know why I painted him in this way, with his face, his whole identity merged into that of Wozzeck. I hadn't consciously intended to do it. Then I remembered that during one of the thirty-four rehearsals we had for *Wozzeck*—instead of the usual two-and-a-half hours with break, he went for short, hour-and-a-quarter, or hour-and-a-half tense, super-concentrated sessions without a break—in the *intermezzo* before the scene with the children he looked as if he was about to cry and asked us *please* to play it with *pain* [*mit Leid*] and that at that moment Kleiber, Alban Berg and Wozzeck became one in my mind."

In July 1974, Kleiber conducted *Tristan und Isolde* at Bayreuth, where he returned for three successive years. Although he had previously conducted the work in Stuttgart in 1967 and in Vienna in 1973, to showers of critical praise, this was one of the greatest triumphs of his career. "I do not think I am exaggerating when I say that Carlos Kleiber is one of the greatest conductors of the present day: his reading was one of the most passionate, fiery and exciting since de Sabata's," wrote Harold Rosenthal in *Opera* magazine. The German and the international press unanimously agreed, and Claudio Abbado invited him to conduct this opera, which he had planned to do himself, during La Scala's bicentennial season, 1977–78. The producer was August Everding who considers Kleiber one of the greatest conductors he knows and states that he would like nothing better than to have him back in Munich, if only he would agree. But his is a dynamic, powerful personality lacking, perhaps, some of the Olympian patience and persistence essential for dealing with Kleiber's chronic indecision:

Kleiber never actually signs a contract if he can possibly help it because then he feels he *has* to do whatever it is. He gives his word and he comes ... or he doesn't. It takes a lot of faith in him and very strong nerves but, as most managements everywhere are willing to acknowledge, the results make it all worthwhile.

But Everding admits that in his purely artistic capacity as a producer he found it difficult to work with Kleiber. "When we did *Tristan* in Bayreuth, Carlos was there from the very first rehearsal, unlike most conductors who only arrive for the last eight, which was wonderful except for the fact that he frustrated and dried me up completely! I sincerely hope that my saying this won't upset him because I greatly enjoy our long discussions together. But at the time, he came up to me looking worried in that special way of his that disarms you before he even opens his mouth, and said: 'It's good, it's good, but Wagner writes that there should be a wall here, why can't we have a wall?' I replied that we didn't really *need* a wall. 'But look, read here, it says in the score that Brangäne is watching over a wall,' he insisted, so I explained that it was not necessary to have an *actual* wall, that we could convey its presence in other ways. He sighed, and looked so unhappy that it made *me* unhappy and, in exasperation, I asked him please to go away! Whenever he is around, I am always bad as a producer, I just can't think any more. He interferes with my instructions to the singers and I get the impression that he would like to be his own producer and just get someone to design the sets and costumes for him."

There may be some truth in this, but usually Kleiber interferes with a producer's instructions only when these interfere with the music! For example, in John Copley's Covent Garden production of *La Bohème*, Musetta sometimes sobs at Mimi's death. But no sob is written in Puccini's score and Kleiber would have none of it. "Must she really do that? It sounds as if she's blowing her nose!" he snapped. He also objected to, and got rid of, Musetta's game of billiards in Act II, because she was taken too far back on the stage for her aria and Kleiber wanted her downstage for musical reasons, which upset Copley a bit, "but one's brief is to keep him happy and to keep him here at all costs, and even though he drives us all nuts for a while, his magical performances make you forget everything!" It is, perhaps, also interesting to mention that in this same production, Kleiber was, and still is, extremely unhappy about another scene in Act IV, in which the Bohemians were playing cricket with a loaf of bread and a herring, because he felt that it was "desecrating the bread and salt of life".

"Bread is holy and the Bohemians are hungry," he explains. But Copley thought that in England nobody would look at it this way.

Three of the most successful productions that Kleiber conducted in Munich were directed by Otto Schenk: *Der Rosenkavalier*, *La traviata* and *Die Fledermaus*, and in all three the unity between the musical and the dramatic elements was so complete, that it seemed as though all the action and the staging was emerging from the score which, according to Schenk, is exactly the result that Kleiber is after:

"He was there from the very first rehearsal and stressed that he wanted me to be a translator of the music in terms of staging and acting. He explained the music to me in great detail, why it was so, what it related to in a previous act and so on and then said, 'Stage it for me, tell them what to do in this pause,' for example. Our collaboration was one of the most fulfilling experiences in my career. I like working with a good conductor, I need a good conductor, when he is not overdoing his job and trying to stop the action in order to get a better musical result. Carlos is one of the greatest talents in the world and it is a pity that he doesn't do more because he could do everything, he could do Mozart like nobody else, he could do more Wagner, everything!"

Lucia Popp, who sang Adele in *Die Fledermaus* and Sophie in *Der Rosenkavalier*, hates singing the latter part with other conductors and always sings it Kleiber's way, which doesn't exactly please them! "He really created this part in me. With Carlos you never feel that he is actually *making* you do something. His personality is so strong that he makes you believe that his way is your way. Musically, rhythm is the thing that he cares most about. But he is also very sensitive about intonation. I think that this *Rosenkavalier* production really works. Otto is a realist but Carlos is more sophisticated and aware of the decadent side of Strauss, so the combination worked well."

Brigitte Fassbänder, who sang Octavian, was as surprised as Otto Schenk was to find that Kleiber follows a production from its first inception to its last breath. "From the very first rehearsal he was there. And had a great deal to say. Sometimes he stopped us after the third word or note and made us repeat, repeat, repeat the same words and phrases for maybe an hour, and always with some new idea about each word! He knew not only Strauss's score and Hofmannsthal's text backwards, but their mentality as well, and as he is a wonderful actor, he sang our parts and showed us exactly how to do everything. He was almost like a producer, except that all his ideas and insights always came out of the unity of words and music. Which is as it should be.

And as you probably know, he is a fanatic! But he never aims solely at the aesthetic perfection of sound; he allows a work to breathe and unfold in its dramatic essence."

An orchestra player, Harold Nash, had also noticed this fundamental feature in Kleiber's approach. "Some conductors always go for beautiful sound. But not Kleiber. Sometimes he demands quite ugly sounds, sometimes exaggerated sounds and effects. His is a much more dramatic approach than most conductors'. When we were rehearsing *Otello*, he stopped in the middle of one of those marvellous rubato bars and said he wanted 'a crazy bar'—very fast, much faster than the tempo, very loud, almost coarse. We tried it a few times, but he said that we were still playing it too nicely, in a sense. Then he added, 'To play this opera properly, you *must* be a little mad. Don't you hate me? Why don't you hate me? Hate, me, hate *me*, take it out on *me*!' And the interesting thing about *that* is that we achieved the result he wanted by thinking of some lesser conductors whom we really do hate!"

Kleiber re-thinks and re-examines works constantly; one of the topics of his marathon discussions with Leonard Bernstein, when the two were fellow guests at Franco Zeffirelli's house in Positano, was Richard Strauss. "I never know where the real climax is in Strauss operas," said Carlos, "because there are so many new climaxes, one after the other, but where is *the* climax?"

Zeffirelli is a producer with whom Kleiber seems to have struck an almost ideal relationship at the moment. They first worked together on a new production of *Otello* at La Scala, with Placido Domingo in the title role. The première, on December 7, 1976, was a dramatic occasion: not only did it make operatic history by being the first performance ever to be televised 'live' from La Scala, but also by having to take place almost under a state of siege! The Theatre was ringed by left-wing demonstrators protesting against its 'anti-proletarian' policies, there were bomb threats, Molotov cocktails, police cordons inside and out, security checks on the audience, in short, pandemonium!

But musically, the evening was an even greater triumph than Kleiber's Scala début with *Der Rosenkavalier* the previous season. "Carlos Kleiber is the most sensational interpreter who has found his way to La Scala in recent years," wrote the *Corriere della Sera*, and all the Italian media were unanimous in their praise. Needless to say, nobody was more surprised than Carlos himself! The television microphones picked up Zeffirelli's congratulations to him during their curtain call: "Well, Maestro, it took a German to show us, Italians, how Verdi should be done." "Franco, please, you shouldn't say things like that," was his embarrassed reply.

Placido Domingo found that working with Kleiber was "an indescribably marvellous experience. The highest compliment I can pay to his inspiring and inspired conducting is to say that he did nothing special! He did exactly what Verdi wrote and followed the score in such a meticulous and penetrating way that I was able to understand exactly how the role should be sung." (*Il Giornale* commented on this very point when *Otello* was revived, in April, 1980: "Kleiber's answer to 'Furtwängler's *Otello*' or 'Toscanini's *Otello*' is not 'Carlos Kleiber's *Otello*', but 'Maestro Giuseppe Verdi's *Otello*'!")

The empathy between Domingo and Kleiber is such that, during performances, they respond to each other's moods and gestures instantaneously and toss spontaneous ideas from pit to stage in a way "that makes it possible for me to fly, to reach the zenith of music!" says Domingo. "Because Carlos is not just making the musicians play the notes. He plays with feelings, and feelings can vary from day to day. I'm sure you noticed that the timings have been different in every performance."

This Scala *Otello* marked the beginning of a close artistic and personal friendship between Zeffirelli, Kleiber and Domingo, and the three came together again for a new production of *Carmen* at the Vienna State Opera in December 1978, which was also televised 'live', this time throughout Europe. Yet he had been nervous for months before first meeting them—"afraid of those big stars", as he put it to friends. When they finally met, he was surprised by their friendliness.

"Carlos is a charming person, and a wonderful, extraordinary talent, a simple talent if you like, in the sense that he is totally unpretentious," says Zeffirelli. "But he is self-destructive most of the time and needs encouragement because he gets so very depressed at times, desperate like a child, while at other times he is all 'up' and excited, again like a child. This is one of his most endearing characteristics. At rehearsals, whenever he gets upset, he throws down his baton and says: 'Oh, I'm going away, I'm tired, I'm a bad conductor.' He does believe it, up to a point, but a lot of it is play-acting!"

On an artistic level, he is ready to believe that every mistake is a personal insult, aimed directly at hurting him, according to Brigitte Fassbänder. "But *why*, what's the *matter*, I don't believe what's happening," he cries, looking mortally wounded, when a singer—and it can happen to the best of them—falls out of time and loses him for a split second. My own feeling is that as he experiences the work in its full perfection so intensely in his mind, that when something goes wrong and disturbs or shatters this image, he feels a deep, sharp, almost physical pain—as Otto Schenk also pointed out—and acute misery and anguish afterwards. Sometimes, he can even stay looking forlorn and dejected for days.

Orchestral players are also aware of this and "we are on a knife edge all the time, trying to sense and anticipate what he is thinking," says Harold Nash. "We, too, have to be extra sensitive in order to please him, because he *needs* to be pleased and we *want* to please him. Also because you find yourself thinking that this is the best performance you have ever been in or are ever likely to be in and it would be dreadful if *you* were the one to spoil it!"

This tendency to get visibly upset and angry during a performance is the only characteristic of Kleiber's that I have heard orchestral players be critical about. "It's always a pity when a conductor gets upset and angry in the pit, because this sets off a chain reaction of nervousness and timidity," says Friedrich Kleinknecht of the Bavarian State Opera. "But Kleiber is sometimes very funny when he gets angry in the pit," says Walter Probst.

"I know I get angry very easily," admitted Kleiber to the orchestra of La Scala with that "mixture of resignation and vulnerability" which according to Carlo Capriata so endears him to the musicians. "I try to fight it by doing mental gymnastics." For a while it works, until something *really* upsets him and he is off again!

Kleiber seldom agrees to conduct without first specifying the number of rehearsals he will require. On very rare occasions—*Der Rosen-kavalier* at the Vienna State Opera in 1974 and *La Bohème* in Munich in January, 1978—he may agree to step in at the last minute and conduct with no rehearsal at all, because the challenge excites him.

But when his demands are not met, when any rehearsals have to be cancelled or when conditions make it completely impossible for him to realize his conception of a work, he simply downs his baton and goes home. (His suitcase is always at hand!) Cancellations have been a characteristic feature of his career. Combined with the unpredictability of his moods and the initial difficulty of getting hold of him and persuading him to agree to conduct in the first place—as he seldom answers letters or returns telephone calls—it makes managements throughout the world acutely nervous.

He claims that his problem is that he doesn't like to work, that he would be quite happy doing nothing and will therefore seize on any excuse to postpone the first rehearsal. (In fact, he is an incorrigible postponer of just about everything!) "I want to be a vegetable," he told Leonard Bernstein. "I want to grow in a garden, I want to have the sun, I want to eat and drink and sleep and make love, and that's it!"

One of his most talked-about cancellations was when he fell ill and could not conduct the Stuttgart Opera's performance of *Wozzeck* at the Edinburgh Festival. Through no fault of his the performance was only cancelled at the last minute, with the audience actually in their seats. There was a great furore, and he later explained the whole story in a letter:

"I cancelled because I was ill.... Return to Stuttgart, followed by lengthy investigation of the 'affair'. The Theatre's solicitor was instructed by Schaefer and Co. to discredit me legally, so as to make my dismissal possible. But unexpectedly their lawyers' approximately hundred-page-long 'opinion' hit the Württemberg Theatre between the eyes: the man stated that an artist who, even subjectively, does not consider himself fit enough to appear, had a right not to do so without fearing reprisals. *When* he cancels is irrelevant. This, for me golden, pamphlet had been hidden by the Theatre Mafia. For what would it lead to? So, as they couldn't dismiss me on legal grounds, grinding their teeth, they paid me further monthly salaries without giving me any work to do. This was supposed to soften me up and provoke me into resigning. It was the most beautiful time of my life: paid for doing nothing and not giving a damn about the Theatre. This is the only truth of the matter. The behaviour of everybody, including Schäfer, Will-nauer, etc. was indescribably horrid. The only Christians were the orchestral players and the children in the *Wozzeck* production, who stood by me. Those in charge were monstrous, as in all eternity, Amen."

A happy result of one of Kleiber's cancellations was his Covent Garden début in June 1974. It happened because Kleiber had cancelled his appearance in a production of *Falstaff* in Hamburg and happened to be free when Covent Garden started looking for a replacement for a suddenly-indisposed James Levine. Not that he agreed straight away! "I have started to teach my son how to swim and wouldn't dream of allowing anything to interfere with this. I could only come if you found me a hotel with a swimming pool!" They did, but he didn't like it and

Seiji Ozawa and his mother, who accompanied the Boston Symphony Orchestra on their historic visit to China in 1978, standing in the courtyard of their old house in Peking, which they abandoned during the war.
BOSTON SYMPHONY ORCHESTRA

Seiji Ozawa at an overnight party he gave for his Boston Symphony Orchestra during their Japanese tour of 1978.
BOSTON SYMPHONY ORCHESTRA

Ozawa and his second wife, Vera, half-Russian, half-Japanese. He has now found a happy way to manage his family life and his career.
BOSTON SYMPHONY ORCHESTRA

"Conducting is very hard work. We use body so much to balance nerve. If you use only nerve, you go crazy." PETER SCHAAF

Sir Georg Solti: At work: intent on his scores, which he learns "step by step, tone by tone, from micro to macro" (*opposite page*). VIVIANNE PURDOM

Right: Solti's are "the wickedest eyes in the world" (Kiri te Kanawa). CLIVE BARDA

Below right: Sir Georg and Lady Solti (BBC TV presenter Valerie Pitts). SIR GEORG SOLTI

... and at play, on holiday at his home on the Italian Riviera (*below*). CHRISTINA BURTON

Klaus Tennstedt: "During the day I work very hard at rehearsals; in the evening, there is the concert—a normal life...." CLIVE BARDA

Carlos Kleiber thanking the orchestra during curtain calls after the triumphant performances of *Elektra* he conducted at Covent Garden in 1977. Next to him, Gwyneth Jones (Chrysothemis). CHRISTINA BURTON

Carlos Kleiber: however hard one might try to pinpoint some of the main characteristics of his conducting there is still something more, something extra, which eludes definition: a Dionysian element, a "divine madness" called a state of "enthusiasm" by the ancient Greeks, which in their language meant a human being not merely inspired, but temporarily taken over, possessed, by the Gods.

SIEGFRIED LAUTERWASSER/DEUTSCHE GRAMMOPHON

Above: Carlos with his sister Veronica in front of the Parthenon in 1937, during a cruise down the Dalmatian coast and Greece with their parents.

Left: Carlos with his father Erich in Berlin. The child's musical talent was apparent very early on....

COURTESY OF THE LATE K. H. RUPPEL

"Carlos Kleiber's personal magnetism is so immense that given three weeks' rehearsal or no rehearsal, he can still do it" (Bram Gay, Orchestra Director, Royal Opera House, Covent Garden).
SABINE TOEPFFER

Below: Vladimir Ashkenazy: "When playing an instrument, you have direct physical contact with sound. And when you play well, you feel a very deep *personal* satisfaction and fulfilment as a human being." CLIVE BARDA

Right: Ashkenazy: "If you are able to communicate, if you have something in your soul and mind, you can make music without a great technique." CLIVE BARDA

Mstislav Rostropovich:
"Slava doesn't interpret,
he *feels*. His music is
really his character. He
is conducting his life."
(Seiji Ozawa.)
CLIVE BARDA

Rostropovich with
Herbert von Karajan:
"My career as a cellist
was the best school for
conducting. I worked
with the best
conductors in the
world. And at every
rehearsal, I watched . . .
watched how they
obtained their results . . .
and I learnt."
SIEGFRIED
LAUTERWASSER/EMI

Above: Riccardo Chailly: "I am a very optimistic person who never wakes up angry, nervoso or hysterical." MIKE EVANS

Below: Simon Rattle: "I have a gift for getting things across which has allowed me to make a career very quickly, much more quickly than I dreamt or wanted." ALAN WOOD

had to be moved.

But his conducting took everybody by storm and the critics raved! Kleiber, incidentally, is very funny about critics. He tries to avoid reading the bad reviews and feels that, good or bad, they are like pornography in that they have as little relation to music as pornography to love!

Three years after this triumphant début, he returned to Covent Garden to conduct a revival of Strauss's *Elektra*. "At last," sighed Birgit Nilsson, who had sung the part umpteen times in her long career. "I could actually *sing* the part!" doubtless referring to the hushed, but nerve-rackingly tense playing that Kleiber drew out of the orchestra. "This was the first time I was working with him, and I was looking forward to it very much," continues Birgit Nilsson. "And I *must say*, I was not disappointed!" To begin with, Kleiber had been nervous about working with her, in case she had rigid ideas about the part. But their great sense of humour came to the rescue and they got on famously.

On the orchestral side, Kleiber achieved his ambition of staying within Strauss's metronome marks, after some initial trouble at rehearsals, during which he felt frustrated because the orchestra couldn't assimilate his tempi, which were very, very fast, straight away. "And Kleiber thinks fast, conducts fast, and wants everything at once," says Marta Szirmay, who sang Klytemnestra. The performances were unforgettable.

So far, Kleiber has not devoted very much time to concert work. There was one concert in Munich back in 1967. The programme included Beethoven's G major Piano Concerto with Alfred Brendel as soloist. "I had known Carlos for years, he is an old friend, and a conductor of extraordinary character. But it was very difficult to arrive at our result, because he has very rigid views, very precise views about every semiquaver of the piece, and one has to struggle and reach some kind of compromise. But I think that the performance was very good!" There was another concert in Prague, which Kleiber considers a failure and kept referring to for years whenever anyone tried to congratulate him for a superb performance in Stuttgart! "Yes," he replied, "but years ago in Prague it went very badly!" According to Dr Schäfer, he clung to this unique failure in his career almost with affection.

In 1972, he conducted a concert with the orchestra of West German Radio in Cologne (Haydn's Symphony No. 94 in G major, Berg's

Three Pieces for Voice and Orchestra from *Wozzeck* with Wendy Fine as soloist, and the Beethoven Seventh) and the North German Radio Orchestra in Hamburg, with the same programme, with such success that he was invited back in 1973, when he conducted Beethoven's *Coriolan* Overture, Strauss's *Tod und Verklärung* and Beethoven's 'Emperor' Piano Concerto, with Arturo Benedetti Michelangeli as soloist. The two seemed ideal for each other, but when they came together again to record this Concerto, they fell out and the recording never materialized.

In October 1978, he made his American début in Chicago, to rave reviews: "Kleiber's recordings had certainly whetted the appetite for the live article. Yet one had to wonder: Is the man as good as everybody says he is? Thursday night provided the answer: No, he is even better!" wrote the *Chicago Tribune*. "Kleiber proved his repute. He will be welcome whenever he returns," said *The Christian Science Monitor*. But so far he hasn't, although he was immediately re-invited. Professor Alfred Altenburger points out that Kleiber is extremely sensitive to atmosphere and surroundings, and it may be that something was amiss in Chicago. In February 1979 he agreed to replace an indisposed Karl Böhm at a concert with the orchestra of the Accademia di Santa Cecilia in Rome.

I was lucky enough to be present at Kleiber's first subscription Concert with the Vienna Philharmonic in Vienna, in December, 1979, one of the most unforgettable concerts I have heard in my life—and both the audience and the critics were ecstatic: "Kleiber came, saw and conquered. If there were such a thing as the ideal conductor for this orchestra, it would be this outstanding, unusual musician," wrote *Die Presse*, and all the Austrian press concurred. Yet he had been painfully nervous before the concert and visibly apprehensive during the first few bars of the Brahms fourth. But the orchestra, who were aware of it, went out of themselves to reassure and please him.

"Kleiber is a unique artist and an exceptional, unusually sensitive and deep-feeling human being who lives in a state of constant tension, created inside him by the music on his mind," says Professor Altenburger. "Because of his extreme sensitivity, he is especially conscientious and does not approach music or arrive at his interpretations lightly. Although this concert took place in December, he came to Vienna for several weeks last July to study Brahms's original manuscript here at the Musikverein, in order to go even deeper into the composer's mind." In fact he had been studying this symphony for well over a year.

"Not for him the quick, pat solutions," continues Professor Altenburger. "He gets so extremely involved in the works he studies, that it becomes absolutely impossible for him to deal with the outside world and practical problems, meetings with managers, correspondence or mundane things. This enhances his reputation of being difficult and hard to get. But we musicians love him because he is totally sincere—true to himself and to the music he conducts—and desires nothing but to serve the music to the best of his and our abilities."

Before each performance he also prepares handwritten notes with comments about details that he would like done differently from the way they were played the last time, and leaves them on the musicians' desks. These, known as 'Kleibergrams', offer an interesting glimpse of his musical thinking. The Orchestra of La Scala presented him with a pack of their own notes, signed by each individual player, asking him to come back soon. They placed them on his desk at the last performance of *Der Rosenkavalier*. Characteristically, he thought they were answering notes telling him what they thought *he* had done wrong! But when he realized what they were, he was very touched.

In everyday life, Kleiber is as unpredictable as in his music-making. He can be shy, reserved and diffident, or elated and gregarious; a passionate romantic who needs outlets for his intense inner emotional life, but also a realist who doesn't suffer fools gladly; despite his moodiness and unpredictability, he possesses a strong sense of duty and adheres to his own strict code of behaviour; although he is quick-tempered, sharply sarcastic and blatantly inconsiderate on occasion, he is basically very kind and goes through patches of intense self-loathing whenever he feels he has hurt anyone. While he hardly ever answers business correspondence, he finds time to write long, funny, multilingual, beautifully written letters to friends; he is lost whenever he has to make travelling arrangements, or any arrangements at all, but is, and expects everyone to be, extremely punctual; in public, he shuns publicity and prefers to be, or to be thought, an enigma, but in private he is friendly and communicative.

Although he is over fifty, there is something very youthful and boyish about him; even childlike at times: he loves riding on the top of London's double-decker buses, packs like a schoolboy (scores, shoes and bottles of whisky find themselves thrown into his suitcase helter

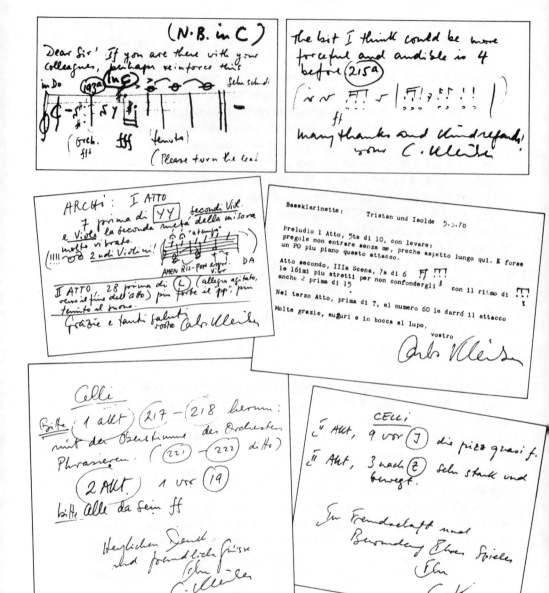

A selection of 'Kleibergrams' from Covent Garden, La Scala
and the Bavarian State Opera.

skelter) and enjoys gadgets of every description—pocket calculators and biorhythm calculators which he takes along to singers' dressing rooms to find out what shape they are in. "Oh, it went 'ping', you must be feeling rotten tonight!" he announced to Ileana Cotrubas.

He is a movie and television addict, which may explain his up-to-date expressions in English, which surprised some of the orchestral musicians at first. He lives in a leafy suburb near Munich—he seems to dislike big cities—with his wife and two children (a teenage son Marko, and a younger daughter Lillian), on whom he dotes and lavishes all the attention that he, himself, had to do without so much of the time. Nothing is too good for them and nothing is ever allowed to interfere with their lives: he may be discussing future plans with La Scala on the telephone, but if it's time for the children's hour on television, he will cut the discussion short. His son, who learnt to read at three and has a flair for mathematics, sometimes accompanies him on short trips, when his schooling permits it. But even when he is away conducting, he rings them every day, spends hours on the telephone helping with their homework, and browses around toy-shops armed with detailed shopping lists from them. On weekends during term time, the children are flown to see a performance of his wherever he happens to be conducting, and he explains each operatic plot to them in detail during the intervals. Obviously they reciprocate his great love, as I observed when I sat in the box opposite theirs at La Scala: when the crowds kept on yelling "Ma-e-stro, Ma-e-stro" for over twenty minutes after a première, his son was jumping up and down excitedly.

Having now said almost everything I could observe or find out about Carlos Kleiber—and here I must make it clear that this chapter was put together without an interview—it seems more appropriate to end with some observations from his fellow artists who know him better than I do:

"With Kleiber, and you have to keep coming back to him as a standard these days, you get the feeling that he cares more for the music than for himself, or for doing the job," says Harold Nash. "You sense that his one desire is to make a great performance. That's all. That he doesn't care about advancing his career or about practical considerations of 'the-show-must-go-on' variety, or even about getting paid. Along with Giulini, he is totally sincere, totally dedicated, and outside, or beyond, himself."

Placido Domingo, who is now slowly embarking on a conducting career himself, says that if he had a fairy godmother, capable of bestowing on him the best quality of each living conductor, he would ask for "the cheering of Jimmy Levine, Claudio Abbado's special way of indicating a legato to the orchestra, Zubin Mehta's incredible facility, but from Carlos Kleiber I would want ... *everything!*"

SOLOIST—
CONDUCTORS

VLADIMIR ASHKENAZY
A Musical Thinker

"I have always found the orchestra mysterious.... As a boy, I spent most of my free time going to orchestral concerts, and loved the sound of orchestral playing. And when I was taken to an opera or a ballet, I hardly ever looked at the stage. I just watched the pit and spent the intervals peering over it at the instruments. But I never thought of conducting at the time. It was never a childhood dream or anything like that. Just being present, listening and enjoying the music was enough.

"Then with the passage of time, as I matured as an artist and as a person, I developed certain discriminating attitudes towards performing. At some point, I started enjoying some of the things I heard less and less, and thinking that I would rather hear them interpreted differently. Yet the idea of actually conducting them myself still never entered my head. But when I saw some people conduct who were not conductors I thought that, perhaps, I should try it, too. Not because of any suppressed desire to stand on a podium in front of an orchestra, but because I felt that, maybe, I could make them play certain music the way I hear it."

Right from the beginning, right from his London début as a conductor—an all-Tchaikovsky concert with the Philharmonia in February 1977—Vladimir ('Vova') Ashkenazy succeeded in obtaining the sound he wanted. Despite inexperience, despite occasional technical clumsiness, it was instantly obvious not only that he could communicate with and inspire his players, but that he also had a great deal *to* communicate. "In short, the celebrated pianist is a real conductor," concluded *The Financial Times*.

And it's true. He feels "totally at home on the podium". Since then, he has been establishing himself as an increasingly respected conductor, conducting approximately thirty-five (out of a total of one hundred and fifteen) concerts a year—mostly in London, Amsterdam, on television and on tour at home and abroad. "Vova is such a good conductor that the fact that I don't resent it is a genuine triumph of close friendship," says André Previn.

Yet the satisfaction he feels after conducting an orchestral concert is totally different from that experienced after a good performance at the piano. "Playing a piano concerto well or giving a good recital produces *for me* a far greater sense of achievement. Because as a conductor you are not actually producing sound. You're hoping that you're communicating, transmitting your ideas and *helping* produce the sound. But when playing an instrument you have direct physical contact with sound. And when you play well, you feel a very deep *personal* satisfaction and fulfilment as a human being. In a good orchestral performance I have a sense of *communal* achievement: I feel part of the group, with all the consequences and achievement this implies."

When Ashkenazy started conducting, he knew almost nothing about technique and the mechanics of beating properly but managed to produce results in spite of it. "I didn't even know where the downbeat was. Having watched conductors all my life, I erroneously thought that the sound should come not *on* but *after* the beat. So I aimed for that, always gave a terribly quick downbeat and jumped up immediately, which was very disconcerting for the players, who need a firm downbeat. Of course there are different kinds of music and some do require very rapid beats. But generally speaking, players do want to be able to *see* a downbeat. And they never could!"

He still knew nothing about proper downbeats when he conducted that much acclaimed all-Tchaikovsky concert. Eventually, he confessed this to some full-time, professional conductors. Their reply was: "If you managed to get through something like *this* not knowing something like *that*, then you really must be a very talented conductor!" The Philharmonia musicians confirm this verdict: "Ashkenazy has got what it takes, he has everything that X [a conductor famous for his technique] has not got, and audiences recognize it no matter *where* you go," says the Assistant Leader, Martin Jones. "And if he has got there with no formal training and only five years' experience, think what he will be like in another five years time." "One of the greatest," adds the Leader, Christopher Warren-Green.

Ashkenazy remembers his first rehearsal with horror: "Terrible. How we managed to play together, I don't know. But I suppose one of the answers must be that if you are able to communicate, if you have something in your soul and mind, you can make music without a great technique. You will probably have horribly bad ensemble, you might have bad balance and so on, which I agree is not good. But the basic message might still be able to get through."

He is a warm, shy, profound man with a sharp, analytical mind on top of his innate ability to move audiences and inspire musicians. He thinks a great deal about music, life and its meaning, society, but most about music: its origins, the people who wrote it and those who presume to interpret it. In fact, an eminent British critic labelled him a "musical thinker"—a particularly apt description not only of the man but also of a quality characteristic of his music-making which, whether emanating from the keyboard or the baton, is always fresh, rousing and deeply felt, yet miraculously free of emotional excesses. "He is a passionate musician, but there is that intelligence behind it which never fails," says André Previn.

Prior to our first meeting, he had been thinking a great deal about the complexities and the mysterious elements involved in producing a good conductor. "I am sure that it is a fallacy to think that someone who is very warm, very friendly and a very good musician to boot, will also necessarily be a good conductor. Because conducting has little to do with all that. It is true that a good rapport with the orchestra sometimes helps. But I've seen some wonderful people, wonderful musicians, who could not conduct very well. And I've seen mean people, nasty people—men whom orchestras hate but cannot resist because of this mesmerizing ability to compel them through their gesture to play almost despite themselves—conduct wonderfully.

"So one cannot generalize about the necessary human qualities required for conducting. But in simple terms, a conductor's perform-ance boils down to two basic ingredients: his understanding of the composer and the work in hand, i.e. his musical qualities, and his ability to communicate. And this is where the mystery begins. He has to communicate with the audience through a hundred people, and it is very difficult to pinpoint why some can and some cannot. Perhaps it has something to do with their temperament, or their complexes, or the ability to free themselves of them. There are thousands of reasons and one could make a real psychological study of the subject.

"But whatever the reasons, this fundamental ability is innate, and however improbable this may seem, applies just as much to something like show business—say the Palladium style—as to conducting. Of course show business does not require a tremendously *profound* knowledge or talent, but it certainly does require an ability to attract, project and communicate, even if in most cases you are communicating little more than mere energy, electricity and are aiming at pure entertainment: it's very simple, it's right on the surface, but the fact that you are able to *project* is what makes you a show-business star.

"Of course, a great deal more than that goes into music-making, especially on a high level—projection is only part of the process, whereas in show-business it is practically everything. But it is dangerous to plunge into generalizations, for the very good reason that conducting is such an intangible and mysterious art. In fact, the only clear thing about it is that it is a mystery!"

Ashkenazy, born in Gorki not far from Moscow, on July 6, 1937, spent most of his early childhood singing. All day long he sang the tunes that his father, a variety-type pianist, practised on his piano, and he sang them "very well, very clean". He sang *so* much that his mother, an ambitious woman who later projected all her ambition through him, suspected that he might be a born musician and took him to a piano teacher when he was only four.

He learnt the piano very, very fast, "so fast that it seemed as though it was something I already knew how to do". (At the age of seven, he was ready to play a Haydn piano concerto with a professional orchestra.) "And the same thing happened later, when I studied the theory of music, harmony and *solfège*. I only had to be given a hint and seemed to know the rest. It all came naturally to me, like remembering something I already knew. People who believe in reincarnation would say that obviously I had done it all before. Maybe."

But in those days, he was always being thrown out of class because the teacher said that there was nothing for him to learn. He would appear only for the examination which he finished in five minutes, and disappear again. This was at the special music school where all exceptionally gifted Russian children are sent between the ages of eight and eighteen and where they are provided with a general education but concentrate chiefly on music. The atmosphere is very serious and disciplined and the youngsters are made to concentrate and work really hard.

In the circumstances, he had "quite a happy childhood", with lots of friends and time for the occasional football game. The family were never in need of money: his education cost nothing, of course, and his father's good connections through the variety circles ensured that they didn't lack many commodities, either. "We could usually get what we needed, but, as always in Russia, after great difficulties.

"But at the time, I didn't even think that there were places where you could live more easily, and if you don't know what your life *could* be compared to somewhere else, you tend to think that it is all right. So I was not discontented from the material point of view. But from the spiritual point of view, as soon as I started to use my brain, so to speak, some time in my teens, I began to feel the constrictions of the System acutely. Although Russia is still an isolated country today, this is nothing compared to what it was then: a completely closed country, closed in principle, because they didn't *want* to absorb anything that might prove detrimental to the Party and the Government's policies. And this also applied to the Arts, which were tightly controlled by the Ministry of Culture.

"For example, I remember the first Russian post-war performance of Debussy's *Nocturnes*, which took place either just before or just after Stalin's death. Nobody ever discovered quite how this came about, but someone must have found a hole in the System. In any case, the excitement and anticipation were such that all of musical Moscow turned up at the performance, to hear the *Nocturnes* performed reasonably, but not particularly, well. But I enjoyed it so enormously that I remember the experience as a cornerstone in my education."

Two or three years later, the Ministry gave permission for *Petrushka* to be performed for the first time since heaven knows when—but only once, during Stravinsky's official visit of 1962, because he had not yet been rehabilitated. Yet growing up as a musician without contact with some of this century's most important works was acutely frustrating.

"The System," explains Ashkenazy, "worked in an all-pervasive but nebulous way. If, for instance, a well-known artist wanted to perform works by composers requiring special clearance, the question would first be taken up by the Director of the Philharmonia, a huge organization responsible for all concerts in Moscow. Nothing would be documented, because nobody wanted to take responsibility for documentation. The Director of the Philharmonia would then telephone or go and see an important man in the Central Committee or maybe in a sub-department in between. But this functionary would also prefer not to be responsible for such a decision and refer the matter up to the Central Committee itself, which has someone special in charge of such cultural matters. But he, too, often did not wish potentially to expose himself. Nor would he like to have it known that he said 'No'. So the answer usually was 'It's up to you. I leave it all to you.' This message would then be relayed down to the Director of the Philharmonia who then told the artist, 'Look, why don't we change the programme? Next time, maybe. But right now, it's a bit difficult.' It was never that the party would not allow it. That's how the System works. And it's impossible. It's Kafka. In the end, you quit trying, because there is nothing you can do against it.

"Of course, if the artist in question were young and unknown, the Director of the Philharmonia would not even bother to ask anyone. He would just say no. I believe that things have changed since then, and that you can now play almost anything, but this does not mean that the intellectual and artistic climate as a whole has improved. It remains stagnant and the official ideology omnipresent and all-pervasive."

After graduating from the special school, Ashkenazy studied at the Moscow Conservatoire and at the age of eighteen won Second Prize at the 1955 Chopin Competition in Warsaw. This was followed by the First Prize at the 1956 Queen Elisabeth International Competition for Piano in Brussels, after which he was allowed to tour in Europe and the United States, accompanied by a "bodyguard" to watch his sayings and movements. As he did not indulge in daily eulogies of the Soviet System and also dared express admiration for contemporary painting and music, he was reported to be "unreliable". Back in Moscow, he was summoned to the Ministry and faced an interrogation which resulted in a three-year ban on foreign travel. As the ban was nearing its end he married a foreigner: an Icelander from England called Thorunn (Dody) Johannsdottir, a former child prodigy who had been so impressed by Russian piano teaching when she participated in the 1958 Tchaikovsky Competition (held every four years) that she returned to Moscow for further study.

The authorities could do nothing to prevent the marriage. But they were not pleased and intimated that it would be "good for his career" if she were to adopt Soviet nationality. They used the potential disfavour with which the marriage could be viewed as a lever to force Ashkenazy to participate in the 1962 Tchaikovsky Competition, against his will. He felt that he was now past this stage, having won two major international competitions in his youth. But Russia badly wanted a win for prestige reasons, as in 1958 the first prize had gone to Van Cliburn from the United States. Reluctantly Ashkenazy agreed—and shared the first prize with John Ogdon from Britain.

As the authorities were now eager to publicize their win, he was allowed to travel abroad again, and gave much-acclaimed and enthusiastically received performances in London. With great difficulty, his wife—who on assumption of Soviet nationality had been congratulated on joining "the freest country in the world"—and baby son Vladimir (Vovka, now in his twenties) were allowed to accompany him a few days later. (The Ashkenazys have since had four more children, now aged nineteen, thirteen, seven and three.)

While staying with his parents-in-law who had lived in London since 1946, he made the crucial decision to stay in the West, "for family reasons", officially because his wife did not want to live in Russia after her recent experiences there. He did not officially "defect" and judiciously avoided any criticism of the country or the System. Amazingly enough, a few weeks later, the Ashkenazys were granted a visa valid for multiple entrances and exits to and from the Soviet Union. They tried it out by paying a short visit to honour some musical commitments, but underwent such traumatic experiences before being allowed out, a month later, that they decided never to return. This was in 1963. For emotional reasons, Ashkenazy did not adopt another nationality and travelled on temporary documents ("halfway to being a stateless person") until 1972 when he became an Icelandic citizen.

Although he was delighted to be back in Britain, it was very hard to adjust to the reality of freedom, the right to make his own decisions and to shed the certainties that come with having limited choices. "It was like a cold shower at first. But I was lucky in my wife, for whom such a life was natural and who helped me a great deal, not by protecting me, but by guiding me along. She knew that the only way to adjustment was being allowed to make my own mistakes—and learning from them."

Whatever his personal problems might have been at the time, they were certainly not reflected in his musical career, which soared. Everywhere he went he was hailed as one of the great pianists of our time. Yet his career as a pianist is only relevant to this book in so far as it affects his life and insights as a conductor. The most obvious influence is on his attitudes to the accompaniment of soloists: "The basis for a good conductor-soloist collaboration is a good understanding of each other's intentions, an in-depth communication between two artists. Ideally, interpreting a concerto should be a two-way affair, because the orchestra has an important part to play between the purely solistic parts, and in some works, like the Brahms concertos, is an almost equal partner. Yet in most cases, conductors tend to accept the soloist's conception as the determining factor in the performance, sometimes at the expense of the music.

"This does happen, from time to time. You are confronted with a situation where you have to go against your own musical insights. But your job as a conductor is to be together with the soloist. You must therefore forget what you hear in your own mind, listen to what *he* is doing, and make sure that you are with him. Many conductors are unwilling to do this. But I find this attitude mean and wrong. You can basically do what you like with your tutti. But in the accompaniments, you should never upset the soloist who is so exposed." This remarkable flexibility of his also applies to his own appearances as a soloist. Normally, he plays his own conception of the work, of course. But should a great conductor say, "Look, why don't we also try it this way?", if the suggestion sounds convincing, he will go home and try it out. "And if, I like it, I may do it. Why not?"

André Previn, with whom he has enjoyed a long and prolifically fruitful collaboration both in the concert hall and the recording studios, remembers the following incident: "We were rehearsing the Brahms second concerto and at the end I went up to the piano and asked if we could take a certain passage more slowly. He said, 'Just a minute, let me see.' And he went backwards and forwards and all that, and finally said, 'Yes, if you tell me why, because I don't actually see the necessity for it because ...' and then went into the reasons why it shouldn't be taken more slowly, with perfect structural reasoning. I then started to laugh and said, 'Vova, I only want it more slowly because it is *so* beautiful that I just wanted a moment longer to enjoy it.' '*That* I can understand,' he said. And on the night we got it a tiny bit slower and I turned around to look at him and he grinned from ear to ear."

Ashkenazy's first-ever appearance as a conductor, in Iceland, where he has made his home since 1970, involved accompanying a pianist: Daniel Barenboim, a close friend, in the first and third Beethoven Piano Concertos. He remembers with a shudder his realization, at the first rehearsal, that he had to control the orchestra and cannot understand how he got through the concert "without ruining everything".

"Then, I started learning. And I'm still learning all the time. Sometimes, I ask friends like Lorin Maazel, André Previn, Colin Davis, Zubin Mehta or Daniel Barenboim for advice about what to do with this or that bar, and I might follow their advice, or I might not. Earlier on, I *always* did because I had no other solutions of my own. Now, I do have different solutions—not an arsenal like Karajan's or Maazel's, needless to say—but various options to choose from, which is great.

"But basically, the only way to learn is by conducting—not by listening to anyone or even by studying scores at home. Because you may think that you have penetrated into the composer's world and solved all the technical conductorial problems in your mind. But the first rehearsal always holds some surprises; how great these may be depends on your experience, or inexperience, as a conductor. But even veteran conductors always find something they had not thought of and which needs working on: some adjustment in the orchestral balance, or some rhythmic point, or a passage that requires new and different gestures."

Ashkenazy learns scores very, very fast. "He can memorize a score in a couple of days," says the Leader of the Philharmonia, Christopher Warren-Green, "which explains why in five years he has managed to conduct a wider repertoire than some of his famous colleagues have in a lifetime." Of course, the familiarity with most composers' styles that comes from his long experience of their music as a pianist means that, in his case, speed does not imply a superficial knowledge.

It is very difficult for him to describe his experiences while studying scores and acquiring his mental image of the sound. "I can only say that I get a feeling, which can be translated into musical images when I need them, but also into other things, which are difficult to express in words. This is why I always refer to a book by the British critic J. W. N. Sullivan called *Beethoven: His Spiritual Development*,* which is not only about Beethoven, but really an introduction to music and what music is about—a crucial question which, I am sure, you will have asked yourself many times. And, for me, this book is the most successful attempt ever to answer that question.

"His basic answer is that as we experience an infinite variety of physical, spiritual and physical-spiritual states, music, although abstract on the surface, in fact describes these innumerable states of mind and body, in its own way. And those composers gifted in a special, transcendental way are able to communicate our most elevated states because, having experienced them, they are in a position to communicate their essence. Perhaps we interpreters have not all experienced the same states of being as these great people and are therefore often inadequate, unable, to reproduce the essence of the composition and communicate the experience of those spiritually advanced states.

* Jonathan Cape, 1927, and Unwin Books, 1964.

Which is why there are so few good performers of the greatest music who are able to proceed, through the music, to the reality, the feeling that inspired it.

"And of course, the greater the music, the more mysteries it contains. Take Mozart and Beethoven, for instance. I have always been puzzled by the fact that Beethoven composed with great difficulty while Mozart did so effortlessly and very, very fast. And most of his music is so incredible, so transcendental, that there are no words to describe it. Beethoven's case seems more understandable because the greatness of the music was the result of so much effort. He certainly had the feeling, the musical idea and the image corresponding to his feeling. But it took a lot of time, anguish and torment before his ideas crystallized into something that could be written on paper, in notes. He did hundreds of sketches. But we know what finally came out. And when it is imperfect or clumsy from the formal point of view, as it very occasionally is, it is still perfect from the point of view of communicating ultimate reality— or in other words, true to life.

"When I say that I can understand Beethoven's case more easily, I am not saying that he is closer to me, but merely that he reflects life in all its states. Mozart, on the other hand, is so elevated, so perfect, that he almost seems removed from life. Because life is not perfect. But Mozart is. Maybe he represents some essence of life, a transcendental essence, the ultimate meaning of life. But I can't explain it. I don't know and can't reconcile the apparently easy process of composition with the unfathomable depth and complete, integral, organic vision contained in his music. Some critics and musical people say that the music was already made up, stamped in his mind all the time. I don't believe this, but cannot provide any answers of my own, either." (Perhaps the only conductor who came close to explaining this mystery was the late Josef Krips who stopped an orchestra during a rehearsal of a Mozart symphony, tapped his baton and said, "Gentlemen, please! Remember: Beethoven *goes* to heaven: Mozart *comes* from heaven!")

Ashkenazy occasionally conducts Mozart concertos from the keyboard, and does not find this particularly difficult from the technical point of view. He makes a circle of four or five principal players who sit around him, can see his hands on the keyboard and who lead their respective sections. The only problem can be that in the effort to be together the sound comes just a little bit too late, which makes everything a little bit slower and heavier, because the cues are given by four or five different people, and nobody wants to risk jumping in too soon. But with time this is easily overcome.

Orchestral players are divided in their opinion on whether it is easier or harder to play under a conductor/pianist, depending on where they sit. The further from the conductor they are, the harder they find it. "Sound doesn't travel as fast as sight, and if you are sitting at the back and relying entirely on your ear, some of your entries are bound to be infinitesimally late, because there is no way of knowing how much you should compensate for this lateness," explains the principal oboe of the Philharmonia, Gordon Hunt.

John Wallace, the principal trumpet, adds that the only problem that can arise when a conductor is playing an instrument at the same time, is the lack of someone detached enough to know when the momentum has gone out of the *tutti* and to get it right again. "It is much easier to do this if one is removed from the simultaneous task of producing sound."

The Leader, Christopher Warren-Green, who sits next to the conductor-pianist, disagrees and finds it easier to play in those circumstances: "If you have two people, the conductor has to wait for his cue from the soloist and then transmit it to us—which means that the preparatory beat is bound to be a trifle late. It's therefore easier to play with someone conducting from the keyboard because the ear reacts faster than the eye, and if you are listening all the time and concentrating really hard, there should be no problems."

As far as Mozart symphonies are concerned, Ashkenazy prefers to perform them with ten first violins and two or three double basses— "that's the right proportion; four basses sound too heavy, even in the 'Jupiter'—although for a big symphony and for concertos like the C minor and D minor he would add an extra two violins.

He has a wide repertoire and can identify with most composers both as a pianist and as a conductor. "I have a very strong love for music and a rather wide basis for identification with various angles of expression. I realize that I can be a medium for many different composers and styles. But a certain kind of second-rate music—a lot of Liszt and Saint-Saëns, for instance—I would never be able to identify with, whereas the greatest composers like Mozart, Beethoven and Brahms, present me with no problems of identification. I have a feeling for them and can play and conduct a lot of their music. I'm not claiming that I can do everything equally well, but that I have the feeling I have something to say, which is important to me. I feel that the area is wide open for exploration, whereas with second-rate music I don't. Yet there is some second-rate *Russian* music—a lot of Rimsky and Balakirev and some Rachmaninov—which I do conduct and play, knowing it to be second-rate, because I know that this music is very much in my blood and I can often find something in it which may lift it from the second-rate to somewhere slightly higher."

A composer whose music Ashkenazy has championed throughout his career is Scriabin. He discovered him in his teens, when he loved his every note, and considers him particularly attractive for young people looking for new dimensions. "They're better off listening to Scriabin than taking a trip on drugs. He is so passionate and exotic, and initiates you into, I don't know, another world.... Take his First Symphony, which I used to love very much in my teens—very beautiful and naïve and romantic and just a bit pompous, too. But he creates an entirely different world and elevates you to new horizons. His idea of ecstasy was to reach spiritual fulfilment through sensual fulfilment."

But although he has few problems of identification with the musical content of most composers' work, from the technical point of view he found everything difficult to conduct at the beginning. "But as you get the hang of it, some of it becomes a bit easier. Now I'm at the stage where it happens naturally, without thinking, except for very few spots where I have to concentrate really hard and consciously think about how I'm going to beat this or that."

He points out that there are certain works in the repertoire which are difficult for everybody, "even for supreme conductors like Karajan and Maazel, I dare say." One of them is Debussy's *Ibéria*, which is always between one and three. The rhythms should always be absolutely clear for the orchestra, otherwise the whole thing would fall to pieces, but at the same time it should sound elegant and totally effortless. Most of Schönberg and Berg, especially *Wozzeck*, is also very hard from the technical point of view—and so is the beginning of Strauss's *Don Juan*, just to give one or two very different examples.

Ashkenazy is not interested in opera and the operatic world, especially not in Italian opera, which he dislikes intensely, because "it seems so foreign to me, so show-businessy. Nothing is really true to life. Everything is overdramatized, one-thousand-per-cent theatrical. Now theatricality could be interesting on occasion, but when it is that overblown I can't stand it. From the purely musical point of view, operas with great music, like Wagner's, Strauss's and Mozart's, would be interesting to do if one were to find some accommodating attitude towards the theatrical side. But as I don't basically like opera, I don't think I ever shall. In any case, my hands are so full with doing the piano and orchestral repertoire which I love, that the question will simply not arise."

On top of his regular appearances in London and Amsterdam, where he is currently recording all the Rachmaninov symphonies with the Concertgebow Orchestra, he has been invited to conduct the Cleveland and the Philadelphia Orchestras during 1983. It is unlikely that he would ever be prepared to consider becoming a full-time Music Director, because of the demands of his career as a pianist.

In fact every spare moment of his day is spent practising at the piano—even the rehearsal breaks, much to the amazement of orchestral players who tend to rush out for tea or coffee and a few minutes' relaxation from the concentration of rehearsing. André Previn remembers an amusing incident during a break in a rehearsal of the Brahms First Piano Concerto in London. "I wanted to go and get a cup of tea, and crossed the empty hall on my way backstage to the artists' bar. As usual, Vova was sitting at the piano, practising throughout the break, and as I didn't want to disturb him, I went past him and when I'd got about five yards past, he played a phrase which I thought was quite unmusical, and was so amazed that my head turned around, automatically. He was smiling at me and said: 'I wanted to catch your attention, but didn't feel like shouting!'"

He practises four or five hours a day, depending on the rest of his schedule, and when on holiday in his house near Epidaurus in Greece, he usually totals six hours. He doesn't consider practising a hardship, he explained when I relayed to him the wide-eyed astonishment of the Philharmonia musicians whom he told this to. Quite the reverse. Sometimes he even experiences the same kind of elation while playing alone that he does at extra-special concerts.

"Those moments can happen when you are practising at home. They can even happen when you are thinking of a certain work. Because all of this is part of music-making, and if you don't enjoy practising, I don't see how you can ever enjoy performing. Music is music, it is not a mechanical thing. And when you learn a new piece you sometimes experience a fantastic sort of ecstasy just by being on intimate terms with it and recreating it.

"Of course there are many meanings to the word ecstasy," he added with his characteristic thoughtfulness and concern for clarity of communication, "but what *I* sometimes experience is a sort of elevation which, I suppose, comes from the realization that I am free, that there are no barriers between myself and the music, no nerves, no feeling of discomfort from playing on a bad piano or any of the millions of niggardly things that can get in the way. Consequently, I am expressing what I feel about the music, reproducing what I hope is the essence of those states I mentioned before when we were discussing Sullivan's book on Beethoven. But as there is a lot of hard, mechanical work going on at the same time, I would prefer to call this experience not ecstasy, but a feeling of controlled contentment."

I didn't see Ashkenazy again until eighteen months after our two talks—when I accidentally ran into him at a television studio where he was recording a documentary with the Philharmonia Orchestra. "Oh," he said eagerly, "I've learnt *so* much since we last talked!" The orchestra's Assistant Leader who overheard us added: "He doesn't get his arms in a tangle any more! And he is one of the few conductors who get up there and, if they make a mistake, are honest enough to put their head in their hands and say: 'Sorry, I've made a mistake.' But it doesn't often happen these days!"

Nothing sums up Ashkenazy the musician more characteristically than yet another story told me by André Previn. "Every soloist says something at the second before we both go on stage to perform, either '*Toi, toi, toi*' or '*Halz und Beinbruch*' or 'Good luck' or whatever. Vova, every one of the hundreds of times we've worked together, has unfailingly looked up at me and said 'All right, let's try'."

MSTISLAV ROSTROPOVICH

An Explosion of Love!

"My career as a cellist has been a wonderful school for conducting," beamed Mstislav Rostropovich—'Slava' to his innumerable friends—stroking the pet dachshund which travels with him almost everywhere in an airline bag. "Because as a cellist I played with the best conductors in the world. The same repertoire with all of them: personalities who were with me all the way, and personalities who were the exact opposite—complementary. Very exciting! And at every rehearsal, I watched ... I watched how they obtained their results; noted their weak points, their strong points; saw how each of them coped with this or that problem ... and I learnt. Maybe I, alone among all my colleagues, had the benefit of such a first-class school for conductors!"

Conductors were his heroes ever since he watched them on the podium while his father played the cello in various orchestras in their home town of Baku on the Caspian coast. He was six at the time, had just begun to play the piano, and had not yet learnt even how to hold a cello. But he told his father that one day he wanted to conduct. Yes, he replied, but conductors should be able to play one or more instruments really well.

"And this is absolutely true. My knowledge of the piano and the cello have proved invaluable to me as a conductor. The piano has given me a sense for harmony and polyphony, and through the cello I got a feeling for string sound, which is so crucial for orchestral expression: different bowings, different fingerings, the way of linking the sound between two notes, all these things make a huge difference to an orchestra's expression and to its overall sound. Being a cellist, it is easy for me to make suggestions about these things to players, because they know that I understand what I am talking about.

"But I must tell you a secret. Teaching conducting is very mysterious.

Because manual technique is not everything. Maybe it is not even thirty-per-cent of the story. What matters is projection, projection of your personality, and this, of course, is like magic. Because if your musical mind is strong and definite, the orchestra understands perfectly and immediately. If you have only technique, if you indicate only tempo, orchestra play boring, very boring." (Rostropovich never uses adverbs. Only adjectives!)

"And something which proved a fantastic tactical help in my conducting is the fact that, as a cellist, I understand that the most difficult things for a player are slow tempi. You may have noticed that some artists play very, very slowly but manage to bring very much texture, energy and feeling into slow tempi—they manage to inject some kind of vitamin inside them so that the public don't feel that they are *that* slow; while other performers may not play all that slowly, but as they do not insert enough personality and backbone to their playing, these slow tempi come across as being *too* slow.

"This feeling is very important for orchestras as well, and is something that the conductor must always bear in mind when deciding what tempo to take. Because this might well have to be different from what he imagined when reading the score, alone in his room. When he comes to rehearse, he will have to go for a tempo which takes into account the individual characteristics of his orchestra.

"Some orchestras, like some soloists, have substance and colour in their slow sound; some have a relaxed, *cantabile* quality; others have brilliance and wonderful attacks but lack this feeling of *cantabile* in their long largos and adagios. So, you must adjust your ears not only to your own feeling, to the sound in your own mind, but also to the orchestra's capacities. Sadly, many conductors don't. They say: 'This is my tempo', and apply it regardless of whether it is too fast or too slow for a particular orchestra."

He cites the finale of the Prokofiev Sixth Symphony as an example of something that needs such adaptability. Normally he likes to take this movement very, very fast. But with some orchestras, he comes up against what he calls "a sound barrier, as with an aircraft", and must therefore modify the tempo to make them comfortable.

"Because I'm not like a puppet who says, 'I'm a power kit, I'm here to produce *my* opinion of a work regardless.' I have to listen to the orchestra first, and then control things so that the result is a mixture of both of us. I have to be flexible. And this quality comes to me mostly because I am a cellist, and therefore understand the difficulties inherent in playing. I *feel* for the players, and have great respect for them, because I know what playing means.

"For example, an oboist in the New York Philharmonic who first played for me at La Scala, played the oboe solo in the slow movement of the Tchaikovsky fourth without breathing and produced a very, very long and beautiful legato, almost like a cello. On the one hand, this was marvellous to hear and I was so happy! But on the other, I worried and was terrible nervous for him because I knew that he was thinking, 'If I breathe now, I might as well be twice dead!'."

This intense human contact that is part of conducting is one of the reasons why he enjoys it so much and why he always longed to be a conductor. "I feel as if my life is just beginning," he announced when he took over the National Symphony in Washington.

"To play the cello, I have to produce sound through an instrument, but this instrument is not alive. As a conductor, I have to make a very deep connection not with instruments, but with human beings. And for this, waving the baton is not enough. I must use my eyes, facial expressions, my whole personality—and not only my musical, but also my human personality."

Rostropovich was born on March 27, 1927 in Baku, to musical parents. His mother, Sofia, was an accomplished pianist and his father Leopold an excellent cellist who, according to his son, "had no luck". Both his parents noticed that he had perfect pitch and his mother started giving him piano lessons when he was five. Three years later, his father insisted that he also learn the cello. Again he made rapid and spectacular progress. His father, who was not a very practical man, then decided to uproot his family and take them to Moscow, so that his children Slava and Veronica—now a violinist with the Moscow Philharmonic Orchestra—could have the benefit of the best possible musical education.

Unfortunately, he never thought of making any arrangements whatsoever before leaving Baku, and the family arrived in Moscow, in the middle of the dour year of 1934, totally destitute apart from an imitation-Persian rug and a mock-Japanese ivory statuette. They knew no one in the capital. With great effort they managed to find a room, from which they were soon evicted by the landlord. Helpless, they wandered in the streets, his father asking strangers for help, his mother and sister in tears. Suddenly an unknown woman approached them, asking how she could help. Zinaida Cherchopova, "Aunt Zina" as she was to become to Slava and his sister, took them to her home: two rooms which she, her husband and son had been allotted in a large communal apartment. The room was so small that there was only space to sleep on the beds at night. But Aunt Zina kept them there for three years, without asking for any rent.

At the beginning of the war, shortages of everything—food, fuel, money—became acute and Slava began to give concerts to help pay the bills. It was one of the coldest winters in Russian history and he remembers practising with woollen gloves from which the fingertips had been cut off. As the Germans advanced on Moscow the family were evacuated to Orenburg in the Urals, where Leopold Rostropovich died of heart failure in 1942, when Slava was only fifteen. He had adored his father and the shock, combined with the intense cold, brought on a serious bronchial illness. He, his mother and sister were now entirely dependent on his godmother, a schoolteacher who was gradually selling all her meagre possessions to keep them. Yet— another of those extraordinary instances of kindness from strangers that have so deeply influenced his own outlook towards people—one day three perfect strangers who had heard about the boy's illness brought a stove, left it in the house and disappeared without making themselves known.

Another such incident has also implanted itself vividly in his memory: when he recovered from his illness, he joined groups of evacuee musicians from Leningrad who were touring the surrounding countryside. One night six of them—three singers, an accompanist, an administrator and Slava—were travelling together by night in a freezing railway compartment, with one blanket per person. Slava's teeth couldn't stop chattering and he remembers lying down, freezing and thinking that, with his father gone, his mother suffering, this would be a good moment to die. He finally fell asleep and woke up warm: his companions had piled all their blankets on top of him.

Experiences like this explain his own warmth, exuberance and open-hearted responsiveness to everyone he comes into contact with. He exudes love and *bonhomie* seemingly towards all. Some people, especially in Britain, tend to be suspicious of his instant assumption that everyone is "my friend". But the spontaneity is sincere, as even those cynics who point out that he is also quite greedy and financially astute, admit. (In any case people who have suffered acute deprivation in their childhood and youth have every right to wish to enjoy the fruits of their labours to the full.) He also feels a profound sense of duty, a debt to life, his country, and its people, which must be repaid through his music-making. Which is why he suffers deeply at the fact that, at present, his countrymen cannot enjoy it. "In fact, most of them probably think I am dead," he mused.

At the end of the war, both he and his sister enrolled at the Moscow Conservatoire, where Slava studied the piano, the cello and composition. By practising extremely hard—and working as a carpenter and frame maker in his spare time—he managed to finish the five-year course in two years.

His professor of composition was Dmitri Shostakovich, who was impressed by this pupil despite the fact that "I composed badly, in the style of Prokofiev", and rang up his mother, asking her to persuade him to give up the cello for composition, which "thank goodness, I didn't". The two men were destined to become close friends and collaborators, and Shostakovich was to write and dedicate numerous works to his erstwhile pupil. One of Rostropovich's fondest memories of the great composer was his passion for being silent—but in the company of someone he liked.

"He would telephone me and say, 'Come quickly, hurry'," Rostropovich reminisced in an interview with *The Observer* after the composer's death. "So, I'd arrive at his flat and he'd say, 'Sit down, and now we can be silent.' We would sit for half an hour, without a word. It was very relaxing, just sitting. Then Shostakovich would get up and say, 'Thank you. Goodbye, Slava.' It was very special, sitting like that with him. When I left I felt as though I'd been through some kind of catharsis; his relaxation was purifying."

Looking back on his education in Russia, he still considers the Soviet system of musical education to be the best in the world, because of the way in which it spots, nurtures and promotes promising talents, assigning them to the best professors in the land, who are made responsible for their progress, and who then have to work their pupils exceedingly hard, "like athletes" and for the same reason: the greater glory of Mother Russia. On the other hand, the omnipresence of politics at every stage of musical life and the constant interference of officialdom with the choice of repertoire and with artists' freedom of movement is a crippling factor.

Rostropovich had his first brush with 'the System' as early as 1948, when Prokofiev and Shostakovich were condemned for the "undemocratic" tendencies expressed in their music, whatever that might mean.

Their music was totally banned for two years and Shostakovich was forbidden to teach at the Conservatoire. The fact that the two composers he most admired should be suddenly crushed into the ground was a profound shock for Rostropovich. Unlike other students, he refused to change his professors, left the Conservatoire and went to live with Prokofiev at his *dacha* outside Moscow until the composer's death in 1953.

He considers his time there to have been "the best school in Russia", since all the great composers had left the Conservatoire after 1948. Prokofiev, who was an eccentric individualist—a flamboyant dresser and a specialist in and collector of French perfumes—taught him a great deal, especially during their long evening walks when he would discuss his music and his favourite composers—but never Shostakovich whom he would not allow others to discuss either.

"Prokofiev and I shared a similar attitude to music. We both approached it as 'life experience,' and tried to find its 'heart'. Because every composition contains the composer's feelings, in code. Your task as an interpreter is to decode them. Take the part just before the second movement of the Schumann Cello Concerto. It always gives me the feeling that Schumann was so tired humanly, so weary at that moment, that he wanted to get out of this world. And I can clearly visualize him going into another room and composing his second movement, all alone. I can actually see him doing it, whenever I come to play this. This attitude to music helped me very much in my friendship with Prokofiev, who had a very similar view—but preferred to talk about orchestral instruments in terms of animals, or insects." (Particularly the sound of the tuba, which he always described as "a million beetles and bugs!")

By the mid-fifties, Rostropovich's career was flourishing and he toured extensively both inside Russia and in the Eastern bloc and made numerous recordings, which eventually established his reputation in the West, too. During one of those tours to Prague he met the beautiful soprano Galina Vishnevskaya, a star of the Bolshoi Opera, whom he had briefly encountered in Moscow, and married her within four days! "It was love, an explosion of love," he explained ("loff" he pronounced it) to *Time* Magazine. "I was happy to be alive!"

It has been a stormy marriage, possibly made worse by his intensely roving eye, but one which has endured through fire and ice and produced two musically gifted daughters, now grown up: Elena, a pianist who sometimes plays with her father, and Olga, who is studying the cello at the Juilliard School of Music in New York.

In the sixties, Rostropovich became a valuable export and was allowed to travel widely to Europe and the United States, and to record for Western companies, with the Soviet establishment smiling on benignly. He and his wife were given a large apartment in Composers' House in Moscow and a luxurious *dacha* on the outskirts, which they filled with treasures amassed from abroad, including three cars, one of them a Mercedes, and an American bar. (Although, of course, they were not allowed to touch their foreign earnings which, as with all Russian artists, have to be paid into a state-run agency.)

Even during these pampered years, the Ministry of Culture kept close watch, and had to be kept informed of all the works he wished to play and where and with whom. If he forgot, he would be summoned for an interview, and after a great deal of pussyfooting, he would be asked why he had told his British manager that he wanted to perform a certain concerto without first informing the Ministry. To remind him of their power, they might, or might not, grant permission. He says that for several years after his move to the West, he had a lingering feeling of having forgotten something all the time—just because he no longer had to report anything to anyone.

In the early sixties (December–January 1962–63) he had a unique experience: for the first time in his life, he played the cello in an orchestra, at the request of Shostakovich, who had revised *Lady Macbeth of Mstensk*, banned by Stalin, into a new version called *Katerina Ismailova*. The authorities had refused permission for it to be performed at the Bolshoi and allocated it to the Stanislavsky Theatre. Shostakovich was worried about the quality of the players in this orchestra, and asked about eight of his friends to help out by playing at the première. "I led the cello section, the only time I have ever played in an orchestra in my life. I was so nervous!" remembered Rostropovich when he subsequently came to record the original version of the work for EMI. The production was a huge, sold-out success, and after the première, they all drank until the early hours of the morning. (His capacity for food and drink is colossal, which might explain why his rotund figure makes him look older than his fifty-five years. Seiji Ozawa, who likes a swill or two himself, says that he didn't know what drinking *meant* until he met Rostropovich. "One night out with Slava, the whole next day gone!")

It was during the late sixties that he scored one of his first great successes as a conductor, a memorable production of *Eugene Onegin* with which the Bolshoi Opera celebrated the centenary of this work, with his wife singing the role of Tatyana. It was an experience that changed his attitude to the study of scores.

"My wife had sung this role many, many times at the Bolshoi, and every time I had been disappointed because I felt sure that many things were interpreted wrongly. The Bolshoi had been performing this work for at least eighty years and many things, including many mistakes, had become part of what they called 'tradition'. If, for example, a singer had made a *fermata* in a certain place eighty years ago—a *fermata* before the highest note, which is very comfortable but wrong—this was blindly followed at every subsequent performance, despite the fact that Tchaikovsky wrote a *fermata* before a *low* note, in Onegin's first-act aria. Evidently, this was not considered 'effective' enough for a cheap public response, so the singer changed it, without any thought for the real musical feeling.

"And once one singer had done this, the next generation who came up thought: if *he* made a three-seconds' *fermata*, I, who am younger and have a fantastic voice, can make a five-seconds' *fermata!* All these stupid things made for a lot of confusion. So I said to myself that I must see the original score. And I looked at it as if it had been given to me by a young composer who had just written it. As a cellist, I had given first performances of more than sixty works, so I was used to studying virgin scores. And as soon as I examined the original of *Eugene Onegin*, I could see at once that it was constantly performed with the wrong tempi and the wrong *fermatas*. So, I thought, why not clean it up and perform it exactly the way it was written?

"I had no political difficulties with the Ministry as yet, so when I informed them of what I planned to do, they said 'yes', with great pleasure. 'But how many rehearsals do you think you will need, considering that the orchestra have known this work for years?' I replied that I didn't know exactly how many but that it would be a lot, and asked the orchestra how many they were prepared to grant me. They said: 'For you, because we love you so much, we can do six.' I replied, 'No, ten.' After a committee meeting, they agreed.

"At the first rehearsal, I changed some bowings and fingerings, and by the time we reached the tenth rehearsal, I said that I was now ready to go on to stage rehearsals. But the orchestra begged please to have more, because they needed such advice and were learning so much. So, we ended up having *twenty-two* orchestral rehearsals! The perform-ance was incredible successful, praised in a fantastic article in *Pravda* and, eventually, taken to Paris and Berlin.

"Since then, I have always approached scores in this meticulous way, be it an opera or a Dvořák symphony, or a work like Penderecki's *Te Deum*, which I will soon perform in New York. And this is the reason why I always have a good success with the Tchaikovsky symphonies: because I go back to the scores. Many, many people think that having those works in your mind and your ears is enough. But you must always go back to the score, and if there are several versions, to the *original* score, to see what is there. Sometimes, you may find a very small but *so* important thing!"

His intensely committed and emotional performances of the Tchaikovsky symphonies at the Royal Festival Hall in London in 1976 (subsequently recorded) were one of the great triumphs of his career, and drew interminable rounds of applause from an audience aroused to a frenzy of enthusiasm; and the critics raved, as they did about his recordings. He loves Tchaikovsky and disagrees with those younger musicians who pooh-pooh him as an inferior composer—an attitude, incidentally, shared by Shostakovich who considered him a mediocre, amateur composer, unlike Prokofiev who greatly admired and loved his works. His own interpretations derive directly from his experience of Russia: its landscape, ("for example, the beginning of Symphony No. 1, 'Winter Dreams', instantly invokes images of winter snow falling slowly over Russia"), its people, their unique temperament.

Having worked closely with so many of the great composers of our time, frequently on works composed specifically for him, he has first-hand experience of a composer's attitudes to changes and modifications to his original score made in the light of performing experience. Shostakovich, for instance, was always happy to accommodate his soloists and gladly agreed to minor adjustments. "'Do you think the tempo should be slightly slower, here?' I would ask him. 'Yes, slow,' he would reply. And if in five minutes I would say about the same passage, 'No, I think that maybe faster was better,' he would agree. 'Yes, you are right. Faster. Whatever you think, Slava.' But only great composers are prepared to do this."

His years of favour with the Soviet System came to an abrupt end over the affair of Alexander Solzhenitsyn, who fell into disgrace after the publication of *The First Circle* and *Cancer Ward* in the West. After he was refused permission to return to Moscow, Rostropovich sheltered him in his *dacha*, and when the official attacks on the writer were intensified after he won the Nobel Prize in 1970, he wrote an open, official letter of protest to the Russian press, who refused to publish it. The foreign press, however, were glad to do so. "That was the greatest step I have ever taken in my life. The greatest. With my whole soul, I said: *Now*, I will not be silent!", he explained to an American magazine after his move to the West, four years later. The letter contained a bitter attack on the Soviet censorship of the Arts, the curtailment of individual freedom, and the placing of incompetent people in positions of power over the Arts. He had no illusions about the outcome of such a move, and even asked his wife if she wanted a quick divorce, to protect her career. She refused.

He was right to expect the worst, though. Soon after the letter was published, the system began a slow, systematic, step-by-step persecution of both of them, aimed at destroying their careers and eradicating their names from public memory. They were not allowed to travel abroad any longer—the State Agency cabled announcing a cancellation due to illness; their recordings were banned from the State radio, and if they featured in a broadcast, their names would be omitted from the credits; they were forbidden to appear on television; if Rostropovich played a recital with another artist, only the other artist's name would appear on the billboards or in the next day's reviews; his wife was given infrequent assignments at the Bolshoi and her name was omitted from the programme even on those rare occasions. The last resort came when, reduced to a series of appearances in some little towns on the shores of the Volga, they arrived in each place only to find that their concerts had been mysteriously cancelled.

In despair Rostropovich wrote a letter to Brezhnev, but got no reply. When, a year later, he was refused permission to participate in a BBC programme in honour of Shostakovich, he felt it was time to try to leave Russia. For the first time, he told a Western journalist of the "artistic quarantine" imposed on him and his wife. His friends abroad reacted immediately. Leonard Bernstein and his wife asked Edward Kennedy to intercede during his forthcoming trip to Moscow, and shortly after that, in 1974, the Rostropoviches were handed back their passports and allowed to leave for America, where he was to receive an Honorary Doctorate of Music at Harvard University. Without officially defecting, they decided not to return to Russia, but retained their Russian passports, hoping the Soviet authorities would gradually change their attitude to them and to artists in general, until they were suddenly stripped of their Soviet citizenship on March 15, 1978.

After their decision to stay in the West, they settled in Paris, in a flat which looked like a miniature corner of Russia. "I cannot live without Russia's spirit running through my blood, so in my home I want to surround myself only with the things that will remind me of my links to my country, to my people," he explained shortly before being stripped of his nationality. He involved himself in numerous Russian charities and was idealistic, or naïve, enough to hope that in the light of so many famous artists' defections, the Authorities would come to their senses, liberalize their policies, and allow the Rostropoviches free movement to and from Russia. The withdrawal of their citizenship came as a deep shock.

Since 1977, Rostropovich has been Music Director of the National Symphony in Washington. He was offered the job immediately after an enthusiastically received concert in Washington in March 1975, and although this had never been anything but a third-rate group, he accepted with alacrity, "twice more excited" than if he had been offered a greater orchestra, because improving them would prove a great challenge and stimulate his creative, educating instincts.

"Guest Conductors come, achieve their concept of sound for one or two concerts, and go, only to be followed by someone who may undo everything they did, whereas Music Directors have a lasting impact. I always liken the two types of conductor to sportsmen: Guest Conductors to athletes who run a hundred metres and Music Directors to marathon runners. Both are very important and have different functions to fulfil. Being a Music Director requires a special kind of talent, because it involves full responsibility for each of the musicians: not only for those who improve during the season, but also for those who deteriorate, which necessitates a deep understanding of human nature. For if, sometimes, a horn or trumpet player is not doing very good work because he is not practising enough at home, which shows almost immediately, you must know *why*. You must ask and find out if he has family or personality problems. Some of my colleagues tell me: 'Slava, what matters is the result. You are like a coachman. If a horse is not running well, you change the horse.' I think this is wrong. You must *care* for the players. Without this human contact, you cannot hope to educate them musically.

"This is why I found it incredible difficult to fire musicians. Only five of the orchestra's new players are replacements—the rest were hired to enlarge it. But replacing even those five was incredible unpleasant. For ten nights before, I didn't sleep. I cried. It was a real problem for me.

Gradually, I persuaded myself that if I weren't strong enough to take the necessary steps to improve the orchestra, I should resign and go. A Guest Conductor's life is much easier," he sighed.

After prevailing upon himself to make these changes, the orchestra improved considerably, although there is still a great deal of work to be done. He especially enjoys his weekly Sunday masterclasses, held in his hotel suite, for the new young players, or any of the other players who care to attend. They play concertos, sonatas, trios, quartets, violin or oboe or clarinet solos for him, and he listens and explains his ideas, his opinions and criticisms, often demonstrating what he means on the piano, "because of my terrible bad English.

"For example, when they play something by Schubert in a strong, military way, I say: 'Children, you sounded like a thousand cows. You know Schubert, you know his face from pictures—that small, round face with sideburns—please play what is there: piano, mezzoforte, but *never* loud; piano, but a piano warm with this feeling of suffering for Schubert. Imagine his face and try to make a very, very deep but very distant sound, like something coming from afar.... Some music is immediate, experienced very much at the present moment. But Schubert's is not. It must sound like a memory, a little bit distant, like an echo, something I hear after it happened, maybe twenty years after it happened. The first time you played it, it sounded like twenty years before!

"Because this kind of thing is what matters most. It's the heart of the music. If I'm conducting some sad music, it can be a deep sadness, or a romantic sort of melancholy, so I try to explain what *kind* of sound I want, principally with my hands, of course, but also with words. Because there are a thousand different *piano* sounds; maybe a million different *piano* sounds. But what kind of *heart* beats through them? That is what matters."

For this reason, he feels that "the sound" of an orchestra should be flexible and depend entirely on the composer—never on the conductor or soloist.

"If I turn on the radio in the middle of a work and immediately recognize the performer, so phenomenal, so fantastic personal that it *must* be so and so, this is wrong, a very big mistake on the performer's part. Because if I instantly recognize the performer, this must be because of technical idiosyncrasies. I would much rather *not* guess who is playing but instantly know that this must be Mozart or Schubert. The performer who makes me know this is a truly great one. Because no performer's identity is as important as the composer's."

Yet the freedom of some of Rostropovich's own interpretations has aroused controversy, especially because of his rubati, which "are Slava's way of being. He doesn't have to follow a dry, metronomic beat. As a string player he knows what it is to form a phrase," Yehudi Menuhin told *Time* after Rostropovich was appointed to the National Symphony. Seiji Ozawa added that "Slava doesn't interpret, he feels. His music is really his character. He is conducting his life." Rostropovich himself would disagree. He feels, but he feels for the composer; he feels, or claims to feel, what the composer felt, as he explained. Which is why Leonard Bernstein finds that his frequent excesses and exaggerations, which shock many, are so very effective; the great love and conviction that go with them make these freedoms acceptable.

Yet although he says that the sound of an orchestra does not depend on the conductor, he admits that he likes a rich string sound, a cold pitch in the woodwinds, with "no vibrato", and, of course, plenty of rubato. This means that some of his performances of the Classics lack finesse and sound more full-bodied than they should. This might change with experience. Because however great an instrumentalist might be, he cannot be expected also to become a great conductor of the entire repertoire overnight.

Rostropovich feels that his career as a cellist has been "incredible helpful" in giving him a feeling for ensemble and instrumental dialogue within the orchestra. "I got used to this kind of dialogue between instruments, because I used to play duets or cello sonatas with other instruments. In many ways, the most uncomfortable instrument to play with was the piano, which has quite another sound-world, more like percussion. The cello has such a different sound, this long legato line which is poles apart. So, when playing a slightly mechanical composition like a fugue, I tried to reproduce this percussion-like sound of the piano with my cello by making my attacks sharper, thus coming a bit closer to a piano sound.

"Playing with an orchestra was always much easier. Because with an orchestra I could have many conversations, a series of dialogues with individual instruments or instrument groups. Sometimes, I made the same colours as the section I was having the dialogue with, to emphasize and continue the musical idea, and sometimes I produced a contrasting sound to make the dialogue more dramatic and dynamic.

"I also try to do this when conducting. Because the orchestra has dialogues between various instruments and instrument groups, too. So, sometimes if the strings are playing pizzicato, I tell the woodwind to play pizzicato also—which, of course, does not exist in woodwind playing, but I mean the *feeling* of pizzicato—and they immediately understand and play what I want. At the end of the third movement of the Mahler fifth, for instance, when the flute repeats a melody just played by the trumpet, I tell the flute to play 'like a crazy trumpet'— very high."

He doesn't accept the accusation that by taking up conducting on such a large scale, he might endanger the excellence of his cello playing—and *that* without becoming a really-top ranking conductor. "But," he explained to a journalist who asked exactly the same question, "once one has achieved a certain level, one must move outside one's own discipline in order to make a leap in imagination—in other words, in order to grow. After a certain point, I could not have gone further with the cello if I hadn't conducted, hadn't heard, seen and *felt* outside my own instrument."

THE YOUNGER GENERATION

RICCARDO CHAILLY
A Sunny Nature that Loves
Living Dangerously!

"When I was six my father took me to my first concert," remembers twenty-nine-year-old Riccardo Chailly, Music Director of the Berlin Radio Orchestra and Principal Guest Conductor of the London Philharmonic. "I was completely shocked! [Chailly always uses this word when he means overwhelmed or bowled over.] This mysterious mixture of people, the different sounds which miraculously came together, that man out there waving a stick! It all made such an impression on me that from then on waving a stick at a group of children assembled in my parents' drawing-room became my favourite game. And I kept pestering my father [Luciano Chailly, the distinguished Italian composer] to take me to more concerts. He did. And I started having ideas. I began to dream of becoming a conductor.

"But my father who knew better than most how difficult the conducting profession is, how easy it is to be mediocre, one of hundreds of anonymous conductors labouring in obscurity, and how frustrating it would be to be the parent of a failed conductor, hoped that I would forget the idea before I had a chance to be disillusioned. I understand his point of view. In fact I rather agree with him in retrospect … there are so many disaster stories of conductors who haven't quite made it."

Chailly most definitely has. For some time he has been considered to be one of today's most promising young conductors. Provided he gives himself enough time and breathing space to mellow and avoids the pitfalls lurking behind early success—and there are indications that he might be falling into some of them—he should become an important conductor in the future. The necessary talent and the right personality are certainly there and were evident from the very first. Wherever he went—the Chicago Lyric Opera, the San Francisco Opera, the Royal and the London Philharmonic, La Scala—he was promptly invited back.

Yet although he considers having a composer for a father a great advantage because "it meant that I was born *into* music and heard notes around me virtually from the day I was born", had Luciano Chailly had his way, his son would have forgotten all about his dream of becoming a conductor. For a while, he tried to, and enrolled at the Istituto Tecnico di Turismo in Rome. "But it was a disaster!" In the end his parents got so desperate about what on earth to do with a son who seemed so stupid and who never worked at school, that they decided to let him have a go at music. His first and strictest composition teacher was his father, "very critical but always in a constructive way which is why I haven't ended up with a bunch of complexes" and later Bruno Bettinelli at the Verdi Conservatoire in Milan. Although he says that he was never any good at composition, the years he spent at it have proved an invaluable help to him as a conductor. "For a conductor's first task is to know the score, from the first note to the last, better than anybody else. For only through a serious, patient and thorough knowledge and analysis of its structure can he arrive at its inner meaning. Otherwise, his interpretation is bound to be superficial."

After graduating from the Verdi Conservatoire, Chailly studied conducting in Perugia with Piero Guarino, who sensed that this pupil was a born conductor, and eventually with Franco Ferrara, "the biggest genius I have met in my life", at the Accademia Chigiana in Siena where he was awarded a *diploma di merito* at the age of nineteen, in 1972. But he had started earning his living even before graduating. His first professional job and his "first money" came from spending three successive summers as a percussion player in a pop group in Trentino, and in 1968 he had made his first public appearance as a conductor with the Solisti Veneti in Padua, at the invitation of the ensemble's director, Claudio Scimone. Two years later, aged only seventeen, he conducted his first concert in Milan, as part of a series at the Teatro Nuovo called 'Musical Afternoons'.

As soon as he got his diploma from Siena, Claudio Abbado engaged him as his assistant at La Scala where he spent two exciting, instructive years that greatly influenced his formation as a conductor. As he was still only nineteen, "this was a big demonstration of trust on Claudio's part," he recently told *Hi Fi News*. For while he didn't conduct at La Scala during that period, Abbado entrusted him with many rehearsals (i.e. preparing the orchestra before the latter took over for the final rehearsals) where he learnt to cope with Brahms and Mozart symphonies as well as impressionistic music like Ravel and Debussy and where he also learned how to work with an orchestra—Italy's best orchestra. Yet unlike most of his famous colleagues who feel that starting in an opera house is the best way for a young conductor to learn his craft, Chailly feels that the other way around is better, "because it makes you treat the orchestration in operatic scores more thoroughly than you otherwise would.

"But learning how to handle an orchestra for the first time from the psychological point of view was just as crucial as my musical apprenticeship. Because musical attributes are only half of a conductor's panoply. The other half are human, psychological qualities—a flair for mass psychology in particular. For he has to dominate large numbers of people and obtain from them the sound image in his mind through sheer force of personality, through his temperament and character. All this is mixed and intertwined with his musical talent, of course, and it's very hard to put your finger on it.... And the strangest, most mysterious and fascinating thing is to watch how the same orchestra changes under different conductors.

"Although there are some notable exceptions to this rule, I believe that conductors are born and not made. For there must be something inside you that flows through your heart, face, hands and eyes and enables you to establish direct contact with orchestras. Of course, at rehearsal a conductor does have to stop the orchestra from time to time and explain what's wrong, verbally. But even then, the best results are often obtained not by stopping, but by transmitting through your eyes and facial expressions, exactly as you would at the concert itself. And the conductor must be very clever in deciding whether to stop or not, and to pick the right moment for doing so. It's a very difficult decision sometimes.... But beyond this point, it all happens through this magnetic contact that goes beyond words—that inborn quality that enables you to express yourself through your hands and physical movements. And needless to say, conducting is a profession that requires a great deal of physical stamina!"

In 1974 Chailly made his début abroad conducting *Madama Butterfly* at the Chicago Lyric Opera, where he has subsequently returned for *Rigoletto* in 1976 and *Cavalleria rusticana* and *I pagliacci* in 1978. He had already made his operatic début at the Teatro Nuovo in Milan—

Werther, with which he was later also to make his recording début—during his year as Abbado's assistant at La Scala. In 1977 came a triumphant début at the San Francisco Opera: Jean-Pierre Ponnelle's production of *Turandot* with Caballé and Pavarotti, "one of the best experiences of my life, an exceptionally convincing production by a director who is very musical, very sensitive, a true artist able to experience the music from the conductor's angle as well—something very, very rare indeed."

We met during the rehearsal period for La Scala's production of Verdi's *I due Foscari* in December 1979 and it was interesting to see how, gradually, all the different artists' interpretations began to come together with his. "This is always so in operatic productions. The final result comes out of the combustion of all of us working together, and is always a compromise. For singers need a lot of help both from the purely vocal and from the musical, interpretational point of view, so I must change and modify the initial sound image in my mind in a way that takes account of the realities of the situation. Every conductor must do this. To be a Mussolini and say this is it, this is the way you will do it, is not only impractical but hateful and terribly old-fashioned. Best to forget it!"

In symphonic work the compromises are not as great. But even then, Chailly finds that a conductor never hears exactly what is in his mind from the first moment. He has to work towards his own sound gradually, and again, take into account the specific qualities of individual orchestras, and their response to him: "For example, conducting early Verdi with American orchestras can be rather dangerous from the stylistic point of view—especially at the beginning—while at La Scala there are no problems, because the orchestra knows this repertoire inside out. But American orchestras are so perfect from the technical point of view that they compensate in other ways for the fact that they are less steeped in Italian tradition than the Scala musicians, who combine great culture and tradition—the heritage of Toscanini, de Sabata and Guarnieri—with a technique that is not quite so perfect. So obviously I spend much longer on obtaining clear playing and don't have to bother with style, which is automatically there. This, of course, is much easier, it's a conductor's normal business." Chailly, whose brilliant handling of both *I masnadieri* and *I due Foscari* was much praised, feels that early Verdi, whom he particularly loves and champions with great zeal, is in fact quite difficult to conduct, "because it's so easy to make those operas sound facile, elementary, banal, scholastic and downright boring unless you really take pains both with the orchestra and with the characterization of every role."

As far as the symphonic repertoire is concerned, Chailly feels a particularly strong affinity for the Romantics—Schumann, Brahms, Mahler, Bruckner, Tchaikovsky—and for Stravinsky. He is honest enough to admit that not only does he listen to colleagues' recordings, but that after doing so he sometimes gets a hankering after a particular score. This is exactly what happened when he heard Böhm's "marvellous record" of the Bruckner seventh which "I dream of conducting someday, but not now, and not in less than five years". But while many conductors admit to listening to colleagues' records, more often than not these tend to be dead colleagues: Furtwängler, Walter, Toscanini or de Sabata. Chailly also listens to Karajan's, Kleiber's and Abbado's recordings because he rightly judges that these offer him an excellent opportunity to learn from and be stimulated by these great artists' ideas and solutions to musical problems. He tends to do his listening a long, long time before actually learning a specific score. "This way it gets my imagination going, but by the time I come to study the score, I have forgotten specific points—which means that I am free to respond to it spontaneously.

"Basically there are two levels of studying and learning scores. Firstly the technical aspects—memorization, subdivision of rhythms, etc.— which are the easiest and most superficial. What helps a lot at this stage is, after first reading it through like a book, to subdivide a score into musical periods, which makes it easier to digest and memorize. Occasionally I might try an odd passage on the piano, bad pianist though I am. Then comes the far more crucial part of your preparation: the musical interpretation, the search for the inner meaning, the inner truth in this score, and concentration on all those harmonic points which may seem secondary but are not."

One of the most difficult scores that Chailly has had to cope with to date was Stravinsky's *The Rake's Progress*, which he conducted at La Scala in the spring of 1980, and which proved one of the two greatest experiences of his career, because of the presence of the London Sinfonietta, "the best orchestra in the world for contemporary music", in the pit. "They were perfect! Like a living record. I had never before come across such quality from the pit. Everybody was in good shape, there was good communication between all of us. I was crazy, gone mad about them! A top experience. And they made light of all the difficulties in the score."

At the time of our meetings, Chailly was busy learning *Le Sacre du printemps*, "one of the hardest pieces to conduct, very difficult and very controversial. Although the music is written in a perfectly clear way, you have to work a lot at the *concertazione*, to ensure that everything sounds. And the rhythms are terribly difficult, too. Every bar is in a different time beat and so *fast*! And it should sound as exact and perfect as a Swiss clock. If one in one hundred and twenty players is even a fraction late, it destroys everything."

He also finds Mahler scores difficult, despite the fact that they are full of verbal instructions for the conductor, because they are so rich and so dense that it is sometimes difficult to achieve absolute clarity in every bar. He particularly loves the last four symphonies and the unfinished Tenth which "from the technical and rhythmical point of view anticipates so much of what Stravinsky was to do later". There are many other areas of the repertoire he would eventually like to explore—*Salome, Otello, Falstaff*—but he is fully aware of the dangers involved in doing them too soon. He had a disastrous experience in 1975, when at the age of twenty-two he accepted an invitation from the Teatro Massimo in Palermo to conduct Gluck's *Iphigénie en Tauride*. "I took up the offer because I was a typical crazy young guy who thoughtlessly committed the deadly sin of youth: thinking I knew everything. And it was one of the sharpest lessons and most shocking contacts I have had in my life: this work was so far from my own musical taste, so classical, so difficult to understand and penetrate, even more difficult than Mozart. This shocked me no end. Because from the technical point of view it was easy, no problems. But musically, I felt that until the last performance, I didn't understand it at all. I was convinced it was a masterpiece, but I couldn't penetrate its inner meaning in a way that could produce a convincing result. I wasn't profound or mature enough, so most of the performances didn't make sense. They did progressively get better, and by the last evening, I had reached the point when I could begin to *start* learning and penetrating it. If anyone were to ask me to do it again, I would say: 'Maybe in twenty years.' I am more cautious now!"

Another major danger facing young conductors today is pressure from the recording companies to record things they are not yet ready for. Chailly's own exclusive contract with Decca has resulted in some carefully chosen and well received recordings—*Guglielmo Tell*, and the first digital album of Rossini Overtures, as well as *Werther* with

Domingo released under the Deutsche Grammophon label—and he hopes to continue being strong-minded about his repertoire. When we talked he felt that one of the beneficial side-effects of the financial crisis in the recording industry might be an urge to make fewer and better records: "For it used to be dreadful a few years ago. Like going to the bakery and choosing yet another loaf from shelvesful of inferior and superficial products on display. And doing things too soon, and only regretting them when it is too late, is one of the biggest dangers facing someone like me. Because one of the most important and precious things for a conductor is time: time not only to learn but to reflect in peace without the pressure of a forthcoming performance." But he could always say 'no'? "Yes, I know ... but the only conductor who actually manages to say 'no' is Carlos Kleiber whom I admire enormously, not only for his marvellous interpretations but also for being unique in taking two, three, four, sometimes six months off work, just to think, to be, to live a normal life. I say it but I don't do it."

Perhaps he should, for in the summer of 1981, he suffered from exhaustion. And while his operatic performances have been justifiably praised, some of the LPO musicians I talked to have begun to feel that he has not yet fulfilled his early promise. But perhaps he will when he settles down as full-time Musical Director with the Berlin Radio Orchestra, a job to which he is looking forward to with great seriousness as well as anticipation.

Apart from musical dangers, another major problem facing a young conductor embarking on a career is how to cope with having a personal life, and in particular, a marriage. Chailly got married at twenty-one and had a daughter shortly afterwards. At the time he felt that combining a marriage and a career was very difficult and that "it is the biggest mistake for a conductor to be married; because you have no time to give to your family. I have a daughter whom I consider the best and biggest mistake of my life: the best because holding her is the greatest emotional experience I have known—yes, even greater than music—and the biggest because she is growing up hardly knowing her father, who has to be away so much of the time. Although I am happy I got married, I still think it was a mistake, I wouldn't do it now. I would just live with a girl. But in those days one was so bogged down by the Italian bourgeois mentality." (He was divorced about a year after our conversations, and has since married again.) Our meeting took place in December 1979 and both at the time and on subsequent occasions he stressed that a young man in his twenties is developing so fast that a great many of his views both about life and about music can change considerably within a relatively short period of time.

A healthy private life is important to every artist and even more so to someone like Chailly who doesn't feel that a successful career is the be-all and end-all of existence. "I love life; I love *living*; I can't just be a professional conductor going around the world—that's too boring. And in a way, I love living dangerously. My favourite sport is motor-cycle racing in the mountains with my Honda and skiing. My parents say I'm crazy because I could so easily break my hands doing either. But I do it all the same.... And I love reading, mostly poetry. I hated it at school, because it was official, it was work, it was awful, because one had to learn it by heart. Then later I came to read Buzzati and Yevtushenko and I was astonished, shocked. I loved it and I love Prévert, too, which is funny because he is so negative and I'm so positive: I am a very optimistic person who never wakes up angry, nervoso or hysterical. I'm always happy when I open my eyes in the morning.

"And I'll tell you another thing about me: I've always had incredibly good luck. Right from the start, everything created at least three new opportunities. Take that *Turandot* in San Francisco for example. The première happened to be broadcast all over the States and afterwards I remember going out with friends and staying up till five in the morning. I always go to bed very late after a performance because after giving it everything I have, I simply cannot go to sleep for hours. And the next day I'm gaga, I must sleep really, really late. (I'm not an early riser at the best of times but on mornings after performances you might as well forget about me altogether!) Anyway, there I was, fast asleep on the morning after *Turandot*, when the telephone rang at nine-thirty. I said to myself who can this bastard be, ringing up so early after a première? It turned out to be Ernest Fleischmann, the Managing Director of the Los Angeles Philharmonic, who said that Zubin Mehta (then Music Director of the LAPO) had heard the broadcast and wanted him to convey his warmest congratulations and to extend an invitation to conduct the LAPO during the coming season. So you see what I mean by luck? If he hadn't happened to be at home that evening and not listened to that broadcast, it might have taken me ten years to get invited there."

Since our meetings, Chailly has not only been appointed Music Director of the RIAS (West Berlin Radio Orchestra) and Principal Guest Conductor of the London Philharmonic, but has also guest conducted the Berlin and the Vienna Philharmonic. At the time, he was "very excited and very afraid" of the challenge. But true to pattern, he has been re-invited back by both orchestras. Dreams for the future include conducting *Tristan und Isolde*—someday. "*Tristan* is the closest music to Latin blood that Wagner ever wrote; the *Ring*, on the other hand, is so far removed from Italian musical taste, culture, blood or whatever you like to call it, that I feel it would be a mistake for an Italian conductor to tackle it. I have always considered *Tristan* to be Wagner's greatest opera. After conducting that you might as well die, because you can't do anything greater. That's why I call it the last, the ultimate dream in my life. In a way, so is *Pelléas et Mélisande*. After *Tristan* and *Pelléas*, where do you go?"

SIMON RATTLE
A Massive Hope for the Future

"I loathe being called 'Maestro' or 'Mr Rattle'. I find it a personal assault. It makes me uncomfortable. Only once you get past this stage, this feudal division between you and the orchestra, does it all start to be fun," announced the engaging, stunningly brilliant Liverpool-born Principal Conductor and Musical Adviser of the City of Birmingham Symphony Orchestra, Artistic Director of the London Choral Society, Music Director of the South Bank Summer Music Festival, Principal Guest Conductor of the Rotterdam Philharmonic, and Principal Guest Conductor of the Los Angeles Philharmonic.

Which is why he particularly enjoys working with the London Sinfonietta and the Nash Ensemble, which consist partly of the same people, who exude "the greatest pleasure in making music that I have ever come across in a professional orchestra.

"And the fact that there is no feudal division makes life much easier for the conductor. Each side can discuss things, criticize the other and say that it was less than efficient, without it being a problem. And their technical standards are extremely high. In fact, they are the only orchestra which complains that I don't rehearse them enough. I say 'okay, that's enough', but they often won't let me go. They say 'no', we want to get this absolutely right, it's not good enough, and stop being so lazy, Simon.' It's lovely. It's almost in danger of getting to be like making music again, instead of this ludicrous power structure which, I think, is very bad for music and which I do everything I can to break down.

"I just don't go back to orchestras who insist on staying aloof, because I can't really respond to them. There is no possibility of my making contact with musicians who won't come up and talk to me. That's why working with the Los Angeles Philharmonic is also great.

They have this tradition of wandering in and out of the conductor's room for a chat, which is wonderful. And it took me only a couple of days to stop them calling me Maestro!"

At twenty-seven, Simon Rattle is undoubtedly the most rivetting conductor to emerge in over a decade. Astonishingly mature, too. Not mature *for his age*. Mature, full stop. Since winning the 1974 John Player Conductors' Competition at the age of nineteen—which gave him two years as Assistant Conductor of the Bournemouth Symphony Orchestra and its Sinfonietta as its prize—his rise has been so meteoric that it has taken even him by surprise.

In 1976, he made his début with the Philharmonia Orchestra at the Royal Festival Hall, at the age of twenty-one; two years later, he was invited to conduct the Los Angeles Philharmonic and the Chicago Symphony; this was followed by guest appearances with the San Francisco and the Toronto Symphony and the Berlin Radio Orchestra as well as several British orchestras and student orchestras like the National Youth and the London Schools' Symphony, before being appointed Assistant Conductor of the BBC Scottish Symphony and Associate Conductor of the Liverpool Philharmonic; in September 1980, he took up his post as Principal Conductor and Musical Adviser in Birmingham.

Everywhere he goes, he makes a winning impression with his lack of arrogance, both musical and personal, his eagerness to learn and his good fortune in possessing a sunny personality that does not arouse antagonism.

"Rattle's ability to communicate sound, phrases and textures with his hands is absolutely astounding," says trumpeter Bram Gay, the Orchestra Director at the Royal Opera House, Covent Garden, where Rattle has not conducted yet but is to make his début in the near future. "There are few conductors in the world now of any age and with any kind of experience who have this knack to a comparable degree. He's the best, the most remarkable conducting talent to emerge in a long, long time. Such a lovely bloke, too. I think that if our Board of Directors is clever, they will snap him up as our Music Director around 1990, when he's had time to develop."

Meanwhile, Rattle is acutely aware of the danger of doing too much too soon. "The danger is that doing too much and studying in a frantic, panic-stricken way results in a superficial understanding of music, sort of filtering down from the top instead of going right to the foundations and working up. Many of us contemporary conductors, including

myself, are guilty of doing things in a superficial way, because it's easy;
the technical expertise of both orchestras and conductors is greater
than it was fifty or even thirty years ago. And the musical understanding is that much less.

"Because in those days, conductors were naturally expected to be
composers—Nikisch was the first one who wasn't, and then it all
changed with Toscanini—and consequently understood the very basis
of the whole business. Sometimes, they were manually disastrous
conductors. But it didn't matter much because they were marvellous
musicians. The whole tragedy of the conducting scene now is that
virtually none of us are composers. We should be, but we're not. And it
shows. You get a glossy style of surface conducting."

But while other conductors of the younger and middle generation are
also aware of those dangers and shortcomings, Simon appears to be the
only one actually prepared to do something in order to avoid them.
And this at a time when his career has really begun to take off, a stage
at which most artists would be at their most insecure, fearing that if
they disappear from view for a few weeks, they might be forgotten or
still worse, surpassed by others.

But not Simon. During the 1980–81 season, he retired to Oxford
University for three terms, to study English and American Literature as
a wandering student. He did do *some* conducting—"I do have a
mortgage to pay and even conductors have to eat"—but only during
the holidays. This was not only financially but also emotionally
necessary, because two months without music were just about as much
as he could take. During term, he made a point of listening to as little
music as possible, even on the gramophone, "with the result that when
I did, the emotional impact was overwhelming. But I wouldn't say that
this was a period of musical starvation—my mind was too full of
things I wanted and needed to explore for that—but more like being on
a diet." For a time, he found the things he was exploring almost as
compulsive as music—especially poetry and the works of James Joyce.
He read his entire output, and that of T. S. Eliot, and found them "a
discovery I can never value too highly. It was like discovering the
Beethoven late Quartets or something of equal value; equal resonance,
anyway."

Yet picking up the baton again during the holidays was not all that
easy. Firstly because of the terrific amount of physical strain involved in
conducting, which people don't realize and which even he didn't realize
until he had to do it again after a two-month gap. "It was like having to

run again, after a period of physical inertia. Every time I started, my arms were *agony* for about a week."

Secondly, although emotionally he was longing to go back to work, he found the switch back to mass communication difficult, because by then he had got used to writing and to dealing with different types of people: academics and literary people "who are much less exuberant than musicians! So having people look you straight in the eye again—which is something one forgets at Oxford, where they always try to look around your nose or at the top of your head or at your feet, depending on the kind of conversation you are having—was something of a shock. And then going away from this and back to writing, trying to still the brain, clear out all those notes and concentrate again, took some time."

In five years' time, he reckons, he will be ready for another sabbatical. It was therefore not surprising to learn that his musical idol is Carlo Maria Giulini—"I worship the man"—a conductor well known for his practice of taking a great deal of time off conducting for several reasons. Simon always made a point of attending all his rehearsals whenever he came to England, and went to visit him in Milan shortly after being invited to conduct Giulini's orchestra, the Los Angeles Philharmonic.

"It was very interesting. We sat there and talked for four or five hours and only in the last hour did we start on music, which I felt was right. I told him about certain pieces—the Beethoven ninth, the Bruckner ninth, the *Missa Solemnis*, the Mozart *Requiem*—which I find impossible to conduct. The time is just not right, yet. He said not to worry, because 'these pieces will come and knock on your door when they want you to conduct them'.

"And I have found this is absolutely true. Now, I'm just not in a position to face those particular pieces or indeed, some other pieces which I previously did conduct but will now allow to rest. Because basically it's not really you who decides whether you want to conduct a score or not. *It* tells you whether you are ready for it or not. Even the fact that you have opened it does not necessarily mean that *you* have selected it. *It* sums *you* up and decides whether it wants you or not.

"For example, there are many, many works which I love to hear conducted by other people. But when I open the scores, they say 'No, you don't know me'.... I suppose that you eventually come to them, very slowly. They sort of filter into your system gradually, through the back door.

"And this gradual acquisition of a real musical understanding is the challenge facing every conductor. Technique is easy, although it obviously takes time to learn. But once you are faced with the real, musical problems, it becomes harder and harder. For instance, I find myself less and less capable of conducting the Beethoven symphonies as I grow older, and they weren't so hot to begin with! But now, as I grow more and more aware of all the different layers, of their unfathomable depth, I am left gasping at the sheer amount that I have to take in.

"It's in those works, the real works, the works of the Classical tradition—Bach, Mozart, Beethoven, Brahms—that the mirror is at its clearest. These works are almost conductor-proof and mirror your weaknesses very strongly. There is always an enormous choice of possibilities in Beethoven and Brahms. In Beethoven, the most difficult thing is those rhythms—you ask any string player and he will tell you that the hardest task in Beethoven is to make the rhythm work, because there is a life-pulse underneath it, and you have to be *in* it. You can't get it right just like that, by skimming the surface, from outside.

"And in a Brahms symphony, one has twenty choices for each phrase as opposed to perhaps two in a work like Stravinsky's *Le Sacre du printemps*. Which is why I'm always staggered that magnificent conductors who can do these extraordinarily difficult things like Brahms, Beethoven and Mozart so beautifully, have problems with Stravinsky and other twentieth-century composers because they find it hard to beat irregular rhythm patterns. Yet twentieth-century music, plus composers like Berlioz, basically all works which are put together more skilfully as orchestral mechanisms, are much easier for us to hide behind, because there is so much to *do*: and you know exactly *what* you have to do, because the shapes are very clear.

"To me, something like *Le Sacre du printemps* is one of the easier works I have conducted, yet you say that many people find it difficult. I honestly can't understand why, because if you can conduct it, they can play it. And if you are able to put down a 5/8 or a 7/8 bar in tempo—which as a percussionist I am able to do—then you can conduct it. There is no rubato in the piece. They just have to play it and, as long as you have a feeling for its shape, it can be extraordinary.

"But I tell you which twentieth-century works *are* difficult: *Petrushka* and Debussy's *Jeux* which, from the purely technical point of view, is almost unconductable. *Terribly* hard. There is an infinity of little chirping things between each beat, and it's as though each bar uncovers a stone under which there are thousands of scampering semi-quavers.

And the rhythms are so subtle, the form is so subtle, like a dream form, one can never quite grab hold of it. I love doing it, but it's always a big challenge.

"In *Petrushka* the difficulties are those rhythms—sevens against threes, fives against threes—which are very hard to get right. There are one or two passages at the end which, nine times out of ten, are chaos at every performance. Yet people consider this work easier to conduct than *Le Sacre*, because it is easy to get away with getting it eighty-per-cent right, whereas *Le Sacre* has got to be a hundred-per-cent right or it shows. But *Petrushka* is also a much more personal piece, there is more puppetry involved in it. Most orchestral players would much rather play this than *Le Sacre*, which is like being involved in an enormous machine, an extraordinary kind of concrete mixer. Yet if you get it right, it can be very impressive."

Simon Rattle's ability to identify so easily and effortlessly with twentieth-century works is partly due to his age and his generation's identification with this music, which is natural to them, and to his quite extraordinary gift for the technical aspects of conducting without which performing such works would be near impossible. But while he explained that there are some Classical and Romantic works which he is not yet ready for, he has now begun to feel at home with several pieces which, a couple of years ago, he found problematic. Beethoven's Fourth Symphony, for example, smiles quite happily on him now, which it used not to. But other works which he then thought he could manage, now seem impossible: "Take the Mozart G minor Symphony (No. 40), I have tapes of every single performance I did, and the first one was the best, because I was only fifteen and didn't realize how difficult it was. So, it cradled me. Each subsequent time, I tried to love it more and more to death, until it finally said 'No'. I did a disastrous performance and gave it up for the time being.

"And all the Brahms symphonies, which I worked very hard on the first time I tackled them, remain excruciatingly difficult. Not technically, but musically. One has to rediscover the culture they encapsule again. As it is, the surface of those works seems to be covered with something, like thin ice on a pond. Which may be why, with three or four exceptions, the performances of Brahms—*and* Beethoven—that one hears today are generally unacceptable, shocking. *Shocking!*

"The two Brahms conductors I deeply admire are Giulini and Boult. I am fascinated by the former's recording of the fourth, which is the 'rightest' in the real sense of right that I have heard, so good that I can no longer accept any others, because they don't give it enough time to breathe. And one wouldn't wish for any note to sound different from the way it does in Boult's recording of the first—yet people abroad just don't know about this man.

"I went to see him the other day and went through the scores of the Brahms symphonies with him. Oddly enough, apart from a few surface things, he didn't have much of interest to say, because whenever we came to something *really* difficult as far as I'm concerned, he said, 'Oh well, naturally, it goes like this, of course.' And, for him, it *does* come naturally, because he's part of that tradition. But for us, conducting Brahms means rediscovering a completely new world.

"Whereas conducting Mahler poses no such problems for me. He is the beginning of my tradition, my generation's tradition, and in his case I, too, find it perfectly obvious that a certain passage should go like this, or that the harmony needs more time here, or that in such and such a spot you need to move faster, or what the mood of the work is. A piece like *Das Lied von der Erde*, for example, comes to me very naturally. For some reason, it's part of my culture."

In 1980, he recorded Deryck Cooke's completed version of the Mahler tenth for EMI, with whom he now has an exclusive contract. Shortly before, he had conducted a deservedly acclaimed performance of this fiendishly difficult and controversial work—arguments are forever raging about the rightness of Cooke's orchestration and about the rightness of finishing and performing this work at all—with the Philharmonia in London. The performance not only convinced many of those who doubted the authenticity of the completed version but was also remarkable for the fact that at no point was one aware that it was being conducted by a twenty-five-year-old.

"The main problem with a work like this is that one is faced with something of the stature of a Brahms or another Mahler or one of the great Bruckner symphonies, but for which there is no performing tradition at all. There is nothing. You have to mine, to goldmine, it for yourself, responding to this raw material with your instincts, exactly like the conductors of Mahler's day had to. And it is very easy to make mistakes, very easy to do something slightly off the mark, purely because there is nothing to guide you.

"This is why I took a great deal of notice of what certain marvellous musicians said after that first performance with the Philharmonia, and spent a lot of time with Berthold Goldschmidt who was very much involved in its initial (1960) orchestration and conducted its first performance. We listened to a tape of the Philharmonia performance together and he gave me some excellent advice: for example, I remember his reaction to a particular passage where I was pushing. 'You are robbing yourself of time for drama,' he said. And it was absolutely true. In the recording, I gave the work a lot more time to speak for itself.

"It was a very, very difficult work to prepare, but I have always loved Mahler, and if you love Mahler, you have to explore the tenth, because it's of enormous importance. At the beginning, I was as cynical as most people. But when I sat down and spent a lot of time with it, I found it irresistible, one of his best symphonies, better than several of the others. It's in a different class, very, very special and forward-looking.

"It gives a clue to what all the other twentieth-century composers were to do: one movement sounds like Berg—the first, which is just like *Lulu*—and another just like Hindemith. It encapsules all that was to come in the future. Everything has been shown a way forward. Many of his contemporaries may not have known the work until the twenties, when the sketches were published and when everyone would have had a chance to see them."

Rattle feels, rightly, that there is much more of Mahler in this symphony than there is of Mozart in the *Requiem*, and yet people seem to listen to what he calls, "that dreadful hackwork by Süssmayr without complaint"; or of Bartók in his Viola Concerto where one has trouble recognizing that this is indeed a work written by this idiosyncratic composer. But does he still miss Mahler or feel frustrated at not having more of him in the tenth?

"Now that I've actually learnt *how* to conduct it and feel that I have started to penetrate some of its secrets, I don't miss him at all. When I didn't understand the piece fully, I missed him a lot more. Now, after spending so much time with it, it poses fewer problems than the Fifth and far fewer than the Seventh. Because although it is very different from most of his other works, what he is doing is very clear. And it's very, very fine music, so you can go with it.

"His intentions, which are very clear, are reflected in the orchestration which, I think, has been done very well. [He, like Kurt Sanderling, who has also conducted this work, has made some amendments to the orchestration, under Goldschmidt's guidance.] I'm sure it would have been incomparably more marvellous if Mahler had lived to do it himself, but I'm also sure that he would have left vast sections intact. Other sections he would have revised. The second movement, for instance, he would probably have revised a lot. It's very bare and very strange and very illogical. Up to then, nobody had experimented with such vast changes of metre. Stravinsky hadn't even started sketching *Le Sacre du printempts* when this symphony was written, and it's much more difficult to conduct this music than anything of Stravinsky's. Technically, it's very nearly the most difficult thing I've ever had to come to grips with, mainly because of the time measures and the immense problem of rhythm and logic.

"You seem surprised that I should use the word logic in this context. But rhythms can be logical; rhythms can be organic. But the rhythms in the second movement of this symphony are definitely *not* organic. Because as far as I can see, he is trying to create something very disturbing indeed, and it is written so that you can't settle down comfortably with it for a minute. It's very dislocating. You're pulled this way and that all the time. The minute you settle down to one rhythm, he will suddenly spurt forward and pull you back again. Very unlike a work like *Le Sacre du printemps*, which we seem to have discussed so much, and which is a very constant, very organic, earthbound piece that stinks of soil and has rhythms that make absolute sense."

The recording of Mahler's tenth was done in three days, digitally, using a two-track machine, which means that, much to his delight, editing facilities were limited—he dislikes recording at the best of times. He found those three days "heaven", because he was allowed to record in long, complete takes. For one of the movements, they used the complete first take, for the last movement they used the complete second take and for the first movement they just did two takes and used bits of the first and bits of the second. It was almost like conducting a performance, with plenty of rehearsal time, which was marvellous. (In fact they finished so early that they had time to record Fauré's *Pelléas et Mélisande* as well.)

The reason why he dislikes recording is the difficulty of keeping the two distinct personalities—the man who rehearses and the man who performs—that every conductor carries inside him, in balance: "The technique of recording inhibits the freedom of the performer, to a certain extent. Yet it is a technique that one must learn. And one must also persuade the orchestra to balance those two elements in its own make-up. This is why I feel that one should only record with the memory, the aftermath, of a performance fresh inside one—otherwise it gets very depressing—and fortunately that was the case with this recording."

The orchestra used in the recording is the Bournemouth Symphony, the very first Simon ever conducted and they did him proud. He has now conducted Mahler's tenth with several orchestras, and found that each experience was like turning a different mirror on his own interpretation. Although his first performance, with the Philharmonia Orchestra, was one of the most unforgettable occasions in his life and he considers that "there is nothing like the actual sound of the Philharmonia strings", to his surprise it was the Bournemouth Symphony that came nearest to the overall sound he wanted.

"Of course, I shouldn't have been surprised, because this was where I had started and where I had learnt a lot of what I consider to be my 'sound world'. And even though I hadn't conducted them for a long time, I realized that a lot of the sound I now want from an orchestra actually stems from that source. Most of the players I knew were still there, so that this particularly biting-forward woodwind sound which is one of this orchestra's specialities and which has become very much a part of my own concept of sound, was still there, and required no persuasion from me."

Rehearsing and performing with different orchestras often requires a different technique. With some orchestras, like the Philharmonia, he can leave a lot for the players to sort out by themselves and know that it will automatically be right on the second or the third time, while with others, like the BBC Scottish Symphony—not one of the most efficient, but definitely one of the most musical groups he has ever worked with—everything must be rehearsed. But he doesn't like orchestras who want to know exactly what is going to happen in a performance.

"I really don't mind telling them whether I'm going to beat in two or four but I do like the freedom of holding one note slightly longer, for example. I want to create an element of chance, even though orchestras look a bit strange when I tell them that in a Haydn symphony a certain passage will be quiet the first time and loud the second time, or possibly the other way round, so just watch me. It takes them a bit of time to get used to this, but then a performance becomes more tense and exciting. Of course, there is such a thing as chemistry, on both sides, and one senses, or has to learn, which orchestras you can have a real contact with.

"Basically, you can't really know until the first concert. I can tell what kind of concert it's going to be after the first few bars. But the first rehearsal is also very interesting. You can only begin to know what kind of communication you are having with them after the interval. The first hour-and-a-half is a purely tribal situation, with both sides walking around each other. No real work ever gets done in the first half of the first rehearsal—ever!—until everyone has had coffee and talked to each other and decided what they are going to think. Then there is a danger that you might actually be able to start working!

"I like orchestras that make every concert an event and are willing to put all their energy at your disposal if you want it. (The Rotterdam Philharmonic, composed almost entirely of Hungarians, do this at almost every concert.) Because I realize more and more that working with an orchestra really boils down to setting up an atmosphere where something can happen. You must get the musicians to be responsive enough to come with you if you suddenly feel like doing something different, something unrehearsed and spontaneous. One of the greatest joys is to be able to have a different phrasing, just by a glance, so that they feel free enough to follow their own spontaneous inclinations. Last night, [the late] Janet Craxton did some outrageous rubatos in Milhaud's *La Création du monde*, which all of us were able to follow and it was rivetting.

"And we also did a super series of concerts with the BBC Scottish Symphony during my last months there—Shostakovitch, Mahler and *the* best *Sacre du printemps* I have ever done. Because we had worked on all the details very painstakingly, and by then we knew and were comfortable with each other. Our very last concert was one of those extraordinary occasions when everything seems to go almost miraculously right, without effort. It reminded me of the Zen saying that only when you don't have to think about whether anything will happen, then there is no chance of it not happening."

Simon, born in Liverpool on January 19, 1955, was the youngest child of musical parents. When he was five, he persuaded his elder sister, who was also musical, to teach him how to read music. A year later, he was given a pair of drums by his parents, which meant an instant end to domestic peace. His father remembers him organizing Sunday-afternoon concerts throughout his childhood, at which family, friends and neighbours were persuaded to provide a live percussion accompaniment to his favourite records.

At the age of eight, he started studying the piano and three years later switched to "a wonderful old teacher, who is now over ninety", who had met Grieg, knew Rachmaninoff and had studied with Godowsky,* one of the "great old Europeans". He treasures the experience, because a teacher like this can transmit certain things, certain traditions which cannot actually be taught in concrete terms; just absorbed from someone who is steeped in them.

Not long afterwards, he became a percussion-player in the Liverpool Philharmonic—his first professional job was the timpani in Handel's *Music for the Royal Fireworks*—and the National Youth Orchestra, with which he went on numerous courses and visits abroad, and occasionally played under Pierre Boulez.

"Boulez has been a vast influence on me, especially because of his way of analysing things, cutting them down to the bone and taking them to pieces—very much a composer's way of looking at music. I probably learnt more of my basic attitudes of mind from him than from anybody else. A lot of them I later rejected. But at the time, I was so wildly pro him, that for a whole year I conducted like him, as best I could, of course, I almost looked like a little imitation, which was ridiculous. In fact, I think that even now a lot of the gestures I make when I want certain sounds, have Boulez at the back. In that way, one has a very strong visual memory."

As it was around this time, at the age of fifteen, that Simon really decided on a conducting career, he sought out Boulez for advice and tuition as often as he possibly could and found him, as everyone who has a chance of meeting and working with him does, "a devastatingly charming, warm-hearted, rather traditional man who always has time for everybody". They first met with the National Youth Orchestra, when Simon had what he calls the insane idea of putting on a concert in Liverpool with friends from various orchestras, with Boulez's *Le Marteau sans maître* in the first half, followed by the Beethoven ninth. "I was only fifteen at the time, but *Le Marteau* would have come off had the singer not gone down with glandular fever. And it would have been an absolutely diabolical performance!"

Sometimes, he felt that Boulez seemed a trifle overconcerned to bring out the structure of a work, especially in Berg, "which is a shame. Because clarity isn't everything. Sometimes I begin to think that clarity isn't anything. Naturally, one wants to be clear about the structure of a work from the point of view of conducting technique, because one wants to help the musicians; one doesn't want to make them more

* Leopold Godowsky, Polish-American pianist (1870–1938).

uncomfortable than necessary. But sometimes, a little discomfort is a good thing. Which is why, every now and then, I try to lose an orchestra, just to create tension and suspense.

"I learnt this from watching Sir Adrian Boult who just before a quiet *tremolo* entry would lose the entire string section, thus drawing a most marvellously tense response from people.... And, of course, Barbirolli always told his pupils to make a few mistakes in the final rehearsal, 'so that the players don't rely on you too much'. What both these conductors were trying to do, in their different ways, was to ensure that they brought the music to life. And you don't do that by repeating a note-perfect rehearsal. For the music to live, you need spontaneity, you need some freedom, and you need to take some risks. In short, you need Furtwängler. Or Beecham. Today, the only man who carries on their tradition is Giulini."

While playing percussion and the piano in those two orchestras, Simon was also preparing for his A levels. At the age of sixteen, he won four grade 'A's and a scholarship to the Royal Academy of Music in London, where he studied the piano, percussion and conducting.

Although conducting is intangible, he doesn't consider it to be a particularly mysterious art—no more so than playing an instrument marvellously. "Conducting requires technique and temperament, much the same things that being able to speak through an instrument does. The only difference is that one cannot actually hear the notes a conductor has in his mind, except through a third channel, the players who make the sound.

"But, in fact, you *can* actually hear how somebody conducts—I mean physically hear—very, very quickly. I don't know if people have learnt to hear how conductors conduct. But the point is that you can conduct wrong notes just as easily as you can play wrong notes. And the minute one is uncertain in intention, this immediately becomes transmitted to the players, because all of us are in a much more highly-charged state of mind while performing. I know that if I'm not entirely convinced by what I'm doing, the orchestra will not play well, however good they are."

Most of what Simon knows about conducting came from John Carewe, the former Principal Conductor of the BBC Welsh Symphony Orchestra, and founder of the New Music Ensemble, who proved his most influential teacher at the Academy. Their very close six-year collaboration started when, one evening, Carewe listened to him "hacking my way through the Mozart E flat Symphony (No. 39), as though it were *The Miraculous Mandarin!*

"He took me for a long drive, during which he tore my performance to shreds. Having done that, he said, 'Right, to make amends, I can help you not to do this again. Are you willing?' I was, and we started our collaboration, during which I was forced to confront my lack of discipline, to study harmony and to work—something which doesn't come naturally to me!

"John saved me ten years of mistakes. Because being gifted is only relative. I have a kind of manual gift of getting things across and being able to communicate—a gift that has allowed me to make a career very quickly, much more quickly than I ever dreamt or wanted, but I don't have other gifts which are equally necessary and more important. I had to learn *what* I wanted to communicate, because I had no idea and that was the problem. For want of anything else, I would just communicate energy—talk about 'a bull in a china shop!' I used to clasp everything to my bosom, and anything that was frail, like Classical music, would be crushed to death. I mean, poor Mozart, he didn't even have a *chance*! He couldn't stand up to that sort of onslaught.

"Everything I know about phrasing and harmony and, of course, style, is also largely due to him. He taught me about Schenker* and that type of harmonic analysis and how to deal with orchestras. I owe him a vast debt of gratitude and affection and it's marvellous occasionally to see a hint of pride in him. At last he seems to think, begrudgingly, that something has penetrated through to my thick skull."

Their continuing friendship is invaluable, because Simon is fully aware that an artist needs to be surrounded by people he can trust. There are very few of those around, and even fewer who can perceive and tell him the truth about himself and his performances. Another such influence is his wife, the American soprano Elise Ross, whom he married in the summer of 1980 after a close relationship. "She is absolutely honest and quicker than I, and can analyse things very well, which is useful!"

Another powerful influence at the Academy was John Streets, an "extraordinary man who ran the operatic department and is also a

---

* Heinrich Schenker (1868–1935), the distinguished Polish-Austrian theorist and teacher, who laid down his extremely minute method of analysing scores in his literary works *Neue Musikalische Theorien und Phantasien* and *Das Meisterwerk in der Musik*.

pianist with the Gabrieli Quartet" and who taught him a great deal about the piano: how to play legato in twenty minutes, or what to do in order to achieve a Fauré sound in ten. "He just said, you do this and that, and left me to it. He is one of the most tasteful men I've ever come across, both musically and technically, and was able to show me that I was playing Fauré like Schumann, which I shouldn't be doing, because it wasn't in the style."

Another influence was Maurice Miles, who taught him an enormous amount about the professional business of being a conductor, about getting through things and cutting corners. In fact, he didn't realize how much he *had* learnt from him until later, when his career had got under way.

After graduating from the Academy, he entered the John Player Conductors' Competition, which he never dreamt of winning, so he "just relaxed and enjoyed myself, which must have got across to the orchestra" who stood up and applauded his reading of *Don Juan*. He won First Prize among 200 applicants who had first been reduced to ten finalists. The Prize included two years as Assistant Conductor of the Bournemouth Symphony and its Sinfonietta, at a salary of £3,000 a year without expenses. Thus, virtually overnight, he was launched into what he always refers to as "the career".

The job involved travelling with the orchestra for twenty-five hours a week and playing for another twenty-five hours. Exhausting, but good training for the wearing and hectic life this profession entails. In addition, there were engagements with other orchestras—the English Chamber Orchestra, the Northern Sinfonia, and the Royal Liverpool Philharmonic whose Associate Conductor he became in 1978, with a commitment to conduct twelve concerts a year.

At the same time, he was named Assistant Conductor of the BBC Scottish Symphony Orchestra, with the much heavier load of forty concerts per season. He made his operatic début at Glyndebourne in 1977—Janáček's *The Cunning Little Vixen*—and has since returned for Haydn's *La fedeltà premiata* (1980), *Ariadne auf Naxos* (1981), and *Der Rosenkavalier* (1982). He has also conducted *Così fan tutte* and *The Rake's Progress* with the Glyndebourne Touring Company.

In 1980, he began his first Principal Conductorship: the City of Birmingham Symphony Orchestra, initially for three years. But he hopes to stay for no less than a decade, unless of course other offers which he can't resist turn up, or unless the orchestra itself wants him to go. He feels that in many ways rehearsal conditions outside London are better for making music, because the musicians are under less pressure. In Birmingham, he has a week before the beginning of each season, just for rehearsing any works he wants from the coming season's repertoire, plus a chance to have split rehearsals and to repeat concerts more than once.

"I look forward to getting to know the players really well and getting down to constant, serious work together. The orchestra has been very well trained, has a good sound and no weak links, thank goodness. I would like to make them a great deal more rhythmic and tight, which up to now they haven't been. But they are very willing to work and get down to things.

"What is tremendously important is that an orchestra should have a good international mix of players and a good balance between men and women. I don't think I want to listen to an all-male orchestra any more. They are sadly lacking. Any orchestra needs a proportion of different types of people: you need the sloggers and you need the sensitive and the hyper-sensitive people to balance each other out.

"In a string section, you often need some of the brute force of a man as well as some of the delicacy, detail and quicker response of women. You need all those different responses. And, interestingly enough, women usually seem to be the more fulfilled members in orchestras, the ones with fewer grouses and less prone to disillusionment. The London Symphony Orchestra, for instance, would be improved by fifty per cent if it had a larger proportion of women, because this necessarily changes the atmosphere—all to the good, I think. In Birmingham, we have a very healthy proportion of female members. And I have just appointed a female trombone player. Yes, this *is* rather rare. But she was by far the best among all the applicants." [She has since resigned, though.]

A year after our first two conversations, this orchestra had become musically the most important thing in his life, the place where he would stay "until they boot me out". It has been fascinating for him to watch them grow into a different class of orchestra within a year. And while he enjoys working elsewhere, he doesn't have the same feeling of rapport, or the endless possibilities for improvement—possibilities which the players want to take up. This, he feels, makes up for all the bad conditions and the bad pay, "for there's no doubt that they work too hard for too little money."

One of the first things that needed improving was the quality of the string sound: "For the English school of string playing is very good and very fluent but not very rich in sonority, which is a problem, and the first thing that hits one when one returns from abroad. But one of the things that struck me when I first went to Birmingham was the fact that their sound was homogeneous, something one could work with. And every time I return to them after a two-month gap, I find that their sound has expanded." During his first season there, they had ninety-seven-per-cent attendance, which is very exciting for him. So is the fact that audiences are getting younger all the time. "As Elgar said, it's a massive hope for the future!"

Rattle has now extended his contract until 1986, which is when, he feels, "the whole thing will just be beginning to settle into what we want it to be. During the first three years, one is merely building a plateau on which one can start painting. At the moment we're just building. But somehow, the thing is coming together much faster than I anticipated. We are already *making music*, and I would rather have that than all the gloss in the world. At the moment, we are like a quartet; we have the same feeling of commitment. And this is the only way forward: old-fashioned fidelity, working with one group. I mean, other places are marvellous too, and I enjoy working there. But I can't help feeling that this group is home.

"And my relationship with them is not feudal. It's a very young orchestra with forty-one people under thirty and okay, sometimes we get cross with each other; but there is no feeling that anything has to be proved; there's no barrier." (Indeed not! I was amused to hear that when Simon appeared at a rehearsal wearing his splendid Miro-inspired T-shirt, one of the clarinettists exclaimed: "*Now* I know what the inside of your brain looks like!" Another day he found the following notice on his stand, placed there by a player who had discovered it on an old bus: "Conductors should report any unnecessary rattles found on the bus"!)

He will aim at a "gentle expansion" of the repertoire towards more twentieth-century classics and contemporary works by Henze, Berio, Boulez and Peter Maxwell Davies, the world première of whose First Symphony he conducted at the composer's request. He was amazed to find that during his first season in Birmingham, a concert that included Boulez's *Rituels* and the Mahler Resurrection Symphony was sold out months in advance, that their performance of Messiaen's Turangalîla Symphony drew a full and wildly enthusiastic house, and that all the far-out things were greeted with far greater joy than the standard repertoire.

In fact Simon's exciting, adventurous and very clever choice of repertoire has been a great asset in his career: apart from the Mahler tenth and Maxwell Davies's First Symphony, he has made a point of conducting rarely performed works, like Janáček's *Glagolitic Mass*, Milhaud's *La Création du monde, Caramel mou* and Clarinet Concerto, among many others. A choice which is sufficiently unusual to arouse interest and which reflects his conviction that no young conductor can possibly have anything interesting to say about the great Classical and Romantic works as yet.

"Doing things for the first time, when you are virgin to them, can never be satisfactory *ever*, but especially not when it comes to the great Classical and Romantic literature. Because everything important only happens in maturing performances. Who wants to listen to a twenty-five-year-old's Beethoven?"

It won't be long before everyone wants to listen to Simon Rattle's Beethoven, *and* Mozart *and* Brahms ("the right age for Brahms is at around fifty," he mused). There is little doubt in my mind that he will prove one of the giants of the future. He himself is more modest:

"My best and worst quality is rashness, I suppose. The good part of it is due to youth, which, of course, is why I am not a great conductor. And I have to learn all those things which have to do with the cerebral part of conducting. I'm a terrible sensualist as far as music is concerned, and that's fifty per cent of the whole thing. An important part, to be sure, but you also need the other side. You can't just go on being sensual, because eventually this will turn in on itself. This other half was entirely missing from my make-up and I am slowly, gradually trying to acquire it. There was just instinct, sensuality and a certain facility for technique. But like many people with instinct I often get things wildly wrong. That's part of the fun, I suppose. It's an unending process, the whole thing. When I was younger, I was terrified of knowing nothing. Now, I know that I know very little," he mused, tucking into heavily garlicked lamb. Sure, he loves his food and drink. "Conductors who don't would be instantly suspect!"

BIBLIOGRAPHY

Bernstein, Leonard, *The Joy of Music* (Simon & Schuster, New York, 1963; White Lion Publishers, London, 1974)
The Infinite Variety of Music (Weidenfeld & Nicolson, London; Simon & Schuster, New York, 1966)
The Unanswered Question: Six Harvard Lectures (Harvard University Press, Cambridge, 1976)
Blyth, Alan, *Colin Davis* (Ian Allan, Shepperton, 1969)
Böhm, Karl, *Ich erinnere mich ganz genau* (autobiography) (Diogenes Verlag, Zurich, 1968)
Bookspan, Martin, & Yockey, Ross, *Zubin: The Zubin Mehta Story* (Harper & Row, New York, 1978; Hale, London, 1980)
Boulez, Pierre, *Conversations with Célestin Deliège* (Eulenburg Books, London, 1976)
Boult, Sir Adrian, *Thoughts on Conducting* (Phoenix House, London, 1963)
My Own Trumpet (autobiography) (Hamish Hamilton, London, 1973; David & Charles, New York, 1979)
A Handbook on the Technique of Conducting (Scholarly, New York, 1951; Paterson's Publications, London, 1968)
Chesterman, Robert (ed.), *Conversations with Conductors* (Robson Books, London; Rowman, New York, 1976)
Fürtwangler, Wilhelm, *Entretiens sur la Musique* (*Concerning Music*, Greenwood, New York, 1977)
Geissmar, Berta, *Two Worlds of Music* (facsimile of 1946 edition of *The Baton and the Jackboot*, Da Capo, London and New York, 1975)
Glotz, Michel, *Révéler Les Dieux* (Robert Laffont, Paris, 1981)
Greenfield, Edward, *André Previn* (Ian Allan, Shepperton, 1973)
Hart, Philip, *Conductors: A New Generation* (Scribner, New York, 1979; Robson Books, London, 1980)
Hauesserman, Ernst, *Herbert von Karajan, Biographie* (C. Bertelsmann Verlag, Munich, 1968)
Herrigel, Eugen, *Zen in the Art of Archery* (translated from the German by R.F.C. Hull) (Random House, New York, 1971; Routledge & Kegan Paul, London, 1972)

Jacobson, Bernard, *Conductors on Conducting* (Macdonald & Jane, London; Columbia Pub., Frenchtown, 1979)

Kenyon, Nicholas, *The BBC Symphony Orchestra 1930–1980* (BBC Publications, London, 1981)

Lobl, Karl, *Das Wunder Karajan* (Wilhelm Heyne Verlag, Munich, 1977)

Peyser, Joan, *Boulez: Composer, Conductor, Enigma* (Cassell, London, 1977; Schirmer, New York, 1978)

Pirie, Peter, *Fürtwangler and the Art of Conducting* (Duckworth, London, 1981)

Previn, André, *Orchestra* (Macdonald & Jane, London, 1979; Doubleday, New York, 1980)

Riess, Curt, *Wilhelm Fürtwangler, A Biography* (translated by Margaret Goldsmith) (Frederick Muller, London, 1955)

Robinson, Paul, *Karajan* (Macdonald & Jane, London; Vanguard, New York, 1976)

Solti (Macdonald & Jane, London; Vanguard, New York, 1979)

Russell, John, *Erich Kleiber* (Da Capo, London, 1981)

Sachs, Harvey, *Toscanini* (Weidenfeld & Nicolson, London; Lippincott, New York, 1978)

Schafer, Walter Erich, *Bühne eines Lebens Erinnerungen* (Deutscher Taschenbuch Verlag, Munich, 1979)

Schonberg, Harold, *The Great Conductors* (Gollancz, London, 1968; Simon & Schuster, New York, 1970)

Sullivan, J.W.N., *Beethoven: His Spiritual Development* (Random House, New York, 1927; Allen & Unwin, London, 1964)

GENERAL INDEX